ANNUAL EDITIONS

Developing World 12/13
Twenty-Second Edition

EDITORS

Robert J. Griffiths
University of North Carolina at Greensboro

Robert J. Griffiths is Associate Professor of Political Science at the University of North Carolina at Greensboro. His teaching and research interests are in the field of comparative and international politics with a focus on Africa. He teaches courses on the politics of the non-western world, African politics, international law and organization, international security, and international political economy. His recent publications include "Democratizing South African Civil-Military Relations: A Blueprint for Post-Conflict Reform?" in *War and Peace in Africa: History, Nationalism, and the State,* edited by Toyin Falola and Raphael C. Njoku (2009) and "Parliamentary Oversight of Defense in South Africa" in *Legislative Oversight and Budgeting: A World Perspective,* Rick Stapenhurst, Riccardo Pelizzo, David Olson, & Lisa von Trapp, edited by World Bank Institute Development Studies (2008).

McGraw-Hill
Connect
Learn
Succeed™

ANNUAL EDITIONS: DEVELOPING WORLD, TWENTY-SECOND EDITION

This book is printed on acid-free paper.

Annual Editions® is a registered trademark of The McGraw-Hill Companies, Inc.

Annual Editions is published by the **Contemporary Learning Series** group within the McGraw-Hill Higher Education division.

1 2 3 4 5 6 7 8 9 0 QDB/QDB 1 0 9 8 7 6 5 4 3 2 1

MHID: 0–07–805100–2
ISBN: 978–0–07–805100–5
ISSN: 1096–4215 (print)
ISSN: 2162–5611 (online)

Managing Editor: *Larry Loeppke*
Developmental Editor II: *Debra A. Henricks*
Permissions Coordinator: *Shirley Lanners*
Senior Marketing Communications Specialist: *Mary Klein*
Project Manager: *Melissa M. Leick*
Design Coordinator: *Margarite Reynolds*
Cover Graphics: *Kristine Jubeck*
Buyer: *Susan K. Culbertson*
Media Project Manager: *Sridevi Palani*

Compositor: Laserwords Private Limited
Cover Photos: United Nations Photos #466634 and 466635/Olivier Chassot, photographer

Editors/Academic Advisory Board

Members of the Academic Advisory Board are instrumental in the final selection of articles for each edition of ANNUAL EDITIONS. Their review of articles for content, level, and appropriateness provides critical direction to the editors and staff. We think that you will find their careful consideration well reflected in this volume.

ANNUAL EDITIONS: Developing World 12/13
22nd Edition

EDITOR

Robert J. Griffiths
University of North Carolina at Greensboro

Preface

The developing world continues to play an increasingly important role in world affairs. It is home to the vast majority of the world's population, and it has an increasingly significant impact on the international economy. From the standpoint of international security, developing countries are not only sites of frequent conflicts and humanitarian crises, but also a source of continuing concern related to international terrorism. Developing countries also play a critical role in the efforts involved to protect the global environment.

The developing world demonstrates considerable ethnic, cultural, political, and economic diversity, thus making generalizations about such a diverse group of countries difficult. Increasing differentiation among developing countries further complicates our comprehension of the challenges of modernization, development, and globalization that they face. A combination of internal and external factors shape the current circumstances throughout the developing world, and issues of peace and security, international trade and finance, debt, poverty, the environment, human rights, and gender illustrate the complexity of these challenges as well as the effects of globalization and the growing interdependence between nations. The ways in which these issues interact demonstrate the importance of greater understanding of the issues and the connections between developing and industrialized countries. There continues to be significant debate about the best way to address the challenges faced by the developing world.

The developing world competes for attention on an international agenda that is often dominated by relations between the industrialized nations. Moreover, the domestic concerns of the industrial countries frequently overshadow the plight of the developing world. The twenty-second edition of *Annual Editions: Developing World* seeks to provide students with an understanding of the diversity and complexity of the developing world and to acquaint them with the challenges that these nations confront. I remain convinced of the need for greater awareness of the problems that confront the developing world and that the international community must make a commitment to effectively address these issues, particularly because of the increasingly important role developing countries are playing in international affairs. I hope that this volume contributes to students' knowledge and understanding of current trends in the developing world and the implications of these developments and serves as a catalyst for further discussion.

Approximately 50 percent of the articles in this edition are new. I chose articles that I hope are both interesting and informative and that can serve as a basis for further student research and discussion. The units deal with what I regard as the major issues facing the developing world. In addition, I have attempted to suggest the similarities and differences between developing countries, the nature of their relationships with the industrialized nations, and the different perspectives that exist regarding the causes of and approaches to meet the issues.

Two new learning features have recently been added to aid students in their study and expand critical thinking about each article topic. Located at the beginning of each unit, *Learning Outcomes* outline the key concepts that students should focus on as they are reading the material. *Critical Thinking* questions, located at the end of each article, allow students to test their understanding of the key concepts. A *Topic Guide* assists students in finding other articles on a given subject within this edition, while a list of recommended *Internet References* guides them to the best sources of additional information on a topic.

I would again like to thank McGraw-Hill for the opportunity to put together a reader on a subject that is the focus of my teaching and research. I would also like to thank those who have offered comments and suggestions. I have tried to take these into account in preparing the current volume. No book on a topic as broad as the developing world can be completely comprehensive. There certainly are additional and alternative readings that might be included. Any suggestions for improvement are welcome. Please complete and return the postage-paid article rating form at the end of the book with your comments.

Robert J. Griffiths
Editor

The Annual Editions Series

VOLUMES AVAILABLE

Adolescent Psychology

Aging

American Foreign Policy

American Government

Anthropology

Archaeology

Assessment and Evaluation

Business Ethics

Child Growth and Development

Comparative Politics

Criminal Justice

Developing World

Drugs, Society, and Behavior

Dying, Death, and Bereavement

Early Childhood Education

Economics

Educating Children with Exceptionalities

Education

Educational Psychology

Entrepreneurship

Environment

The Family

Gender

Geography

Global Issues

Health

Homeland Security

Human Development

Human Resources

Human Sexualities

International Business

Management

Marketing

Mass Media

Microbiology

Multicultural Education

Nursing

Nutrition

Physical Anthropology

Psychology

Race and Ethnic Relations

Social Problems

Sociology

State and Local Government

Sustainability

Technologies, Social Media, and Society

United States History, Volume 1

United States History, Volume 2

Urban Society

Violence and Terrorism

Western Civilization, Volume 1

Western Civilization, Volume 2

World History, Volume 1

World History, Volume 2

World Politics

Contents

UNIT 1
Understanding the Developing World

1. **The New Face of Development,** Carol Lancaster, *Current History,*
January 2008
The nature and emphasis of development has shifted as some progress on reducing poverty has been achieved. While poverty continues to be a challenge, especially in sub-Saharan Africa, development has increasingly come to be identified with human development, civil and political rights, security, and sustainability. Government to government aid programs are increasing through the efforts of civil society organizations, philanthropists, and multinational corporations. Technology has also helped shift development emphases.   **3**

2. **How Development Leads to Democracy: What We Know about
Modernization,** Ronald Inglehart and Christian Welzel, *Foreign Affairs,*
March/April 2009
A reinterpretation of modernization theory in a way that emphasizes the cultural changes that accompany this process helps to explain how pressures for democracy push societies toward greater openness and political participation. A key component is the connection between economic development and changes in society, culture, and politics that promotes tolerance, encourages self-expression, and fosters political participation.   **7**

3. **The New Population Bomb: The Four Megatrends That Will Change the
World,** Jack A. Goldstone, *Foreign Affairs,* January/February 2010
Declining fertility rates will stabilize world population in the middle of the twenty-first century. *Shifting demographics will bring about significant changes in both rich and poor countries, however.* The industrial countries will account for less of the world's population, their economic influence will diminish, and they will need more migrant workers. Meanwhile, most of the world's population growth will take place in the developing world, especially the poorest countries. Those populations will also be increasingly urban.   **13**

4. **Best. Decade. Ever.** Charles Kenny, *Foreign Policy,* September/October
2010
Despite being bracketed by the September 11th attacks and the global financial crisis, the first decade of the 21st century brought significant gains for the developing world. **From economic growth and a reduction in the number of people living in poverty, to progress on infectious diseases and fewer conflicts, living conditions improved for many citizens of the developing world.** Serious challenges such as environmental degradation remain, however.   **18**

5. **And Justice for All: Enforcing Human Rights for the World's Poor,** Gary
Haugen and Victor Boutros, *Foreign Policy,* May/June 2010
There has been significant progress on human rights law since the end of WWII. **Although the body of human rights law has expanded, poor people often find that the laws are not enforced and their access to legal protection and representation is very limited.** This absence of the rule of law also undermines development efforts.   **20**

The concepts in bold italics are developed in the article. For further expansion, please refer to the Topic Guide.

UNIT 2
Political Economy and the Developing World

The concepts in bold italics are developed in the article. For further expansion, please refer to the Topic Guide.

The concepts in bold italics are developed in the article. For further expansion, please refer to the Topic Guide.

UNIT 3
Conflict and Instability

The concepts in bold italics are developed in the article. For further expansion, please refer to the Topic Guide.

UNIT 4
Political Change in the Developing World

The concepts in bold italics are developed in the article. For further expansion, please refer to the Topic Guide.

The concepts in bold italics are developed in the article. For further expansion, please refer to the Topic Guide.

UNIT 5
Population, Resources, Environment, and Health

The concepts in bold italics are developed in the article. For further expansion, please refer to the Topic Guide.

UNIT 6
Women and Development

The concepts in bold italics are developed in the article. For further expansion, please refer to the Topic Guide.

The concepts in bold italics are developed in the article. For further expansion, please refer to the Topic Guide.

Correlation Guide

The *Annual Editions* series provides students with convenient, inexpensive access to current, carefully selected articles from the public press. **Annual Editions: Developing World 12/13** is an easy-to-use reader that presents articles on important topics such as *democracy, foreign aid, human rights,* and many more. For more information on *Annual Editions* and other *McGraw-Hill Contemporary Learning Series* titles, visit www.mhhe.com/cls.

This convenient guide matches the units in **Annual Editions: Developing World 12/13** with the corresponding chapters in one of our best-selling McGraw-Hill Political Science textbooks by Rourke/Boyer.

Annual Editions: Developing World, 12/13	International Politics on the World Stage, Brief, 8/e by Rourke/Boyer
Unit 1: Understanding the Developing World	**Chapter 1:** Thinking and Caring about World Politics **Chapter 2:** The Evolution of World Politics **Chapter 4:** Nationalism: The Traditional Orientation **Chapter 5:** Globalism: The Alternative Orientation
Unit 2: Political Economy and the Developing World	**Chapter 3:** Levels of Analysis and Foreign Policy **Chapter 5:** Globalism: The Alternative Orientation **Chapter 11:** International Economics: The Alternative Road
Unit 3: Conflict and Instability	**Chapter 9:** Pursuing Security
Unit 4: Political Change in the Developing World	**Chapter 6:** Power, Statecraft, and the National State: The Traditional Structure **Chapter 7:** Intergovernmental Organizations: Alternative Governance
Unit 5: Population, Resources, Environment, and Health	**Chapter 8:** International Law and Human Rights **Chapter 10:** National Economic Competition: The Traditional Road **Chapter 11:** International Economics: The Alternative Road **Chapter 12:** Preserving and Enhancing the Biosphere
Unit 6: Women and Development	**Chapter 8:** International Law and Human Rights

Topic Guide

This topic guide suggests how the selections in this book relate to the subjects covered in your course. You may want to use the topics listed on these pages to search the Web more easily.

On the following pages a number of websites have been gathered specifically for this book. They are arranged to reflect the units of this Annual Editions reader. You can link to these sites by going to www.mhhe.com/cls.

All the articles that relate to each topic are listed below the bold-faced term.

Internet References

The following Internet sites have been selected to support the articles found in this reader. These sites were available at the time of publication. However, because websites often change their structure and content, the information listed may no longer be available. We invite you to visit www.mhhe.com/cls for easy access to these sites.

Annual Editions: Developing World 12/13

General Sources

Council on Foreign Relations
www.cfr.org

Independent, non-partisan membership and research organization providing information on world affairs and United States Foreign policy.

Foreign Policy in Focus (FPIF): Progressive Response Index
http://fpif.org/progresp/index_body.html

This index is produced weekly by FPIF, a "think tank without walls," which is an international network of analysts and activists dedicated to "making the U.S. a more responsible global leader and partner by advancing citizen movements and agendas." This index lists volume and issue numbers, dates, and topics covered by the articles.

Nordic Africa Institute
www.nai.uu.se

Center for research, documentation, and information on Africa.

People & Planet
www.peopleandplanet.org

People & Planet is an organization of student groups at universities and colleges across the United Kingdom. Organized in 1969 by students at Oxford University, it is now an independent pressure group campaigning on world poverty, human rights, and the environment.

United Nations System Web Locator
www.unsystem.org

This is the website for all the organizations in the United Nations family. According to its brief overview, the United Nations, an organization of sovereign nations, provides the machinery to help find solutions to international problems or disputes and to deal with pressing concerns that face people everywhere, including the problems of the developing world, through the UN Development Program at www.undp.org and UNAIDS at www.unaids.org.

United States Census Bureau: International Summary Demographic Data
www.census.gov/ipc/www/idb

The International Data Base (IDB) is a computerized data bank containing statistical tables of demographic and socioeconomic data for all countries of the world.

UNIT 1: Understanding the Developing World

Africa Index on Africa
www.afrika.no/index

A complete reference source on Africa is available on this website.

African Studies WWW (U. Penn)
www.sas.upenn.edu/African_Studies/AS.html

The African Studies Center at the University of Pennsylvania supports this ongoing project that lists online resources related to African Studies.

United Nations Development Program
http://undp.org

The UN's global development network advocating change and connecting countries to knowledge, experience, and resources.

UNIT 2: Political Economy and the Developing World

Center for Third World Organizing
www.ctwo.org

The Center for Third World Organizing (CTWO, pronounced "C-2") is a racial justice organization dedicated to building a social justice movement led by people of color. CTWO is a 20-year-old training and resource center that promotes and sustains direct action organizing in communities of color in the United States.

ENTERWeb
www.enterweb.org

ENTERWeb is an annotated meta-index and information clearinghouse on enterprise development, business, finance, international trade, and the economy in this age of cyberspace and globalization. The main focus is on micro-, small-, and medium-scale enterprises, cooperatives, and community economic development both in developed and developing countries.

International Monetary Fund (IMF)
www.imf.org

The IMF was created to promote international monetary cooperation, to facilitate the expansion and balanced growth of international trade, to promote exchange stability, to assist in the establishment of a multilateral system of payments, to make its general resources temporarily available under adequate safeguards to its members experiencing balance of payments difficulties, and to shorten the duration and lessen the degree of disequilibrium in the international balances of payments of members.

TWN (Third World Network)
www.twnside.org.sg

The Third World Network is an independent, nonprofit international network of organizations and individuals involved in issues relating to development, the Third World, and North-South issues.

U.S. Agency for International Development (USAID)
www.usaid.gov

USAID is an independent government agency that provides economic development and humanitarian assistance to advance U.S. economic and political interests overseas.

The World Bank
www.worldbank.org

The International Bank for Reconstruction and Development, frequently called the World Bank, was established in July 1944 at the UN Monetary and Financial Conference in Bretton Woods, New Hampshire. The World Bank's goal is to reduce poverty and improve living standards by promoting sustainable growth and investment in people. The bank provides loans, technical assistance, and policy guidance to developing country members to achieve this objective.

Internet References

World Trade Organization (WTO)
www.wto.org

The WTO is promoted as the only international body dealing with the rules of trade between nations. At its heart are the WTO agreements and the legal ground rules for international commerce and for trade policy.

UNIT 3: Conflict and Instability

The Carter Center
www.cartercenter.org

The Carter Center is dedicated to fighting disease, hunger, poverty, conflict, and oppression through collaborative initiatives in the areas of democratization and development, global health, and urban revitalization.

Center for Strategic and International Studies (CSIS)
www.csis.org

For four decades, the Center for Strategic and International Studies (CSIS) has been dedicated to providing world leaders with strategic insights on, and policy solutions to, current and emerging global issues.

Conflict Research Consortium
http://conflict.colorado.edu

The site offers links to conflict- and peace-related Internet sites.

Institute for Security Studies
www.iss.co.za

This site is South Africa's premier source for information related to African security studies.

International Crisis Group
www.crisisgroup.org

A leading independent, non-partisan research organization focused on the prevention and resolution of conflict.

PeaceNet
www.igc.org/peacenet

PeaceNet promotes dialogue and sharing of information to encourage appropriate dispute resolution, highlights the work of practitioners and organizations, and is a proving ground for ideas and proposals across the range of disciplines within the conflict resolution field.

Refugees International
www.refintl.org

Refugees International provides early warning in crises of mass exodus. It seeks to serve as the advocate of the unrepresented—the refugee. In recent years, Refugees International has moved from its initial focus on Indochinese refugees to global coverage, conducting almost 30 emergency missions in the last four years.

UNIT 4: Political Change in the Developing World

Center for Research on Inequality, Human Security, and Ethnicity
www.crise.ox.ac.uk

Information on multiethnic societies and the conditions that promote human security.

Latin American Network Information Center—LANIC
www.lanic.utexas.edu

According to Latin Trade, LANIC is "a good clearinghouse for Internet-accessible information on Latin America."

ReliefWeb
www.reliefweb.int/w/rwb.nsf

ReliefWeb is the UN's Department of Humanitarian Affairs clearinghouse for international humanitarian emergencies.

UNIT 5: Population, Resources, Environment, and Health

Earth Pledge Foundation
www.earthpledge.org

The Earth Pledge Foundation promotes the principles and practices of sustainable development—the need to balance the desire for economic growth with the necessity of environmental protection.

EnviroLink
http://envirolink.org

EnviroLink is committed to promoting a sustainable society by connecting individuals and organizations through the use of the World Wide Web.

Greenpeace
www.greenpeace.org

Greenpeace is an international NGO (nongovernmental organization) that is devoted to environmental protection.

Linkages on Environmental Issues and Development
www.iisd.ca/linkages

Linkages is a site provided by the International Institute for Sustainable Development. It is designed to be an electronic clearinghouse for information on past and upcoming international meetings related to both environmental issues and economic development in the developing world.

Population Action International
www.populationaction.org

According to its mission statement, Population Action International is dedicated to advancing policies and programs that slow population growth in order to enhance the quality of life for all people.

World Health Organization (WHO)
www.who.ch

The WHO's objective, according to its website, is the attainment by all peoples of the highest possible level of health. Health, as defined in the WHO constitution, is a state of complete physical, mental, and social well-being and not merely the absence of disease or infirmity.

The Worldwatch Institute
www.worldwatch.org

The Worldwatch Institute advocates environmental protection and sustainable development.

UNIT 6: Women and Development

WIDNET: Women in Development NETwork
www.focusintl.com/widnet.htm

This site provides a wealth of information about women in development, including the Beijing '95 Conference, WIDNET statistics, and women's studies.

Women Watch/Regional and Country Information
www.un.org/womenwatch

The UN Internet Gateway on the Advancement and Empowerment of Women provides a rich mine of information.

UNIT 1

Understanding the Developing World

Unit Selections

1. **The New Face of Development,** Carol Lancaster
2. **How Development Leads to Democracy: What We Know about Modernization,** Ronald Inglehart and Christian Welzel
3. **The New Population Bomb: The Four Megatrends That Will Change the World,** Jack A. Goldstone
4. **Best. Decade. Ever.,** Charles Kenny
5. **And Justice for All: Enforcing Human Rights for the World's Poor,** Gary Haugen and Victor Boutros
6. **The Case against the West: America and Europe in the Asian Century,** Kishore Mahbubani

Learning Outcomes

After reading this unit, you should be able to:

- Discuss the complexity and diversity of developing countries.

- Describe the changes in the emphasis of development over time.

- Outline the connection between democracy and development.

- Explain the ways that demographic and economic changes are likely to have an impact on the power and influence of both developing and industrialized countries.

- Discuss the reasons why living conditions for many in the developing world have improved.

- Explain why the poor often lack access to legal protection and how this has an impact on development.

- Analyze the argument that the West's global influence is declining.

Student Website

www.mhhe.com/cls

Internet References

Africa Index on Africa
www.afrika.no/index
African Studies WWW (U. Penn)
www.sas.upenn.edu/African_Studies/AS.html
United Nations Development Program
http://undp.org

The diversity of the countries that make up the developing world has always made it difficult to characterize and understand these countries and their role in international affairs. The task has become even more difficult as further economic, political, and social differentiation among developing countries has occurred. "Developing world" has always been a catchall term that lacks precision and explanatory power. It is used to describe societies that are desperately poor as well as those rich in resources. The term also refers to societies ranging from traditional to modern and from authoritarian to democratic. To complicate things even further, there is also debate over what actually constitutes development. For some, it is economic growth or progress toward democracy, while for others it involves greater empowerment and dignity. There are also differing views on why progress toward development has been uneven. The West tends to see the problem as stemming from poor governance, institutional weakness, and failure to embrace free-market principles. Critics from the developing world cite the legacy of colonialism and the nature of the international political and economic structures as the reasons for the lack of development. Not only are there differing views on the causes of lagging development, but there is also considerable debate on how best to tackle these issues. The Millennium Development Goals (MDGs) seek to eradicate extreme poverty and hunger and address issues of education, health, gender, and the environment. Progress in this effort so far has been uneven. This has contributed to the debate on the best way to achieve development. Critics maintain that the top-down ideology of development epitomized in the MDGs focuses attention at the macro level of development and impedes the emergence of local, grassroots solutions. The emphasis of development has shifted as well; it now extends beyond the traditional focus on poverty reduction to include issues like civil and political rights, human security, and environmental sustainability. Reflecting this broader emphasis is a growing list of actors that includes non-governmental organizations and philanthropic organizations involved in development efforts. In any case, lumping together the 120-plus nations that make up the developing world obscures the disparities in size, population, resources, forms of government, level of industrialization, distribution of wealth, ethnicity, and a host of other indicators that makes it difficult to categorize and generalize about this large, diverse group of countries.

Despite their diversity, most nations of the developing world share some characteristics. Many developing countries have large populations, with annual growth rates that often exceed 2 percent. Although there has been some improvement, poverty continues to be widespread in both rural and urban areas, with rural areas often containing the poorest of the poor. While the majority of the developing world's inhabitants continue to live in the countryside, there is a massive rural-to-urban migration under way, cities are growing rapidly, and some developing countries are approaching urbanization rates similar to those of

© Melba Photo Agency/Punchstock

industrialized countries. Wealth is unevenly distributed, making education, employment opportunities, and access to health care and legal protection luxuries that only a few enjoy. Corruption and mismanagement are also common. With very few exceptions, these nations share a colonial past that has affected them both politically and economically. A critical perspective from the developing world charges that the neocolonial structure of the international economy and the West's political, military, and cultural links with the developing world amount to continued domination.

The roots of the diverging views between the rich and the poor nations on development emerged shortly after the beginning of the independence era. The neocolonial viewpoint encouraged efforts to alter the international economic order during the 1970s. While the New International Economic Order (NIEO) succumbed to neo-liberalism in the 1980s, developing countries still frequently seek solidarity in their interactions with the West. The ability of developing countries to cooperate against the West threatens to diminish as the more successful countries begin to map out their development strategies.

Moreover, developing countries still view Western prescriptions for development skeptically and chafe under the Washington Consensus, which dictates the terms for the access to funds from international financial institutions and foreign aid. Furthermore, some critics suggest that Western development models result in inequitable development and give rise to cultural imperialism. In contrast to the developing world's criticism of the West, industrial countries continue to maintain the importance of institution-building and following the Western model that emphasizes a market-oriented approach to development. As the developing world comes to play a more prominent role in economic, security, and environmental issues, the West's ability to dictate the terms on which development occurs will diminish.

There is a clear difference of opinion between the industrialized countries and the developed world on issues ranging from economic development to governance. While the West has always had an advantage in determining the agenda for development, the influence of the industrialized countries may wane as demographic and economic changes bring about a shift in power. China's successful economic growth presents an alternative model of development that differs significantly from the one advanced by the West. Ultimately, the development process will be shaped primarily by the countries experiencing it. The industrialized countries can, however, continue to contribute to this process, although it may require re-evaluation of policies on trade and technology transfer, along with more emphasis on innovative and effective aid.

The New Face of Development

As the traditional development challenge of reducing poverty is increasingly met, a new challenge for the twenty-first century emerges: that of ensuring a livable, peaceful, and prosperous world.

CAROL LANCASTER

A number of trends in international development that were already emerging at the end of the last millennium—including the introduction of new actors and technologies, the increasing role of private investment, and the remarkable reduction in poverty in countries such as China and India—have become even more apparent as we approach the end of the current decade. These trends go to the core of what development is, how it is achieved, and who is involved in promoting it. In combination, they suggest that international development in the future will likely be very different from what it has been in the past.

The world first turned its attention to the challenge of international development in the decades immediately after World War II, as the cold war began and decolonization got under way. How, the international community asked itself, could growth be accelerated and poverty reduced in newly independent, less developed nations? Wealthy countries increasingly engaged in promoting economic progress in developing countries (primarily through foreign aid), and also established professional agencies, both bilateral and multilateral, to allocate and manage development assistance. The motives for the developed countries' actions, of course, were not purely altruistic. They sought to promote their national interests (such as the containment of Soviet influence); to ensure that decolonization proceeded smoothly; to preserve spheres of influence in former colonies; to expand their own exports; and to secure sources of raw materials abroad.

During the 40 years between 1960 and 2000, the international aid and development regime depended on rich countries' providing concessional economic assistance. They provided such assistance either directly to recipient governments, or indirectly, through international institutions. The aid was targeted toward agreed-upon projects like roads, government-provided agricultural services, primary education, and health care. Rich countries' trade and investment policies were understood to be an important part of the development equation, but they tended to be much less prominent than development aid itself, since trade and investment usually involved powerful domestic interests

within rich countries, a circumstance that constrained their use for development purposes.

Over the same period, the ways in which aid was used to promote development underwent an evolution. In the 1960s, the primary emphasis was on encouraging economic growth by providing funds for infrastructure and other projects meant to expand national production. In the 1970s, the main focus was direct action to alleviate poverty, with aid devoted to projects that would meet the basic needs of the poor in developing countries (including basic education, primary health care, and development of small farms). In the 1980s, the emphasis was on fostering growth through budgetary support for economic reforms and "structural adjustment."

The 1990s turned out to be a transition decade for development. With the end of the cold war and the breakup of the Soviet Union, many of the former communist bloc countries began a transition to free markets and democratic governance. Aid-giving governments turned their attention, and their aid, to furthering this transition. A wave of democratization washed over other parts of the world as well, including sub-Saharan Africa, and democracy became increasingly linked with development in the minds of many development practitioners. Democracy, it was now argued, was a key facilitator of development, and thus foreign aid was increasingly used to promote political development.

At the same time, rising concerns over transnational problems, such as environmental deterioration and infectious diseases (especially HIV/AIDS), expanded the development discourse. Conflict prevention and mitigation became part of the broadening framework of international development as civil conflicts erupted in a number of countries, especially in Africa, and it became obvious that economic progress required peaceful conditions. Finally, the development dialogue renewed its emphasis on poverty reduction, partly because of the "associational revolution"—an explosion of civil society organizations, in both rich and poor countries. Many of these organizations were interested in bettering the human condition.

The continued evolution of information technologies will empower the poor, probably in ways we cannot foresee.

And so, between the postwar period and the year 2000, much changed. In particular, the notion of development expanded to include a much wider range of issues. Yet the core focus remained poverty reduction, and the primary instrument for achieving it remained government-based economic assistance.

An Elastic Idea

Today, international development has become an even more elastic concept, as ideas about what constitutes development, how it is best achieved, and who should be part of the process continue to evolve. Starting from the early years of the international development era a half-century ago, development was thought of as a means to improve the material conditions of life. That is, public and private investment would promote growth, which in turn would eventually reduce or even eliminate poverty. This basic concept remains at the heart of development, but there have been some important additions.

"Human development" is now part of the equation, meaning that education, health, life expectancy, and other indicators of well-being are given greater attention. Political rights are also considered a key aspect of development, in part to ensure that the poor and excluded have a political voice. Some have incorporated "human security," as well, including security against economic deprivation and against physical violence, actual or threatened. "Sustainable development," or economic progress that does not affect the environment too harshly, is another element in the welter of ideas that currently define development. Some in recent years have defined development as the freedom to choose a fulfilling life.

This trend is likely to continue. Development will have at its core the reduction of severe poverty as long as that problem endures; but it will also continue to evolve to reflect changing global beliefs about the basic requirements of a decent human life and about how to meet those requirements.

Western economists have always believed that the driver of development is private investment—on the theory that because it increases productivity, production, growth, incomes, and jobs, it will ultimately eliminate poverty. Others, however, have taken the view that the market is unable to create equitable development and that state intervention is necessary to direct and hasten economic progress. This state-versus-market tension was evident during the cold war, with the socialist and capitalist models doing battle. The same philosophical difference is part of the debate between those who emphasize macroeconomic growth (for example, through structural adjustment) and those who emphasize direct interventions to reduce poverty. From an institutional perspective, this tension has been reflected in the often differing approaches of the World Bank and nongovernmental organizations (NGOs) toward promoting development.

In recent years, something of a consensus has emerged. It is now broadly accepted that private investment and well functioning markets are essential to sustaining long-term growth, and that the state cannot do it alone. But it is also generally recognized that without a well-functioning state, markets cannot produce sustained growth and reduce poverty.

When the era of international development began, the major actors were states, along with international institutions like the World Bank. Rich states shaped world trade policies and the special trade arrangements (for example, the Generalized System of Preferences) that affected the trade of poor countries. Not much foreign investment in poor countries was carried out, and even then it was sometimes unwelcome. Essentially, the governments of rich countries provided aid to the governments of poor countries. It was, in the language of telecommunications, a "one-to-one" world.

This has changed. Governments still play a major role but they are joined by civil society organizations, both in developed and developing countries. These groups deliver services, funded both by governments and through private giving, and advocate for more action to improve the lives of the poor. Growing numbers of corporations are investing large amounts in poor countries. They are also funding development activities on their own, often in public-private partnerships that also involve governments of rich countries and NGOs. These activities are part of corporate social responsibility programs, or even part of businesses' marketing strategies.

The scale of global philanthropy has grown over time, and the number of philanthropic organizations funding development activities has also grown. The Gates Foundation is the most prominent of the new foundations but there are many others. Countless so-called social entrepreneurs have come on the scene as well. These are individuals in developed and developing countries who create NGOs to tackle development problems—as well as "venture philanthropists" who create enterprises with double and triple bottom lines, enterprises that aim to do good while doing well. (An example would be an equity fund that combines investing with providing technical assistance to small enterprises that have few alternatives for capital or training.)

These actors have created a "many-to-many" development space that promises to grow in the coming decades. Also contributing to many-to-many development is the growing flow of remittances from immigrants working in rich countries to their families in poor countries. Indeed, the flow of remittances exceeds the global total of foreign aid by a considerable amount.

The Technology Revolution

All these trends have been facilitated by new information technologies. We are living, in fact, in the midst of several technology revolutions—information technology, biotechnology, nanotechnology, and materials technology. All of these hold the promise of radically changing not only our lives but also the lives of the poor in developing countries.

Information technology is already connecting many inhabitants of developing nations to the internet, as computers become increasingly affordable in poor countries. Cell phones are being used for banking, medical investigations, market updates, and obtaining all manner of otherwise out-of-reach information (as well as for political networking). The continued evolution of information technologies will empower the poor, probably in ways we cannot foresee. It has already provided new means for financial support to reach the poor through NGOs operating in developing countries, as wealthy people contribute through internet portals. This innovation cuts out middlemen and encourages direct giving. The internet has also facilitated the transfer of remittances from rich to poor countries. And it permits the poor to network as never before, an opportunity that will surely be seized even more in the future as cell phones come to resemble computers and become more affordable for all.

The biological revolution promises gains in medicine and agriculture, though these are not without controversy. The benefits have not yet reached a large enough scale to have a major impact on the lives of the poor, but this seems only a matter of time. Nanotechnology fosters miniaturization that, among other things, will make more powerful and cheaper cell phones possible. And advances in materials technology could lead to the production of commodities especially designed for difficult environments, an encouraging prospect for the poor living in those environments.

The Third World's End

During much of the past 40 years, people spoke and wrote about the "Third World"—the many developing countries that were an arena of competition between the United States and the Soviet Union. The Soviet Union, of course, is gone. But so is any semblance of shared poverty among the 150 or so countries comprising Asia, Africa, and Latin America. China has provided the most dramatic example of a poor country achieving rapid growth through manufacturing and exporting. In the past 25 years, China's development has lifted a quarter of a billion people out of poverty. This is a degree of economic progress, even with all of its accompanying problems, that is historically unprecedented. China is in fact now a major source of trade, aid, and investment for countries in Africa, Latin America, and elsewhere in Asia.

Economic progress in India—the other country with large-scale poverty and a population in excess of a billion—is increasingly evident as well. There, development is based to a large extent on the export of services. Poverty has fallen somewhat in Latin America, too, as many economies there diversify and grow. This means that the world's hard-core poverty and development problem is now concentrated in sub-Saharan Africa.

In many countries in sub-Saharan Africa, little economic progress has been achieved since independence. The difficulties standing in the way of the region's advancement include a difficult climate and the heavy disease load that comes with being located in the tropics. Also, many sub-Saharan nations are small and landlocked. Others are resource-rich but have found these resources to be a curse (Nigeria with its oil; Sierra Leone with its diamonds; the Democratic Republic of Congo [DRC] with its copper, cobalt, and other minerals).

One discerns a real opportunity—for the first time in history—to eradicate severe poverty worldwide.

Governments in these countries have long exhibited incompetence and corruption, and their resources have made it possible for them to provide little accountability to their citizens. Discontent has often led to violent conflict, which has been further stoked by competition for the control of resources. Civil conflicts in the DRC, Sierra Leone, and elsewhere have killed large numbers of people, created even more refugees and displaced persons, and destroyed national assets. Nigeria continues to teeter on the brink of a political abyss, the DRC continues to be plagued by internal war, and Somalia is still a collapsed state—with predictable effects on development.

But not all the news out of Africa is gloomy. Economic growth in India and China has increased demand, and thus prices, for the raw materials that many African countries export. Economic management in Africa, at least in most places, is better than it has been in several decades. Democratic development—or political openness, anyway—is greater than it has been during much of the period since independence.

Corruption, on the other hand, remains a major problem in many African countries. Additionally, China's extraordinary success in producing cheap manufactured goods appears to have left African countries—which lack the cheap, productive labor that China has—with few opportunities to attract the investment that might lead them into world manufacturing markets. In short, Africa is experiencing some new economic opportunities but also some new challenges.

Global Challenges

Beginning in the 1990s, major powers began to take greater note of global and transnational problems when they calculated their foreign policy and foreign aid policies. For much of that decade, the focus of this set of concerns, known as global public goods, was the environment—pollution, loss of plant and animal species, and loss of the ozone layer. While these transnational concerns (other than the ozone layer) have not abated, two more have joined them: infectious disease (above all HIV/AIDS) and climate change (which was not yet such a prominent concern in the 1990s).

The Bush administration has promised an extraordinary amount of aid to fight HIV/AIDS worldwide—$30 billion over the coming five years. Concern over this disease has risen in the United States as its global impact has become ever more evident, above all in Africa. The American religious right—long skeptical of the appropriateness and efficacy of foreign aid—has embraced fighting HIV/AIDS as the duty of Christians to aid those, especially women and children, who are suffering through no fault of their own. Although allocations of assistance so far have not kept pace with pledges, it is possible that fighting this disease will become the largest element in US foreign aid in the future.

But the next US president will also need to confront the issue of climate change, the reality and probable impact of which can no longer be ignored. That impact, incidentally, is expected to be particularly damaging to many of the world's poor countries. It seems likely, given that the governments of rich countries only have so much money to spend on development, that some development money will be shifted over the coming decades to fund activities intended to combat global warming—perhaps some of it as incentive payments to encourage governments to reduce greenhouse gas emissions.

Beyond climate change, two other trends may produce major development challenges in decades to come: the continuing growth of the world's population and the economic growth in China, India, and elsewhere. Global population is expected to continue expanding over the coming years—with nearly all of the growth taking place in the world's poor countries. Increased population will mean additional greenhouse gas emissions, as well as additional pressure on supplies of food, water, and energy. Economic growth, though it is hoped for and expected, will exacerbate those pressures, especially as demand for superior foods—meats instead of grains—increases. (A widely observed growth pattern is that as people's incomes rise they demand more protein in their diets in the form of meat and fish. But producing one pound of beef requires eight pounds of grain, and this increases pressures on food production systems.)

As for water, pressures on supply are already evident in Africa, the Middle East, northern China, and the Indian subcontinent. Where adequate water supplies cannot be procured, threats to human health and well-being emerge, along with threats to peace, stability, and income growth. Severe tensions over water already exist in the Middle East, and such situations are likely to become more common as population continues to increase. Meanwhile, a growing world population will use more fossil fuels, which will not only lead to progressively higher petroleum prices but will also exacerbate global warming.

These trends suggest that the combination of worldwide population growth and income growth needs to be managed carefully if the planet is to remain livable for our children and grandchildren. This challenge may prove the greatest of the twenty-first century.

An additional problem affecting development worldwide will be movements of people. The populations of many rich countries, and China as well, are growing at or below the replacement rate (with the United States, for reasons that are not entirely clear, a notable exception). The average age of people in these countries is rising, and this means that the dependency ratio is rising as well—each worker is in effect supporting more people. Unsurprisingly, the demand for additional workers is growing in these economies, and immigration from poorer countries to richer ones—from China to Japan, from North Africa and sub-Saharan Africa to Europe, and from Latin America to the United States—has exploded. Much of this immigration is illegal.

This movement of people has delivered benefits both to host countries and to countries of origin. It allows necessary work to be carried out in host countries while immigrants are able to send home remittances that finance consumption and investment there. This seems like a win-win arrangement—except that some citizens of the host countries experience the arrangement as a threat to their identities and ways of life. Even in the United

States, where national identity is based on the idea of republican democracy rather than ethnicity, religion, or language, tensions surrounding immigration are increasingly evident.

Such tensions, in the United States and also in Japan and Europe, threaten sometimes to erupt into social strife (as indeed has occurred in recent years in France). It is not clear what will happen as the irresistible force of immigration continues to collide with the immovable object of host-country resistance, but certainly if the remittance economy and access to labor are constrained, international development will suffer a setback.

After Poverty

Since the end of the cold war, because we no longer live in a bipolar world, we have lacked a certain clarity that allowed us to order our international relations and forge domestic consensus on urgent problems. Today's world has a single major power—and many complex problems that are beyond that power's ability to resolve. International development is one of them.

Nevertheless, within this complex and fluid world, one discerns a real opportunity—for the first time in history—to eradicate severe poverty worldwide. The resources and know-how are available and much progress has already been made, especially in China and, increasingly, in India. It will not be easy to "make poverty history" over the coming decades. A great deal needs to be achieved in education, investment, and governance, and in addition we must address the issue of migrations of people away from areas of the world with too few resources to sustain a minimally acceptable standard of living. The obstacles may be insuperable in some cases. But the opportunities are there.

Meanwhile, as the traditional development challenge of reducing poverty is increasingly met, a new development challenge for the twenty-first century emerges: that of ensuring a livable, peaceful, and prosperous world. This will require addressing the global problems that arise when growing populations and rising incomes collide with limited resources.

Critical Thinking

1. What trends account for the current perspective on international development?
2. How has the view of international development changed over the past five decades?
3. How would you define the terms human development, human security, and sustainable development?
4. What actors have increasingly come to play a role in development?
5. What global challenges are likely to affect development in the future?

CAROL LANCASTER is an associate professor at Georgetown University's Walsh School of Foreign Service and director of the university's Mortara Center for International Studies. A former deputy administrator of the US Agency for International Development, she is author of the forthcoming *George Bush's Foreign Aid: Revolution or Chaos?* (Center for Global Development, 2008).

From *Current History*, January 2008. Copyright © 2008 by Current History, Inc. Reprinted by permission.

How Development Leads to Democracy
What We Know about Modernization

Ronald Inglehart and Christian Welzel

In the last several years, a democratic boom has given way to a democratic recession. Between 1985 and 1995, scores of countries made the transition to democracy, bringing widespread euphoria about democracy's future. But more recently, democracy has retreated in Bangladesh, Nigeria, the Philippines, Russia, Thailand, and Venezuela, and the Bush administration's attempts to establish democracy in Afghanistan and Iraq seem to have left both countries in chaos. These developments, along with the growing power of China and Russia, have led many observers to argue that democracy has reached its high-water mark and is no longer on the rise.

That conclusion is mistaken. The underlying conditions of societies around the world point to a more complicated reality. The bad news is that it is unrealistic to assume that democratic institutions can be set up easily, almost anywhere, at any time. Although the outlook is never hopeless, democracy is most likely to emerge and survive when certain social and cultural conditions are in place. The Bush administration ignored this reality when it attempted to implant democracy in Iraq without first establishing internal security and overlooked cultural conditions that endangered the effort.

The good news, however, is that the conditions conducive to democracy can and do emerge—and the process of "modernization," according to abundant empirical evidence, advances them. Modernization is a syndrome of social changes linked to industrialization. Once set in motion, it tends to penetrate all aspects of life, bringing occupational specialization, urbanization, rising educational levels, rising life expectancy, and rapid economic growth. These create a self-reinforcing process that transforms social life and political institutions, bringing rising mass participation in politics and—in the long run—making the establishment of democratic political institutions increasingly likely. Today, we have a clearer idea than ever before of why and how this process of democratization happens.

The long-term trend toward democracy has always come in surges and declines. At the start of the twentieth century, only a handful of democracies existed, and even they fell short of being full democracies by today's standards. There was a major increase in the number of democracies following World War I, another surge following World War II, and a third surge at the end of the Cold War. Each of these surges was followed by a

decline, although the number of democracies never fell back to the original base line. By the start of the twenty-first century, about 90 states could be considered democratic.

Although many of these democracies are flawed, the overall trend is striking: in the long run, modernization brings democracy. This means that the economic resurgence of China and Russia has a positive aspect: underlying changes are occurring that make the emergence of increasingly liberal and democratic political systems likely in the coming years. It also means that there is no reason to panic about the fact that democracy currently appears to be on the defensive. The dynamics of modernization and democratization are becoming increasingly clear, and it is likely that they will continue to function.

The Great Debate

The concept of modernization has a long history. During the nineteenth and twentieth centuries, a Marxist theory of modernization proclaimed that the abolition of private property would put an end to exploitation, inequality, and conflict. A competing capitalist version held that economic development would lead to rising living standards and democracy. These two visions of modernization competed fiercely throughout much of the Cold War. By the 1970s, however, communism began to stagnate, and neither economic development nor democratization was apparent in many poor countries. Neither version of utopia seemed to be unfolding, and critics pronounced modernization theory dead.

Since the end of the Cold War, however, the concept of modernization has taken on new life, and a new version of modernization theory has emerged, with clear implications for our understanding of where global economic development is likely to lead. Stripped of the oversimplifications of its early versions, the new concept of modernization sheds light on ongoing cultural changes, such as the rise of gender equality the recent wave of democratization, and the democratic peace theory.

For most of human history, technological progress was extremely slow and new developments in food production were offset by population increases—trapping agrarian economies in a steady-state equilibrium with no growth in living standards. History was seen as either cyclic or in long-term decline from a past golden age. The situation began to change with the Industrial Revolution and the advent of sustained economic growth—which led to both the capitalist and the communist visions of modernization. Although the ideologies competed fiercely, they were both committed to economic growth and social progress and brought mass participation in politics. And each side believed that the developing nations of the Third World would follow its path to modernization.

At the height of the Cold War, a version of modernization theory emerged in the United States that portrayed underdevelopment as a direct consequence of a country's psychological and cultural traits. Underdevelopment was said to reflect irrational traditional religious and communal values that discouraged achievement. The rich Western democracies, the theory went, could instill modern values and bring progress to "backward" nations through economic, cultural, and military assistance. By the 1970s, however, it had become clear that assistance had not brought much progress toward prosperity or democracy—eroding confidence in this version of modernization theory, which was increasingly criticized as ethnocentric and patronizing. It came under heavy criticism from "dependency theorists," who argued that trade with rich countries exploits poor ones, locking them into positions of structural dependence. The elites in developing countries welcomed such thinking, since it implied that poverty had nothing to do with internal problems or the corruption of local leaders; it was the fault of global capitalism. By the 1980s, dependency theory was in vogue. Third World nations, the thinking went, could escape from global exploitation only by withdrawing from global markets and adopting import-substitution policies.

More recently, it has become apparent that import-substitution strategies have failed: the countries least involved in global trade, such as Cuba, Myanmar (also called Burma), and North Korea, have not been the most successful—they have actually grown the least. Export-oriented strategies have been far more effective in promoting sustained economic growth and, eventually, democratization. The pendulum, accordingly, has swung back, and a new version of modernization theory has gained credibility. The rapid economic development of East Asia, and the subsequent democratization of South Korea and Taiwan, seem to confirm its basic claims: producing for the world market enables economic growth; investing the returns in human capital and upgrading the work force to produce high-tech goods brings higher returns and enlarges the educated middle class; once the middle class becomes large and articulate enough, it presses for liberal democracy—the most effective political system for advanced industrial societies. Nevertheless, even today, if one mentions modernization at a conference on economic development, one is likely to hear a reiteration of dependency theory's critique of the "backward nations" version of modernization theory, as if that were all there is to modernization theory—and as if no new evidence had emerged since the 1970s.

The New Modernization

In retrospect, it is obvious that the early versions of modernization theory were wrong on several points. Today, virtually nobody expects a revolution of the proletariat that will abolish private property, ushering in a new era free from exploitation and conflict. Nor does anyone expect that industrialization will automatically lead to democratic institutions; communism and fascism also emerged from industrialization. Nonetheless, a massive body of evidence suggests that modernization theory's central premise was correct: economic development does tend to bring about important, roughly predictable changes in society, culture, and politics. But the earlier versions of modernization theory need to be corrected in several respects.

First, modernization is not linear. It does not move indefinitely in the same direction; instead, the process reaches inflection points. Empirical evidence indicates that each phase of modernization is associated with distinctive changes in people's worldviews. Industrialization leads to one major process of change, resulting in bureaucratization, hierarchy, centralization of authority, secularization, and a shift from traditional to secular-rational values. The rise of postindustrial society brings another set of cultural changes that move in a different direction: instead of bureaucratization and centralization, the new trend is toward an increasing emphasis on individual autonomy and self-expression values, which lead to a growing emancipation from authority.

Thus, other things being equal, high levels of economic development tend to make people more tolerant and trusting, bringing more emphasis on self-expression and more participation in decision-making. This process is not deterministic, and any forecasts can only be probabilistic, since economic factors are not the only influence; a given country's leaders and nation-specific events also shape what happens. Moreover, modernization is not irreversible. Severe economic collapse can reverse it, as happened during the Great Depression in Germany, Italy, Japan, and Spain and during the 1990s in most of the Soviet successor states. Similarly, if the current economic crisis becomes a twenty-first-century Great Depression, the world could face a new struggle against renewed xenophobia and authoritarianism.

Second, social and cultural change is path dependent: history matters. Although economic development tends to bring predictable changes in people's worldviews, a society's heritage—whether shaped by Protestantism, Catholicism, Islam, Confucianism, or communism—leaves a lasting imprint on its worldview. A society's value system reflects an interaction between the driving forces of modernization and the persisting influence of tradition. Although the classic modernization theorists in both the East and the West thought that religion and ethnic traditions would die out, they have proved to be highly resilient. Although the publics of industrializing societies are becoming richer and more educated, that is hardly creating a uniform global culture. Cultural heritages are remarkably enduring.

Third, modernization is not westernization, contrary to the earlier, ethnocentric version of the theory. The process of industrialization began in the West, but during the past few decades, East Asia has had the world's highest economic growth rates, and Japan leads the world in life expectancy and some other aspects of modernization. The United States is not the model for global cultural change, and industrializing societies in general are not becoming like the United States, as a popular version of modernization theory assumes. In fact, American society retains more traditional values than do most other high-income societies.

Fourth, modernization does not automatically lead to democracy. Rather, it, in the long run, brings social and cultural changes that make democratization increasingly probable. Simply attaining a high level of per capita GDP does not produce democracy: if it did, Kuwait and the United Arab Emirates would have become model democracies. (These countries have not gone through the modernization process described above.) But the emergence of postindustrial society brings certain social and cultural changes that are specifically conducive to democratization. Knowledge societies cannot function effectively without highly educated publics that have become increasingly accustomed to thinking for themselves. Furthermore, rising levels of economic security bring a growing emphasis on a syndrome of self-expression values—one that gives high priority to free choice and motivates political action. Beyond a certain point, accordingly, it becomes difficult to avoid democratization, because repressing mass demands for more open societies becomes increasingly costly and detrimental to economic effectiveness. Thus, in its advanced stages, modernization brings social and cultural changes that make the emergence and flourishing of democratic institutions increasingly likely.

The core idea of modernization theory is that economic and technological development bring a coherent set of social, cultural, and political changes. A large body of empirical evidence supports this idea. Economic development is, indeed, strongly linked to pervasive shifts in people's beliefs and motivations, and these shifts in turn change the role of religion, job motivations, human fertility rates, gender roles, and sexual norms. And they also bring growing mass demands for democratic institutions and for more responsive behavior on the part of elites. These changes together make democracy increasingly likely to emerge, while also making war less acceptable to publics.

Evaluating Values

New sources of empirical evidence provide valuable insights into how modernization changes worldviews and motivations. One important source is global surveys of mass values and attitudes. Between 1981 and 2007, the World Values Survey and the European Values Study carried out five waves of representative national surveys in scores of countries, covering almost 90 percent of the world's population. (For the data from the surveys, visit www.worldvaluessurvey.org.) The results show large cross-national differences in what people believe and value. In some countries, 95 percent of the people surveyed said that God was very important in their lives; in others, only 3 percent did. In some societies, 90 percent of the people surveyed said they believed that men have more of a right to a job than women do; in others, only 8 percent said they thought so. These cross-national differences are robust and enduring, and they are closely correlated with a society's level of economic development: people in low-income societies are much likelier to emphasize religion and traditional gender roles than are people in rich countries.

These values surveys demonstrate that the worldviews of people living in rich societies differ systematically from those of people living in low-income societies across a wide range of political, social, and religious norms. The differences run along two basic dimensions: traditional versus secular-rational values and survival versus self-expression values. (Each dimension reflects responses to scores of questions asked as part of the values surveys.)

The shift from traditional to secular-rational values is linked to the shift from agrarian to industrial societies. Traditional societies emphasize religion, respect for and obedience to authority, and national pride. These characteristics change as societies become more secular and rational. The shift from survival to self-expression values is linked to the rise of postindustrial societies. It reflects a cultural shift that occurs when younger generations emerge that have grown up taking survival for granted. Survival values give top priority to economic and physical security and conformist social norms. Self-expression values give high priority to freedom of expression, participation in decision-making, political activism, environmental protection, gender equality, and tolerance of ethnic minorities, foreigners, and gays and lesbians. A growing emphasis on these latter values engenders a culture of trust and tolerance in which people cherish individual freedom and self-expression and have activist political orientations. These attributes are crucial to democracy—and thus explain how economic growth, which takes societies from agrarian to industrial and then from industrial to postindustrial, leads to democratization. The unprecedented economic growth of the past 50 years has meant that an increasing share of the world's population has grown up taking survival for granted. Time-series data from the values surveys indicate that mass priorities have shifted from an overwhelming emphasis on economic and physical security to an emphasis on subjective well-being, self-expression, participation in decision-making, and a relatively trusting and tolerant outlook.

Both dimensions are closely linked to economic development: the value systems of high-income countries differ dramatically from those of low-income countries. Every nation that the World Bank defines as having a high income ranks relatively high on both dimensions—with a strong emphasis on both secular-rational and self-expression values. All the low-income and lower-middle-income countries rank relatively low on both dimensions. The upper-middle-income countries fall somewhere in between. To a remarkable degree, the values and beliefs of a given society reflect its level of economic developments—just as modernization theory predicts.

This strong connection between a society's value system and its per capita GDP suggests that economic development tends to produce roughly predictable changes in a society's beliefs and values, and time-series evidence supports this hypothesis. When one compares the positions of given countries in successive waves of the values surveys, one finds that almost all the countries that experienced rising per capita GDPs also experienced predictable shifts in their values.

The values survey evidence also shows, however, that cultural change is path dependent; a society's cultural heritage also shapes where it falls on the global cultural map. This map shows distinctive clusters of countries: Protestant Europe, Catholic Europe, ex-communist Europe, the English-speaking countries, Latin America, South Asia, the Islamic world, and Africa. The values emphasized by different societies fall into a remarkably coherent pattern that reflects both those societies' economic development and their religious and colonial heritage. Still, even if a society's cultural heritage continues to shape its prevailing values, economic development brings changes that have important consequences. Over time, it reshapes beliefs and values of all kinds—and it brings a growing mass demand for democratic institutions and for more responsive elite behavior. And over the quarter century covered by the values surveys, the people of most countries placed increasing emphasis on self-expression values. This cultural shift makes democracy increasingly likely to emerge where it does not yet exist and increasingly likely to become more effective and more direct where it does.

Development and Democracy

Fifty years ago, the sociologist Seymour Martin Lipset pointed out that rich countries are much more likely than poor countries to be democracies. Although this claim was contested for many years, it has held up against repeated tests. The causal direction of the relationship has also been questioned: Are rich countries more likely to be democratic because democracy makes countries rich, or is development conducive to democracy? Today, it seems clear that the causality runs mainly from economic development to democratization. During early industrialization, authoritarian states are just as likely to attain high rates of growth as are democracies. But beyond a certain level of economic development, democracy becomes increasingly likely to emerge and survive. Thus, among the scores of countries that democratized around 1990, most were middle-income countries: almost all the high-income countries already were democracies, and few low-income countries made the transition. Moreover, among the countries that democratized between 1970 and 1990, democracy has survived in every country that made the transition when it was at the economic level of Argentina today or higher; among the countries that made the transition when they were below this level, democracy had an average life expectancy of only eight years.

The strong correlation between development and democracy reflects the fact that economic development is conducive to democracy. The question of why, exactly, development leads to democracy has been debated intensely, but the answer is beginning to emerge. It does not result from some disembodied force that causes democratic institutions to emerge automatically when a country attains a certain level of GDP. Rather, economic development brings social and political changes only when it changes people's behavior. Consequently, economic development is conducive to democracy to the extent that it, first, creates a large, educated, and articulate middle class of people who are accustomed to thinking for themselves and, second, transforms people's values and motivations.

Today, it is more possible than ever before to measure what the key changes are and how far they have progressed in given countries. Multivariate analysis of the data from the values surveys makes it possible to sort out the relative impact of economic, social, and cultural changes, and the results point to the conclusion that economic development is conducive to democracy insofar as it brings specific structural changes (particularly the rise of a knowledge sector) and certain cultural changes (particularly the rise of self-expression values). Wars, depressions, institutional changes, elite decisions, and specific leaders also influence what happens, but structural and cultural change are major factors in the emergence and survival of democracy.

Modernization brings rising educational levels, moving the work force into occupations that require independent thinking and making people more articulate and better equipped to intervene in politics. As knowledge societies emerge, people become accustomed to using their own initiative and judgment on the job and are also increasingly likely to question rigid and hierarchical authority.

Modernization also makes people economically more secure, and self-expression values become increasingly widespread when a large share of the population grows up taking survival for granted. The desire for freedom and autonomy are universal aspirations. They may be subordinated to the need for subsistence and order when survival is precarious, but they take increasingly high priority as survival becomes more secure. The basic motivation for democracy—the human desire for free choice—starts to play an increasingly important role. People begin to place a growing emphasis on free choice in politics and begin to demand civil and political liberties and democratic institutions.

Effective Democracy

During the explosion of democracy that took place between 1985 and 1995, electoral democracy spread rapidly throughout the world. Strategic elite agreements played an important role in this process, facilitated by an international environment in which the end of the Cold War opened the way for democratization. Initially, there was a tendency to view any regime that held free and fair elections as a democracy. But many of the new democracies suffered from massive corruption and failed to apply the rule of law, which is what makes democracy effective. A growing number of observers today thus emphasize the inadequacy of "electoral demomcy," "hybrid democracy," "authoritarian democracy," and other forms of sham democracy in which mass preferences are something that political elites can largely ignore and in which they do not decisively influence government decisions. It is important, accordingly, to distinguish between effective and ineffective democracies.

The essence of democracy is that it empowers ordinary citizens. Whether a democracy is effective or not is based on not only the extent to which civil and political rights exist on paper but also the degree to which officials actually respect these rights. The first of these two components—the existence of rights on paper—is measured by Freedom House's annual rankings: if a country holds free elections, Freedom House tends to rate it as "free," giving it a score at or near the top of its scale. Thus, the new democracies of eastern Europe receive scores as high as those of the established democracies of western Europe, although in-depth analyses show that widespread corruption makes these new democracies far less effective in responding to their citizens' choices. Fortunately, the World Bank's governance scores measure the extent to which a country's democratic institutions are actually effective. Consequently, a rough index of effective democracy can be obtained by multiplying these two scores: formal democracy, as measured by Freedom House, and elite and institutional integrity, as measured by the World Bank.

Effective democracy is a considerably more demanding standard than electoral democracy. One can establish electoral democracy almost anywhere, but it will probably not last long if it does not transfer power from the elites to the people. Effective democracy is most likely to exist alongside a relatively developed infrastructure that includes not only economic resources but also widespread participatory habits and an emphasis on autonomy. Accordingly, it is closely linked to the degree to which a given public emphasizes self-expression values. Indeed, the correlation between a society's values and the nature of the country's political institutions is remarkably strong.

Virtually all the stable democracies show strong self-expression values. Most Latin American countries are underachievers, showing lower levels of effective democracy than their publics' values would predict. This suggests that these societies could support higher levels of democracy if the rule of law were strengthened there. Iran is also an underachiever—a theocratic regime that allows a much lower level of democracy than that to which its people aspire. Surprising as it may seem to those who focus only on elite-level politics, the Iranian public shows relatively strong support for democracy. Conversely, Cyprus, Estonia, Hungary, Poland, Latvia, and Lithuania are overachievers, showing higher levels of democracy than their publics' values would predict—perhaps reflecting the incentives to democratize provided by membership in the European Union.

But do self-expression values lead to democracy, or does democracy cause self-expression values to emerge? The evidence indicates that these values lead to democracy. (For the full evidence for this claim, see our book *Modernization, Cultural Change, and Democracy*.) Democratic institutions do not need to be in place for self-expression values to emerge. Time-series evidence from the values surveys indicates that in the years preceding the wave of democratization in the late 1980s and early 1990s, self-expression values had already emerged through a process of an intergenerational change in values—not only in the Western democracies but also within many authoritarian societies. By 1990, the publics of East Germany and Czechoslovakia—which had been living under two of the most authoritarian regimes in the world—had developed high levels of self-expression values. The crucial factor was not the political system but the fact that these countries were among the most economically advanced countries in the communist world, with high levels of education and advanced social welfare systems. Thus, when the Soviet leader Mikhail Gorbachev renounced the Brezhnev Doctrine, removing the threat of Soviet military intervention, they moved swiftly toward democracy.

In recent decades, self-expression values have been spreading and getting stronger, making people more likely to directly intervene in politics. (Indeed, unprecedented numbers of people took part in the demonstrations that helped bring about the most recent wave of democratization.) Does this mean that authoritarian systems will inevitably crumble? No. A rising emphasis on self-expression values tends to erode the legitimacy of authoritarian systems, but as long as determined authoritarian elites control the army and the secret police, they can repress pro-democratic forces. Still, even repressive regimes find it costly to check these tendencies, for doing so tends to block the emergence of effective knowledge sectors.

Modern Strategy

This new understanding of modernization has broad implications for international relations. For one thing, it helps explain why advanced democracies do not fight one another. Recent research provides strong empirical support for the claim that they do not, which goes back to Adam Smith and Immanuel Kant. Since they emerged in the early nineteenth century, liberal democracies have fought a number of wars, but almost never against one another. This new version of modernization theory indicates that the democratic peace phenomenon is due more to cultural changes linked to modernization than to democracy per se.

In earlier periods of history, democracies fought one another frequently. But the prevailing norms among them have evolved over time, as is illustrated by the abolition of slavery, the gradual expansion of the franchise, and the movement toward gender equality in virtually all modern societies. Another cultural change that has occurred in modern societies—which tend to be democracies—is that war has become progressively less acceptable and people have become more likely to express this preference and try to affect policy accordingly. Evidence from the World Values Survey indicates that the publics of high-income countries have much lower levels of xenophobia than do the publics of low-income countries, and they are much less willing to fight for their country than are the publics of low-income countries. Moreover, economically developed democracies behave far more peacefully toward one another than do poor democracies, and economically developed democracies are far less prone to civil war than are poor democracies.

Modernization theory has both cautionary and encouraging implications for U.S. foreign policy. Iraq, of course, provides a cautionary lesson. Contrary to the appealing view that democracy can be readily established almost anywhere, modernization theory holds that democracy is much more likely to flourish under certain conditions than others. A number of factors made it unrealistic to expect that democracy would be easy to establish in Iraq, including deep ethnic cleavages that had been exacerbated by Saddam Hussein's regime. And after Saddam's defeat, allowing physical security to deteriorate was a particularly serious mistake. Interpersonal trust and tolerance flourish when people feel secure. Democracy is unlikely to survive in a society torn by distrust and intolerance, and Iraq currently manifests the highest level of xenophobia of any society for which data are available. A good indicator of xenophobia is the extent to which people say they would not want to have foreigners as neighbors. Across 80 countries, the median percentage of those surveyed who said this was 15 percent. Among Iraqi Kurds, 51 percent of those polled said they would prefer not to have foreigners as neighbors. Among Iraqi Arabs, 90 percent of those polled said they would not want foreigners as neighbors. In keeping with these conditions, Iraq (along with Pakistan and Zimbabwe) shows very low levels of both self-expression values and effective democracy.

Modernization theory also has positive implications for U.S. foreign policy. Supported by a large body of evidence, it points to the conclusion that economic development is a basic driver of democratic change—meaning that Washington should do what it can to encourage development. If it wants to bring democratic change to Cuba, for example, isolating it is counterproductive. The United States should lift the embargo, promote economic development, and foster social engagement with, and other connections to, the world. Nothing is certain, but empirical evidence suggests that a growing sense of security and a growing emphasis on self-expression values there would undermine the authoritarian regime.

Similarly, although many observers have been alarmed by the economic resurgence of China, this growth has positive implications for the long term. Beneath China's seemingly monolithic political structure, the social infrastructure of democratization is emerging, and it has progressed further than most observers realize. China is now approaching the level of mass emphasis on self-expression values at which Chile, Poland, South Korea, and Taiwan made their transitions to democracy. And, surprising as it may seem to observers who focus only on elite-level politics, Iran is also near this threshold. As long as the Chinese Communist Party and Iran's theocratic leaders control their countries' military and security forces, democratic institutions will not emerge at the national level. But growing mass pressures for liberalization are beginning to appear, and repressing them will bring growing costs in terms of economic inefficiency and low public morale. On the whole, increasing prosperity for China and Iran is in the United States' national interest.

More broadly, modernization theory implies that the United States should welcome and encourage economic development around the world. Although economic development requires difficult adjustments, its long-term effects encourage the emergence of more tolerant, less xenophobic, and ultimately more democratic societies.

Critical Thinking

1. What is modernization? How does this process make democratization more likely?
2. How has modernization theory evolved over time?
3. What changes in emphasis need to be made to ensure modernization's continued relevance?
4. What values are important to democracy?
5. What is the connection between economic development and democracy?

RONALD INGLEHART is Professor of Political Science at the University of Michigan and Director of the World Values Survey. **CHRISTIAN WELZEL** is Professor of Political Science at Jacobs University Bremen, in Germany. They are the co-authors of *Modernization, Cultural Change, and Democracy*.

The New Population Bomb
The Four Megatrends That Will Change the World

JACK A. GOLDSTONE

Forty-two years ago, the biologist Paul Ehrlich warned in *The Population Bomb* that mass starvation would strike in the 1970s and 1980s, with the world's population growth outpacing the production of food and other critical resources. Thanks to innovations and efforts such as the "green revolution" in farming and the widespread adoption of family planning, Ehrlich's worst fears did not come to pass. In fact, since the 1970s, global economic output has increased and fertility has fallen dramatically, especially in developing countries.

The United Nations Population Division now projects that global population growth will nearly halt by 2050. By that date, the world's population will have stabilized at 9.15 billion people, according to the "medium growth" variant of the UN's authoritative population database World Population Prospects: The 2008 Revision. (Today's global population is 6.83 billion.) Barring a cataclysmic climate crisis or a complete failure to recover from the current economic malaise, global economic output is expected to increase by two to three percent per year, meaning that global income will increase far more than population over the next four decades.

But twenty-first-century international security will depend less on how many people inhabit the world than on how the global population is composed and distributed: where populations are declining and where they are growing, which countries are relatively older and which are more youthful, and how demographics will influence population movements across regions.

These elements are not well recognized or widely understood. A recent article in *The Economist,* for example, cheered the decline in global fertility without noting other vital demographic developments. Indeed, the same UN data cited by *The Economist* reveal four historic shifts that will fundamentally alter the world's population over the next four decades: the relative demographic weight of the world's developed countries will drop by nearly 25 percent, shifting economic power to the developing nations; the developed countries' labor forces will substantially age and decline, constraining economic growth in the developed world and raising the demand for immigrant workers; most of the world's expected population growth will increasingly be concentrated in today's poorest, youngest, and most heavily Muslim countries, which have a dangerous lack of quality education, capital, and employment opportunities; and, for the first time in history, most of the world's population will become urbanized, with the largest urban centers being in the world's poorest countries, where policing, sanitation, and health care are often scarce.

Taken together, these trends will pose challenges every bit as alarming as those noted by Ehrlich. Coping with them will require nothing less than a major reconsideration of the world's basic global governance structures.

Europe's Reversal of Fortunes

At the beginning of the eighteenth century, approximately 20 percent of the world's inhabitants lived in Europe (including Russia). Then, with the Industrial Revolution, Europe's population boomed, and streams of European emigrants set off for the Americas. By the eve of World War I, Europe's population had more than quadrupled. In 1913, Europe had more people than China, and the proportion of the world's population living in Europe and the former European colonies of North America had risen to over 33 percent.

But this trend reversed after World War I, as basic health care and sanitation began to spread to poorer countries. In Asia, Africa, and Latin America, people began to live longer, and birthrates remained high or fell only slowly. By 2003, the combined populations of Europe, the United States, and Canada accounted for just 17 percent of the global population. In 2050, this figure is expected to be just 12 percent—far less than it was in 1700. (These projections, moreover, might even understate the reality because they reflect the "medium growth" projection of the UN forecasts, which assumes that the fertility rates of developing countries will decline while those of developed countries will increase. In fact, many developed countries show no evidence of increasing fertility rates.)

The West's relative decline is even more dramatic if one also considers changes in income. The Industrial Revolution made Europeans not only more numerous than they had been but also considerably richer per capita than others worldwide. According to the economic historian Angus Maddison, Europe, the United States, and Canada together produced about 32 percent of the world's GDP at the beginning of the nineteenth century. By 1950, that proportion had increased to a remarkable 68 percent of the world's total output (adjusted to reflect purchasing power parity).

This trend, too, is headed for a sharp reversal. The proportion of global GDP produced by Europe, the United States, and Canada fell from 68 percent in 1950 to 47 percent in 2003 and will decline even more steeply in the future. If the growth rate of per capita income (again, adjusted for purchasing power parity) between 2003 and 2050 remains as it was between 1973 and 2003—averaging 1.68 percent annually in Europe, the United States, and Canada and 2.47 percent annually in the rest of the world—then the combined GDP of Europe, the United States, and Canada will roughly double by 2050, whereas the GDP of the rest of the world will grow by a factor of five. The portion of global GDP produced by Europe, the United States, and Canada in 2050 will then be less than 30 percent—smaller than it was in 1820.

These figures also imply that an overwhelming proportion of the world's GDP growth between 2003 and 2050—nearly 80 percent—will occur outside of Europe, the United States, and Canada. By the middle of this century, the global middle class—those capable of purchasing durable consumer products, such as cars, appliances, and electronics—will increasingly be found in what is now considered the developing world. The World Bank has predicted that by 2030 the number of middle-class people in the developing world will be 1.2 billion—a rise of 200 percent since 2005. This means that the developing world's middle class alone will be larger than the total populations of Europe, Japan, and the United States combined. From now on, therefore, the main driver of global economic expansion will be the economic growth of newly industrialized countries, such as Brazil, China, India, Indonesia, Mexico, and Turkey.

Aging Pains

Part of the reason developed countries will be less economically dynamic in the coming decades is that their populations will become substantially older. The European countries, Canada, the United States, Japan, South Korea, and even China are aging at unprecedented rates. Today, the proportion of people aged 60 or older in China and South Korea is 12–15 percent. It is 15–22 percent in the European Union, Canada, and the United States and 30 percent in Japan. With baby boomers aging and life expectancy increasing, these numbers will increase dramatically. In 2050, approximately 30 percent of Americans, Canadians, Chinese, and Europeans will be over 60, as will more than 40 percent of Japanese and South Koreans.

Over the next decades, therefore, these countries will have increasingly large proportions of retirees and increasingly small proportions of workers. As workers born during the baby boom of 1945–65 are retiring, they are not being replaced by a new cohort of citizens of prime working age (15–59 years old). Industrialized countries are experiencing a drop in their working-age populations that is even more severe than the overall slowdown in their population growth. South Korea represents the most extreme example. Even as its total population

is projected to decline by almost 9 percent by 2050 (from 48.3 million to 44.1 million), the population of working-age South Koreans is expected to drop by 36 percent (from 32.9 million to 21.1 million), and the number of South Koreans aged 60 and older will increase by almost 150 percent (from 7.3 million to 18 million). By 2050, in other words, the entire working-age population will barely exceed the 60-and-older population. Although South Korea's case is extreme, it represents an increasingly common fate for developed countries. Europe is expected to lose 24 percent of its prime working-age population (about 120 million workers) by 2050, and its 60-and-older population is expected to increase by 47 percent. In the United States, where higher fertility and more immigration are expected than in Europe, the working-age population will grow by 15 percent over the next four decades—a steep decline from its growth of 62 percent between 1950 and 2010. And by 2050, the United States' 60-and-older population is expected to double.

All this will have a dramatic impact on economic growth, health care, and military strength in the developed world. The forces that fueled economic growth in industrialized countries during the second half of the twentieth century—increased productivity due to better education, the movement of women into the labor force, and innovations in technology—will all likely weaken in the coming decades. College enrollment boomed after World War II, a trend that is not likely to recur in the twenty-first century; the extensive movement of women into the labor force also was a one-time social change; and the technological change of the time resulted from innovators who created new products and leading-edge consumers who were willing to try them out—two groups that are thinning out as the industrialized world's population ages.

Overall economic growth will also be hampered by a decline in the number of new consumers and new households. When developed countries' labor forces were growing by 0.5–1.0 percent per year, as they did until 2005, even annual increases in real output per worker of just 1.7 percent meant that annual economic growth totaled 2.2–2.7 percent per year. But with the labor forces of many developed countries (such as Germany, Hungary, Japan, Russia, and the Baltic states) now shrinking by 0.2 percent per year and those of other countries (including Austria, the Czech Republic, Denmark, Greece, and Italy) growing by less than 0.2 percent per year, the same 1.7 percent increase in real output per worker yields only 1.5–1.9 percent annual overall growth. Moreover, developed countries will be lucky to keep productivity growth at even that level; in many developed countries, productivity is more likely to decline as the population ages.

A further strain on industrialized economies will be rising medical costs: as populations age, they will demand more health care for longer periods of time. Public pension schemes for aging populations are already being reformed in various industrialized countries—often prompting heated debate. In theory, at least, pensions might be kept solvent by increasing the retirement age, raising taxes modestly, and phasing out benefits for the wealthy. Regardless, the number of 80- and 90-year-olds—who are unlikely to work and highly likely to require nursing-home and other expensive care—will rise dramatically. And even if 60- and 70-year-olds remain active and employed, they will require procedures and medications—hip replacements, kidney transplants, blood-pressure treatments—to sustain their health in old age.

All this means that just as aging developed countries will have proportionally fewer workers, innovators, and consumerist young households, a large portion of those countries' remaining economic growth will have to be diverted to pay for the medical bills and pensions of their growing elderly populations. Basic services, meanwhile, will be increasingly costly because fewer young workers will be available for strenuous and labor-intensive jobs. Unfortunately, policymakers seldom reckon with these potentially disruptive effects of otherwise welcome developments, such as higher life expectancy.

Youth and Islam in the Developing World

Even as the industrialized countries of Europe, North America, and Northeast Asia will experience unprecedented aging this century, fast-growing countries in Africa, Latin America, the Middle East, and Southeast Asia will have exceptionally youthful populations. Today, roughly nine out of ten children under the age of 15 live in developing countries. And these are the countries that will continue to have the world's highest birthrates. Indeed, over 70 percent of the world's population growth between now and 2050 will occur in 24 countries, all of which are classified by the World Bank as low income or lower-middle income, with an average per capita income of under $3,855 in 2008.

Many developing countries have few ways of providing employment to their young, fast-growing populations. Would-be laborers, therefore, will be increasingly attracted to the labor markets of the aging developed countries of Europe, North America, and Northeast Asia. Youthful immigrants from nearby regions with high unemployment—Central America, North Africa, and Southeast Asia, for example—will be drawn to those vital entry-level and manual-labor jobs that sustain advanced economies: janitors, nursing-home aides, bus drivers, plumbers, security guards, farm workers, and the like. Current levels of immigration from developing to developed countries are paltry compared to those that the forces of supply and demand might soon create across the world.

These forces will act strongly on the Muslim world, where many economically weak countries will continue to experience dramatic population growth in the decades ahead. In 1950, Bangladesh, Egypt, Indonesia, Nigeria, Pakistan, and Turkey had a combined population of 242 million. By 2009, those six countries were the world's most populous Muslim-majority countries and had a combined population of 886 million. Their populations are continuing to grow and indeed are expected to increase by 475 million between now and 2050—during which time, by comparison, the six most populous developed countries are projected to gain only 44 million inhabitants. Worldwide, of the 48 fastest-growing countries today—those with annual population growth of two percent or more—28 are majority Muslim or have Muslim minorities of 33 percent or more.

It is therefore imperative to improve relations between Muslim and Western societies. This will be difficult given that many Muslims live in poor communities vulnerable to radical appeals and many see the West as antagonistic and militaristic. In the 2009 Pew Global Attitudes Project survey, for example, whereas 69 percent of those Indonesians and Nigerians surveyed reported viewing the United States favorably, just 18 percent of those polled in Egypt, Jordan, Pakistan, and Turkey (all U.S. allies) did. And in 2006, when the Pew survey last asked detailed questions about Muslim-Western relations, more than half of the respondents in Muslim countries characterized those relations as bad and blamed the West for this state of affairs.

But improving relations is all the more important because of the growing demographic weight of poor Muslim countries and the attendant increase in Muslim immigration, especially to Europe from North Africa and the Middle East. (To be sure, forecasts that Muslims will soon dominate Europe are outlandish: Muslims compose just three to ten percent of the population in the major European countries today, and this proportion will at most double by midcentury.) Strategists worldwide must consider that the world's young are becoming concentrated in those countries least prepared to educate and employ them, including some Muslim states. Any resulting poverty, social tension, or ideological radicalization could have disruptive effects in many corners of the world. But this need not be the case; the healthy immigration of workers to the developed world and the movement of capital to the developing world, among other things, could lead to better results.

Urban Sprawl

Exacerbating twenty-first-century risks will be the fact that the world is urbanizing to an unprecedented degree. The year 2010 will likely be the first time in history that a majority of the world's people live in cities rather than in the countryside. Whereas less than 30 percent of the world's population was urban in 1950, according to UN projections, more than 70 percent will be by 2050.

Lower-income countries in Asia and Africa are urbanizing especially rapidly, as agriculture becomes less labor intensive and as employment opportunities shift to the industrial and service sectors. Already, most of the world's urban agglomerations—Mumbai (population 20.1 million), Mexico City (19.5 million), New Delhi (17 million), Shanghai (15.8 million), Calcutta (15.6 million), Karachi (13.1 million), Cairo (12.5 million), Manila (11.7 million), Lagos (10.6 million), Jakarta (9.7 million)—are found in low-income countries. Many of these countries have multiple cities with over one million residents each: Pakistan has eight, Mexico 12, and China more than 100. The UN projects that the urbanized proportion of sub-Saharan Africa will nearly double between 2005 and 2050, from 35 percent (300 million people) to over 67 percent (1 billion). China, which is roughly 40 percent urbanized today, is expected to be 73 percent urbanized by 2050; India, which is less than 30 percent urbanized today, is expected to be 55 percent urbanized by 2050. Overall, the world's urban population is expected to grow by 3 billion people by 2050.

This urbanization may prove destabilizing. Developing countries that urbanize in the twenty-first century will have far lower per capita incomes than did many industrial countries when they first urbanized. The United States, for example, did not reach 65 percent urbanization until 1950, when per capita income was nearly $13,000 (in 2005 dollars). By contrast, Nigeria, Pakistan, and the Philippines, which are approaching similar levels of urbanization, currently have per capita incomes of just $1,800–$4,000 (in 2005 dollars).

According to the research of Richard Cincotta and other political demographers, countries with younger populations are especially prone to civil unrest and are less able to create or sustain democratic institutions. And the more heavily urbanized, the more such countries are likely to experience Dickensian poverty and anarchic violence. In good times, a thriving economy might keep urban residents employed and governments flush with sufficient resources to meet their needs. More often, however, sprawling and impoverished cities are vulnerable to crime lords, gangs, and petty rebellions. Thus, the rapid urbanization of the developing world in the decades ahead might bring, in exaggerated form, problems similar to those that urbanization brought to nineteenth-century Europe. Back then, cyclical employment, inadequate policing, and limited sanitation and education often spawned widespread labor strife, periodic violence, and sometimes—as in the 1820s, the 1830s, and 1848—even revolutions.

International terrorism might also originate in fast-urbanizing developing countries (even more than it already does). With their neighborhood networks, access to the Internet and digital communications technology, and concentration of valuable targets, sprawling cities offer excellent opportunities for recruiting, maintaining, and hiding terrorist networks.

Defusing the Bomb

Averting this century's potential dangers will require sweeping measures. Three major global efforts defused the population bomb of Ehrlich's day: a commitment by governments and nongovernmental organizations to control reproduction rates; agricultural advances, such as the green revolution and the spread of new technology; and a vast increase in international trade, which globalized markets and thus allowed developing countries to export foodstuffs in exchange for seeds, fertilizers, and machinery, which in turn helped them boost production. But today's population bomb is the product less of absolute growth in the world's population than of changes in its age and distribution. Policymakers must therefore adapt today's global governance institutions to the new realities of the aging of the industrialized world, the concentration of the world's economic and population growth in developing countries, and the increase in international immigration.

During the Cold War, Western strategists divided the world into a "First World," of democratic industrialized countries; a "Second World," of communist industrialized countries; and a "Third World," of developing countries. These strategists focused chiefly on deterring or managing conflict between the First and the Second Worlds and on launching proxy wars and diplomatic initiatives to attract Third World countries into the First World's camp. Since the end of the Cold War, strategists have largely abandoned this three-group division and have tended to believe either that the United States, as the sole superpower, would maintain a Pax Americana or that the world would become multipolar, with the United States, Europe, and China playing major roles.

Unfortunately, because they ignore current global demographic trends, these views will be obsolete within a few decades. A better approach would be to consider a different three-world order, with a new First World of the aging industrialized nations of North America, Europe, and Asia's Pacific Rim (including Japan, Singapore, South Korea, and Taiwan, as well as China after 2030, by which point the one-child policy will have produced significant aging); a Second World comprising fast-growing and economically dynamic countries with a healthy mix of young and old inhabitants (such as Brazil, Iran, Mexico, Thailand, Turkey, and Vietnam, as well as China until 2030); and a Third World of fast-growing, very young, and increasingly urbanized countries with poorer economies and often weak governments.

To cope with the instability that will likely arise from the new Third World's urbanization, economic strife, lawlessness, and potential terrorist activity, the aging industrialized nations of the new First World must build effective alliances with the growing powers of the new Second World and together reach out to Third World nations. Second World powers will be pivotal in the twenty-first century not just because they will drive economic growth and consume technologies and other products engineered in the First World; they will also be central to international security and cooperation. The realities of religion, culture, and geographic proximity mean that any peaceful and productive engagement by the First World of Third World countries will have to include the open cooperation of Second World countries.

Strategists, therefore, must fundamentally reconsider the structure of various current global institutions. The G-8, for example, will likely become obsolete as a body for making global economic policy. The G-20 is already becoming increasingly important, and this is less a short-term consequence of the ongoing global financial crisis than the beginning of the necessary recognition that Brazil, China, India, Indonesia, Mexico, Turkey, and others are becoming global economic powers. International institutions will not retain their legitimacy if they exclude the world's fastest-growing and most economically dynamic countries. It is essential, therefore, despite European concerns about the potential effects on immigration, to take steps such as admitting Turkey into the European Union. This would add youth and economic dynamism to the EU—and would prove that Muslims are welcome to join Europeans as equals in shaping a free and prosperous future. On the other hand, excluding Turkey from the EU could lead to hostility not only on the part of Turkish citizens, who are expected to number 100 million by 2050, but also on the part of Muslim populations worldwide.

NATO must also adapt. The alliance today is composed almost entirely of countries with aging, shrinking populations and relatively slow-growing economies. It is oriented toward the Northern Hemisphere and holds on to a Cold War structure that cannot adequately respond to contemporary threats. The young and increasingly populous countries of Africa, the Middle East, Central Asia, and South Asia could mobilize insurgents much more easily than NATO could mobilize the troops it would need if it were called on to stabilize those countries. Long-standing NATO members should, therefore—although it would require atypical creativity and flexibility—consider the logistical and demographic advantages of inviting into the alliance countries such as Brazil and Morocco, rather than countries such as Albania. That this seems far-fetched does not minimize the imperative that First World countries begin including large and strategic Second and Third World powers in formal international alliances.

The case of Afghanistan—a country whose population is growing fast and where NATO is currently engaged—illustrates the importance of building effective global institutions. Today, there are 28 million Afghans; by 2025, there will be 45 million; and by 2050, there will be close to 75 million. As nearly 20 million additional Afghans are born over the next 15 years, NATO will have an opportunity to help Afghanistan become reasonably stable, self-governing, and prosperous. If NATO's efforts fail and the Afghans judge that NATO intervention harmed their interests, tens of millions of young Afghans will become more hostile to the West. But if they come to think that NATO's involvement benefited their society, the West will have tens of millions of new friends. The example might then motivate the approximately one billion other young Muslims growing up in low-income countries over the next four decades to look more kindly on relations between their countries and the countries of the industrialized West.

Creative Reforms at Home

The aging industrialized countries can also take various steps at home to promote stability in light of the coming demographic trends. First, they should encourage families to have more children. France and Sweden have had success providing child care, generous leave time, and financial allowances to families with young children. Yet there is no consensus among policymakers—and certainly not among demographers—about what policies best encourage fertility.

More important than unproven tactics for increasing family size is immigration. Correctly managed, population movement can benefit developed and developing countries alike. Given the dangers of young, underemployed, and unstable populations in developing countries, immigration to developed countries can provide economic opportunities for the ambitious and serve as a safety valve for all. Countries that embrace immigrants, such as the United States, gain economically by having willing laborers and greater entrepreneurial spirit. And countries with high levels of emigration (but not so much that they experience so-called brain drains) also benefit because emigrants often send remittances home or return to their native countries with valuable education and work experience.

One somewhat daring approach to immigration would be to encourage a reverse flow of older immigrants from developed to developing countries. If older residents of developed countries took their retirements along the southern coast of the Mediterranean or in Latin America or Africa, it would greatly reduce the strain on their home countries' public entitlement systems. The developing countries involved, meanwhile, would benefit because caring for the elderly and providing retirement and leisure services is highly labor intensive. Relocating a portion of these activities to developing countries would provide employment and valuable training to the young, growing populations of the Second and Third Worlds.

This would require developing residential and medical facilities of First World quality in Second and Third World countries. Yet even this difficult task would be preferable to the status quo, by which low wages and poor facilities lead to a steady drain of medical and nursing talent from developing to developed countries. Many residents of developed countries who desire cheaper medical procedures already practice medical tourism today, with India, Singapore, and Thailand being the most common destinations. (For example, the international consulting firm Deloitte estimated that 750,000 Americans traveled abroad for care in 2008.)

Never since 1800 has a majority of the world's economic growth occurred outside of Europe, the United States, and Canada. Never have so many people in those regions been over 60 years old. And never have low-income countries' populations been so young and so urbanized. But such will be the world's demography in the twenty-first century. The strategic and economic policies of the twentieth century are obsolete, and it is time to find new ones.

Critical Thinking

1. What demographic and economic shifts are currently under way worldwide?

2. What helps to explain economic shifts in the industrialized countries?

3. Where is population growing most rapidly? What are the implications of this growth?

4. What will be the impact of increasing urbanization?

5. What effect will demographic changes have on international institutions?

JACK A. GOLDSTONE is Virginia E. and John T. Hazel, Jr., Professor at the George Mason School of Public Policy.

From *Foreign Affairs*, vol. 89, no. 1, January/February 2010, pp. 31–43. Copyright © 2010 by Council on Foreign Relations, Inc. Reprinted by permission of Foreign Affairs. www.ForeignAffairs.com

Best. Decade. Ever.

The first 10 years of the 21st century were humanity's finest—even for the world's bottom billion.

CHARLES KENNY

The past 10 years have gotten a bad rap as the "Naughty Aughties"—and deservedly so, it seems, for a decade that began with 9/11 and the Enron scandal and closed with the global financial crisis and the Haiti earthquake. In between, we witnessed the Asian tsunami and Hurricane Katrina, SARS and swine flu, not to mention vicious fighting in Sudan and Congo, Afghanistan and, oh yes, Iraq. Given that our brains seem hard-wired to remember singular tragedy over incremental success, it's a hard sell to convince anyone that the past 10 years are worthy of praise.

But these horrific events, though mortal and economic catastrophes for many millions, don't sum up the decade as experienced by most of the planet's 6-billion-plus people. For all its problems, the first 10 years of the 21st century were in fact humanity's finest, a time when more people lived better, longer, more peaceful, and more prosperous lives than ever before.

Consider that in 1990, roughly half the global population lived on less than $1 a day; by 2007, the proportion had shrunk to 28 percent—and it will be lower still by the close of 2010. That's because, though the financial crisis briefly stalled progress on income growth, it was just a hiccup in the decade's relentless GDP climb. Indeed, average worldwide incomes are at their highest levels ever, at roughly $10,600 a year—and have risen by as much as a quarter since 2000. Some 1.3 billion people now live on more than $10 a day, suggesting the continued expansion of the global middle class. Even better news is that growth has been faster in poor places like sub-Saharan Africa than across the world as a whole.

There are still 1 billion people who go to bed each night desperately hungry, but cereal prices are now a fraction of what they were in the 1960s and 1970s. That, alongside continued income growth, is why the proportion of the developing world's population classified as "undernourished" fell from 34 percent in 1970 to 17 percent in 2008, even at the height of a global spike in food prices. Agricultural productivity, too, continues to climb: From 2000 to 2008, cereal yields increased at nearly twice the rate of population growth in the developing world. And though famine continues to threaten places such as Zimbabwe, hundreds of millions of people are eating more—and better—each day.

We're also winning the global battle against infectious disease. The 2009 swine flu has killed more than 18,000 people so far, according to the World Health Organization. But its impact has been far less severe than the apocalyptic forecasts of a few years ago, fueled by nightmare scenarios of drug-resistant, Airbus-hopping viruses overwhelming a hot, flat, and crowded world. The truth is that pandemics are on the wane. Between 1999 and 2005, thanks to the spread of vaccinations, the number of children who died annually from measles dropped 60 percent. The proportion of the world's infants vaccinated against diphtheria, whooping cough, and tetanus has climbed from less than half to 82 percent between 1985 and 2008.

There are dark spots still, not least the continuing tragedy of the HIV/AIDS epidemic. But though the 15 countries with the highest HIV prevalence still see life expectancies more than three years lower than their 1990 peak, at least the trend has started ticking back up in the last decade. The overwhelming global picture is of better health: From 2000 to 2008, child mortality dropped more than 17 percent, and the average person added another two years to his or her life expectancy, now just one shy of the biblical standard of three score and 10.

We can thank improved literacy, which has played a role in spreading vital knowledge in low-income societies, for some of these health gains. More than four-fifths of the world's population can now read and write—including more than two-thirds of Africans. The proportion of the world's young people who go on to university climbed from below one-fifth to above a quarter from 2000 to 2007 alone. And progress in education has been particularly rapid for women, one sign of growing gender equity. Although no one would argue the struggle is complete, the gains are striking—the worldwide proportion of women parliamentarians, for instance, increased from 11 percent in 1997 to 19 percent in 2009.

If you had to choose a decade in history in which to be alive, the first of the 21st century would undoubtedly be it.

Even the wars of the last 10 years, tragic as they have been, are minor compared with the violence and destruction of decades and centuries past. The number of armed conflicts—and their death toll—has continued to fall since the end of the Cold War. Worldwide, combat casualties fell 40 percent from 2000 to 2008. In sub-Saharan Africa, some 46,000 people died in battle in 2000. By 2008, that number had dropped to 6,000. Military expenditures as a percentage of global GDP are about half of their 1990 level. In Europe, so recently divided into two armed camps, annual military budgets fell from $744 billion in 1988 to $424 billion in 2009. The statistical record doesn't go back far enough for us to know with absolute certainty whether this was the most peaceful decade ever in terms of violent deaths per capita, but it certainly ranks as the lowest in the last 50 years.

On the other hand, humanity's malignant effect on the environment has accelerated the rate of extinction for plants and animals, which now reaches perhaps 50,000 species a year. But even here there was some good news. We reversed our first man-made global atmospheric crisis by banning chlorofluorocarbons—by 2015, the Antarctic ozone hole will have shrunk by nearly 400,000 square miles. Stopping climate change has been a slower process. Nonetheless, in 2008, the G-8 did commit to halving carbon emissions by 2050. And a range of technological advances—from hydrogen fuel cells to compact fluorescent bulbs—suggests that a low-carbon future need not require surrendering a high quality of life.

Technology has done more than improve energy efficiency. Today, there are more than 4 billion mobile-phone subscribers, compared with only 750 million at the decade's start. Cell phones are being used to provide financial services in the Philippines, monitor real-time commodity futures prices in Vietnam, and teach literacy in Niger. And streaming video means that fans can watch cricket even in benighted countries that don't broadcast it—or upload citizen reports from security crackdowns in Tehran.

Perhaps technology also helps account for the striking disconnect between the reality of worldwide progress and the perception of global decline. We're more able than ever to witness the tragedy of millions of our fellow humans on television or online. And, rightly so, we're more outraged than ever that suffering continues in a world of such technological wonder and economic plenty.

Nonetheless, if you had to choose a **decade** in history in which to be alive, the first of the 21st century would undoubtedly be it. More people lived lives of greater freedom, security, longevity, and wealth than ever before. And now, billions of them can tweet the good news. Bring on the 'Teenies.

Critical Thinking

1. Why does Kenny think the first decade of the 21st century is the best?

2. In what ways have conditions in the developing world improved?

3. What challenges remain?

4. Why do the reality and perceptions of global decline continue to be at odds?

CHARLES KENNY, a contributing editor to *Foreign Policy* is author of the forthcoming book *Getting Better: Why Global Development Is Succeding and How We Can Improve the World Even More.*

And Justice for All

Enforcing Human Rights for the World's Poor

GARY HAUGEN AND VICTOR BOUTROS

For a poor person in the developing world, the struggle for human rights is not an abstract fight over political freedoms or over the prosecution of large-scale war crimes but a matter of daily survival. It is the struggle to avoid extortion or abuse by local police, the struggle against being forced into slavery or having land stolen, the struggle to avoid being thrown arbitrarily into an overcrowded, disease-ridden jail with little or no prospect of a fair trial. For women and children, it is the struggle not to be assaulted, raped, molested, or forced into the commercial sex trade.

Efforts by the modern human rights movement over the last 60 years have contributed to the criminalization of such abuses in nearly every country. The problem for the poor, however, is that those laws are rarely enforced. Without functioning public justice systems to deliver the protections of the law to the poor, the legal reforms of the modern human rights movement rarely improve the lives of those who need them most. At the same time, this state of functional lawlessness allows corrupt officials and local criminals to block or steal many of the crucial goods and services provided by the international development community. These abuses are both a moral tragedy and wholly counterproductive to the foreign aid programs of countries in the developed world. Helping construct effective public justice systems in the developing world, therefore, must become the new mandate of the human rights movement in the twenty-first century.

Cold Cases

In a June 2008 report, the United Nations estimated that four billion people live outside the protection of the rule of law. As the report concluded, "Most poor people do not live under the shelter of the law"; instead, they inhabit a world in which perpetrators of abuse and violence are unrestrained by the fear of punishment. In this world, virtually every component of the public justice system—police, defense lawyers, prosecutors, and courts—works against, not with, the poor in providing the protections of the law. Take, for example, the police. For most of the world's poor, the local police force is their primary contact with the public justice system. The average poor person in the developing world has probably never met a police officer who is not, at best, corrupt or, at worst, gratuitously brutal. In fact, the most pervasive criminal presence for the global poor is frequently their own police forces. A 2006 study in Kenya, for example, revealed that 65 percent of those citizens polled reported difficulty obtaining help from the police, and 29 percent said they had to make "extraordinary efforts" to avoid problems with the police in the past year. According to a 1999 World Bank study, poor people in the developing world view the police as a group of "vigilantes and criminals" who actively harass, oppress, and brutalize them. Making matters worse is that in the cases in which local police officers are inclined to protect the poor, they frequently lack the training, resources, and mandate to conduct proactive investigations. As a result, when faced with danger or a crisis, the poor do not run to the police—they run away from them.

When a poor person does come into contact with the public justice system beyond the police, it is frequently because he or she has been charged with a crime. With incomes for the global poor hovering around $1–$2 a day, the average poor person cannot hope to pay legal fees. Many countries in the developing world do not recognize a right to indigent legal representation, leaving those who cannot afford a lawyer to navigate the legal process without an advocate. This means that a local official—or, for that matter, anyone in the community—can make an unsubstantiated accusation against a poor person that could put his or her liberty at risk without legal representation.

This problem is made worse by the simple scarcity of lawyers in the developing world. The average person in the developing world has never met a lawyer in his or her life. In the United States, there is approximately one lawyer for every 749 people. In Zambia, by contrast, there is only one lawyer for every 25,667 people; in Cambodia, there is one for every 22,402 people. There are more lawyers in the New York offices of some major law firms than there are in all of Zambia or Cambodia. Of this small class of lawyers, prosecutors represent an even tinier subset—and some of these are not even trained lawyers, and others, much like the police, extract bribes to drop cases. When cases are reported and referred for trial, there are frequently too few public prosecutors to handle the volume.

This creates an enormous backlog, allowing cases to languish indefinitely on overloaded dockets.

The great legal reforms of the modern human rights movement often deliver only empty parchment promises to the poor.

Some experts, for example, have estimated that at the current rate, it would take 350 years for the courts in Mumbai, India, to hear all the cases on their books. According to the UN Development Program, India has 11 judges for every one million people. There are currently more than 30 million cases pending in Indian courts, and cases remain unresolved for an average of 15 years. Someone who is detained while awaiting trial in India often serves more than the maximum length of his or her prospective sentence even before a trial date is set. The International Center for Prison Studies at King's College London found that nearly 70 percent of Indian prisoners have never been convicted of any crime. Even those who are not held in custody before trial face difficulties: some courts are so far away that it is too costly or logistically challenging for the poor to reach them, and the cases are decided in their absence. In India, like in many countries in the developing world, judges and magistrates sometimes solicit bribes in exchange for favorable verdicts or, in other cases, to continue the case indefinitely. Some courts do not even have access to the applicable legal texts, and judges consequently reach decisions without consulting the relevant legal standards.

In communities where de facto lawlessness reigns, even if a poor person is aware that he or she is being illegally abused, it is unlikely that such a person has ever seen a law against such abuse enforced on behalf of someone of similar social status. On the contrary, a poor person in the developing world is far more likely to know someone who has been a victim of the public justice system than a beneficiary of it. As a result, the idea of "law enforcement" is not one of the social mechanisms that most poor people in the developing world consider useful for navigating the threats of daily life.

A Third Era?

The modern human rights movement began in the years following World War II, when a number of scholars and diplomats began an effort to articulate and codify international standards on fundamental rights. Documents such as the Universal Declaration of Human Rights, the International Covenant on Civil and Political Rights, and the International Covenant on Economic, Social and Cultural Rights—as well as conventions on discrimination, torture, children's rights, and women's rights—are the products of this movement. Over time, it produced a body of rights and norms to which all people of the world can lay claim. This work continues today, as international organizations and countries draft and amend treaties, conventions, and protocols that obligate states to extend fundamental legal protections to those within their borders.

If the first stage of the modern human rights movement was largely intellectual, the second was political. During this stage, the movement worked to embed the growing body of international norms into national law. Individual governments throughout the developing world began to enact reforms that protected political, civil, and economic rights. South Asian countries, for example, passed laws outlawing bonded slavery; African countries threw off centuries of traditional cultural practice and gave women the right to own and inherit land and to be free of ritual genital mutilation; Southeast Asian governments elevated the status of women and girls, creating new laws to protect them from sexual exploitation and trafficking; and Latin American countries adopted international standards for arrest and detention procedures and codified land reform rights. As a result of this global political movement, hundreds of millions of vulnerable and abused people became entitled to global standards of justice and equity under local law.

The tragic irony, however, is that the enforcement of these rights was left to utterly dysfunctional national law enforcement institutions. Most public justice systems in the developing world have their roots in the colonial era, when their core function was to serve those in power—usually the colonial state. As the colonial powers departed, authoritarian governments frequently took their place. They inherited the public justice systems of the colonial past, which they proceeded to use to protect their own interests and power, in much the same way that their colonial predecessors had. Rather than fulfill the post-colonial mandate of broad public service, the police and the judiciaries of the developing world often serve a narrow set of elite interests. The public justice systems of this part of the world were never designed to serve the poor, which means that there is often no credible deterrent to restrain those who commit crimes against them.

In the absence of functioning justice systems, the private sector has developed substitutes: instead of relying on the police for security, companies and wealthy individuals hire private security forces; instead of submitting commercial disputes to clogged and corrupt courts, they establish alternative dispute-resolution systems; and instead of depending on lawyers to push legal matters through the system, those with the financial means may seek and, in some cases, purchase political influence.

Without pressure from other powerful actors in society, elites have little or no incentive to build legal institutions that serve the poor. A properly functioning legal system would only limit their power—and require a substantial commitment of financial and human resources. At the moment, they see no serious benefits to justify the effort: for them, a functioning public justice system might, in fact, be a problem.

Two generations of global human rights efforts have been predicated—consciously or unconsciously—on assumptions about the effectiveness of the public justice systems in the developing world. But those systems clearly lack effective enforcement tools; as a result, the great legal reforms of the modern human rights movement often deliver only empty parchment promises to the poor. In large part, the human rights community—which includes various UN bodies and agencies, government offices, nongovernmental organizations, and individual jurists and scholars—exists to defend the victimized, particularly where more powerful actors have little incentive to act on their behalf. Yet throughout the history of the modern human rights movement, this community has largely neglected the task of helping build public justice systems in the developing world that work for the poor.

The High Costs of Low Enforcement

The unrealized potential of the human rights movement should not eclipse the significance of its enormous contributions over the last half century. Suppose that scientists had worked feverishly for two generations to develop and fill warehouses with miracle vaccines that hundreds of millions of vulnerable people desperately needed—but could not access. Theirs would be a great achievement, but the absence of an effective delivery system would present an urgent new priority for the international public health community. Similarly, after 60 years of developing and refining human rights law, few of the gains are reaching the people who need them most.

The absence of functioning public justice systems for the poor also jeopardizes half a century of development work, because there is no effective mechanism to prevent those in power from taking away or blocking access to the goods and services the development community is providing. Resources earmarked for aid efforts often never reach their intended beneficiaries. A World Bank study found that as much as 85 percent of aid flows are diverted away from their intended targets. To be sure, a considerable amount of the money and materials that go missing is siphoned off by corrupt leaders and high-level officials. But those resources that do reach local communities do not fare much better. Farming tools are of no use to widows whose land has been stolen, vocational training is not helpful for people who have been thrown in jail for refusing to pay a bribe, local medical clinics cannot treat bonded slaves who are not allowed to leave the factory even when they are sick, and microloans for new sewing machines do not benefit the poor if the profits are stolen by local police.

Similarly, a culture of impunity for such abuses undermines attempts to improve the health of the poor in the developing world. Take, for example, the damaging public health consequences of sex crimes. A 1994 World Bank report estimated that women in the developing world are as likely to die at the hands of an abuser as they are from cancer, and it found that their chances of being incapacitated by abuse are greater than their combined chances of being incapacitated by traffic accidents or malaria. A 2002 World Health Organization report, meanwhile, showed that in some countries, nearly two out of three women reported having been physically assaulted, and nearly half reported that their first instance of sexual intercourse was forced. The problem is pervasive. Surveys of villages in India cited by the United Nations reveal that in the 1990s, 16 percent of all maternal deaths during pregnancy came from domestic abuse. In Peru, about 40 percent of girls will be victims of rape or attempted rape by the age of 14. In parts of southern Africa, 78 percent of HIV-infected women

and girls report having been raped—AIDS-education programs do little to help these women and children. As the sad facts surrounding sex crimes show, the unchecked violation of human rights in many parts of the developing world reflects an enforcement gap with disastrous effects on health, economic productivity, and stability.

Pulling Up Short

Few, if any, international human rights or development organizations focus on building public justice systems that work for the poor. Although the United Nations, some government agencies, and human rights organizations do important work in calling attention to human rights violations and lobbying for legal reforms, none measures its success by its ability to bring effective law enforcement to local communities in the developing world.

The problem is not that these groups fail to see the dysfunction of public justice systems in the developing world. Indeed, some of their researchers have been meticulously documenting this problem for decades. Why, then, have none of these agencies made the effectiveness of public justice systems a fundamental priority?

First, international human rights and development agencies may fear that building functioning public justice systems in the developing world is impossible. The evolution of these systems in the developed world suggests that such fear is unwarranted. A century ago, police and courts in the United States were nothing like the professional—albeit imperfect—U.S. law enforcement system that is now taken for granted. Instead, they resembled public justice systems in the developing world today. In 1894 and 1895, for example, the Lexow Committee in the New York State Senate collected testimony from hundreds of witnesses regarding pervasive extortion, bribery, counterfeiting, voter intimidation, election fraud, torture, and general brutality by the New York City Police Department. Police officers spoke openly of purchasing appointments to a particular rank or duty. The most lucrative assignments were in the red-light districts, where officers could extract hefty bribes in exchange for ignoring the criminal enterprises of brothel owners. This culture was challenged by a relatively small band of local crusaders and outsiders, who gained federal support to establish police and courts in New York City that were not controlled by patronage and corruption. Similar movements took place in other cities across the United States, and the deficiencies in public justice systems in the developing world today can be overcome in much the same way. Justice systems ruled by corruption, cronyism, and theft do not change by themselves—they need external pressure and resources.

Second, international human rights and development agencies may sense that larger bodies, such as the United Nations and the World Bank, are already undertaking such efforts. But sustained efforts to develop functioning public justice systems in poor countries have rarely been tried. Recently, there have been some attempts to build them as part of larger nation-building strategies in postconflict environments such as Afghanistan and Iraq. These efforts reflect a growing—if not desperate—recognition that public justice systems are fundamental to socioeconomic progress. To date, however, there have not yet been similar investments in more stable developing countries, such as Bolivia, India, Indonesia, Kenya, or the Philippines, to name a few.

Much more money, intellectual effort, professional investment, and political and diplomatic capital have been poured into traditional development activities—fixing health care, distributing food, providing access to water, strengthening financial systems, and so on—than into supporting public justice systems. For example, excluding Afghanistan and Iraq, the United States allocated less than 1.5 percent of last year's foreign aid budget to rule-of-law programs.

When donor countries have invested in law enforcement training in the developing world, they have largely focused on transnational criminal issues, such as narcotics, arms trafficking, and terrorism. Such initiatives largely ignore the daily struggles that stem from the lack of legal protections for the global poor. And the little funding that has supported rule-of-law, anticorruption, and good governance programs has generally focused on reducing the theft or misappropriation of aid dollars or on strengthening legal protections for business and commerce. On those rare occasions when donors have invested in public justice systems with the goal of serving the indigenous public, the investments have been small, isolated, and ineffective.

Caseworkers for the Poor

The modern human rights movement must enter into a new era, shifting its focus from legal reform to law enforcement. In other words, the time has come to move human rights from wholesale to retail—to take the human rights promises stored in the warehouses of national law and deliver them to the poor standing in line for justice.

Admittedly, creating functioning public justice systems in the developing world will be difficult. It will require political will, steadfastness, and local knowledge and creativity. On the local level, approaches must focus on directly cultivating the political will and capacity of the police, prosecutors, and judges who are supposed to enforce the law on behalf of the poor. This could include providing financial assistance to build police and judicial units with salaries high enough to make petty corruption less likely; material resources that give police, prosecutors, social workers, and judges the basic tools of their trade; practical on-the-ground casework training; and legal aid and social services to the poor. These would be expensive investments, but they would represent a small fraction of the trillions of dollars that governments have spent on development aid—much of which has been of questionable long-term value given the absence of effective law enforcement systems for the poor. Indeed, rule-of-law aid and development aid are mutually reinforcing: as functioning public justice systems in the developing world mature, the poor will begin to fully reap the benefits of the enormous investments in development being made on their behalf.

At the state level, aid must focus on developing both the political will and the capacity of government elites to enforce existing laws. This aid should target the diplomats, politicians, and policymakers who set the agendas for the large cadres of enforcement personnel under their authority. To push this along, developed-country governments should link their international development assistance to the willingness of developing-country governments to improve their public justice systems. One example of such a strategy is already working its way through the U.S. Congress: the Child Protection Compact Act would authorize U.S. government grants to developing countries that have demonstrated a commitment to combating child trafficking with effective tools, measured by concrete benchmarks. Likewise, the United States and other governments in the developed world should cut off or limit foreign aid to countries that are unwilling to improve their capacity to protect the poor from abuse and violence—especially since rampant lawlessness is likely to make any such assistance unproductive in the first place.

Rule-of-law aid and development aid are mutually reinforcing.

In places where central and local governments do show a willingness to reform, international agencies should be prepared to help. One promising model is called "collaborative casework." In such programs, human rights lawyers and law enforcement professionals work with local officials to identify individual victims of violent abuse, extricate them from oppressive criminal enterprises, and support the prosecution of the perpetrators in the local public justice system. The International Justice Mission (IJM) has helped pioneer the collaborative-casework approach over the last decade and has worked with local authorities to prosecute thousands of cases of violence against the poor.

A case-driven agency—whether it is a nongovernmental organization such as IJM or an office within the United Nations or within a national government—could select a particular geographic area and focus on a single abuse that is relatively uncontroversial and the targeting of which would not threaten the local political establishment—helping authorities in one city fight sexual violence against children, for example.

As part of this collaborative process, a case-driven agency builds the crime-fighting and judicial capacity of local police, prosecutors, and court officials. It identifies, for example, case after case of child rape and works with the relevant authorities to overcome any obstacles or chokepoints in the justice system. It does not publicly embarrass officials if they lack competence or integrity, except as a last resort—rather, it trains them in professional methods and facilitates their getting public credit for good work.

It is simply not true that all public authorities in the developing world are hopelessly corrupt, apathetic, and brutish. In places where the case-driven model has succeeded—such as in Cebu, in the Philippines, where two years of collaborative casework led by IJM resulted in a 70 percent reduction in the victimization of children in the commercial sex trade—it has required the courage and competence of local authorities. Such partners exist; they just need political support, training, and resources. When empowered, local law enforcement officials no longer treat serious crimes, such as child rape, as peripheral offenses. Instead, the effort to combat such crimes receives special training, international resources, and professional regard. As the authorities successfully solve and prosecute the kinds of cases that were once ignored, the poor and the underrepresented start to demand more justice. At the same time, dormant demands for the rule of law among the middle class are reignited, local leaders encouraged by these demands begin to emerge, and obstructionists begin to be marginalized.

Over the last decade, IJM has used this model to provide legal assistance to nearly 15,000 individual clients in poor countries throughout Africa, Asia, and Latin America. There is no reason this approach cannot work on a larger scale with greater resources and investment. Working with local officials to protect against one category of abuse provides those officials with experience, allies, assets, and self-confidence, which then allow the justice system to work against other types of abuse—whether land seizures, forced labor, domestic violence, illegal detention, or police abuse.

To accomplish this goal, the human rights and development communities will have to restructure themselves to include those with the backgrounds and technical skills to diagnose and repair the ailments of broken public justice systems. Of course, these experts will not come with ready answers or quick solutions—but they will know where to start looking and will recognize what matters and what does not. And given even a small fraction of the time and money that have been devoted to fixing roads, improving health systems, providing clean water, and building schools in developing countries, they will begin to enable the poor to retain the benefits of such development assistance. On behalf of the billions of poor people in this world who are made small under the vast shadow of lawlessness, the time has come to construct a shelter of justice.

Critical Thinking

1. What obstacles do the poor face in obtaining legal protection?
2. Why are public justice and law enforcement so weak in developing countries?
3. How does a lack of legal protection undermine development efforts?
4. Why is there not more effort devoted to building public justice systems?

GARY HAUGEN is President and CEO of International Justice Mission. **VICTOR BOUTROS** is a Federal Prosecutor in the Civil Rights Division of the U.S. Department of Justice. Both are lecturers at the University of Chicago Law School. The views expressed here are their own and not those of the U.S. Department of Justice.

The Case against the West
America and Europe in the Asian Century

KISHORE MAHBUBANI

There is a fundamental flaw in the West's strategic thinking. In all its analyses of global challenges, the West assumes that it is the source of the solutions to the world's key problems. In fact, however, the West is also a major source of these problems. Unless key Western policymakers learn to understand and deal with this reality, the world is headed for an even more troubled phase.

The West is understandably reluctant to accept that the era of its domination is ending and that the Asian century has come. No civilization cedes power easily, and the West's resistance to giving up control of key global institutions and processes is natural. Yet the West is engaging in an extraordinary act of self-deception by believing that it is open to change. In fact, the West has become the most powerful force preventing the emergence of a new wave of history, clinging to its privileged position in key global forums, such as the UN Security Council, the International Monetary Fund, the World Bank, and the G-8 (the group of highly industrialized states), and refusing to contemplate how the West will have to adjust to the Asian century.

Partly as a result of its growing insecurity, the West has also become increasingly incompetent in its handling of key global problems. Many Western commentators can readily identify specific failures, such as the Bush administration's botched invasion and occupation of Iraq. But few can see that this reflects a deeper structural problem: the West's inability to see that the world has entered a new era.

Apart from representing a specific failure of policy execution, the war in Iraq has also highlighted the gap between the reality and what the West had expected would happen after the invasion. Arguably, the United States and the United Kingdom intended only to free the Iraqi people from a despotic ruler and to rid the world of a dangerous man, Saddam Hussein. Even if George W. Bush and Tony Blair had no malevolent intentions, however, their approaches were trapped in the Western mindset of believing that their interventions could lead only to good, not harm or disaster. This led them to believe that the invading U.S. troops would be welcomed with roses thrown at their feet by happy Iraqis. But the twentieth century showed that no country welcomes foreign invaders. The notion that any Islamic nation would approve of Western military boots on its soil was ridiculous. Even in the early twentieth century, the British invasion and occupation of Iraq was met with armed resistance. In 1920, Winston Churchill, then British secretary for war and air, quelled the rebellion of Kurds and Arabs in British-occupied Iraq by authorizing his troops to use chemical weapons. "I am strongly in favor of using poisoned gas against uncivilized tribes," Churchill said. The world has moved on from this era, but many Western officials have not abandoned the old assumption that an army of Christian soldiers can successfully invade, occupy, and transform an Islamic society.

Many Western leaders often begin their speeches by remarking on how perilous the world is becoming. Speaking after the August 2006 discovery of a plot to blow up transatlantic flights originating from London, President Bush said, "The American people need to know we live in a dangerous world." But even as Western leaders speak of such threats, they seem incapable of conceding that the West itself could be the fundamental source of these dangers. After all, the West includes the best-managed states in the world, the most economically developed, those with the strongest democratic institutions. But one cannot assume that a government that rules competently at home will be equally good at addressing challenges abroad. In fact, the converse is more likely to be true. Although the Western mind is obsessed with the Islamist terrorist threat, the West is mishandling the two immediate and pressing challenges of Afghanistan and Iraq. And despite the grave threat of nuclear terrorism, the Western custodians of the nonproliferation regime have allowed that regime to weaken significantly. The challenge posed by Iran's efforts to enrich uranium has been aggravated by the incompetence of the United States and the European Union. On the economic front, for the first time since World War II, the demise of a round of global trade negotiations, the Doha Round, seems imminent. Finally, the danger of global warming, too, is being mismanaged.

Yet Westerners seldom look inward to understand the deeper reasons these global problems are being mismanaged. Are there domestic structural reasons that explain this? Have Western democracies been hijacked by competitive populism and structural short-termism, preventing them from addressing long-term challenges from a broader global perspective?

Fortunately, some Asian states may now be capable of taking on more responsibilities, as they have been strengthened by implementing Western principles. In September 2005, Robert Zoellick, then U.S. deputy secretary of state, called on China to become a "responsible stakeholder" in the international system. China has responded positively, as have other Asian states. In recent decades, Asians have been among the greatest beneficiaries of the open multilateral order created by the United States and the other victors of World War II, and few today want to destabilize it. The number of Asians seeking a comfortable middle-class existence has never been higher. For centuries, the Chinese and the Indians could only dream of such an accomplishment; now it is within the reach of around half a billion people in China and India. Their ideal is to achieve what the United States and Europe did. They want to replicate, not dominate, the West. The universalization of the Western dream represents a moment of triumph for the West. And so the West should welcome the fact that the Asian states are becoming competent at handling regional and global challenges.

The Middle East Mess

Western Policies have been most harmful in the Middle East. The Middle East is also the most dangerous region in the world. Trouble there affects not just seven million Israelis, around four million Palestinians, and 200 million Arabs; it also affects more than a billion Muslims worldwide. Every time there is a major flare-up in the Middle East, such as the U.S. invasion of Iraq or the Israeli bombing of Lebanon, Islamic communities around the world become concerned, distressed, and angered. And few of them doubt the problems origin: the West.

The invasion and occupation of Iraq, for example, was a multidimensional error. The theory and practice of international law legitimizes the use of force only when it is an act of self-defense or is authorized by the UN Security Council. The U.S.-led invasion of Iraq could not be justified on either count. The United States and the United Kingdom sought the Security Council's authorization to invade Iraq, but the council denied it. It was therefore clear to the international community that the subsequent war was illegal and that it would do huge damage to international law.

This has created an enormous problem, partly because until this point both the United States and the United Kingdom had been among the primary custodians of international law. American and British minds, such as James Brierly, Philip Jessup, Hersch Lauterpacht, and Hans Morgenthau, developed the conceptual infrastructure underlying international law, and American and British leaders provided the political will to have it accepted in practice. But neither the United States nor the United Kingdom will admit that the invasion and the occupation of Iraq were illegal or give up their historical roles as the chief caretakers of international law. Since 2003, both nations have frequently called for Iran and North Korea to implement UN Security Council resolutions. But how can the violators of UN principles also be their enforcers?

One rare benefit of the Iraq war may be that it has awakened a new fear of Iran among the Sunni Arab states. Egypt, Jordan, and Saudi Arabia, among others, do not want to deal with two adversaries and so are inclined to make peace with Israel. Saudi Arabia's King Abdullah used the opportunity of the special Arab League summit meeting in March 2007 to relaunch his long-standing proposal for a two-state solution to the Israeli-Palestinian conflict. Unfortunately, the Bush administration did not seize the opportunity—or revive the Taba accords that President Bill Clinton had worked out in January 2001, even though they could provide a basis for a lasting settlement and the Saudis were prepared to back them. In its early days, the Bush administration appeared ready to support a two-state solution. It was the first U.S. administration to vote in favor of a UN Security Council resolution calling for the creation of a Palestinian state, and it announced in March 2002 that it would try to achieve such a result by 2005. But here it is 2008, and little progress has been made.

The United States has made the already complicated Israeli-Palestinian conflict even more of a mess. Many extremist voices in Tel Aviv and Washington believe that time will always be on Israel's side. The pro-Israel lobby's stranglehold on the U.S. Congress, the political cowardice of U.S. politicians when it comes to creating a Palestinian state, and the sustained track record of U.S. aid to Israel support this view. But no great power forever sacrifices its larger national interests in favor of the interests of a small state. If Israel fails to accept the Taba accords, it will inevitably come to grief. If and when it does, Western incompetence will be seen as a major cause.

Never Say Never

Nuclear nonproliferation is another area in which the West, especially the United States, has made matters worse. The West has long been obsessed with the danger of the proliferation of weapons of mass destruction, particularly nuclear weapons. It pushed successfully for the near-universal ratification of the Biological and Toxin Weapons Convention, the Chemical Weapons Convention, and the Nuclear Nonproliferation Treaty (NPT).

But the West has squandered many of those gains. Today, the NPT is legally alive but spiritually dead. The NPT was inherently problematic since it divided the world into nuclear haves (the states that had tested a nuclear device by 1967) and nuclear have-nots (those that had not). But for two decades it was reasonably effective in preventing horizontal proliferation (the spread of nuclear weapons to other states). Unfortunately, the NPT has done nothing to prevent vertical proliferation, namely, the increase in the numbers and sophistication of nuclear weapons among the existing nuclear weapons states. During the Cold War, the United States and the Soviet Union agreed to work together to limit proliferation. The governments of several countries that could have developed nuclear weapons, such as Argentina, Brazil, Germany, Japan, and South Korea, restrained themselves because they believed the NPT reflected a fair bargain between China, France, the Soviet Union, the United Kingdom, and the United States (the five official nuclear weapons states and five permanent members of the UN Security Council) and the rest of the world. Both sides agreed that the world would be safer if the five nuclear states took steps to reduce their arsenals and worked toward the eventual goal of universal disarmament and the other states refrained from acquiring nuclear weapons at all.

So what went wrong? The first problem was that the NPT's principal progenitor, the United States, decided to walk away from the postwar rule-based order it had created, thus eroding the infrastructure on which the NPT's enforcement depends. During the time I was Singapore's ambassador to the UN, between 1984 and 1989, Jeane Kirkpatrick, the U.S. ambassador to the UN, treated the organization with contempt. She infamously said, "What takes place in the Security Council more closely resembles a mugging than either a political debate or an effort at problem-solving." She saw the postwar order as a set of constraints, not as a set of rules that the world should follow and the United States should help preserve. This undermined the NPT, because with no teeth of its own, no self-regulating or sanctioning mechanisms, and a clause allowing signatories to ignore obligations in the name of "supreme national interest," the treaty could only really be enforced by the UN Security Council. And once the United States began tearing holes in the fabric of the overall system, it created openings for violations of the

NPT and its principles. Finally, by going to war with Iraq without UN authorization, the United States lost its moral authority to ask, for example, Iran to abide by Security Council resolutions.

Another problem has been the United States'—and other nuclear weapons states'—direct assault on the treaty. The NPT is fundamentally a social contract between the five nuclear weapons states and the rest of the world, based partly on the understanding that the nuclear powers will eventually give up their weapons. Instead, during the Cold War, the United States and the Soviet Union increased both the quantity and the sophistication of their nuclear weapons: the United States' nuclear stockpile peaked in 1966 at 31,700 warheads, and the Soviet Union's peaked in 1986 at 40,723. In fact, the United States and the Soviet Union developed their nuclear stockpiles so much that they actually ran out of militarily or economically significant targets. The numbers have declined dramatically since then, but even the current number of nuclear weapons held by the United States and Russia can wreak enormous damage on human civilization.

The nuclear states' decision to ignore Israel's nuclear weapons program was especially damaging to their authority. No nuclear weapons state has ever publicly acknowledged Israel's possession of nuclear weapons. Their silence has created a loophole in the NPT and delegitimized it in the eyes of Muslim nations. The consequences have been profound. When the West sermonizes that the world will become a more dangerous place when Iran acquires nuclear weapons, the Muslim world now shrugs.

India and Pakistan were already shrugging by 1998, when they tested their first nuclear weapons. When the international community responded by condemning the tests and applying sanctions on India, virtually all Indians saw through the hypocrisy and double standards of their critics. By not respecting their own obligations under the NPT, the five nuclear states had robbed their condemnations of any moral legitimacy; criticisms from Australia and Canada, which have also remained silent about Israel's bomb, similarly had no moral authority. The near-unanimous rejection of the NPT by the Indian establishment, which is otherwise very conscious of international opinion, showed how dead the treaty already was.

The world has lost its trust in the five nuclear weapons states and now sees them as the NPT's primary violators.

From time to time, common sense has entered discussions on nuclear weapons. President Ronald Reagan said more categorically than any U.S. president that the world would be better off without nuclear weapons. Last year, with the NPT in its death throes and the growing threat of loose nuclear weapons falling into the hands of terrorists forefront in everyone's mind, former Secretary of State George Shultz, former Defense Secretary William Perry, former Secretary of State Henry Kissinger, and former Senator Sam Nunn warned in *The Wall Street Journal* that the world was "now on the precipice of a new and dangerous nuclear era." They argued, "Unless urgent new actions are taken, the U.S. soon will be compelled to enter a new nuclear era that will be more precarious, psychologically disorienting, and economically even more costly than was Cold War deterrence." But these calls may have come too late. The world has lost its trust in the five

nuclear weapons states and now sees them as the NPT's primary violators rather than its custodians. Those states' private cynicism about their obligations to the NPT has become public knowledge.

Contrary to what the West wants the rest of the world to believe, the nuclear weapons states, especially the United States and Russia, which continue to maintain thousands of nuclear weapons, are the biggest source of nuclear proliferation. Mohamed ElBaradei, the director general of the International Atomic Energy Agency, warned in *The Economist* in 2003, "The very existence of nuclear weapons gives rise to the pursuit of them. They are seen as a source of global influence, and are valued for their perceived deterrent effect. And as long as some countries possess them (or are protected by them in alliances) and others do not, this asymmetry breeds chronic global insecurity." Despite the Cold War, the second half of the twentieth century seemed to be moving the world toward a more civilized order. As the twenty-first century unfurls, the world seems to be sliding backward.

Irresponsible Stakeholders

After leading the world toward a period of spectacular economic growth in the second half of the twentieth century by promoting global free trade, the West has recently been faltering in its global economic leadership. Believing that low trade barriers and increasing trade interdependence would result in higher standards of living for all, European and U.S. economists and policymakers pushed for global economic liberalization. As a result, global trade grew from seven percent of the world's GDP in 1940 to 30 percent in 2005.

But a seismic shift has taken place in Western attitudes since the end of the Cold War. Suddenly, the United States and Europe no longer have a vested interest in the success of the East Asian economies, which they see less as allies and more as competitors. That change in Western interests was reflected in the fact that the West provided little real help to East Asia during the Asian financial crisis of 1997–98. The entry of China into the global marketplace, especially after its admission to the World Trade Organization, has made a huge difference in both economic and psychological terms. Many Europeans have lost confidence in their ability to compete with the Asians. And many Americans have lost confidence in the virtues of competition.

There are some knotty issues that need to be resolved in the current global trade talks, but fundamentally the negotiations are stalled because the conviction of the Western "champions" of free trade that free trade is good has begun to waver. When Americans and Europeans start to perceive themselves as losers in international trade, they also lose their drive to push for further trade liberalization. Unfortunately, on this front at least, neither China nor India (nor Brazil nor South Africa nor any other major developing country) is ready to take over the West's mantle. China, for example, is afraid that any effort to seek leadership in this area will stoke U.S. fears that it is striving for global hegemony. Hence, China is lying low. So, too, are the United States and Europe. Hence, the trade talks are stalled. The end of the West's promotion of global trade liberalization could well mean the end of the most spectacular economic growth the world has ever seen. Few in the West seem to be reflecting on the consequences of walking away from one of the West's most successful policies, which is what it will be doing if it allows the Doha Round to fail.

At the same time that the Western governments are relinquishing their stewardship of the global economy, they are also failing to take the lead on battling global warming. The awarding of the Nobel Peace Prize to former U.S. Vice President Al Gore, a longtime environmentalist, and the UN's Intergovernmental Panel on Climate Change confirms there is international consensus that global warning is a real threat. The most assertive advocates for tackling this problem come from the U.S. and European scientific communities, but the greatest resistance to any effective action is coming from the U.S. government. This has left the rest of the world confused and puzzled. Most people believe that the greenhouse effect is caused mostly by the flow of current emissions. Current emissions do aggravate the problem, but the fundamental cause is the stock of emissions that has accumulated since the Industrial Revolution. Finding a just and equitable solution to the problem of greenhouse gas emissions must begin with assigning responsibility both for the current flow and for the stock of greenhouse gases already accumulated. And on both counts the Western nations should bear a greater burden.

The West has to learn to share power and responsibility for the management of global issues with the rest of the world.

When it comes to addressing any problem pertaining to the global commons, such as the environment, it seems only fair that the wealthier members of the international community should shoulder more responsibility. This is a natural principle of justice. It is also fair in this particular case given the developed countries' primary role in releasing harmful gases into the atmosphere. R. K. Pachauri, chair of the Intergovernmental Panel on Climate Change, argued last year, "China and India are certainly increasing their share, but they are not increasing their per capita emissions anywhere close to the levels that you have in the developed world." Since 1850, China has contributed less than 8 percent of the world's total emissions of carbon dioxide, whereas the United States is responsible for 29 percent and western Europe is responsible for 27 percent. Today, India's per capita greenhouse gas emissions are equivalent to only 4 percent of those of the United States and 12 percent of those of the European Union. Still, the Western governments are not clearly acknowledging their responsibilities and are allowing many of their citizens to believe that China and India are the fundamental obstacles to any solution to global warming.

Washington might become more responsible on this front if a Democratic president replaces Bush in 2009. But people in the West will have to make some real concessions if they are to reduce significantly their per capita share of global emissions. A cap-and-trade program may do the trick. Western countries will probably have to make economic sacrifices. One option might be, as the journalist Thomas Friedman has suggested, to impose a dollar-per-gallon tax on Americans' gasoline consumption. Gore has proposed a carbon tax. So far, however, few U.S. politicians have dared to make such suggestions publicly.

Temptations of the East

The Middle East, nuclear proliferation, stalled trade liberalization, and global warming are all challenges that the West is essentially failing to address. And this failure suggests that a systemic problem is emerging in the West's stewardship of the international order—one that Western minds are reluctant to analyze or confront openly. After having enjoyed centuries of global domination, the West has to learn to share power and responsibility for the management of global issues with the rest of the world. It has to forgo outdated organizations, such as the Organization for Economic Cooperation and Development, and outdated processes, such as the G-8, and deal with organizations and processes with a broader scope and broader representation. It was always unnatural for the 12 percent of the world population that lived in the West to enjoy so much global power. Understandably, the other 88 percent of the world population increasingly wants also to drive the bus of world history.

First and foremost, the West needs to acknowledge that sharing the power it has accumulated in global forums would serve its interests. Restructuring international institutions to reflect the current world order will be complicated by the absence of natural leaders to do the job. The West has become part of the problem, and the Asian countries are not yet ready to step in. On the other hand, the world does not need to invent any new principles to improve global governance; the concepts of domestic good governance can and should be applied to the international community. The Western principles of democracy, the rule of law, and social justice are among the world's best bets. The ancient virtues of partnership and pragmatism can complement them.

Democracy, the foundation of government in the West, is based on the premise that each human being in a society is an equal stakeholder in the domestic order. Thus, governments are selected on the basis of "one person, one vote." This has produced long-term stability and order in Western societies. In order to produce long-term stability and order worldwide, democracy should be the cornerstone of global society, and the planet's 6.6 billion inhabitants should become equal stakeholders. To inject the spirit of democracy into global governance and global decision-making, one must turn to institutions with universal representation, especially the UN. UN institutions such as the World Health Organization and the World Meteorological Organization enjoy widespread legitimacy because of their universal membership, which means their decisions are generally accepted by all the countries of the world.

The problem today is that although many Western actors are willing to work with specialized UN agencies, they are reluctant to strengthen the UN's core institution, the UN General Assembly, from which all these specialized agencies come. The UN General Assembly is the most representative body on the planet, and yet many Western countries are deeply skeptical of it. They are right to point out its imperfections. But they overlook the fact that this imperfect assembly enjoys legitimacy in the eyes of the people of this imperfect world. Moreover, the General Assembly has at times shown more common sense and prudence than some of the most sophisticated Western democracies. Of course, it takes time to persuade all of the UN's members to march in the same direction, but consensus building is precisely what gives legitimacy to the result. Most countries in the world respect and abide by most UN decisions because they believe in the authority of the UN. Used well, the body can be a powerful vehicle for making critical decisions on global governance.

The world today is run not through the General Assembly but through the Security Council, which is effectively run by the five permanent member states. If this model were adopted in the United States, the U.S. Congress would be replaced by a selective council comprised of only the representatives from the country's five most powerful states. Would the populations of the other 45 states not deem any such proposal absurd? The West must cease its efforts to prolong its undemocratic management of the global order and find ways to effectively engage the majority of the world's population in global decision-making.

Another fundamental principle that should underpin the global order is the rule of law. This hallowed Western principle insists that no person, regardless of his or her status, is above the law. Ironically, while being exemplary in implementing the rule of law at home, the United States is a leading international outlaw in its refusal to recognize the constraints of international law. Many Americans live comfortably with this contradiction while expecting other countries to abide by widely accepted treaties. Americans react with horror when Iran tries to walk away from the NPT. Yet they are surprised that the world is equally shocked when Washington abandons a universally accepted treaty such as the Comprehensive Test Ban Treaty.

The Bush administration's decision to exempt the United States from the provisions of international law on human rights is even more damaging. For over half a century, since Eleanor Roosevelt led the fight for the adoption of the Universal Declaration of Human Rights, the United States was the global champion of human rights. This was the result of a strong ideological conviction that it was the United States' God-given duty to create a more civilized world. It also made for a good ideological weapon during the Cold War: the free United States was fighting the unfree Soviet Union. But the Bush administration has stunned the world by walking away from universally accepted human rights conventions, especially those on torture. And much as the U.S. electorate could not be expected to tolerate an attorney general who broke his own laws from time to time, how can the global body politic be expected to respect a custodian of international law that violates these very rules?

Finally, on social justice, Westerns nations have slackened. Social justice is the cornerstone of order and stability in modern Western societies and the rest of the world. People accept inequality as long as some kind of social safety net exists to help the dispossessed. Most western European governments took this principle to heart after World War II and introduced welfare provisions as a way to ward off Marxist revolutions seeking to create socialist societies. Today, many Westerners believe that they are spreading social justice globally with their massive foreign aid to the developing world. Indeed, each year, the members of the Organization for Economic Cooperation and Development, according to the organization's own estimates, give approximately $104 billion to the developing world. But the story of Western aid to the developing world is essentially a myth. Western countries have put significant amounts of money into their overseas development assistance budgets, but these funds' primary purpose is to serve the immediate and short-term security and national interests of the donors rather than the long-term interests of the recipients.

Some Asian countries are now ready to join the West in becoming responsible custodians of the global order.

The experience of Asia shows that where Western aid has failed to do the job, domestic good governance can succeed. This is likely to be Asia's greatest contribution to world history. The success of Asia will inspire other societies on different continents to emulate it. In addition, Asia's march to modernity can help produce a more stable world order. Some Asian countries are now ready to join the West in becoming responsible custodians of the global order; as the biggest beneficiaries of the current system, they have powerful incentives to do so. The West is not welcoming Asia's progress, and its short-term interests in preserving its privileged position in various global institutions are trumping its long-term interests in creating a more just and stable world order. Unfortunately, the West has gone from being the world's primary problem solver to being its single biggest liability.

Critical Thinking

1. According to Kishore Mahbubani, how is the West's strategic thinking flawed?

2. How did the U.S. invasion of Iraq affect the Middle East region? What was its impact on international law?

3. How has western policy contributed to the undermining of the Nuclear Nonproliferation Treaty?

4. How do recent western trade and environmental policies affect prospects for progress on these issues?

5. What does Mahbubani argue the West must do to address the challenges that face the international system?

KISHORE MAHBUBANI is Dean of the Lee Kuan Yew School of Public Policy at the National University of Singapore. This essay is adapted from his latest book, *The New Asian Hemisphere: The Irresistible Shift of Global Power to the East* (Public Affairs, 2008).

From *Foreign Affairs*, May/June 2008, pp. 111–124. Copyright © 2008 by Council on Foreign Relations, Inc. Reprinted by permission of Foreign Affairs. www.ForeignAffairs.com

UNIT 2

Political Economy and the Developing World

Unit Selections

Learning Outcomes

After reading this unit, you should be able to:

- Discuss the challenges to the Washington Consensus
- Outline the impact of the recent financial crisis on developing countries.
- Trace the obstacles to reform in India.
- Explain China's impact on developing countries.
- Discuss the nature of the international trade system and describe the differences between industrialized and developing countries on trade issues.
- Describe the factors that have helped improve Africa's economic prospects.
- Recognize the changes in funding and disbursement of development aid and the issues associated with these activities.
- Analyze the advantages and disadvantages of microfinance.
- Assess the prospects for reducing corruption in developing countries.

Student Website

www.mhhe.com/cls

Internet References

Center for Third World Organizing
www.ctwo.org

ENTERWeb
www.enterweb.org

International Monetary Fund (IMF)
www.imf.org

TWN (Third World Network)
www.twnside.org.sg

U.S. Agency for International Development (USAID)
www.usaid.gov

The World Bank
www.worldbank.org

World Trade Organization (WTO)
www.wto.org

Economic issues are among the most pressing concerns of the developing world. Economic growth and stability are essential to tackle the various problems confronting developing countries. Even though the developing world is beginning to play a larger role in the global economy and there have been significant increases in living standards, many countries still continue to struggle to achieve consistent economic growth. Economic inequality between the industrial countries and much of the developing world also persists. This is especially true of the poorest countries that have become further marginalized due to their limited participation in the global economy. Substantial inequality within developing countries is also obvious. The elite's access to education, capital, and technology has significantly widened the gap between the rich and the poor. Since their incorporation into the international economic system during colonialism, the majority of developing countries have been primarily suppliers of raw materials, agricultural products, and inexpensive labor. Dependence on commodity exports means that developing countries have had to deal with fluctuating, and frequently declining, prices for their exports. At the same time, prices for imports have remained constant or have increased. At best, this decline in terms of trade has made development planning difficult; at worst, it has led to economic stagnation and decline. Although industrialization in China and India boosted demand for primary products over the past few years, the recent global economic decline has resulted in falling demand and lower prices, clearly demonstrating that dependence on the export of raw materials is not an ideal long-term strategy for economic success. Domestic constraints may also prevent India from further boosting its economic growth.

With a few exceptions, most of the developing nations have had limited success in breaking out of this dilemma through the diversification of their economies. Efforts at industrialization and export of light manufactured goods have led to competition with the less efficient industries of the industrialized world. The response of industrialized countries has often been protectionism and demands for trade reciprocity, which can overwhelm the markets of the developing countries. The economic situation in the developing world, however, is not entirely attributable to colonial legacy and protectionism on the part of industrialized countries. Developing countries have sometimes constructed their own trade barriers. In addition, industrialization schemes involving heavy government direction were often ill-conceived or have resulted in corruption and mismanagement. Industrialized countries frequently point to these inefficiencies in calling for market-oriented reforms, but the emphasis on privatization does not adequately recognize the role of the state in developing countries' economies; and privatization may result in foreign control of important sectors of the economy, as well as a loss of jobs. Moreover, developing countries charge that the industrialized countries are selective in their efforts to dismantle trade barriers and emphasize only those trade issues that reflect their interests. Delegates from poor countries walked out of the 2003 WTO ministerial meeting in Cancún, Mexico, protesting the rich countries' reluctance to eliminate agricultural subsidies and their efforts to dominate the agenda. Neither the 2005 Hong Kong

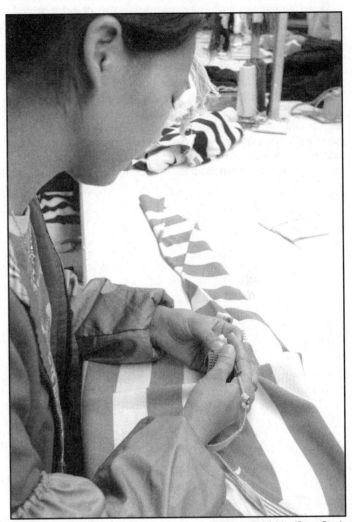

© Ingram Publishing/SuperStock

WTO ministerial meeting nor the 2006 talks in Geneva made much progress on forming a comprehensive international trade agreement. Further talks in 2007 and 2008 also failed to produce an agreement, largely due to disagreement over agricultural trade. It seems increasingly unlikely that the Doha round will produce a broad agreement further liberalizing trade.

During the 1970s, developing countries' prior economic performance and the availability of petrodollars encouraged extensive commercial lending. The worldwide recession in the early 1980s left many developing countries unable to meet their debt obligations and international financial institutions became the lenders of last resort. Access to the World Bank and International Monetary Fund became conditional on the adoption of structural adjustment programs that involved steps such as reduced public expenditures, devaluation of currencies, and export promotion, all geared to debt reduction. The consequences of these programs have been painful for developing countries, resulting in declining public services, higher prices, and greater reliance on primary production.

However, the global economic crisis has undermined the Washington Consensus, which was the basis for many of these policy prescriptions. As a result, developing countries are much more likely to be skeptical of the western model of development.

Despite a renewed interest in foreign aid after the September 11th attacks, the effectiveness of this assistance remains uneven. Some are calling for a re-evaluation of aid that takes into account broader goals and the greater number of actors involved and provides better ways to measure effectiveness. Efforts to raise more revenue for development aid have led to innovative financing schemes. The money raised by small taxes on airline tickets and voluntary contributions associated with the sale of certain products can then be channeled to developing countries to help fight disease and boost economic activity. In the meantime, the emergence of non-governmental organizations as major players in the disbursement of aid has become a controversial trend. Critics argue that this lets incompetent governments escape responsibility and scrutiny. While microloans have been credited with helping to reduce poverty, criticism has emerged regarding the cost of these loans and the emergence of large banks and financial institutions as providers of these funds. The amount of development aid available as well as its effectiveness and administration continue to be controversial topics. Globalization has produced differing views regarding the benefits and costs of this trend for the developing world. Advocates claim that closer economic integration, especially through trade and financial liberalization, increases economic prosperity in developing countries and encourages good governance, transparency, and accountability. Critics respond that globalization favors the powerful nations and through the international financial institutions, imposes difficult and perhaps counterproductive policies on the struggling economies. They also charge that globalization undermines workers' rights and causes environmental degradation. Moreover, most of the benefits of globalization have gone to those countries that are already growing—leaving the poorest even further behind.

The Post-Washington Consensus
Development after the Crisis

Nancy Birdsall and Francis Fukuyama

The last time a global depression originated in the United States, the impact was devastating not only for the world economy but for world politics as well. The Great Depression set the stage for a shift away from strict monetarism and laissez-faire policies toward Keynesian demand management. More important, for many it delegitimized the capitalist system itself, paving the way for the rise of radical and antiliberal movements around the world.

This time around, there has been no violent rejection of capitalism, even in the developing world. In early 2009, at the height of the global financial panic, China and Russia, two formerly noncapitalist states, made it clear to their domestic and foreign investors that they had no intention of abandoning the capitalist model. No leader of a major developing country has backed away from his or her commitment to free trade or the global capitalist system. Instead, the established Western democracies are the ones that have highlighted the risks of relying too much on market-led globalization and called for greater regulation of global finance.

Why has the reaction in developing countries been so much less extreme after this crisis than it was after the Great Depression? For one, they blame the United States for it. Many in the developing world agreed with Brazilian President Luiz Inácio Lula da Silva when he said, "This is a crisis caused by people, white with blue eyes." If the global financial crisis put any development model on trial, it was the free-market or neoliberal model, which emphasizes a small state, deregulation, private ownership, and low taxes. Few developing countries consider themselves to have fully adopted that model.

Indeed, for years before the crisis, they had been distancing themselves from it. The financial crises of the late 1990s in East Asia and Latin America discredited many of the ideas associated with the so-called Washington consensus, particularly that of unalloyed reliance on foreign capital. By 2008, most emerging-market countries had reduced their exposure to the foreign financial markets by accumulating large foreign currency reserves and maintaining regulatory control of their banking systems. These policies provided insulation from global economic volatility and were vindicated by the impressive rebounds in the wake of the recent crisis: the emerging markets have posted much better economic growth numbers than their counterparts in the developed world.

Thus, the American version of capitalism is, if not in full disrepute, then at least no longer dominant. In the next decade, emerging-market and low-income countries are likely to modify their approach to economic policy further, trading the flexibility and efficiency associated with the free-market model for domestic policies meant to ensure greater resilience in the face of competitive pressures and global economic trauma. They will become less focused on the free flow of capital, more concerned with minimizing social disruption through social safety net programs, and more active in supporting domestic industries. And they will be even less inclined than before to defer to the supposed expertise of the more developed countries, believing—correctly—that not only economic but also intellectual power are becoming increasingly evenly distributed.

The Foreign Finance Fetish

One of the central features of the old, pre-crisis economic consensus was the assumption that developing countries could benefit substantially from greater inflows of foreign capital—what the economist Arvind Subramanian has labeled "the foreign finance fetish." The idea that the unimpeded flow of capital around the globe, like the free flow of goods and services, makes markets more efficient was more or less taken for granted in policy circles. In the 1990s, the United States and international financial institutions such as the International Monetary Fund (IMF) pushed developing-country borrowers to open up their capital markets to foreign banks and dismantle exchange-rate controls.

Although the benefits of free trade have been well documented, the advantages of full capital mobility are much less clear. The reasons for this have to do with the fundamental differences between the financial sector and the "real" economy. Free capital markets can indeed allocate capital efficiently. But large interconnected financial institutions can also take risks that impose huge negative externalities on the rest of the economy in a way that large manufacturing firms cannot.

One of the paradoxical consequences of the 2008–9 financial crisis may thus be that Americans and Britons will finally learn what the East Asians figured out over a decade ago, namely, that open capital markets combined with unregulated financial sectors is a disaster in the waiting. At the conclusion of the Asian financial crisis, many U.S. policymakers and economists walked back their previous stress on quick liberalization and started promoting "sequencing," that is, liberalization only after a strong regulatory system with adequate supervision of banks has been put in place. But they devoted little thought to whether certain developing countries were capable of enacting such regulation quickly or what an appropriate regulatory regime would look like. And they overlooked the relevance of their new message to their own case, failing to warn against the danger of the huge, unregulated, and overleveraged shadow financial sector that had emerged in the United States.

The first clear consequence of the crisis has thus been the end of the foreign finance fetish. The countries that pursued it the most enthusiastically, such as Iceland, Ireland, and those in eastern Europe, were the hardest hit and face the toughest recoveries. Just as for Wall Street, the strong growth records these countries amassed from 2002 to 2007 proved to be partly a mirage, reflecting the easy availability of credit and high leverage ratios rather than strong fundamentals.

Caring about Caring

The second consequence is a new respect among developing countries for the political and social benefits of a sensible social policy. Before the crisis, policymakers tended to downplay social insurance and safety net programs in favor of strategies that emphasized economic efficiency. U.S. President Ronald Reagan and British Prime Minister Margaret Thatcher had come to power in the late 1970s and 1980s attacking the modern welfare state, and many of their critiques were well taken: state bureaucracies had become bloated and inefficient in many countries, and an entitlement mentality had taken hold. The Washington consensus did not necessarily reject the use of social policy, but its focus on efficiency and fiscal discipline often led to cuts in social spending.

What the crisis did, however, was to underscore the instability inherent in capitalist systems—even ones as developed and sophisticated as the United States. Capitalism is a dynamic process that regularly produces faultless victims who lose their jobs or see their livelihoods threatened. Throughout the crisis and its aftermath, citizens have expected their governments to provide some level of stability in the face of economic uncertainty. This is a lesson that politicians in developing-country democracies are not likely to forget; the consolidation and legitimacy of their fragile democratic systems will depend on their ability to deliver a greater measure of social protection.

Consider how continental Europe has reacted in comparison to the United States. Until now, with the eurozone crisis, western Europe experienced a far less painful recovery, thanks to its more developed system of automatic countercyclical social spending, including for unemployment insurance. In contrast, the jobless recovery in the United States makes the U.S. model even less attractive to policymakers in the developing world, particularly those who are increasingly subject to political pressure to attend to the needs of the middle class.

A good example of the new stress on social policy can be found in China. Reacting to the country's rapidly aging population, its leadership is struggling behind the scenes to build a modern pension system, something that represents a shift from the traditional tactic of concentrating solely on generating new jobs to maintain social and political stability. In Latin America, the same pressures are playing out differently. After experiencing fatigue in the wake of liberalizing reforms in the 1990s that did not seem to produce the growth that was expected, the region has moved to the left in this century, and the new governments have increased social spending to reduce poverty and inequality. Many countries have followed the successful example of Brazil and Mexico and instituted cash transfer schemes targeted to poor households (which require beneficiaries to keep their children in school or meet other conditions). In Brazil and Mexico, the approach has contributed to the first visible declines in income inequality in many years and helped shelter the poorest households from the recent crisis.

The question, of course, is whether programs like these that target the poor (and thus keep fiscal outlays surprisingly low) will have difficulty attracting long-term support from the region's growing middle class, and how these and other emerging economies, including China, will manage the fiscal costs of more universal health, pension, and other social insurance programs. Will they be better at handling the problems associated with these unfunded universal entitlement programs, the kinds of problems now facing Europe and the United States as their populations age?

The Visible Hand

The third consequence of the crisis has been the rise of a new round of discussions about industrial policy—a country's strategy to develop specific industrial sectors, traditionally through such support as cheap credit or outright subsidies or through state management of development banks. Such policies were written off as dangerous failures in the 1980s and 1990s for sustaining inefficient insider industries at high fiscal cost. But the crisis and the effective response to it by some countries are likely to bolster the notion that competent technocrats in developing countries are capable of efficiently managing state involvement in the productive sectors. Brazil, for example, used its government-sponsored development bank to direct credit to certain sectors quickly as part of its initial crisis-driven stimulus program, and China did the same thing with its state-run banks.

However, this new industrial policy is not about picking winners or bringing about large sectoral shifts in production. It is about addressing coordination problems and other barriers that discourage private investment in new industries and technologies, difficulties that market forces alone are unlikely to overcome. To promote an innovative clothing industry in West Africa, for example, governments might ensure a constant supply of textiles or subsidize the construction of ports to avoid export bottlenecks. The idea is that by bearing some of the initial financial or other risks and more systematically targeting public infrastructure, governments can help private investors overcome the high costs of being the first movers and innovators in incipient sectors.

For the last three decades, Washington-based development institutions have taken the view that growth is threatened more by government incompetence and corruption than by market failures. Now that American-style capitalism has fallen from its pedestal, might this view begin to shift? Might the idea that the state can take a more active role get far more traction? The answer depends, for any single developing country, on an assessment of its state capacity and overall governance. This is because the most significant critique of industrial policy was never economic but political, contending that economic decision-making in developing countries could not be shielded from political pressure. Critics argued that policymakers would retain protectionist measures long after they had fulfilled their original purpose of jump-starting domestic industries. Industrial policies such as reducing dependency on imports and promoting infant industries, although later derided in Washington, did in fact produce impressive rates of economic growth in the 1950s and 1960s in East Asia and Latin America. The problem, however, was that governments in the latter region were politically unable to unwind that protection, and so their domestic industries failed to become globally competitive.

Therefore, technocrats in developing countries contemplating the use of industrial policies must consider the politics of doing so. Does a bureaucracy exist that is sufficiently capable and autonomous from political pressure? Is there enough money to sustain such an agenda? Will it be possible to make hard political decisions, such as eliminating the policies when they are no longer needed? Most of the successful uses of industrial policy have been in East Asia, which has a long tradition of strong technocratic bureaucracies. Countries without such a legacy need to be more careful.

Making Bureaucracy Work

If countries are to promote industrial development and provide a social safety net, they will need to reform their public sectors; indeed, the fourth consequence of the crisis has been a painful reminder of the costs of not doing so. In the United States, regulatory agencies were underfunded, had difficulty attracting high-quality personnel, and faced political opposition. This was not surprising: implicit in the Reagan-Thatcher doctrine was the belief that markets were an acceptable substitute for efficient government. The crisis demonstrated that unregulated or poorly regulated markets can produce extraordinary costs.

Leaders in both the developing world and the developed world have marveled at China's remarkable ability to bounce back after the crisis, a result of a tightly managed, top-down policymaking machine that could avoid the delays of a messy democratic process. In response, political leaders in the developing world now associate efficiency and capability with autocratic political systems. But there are plenty of incompetent autocratic regimes. What sets China apart is a bureaucracy that, at its upper levels at least, is capable of managing and coordinating sophisticated policies. Among low-income countries, that makes China an exception.

Promoting effective public sectors is one of the most daunting development challenges that the world faces. Development institutions such as the World Bank and the United Kingdom's Department for International Development have supported programs that strengthen public sectors, promote good governance, and combat corruption for the last 15 years with little to show for it. The fact that even financial regulators in the United States and the United Kingdom failed to use their existing powers or to keep pace with rapidly evolving markets is a humbling reminder that effective public sectors are a challenge to maintain in even the most developed countries.

Why has so little progress been made in improving developing countries' public sectors? The first problem is that their bureaucracies often serve governments that are rent-seeking coalitions acting according to self-interest, instead of an ideal of impersonal public service. Outside donors typically do not have the leverage to force them to change, with the partial exception of mechanisms such as the European Union's accession process. Second, effective institutions have to evolve indigenously, reflecting a country's own political, social, and cultural realities. The development of impersonal bureaucracies in the West was the product of a long and painful process, with factors exogenous to the economy (such as the need to mobilize for war) playing a large part in creating strong state institutions (such as Prussia's famously efficient bureaucracy). Institutions such as the rule of law will rarely work if they are simply copied from abroad; societies must buy into their content. Finally, public-sector reform requires a parallel process of nation building. Unless a society has a clear sense of national identity and a shared public interest, individuals will show less loyalty to it than to their ethnic group, tribe, or patronage network.

Moving to Multipolarity

Years from now, historians may well point to the financial crisis as the end of American economic dominance in global affairs. But the trend toward a multipolar world began much earlier, and the implosion of Western financial markets and their weak recoveries have merely accelerated the process. Even before the crisis, the international institutions created after World War II to manage economic and security challenges were under strain and in need of reform. The IMF and the World Bank suffered from governance structures that reflected outdated economic realities. Starting in the 1990s and continuing into the new century, the Bretton Woods institutions have come under increasing pressure to grant more voting power to emerging-market countries such as Brazil and China. Meanwhile, the G-7, the elite group of the six most economically important Western democracies plus Japan, remained the world's informal steering committee when it came to issues of global economic coordination, even as other power centers emerged.

The financial crisis finally led to the demise of the G-7 as the primary locus of global economic policy coordination and its replacement by the G-20. In November 2008, heads of state from the G-20 gathered in Washington, D.C., to coordinate a global stimulus program—a meeting that has since grown into an established international institution. Since the G-20, unlike the G-7, includes emerging countries such as Brazil, China, and India, the expansion of economic coordination represents an overdue recognition of a new group of global economic players.

The crisis also breathed new life and legitimacy into the IMF and the World Bank. Beforehand, the IMF had looked like it was rapidly becoming obsolete. Private capital markets provided countries with financing on favorable terms without the conditions often attached to IMF loans. The organization was having trouble funding its own activities and was in the process of reducing its staff.

But the outlook changed in 2009, when the G-20 leaders agreed to ensure that the Bretton Woods institutions would have as much as $1 trillion in additional resources to help countries better weather future financing shortfalls. Countries such as Brazil and China were among the contributors to the special funds, which have ended up supporting Greece, Hungary, Iceland, Ireland, Latvia, Pakistan, and Ukraine.

By requesting that emerging markets take on a bigger leadership role in global affairs, the Western democracies are implicitly admitting that they are no longer able to manage global economic affairs on their own. But what has been called "the rise of the rest" is not just about economic and political power; it also has to do with the global competition of ideas and models. The West, and in particular the United States, is no longer seen as the only center for innovative thinking about social policy. Conditional cash transfer schemes, for example, were first developed and implemented in Latin America. As for industrial policy, the West has contributed little innovative thinking in that realm in the last 30 years. One has to turn to emerging-market countries, rather than the developed world, to see successful models in practice. And when it comes to international organizations, the voices and ideas of the United States and Europe are becoming less dominant. Those of emerging-market countries—states that have become significant funders of the international financial institutions—are being given greater weight.

All this signals a clear shift in the development agenda. Traditionally, this was an agenda generated in the developed world that was implemented in—and, indeed, often imposed on—the developing world. The United States, Europe, and Japan will continue to be significant sources of economic resources and ideas, but the emerging markets are now entering this arena and will become significant players. Countries such as Brazil, China, India, and South Africa will be both donors and recipients of resources for development and of best practices for how to use them. A large portion of the world's poor live within their borders, yet they have achieved new respect on the global scene in economic, political, and intellectual terms. In fact, development has never been something that the rich bestowed on the poor but rather something the poor achieved for themselves. It appears that the Western powers are finally waking up to this truth in light of a financial crisis that, for them, is by no means over.

Critical Thinking

1. How did the financial crisis affect attitudes about capital mobility?

2. Why are emerging economies more likely to favor social spending in the aftermath of the crisis?

3. What is the emerging attitude about industrial policy?

4. What will countries need to effectively implement social and industrial policies?

5. How has the financial crisis changed developing countries' influence on international economic policy?

NANCY BIRDSALL is President of the Center for Global Development. **FRANCIS FUKUYAMA** is Olivier Nomellini Senior Fellow at the Freeman Spogli Institute for International Studies at Stanford University. They are the editors of *New Ideas in Development After the Financial Crisis* (Johns Hopkins University Press, 2011), from which this essay is adapted.

From *Foreign Affairs*, March/April 2011, pp. 45–53. Copyright © 2011 by Council on Foreign Relations, Inc. Reprinted by permission of Foreign Affairs. www.ForeignAffairs.com

The Poor Man's Burden

Eighty years ago, a depression changed the way we think about poverty. It took decades for the world to recover and to remember that if people are given freedom, they will prosper. Now, in the wake of another massive meltdown, the fear that shocked us into depending on government to fix poverty is spreading once again—and threatening to undo many of the gains we've made.

WILLIAM EASTERLY

Will Richard Fuld, the disgraced CEO of the now defunct Lehman Brothers, go down in history as the father of Bolivian socialism? If we learn the wrong lessons from the global financial Crash of 2008, he very well could.

That's because the crash arrived at a crucial moment in the global fight to reduce poverty. For Bolivia—and so many other countries like it—the crash represents much more than a temporary downturn; it could mean the end of one of the greatest openings for prosperity in decades. Amid today's gloom, it is easy to forget we have just witnessed half a century of the greatest mass escape from poverty in human history. The proportion of the world's population living in extreme poverty in 2008 (those earning less than a $1 a day) was a fifth of what it was in 1960. In 2008, the income of the average citizen of the world was nearly three times higher than it was in 1960. But those tremendous gains are now in peril. For this crash hit many poor countries from Asia to Africa to Latin America that are still experimenting with political and economic freedom—but have yet to fully embrace it and experience its benefits. For decades, these countries have struggled tremendously to realize the potential of individual creativity as opposed to the smothering hand of the state. And it even seemed that the power of individual liberty might be winning.

It wasn't happening because experts had handed out some blueprint for achieving economic growth to governments and then down to their people. What happened instead was a Revolution from Below—poor people taking initiative without experts telling them what to do. We saw such surprising success stories as the family grocer in Kenya who became a supermarket giant, the Nigerian women who got rich making tie-dyed garments, the Chinese schoolteacher who became a millionaire exporting socks, and the Congolese entrepreneur who started a wildly successful cellphone business in the midst of his country's civil war. Perhaps not coincidentally, the share of countries enjoying greater levels of economic and political freedom steadily and simultaneously shot upward.

Then came the crash.

Today, global economic calamity risks aborting that hopeful Revolution from Below. As India's Prime Minister Manmohan Singh warned late last fall, "It would be a great pity if this growing support for open policies in the developing world is weakened" because of the crash. Singh understands that the risk of a backlash against individual freedom is far more dangerous than the direct damage to poor countries caused by a global recession, falling commodity prices, or shrinking capital flows. We're already seeing this dangerous trend in Latin America. In Bolivia, President Evo Morales has openly crowed about the failure of Fuld's Lehman Brothers and other Wall Street giants: The capitalist "models in place are not a good solution for humanity . . . because [they are] based on injustice and inequality." Socialism, he said, will be the solution—in Bolivia, the state "regulates the national economy, and not the free market." The leaders of Argentina, Bolivia, Brazil, Ecuador, Nicaragua, Honduras, Paraguay, Venezuela, and even tiny Dominica to varying degrees align with these anticapitalist pretensions, all seemingly vindicated by the Crash of 2008. And it's not confined to Latin America: Vladimir Putin blamed the U.S. financial system for his own populist mismanagement of Russia's even more catastrophic crisis. A spreading fire of statism would find plenty of kindling already stacked in the Middle East, the former Soviet Union, Africa, and Asia. And there are many Western "development" experts who would eagerly fan the flames with their woolly, paternalistic thinking.

To Jeffrey Sachs, perhaps the foremost of these experts, the crash is an opportunity to gain support for the hopelessly utopian Millennium Development Goals of reducing poverty, achieving gender equality, and improving the general state of the planet through a centrally planned, government-led Big Push. "The US could find $700 billion for a bailout of its corrupt and errant banks but couldn't find a small fraction of that for the world's poor and dying," he wrote in September. "The laggards in the struggle for the [goals] are not the poor countries . . . the laggards are the rich world." To Sachs and his acolytes, poor people can't prosper without Western-country plans—and the crash only serves to turn Western governments inward. Therefore, progress on poverty is bound to suffer. To governments of poor countries that have failed to give their people the freedom needed to prosper, the neglect of Western governments is an easy excuse. So the gospel of Sachs and his disciples, though terribly condescending and wrong-headed, could attract many converts in the coming months.

A Depressing History

At least we've been here before—and we have a chance to avoid the philosophical traps we fell into after the last calamity that did so much harm to our economic system. But so far, there have been strikingly similar reactions to the crashes of 1929 and 2008. In both cases, when stocks registered some of their largest percentage declines on record, highly leveraged firms and individuals who had placed large bets using complex financial securities that few understood lost everything. The failure of gigantic financial firms spread panic. Complaints about the greedy and reckless rich escalated; a shift toward protectionism and government interventionism appeared inevitable even where free markets once reigned supreme. Authoritarian populists abroad mocked the U.S. system. The catastrophe seemed to threaten democratic capitalism everywhere.

So far, there have been strikingly similar reactions to the crashes of 1929 and 2008.

The difference is today we know that after a long and scary Great Depression, democratic capitalism did survive. And the U.S. economy returned to exactly the same long-run trend path it was on before the Depression.

We also know that, for another important part of the world, democratic capitalism did not hold up so well. In many ways, that failure stemmed from a misguided overreaction on the part of a new, influential field of economics that was highly skeptical of capitalism, was deeply traumatized by economic calamity, and considered much of the world "underdeveloped." Born in the aftermath of the Depression, "development economics" grew on a foundation of bizarre misconceptions and dangerous assumptions.

This approach to poor-country development, promulgated by the economists who took up its cause in the 1950s, had four unfortunate lasting consequences, the effects of which we're still reckoning with today in the midst of the latest big crash.

First, seeing Depression-style unemployment in every part of the world led these economists to assume that poor countries simply had too many people who were literally producing nothing. A U.N. report in 1951, produced by a group of economists, including future Nobel laureate Arthur Lewis, estimated that fully half of the farming population of Egypt produced

nothing. The insulting assumption that poor people had "zero" productivity led these economists to think that individual freedoms for the poor should not be the foundation for wealth creation, as they had been during the Industrial Revolution, when the state had played a secondary, supportive role. And because governments seemed to successfully take on a larger role during the Depression, development economists assumed that granting extensive powers to the state was the surest path to progress. A 1947 U.N. report on development gave equivalent approval to state action in democratic capitalist countries like Chile, enslaved Soviet satellites like Poland, African colonies of the British and French, and apartheid South Africa, ignoring the vast differences in individual liberty between these places.

Second, these thinkers lost faith in bottom-up economic development that was "spontaneous, as in the classical capitalist pattern" (as a later history put it), preferring instead development "consciously achieved through state planning." After all, the Five-Year Plans of the 1930s Soviet Union had avoided the Depression, at an appalling but then ignored cost in lives and human rights. This thinking was so universal that Gunnar Myrdal (who would later win a Nobel Prize in economics) claimed in 1956: "Special advisors to underdeveloped countries who have taken the time and trouble to acquaint themselves with the problem . . . all recommend central planning as the first condition of progress."

Third, these economists grew to believe that the most important factor in reducing poverty was the amount of money invested in the tools to do so. After all, if there were simply too many people, they reasoned, the binding constraint on growth must be the lack of physical equipment. As a result, this line of economic philosophy would forever stress the volume of investment over the efficiency of using those resources; would be stubbornly indifferent as to whether it was the state or individuals who made the investments; would always stress the total amount of aid required to finance investment as the crucial ingredient in escaping poverty; and would ignore the role of a dynamic financial system in allocating investment resources to those private uses where they would get the highest return.

Fourth, the collapse of international trade during the Depression made development economists skeptical about trade as an engine of growth. So in Africa, for example, they pushed for heavy taxes on export crops like cocoa to finance domestic industrialization. In Latin America, Raúl Prebisch pushed import-substituting industrialization instead of export-led growth. This strategy was supposed to help developing countries in Africa and Latin America escape a presumed "poverty trap." But the only "trap" it kept them out of was the greatest global trade boom in history following World War II, which fueled record growth in Asia, Europe, and the United States.

By the 1980s, the state-led plans had clearly failed. The wreckage of unsuccessful state enterprises, bankrupt state banks, and inefficient hothouse industries behind protectionist walls—all of which culminated in African and Latin American debt crises that destroyed growth—became too obvious to ignore. These factors, plus East Asia's rise to power in global markets, finally fueled a counterrevolution in development thinking that favored free markets and individual liberty. By the new millennium, the long record of failure of the top-down development experts triggered a well-deserved collapse of confidence in top-downplanning. It had taken nearly 50 years for the world to recognize the damage that the state-led, expert-directed, antifreedom agenda had done to the world's poor. Today, the only remaining holdouts among the top-down experts are so utopian that they are safely insulated from reality.

A 5(0)-Year Plan

Today, just when we were getting over the long, toxic legacy of the Depression and its misguided emphasis on statist plans to fight poverty, this financial crash threatens to take us back to the bad old days. To avoid such a return, we must keep some principles in mind.

First, we must not fall into the trap of protectionism—neither unilaterally nor multilaterally, neither in rich countries nor poor. Protectionism will just make the recession spread further and deeper, as it did during the Depression.

Second, when changing financial regulations to repair the excesses of the past several years, don't strangle the financial system altogether. You can't have a Revolution from Below without it. This lesson is especially salient as Washington bails out Wall Street banks and failing industries and intervenes in the U.S. financial sector to an unprecedented degree. This bailout might turn out to be the bitter medicine that saves "finance capitalism" from a stronger form of anticapitalism, but in developing countries, open economies are still an open question.

Third, keep slashing away at the enormous red tape that is left over from previous harebrained attempts at state direction of the economy. Learn from the combined dismal track record of state-owned enterprises but also from the unexpected success stories: Private entrepreneurs are far better than the government at picking industries that can be winners in the global economy. Although fierce opposition will be inevitable, to adopt these policies would be to turn the bad hand we've been dealt into an outright losing one.

Fourth, don't look to economists to create "development strategies," and don't back up such experts with external coercion like IMF and World Bank conditions on loans. Such efforts will be either a waste of local politicians' time or positively harmful. Jeffrey Sachs alone can take partial credit for the rise of two xenophobic rulers hostile to individual liberty—Evo Morales and Vladimir Putin—after his expert advice backfired in Bolivia and Russia. If like-minded experts couldn't get it done in the 50 years after the Great Depression, they can't do it in the next 50 years. Nothing in the current crash changes these common-sense principles.

Driving the Right Way

In the coming months and years, the world's economists, politicians, and average consumers could find it incredibly easy to fall again for the wrongheaded policies of the past century. But if we are truly to continue the miraculous exodus from poverty that was under way before this traumatic crash, we ought to keep in mind stories like that of Chung Ju-yung.

The son of North Korean peasant farmers, Chung had to leave school at 14 to support his family. He held jobs as a railway construction laborer, a dockworker, a bookkeeper, and a deliveryman for a rice shop in Seoul. At 22, he took over the rice shop, but it failed. He then started A-Do Service garage, but that failed, too. In 1946, at age 31, Chung tried once again to start an auto repair service in Seoul. At last, his enterprise succeeded, largely through the contracts he won to repair U.S. Army vehicles. As his success continued, Chung diversified into construction, and his company kept growing rapidly. In 1968, he started manufacturing cars.

He named his company Hyundai. It became one of the largest companies contributing to South Korea's rise. His first effort to export cars to the United States in 1986 brought ridicule because of the cars' poor quality. The Asian crisis of 1997–98 led to a partial breakup of the Hyundai Group, but the Hyundai Motor Company continues to thrive. Chung died in 2001, but his dreams for the U.S. market came true. By 2008, Hyundai cars had received awards in the United States for the highest level of quality from *Consumer Reports*.

However terrifying the latest crash may be, let's never forget that it is the Chungs of the world that will end poverty—not the Depression-inspired regression into statism.

Want to Know More?

William Easterly's most recent book, *The White Man's Burden: Why the West's Efforts to Aid the Rest Have Done So Much Ill and So Little Good* (New York: Oxford University Press, 2006), criticizes Western approaches to global poverty. In **"The Ideology of Development"** (*Foreign Policy* July/August 2007), Easterly warns of the dangers of "Developmentalism."

Easterly's chief economic adversaries, Jeffrey Sachs and Paul Collier, take a more aid-oriented approach. Sachs's *Common Wealth: Economics for a Crowded Planet* (New York: Penguin Press, 2008) and Collier's *The Bottom Billion: Why the Poorest Countries Are Failing and What Can Be Done About It* (New York: Oxford University Press, 2008) offer policy solutions for the world's most pressing problems.

For a look at one of the earliest and most prescient (and now forgotten) economists to advocate the potential of free markets as a tool for development, read S. Herbert Frankel's *Some Conceptual Aspects of International Economic Development of Underdeveloped Territories* (Princeton: Princeton University, 1952). For a more well-known early critique of development, see P.T. Bauer's *Dissent on Development* (Cambridge: Harvard University Press, 1976).

Critical Thinking

1. What impact might the 2008–2009 global financial crisis have on developing countries?
2. According to William Easterly, what accounts for the rapid decline in poverty rates in developing countries?
3. How might the economic slowdown affect open economic policies?
4. What steps must be taken to avoid a return to statist plans geared toward fighting poverty?

WILLIAM EASTERLY is professor of economics at New York University.

A Tiger Despite the Chains
The State of Reform in India

Powerful political interests still stand in the way of India's realizing its economic potential.

Rahul Mukherji

India's rapid and sustained economic growth since 1991 has occurred in an environment in which industrialists, trade unions, bureaucrats, farmers, and nongovernmental organizations wield considerable political power. Two decades ago, India was stereotyped as a "soft" state, quite unlike the fast-growing "tiger" economies of East Asia. India was deemed incapable of disciplining powerful social actors in order to promote its competitiveness.

This perception seemed confirmed when the economic growth that the country enjoyed in the 1980s, which was fueled by greater opportunities for private companies in a closed economy, became unsustainable in 1991 amid a balance of payments crisis. That crisis was driven by fiscal profligacy, a rise in the price of oil during the Gulf War in 1990, and India's heavy dependence on foreign commercial borrowings.

And yet, substantial economic reforms did occur after 1991, and they helped transform India's economy. How did this happen? New policy ideas gradually replaced old ones, which had emphasized economic self-sufficiency and trade pessimism. Also, reforming statesmen such as Prime Minister P. V. Narasimha Rao and Finance Minister (now Prime Minister) Manmohan Singh, along with reforming technocrats like Montek Ahluwalia and Chakravarthy Rangarajan, took advantage of the balance of payments crisis to alter fundamentally the rules of economic engagement in India.

Since 1991, the Indian economy has experienced an average growth rate in excess of 6 percent per year. Between 2003 and 2007, the economy grew at an average rate of 9 percent. It weathered the recent global financial crisis with greater ease than most countries' economies, and it continued to grow at a 6.7 percent clip in 2008–2009. India's current finance minister, Pranab Mukherjee, expects the figure to be 7.2 percent in 2009–2010. After the global downturn has ended, a return to a 9 percent growth rate seems likely.

But why does the Indian economy not grow at double-digit rates like China's does? It is because numerous political challenges still get in the way. Powerful constituencies such as trade unions, rich farmers, and politicians and bureaucrats still pose substantial obstacles to investment.

Trade unions, rich farmers, and politicians and bureaucrats still pose obstacles to investment.

In addition, economic reform has not yet benefited enough Indians for the country to harness the potential of its youthful workforce. Substantial resources have been pledged in areas such as literacy promotion and employment generation, yet the government so far has been unable to reach targeted populations efficiently. For India, which has more poverty than any other nation in the world, improvement in the human condition is not just an end in itself—it is a means toward sustaining a high-growth trajectory.

Reform and Rejuvenation

The government's response to the foreign exchange crisis in July and August of 1991 constituted a watershed in India's economic history. A number of significant policy decisions taken at that time subsequently improved the country's competitiveness in the global economy.

First, India devalued the rupee by about 20 percent, thereby making Indian exports cheaper in the world market. (In 1994, the rupee was made fully convertible in the capital account, which meant that exporters could easily access foreign exchange at the market rate.) Second, the government overturned an intrusive regulatory framework that had evolved since 1951, a framework that required industrialists to seek state permission before embarking on commercial enterprises. Third, the government abolished stringent regulations on capacity expansion in any company worth more than 1 billion rupees. Fourth, the foreign investment limit in most sectors was raised from 40 percent to 51 percent.

India's growth story owes a great deal to entrepreneurs who took advantage of the new industrial deregulation and export orientation of the 1990s. The country's ratio of trade to gross domestic product (GDP), which had been constant at about 16 percent between 1980–81 and 1990–91, jumped to 54 percent by 2008. Information technology exports surged from $194 million in 1991–92 to $6.54 billion in 2001–02, and to $50.4 billion in 2008–09.

The information technology service company Infosys, which began with an initial investment of $250 in 1981, was worth $4 billion in 2008. Tata Steel retrenched its workforce and invested $2.5 billion to transform itself from a top-fifty steel company in the world to one of the leading five. The Tata Group, in search of technology and markets, bought the Anglo-Dutch steel maker Corus Group in 2007 for $12.1 billion.

Successful companies have generated substantial personal wealth for a few individuals. Mukesh Ambani, a tycoon in several industries, is the fourth-richest person in the world, with a fortune of $29 billion. According to the latest rankings in *Forbes*, four other Indian entrepreneurs rank among the top fifty billionaires.

Linking domestic competitiveness with global acquisitions has become characteristic of many of India's best companies. These include Bharat Forge (automobile parts), Tata Motors (cars), Wipro (information technology), Dr. Reddy's (pharmaceuticals), and Tata Tea (fast-moving consumer goods).

In 2006–07, Indian companies spent $12.8 billion on acquisitions of overseas companies, compared with China's $16.1 billion. This represented a substantial amount, considering that the Chinese economy is two and a half times the size of the Indian economy. Moreover, a large share of Chinese investment was accounted for by state-owned companies pursuing natural resources, whereas India's investments were made by private companies in search of technology, brand names, and markets.

Financial Returns

The government also successfully reformed India's banks and stock markets to create the financial environment necessary for growth. The Reserve Bank of India improved the supervision of banks and systematically subjected them to international best practices. This led to a substantial reduction in bad debts and an improvement in profitability. Indeed, India's banking system is today better regulated than China's.

The government viewed stock markets as critical for raising resources for Indian companies. So, when the brokers of the Bombay Stock Exchange refused to accept international best practices, the Ministry of Finance in 1993 created a modern and computerized national stock exchange. Competition from the national exchange forced the Bombay exchange to acquiesce to the reforms suggested by the Ministry of Finance. Substantial reforms in trading norms followed, in 2003.

The booming markets quickly became an attractive investment proposition for Indians and foreigners alike. India's stock markets attracted $24.2 billion from foreign institutional investors between 1992–93 and 2002–03. This figure was a little higher than the foreign direct investment ($24.1 billion) registered during the same period.

Foreign investment was impaired because the business environment for multinational companies was more hostile in India than in China. India had enormous entrepreneurial potential waiting to be unleashed in 1991, whereas China had no private sector when it initiated its economic reforms. Partly as a result, India's government and companies were more cautious than China about allowing foreign investment. In 1993, an informal group of industrialists calling themselves the Bombay Club made the case that foreign investment was detrimental to India. Many a productive investment was blocked by regulations governing joint ventures with foreign partners and by the need for state-level intervention in matters related to obtaining land, water, electricity, road infrastructure, and a variety of such amenities.

This business environment for foreign investors is changing gradually. Successful Indian businesses that began as relatively small entrepreneurial endeavors have needed foreign capital and technology to compete with larger companies. For example, the Hero Group, a bicycle manufacturer, partnered with Honda to become a leading producer of motorized two-wheelers. Bharti's partnership with SingTel helped it become India's leading telecom service provider. Whereas India attracted $24.1 billion in foreign direct investment between 1992–93 and 2002–03, in a single recent year (2008–09) it attracted $27.3 billion.

The Telecom Boom

It is well known that India's telecom boom has contributed substantially to the country's growth. Less widely known perhaps has been the impact of government actions on telecommunications. India has more than 500 million telephone lines and is adding between 8 and 10 million lines every month, in what is considered the world's fastest-growing telecom market. Indian companies offer the cheapest rates in the world. But it was the Indian state's response to the balance of payments crisis of 1991 that created conditions favorable for private sector participation and growth in the telecom field. The government proved it was serious about withdrawing from commercially viable sectors in order to reduce substantial fiscal deficits.

In the early 1990s, private sector activity in the absence of appropriate regulation sowed the seeds for companies to experience investment crises later in the decade. This could have driven telecom service providers to bankruptcy. But the government again responded, first in 1997, by creating the Telecom Regulatory Authority of India, then in 2000 by further empowering the regulators.

The success of Indian telecommunications owes much to the spread of wireless telephone. By 2008, 90 percent of the Indian market was using wireless technology. Two principal factors made this possible. First, the sector's transformation from a government monopoly in 1991 to one in which 80 percent of the market is now served by private companies drove telecommunications providers to become more efficient. Technological advances in mobile technology further fueled growth. (Private companies enjoyed the first mover's advantage in cellular services because the government had not predicted the potential of this technology in the early 1990s.)

Second, competent regulation promoted competition among service providers, which exerted downward pressure on tariffs. Today the penetration of mobile telephones in the smaller cities and villages holds great promise of opening up new opportunities for the poorer people of India.

Remaining Fetters

Notwithstanding India's economic performance over the past two decades, powerful interest groups—in particular, trade unions, wealthy farmers, and government bureaucracies—continue to present substantial challenges to the promotion of the nation's competitiveness and overall development. They constitute the principal reasons that India is unable to grow as rapidly as China.

India's labor unions, though they represent less than 10 percent of the workforce, have successfully thwarted a social contract that would benefit the majority of Indian workers and boost the country's productivity. Trade unions in many European countries, with memberships that protect more than 70 percent of the labor force, have promoted a business environment in which labor is productive and contributes to the industrial sector's competitiveness. Labor laws in India, on the other hand, protect a minority of workers and turn a blind eye to the majority in the unorganized sector who work under exploitative conditions.

Legal protection for labor, moreover, increases with the size of the enterprise. The government's regulatory framework thus forces industrial enterprises either to reduce their scale or become more capital-intensive. This is a disincentive for reaping economies of scale in a labor-abundant economy like India's.

The political power of the unions can be judged from the fact that even severe economic crises and fiscal and external pressures have not made an impact on laws that create perverse incentives. India is in dire need of more widely inclusive unions that pledge productivity in return for social protection. This represents a significant challenge for promoting competitiveness in labor-intensive activities, an essential condition for generating more employment.

India's rich farmer lobby is another potent political force and hindrance to growth and development. This lobby benefits from fertilizer and power subsidies that do not help marginal farmers and that crowd out public investments in areas such as irrigation and rural roads. The subsidies also contribute handsomely to India's fiscal deficits.

To be sure, public investment is essential in a sector that constitutes less than 20 percent of GDP yet employs a majority of the population. Average annual growth in the country's agricultural sector dipped from 3.4 percent in the 1980s to 2.9 percent in the 1990s. The sector witnessed zero or negative growth in three of the first four years of the new millennium. Policy makers have tried to give agriculture serious attention since 2004.

But the political power of the wealthy farmers has stalled reforms, particularly in the power sector. Farmers in many Indian states do not pay electricity bills. In states such as Andhra Pradesh and Tamil Nadu, the agricultural lobby can bring down governments that seek to impose even a subsidized tariff. Consequently, the losses of state-owned power companies have increased from $4.8 billion in 2005–06 to $7.1 billion in 2008–09.

The private sector hesitates to play an enthusiastic role in a business environment in which obtaining revenues is a major challenge. And the power sector's losses not only impose a burden on the public treasury; they also increase costs for industry, which has to subsidize the free power delivered to farmers.

India's poorer farmers, meanwhile, are unable to benefit from these subsidies because their farms depend on canal irrigation and diesel pumps. Farmers who consume free electricity to run electric hand pumps pay a price anyway, in the form of poor power quality and frequent transformer burnouts.

Land acquisition can also be a major bottleneck for productive investment in India. Political mobilization at the local level often impedes acquisition of land for industrial enterprises. To give one example, Tata Motors faced a slew of challenges when it wanted to make an iconic investment in the world's cheapest car, the Nano. Such was the level of politically motivated opposition to the setting up of a Nano factory in Singur, in the eastern state of West Bengal, that one of the most highly respected captains of Indian industry, Ratan Tata, had to shift the location of the factory from Singur to Pantnagar, in the northern state of Uttarakhand.

Laws that govern the acquisition of land contain serious flaws. The colonial-era Land Acquisition Act gives the government absolute power to acquire any piece of land. But protests in places like Singur and Nandigram in West Bengal point to the need to win the consent of the local population. The government needs to devise a regulatory framework that allows for adequate compensation and makes the acquirers of land work toward improving the living conditions of those who will be displaced as a result of commercial activity.

Within an appropriate regulatory framework, productive investment can be a win-win situation for the investor and for displaced people. Investment-friendly states such as Gujarat, Tamil Nadu, Haryana, and Andhra Pradesh have found ways to win consent for land acquisitions in the absence of a national regulatory framework; as a result, they have been able to attract more investment and grow rapidly.

Government in the Way

Even more than trade unions and obstructive rural interests, the government itself is often the worst enemy of competitiveness in India. For example, the ports that carry 95 percent of the country's trade by volume could benefit from better regulation of private investment. India's ports charge higher fees and take a longer time to provide services than do ports in Dubai, Colombo, and Singapore. Larger vessels often dock in other countries' more efficient ports and use smaller vessels to ship merchandise to India because of the inadequacy of that nation's port infrastructure. Indian ports thus lose business, and Indian exports and imports face higher transaction costs.

The government's regulation of private sector participation in ports is primitive compared to its regulation of the telecom sector. Bidding procedures regarding ports, for example, encourage private players to make unreasonably high bids to secure contracts that may not be commercially viable. Tariff-making procedures do not aid the realization of scale economies. And the governance of most major ports is controlled by port trusts, which are run by government servants who do not respect commercial considerations. The terminal charges for private operators are competitive, but high port costs result from additional charges levied by the port trusts.

The government has dragged its feet in other areas as well. The civil aviation sector lacks an independent regulator, and Air India continues to lose money. The United Progressive Alliance government, in office since 2004, has been averse to the privatization of a loss-making airline. As a consequence, precious taxpayers' money is diverted from developmental projects. The case of Air India reflects a trend in which disinvestment in loss-making public companies has taken a back seat in recent years.

In contrast, allowing a greater role for commercial considerations in Indian Railways six years ago catapulted the rail system from bankruptcy to substantial profits. Yet the populist inclinations of the government's new railway minister may overturn this legacy. Likewise, the development of national highways and private sector participation in roads have also slowed in recent years. These infrastructure areas are vital for India's economic growth, and the government is constricting their development.

Sharing Growth

India's rapid economic growth needs to involve a larger proportion of the citizenry. The government's inattention to areas such as literacy promotion and employment generation has helped produce unacceptable levels of absolute poverty. Most economists believe that about 26 percent of the Indian people in 1999 lived below the poverty line, under unacceptable conditions, when the same figure for China was about 10 percent.

The economic reforms of the early 1990s clearly reduced poverty levels from what they would have been without the reforms. But it is also apparent that the benefits of rapid economic growth trickle down too slowly in India. Moreover, it may not be politically feasible to sustain a social environment in which a few of the richest individuals in the world coexist with a vast population that lives on less than $2 a day.

India produces more engineers than the United States, but its literacy rate in 2001 was 61 percent, far lower than in China—or, for that matter, in Sri Lanka, where more than 90 percent of the population is literate. India's policy elite during the 1990s ignored the need to abolish child labor and promote literacy. The prevailing view was that poor people could keep their children at work to augment their family incomes, and that literacy for such Indians was not critical.

This view has changed over time. India's Supreme Court linked the right to education and the right to life in 1993.

In the new millennium, the government has pledged substantially greater resources for literacy promotion, a commitment that was evident in the Right to Education Act of 2009. More than 96 percent of Indian children aged 6 to 14 years were enrolled in school in 2006–07. This suggests that the literacy picture in India is undergoing a belated transformation.

The major challenge facing literacy promotion is the low quality of government schools. Teacher absenteeism rates in India's public schools are among the highest in the world. And the children of poor parents have no exit options. Cheap private schools serve the lower middle class and the relatively better off among the poor. Policy makers are debating whether school vouchers for the poor may be a better option than spending large sums of money on government schools that are largely dysfunctional. States like Madhya Pradesh have been able to reduce teacher absenteeism by involving village governments in the governance of schools and by keeping teachers on renewable contracts.

High levels of unemployment and underemployment also pose a significant challenge for poverty alleviation. The Mahatma Gandhi National Rural Employment Guarantee Act (NREGA) of 2005 is the most ambitious welfare program in India. It guarantees 100 days of paid work to all who seek employment. Employment is generated by the creation of public goods such as water tanks, roads, and schools, especially in rural areas. Public works are monitored by local village governments.

According to NREGA, 47.2 million families have benefited so far from this scheme, over 50 percent of whom are from socially and economically marginalized castes and tribes, and 48 percent of the beneficiaries are women. Rajasthan has the best implementation record, and India's poorest states—including Bihar, Chhattisgarh, and Madhya Pradesh—are among NREGA's top five beneficiaries. This program seems to be making a dent in poverty, notwithstanding some corruption problems.

Corruption has been the bane of India's poverty reduction efforts. Funds provided for employment generation schemes are often siphoned off to benefit richer families. In 2003–04, over $90 million out of a $158 million food subsidy did not reach a single family whose economic status was considered below the official poverty line. Meanwhile, teacher absenteeism impairs literacy initiatives, and health worker absenteeism weakens health programs.

The current government has taken two significant steps in an effort to improve service delivery for Indian citizens. First, the Right to Information Act of 2005 replaced the Official Secrets Act of 1923, which had made it legally impossible to obtain information vital for punishing corruption within the government. Social activists such as Aruna Roy helped bring about this reform. Roy had resigned from the civil service and started a "social audit," whereby poorer people who were supposed to benefit from public services began to assess government programs. The Right to Information Act is a powerful weapon that has been successfully deployed to catch corruption in high places.

Second, the Unique Identification Authority of India, initiated in 2009, will provide every resident with a card that will carry essential data about the individual. The card is designed to empower citizens such that they should easily be able to access essential public services. The authority is headed by Nandan Nilekani, who gave up his chief executive's job at Infosys to help devise the system. The new card will eliminate the need for multiple identification cards, such as one card for NREGA employment benefits and another that certifies a person's status as living below the official poverty line.

The Road Ahead

India's growth story has largely been driven by the gradual development of new policy ideas—ideas whose value became more apparent during financial crises, which facilitated their consolidation. Gaining political support for new ideas has taken time; indeed, ideas such as autarkic development and public control over the economy could not be quickly or easily replaced by ones that emphasize the role of private companies and international trade. New ideas have also been resisted by political constituencies that benefited from the old ideas.

The transformation of policy ideas and politics has made India's corporate sector more efficient. It has engendered better service provision in appropriately regulated areas such as telecommunications, banks, and stock markets. In these arenas, the government's role has contributed to India's rise as a rapidly emerging economy.

Predatory propensities within the government hinder the development of roads, railways, and airlines.

But powerful political interests still stand in the way of India's realizing its economic potential. The country's trade unions have successfully opposed a legal framework that could benefit more workers and spur labor-intensive industrialization. Rich farmers make unreasonable demands for power and fertilizer subsidies that crowd out essential public investment in rural areas. The predatory propensities of politicians and bureaucrats prevent India's ports from achieving their potential.

Similar predatory propensities within the government hinder the development of vital infrastructure such as roads, railways, and airlines.

Growth has made welfare more affordable, and democratic pressures are making it essential.

India's growth has preceded the creation of a welfare state. Growth has made welfare more affordable, and democratic pressures are making it essential. In advanced industrial welfare states, capitalism arrived before democracy. The welfare state was born because of democratic pressures on the propertied classes after substantial surplus accumulation had already occurred. A similar phenomenon is occurring now in India.

Legal and institutional developments such as the Right to Education Act, the Mahatma Gandhi National Rural Employment Guarantee Act, the Right to Information Act, and the Unique Identification Authority of India point to the pressures from below that are today demanding redistribution of wealth and consolidating the idea that the Indian citizen has certain rights to services, which the state is obliged to provide. Going forward, efforts to reduce poverty could have a significant impact, not only in spreading the benefits of growth more widely, but also in sustaining India's rapid economic development.

Critical Thinking

1. What accounts for India's rapid and sustained recent economic growth?
2. What factors prevent India from matching China's dramatic economic growth?
3. What role does the government play in limiting competitiveness in India?
4. How might India's growth benefits be more widespread?

RAHUL MUKHERJI, an associate professor at the National University of Singapore, is the editor of *India's Economic Transition: The Politics of Reforms* (Oxford University Press, 2007).

From *Current History*, April 2010, pp. 144–146, 148–150. Copyright © 2010 by Current History, Inc. Reprinted by permission.

Welcome to Minegolia

How the land of Genghis Khan became a new gold rush san francisco on the steppe.

RON GLUCKMAN

For the first time in as long as anyone can seem to remember, there have been traffic jams in Ulan Bator—a place previously known mainly either as the answer to a trivia question (Which capital city has the coldest average temperature?) or as a historical curiosity: Asia's Timbuktu, the fabled homeland of Genghis Khan. Until recently, the Mongolian capital had more horses than cars.

No longer. Mongolia is in the middle of an epic gold rush—think San Francisco in 1849—but it's copper and coal that have enticed businessmen, investment bankers, and miners from London, Dallas, and Toronto by the planeload. Today, Ulan Bator is abuzz with talk of options and percentages, yields and initial public offerings. Not since the 13th century, when Genghis Khan consolidated the nomadic tribes of these remote steppes and established an empire that eventually spanned from Eastern Europe to Vietnam, has Mongolia seen so much action. The country's stock exchange (though still the world's smallest) rose 125 percent last year, and the IMF forecasts double-digit GDP growth rates for years to come. Others aren't nearly so pessimistic: Renaissance Capital—an investment bank that specializes in emerging markets, one of many that have recently set up shop in Mongolia—notes that overall economic output could quadruple by 2013.

"Mongolia is about to boom. Of that, there is no longer any doubt," says John P. Finigan, the Irish CEO of one of Mongolia's largest banks. A veteran of developing markets in scores of countries, he says the only comparable growth potential he has seen has been in the Persian Gulf oil states.

The reason for the boom can be summed up in a word: China. Mongolia has some of the world's largest undeveloped fields of coal, vital for its southern neighbor's hungry steel mills and power plants. Mongolia is also rich in copper, needed for the power-transmission lines being strung at record rates in fast-growing Chinese cities and for the production of batteries, especially those for the booming market in electric cars. China currently consumes nearly 7 million tons of copper each year (about 40 percent of global demand), but it's on track to triple its copper needs within 25 years, according to CRU Strategies, a London-based mining and metals consultancy.

Twenty years ago, when I first visited Mongolia, it had just emerged from seven decades under the Soviet umbrella.

Ulan Bator had a shellshocked otherworldliness about it. There were a few grimy hotels fronting Sukhbaatar Square, named for the leader of the 1921 revolution that transformed Mongolia into the world's second socialist state. After decades of decline, the city looked like a set for an apocalyptic movie, especially in the crush of winter, when the sky was a perpetual charcoal gray.

Nowadays, Ulan Bator looks increasingly like a Chinese boomtown, with all the same trappings—exploding property prices, huge capital inflows, rising concerns about corruption, widening gaps in income disparity, and a flood of flashy automobiles on the roads. A year ago, a Louis Vuitton boutique opened for business in the posh Central Tower building near Sukhbaatar Square. A glass cabinet holds a horse saddle encrusted in gems. "It's one of a kind, custom-made for Mongolia," the manager notes. Downstairs, the offerings are more conventional. A crocodile purse fetches $20,000; watches run $17,000. The sums are astounding in a country that is still among the world's poorest. Per capita GDP in 2008 was about $3,100, making Mongolia the world's 166th-poorest country—just ahead of the West Bank. Yet that hasn't stopped Ermenegildo Zegna, Hugo Boss, and Burberry from opening up. "There's lots of new money here," says Zoljargal, marketing manager for Shangri-La Ulaanbaatar, which is rushing to finish a new shopping plaza, along with Mongolia's first luxury hotel.

The reason for Mongolia's boom can be summed up in a word: China.

The luxury disappears as soon as you leave the capital. On the town's outskirts lie *ger* camps, nomadic tent communities where tens of thousands of people live in poverty; beyond, there is little sign of civilization, just the vastness of the Gobi Desert. The harsh conditions and lack of infrastructure have hampered habitation and development for centuries.

But this inhospitable terrain is also key to the boomtown future. For here is Ovoot Tolgoi, a coal mine 30 miles from the Chinese border run by a Canadian company called SouthGobi. The company has invested $200 million in a state-of-the-art facility that is on pace to sell 4 million tons of coal to China annually, with plans to double production by 2012. "Mongolia: the Saudi Arabia of Coal," reads the slogan on the firm's website.

The optimism becomes understandable as I tour the site, where an ocean of coal covers the surface of the sandy earth. The seam averages more than 50 meters wide—one of the world's thickest—and 250 meters deep, though portions of it go down at least 600 meters. Ovoot Tolgoi has proven initial reserves of 114 million tons, enough to last up to 16 years, but that's a conservative estimate and that's just the one mine in production. SouthGobi also has licenses for two other sites. Layton Croft, a vice president at SouthGobi, compares the rush to the heady days of the dotcom era. "It is a bit like Minegolia .com," he says. "The difference is, this boom is for real, and it's going to last a long, long time."

There are obstacles in the way, not least a government that is prone to corruption and more accustomed to reeling from regular shortages of fuel and food than managing a sudden windfall. "Of course, the worry is this revenue will lead to bad political decisions," says S. Oyun, a member of parliament and head of the Zorig Foundation, a government watchdog group. But President Tsakhia Elbegdorj brushes away concerns that

Mongolia could end up the next poster child of the resource curse. "We are very much aware of the Nigeria case, the Dutch disease phenomenon, and so on," Elbegdorj tells me. "Mongolia is a democratic country of educated people. Our people and democracy are the guarantees that our country will not become another Nigeria."

It's hard to root against a people who've long had so little finally getting a slice of the pie. But in this stark land of fabled warriors, something will inevitably be lost if Mongolia becomes north Asia's Saudi Arabia. Genghis Khan wouldn't be caught dead wearing Prada.

Critical Thinking

1. What accounts for Mongolia's booming economy?
2. How has the influx of money changed the capital, Ulan Bator?
3. What are the concerns about the country's new-found prosperity?

RON GLUCKMAN is a Beijing-based correspondent.

Reprinted in entirety by McGraw-Hill with permission from *Foreign Policy*, January/February 2011, pp. 44–45. www.foreignpolicy.com. © 2011 Washingtonpost.Newsweek Interactive, LLC.

The African Miracle

How the world's charity case became its best investment opportunity.

NORBERT DÖRR, SUSAN LUND, AND CHARLES ROXBURGH

Not so long ago, the world lamented its broken continent. "The state of Africa is a scar on the conscience of the world," declared British Prime Minister Tony Blair in 2001—and his was a common refrain. Civil war, economic stagnation, and a high disease burden seemed irreversible, condemning the region to perpetual poverty.

A decade later, however, Africa has outgrown the gloom and doom. Far from the misery-stricken place so often portrayed, Africa today is alive with rising urban centers, a growing consumer class, and sizzling business deals. It's a land of opportunity.

Africa, in fact, is now one of the world's fastest-growing economic regions. Between 2000 and 2008, the continent's collective GDP grew at 4.9 percent per year—twice as fast as in the preceding two decades. By 2008, that put Africa's economic output at $1.6 trillion, roughly on par with Russia and Brazil. Africa was one of only two regions—Asia being the other—where GDP rose during 2009's global recession. And revenues from natural resources, the old foundation of Africa's economy, directly accounted for just 24 percent of growth during the last decade; the rest came from other booming sectors, such as finance, retail, agriculture, and telecommunications. Not every country in Africa is resource rich, yet GDP growth accelerated almost everywhere.

Government reforms, greater political stability, improved macroeconomics, and a healthier business environment are now taking hold in a region long dismissed as hopeless. Inflation fell to an average of 8 percent in the 2000s after a decade during which it hovered at 22 percent. African countries have lowered trade barriers, cut taxes, privatized companies, and liberalized many sectors, including banking. Africa now boasts more than 100 domestic companies with revenue greater than $1 billion. And capital flows to the continent increased from just $15 billion in 2000 to $87 billion in 2007. With good reason: Africa offers the highest rate of return on investment of any region in the world.

Pockets of great risk and instability certainly remain, but the long-term trends look good. Global demand for commodities is rising, and Africa is well positioned to profit. The fastest-growing demand for these raw inputs comes from the world's emerging economies, with which sub-Saharan Africa now conducts half its trade. Africa's production of oil, gas, minerals, and other resources is projected to grow at 2 to 4 percent per year for the next 10 years. At current prices, this will raise the value of resource production to $540 billion by 2020—and possibly much higher depending on how commodity prices rise.

An even bigger source of growth will be the rise of the urban African consumer. In 1980, just 28 percent of Africans lived in cities. Today, 40 percent of the continent's 1 billion do, a portion close to China's, larger than India's, and likely to keep growing in the coming years. The number of households with discretionary income is projected to grow 50 percent over the next 10 years to 128 million. Already, Africa's household spending tops $860 billion a year, more than that of India or Russia. And consumer spending in Africa is growing two to three times faster than in the wealthy developed countries and could be worth $1.4 trillion in annual revenue within a decade.

Nothing spawns growth like growth, and Africa's urbanization is also increasing demand for new roads, rail systems, clean water, power generation, and other infrastructure. Even agriculture, in which Africa has long lagged, is poised for takeoff. The continent is home to 60 percent of the world's uncultivated arable land. So if farmers brought more of it into use, raised the yields on key crops to 80 percent of the world average, and shifted cultivation to higher-value crops, the continent's famers could increase the value of their annual agricultural output from $280 billion today to around $500 billion by 2020.

Multinational companies have already shifted their mindsets, even if the political world is still used to thinking of Africa as a charity case. Telecom firms have signed up 316 million new African subscribers since 2000, more than the population of the United States. Walmart recently bid $4.6 billion for one of the region's largest retailers, confirmation that global businesses think Africa holds commercial potential on a scale not seen since China opened up more than 20 years ago. Those prospects will only grow as Africa urbanizes; already, the continent is home to 52 cities with populations of at least 1 million, as many as in Western Europe today.

While challenges remain, Africa has a bright future—you can bet on it, as countless businesses are doing every day.

Critical Thinking

1. Why have Africa's economic growth rates improved?
2. What changes in demographic patterns have contributed to growth?
3. How are these gains likely to spur even more growth in the future?

NORBERT DÖRR is the managing partner for McKinsey Sub-Saharan Africa in Johannesburg. SUSAN LUND is the director of research and CHARLES ROXBURGH is the London-based director of the McKinsey Global Institute.

Reprinted in entirety by McGraw-Hill with permission from *Foreign Policy,* December 2010, pp. 80–81. www.foreignpolicy.com. © 2010 Washingtonpost.Newsweek Interactive, LLC.

The New Mercantilism: China's Emerging Role in the Americas

Beijing offers to the countries of Latin America and the Caribbean the opportunity to forge a path independent of the United States and liberal economic orthodoxy.

Eric Farnsworth

My first visit to China was in 1986; my second was in 2010. The difference between the two visits was profound. Within one generation, it seemed as if everything except the Forbidden City and the Great Wall had changed. Cars had replaced bicycles, shining office towers had replaced ramshackle tenements, and consumerism had replaced the dreary economic hopelessness that many Chinese previously endured.

Which is not to say all is well there. Newly acquired wealth exists side by side with abject poverty. Stunning natural beauty contrasts with choking pollution. And overseeing the country's dramatic change is the Communist Party leadership, which remains jealous of its 60-year monopoly on political power and is unwilling to tolerate any challenge to its rule.

To maintain legitimacy and power, the government has made a strategic bet—that it can keep political control by allowing and even encouraging economic liberalization. Growth and job creation are the keys to making this strategy work, and have become a virtual obsession of Chinese leaders. According to the International Monetary Fund, China accounted for almost a fifth of world growth in 2010. Exports have been and continue to be critical to this success; China uses an undervalued currency as a tool to keep global demand for its exports high.

Production, however, requires inputs, and exports require raw materials. Thus, over the past 10 years, China has been on a global hunt for the raw materials that it needs to keep its production lines humming and its people employed, including the additional millions who join the work force every year. Coal, oil and gas, ores and minerals, soy and other agricultural goods: Chinese demand for these has caused a secular shift in global commodities markets.

China's leaders, moreover, are not content to leave their procurement efforts to the vagaries of global markets. Rather, they seek long-term, guaranteed access to raw materials, in some cases even looking to control the means of production and in-country infrastructure such as ports and rail. Raw materials are then turned into value-added products and re-exported from China around the world.

This is a transparently mercantilist strategy, with domestic political requirements at its core. It is a strategy designed, fundamentally, to keep the ruling party in power. It is not a strategy to project power or to contribute to the development of the impoverished abroad. Nor is it a strategy primarily to build political alliances, though political influence will naturally increase with enhanced trade linkages. (China has asked trading partners, for instance, to support the diplomatic isolation of Taiwan.)

It is a strategy, however, that is changing the world. In Latin America, in particular, the impact has been significant, with game-changing implications for economic growth, long-term development, governance, and US policy.

The Dragon Enters

Traditionally, China had virtually no footprint in Latin America or the Caribbean. It was a region that Chinese leaders considered the "backyard" of the United States and were reluctant to enter. Similarly, Latin American and Caribbean leaders gave almost no thought to China, the exceptions being smaller nations that recognized Taiwan as a result of Taiwanese financial incentives, and extralegal groups like Peru's Shining Path that purposefully fashioned themselves after Maoist revolutionaries.

Latin American and Caribbean trade and investment generally flowed on a north-south axis, with European connections also playing an important role, particularly in economic relations with Brazil and South America's Southern Cone. Japan, too, played an important, though tertiary, trade role.

In recent years, however, China has entered the region forcefully. Between 2000 and 2009, China's imports from Latin America and the Caribbean ballooned from approximately $5 billion to $44 billion. Exports to the region have followed a similar trajectory, rising from $4.5 billion to $42 billion over the same time period. China is now Brazil and Chile's largest trade partner, and may soon be Peru's as well. The United Nations Economic Commission for Latin America and the Caribbean estimates that China will displace the European Union as the second-largest regional trading partner by 2015, and will trail only the United States.

The US share of regional trade, meanwhile, is declining. From 2002 to 2008, the US share of exports to the region fell from 48 to 37 percent, while China's grew from 4 to 10 percent. This trend is likely to continue, especially as China locks in trade arrangements for the long term. Bilateral free trade agreements are now in force between China and Chile, Costa Rica, and Peru. Additional agreements are just a matter of time.

China buys primarily raw materials from Latin America. In fact, commodities make up fully 80 percent of Chinese purchases—driven, again, by China's domestic development needs. As a result of China's dash for growth, cyclical commodities markets have stabilized and prices have remained at historic highs. Conversely, most of what China sends back to Latin America and the Caribbean is in the form of competitively priced manufactured goods, actually threatening the manufacturing base of countries like Mexico, the Central American states, and even Brazil.

This is the very definition of mercantilism. China buys raw materials from the region, engages in value-added production at home, and then re-exports the finished products to Latin America and the Caribbean, thereby undercutting the region's own efforts at value-added production.

China promises only a commercial relationship without political or policy interference.

At the same time, Latin America and the Caribbean have clearly benefited from selling to China over the past decade. Weak economic growth, averaging little more than 1 percent per year in the 1980s and 1990s, has given way to regional growth rates in the range of 4 to 6 percent. Brazil's growth alone has risen from an average of 1.7 percent annually in the 1998–2003 period to 4.2 percent since 2004. In 2010, Brazil's economy grew an estimated 7.5 percent; projections suggest a sustainable rate of 5.5 percent through 2014. Much of this is a result of trade with China. And the rest of the commodities-exporting nations in the region have experienced similar growth.

Taking Advantage

Those countries without much in the way of commodities sales to China, including Mexico and nations in Central America and the Caribbean Basin, have not done as well. In addition to having only limited commodities to sell in the first place, these countries are truly dependent on the US economy as their primary export market for both goods and services, and also the primary economy from which remittances are sent.

Sluggish recovery in the United States will continue to limit Mexican, Central American, and Caribbean Basin growth rates for the foreseeable future, especially as manufacturers from the region come under continuing pressure from Chinese imports.

On the other hand, for those nations, primarily in South America, that have been in a position to take advantage, exports of primary goods to China have been one of the key factors keeping their economies out of the depths of the recent recession and leading them to rapid recovery.

It has also had the effect, however, of shielding such countries from the need to reform their economies to promote broad-based development and to position themselves more competitively for the long run. When nations are able to sell as much as they can produce of any particular product, the thinking is generally to continue doing so and reap the rewards. When economies are growing, there is little political imperative or incentive for reform.

Yet Latin America continues to lack knowledge-based, value-added innovation and production. Education rates remain comparatively low. Workforce development and the liberalization of labor codes have lagged. Investment in research and development barely registers in most countries. And national development strategies are virtually nonexistent.

Of course, China has aggressively and successfully promoted its own value-added production, in part by insisting on technology transfer and other capacity-building measures whenever Western companies look to gain access to the Chinese marketplace. It is a strategy that has paid off handsomely for the Chinese, who are starting to compete head to head with others on highly sophisticated products.

There is no reason at all why Latin America should not replicate this model (abstaining, of course, from obviously negative aspects of Chinese practices, such as theft of intellectual property). Brazil is beginning to take this approach, insisting on in-country investments, technology transfer, joint research and development platforms that help to develop local valued-added capabilities and expertise. Others should, too. For example, Bolivia, South America's poorest nation, should refuse to give Beijing access to its massive deposits of lithium unless the Chinese first agree to joint research and development of the technology needed to build the car batteries for which the lithium is intended. Rather than merely mining lithium, Bolivia might then aspire to become a developer of battery technology, reaping rewards from a potentially huge demand for clean energy transportation alternatives.

The ability to promote labor and environmental protections, human rights, and the rule of law is being commensurately reduced.

Let's Make a Deal

Expanding trade always attracts attention, but headlines are drawn by investment deals—including blockbuster announcements by Chinese officials detailing massive regional investments that they intend to make. The reality of China's investments in the region is, however, somewhat more complex than the headlines would indicate. The actual flow of money has been limited despite announced figures, as China takes steps to learn about and understand markets before actually committing funds. Even so, investments and acquisitions have begun to surge.

Oil and gas deals have been leading the charge, hitting over $13 billion in 2010, up from zero in 2009. China's oil giant Sinopec has been particularly active, announcing in December 2010 that it would acquire Occidental Petroleum Corporation's assets in Argentina for $2.45 billion. This followed hard on Sinopec's October announcement that it would buy 40 percent of the Spanish company Repsol's Brazilian assets for $7.1 billion, the biggest acquisition by a Chinese firm in Latin America to date. Additional significant announcements are on the horizon, as Sinopec, China National Offshore Oil Company, and others vie for assets.

Oil and gas are not the only sectors involved, of course. Mining, power generation, fishing, and agriculture deals have also recently occurred and will continue to occur given China's strategic play to lock in access to raw materials. Because they are commodities producers, Argentina, Brazil, Chile, and Peru have benefited handsomely, while Colombia is also on track to benefit and is currently negotiating a free trade agreement with China.

Infrastructure projects are next in line, given Latin America's significant underinvestment in the infrastructure required to take advantage of its emerging role in the global economy. Roads, bridges, railways, ports, and information technology and telecommunications, for example, will all require huge investments in the near term to help make the region more competitive. As well, signature projects in Brazil, as that nation gets ready to host the World Cup in 2014 and the Olympic Summer Games in 2016, will soon come on line.

The Chinese government is supportive of overseas projects generally, and the Bank of China offers attractive finance. With such backing, Chinese companies have been known to make above-market offers on infrastructure projects and for assets such as oil and gas and mineral deposits that otherwise have attracted little attention, guaranteeing that China will be in position to bid successfully.

China has also done investment deals with Venezuela, Ecuador, Cuba, and Bolivia—leftist-run countries that one would predict, if ideology were an overriding factor in Chinese decisions, might attract the lion's share of investment. To date, however, China's commercial relations with Ecuador have been rocky. An April 2010 promise by Beijing to loan $20 billion to Venezuela in order to lock in access to that country's heavy oil remains pending. And Bolivia's takeover of its gas fields did not impress the Chinese, who are looking for long-term certainty in their investments.

In fact, Chinese companies have no problem dealing with populist or authoritarian leaders, but neither are they unduly attracted to doing business in countries ruled by them. With them, it is strictly business. If a decent, risk-adjusted return can be made, and access to a necessary resource guaranteed, the investment will likely be made. Otherwise, it will not. This is a matter not of charity or ideology, but of China's need to meet its domestic demands in the most efficient and effective manner possible.

It must be said that total Chinese foreign direct investment (FDI) in Latin America and the Caribbean is dwarfed by the stock of US investment in the region, and will be for some time. But Chinese investment is increasing rapidly. In 2009, for example, some 17 percent of total Chinese FDI went to Latin America. And Chinese investment is just at the beginning of the curve as the nation pursues its strategy of locking in access to raw materials.

China appears to be less interested in majority control of enterprises than in taking significant minority stakes, which allow Chinese investors to learn the ins and outs of a heretofore unknown marketplace while guaranteeing long-term access to raw materials. Chinese portfolio investment, on the other hand, has only just begun, but it will play an increasingly important role in the region as Chinese investors, like their Western counterparts, seek higher returns in emerging markets in an era of slow growth elsewhere.

Returns on Investment

As investment increases, the quality of FDI is important to consider. Not all investment is the same. For example, US investors and corporations operating abroad generally follow anticorruption provisions codified in the Foreign Corrupt Practices Act. They abide by corporate governance and reporting requirements. They comply with US and local labor laws and human resources requirements. They transfer technology and management expertise to local markets. They provide access to the global marketplace for local production. They source locally. They pay taxes, even when tax laws, as in Brazil, are complex and impenetrable.

US businesses often pursue corporate social responsibility activities, including humanitarian relief, thereby contributing to local economies and social development. They hire from the local economy, using a limited number of expatriates to manage operations while building businesses from local hires. And they abide by US government foreign policies—for example, when countries like Myanmar (formerly Burma), Cuba, or Iran are sanctioned.

Of course, not every company is perfect, and nongovernmental organizations have aggressively highlighted instances in which they believe corporate malfeasance has occurred. To the extent it has, wrongdoers should be held accountable. But in the main, US investors are required by their boards to follow these general guidelines as a matter of course.

Chinese companies, on the other hand, are less likely to abide by these guidelines, though their record is not as lengthy or detailed as that for US investors. One issue that almost universally galls observers of Beijing's investment in the region is China's lack of interest in hiring local workers. Labor forces for construction and operations are routinely brought from China to Latin America and the Caribbean. Many if not most of the jobs that could go to locals are reserved for Chinese nationals.

It is a difficult case to make, as a result, that one of Chinese investment's primary benefits to the region has been job creation. Disgruntlement over this trend can be expected to rise as investment increases, unless active steps are taken to reverse course.

More broadly, the political implications of different investment models are important. The United States and other like-minded nations have traditionally used economic and financial incentives to encourage reforms in Latin America and the Caribbean. Tools have included bilateral and regional trade agreements, market access agreements, defense and security relations, equipment sales and transfer, training and capacity building, and foreign assistance. Areas of interest to US policy makers run the gamut from democracy to human rights, from labor rights to the environment, from investor protections to intellectual property provisions.

The US trade agreement with Colombia, for example, was signed in 2006 but remains pending, given Washington's expressed concerns over labor rights and protections in Colombia. A trade agreement with Peru was held up pending the resolution of environmental concerns. The North American Free Trade Agreement required side agreements on both labor and environmental issues before Congress approved it. A unilateral Andean trade preferences program requires that recipient nations cooperate fully on counter-narcotics and also maintain appropriate investment climates. And so on.

China, on the other hand, promises a commercial relationship without political or policy interference in the nations in question. Chinese investors are not hung up on whether a host nation's government is capitalist or populist, authoritarian or democratic, corrupt or not. They certainly do not care if the government is pro–United States or anti–United States.

The Chinese do not care if their investments prop up local bad guys or undercut collective international efforts to enforce norms of behavior. Their emphasis is on doing business effectively and undisturbed. For domestic purposes, they have pursued a strategy of business for business's sake in Latin America and the Caribbean, as they have around the world; they are not attempting to *change* the world.

China is now Brazil and Chile's largest trade partner, and may soon be Peru's as well.

Conquistadors

And yet, the world is changing, because by acting in this manner, Beijing offers to the countries of Latin America and the Caribbean the opportunity to forge a path independent of the United States and liberal economic orthodoxy. This is attractive to them, particularly when the US economy is struggling, and to the extent that US leaders at times have been overbearing and self-interested in their actions toward the region. Regional elites have often chafed at what they consider to be the United States' patronizing tendency to use trade and investment to leverage sensitive domestic political changes.

At the same time, the ability of the United States and other Western nations to promote labor and environmental protections, human rights, and the rule of law in Latin America and the Caribbean is being commensurately reduced by the increase in Chinese economic activity. The region is beginning to have other options, a trend cheered by those who most disdain the perceived historic role that the United States has played in the region, and by those who mistakenly view trade itself as an exploitative mechanism that primarily benefits the United States. (This view is particularly pronounced within the human rights and development communities, without the recognition that trade and investment are among the most potent tools that the United States has for promoting the agendas that they themselves hold dear.)

This is ironic. For years, Latin American and Caribbean elites and observers have railed against the United States for its alleged exploitation of Latin America's natural resources, claiming that the North Americans came to conquer, despoil the landscape, impoverish the region, and make off with the riches of the continent.

An entire literature has arisen around these themes, the most famous example of which, perhaps, is Uruguayan journalist Eduardo Galeano's *Open Veins of Latin America: Five Centuries of the Pillage of a Continent.* Though it was written in 1971, the book remains popular with a new generation of leaders, including Venezuelan President Hugo Chávez, who mischievously presented a copy to President Barack Obama at the Summit of the Americas in Trinidad and Tobago in April 2009.

Even Hollywood has gotten into the act. Filmmaker Oliver Stone's 2010 documentary "South of the Border" purports to show that the United States, global capitalism, and the corporate media have caused the ills of the Western Hemisphere. The primary explanation for a lack of development and opportunity in Latin America is the predatory and exploitative behavior of the developed world, with the private sector at the vanguard, supported by the raw military, financial, and political muscle of a hegemonic United States.

This line of thinking is a tired and tiresome approach to analyzing the Americas, and has been widely and repeatedly debunked. At the same time, one often hears across Latin America—including from populist, anti-US leaders—that building relations with China and welcoming Chinese trade and investment are national priorities.

For countries such as Brazil, Chile, and Peru, links with China are intended to help build economies. For the new administration of President Juan Manuel Santos in Colombia, China links provide a means to develop a healthier, less dependent relationship with the United States. For others, they are seen as a means of diversifying relations away from traditional trade and investment patterns and the political connections that develop alongside them, while providing new economic options that will allow greater flexibility in governing.

Venezuela's Chávez is the best example of this latter category, particularly regarding the president's desire to diversify the markets for his country's heavy crude away from the United States. Accomplishing this will require massive investments in infrastructure, including specially built refineries, along the Venezuela-to-China supply chain. Economically, this makes zero sense. Politically, it makes a great deal of sense to Chávez. And if it guarantees the Chinese access to Venezuelan crude over the long term, it is win-win, even though the arrangement may take years to materialize fully.

Hard Thinking

At a time when Latin American economies are growing, and when many countries are gaining a new sense of confidence and of a direction apart from the United States, the region is running headlong into an economic embrace of China. This is not to suggest that China will supplant the United States in investment any time soon, or that Chinese economic linkages will lead to political meddling or adventurism from Beijing.

In fact, neither the pronouncements nor the behavior of the Chinese to this point supports the contentions of conservative US commentators that Beijing entertains strategic political or military designs on the Western Hemisphere. There is no evidence that China aspires to take over the Panama Canal or otherwise project power into the region. The United States will remain the strongest nation in the Western Hemisphere, albeit less able over time to determine the outcome of regional events.

Still, as economic links with China proliferate, it must be asked whether China is good for the Americas beyond the short-term economic gain it provides, no matter how beneficial this has been and will continue to be for the foreseeable future. One wonders why regional leaders and observers, so quick to condemn the United States for its alleged pillaging of the continent, have not seen fit to raise their voices to question the Chinese approach—an approach that is straightforwardly mercantilist and is lacking in any of the benevolent or pro-development impulses that can be found in US engagement with the region, including the promotion of international norms and Western values.

China's involvement in the region is not illegitimate, illegal, or even necessarily threatening, despite being economically unbalanced. But people in the region do need to think hard about the best means to ensure that Chinese engagement benefits the region over the long term, and not just in the short run.

Correspondingly, the United States needs to meet its own obligations in the hemisphere—from passing pending trade agreements to engaging with the people of the region in a manner that is conducive to cooperation and mutual respect. Perhaps then the silly idea so frequently heard in policy circles and around the region—that Chinese economic engagement is unquestionably positive for the Americas, while US economic engagement is exploitative and should be resisted—can be put to rest. The outcome of this debate will, in any event, help determine Latin America and the Caribbean's political direction, as well as its development prospects, for many years to come.

Critical Thinking

1. What accounts for China's interest in Latin America?
2. What has been the immediate impact of the booming trade with China?
3. What are the advantages of this trade?
4. How does increased trade with China affect U.S. relations with the region?

ERIC FARNSWORTH is vice president of the Council of the American.

Cotton: The Huge Moral Issue

World cotton prices have dropped to an historic low: the reason being the immoral continuation of EU and US trade subsidies that allow non-competitive and inefficient farming to continue. While the recent WTO meeting in Hong Kong failed to resolve the issue, the livelihoods of West Africa's 12 million cotton farmers will soon be destroyed if subsidies are not slashed. This is a huge moral issue.

KATE ESHELBY

Seydou, dressed in a ripped T-shirt that hangs off his shoulders, looked at me blankly as I questioned him about the effects of US subsidies on his only source of income, cotton farming. "I don't know about cotton in the US but I know cotton prices have fallen here in Burkina Faso," he lamented.

The farmers working in the cotton fields of Burkina Faso, often in remote locations, have little knowledge of the intricacies of world markets. What they do know is that the price they receive for their cotton harvests—essential for basic necessities such as medicines and school fees—is dropping fast.

The end of cotton farming in Burkina Faso and other cotton producing West African countries is rapidly approaching. World cotton prices have dropped to an historic low: the reason being the immoral continuation of EU and US trade subsidies that allow non-competitive and inefficient farming to continue.

Cotton subsidies in richer countries cause over production, artificially distorting world markets. And who suffers? The poor countries, whose economies are wholly dependent on the cotton trade.

In Burkina Faso, a former French colony in West Africa, cotton is the country's main cash crop. It is the primary source of foreign income, making up one-third of export earnings, and the lifeblood for the majority of farmers. Here cotton is grown on small, family-owned farms, seldom bigger than five hectares. One farmer, called Yacouba, explains: "I also grow maize and groundnuts on the farm, to feed my family, but cotton is my only source of cash."

In contrast, US cotton operations are enormous and yet, unlike Burkina Faso, cotton is a minimal proportion of its GDP. Ironically, the US subsidies are concentrated on the biggest, and richest, farms. One such farm based in Arkansas has 40,000 acres of cotton and receives subsidies equivalent to the average income of 25,000 people in Burkina Faso.

The benefits of subsidies only reach a small number of people in the US and other Western countries, whereas two million people in Burkina Faso, one of the world's poorest countries with few other natural resources, depend on cotton for survival.

The farms in Burkina Faso are very productive, it is cheaper and more economical to grow cotton there than in the US. "I have to take out loans each year to buy enough insecticides and fertilisers for my cotton," says Yacouba. "They are very expensive so we have to work hard to ensure we get a good harvest. Each year I worry whether I will earn enough to pay back the loans." Burkinabe farmers are forced to be efficient, also prevailing against climatic uncertainties and limited infrastructure—all this, with no support from subsidies.

Fields are prepared by plough and both seed planting and picking are done by hand, which explains why cotton is also vital for providing jobs—being very labour intensive. Yacouba explains: "My family works on the farm throughout the year, but during harvesting we bring in extra help." Pickers are dotted around the fields surrounding him, plucking the cotton balls from the shoulder-high plants. Some of the women have children tied to their backs and the sacks of cotton are steadily placed under the shade of a giant baobab tree. This scene is in stark contrast to the US where huge, computerised harvesters pick the cotton and aerial spraying administers the chemicals required.

The meeting (in mid-December 2005) of the World Trade Organisation (WTO) in Hong Kong was to address this farcical situation as part of the Doha "development" talks. But nothing much came out of it. Burkina Faso is still resting its hopes on cotton subsidies being eliminated, or at least reduced, in order to save its fundamental crop from demise. The Doha negotiations, launched in 2001, are intended to show that trade could benefit the world's poor. But subsidies are a global injustice, and create major imbalances in world trade—it is argued they should only be available for products that are not exported, and targeted towards family and small-scale farmers.

The US gives approximately $3.4bn a year in subsidies to its 25,000 cotton farmers; this is more than the entire GDP of Burkina Faso. Subsidies dramatically increased in the US after the 2002 Farm Act and as a result US cotton production has recently reached historic highs. It is now the world's second largest cotton producer, after China, and the biggest exporter—an easy achievement because US cotton prices no longer bear any relation to production costs.

Current world cotton prices are in decline due to global over-production, fuelled by agricultural subsidies. EU and US taxpayers and consumers pay farmers billions of dollars to overproduce for a stagnant market. These surpluses are then dumped overseas, often in developing countries, destroying their markets and driving down world prices.

The livelihoods of West Africa's 12 million cotton farmers will soon be destroyed if subsidies are not slashed. This is a huge moral issue. It is simple—Burkina Faso cannot compete against heavily subsidised exports.

In March 2004, a WTO panel ruled that the majority of US cotton subsidies were illegal. The WTO agreements state that "domestic support should have no, or at most minimal trade-distorting effects on production." The US tried to appeal against this decision but it was overruled.

If Africa took just 1% more in world trade, it would earn $70bn more annually—three times what it now receives in aid. In 2003, Burkina Faso received $10m in US aid, but lost $13.7m in cotton export earnings, as a result of US subsidies. No country ever grew rich on charity, it is trade that holds the key to generating wealth. Fair trade would give the Burkinabe cotton farmers a decent opportunity to make a living by selling their produce, at a decent price, to the richer world; enabling them to work their way out of poverty.

The US was legally required to eliminate all trade-distorting subsidies by 21 September 2005, according to a WTO ruling. President George Bush keeps saying he will cut subsidies, but actions are louder than words. The delay is partly due to a long-standing arm wrestle between the US and the EU, neither of whom will budge. The British prime minister, Tony Blair, does seem to want to abolish EU subsidies, but the French argue that subsidies are not even negotiable. Despite four years of haggling, negotiators are still at loggerheads. Numerous reports have been compiled, many meetings held and yet scant progress has been made—and things are only getting worse for the Burkinabe cotton farmers.

"Both the US and EU brag about their boldness, but the actual reform they propose is minuscule, tiny fractions of their massive farm support. The negotiations have recently moved into the finger-pointing phase in which rich countries criticise the inadequacy of each other's proposals. Meanwhile, poor countries await something real," says Issaka Ouandago, from Oxfam's office in Burkina Faso.

Oxfam has been supporting the struggle of African cotton farmers in their campaign known as the "Big Noise", and are hoping to gather a petition of one million signatures against cotton subsidies. "We can only hope the US reform their subsidy programmes and stop dumping cheap cotton onto the world market," Ouandago continues. "Despite their WTO commitments to reduce trade-distorting subsidies, the EU and US have used loopholes and creative accounting to continue. Such practices are undermining the fragile national economics of countries that depend on cotton."

The rich countries have to come forward with more, otherwise the Doha Round will achieve nothing, as the meeting in Hong Kong proved—although developing countries have less political power, they are still capable of blocking the negotiations if they don't get what they want. In the last WTO meeting, held in Geneva, July 2004,

negotiations on US cotton subsidies were supposed to be kept separate from broader agricultural negotiations—this did not happen. It was a blow for Burkina Faso and other West Africa countries who produce mainly cotton and are less interested in other commodities. A subcommittee on cotton was set up to "review" the situation, but the EU and US have not taken this committee seriously.

With the emergence of the G20 alliance, some developing countries, such as India and Brazil, are now powerful enough to resist pressures, but African countries have previously never been centre stage. West African cotton producers are, however, becoming far stronger as a group. "We have become more united to make our voice heard. Our aim is to gather all African cotton producers together," explains Yao, a member of the National Union of Cotton Producers in Burkina Faso.

The only reason Burkinabe cotton farmers are still surviving is that producer prices have been maintained at a minimum level—175 CFA per kg of cotton seed is the minimum price the farmers need to break even, prices never go below this, despite being above current world prices.

In recent years, the Burkinabe cotton companies used their profits from previous harvests to support the farmers; these savings are now depleted. The full effects of world prices have, therefore, not yet been felt by the farmers, the worst is to come—once the prices are forced to drop below this minimum, the farmers can no longer survive.

Leaving the house of Seydou, I wonder about his fate. A pile of bright-white cotton sits drying in the glaring sun, in front of his mud house. Inside the walls are bare, except for a single cross; a bundle of clothes hang from a rope and a pile of maize is stacked in the corner. "I cannot afford to buy things because cotton prices keep fluctuating," he says. "I know cotton grows well here but prices are down so I cannot send my youngest son to school. This makes me sad. I know his only chance of a good future is school."

In Burkina Faso, cotton is the country's biggest interest and essential to its economy, so it prays that cotton is addressed more seriously and given the attention it deserves. As the sun sets, the workers leave the fields, holding sacks of cotton above their heads. A donkey cart trundles by, carrying a mound of cotton—kicking up a trail of red earth. Their livelihoods depend on the decisions made at the WTO.

Critical Thinking

1. How do subsidies hurt cotton producers in poor countries?

2. In what ways do subsidies push down prices?

3. How might elimination of subsidies boost African trade and prosperity prospects?

4. What has allowed Burkina Faso's cotton producers to survive? Can this be sustained?

From *New African*, January 2006, pp. 26–28. Copyright © 2006 by IC Publications Ltd. Reprinted by permission.

Taking the Measure of Global Aid

International development assistance has in effect been assigned a new grand purpose: managing interdependencies in a globalized world.

JEAN-MICHEL SEVERINO AND OLIVIER RAY

"Official development assistance"—the standard measure of aid that governments and multilateral institutions provide to developing countries—is dying. Not that it ever really existed, in the sense of neatly representing a global fight against poverty that comprised common objectives and means. And not that international solidarity itself has diminished: More money, not less, is being poured each year into what can be called global development policies.

Still, an outdated concept of development—one based on illusions about the unity, clarity, and purity of the international community's goals—is giving way to a complex new mix of public policies that attempts to promote global public goods and confront the development challenges of a globalized world. The aid deck has been reshuffled by a triple revolution in objectives, players, and instruments.

This sudden metamorphosis of international development aid presents a problematic question: What is the relevance of global standards such as the widely cited objective of allocating 0.7 percent of donor countries' gross domestic product (GDP) to official development assistance (ODA)? Understanding why this benchmark is senseless may give us a clue as to why it is not reached. In any case, it is high time for new measures to guide development assistance policies.

The New World Order

The first of the revolutions that have recently swept through international development aid is a drastic expansion of the goals assigned to assistance. Development aid has always served a wide range of economic, political, social, and cultural objectives. Yet, for most of its existence, its main driving force was geopolitical. The initiators of aid were nation-states: European nations, by financing expensive economic development projects, retained some say in the political and economic lives of their former colonies. During the cold war, too, development aid served to purchase influence in the global south. Indeed, a race for influence ran parallel to the global arms race. Vast sums were disbursed to keep regions in the right camp.

Then came the fall of the Berlin Wall and the collapse of most communist states. In this new world order, economic liberalism prevailed on all continents and in virtually all countries. The widespread embrace of trade and markets as the engines of development created a major identity crisis for official development assistance, and this period was characterized by large decreases in official development flows. ODA for the United States, France, and the United Kingdom was halved in the space of seven years.

For much of the 1990s, development assistance budgets were used largely to refinance developing countries' public debts, contain humanitarian crises, and address the most troubling social consequences of structural adjustment programs. Aid became much more people-centered and much less growth-oriented. An increasing share of ODA went to social sectors, while budgets for infrastructure and agriculture were sliced. And because north-south relations were no longer perceived as strategic, states happily gave up the monopoly over aid they once enjoyed—such that decreases in public aid flows were partly compensated for by increases in private aid.

Since the turn of the century, however, the international community has come to discover other, less appealing characteristics of the "new world order." For many, the terrorist attacks of September 11, 2001, manifested the interdependency between developed and developing nations in terms of global security. Since then, much ODA has been poured into the Iraqs and Afghanistans of the world. Vast amounts of money have been dedicated to "failed" states. Conflict prevention and conflict management have become high-level items on the international development agenda.

Globalization has introduced other challenges as well. It has increased the risk that transmittable diseases will spread via commercial trade and international travel. It has accelerated global warming and the loss of biodiversity. In recent years it helped provoke an international food crisis and a period of soaring energy prices. The global financial meltdown that began in America illustrated that, in an integrated world economy, misguided policy choices in one country can penalize the system as a whole.

> ## The global has not subsumed or transcended the local. Rather, local challenges have become an integral part of global stakes.

This new set of global problems has compounded the historic challenges of poverty and inequality. Contrary to what many early analysts of globalization expected, transcended the local. Rather, local challenges have become an integral part of global stakes. For all of these reasons, international development assistance has in effect been assigned a new grand purpose: managing interdependencies in a globalized world.

Everyone's an Actor

A second revolution in development assistance is an impressive expansion, in both number and range, of the players involved in the "market" for aid. The end of the state monopoly has sparked a boom in private giving. Nongovernmental organizations (NGOs)—left-wing and conservative, secular and faith-based, small and large—have mushroomed in all industrialized countries, and have come to represent a considerable proportion of north-south financial transfers. Businesses have also emerged as a growing component of international transfers.

Organizations and special funds dedicated to development have flourished and proliferated as never before. Behind each of these lies a respectable international concern, but many of them also represent lobbies that resist aid restructuring and streamlining. And because overall cash transfers have not increased as fast as have the entities involved, the average size of projects and operations has decreased sharply.

Recipient states too have contributed to making the international landscape more complex. Political liberalization in many developing countries has led to the birth of civil society organizations, themselves on the receiving end of an increasing share of development funds. Local governments are also taking on a greater role as political decentralization—enabled by democratization, urbanization, and demographic growth—advances throughout the world. Local businesses and financial institutions have likewise been increasingly involved.

This changing and ever-denser institutional environment is commonly considered a problem for both the efficiency and the coherence of public policy. Indeed, the costs of coordinating the activities of multiple stakeholders with differing agendas have skyrocketed over the past decade. In some cases, the gains realized from having more actors involved are outweighed by policy incoherence and coordination costs.

But the bustling creativity of new development actors has also unleashed forms of innovation that would probably not have come about had conservative public administrations continued to monopolize policy. For instance, philanthropic foundations have brought modern business practices to international development. In any case, this change is not something that can be curbed significantly: Whether we applaud or lament it, the genie is out of the bottle. Tomorrow's major development challenges will need to be resolved in this new, tumultuous environment.

A New Tool Kit

The third revolution that has swept through development assistance involves the tools with which problems are addressed. In the days when aid was about geopolitics and states, the lion's share of ODA was accounted for by sovereign grants and loans. These were largely channeled to infrastructure and agriculture projects. When compassion and private solidarity came to drive the field, smaller-scale projects in the social sector grew in importance, along with large-scale debt relief.

A section of the international aid community, tasked with finding solutions to increasingly globalized ills and representing new and diverse combinations of actors, has already moved far beyond "old school" development aid. Over the space of a decade, international development assistance has witnessed an astonishing proliferation of complex instruments: new taxation or quasi-taxation mechanisms (such as taxes on airline tickets); increased investment in risk capital; countercyclical/contingent lending instruments; and so forth.

Moreover, the way in which projects are evaluated has undergone a dramatic shift. Old school ODA typically consisted of loans and grants that subsidized the start-up costs of projects whose recurrent operational costs were meant to be borne by the beneficiaries. The idea was to avoid donor dependency. This principle, that projects needed to be financially and economically viable, became one of the cornerstones of development assistance. Although projects conceived in this way continue to exist—and justly so, since the needs to which they respond have not disappeared—economic viability and discrete transfers have often been set aside in recent years to allow for longer-term, recurrent transfers.

> ## Today no one asks whether projects funding the education of Mali's children or providing access to clean water for Haiti's urban dwellers are economically viable.

Today no one asks whether projects funding the education of Mali's children or providing access to clean water for Haiti's urban dwellers are economically viable. The efficiency of a program is now evaluated according to the improvements brought to a targeted population's basic living standard. In a way, the logic of economic investment has been replaced by one of long-term social redistribution.

A similar paradigmatic shift in the instruments of aid has occurred because of the need to protect and finance global public goods. International health, for example, responds to the logic of the weakest link: Pandemics tend to break out in countries with the lowest capacity for prevention, early warning, and emergency treatment. If the world is to defend itself from global pandemics, it will need to strengthen the weakest links. The same goes for certain climate change efforts. Thus, nations cooperate to achieve a global public good, sharing the burden of action according to actors' capacity to pay. This requires mobilizing more stable sources of funding and finding appropriate disbursement mechanisms.

Let us be clear: This new creativity in development aid should not—cannot—aspire to replace traditional aid channels and resources. Many traditional development problems require traditional development solutions. But the diversification of tools and resources is both vital and natural.

Sins of Mismeasurement

This triple revolution in goals, actors, and instruments amounts to enormous change. But surprisingly, it has not yet affected the way that the international development community measures financial volumes dedicated to development aid. The new daily practice of aid in the twenty-first century is now well established, yet assessment of national contributions and their impacts has largely stuck to old school methods.

The problem in a nutshell is that the Development Assistance Committee (DAC) of the Organization for Economic Cooperation and Development (OECD) continues to measure development assistance by adding up OECD member states' grants, certain types of loans, and a whole series of "other" expenses whose link to development financing is at times tenuous. Indeed, it is hard to find other examples of public policies whose performance is assessed so little on the basis of results and so much on the basis of expenses, themselves measured so imperfectly. Still, the DAC's figures continue to serve as the basis for official and highly publicized promises of development aid.

The OECD's measure of ODA, which was created to gauge a relatively narrow set of activities aimed at promoting the convergence of former colonies' economies with their former masters', has become the only benchmark to assess official north-south financial flows. Yet it suffers from three deadly sins: It measures expenditures not remotely relevant to what really matters; it fails to capture the resources that are dedicated to specific ends; and it does not align costs with outcomes. In fact, only a minority of expenses included under ODA actually translates into fresh funds for development programs in the world's poorest nations.

To start with, the administrative overhead of donor states counts as aid—which clearly is not the best incentive for achieving resource-efficient aid bureaucracies. ODA figures include items such as grants offered to students from the developing world who study in a donor nation—even when they never return to their home countries to work. Also included are the costs of caring for political refugees from developing nations, and emergency relief and food aid sent to zones of natural disaster or conflict. The importance of such expenses is undeniable, but their link to countries' long-term economic and social development is very indirect.

Debt relief is also included: In 2005 it represented a record-high 25 percent of ODA. While it is true that debt restructuring has been helpful to many developing nations, allowing them to recover essential margins of maneuver in their national budgets, debt forgiveness sometimes does not represent a real budgetary cost to donors, since they do not actually expect to be paid back. There is also something awkward about counting the cancellation of loans that at the time they were granted would not have counted as ODA—as is the case with Iraq's sovereign debt, which was largely amassed to pay for weaponry during the Iran-Iraq War.

Conversely, ODA's second sin is that it misses a whole range of items that contribute meaningfully to financing development assistance. For one thing, development aid from non-OECD countries appears nowhere in statistics on international development—other than in very approximate and unofficial estimates. Yet non-OECD states represent a growing share of development aid.

China's aid to Africa is a case in point. Beijing has become one of the major contributors to the financing of infrastructure in sub-Saharan Africa. The very generous aid policies of oil-rich Arab states are not included either. In the same vein, although private giving to development efforts is now estimated as equal to half of (the inflated) official totals of official development assistance, this contribution does not appear in official measures of development aid.

Moreover, many of the innovative tools that have been designed in recent decades to finance development do not count toward ODA, which only takes into consideration grants and loans with a grant element of at least 25 percent. Failing to include new tools in measures of development assistance reduces the incentive for countries to use them. Likewise, many activities are not captured because they are deemed too remote from the so-called core of the development agenda expressed in the Millennium Development Goals. This is the case, for instance, with some peace-building and post-conflict activities, the training of international police forces, and the construction of prisons.

Costs and Benefits

The third deadly sin of ODA is its failure to address a number of crucial types of questions, thereby preventing a better appraisal of donor efforts and a more efficient alignment of expenditures with outcomes. First, what are the overall funds mobilized to finance global development policy—regardless of their origin and delivery method? The international community is ill-equipped today to assess its own efforts according to this most basic benchmark.

Second, what outputs and impacts are achieved through the projects and programs that are financed? How many children gain access to vaccinations? How many square kilometers of rain forest are saved from destruction? Because ODA measures only financial inputs, and because it does not identify the policy goals that are sought, it is absolutely mute on the question of impacts.

Third, what are the budgetary costs to donor states of development aid? Although this seems the most logical benchmark for comparing states' contributions to international development, such figures are nowhere to be found. Grants of course relate directly to budgetary costs, but official data do not capture the fiscal expenditures represented by tax exemptions that help NGOs and foundations appeal to public generosity (and the desire to avoid inheritance taxes).

Finally, what are the administrative costs of delivering development policies? DAC standards allow for declaring administrative costs, but these figures are then mixed into the broader hodgepodge of ODA. And no one is able to identify clearly how much money is spent in the field and how much is spent outside developing countries.

The Name's the Thing

What are our options for escaping the current impasse and steering global development policy as efficiently as possible? Four goals can be identified: first, giving things appropriate names, since proper naming and counting are crucial to building a sound foundation for global policies; second, devising estimates of the overall funding made available for particular goals, whatever the provenance of the funding; third, aligning policy goals with measures of results, laying aside for good the bureaucratic focus on expenditures; and fourth, assessing the budgetary costs of official aid so that we can benchmark governments' efforts.

To address the first goal, we suggest forgetting about ODA. Why not move toward a new concept: global policy finance (GPF)? This measure would include all funding devoted to the three core components of sustainable development: achieving convergence between northern and southern economies; providing better access to essential services across the world; and providing global public goods (environmental protection, international health, and so on).

Although GPF would encompass activities that go beyond old school economic development objectives and delivery methods, it would in no way exclude them. This broader scope would recognize that the nature of what the international community is undertaking has changed, and thus what needs to be measured has changed.

Regarding the second goal, our statistics should estimate the overall financing provided toward an agreed set of objectives for international development assistance. These figures should disregard financing's provenance and the share of grant money, and give us a measure of the overall sum that can be invested in the policy. Such a measure would provide a first yardstick of the financing gap for each type of policy goal (such as fighting climate change, or eradicating a given disease).

As to the third goal, we should devise a way to measure the development results of specific development activities or other global public policies. This would encourage innovation and allow us to concentrate on what ultimately matters: impact. An agreed methodology would allow us to compare the results of very different actions, be they systemic, programmatic, or project-oriented. Each actor in development aid, whatever its

nature (public or private, from a traditional or an emerging donor nation, and so on), would be able to report the results of its development activities according to this methodology. Results would be open to verification.

Regarding the fourth goal, we could establish a metric such as "official global public finance" that would tabulate states' budgetary efforts toward a set of agreed global causes. This would measure public resources earmarked for financing global policies—no matter the instruments through which they are channeled. This approach would encourage countries to leverage their instruments so as to enhance the impact per dollar spent.

Times Change

These are bold changes in policy formulation and measurement, and implementing them would have important consequences on, among other things, communications. The target of spending 0.7 percent of GDP on development assistance has played an important role in public debates, and it has helped in the naming and shaming of countries that perform badly. Defining a policy objective according to its budgetary inputs is, as we have suggested, problematic. However, preserving some sort of easy-to-communicate minimum benchmark is important.

Thus, one could retain the figure of 0.7 percent, but, for example, specify that it should be applied only to a certain category of actions (for instance, promoting access to essential services). Alternately, we could alter the target (for instance, to 1 percent or 1.5 percent of GDP) and include all the development objectives—promoting economic growth, human welfare, and global public goods.

Another question is whether the DAC should continue to exist. It should, but its scope should be extended. Many countries and organizations that currently do not want to or cannot join the OECD would be willing to participate in a forum where global development policies are debated, standards set, and evaluations processed.

Such a group would probably look very different from the current DAC. It would therefore need a new name, such as "Global Policy Funding Forum." The UN would have a crucial role to play in this reorganization: A joint venture between the DAC and the UN Development Program might provide the best platform for such global engagement. The Bretton Woods institutions would also have an active role to play.

Changes such as these will not happen overnight, nor will they happen by themselves. At some stage, a set of actors will need to take the initiative and clarify the emerging global policy of development assistance by making it more inclusive—and better measured, evaluated, and communicated. To declare the death of ODA is neither to claim victory over poverty nor to admit defeat. Rather it is a statement of reality, an admission that times change. Moving from ODA to GPF would be to recognize that policies, actors, and instruments also change over time—and that an administrative measuring instrument created several decades ago needs serious revamping if we are to face effectively the global policy challenges of this century.

Critical Thinking

1. What three developments are changing the nature of development aid?
2. How has the agenda of development expanded?
3. What important new actors are now involved in international development?

4. What are the new sources of development assistance?
5. How should the effectiveness of international development aid be evaluated?

JEAN-MICHEL SEVERINO is managing director of France's international development agency, and was formerly vice president for Asia at the World Bank. **OLIVIER RAY** is his adviser in charge of research. This article is adapted from a Center for Global Development working paper.

The New Colonialists

Only a motley group of aid agencies, international charities, and philanthropists stands between some of the world's most dysfunctional states and collapse. But for all the good these organizations do, their largesse often erodes governments' ability to stand up on their own. The result: a vicious cycle of dependence and too many voices calling the shots.

MICHAEL A. COHEN, MARIA FIGUEROA KÜPÇÜ, AND PARAG KHANNA

Even on their best days, the world's failed states are difficult to mistake for anything but tragic examples of countries gone wrong. A few routinely make the headlines—Somalia, Iraq, Congo. But alongside their brand of extreme state dysfunction exists an entirely separate, easily missed class of states teetering on the edge. In dozens of countries, corrupt or feeble governments are proving themselves dangerously incapable of carrying out the most basic responsibilities of statehood. These countries—nations such as Botswana, Cambodia, Georgia, and Kenya—might appear to be recovering, even thriving, developing countries, but like their failed-state cousins, they are increasingly unable, and perhaps unwilling, to fulfill the functions that have long defined what it means to be a state.

What—or who—is keeping these countries from falling into the abyss? Not so long ago, former colonial masters and superpower patrons propped them up. Today, however, the thin line that separates weak states from truly failed ones is manned by a hodgepodge of international charities, aid agencies, philanthropists, and foreign advisors. This armada of nonstate actors has become a powerful global force, replacing traditional donors' and governments' influence in poverty-stricken, war-torn world capitals. And as a measure of that influence, they are increasingly taking over key state functions, providing for the health, welfare, and safety of citizens. These private actors have become the "new colonialists" of the 21st century.

In much the same way European empires once dictated policies across their colonial holdings, the new colonialists—among them international development groups such as Oxfam, humanitarian nongovernmental organizations (NGOs) like Doctors Without Borders, faith-based organizations such as Mercy Corps, and megaphilanthropies like the Bill & Melinda Gates Foundation—direct development strategies and craft government policies for their hosts. But though the new colonialists are the glue holding society together in many weak states, their presence often deepens the dependency of these states on outsiders. They unquestionably fill vital roles, providing lifesaving healthcare, educating children, and distributing food in countries where the government can't or won't. But, as a consequence, many of these states are failing to develop the skills necessary to run their countries effectively, while others fall back on a global safety net to escape their own accountability. Have the new colonialists gone too far in attempting to manage responsibilities that should be those of governments alone? And given the dependency they have nurtured, can the world afford to let them one day walk away?

A Shift of Money and Power

Dependency is not a new phenomenon in the world's most destitute places. But as wealthy governments have lost their appetite for the development game, the new colonialists have filled the breach. In 1970, seven of every 10 dollars given by the United States to the developing world came from official development assistance (ODA). Today, ODA is a mere 15 percent of such flows, with the other 85 percent coming from private capital flows, remittances, and NGO contributions. Nor is this trend strictly an American phenomenon. In 2006, total aid to the developing world from countries of the Organisation for Economic Co-operation and Development (OECD) amounted to $325 billion. Just a third of that sum came from governments.

The expanding budgets of humanitarian NGOs are indicative of the power shift taking place. During the 1990s, the amount of aid flowing through NGOs in Africa, rather than governments, more than tripled. Spending by the international relief and development organization CARE has jumped 65 percent since 1999, to $607 million last year. Save the Children's budget has tripled since 1998; Doctors Without Borders' budget has doubled since 2001; and Mercy Corps' expenditures have risen nearly 700 percent in a decade.

The shift is equally apparent on the receiving end. When aid reaches developing countries, it increasingly bypasses the host governments altogether, often going straight into the coffers of the new colonialists on the ground. In 2003, the USAID Office of U.S. Foreign Disaster Assistance distributed two thirds of its budget through NGOs rather than affected governments. Between 1980 and 2003, the amount of aid from OECD countries channeled through NGOs grew from $47 million to more than $4 billion. One reason for the shift is the growing reluctance of rich countries to route aid through corrupt foreign officials. That has created an increasing reliance on new colonialists to deliver assistance—and produce results.

But the new colonialists are doing far more than simply carrying out the mandates of wealthy benefactors back home. They often tackle challenges that donors and developing-country governments either ignore or have failed to address properly. International Alert, a London-based peace-building organization, monitors corruption in natural-resource management in unstable countries such as the Democratic Republic of the Congo and serves as an early warning system to Western governments about impending conflicts. The Gates Foundation, which has spent more in the past decade on neglected-disease research than all the world's governments combined, has been so dissatisfied with existing international health indexes that it is funding the development of brand-new metrics for ranking developing-world health systems.

Seeing jobs that need to be done, the new colonialists simply roll up their sleeves and go to work, with or without the cooperation of states. That can be good for the family whose house needs rebuilding or the young mother who needs vaccinations for her child. But it can be a blow to the authority of an already weak government. And it may do nothing to ensure that a state will be able to provide for its citizens in the future.

The Power behind the Throne

The responsibilities the new colonialists assume are diverse—improving public health, implementing environmental initiatives, funding small businesses, providing military training, even promoting democracy. But whatever the task, the result is generally the same: the slow and steady erosion of the host state's responsibility and the empowerment of the new colonialists themselves.

The extent of the new colonialists' influence is perhaps best illustrated in Afghanistan. The government possesses only the most rudimentary control over its territory, and President Hamid Karzai has made little progress in combating corruption and narcotics trafficking. The result is a shell of a government, unable to provide basic services or assert its authority. Today, 80 percent of all Afghan services, such as healthcare and education, are delivered by international and local NGOs. According to its own estimates, the Afghan government administers only a third of the several billion dollars of aid flowing into the country each year. The rest is managed directly by private contractors, development agencies, and humanitarian aid groups. Major donors such as Britain only briefly include the Afghan government in their aid agendas: Although 80 percent of Britain's $200 million in annual aid to Afghanistan is dedicated to state ministries, as soon as the money arrives, it is swiftly handed over to NGOs like Oxfam or CARE for the actual construction of schools and hospitals. The transfers simply reflect many donors' lack of confidence in Afghan ministries to distribute funds competently and implement aid mandates on their own.

Many of the gains that Afghanistan has made since the fall of the Taliban can undoubtedly be attributed to the efforts and largesse of the many thousands of NGOs that have set up shop in Kabul. But not everyone is thankful for their labor. Karzai has derided the wasteful overlap, cronyism, and unaccountability among foreign NGOs in Afghanistan as "NGOism," just another "ism," after communism and Talibanism, in his country's unfortunate history. In 2005, Ramazan Bashardost, a parliamentary candidate in Kabul, sailed to electoral victory by running on an anti-NGO platform, threatening to expel nearly 2,000 NGOs that he claimed were corrupt, for-profit ventures providing little service to the country.

Many NGOs understandably resent such criticism, particularly as it lumps together a diverse lot—private contractors, international aid agencies, local NGOs—and ignores the important contributions some have made. But none of these groups is anxious to perform so well that it works itself out a job. No matter how well-intentioned, these new colonialists need weak states as much as weak states need them.

None of the new colonialists is anxious to perform so well that it works itself out of a job. They need weak states as much as weak states need them.

This kind of perverse dependency is on display in Georgia, where new colonialists have come to wield an inordinate amount of influence since the country emerged from Soviet rule. Today, its pro-Western president is supported by a steady dose of financial and political aid from abroad, and many state functions are financed or managed by outside help. In advance of the country's Rose Revolution, foreign political consultants advised the opposition's campaign strategy. The American consulting firm Booz Allen Hamilton has been hired to help rebuild state ministries from the ground up, recruiting new staff and retraining bureaucrats. These foreign technocrat-consultants participate in the day-to-day decision-making on critical national matters, such as political reform and intelligence sharing. But in Georgia, as well as other countries where these consultants operate, as they help mold state functions and prioritize development policies, they also write the complex grant applications that their home governments consider—grants that effectively extend their own positions of influence. The result is a vicious cycle of dependency as new colonialists vie for the contracts that will keep them in business.

That isn't to say that the new colonialists don't get results—many do. And in few areas are the efforts of the new colonialists more impressive than in the public-health arena. When Cambodia emerged from more than a decade of civil war in 1991, the public healthcare system was nonexistent. Since 1999, the government has outsourced much of the country's healthcare to international NGOs such as HealthNet and Save the Children. Today, it is estimated that 1 in 10 Cambodians receives Healthcare from such groups, which run hundreds of hospitals and clinics throughout the country and often provide far better care than government institutions. So reliable are these NGOs in providing quality care that it is difficult to imagine the government taking over responsibilities anytime soon—if ever.

Many aid organizations will say that their ultimate goal is to ensure their services are no longer needed. But aid organizations and humanitarian groups need dysfunction to maintain their relevance. Indeed, their institutional survival depends on it. Although aid groups occasionally have pulled out of countries because of security concerns or to protest the manipulation of aid, it is difficult to find examples where these groups have pulled up stakes because the needs they seek to address are no more. And as these groups deepen their presence in weak states, they often bleed the country of local talent. The salaries they offer are not only better and the work more effective, but there are often no comparable opportunities for well-educated locals in their country's civil service or private sector. The new colonialists may depend on this talent to ensure their legitimacy and local expertise, but it further weakens the host government's ability to attract their own best and brightest, ensuring that they remain reliant on new colonialists for know-how and results.

An Unbroken Cycle

There is no single global clearinghouse that coordinates, or even tracks, how these actors behave around the world. If new colonialists only pay lip service to local ownership and democracy, there is little to suggest that the cycle of mutual dependence will ever be broken. And if that is the case, the new-colonialist crutch may enable corrupt governments to continue to avoid their responsibilities in perpetuity.

Of course, there is another disturbing possibility that many observers do not like to countenance: Without the new colonialists, today's weak states could be tomorrow's basket cases. It speaks to the ubiquity of the new colonialists that this prospect seems remote. Nor can most weak states successfully resist their influence. When Cyclone Nargis struck Burma in May, the governing military junta initially resisted outside assistance. But state incapacity, corruption, and incompetence often make a defiant stance impossible. After several weeks, the regime's leaders had little choice but to accept the help of aid workers who were clamoring to gain access to the people in greatest need.

How then should the international community respond to the increasing influence of the new colonialists? Some observers argue that the market should take the lead in solving development challenges. Unfortunately, new investment often avoids failing states, and aid groups can rightly say that they do the work no one else is willing to do. Other observers think it is time to restore the centrality of the United Nations, at least as a coordinating force among these actors. But globalization resists the centralization of power, and the United Nations lacks the support of member states to take on such ambitious and expensive goals.

The fundamental challenge in this messy new landscape will be to establish a system of accountability. To earn a place at the table of global governance, the new colonialists will have to keep their promises not only to their donors and benefactors but to the citizens of failing states themselves. Competition among aid groups might actually serve to improve this accountability in the future. In many ways, the new colonialists are building a genuine global constituency, and, for better or worse, they may be the first—and last—line of defense for states sliding toward failure.

Want to Know More?

In *Global Development 2.0: Can Philanthropists, the Public, and the Poor Make Poverty History?* (Washington: Brookings Institution Press, 2008), economists and NGO experts debate whether the incredible proliferation of development players can work together to improve life for the world's poor. Ann Florini argues that only collective action by civil society, national governments, and private enterprise can tackle the challenges of the 21st century in *The Coming Democracy: New Rules for Running a New World* (Washington: Island Press, 2003). For an influential analysis of the rise of global civil society, see Jessica T. Mathews's "**Power Shift**" (*Foreign Affairs*, January/February 1997).

Several organizations produce rankings on the performance of global development players. The Hudson Institute's **Index of Global Philanthropy** tracks the scale of private giving to the developing world with case studies of its effectiveness. The One World Trust, established by a group of British parliamentarians, assesses the operations of some of the world's most powerful NGOs in the **2007 Global Accountability Report.**

Sebastian Mallaby exposes the often contentious relations between NGOs and international aid agencies—and the poor who get lost in the shuffle—in "**NGOs: Fighting Poverty, Hurting the Poor**" (*Foreign Policy*, September/October 2004). Erika Check reports on the fight to get lifesaving medicines to the world's poor and the growing influence of the Gates Foundation on global public health priorities in "**Quest for the Cure**" (*Foreign Policy*, July/August 2006).

For links to relevant websites, access to the *FP* Archive, and a comprehensive index of related *Foreign Policy* articles, go to ForeignPolicy.com.

Critical Thinking

1. Who are the "new colonialists"?
2. What roles do these actors play?
3. What impact might they have on the state?
4. How do aid agencies come to depend on dysfunction and how does this affect weak states?
5. What is the challenge in dealing with aid agencies?

MICHAEL A. COHEN, MARIA FIGUEROA KÜPÇÜ, and **PARAG KHANNA** are senior research fellows at the New America Foundation.

Reprinted in entirety by McGraw-Hill with permission from *Foreign Policy,* July/August 2008, pp. 74–79. www.foreignpolicy.com. © 2008 Washingtonpost.Newsweek Interactive, LLC.

A Few Dollars at a Time
How to Tap Consumers for Development

PHILIPPE DOUSTE-BLAZY AND DANIEL ALTMAN

Starting in this quarter, hundreds of millions of people will have an unprecedented opportunity to help the world's most unfortunate inhabitants. When purchasing airline tickets through most major reservation websites or through a travel agent, consumers will be asked if they want to make a direct contribution to the fight against the world's three deadliest epidemics: HIV/AIDS, malaria, and tuberculosis. Part of a movement called innovative financing, the project is a new kind of aid that could fundamentally change the relationship between the rich and the poor throughout the world, a few dollars at a time.

Awareness about the epidemics that rage throughout the developing world occasionally crests in the international media when there is an outbreak, as there was of the Ebola virus in the 1990s and of dengue fever in the first years of this century. These periodic outbreaks usually subside within a year or two, or at least are contained before they become pandemics. The HIV/AIDS, malaria, and tuberculosis epidemics have shown more staying power, however, and even now, after years of attention and treatment, each of these diseases still causes more deaths in developing countries than any other single disease, according to the World Health Organization. In 2004, the last year for which statistics were available at the time of this writing, together these three diseases caused one in eight deaths in low-income countries.

Part of the reason these diseases are so harmful is that they reinforce one another. Hundreds of millions of people around the world have latent tuberculosis infections. In most cases, tuberculosis never becomes active, but the disease is much more likely to explode into a full-blown infection, and the infection tends to be much more severe, in people who also have HIV/AIDS. Even those without latent tuberculosis are more susceptible to getting the disease if they already have HIV/AIDS. This is partly because HIV/AIDS suppresses the immune system—which also means that it is harder for people with HIV/AIDS to fight off malaria. And completing the vicious circle, malaria seems to make HIV/AIDS worse: studies by researchers at the Centers for Disease Control suggest that the body encourages HIV to replicate when it creates antigens to fight malaria. Not surprisingly, patients in the developing world—especially in the tropical zones of Latin America, the Caribbean, Africa, and

Southeast Asia—are often diagnosed with two or three of these diseases. It makes sense, then, to fight all three together.

Why make them a priority? Worldwide, the mortality rate for heart disease and cancer combined is five times as high as the mortality rate for HIV/AIDS, malaria, and tuberculosis combined. But unlike HIV/AIDS and tuberculosis, heart disease and cancer are not contagious. Heart disease and cancer also tend to prey on the aged, whereas HIV/AIDS, malaria, and tuberculosis kill millions of young adults, children, and babies every year. The World Health Organization estimates that HIV/AIDS and malaria together kill more children under the age of five than all forms of cancer and heart disease combined. By contrast, the American Heart Association reports that 83 percent of people who die from coronary heart disease in the United States are 65 or older. Tuberculosis kills across all ages, but the average age at death is dropping in many countries because of the disease's association with HIV/AIDS.

Stopping HIV/AIDS, malaria, and tuberculosis does not just add a few years to someone's life; it adds a lifetime. Moreover, these lifetimes add real value to the world, and not just in moral terms. Every life lost to infectious disease represents lost economic activity and lost economic development. For example, the death of all the world's poorest people—those destined to earn just $2 a day for 30 working years (with weekends off)—would mean a loss to the world's future economic output of more than $50 billion every year. And that is not counting the loss to overall economic development in poor countries ravaged by these infectious diseases.

There are economic costs to rich countries, too. Disease-stricken states cannot afford to import as much from wealthier ones as they otherwise would. In addition, the desperation caused by these diseases is a source of instability that can devolve into conflict, sometimes pulling neighboring countries and even global powers into difficult situations. As early as 1987, a CIA report discussed how HIV/AIDS could exacerbate conflict in sub-Saharan Africa. A 2006 study by the Institute for the Theory and Practice of International Relations at the College of William and Mary showed that the prevalence of HIV/AIDS in developing countries was strongly associated with higher levels of civil conflict and more human rights abuses. Recent research by Andrew Price-Smith of Colorado

College has suggested that epidemics can distort demographics by reducing the working-age population, weaken governments, and reduce the state's ability to take care of its people, all effects that in turn can breed conflict. If the world could better control these diseases, the benefits—economic, social, and otherwise—would be remarkable.

The good news is that HIV/AIDS, malaria, and tuberculosis are completely controllable diseases; successful treatments are available for all three. The hard part is purchasing and delivering the treatments. The United Nations took up this challenge when its members set the Millennium Development Goals and committed themselves to reversing the spread of these three diseases and to making treatments available to everyone who needed them by 2015. In 2002, the UN's members founded the Global Fund to Fight AIDS, Tuberculosis and Malaria as a central source of financing. The deadline is only five years away, however, and the effort is running tragically behind schedule.

This is largely for lack of money. In 2007, according to the Organization for Economic Cooperation and Development, 22 wealthy countries on its Development Assistance Committee gave $118 billion in direct aid to the developing world but earmarked only $5.3 billion of this for health programs. (Much greater sums went to education, infrastructure, industrial assistance, and debt restructuring.) At the beginning of 2007, according to the World Health Organization, more than five million HIV-positive people in developing countries needed antiretroviral treatment but were not receiving it. To treat all of them every day for a year with just the most basic regimen of drugs would have required raising global aid for health by 20–30 percent. To treat them with the latest generation of antiretroviral drugs would have required more than doubling health-related aid—and that would have been for just HIV/AIDS. There is an enormous gap in the funding for the fight against infectious diseases. The pressing question of how to close it is a matter of life or death for hundreds of thousands of people every year.

A Penny for Your Tickets

One of the most promising methods for closing the gap is innovative financing. The goal of this kind of development aid is to harness markets in an intense effort to quickly raise hundreds of millions, perhaps even billions, of dollars—the kind of money that can make a real difference in the development, purchasing, and delivery of life-saving treatments. Starting big and front-loading investments creates incentives for researchers to look for new treatments, encourages pharmaceutical companies to design the resulting drugs so that they are easy to distribute and administer in poor countries, and reduces the drugs' prices by guaranteeing bulk orders.

A handful of such programs have sprung up in the past several years. For example, the International Finance Facility for Immunization, a charitable corporation set up in 2006 under the auspices of the British government, issues bonds guaranteed by the governments of wealthy countries to raise hundreds of millions of dollars a year for vaccines. The governments repay the bonds over time. So far, the International Finance Facility for Immunization has collected $1.6 billion in up-front cash.

Another initiative, (Red), collects donations from companies that sell goods and services under its (Product) Red brand, which is advertised to consumers as a charitable endeavor. Participating brands include household names such as American Express, Apple, Converse, Gap, and Hallmark. Together, they have raised $130 million in three years.

And then there is UNITAID. The program, under the auspices of the World Health Organization, stands apart for collecting money directly from consumers and businesses through the worldwide market for airline tickets. The idea is to share a tiny fraction of globalization's enormous economic gains with sick people in poor countries. UNITAID does not require consumers to buy any particular brand. In 13 countries, whenever consumers purchase an airline ticket, a small tax—sometimes as little as $1—is set aside for the fight against the three major epidemics. With this simple model, UNITAID raised $1.2 billion in the first three years of its existence. And it has begun to finance the antiretroviral treatments of three out of four children who receive treatment for HIV/AIDS, help treat over one million people for tuberculosis, buy 20 million bed nets to protect against malaria-carrying mosquitoes, and more.

Innovative financing sprang from the recognition by former French President Jacques Chirac, Brazilian President Luiz Inácio Lula da Silva, and former Chilean President Ricardo Lagos that the Millennium Development Goals could not be met with official aid alone. A commission of academics and policy experts established by Chirac to investigate other options released scores of ideas in late 2004. The one that grabbed Chirac's attention called for collecting revenue from a tiny tax on transactions in some major industry—currency exchange, carbon-emissions trading, cars, air travel—and committing it to one or more of the Millennium Development Goals.

The three leaders eventually settled on the idea of an airline-ticket tax, and one of us, Philippe Douste-Blazy, then the French foreign minister, proposed that he and his staff turn the idea into reality. The genius of the tax was not only that it would be a tiny levy on a very broad base but also that it would not significantly affect the flow of travelers to the countries that instituted it. If the French government implemented the tax, for example, it would apply only to tickets purchased in France. As a result, French people might be marginally discouraged from flying, but not foreigners traveling to France, unless they bought their tickets in countries that also had the tax. It would be the first time in modern history that countries would be levying a tax on their own citizens exclusively for the benefit of citizens of other countries.

The French and Chilean governments began collecting the tax within a year. South Korea and nine African countries soon followed suit. Before Chirac left office in 2007, the program was housed at the World Health Organization under the name UNITAID, derived from the French "tous unis pour aider" (everyone united to help). The board of UNITAID was composed of representatives from its founding countries—Brazil, Chile, France, Norway, and the United Kingdom—with additional seats for representatives from Africa, Asia, international health groups, and nongovernmental organizations, including patients' rights groups.

Soon, the organization began to receive direct contributions from a few European governments and from the Bill and Melinda Gates Foundation. These were motivated not just by UNITAID's pioneering role in innovative financing but also by its novel approach to spending. UNITAID's board remains committed to financing programs that will have a major impact on HIV/AIDS, malaria, and tuberculosis all at once: creating the first child-sized doses of antiretroviral medicines, lowering the prices of the most cutting-edge malaria treatments to match those of old-fashioned quinine pills, and commercializing the first child-specific drug for tuberculosis. It has also undertaken to finance these treatments as long as the patients need them, something that governments, which allot foreign aid on a yearly basis through an onerous political process, can rarely do. UNITAID can achieve these things because its immense spending power allows it to purchase hundreds of millions of dollars' worth of treatments. Pharmaceutical companies thus have an incentive to reformat medicines—creating, for example, pediatric doses and transforming difficult-to-measure syrups into pills—and to reprice them for underserved populations in the developing world.

One by one, countries began adopting the tax. By the end of 2007, 17 states had passed a law that would implement it and 17 more were considering doing so.

Good Travels

But there was limited enthusiasm in the world's biggest market for airline tickets, the United States. And so it seemed clear that if UNITAID was to become truly global, it would need a complementary approach: voluntary contributions. This idea was the brainchild of Jean-François Rial, a French entrepreneur who heads Voyageurs du Monde, France's leading tourism agency. Realizing that only three companies (Sabre, Amadeus, and Travelport) controlled the reservation systems for two billion plane tickets issued each year—roughly 80 percent of the world's total—he reasoned that if those three companies incorporated a voluntary-contribution mechanism into their reservation software, travelers around the world would have a chance to directly fund the fight against HIV/AIDS, malaria, and tuberculosis.

After two years of development, the mechanism is expected to launch on all three systems this quarter. Travelers from any country who book a trip with Expedia, Opodo, or Travelocity, among many other websites, will be asked during checkout whether they would like to contribute two dollars, two euros, or two pounds to save the lives of poor people. The prompt will be seamlessly integrated into the booking experience—a pop-up window on the computer screen, a box for the travel agent to check. Within weeks, it will become a routine part of life for millions of travelers around the globe—a routine with the potential to help save as many as three million lives every year and prevent the loss of tens of billions of dollars annually in new economic activity, increasing opportunities for growth in poor countries and limiting some of the causes of instability and conflict. The contributors will also have a chance to interact with one another and possibly with the people they

are helping through an associated online social initiative called Massive Good. Such communication will enable participants to make the program even more effective: they will be able to encourage businesses where they live to opt for the voluntary contribution when those businesses book travel, and they will be able to check that the treatments arrived at their destinations.

A preliminary study conducted by McKinsey & Company in 2007 suggested that the new mechanism could raise $1 billion in its first four years, almost doubling UNITAID's budget from the airline-ticket tax and other contributions. With this money, UNITAID is now helping manufacturers of generic drugs roll the various medicines needed to treat an epidemic into a single pill. To achieve this, UNITAID is trying to persuade the pharmaceutical companies that developed those medicines to pool their intellectual property and offer it as a package to generic-drug manufacturers. Creating a single pill would greatly simplify the treatment of all three major epidemics—an unprecedented move in public health. UNITAID also hopes to launch a satellite tracking mechanism so that contributors can follow the journey of the treatments they purchase from the factories to the patients, thereby reinforcing solidarity between the world's rich and the world's poor.

Supplements, Not Replacements

Voluntary contributions come with some downsides, however. Most notably, if the program succeeds, the governments of wealthy countries might feel less obligated to send official aid overseas. This possibility could become especially likely during an economic downturn, when governments might be looking for excuses to cut foreign aid—even as they hand out hundreds of billions of dollars to save their troubled banks and insurance companies. Conversely, if the voluntary-contribution scheme were to founder, these governments might take that as a popular verdict against the Millennium Development Goals and use it as a pretext to reduce their official aid.

Some of the nongovernmental organizations that fight HIV/AIDS, malaria, and tuberculosis also might have reason for concern. These groups depend on official aid, in addition to private donations, for a large part of their funding, and they might resent seeing heads of state celebrate the launch of a voluntary-contribution scheme while they freeze or trim that support. Because UNITAID and the other innovative financing mechanisms channel most of their spending through a few big delivery organizations, such as UNICEF and the Clinton HIV/AIDS Initiative, they cannot replace the efforts of hundreds of smaller groups working on locally targeted programs.

This concern is of paramount importance for all innovative financing mechanisms, which were intended as supplements, not replacements, to help close the gap between official aid and the huge sums necessary to turn the tide against the three big epidemics once and for all. If governments invoke these financing schemes as substitutes for official aid, then those funds' very purpose will be defeated. To avoid this, the Millennium Foundation for Innovative Finance for Health, which is a UNITAID partner, and other independent or quasi-independent entities will have to hold governments to account, by shaming them publicly for cutting aid budgets when they do and by holding them to their promises that they will increase aid at least enough to keep up with inflation. The backers of innovative financing mechanisms, such as UNITAID, have two main responsibilities: to help fight diseases through novel ways of raising money and also to ensure that their success does not undermine the existing efforts they set out to strengthen.

Critical Thinking

1. What is helping to finance the campaign against HIV/AIDS, malaria, and tuberculosis?

2. Why are these diseases so harmful? Why target them in particular?

3. What are the potential costs to the rich states of these diseases?

4. What is the goal of innovative financing?

5. What are the downsides of voluntary contributions?

PHILIPPE DOUSTE-BLAZY, who served as France's Foreign Minister from 2005 to 2007, is currently the United Nations' Special Adviser for Innovative Financing for Development and Chair of UNITAID. **DANIEL ALTMAN** is President of North Yard Economics, a not-for-profit consulting firm serving developing countries. This article is adapted from their book on innovative financing, which will be published in January 2010 by PublicAffairs.

The Fertile Continent

Africa, Agriculture's Final Frontier

Roger Thurow

Throughout this past summer, in the long-suffering hills of western Rwanda, legions of farmers toiled at their sloped plots. With hoes and axes, they crafted flat, wide terraces and a simple water-management system that would keep valuable topsoil in place. Their efforts were part of a $800 million investment program supported by the United States and other international donors that is meant to boost Rwanda's agricultural production and reduce its dependence on food aid. The farmers were reshaping their land in the hope that a new watershed, along with better-quality seeds and fertilizer, would double or triple their harvests of corn, potatoes, beans, and rice by the next season.

As he patrolled the hillsides one day last June, Innocent Musabyimana, the project's manager in the Ministry of Agriculture, expressed a kind of desperate optimism. "To make our agriculture sustainable, we have to do this," he said. "Ninety percent of the country is like this, all hills. If we don't do anything, in 40 years, with the erosion, the farms will be gone." Musabyimana opened his arms wide. "This," he said, taking in the sweeping panorama, "is our future."

He meant the future of Rwanda and the future of Africa. But he might as well have been talking about the future of the world, too. For what is happening on the hills near Lake Kivu is at the vanguard of an effort to reverse years of neglect in agricultural development, tackle widespread chronic hunger, and satisfy the world's ever-expanding appetite.

Malthusian predictions that relentless population growth will outstrip food production and trigger starvation worldwide have recurred over the centuries. They have come and then gone as farmers have deployed new technologies to increase food output. Even now, enough food is being produced to adequately feed every person on the planet; the fact that nearly one billion people are nonetheless going hungry is a damning indictment of the world's food-distribution system. But since demand is growing, production will also have to increase in the years ahead. With the world's population expected to expand to more than nine billion by 2050 and much of that growth occurring in China, India, and other countries where living standards are rising fast, global food production will need to increase by 70–100 percent in order to keep pace and feed the already chronically hungry. This is a mighty challenge: all the more so because given current soil technology and environmental concerns, more food will have to be produced on roughly the same amount of arable land—and with less water than is used now and at a time when both growing demand for biofuels and changing climate patterns are also putting pressure on production. Where will the needed rise in food supplies come from, and how quickly can the distribution problems be solved?

The countries that managed quantum leaps in agricultural production in the past cannot be counted on for repeat performances, unless great leaps in technology introduce new strains of seeds or suddenly turn unproductive lands into fertile soil. The United States, long the breadbasket of the world, led the way in agricultural innovation and productivity after World War II. Advances in seed breeding—first with hybrids, then with genetically modified crops—spurred huge jumps in the yields of several staples: from 1950 to 1990, corn and rice yields in the United States grew by an average of more than two percent annually, with gains in wheat yields close behind. But in recent years, yields for these crops have grown by less than 1.5 percent. Crop yields throughout the rest of the developed world have followed the same trend.

Likewise, future productivity gains in the grain-belt fields of the former Soviet states and in Brazil, China, and India—once hungry countries that turned into agricultural powerhouses thanks to advances made in the 1960s and 1970s, lifting hundreds of millions of people out of poverty—depend on continued investment in infrastructure and research. Under some scenarios, water scarcity in China and India could cut wheat and rice production in these countries by 30–50 percent by 2050, even as demand for these grains there is expected to rise by as much over the same period.

Thus, more and more eyes are turning to Africa, agriculture's final frontier. Africa was largely left out of the green revolution, the postwar movement to push up crop yields in the hungriest parts of the world by promoting the use of new seeds and new farming technology. And so agricultural production on the continent could jump quickly if farmers there simply used existing seed, fertilizer, and irrigation technology. And if more efficient networks were developed to distribute and sell the harvests, boosting agricultural yields in Africa could be a major step toward feeding not just the continent but also the rest of the world.

Ripe for Revolution

How did Africa get so far behind? How can hunger be spreading this century when the green revolution was one of the great technological and scientific achievements of the last?

"The Green Revolution has not yet been won," warned Norman Borlaug, the American plant breeder credited with starting it, as he accepted the Nobel Peace Prize in 1970. "Tides have a way of flowing and then ebbing again. We may be at high tide now, but ebb tide could soon set in if we become complacent and relax our efforts." Some 40 years later, more than one in seven people are going hungry, and as Borlaug feared, that failure was largely born of success. The green revolution beat back famine in Asia and Latin America, disproving the dire Malthusian predictions. Between 1975 and 1985, the world's production of corn, wheat, and rice grew more than twice as fast as the world's population. Surpluses replaced shortages. The gluts depressed prices in the United States and Europe, creating a false sense of accomplishment and security there. The rich world's awareness of the wretchedly poor and hungry receded. Yet the green revolution had not come to Africa.

By the late 1970s, Borlaug's simple idea of helping the world's small farmers—also the world's hungriest people—feed themselves had become more complicated to implement. Environmentalists criticized the green revolution for introducing fertilizers and pesticides to hundreds of millions of acres of land; their overuse was creating a new kind of pollution. Social scientists worried that bringing the notion of surpluses and profits to smallholder farmers would upset the harmony of rural villages by creating debt and prompting land grabs. Research for new breeds of seeds and better soil nourishment to improve the yields of the world's poorest farmers dwindled; priorities shifted to producing safer food in environmentally friendly ways for the world's well-fed.

Overall funding from rich nations for agricultural projects in the developing world also collapsed. According to the World Bank, official development assistance for agriculture from rich countries to poor ones plummeted from its peak of $8 billion in 1984 to $3.4 billion in 2004 (measured in 2004 dollars). Over the same period, the share of aid devoted to agriculture relative to total assistance crashed from about 18 percent to less than four percent. Agricultural assistance to sub-Saharan Africa briefly exceeded $3 billion in the mid-1980s, but it soon sank back to $1.2 billion, its 1975 level. The U.S. government's retreat was particularly dramatic: annual U.S. aid to agriculture in sub-Saharan Africa declined from more than $400 million in 1984 to just $60 million in 2006.

Uneven Plowing Fields

This precipitous drop in research and aid came just as international development theory began to doubt whether helping farmers in poor nations was the most effective way to fight hunger and poverty. In the 1980s, the World Bank and other international development institutions promoted "structural adjustment," a policy that required central governments to exercise fiscal discipline and reduce their debt. Governments in Africa were instructed to get out of the agricultural sector, among other areas, and let the private sector take over.

But in most African countries, the private sector was too small, too weak, and too undercapitalized to lead agricultural development; supply enough seeds and fertilizers; buy, transport, and store harvests; or build domestic and export markets. Starved of assistance, the continent's agricultural infrastructure—research institutions, the roads connecting farms to markets, the network of so-called extension agents who carry new information and technology to farmers, post-harvest storage and distribution capability—fell into a woeful state (refuting, it seems, the arguments of those who insisted that Africa would be better off without foreign aid).

Meanwhile, the international development community was asking African governments to stop subsidizing African farmers to encourage them to plant as much as possible. Many African governments were happy to follow this lead: even though small farmers made up a majority of the population in much of Africa, it was the urban voters who kept governments in power. But that left the continent's farmers bearing 100 percent of the risk of a very risky business. They were being asked to perform a high-wire act without a safety net, and they were the only farmers in the world who had to do so. The countries of the Organization for Economic Cooperation and Development continued to lavish subsidies on their own farmers—more than $250 billion annually—making it impossible for unsubsidized farmers to compete in world food markets. On top of all this, conflict in several African countries turned farmers' fields into battlefields: once productive lands such as Sudan and Zimbabwe became big recipients of food aid.

Still, at the time, the prevailing idea was that Africa's smallholder farmers could not, and therefore should not, compete. Since food produced on large-scale farms in the rich, developed countries was cheaper, the poor countries would benefit from developing their industrial sectors so that, rather than grow their own food, they could earn money to import some. This, ostensibly, was their comparative advantage: where local labor was cheap, better to invest in manufacturing than in agriculture—better to produce underwear than maize. If Africa's peasants went hungry, they could be fed with food aid from the rich world's overflowing warehouses.

What happened was that imported crops displaced locally grown food throughout the developing world, crushing both the incentives of poor peasants to farm and Africa's hopes of food self-sufficiency, the best long-term barrier against famine. All these development missteps were made cruelly manifest during the famine that struck Ethiopia in 2003. In the two previous years, Ethiopian farmers had had the best harvests of their lives thanks to Borlaug's attempts to ignite a green revolution there and provide better access to seeds and fertilizers. But these efforts' single-minded goal had been to produce, produce, produce; developing the infrastructure to store any resulting surpluses and bring them to the market was considered a problem to be addressed later. By the end of 2002, Ethiopia's underdeveloped markets could not absorb the excess production. As a result, prices collapsed by 80 percent, to levels far below production costs. Farmers and grain traders filled whatever warehouses existed, hoping to hold on to their crops until prices improved. Storage capacity was insufficient, however, which meant massive spoilage on the farms (a total of 300,000 tons were wasted, by some estimates). As Ethiopian farmers entered the planting season of 2002–03, their incentive to produce choked by the low prices, they cut back on expenses, used cheaper seeds, shunned fertilizers, shut off irrigation systems, and took some land out of production. They knew they were likely limiting their harvests, but they hoped to keep them large enough to feed their families. They looked heavenward for rain. But that season the rains failed, causing a drought and then a famine. Farmers who one year before had carried surplus grain to village markets were now carrying starving children to emergency feeding centers. Economics had failed them even before the weather did.

U.S. policy failed them next. During the 2003 famine, the U.S. government spent more than $500 million on food aid to help the 14 million Ethiopians who were starving, but it spent less than $5 million on agricultural development aid to prevent Ethiopian farmers from starving the next time around. U.S. policy also mandated—and it still does—that U.S. food aid take the form of crops grown in the United States rather than cash with which recipients could buy local crops. The result was perverse: U.S.-grown food streamed in, rolling past warehouses still filled with Ethiopian-grown grain. Although Ethiopian farmers had no market in Ethiopia, U.S. farmers had a very big one. The U.S. food-aid industry had morphed from Band-Aid into big business.

Soon, the drought that had struck Ethiopia spread from the Horn of Africa down the continent's east coast and into its southern savannas, where the HIV/AIDS epidemic was already wreaking havoc on agriculture by killing millions of farmers. A few years into the twenty-first century, Africa was hungrier than ever before.

From Breadbasket to Basket Case

On the tail of the 2003 famine, African governments got fed up with the prevailing doctrine. At a meeting in Maputo, Mozambique, during the summer of 2003, the continent's leaders embraced the goal of increasing their spending on agricultural development to ten percent of their national budgets. In 2004, Kofi Annan, a son of Africa and then secretary-general of the United Nations, called for an African green revolution. New generals enlisted in the fight against hunger. The freshly elected president of Malawi, Bingu wa Mutharika, subsequently announced that his government would start providing subsidies to farmers to help them obtain seeds and fertilizers. Rwanda's president, Paul Kagame, said that he would do the same, to boost agricultural production in his country. The World Bank also eventually reversed course, retreating from the dogma of structural adjustment. In its *World Development Report 2008,* it hailed the role of small farmers in leading the way out of hunger and poverty and recognized the importance of state investment in agriculture and of some subsidies.

To those who did not heed the African famine of 2003, the global food crisis of 2008 should have been a wake-up call. By then, it was clear that if Borlaug had managed for a time to give the world a lead in the race to keep food production ahead of population growth, the global food supply was now far less

secure. With the world's population getting bigger and wealthier, the demand for grain-fed meat and dairy products was escalating. At the same time, the continued volatility of oil prices was driving a major rise in the production of alternative sources of fuel, many made from foodstuffs. (By 2009, about 30 percent of the United States' corn crop went to producing ethanol, roughly twice as much as in 2006.) This caused food supplies to dwindle and made harvests more vulnerable to disruptions caused by natural disasters. Global grain reserves plummeted in 2007 and 2008 to their lowest levels in three decades, and the prices of many staples doubled. Countries shut off food exports; trade was interrupted. The food that poor countries were supposed to buy for cheap rather than grow themselves suddenly no longer was so cheap or even so available. As shortages spread and prices skyrocketed, rioting erupted, escalating global security concerns. The global financial meltdown that soon followed did bring crop prices down but only to levels that were still historically high. Meanwhile, the conditions that had pushed up food demand remained in place—they still remain today and are likely to intensify as the world economy recovers. In fact, scenes from the 2008 food crisis replayed at the end of this past summer: a drought choked the wheat crop in Russia, triggering higher wheat prices on the world market, and rioting broke out in Mozambique over bread shortages. As the twenty-first century advances, so, too, must the work on doubling the world's food production.

Harvesting Potential

Africa is so far behind the rest of the world agriculturally that it would make great gains simply by applying existing technology and developing the infrastructure that is common in the rest of the world, such as farm-to-market roads, basic irrigation systems, crop-storage facilities, and commodities exchanges. The hybrid seeds that revolutionized agriculture in the developed world several decades ago are still scarce in Africa. According to the International Maize and Wheat Improvement Center, the base of Borlaug's work, such seeds account for less than 30 percent of the corn grown in Africa, and in some countries, such as Ghana, for less than five percent. Farmers who adopt these higher-yielding seeds typically see their harvests increase two-, three-, or fourfold.

Also in contrast to much of the rest of the world, land and water resources in Africa have been largely underused. More than half of the earth's unused arable land that can still be exploited without endangering forests and other ecosystems is in Africa. And less than five percent of Africa's arable land is irrigated; abundant water sources, such as the Blue Nile River in Ethiopia, are largely untapped for farming. The continent's soil has been depleted over the decades, but it could readily be replenished: African farmers use less than one-tenth the amount of fertilizer deployed by farmers in Asia and Latin America. Of the harvests that are reaped in Africa, one-third to one-half are routinely wasted, spoiled by pests, moisture, or disease. Climate-controlled, vermin-secure storage facilities are rare; many smallholder farmers store their harvests in flimsy wooden shelters or pile them up in their mud-brick homes. And as the 2003 famine in Ethiopia showed, the continent's prime agricultural regions do not have modern markets capable of absorbing and distributing the harvests quickly.

Remedying these problems, and tapping Africa's farming potential, has become a central focus of many governments and research and development institutions, and of the world's most generous philanthropists. Countries such as China, India, and Saudi Arabia, which face limitations on food production at home because of land, water, and climate constraints, are looking to invest in and buy land in Africa to grow food for their own people. Partly as a result, African governments are beginning to recognize the importance of taking the reins in developing their own agricultural sectors (some fear a form of postcolonial colonization). As soon as Mutharika, the president of Malawi, became chair of the African Union earlier this year, he pledged to champion greater investment in agriculture: "Africa must feed Africa," he said.

But others can help. The scientific institutes that transformed Brazil's savanna from an idle bush land into verdant fields of soybeans, rice, and maize in the 1970s and 1980s are beginning to work on areas in Africa with familiar ecological and agricultural conditions. Support from the United States will also be crucial to improving African farming, just as it was in helping ignite the agricultural boom in Asia and Latin America in the 1950s and 1960s, when it convinced several governments in those regions to trust Borlaug's ideas and back the green revolution.

Helping Hands

U.S. President Barack Obama, whose relatives still till the soil of Kenya, has recognized this challenge and set out to make agricultural development a pillar of American soft power. In his inaugural address last year, he proclaimed, "To the people of poor nations, we pledge to work alongside you to make your farms flourish and let clean waters flow, to nourish starved bodies and feed hungry minds." Those 30 words have since grown into Feed the Future, a program involving most departments of the administration—from the Department of State and the Department of Agriculture to the Treasury Department and the National Security Council. Its goal is to help the world's poorest farmers grow enough to feed themselves and to have surpluses to sell on the market rather than have to rely on emergency food aid to survive. Obama has asked for $3.5 billion over three years to support agricultural development programs that the governments of low-income countries would draw up themselves.

The U.S. government has rallied international support for Feed the Future by citing global security concerns, pointing, for example, to the rioting that struck dozens of countries during the 2008 food crisis. At Washington's prodding, in 2009, the leaders of the G-8 countries pledged $22 billion over three years for agricultural development in the world's poorest countries. Then the G-20 called for the creation of a multidonor trust fund to help finance those efforts. The Global Agriculture and Food Security Program (GAFSP) was launched this April, with an initial commitment from Canada, Spain, South Korea, and the United States, as well as the Bill & Melinda Gates Foundation, that totaled $880 million. As he announced this new fund,

U.S. Treasury Secretary Timothy Geithner spoke of security. "A world where more than one billion people suffer from hunger is not a strong or stable world. A world where more than two billion people in rural areas struggle to secure a livelihood is not a balanced one," he said. He continued: "Promoting economic growth abroad increases prosperity and security at home."

Standing beside Geithner that spring day was Bill Gates, whose foundation contributed $30 million to starting up GAFSP—and has invested well over $1.5 billion in agricultural development over the past five years. The Bill & Melinda Gates Foundation has teamed up with the Rockefeller Foundation (a main backer of Borlaug's work) to form the Alliance for a Green Revolution in Africa, partly because it has determined that ending malnutrition is key to the success of any poverty-reduction efforts in Africa. And Africa's smallholder farmers, who make up two-thirds to three-quarters of the population in many African countries, are the key to that. "Helping the poorest smallholder farmers grow more crops and get them to market is the world's single most powerful lever for reducing hunger and poverty," Gates said at the World Food Prize symposium in Des Moines, Iowa, last year.

According to the McKinsey Global Institute, if a green revolution ignites in Africa, the continent's agricultural output could increase from the current value of $280 billion per year to as much as $880 billion per year by 2030. Such growth is possible, the institute calculates, if Africa raises yields on key crops to 80 percent of the world average and brings more of its potential farmland into cultivation. Such measures would increase demand for fertilizers, seeds, and pesticides and spur a boom in postharvest processing, all of which could be worth another $275 billion in global revenue by 2030.

In addition to security concerns and business opportunities, there is, of course, the moral imperative to promote an African agricultural revolution. In its latest report on hunger trends, the U.S. Department of Agriculture warned that without an improvement in local agriculture, the number of "food insecure" people—those who consume less than 2,100 calories per day—in sub-Saharan Africa will exceed 500 million by 2020, or half the region's population. According to the USDA's report, which studied 70 developing countries, sub-Saharan Africa would in that case account for just 27 percent of the total population of the countries studied but for 59 percent of the total number of food-insecure people in those states.

Getting to Growth

Nongovernmental organizations are also zeroing in on agriculture as the key way to reduce hunger and poverty in Africa. One day last July, in a small, dimly lit bungalow in Bungoma, in western Kenya, Andrew Youn, the founder and director of the nonprofit organization One Acre Fund, told me, "Agriculture is the fundamental humanitarian problem of our time." Africa's farmers, he added, "need to be producing way more, or we'll have a serious food crisis in the world."

A few years ago, fresh from Northwestern University's Kellogg School of Management, Youn noticed while traveling in Kenya that two neighboring farmers had very different crop yields on their respective plots. The one with the bigger harvest was using better-quality seeds and fertilizers and had access to training; the other one did not. And so, as the next planting season rolled around, Youn began working with about 40 Kenyan farmers who were struggling to feed their families. Rather than give farmers handouts, One Acre Fund provides seeds and fertilizers and draws up repayment plans. It provides training on planting techniques and, once the harvest is in, on drying and storage practices. When needed, the organization also links farmers to markets. And it offers innovative insurance coverage to protect them against failed harvests due to weather. In just four years, One Acre Fund has gone from helping 40 families in Kenya to working with close to 30,000 in both Kenya and Rwanda, doubling or tripling harvests on almost every field. The organization plans to roughly double the number of farmers it assists every year, aiming to work with one million within a decade.

Often, the efforts of social entrepreneurs naturally complement the official actions of governments, even when there are no direct ties between the two. In Rwanda, for instance, One Acre Fund's work coincides with the government's efforts to end hunger through agricultural development. The government in Kigali has increased its spending on agriculture from just three percent of the national budget a few years ago to seven percent today, and, according to both Rwandan officials and the World Food Program, the country has largely freed itself from any dependence on food aid. Thanks to the government's Crop Intensification Program, which seeks to raise farmers' yields by giving them access to better seeds and fertilizer, corn production has quadrupled in the last five years. Now, the agriculture minister, Agnes Kalibata, is counting on the U.S. government and other international donors to help keep up the momentum. Because of its own investment plans for agriculture, Rwanda has emerged as a model country in the Feed the Future program. It received $50 million in the first round of GAFSP funding, including for the terracing and water-management project on the hillsides near Lake Kivu.

Many obstacles will have to be overcome before an agricultural revolution can be sown in Africa. On a visit to cornfields in Rwanda's Eastern Province last June, Kalibata said, "We need to build warehouses; we need markets." She noticed the bumper harvest piling up in farmers' houses and heard their worries that the surplus would push prices below farming costs. "Unless we sell this, how we can we get them to grow more?" Kalibata asked, looking around at the surpluses. "That's the challenge of creating food security."

After several decades of neglect by the continent's own governments and the outside world, Africa's rural infrastructure all along the production chain has fallen into great disrepair. Sub-Saharan Africa is so diverse that it will need not one green revolution but dozens, one for each ecological zone and one for each of the myriad staple crops. The region will also need political and social stability. And holding the world's interest in its progress will be an immense challenge. The U.S. Congress has already been whittling away at the Feed the Future and GAFSP budgets, threatening to starve the programs of adequate funding before they have had a chance to really get going.

But the rich world neglects Africa's development at its own peril. It will be impossible to multiply global food production—that is, to reduce hunger in poor countries while meeting growing demand in emerging ones—in the coming decades if Africa's farmers are not given the means to grow as much food as they possibly can. As Borlaug liked to say, "You can't eat potential." The continent that has been fed by the world's food aid must now help feed the world.

Critical Thinking

1. Why has agricultural production in Africa lagged behind?
2. What impact did structural adjustment have on African agricultural production?
3. How could African farmers be more productive?
4. How can western governments and NGOs contribute to increasing African agricultural production?

ROGER THUROW is Senior Fellow on Global Agriculture and Food Policy at the Chicago Council on Global Affairs. He is a co-author, with Scott Kilman, of *Enough: Why the World's Poorest Starve in an Age of Plenty*.

From *Foreign Affairs*, November/December 2010, pp. 102–110. Copyright © 2010 by Council on Foreign Relations, Inc. Reprinted by permission of Foreign Affairs. www.ForeignAffairs.com

The Micromagic of Microcredit

KAROL BOUDREAUX AND TYLER COWEN

Microcredit has star power. In 2006, the Nobel Committee called it "an important liberating force" and awarded the Nobel Peace Prize to Muhammad Yunus, the "godfather of microcredit." The actress Natalie Portman is a believer too; she advocates support for the Village Banking Campaign on its MySpace page. The end of poverty is "just a mouse click away," she promises. A button on the site swiftly redirects you to paypal.com, where you can make a contribution to microcredit initiatives.

After decades of failure, the world's aid organizations seem to think they have at last found a winning idea. The United Nations declared 2005 the "International Year of Microcredit." Secretary-General Kofi Annan declared that providing microloans to help poor people launch small businesses recognizes that they "are the solution, not the problem. It is a way to build on their ideas, energy, and vision. It is a way to grow productive enterprises, and so allow communities to prosper."

Many investors agree. Hundreds of millions of dollars are flowing into microfinance from international financial institutions, foundations, governments, and, most important, private investors—who increasingly see microfinance as a potentially profitable business venture. Private investment through special "microfinance investment vehicles" alone nearly doubled in 2005, from $513 million to $981 million.

On the charitable side, part of microcredit's appeal lies in the fact that the lending institutions can fund themselves once they are launched. Pierre Omidyar, the founder of eBay, explains that you can begin by investing $60 billion in the world's poorest people, "and then you're done!"

But can microcredit achieve the massive changes its proponents claim? Is it the solution to poverty in the developing world, or something more modest—a way to empower the poor, particularly poor women, with some control over their lives and their assets?

On trips to Africa and India we have talked to lenders, borrowers, and other poor people to try to understand the role microcredit plays in their lives. We met people like Stadile Menthe in Botswana. Menthe is, in many ways, the classic borrower. A single mother with little formal education, she borrowed money to expand the small grocery store she runs on a dusty road on the outskirts of Botswana's capital city, Gaborone. Menthe's store has done well, and she has expanded into the lucrative business of selling phone cards. In fact, she's been successful enough that she has built two rental homes next to her store. She has diversified her income and made a better life for herself and her daughter. But how many borrowers are like Menthe? In our judgment, she is the exception, not the norm. Yes, microcredit is mostly a good thing. Very often it helps keep borrowers from even greater catastrophes, but only rarely does it enable them to climb out of poverty.

The modern story of microcredit began 30 years ago, when Yunus—then an economics professor at Chittagong University in southeastern Bangladesh—set out to apply his theories to improving the lives of the poor in the nearby village of Jobra. He began in 1976 by lending $27 to a group of 42 villagers, who used the money to develop informal businesses, such as making soap or weaving baskets to sell at the local market. After the success of the first experiment, Yunus founded Grameen Bank. Today, the bank claims more than five million "members" and a loan repayment rate of 98 percent. It has lent out some $6.5 billion.

At the outset, Yunus set a goal that half of the borrowers would be women. He explained, "The banking system not only rejects poor people, it rejects women. . . . Not even one percent of their borrowers are women." He soon discovered that women were good credit risks, and good at managing family finances. Today, more than 95 percent of Grameen Bank's borrowers are women. The UN estimates that women make up 76 percent of microcredit customers around the world, varying from nearly 90 percent in Asia to less than a third in the Middle East.

While 70 percent of microcredit borrowers are in Asia, the institution has spread around the world; Latin America and sub-Saharan Africa account for 14 and 10 percent of the number of borrowers, respectively. Some of the biggest microfinance institutions include Grameen Bank, ACCION International, and Pro Mujer of Bolivia.

The average loan size varies, usually in proportion to the income level of the home country. In Rwanda, a typical loan might be $50 to $200; in Romania, it is more likely to be $2,500 to $5,000. Often there is no explicit collateral. Instead, the banks lend to small groups of about five people, relying on peer pressure for repayment. At mandatory weekly meetings, if one borrower cannot make her payment, the rest of the group must come up with the cash.

The achievements of microcredit, however, are not quite what they seem. There is, for example, a puzzling fact at the heart of the enterprise. Most microcredit banks charge interest rates of 50 to 100 percent on an annualized basis (loans, typically, must be paid off within weeks or months). That's not as scandalous as it sounds—local moneylenders demand much higher rates. The puzzle is a matter of basic economics: How can people in new businesses growing at perhaps 20 percent annually afford to pay interest at rates as high as 100 percent?

The answer is that, for the most part, they can't. By and large, the loans serve more modest ends—laudable, but not world changing.

Microcredit does not always lead to the creation of small businesses. Many microlenders refuse to lend money for start-ups; they insist that a business already be in place. This suggests that the business was sustainable to begin with, without a microloan. Sometimes lenders help businesses to grow, but often what they really finance is spending and consumption.

That is not to say that the poor are out shopping for jewelry and fancy clothes. In Hyderabad, India, as in many other places, we saw that loans are often used to pay for a child's doctor visit. In the Tanzanian capital of Dar es Salaam, Joel Mwakitalu, who runs the Small Enterprise Foundation, a local microlender, told us that 60 percent of his loans are used to send kids to school; 40 percent are for investments. A study of microcredit in Indonesia found that 30 percent of the borrowed money was spent on some form of consumption.

Sometimes consumption and investment are one and the same, such as when parents send their children to school. Indian borrowers often buy mopeds and motorbikes—they are fun to ride but also a way of getting to work. Cell phones are used to call friends but also to run businesses.

For better or worse, microborrowing often entails a kind of bait and switch. The borrower claims that the money is for a business, but uses it for other purposes. In effect, the cash allows a poor entrepreneur to maintain her business without having to sacrifice the life or education of her child. In that sense, the money is for the business, but most of all it is for the child. Such lifesaving uses for the funds are obviously desirable, but it is also a sad reality that many microcredit loans help borrowers to survive or tread water more than they help them get ahead. This sounds unglamorous and even disappointing, but the alternative—such as no doctor's visit for a child or no school for a year—is much worse.

Commentators often seem to assume that the experience of borrowing and lending is completely new for the poor. But moneylenders have offered money to the world's poor for millennia, albeit at extortionate rates of interest. A typical moneylender is a single individual, well-known in his neighborhood or village, who borrows money from his wealthier connections and in turn lends those funds to individuals in need, typically people he knows personally. But that personal connection is rarely good for a break; a moneylender may charge 200 to 400 percent interest on an annualized basis. He will insist on collateral (a television, for instance), and resort to intimidation and sometimes violence if he is not repaid on time. The moneylender operates informally, off the books, and usually outside the law.

So compared to the alternative, microcredit is often a very good deal indeed. Microcredit critics often miss this point. For instance, Aneel Karnani, who teaches at the University of Michigan's business school, argues that microfinance "misses its mark." Karnani says that in some cases microcredit can make life for the planet's bottom billion even worse by reducing their cash flow. Karnani cites the high interest rates that microlenders charge and points out that "if poor clients cannot earn a greater return on their investment than the interest they must pay, they will become poorer as a result of microcredit, not wealthier." But the real question has never been credit vs. no credit; rather, it is moneylender vs. modern microcredit. Credit can bring some problems, but microcredit is easing debt burdens more than it is increasing them.

At microlender SERO Lease and Finance in Tanzania, borrower Margaret Makingi Marwa told us that she prefers working with a microfinance institution to working with a moneylender. Moneylenders demand quick repayment at high interest rates. At SERO, Marwa can take six months or a year to pay off her lease contract. Given that her income can vary and that she may not have money at hand every month, she prefers to have a longer-term loan.

Moneylenders do offer some advantages, especially in rural areas. Most important, they come up with cash on the spot. If your child needs to go to the doctor right now, the moneylender is usually only a short walk away. Even under the best of circumstances, a microcredit loan can take several days to process, and the recipient will be required to deal with many documents, not to mention weekly meetings.

There is, however, an upside to this "bureaucracy." In reality, it is the moneylender who is the "micro" operator. Microcredit is a more formal, institutionalized business relationship. It represents a move up toward a larger scale of trade and business organization. Microcredit borrowers gain valuable experience in working within a formal institution. They learn what to expect from lenders and fellow borrowers, and they learn what is expected of themselves. This experience will be a help should they ever graduate to commercial credit or have other dealings with the formal financial world.

The comparison to moneylending brings up another important feature of microcredit. Though its users avoid the kind of intimidation employed by moneylenders, microcredit could not work without similar incentives. The lender does not demand collateral, but if you can't pay your share of the group loan, your fellow borrowers will come and take your TV. That enforcement process can lead to abuses, but it is a gentler form of intimidation than is exercised by the moneylender. If nothing else, the group members know that at the next meeting any one of them might be the one unable to repay her share of the loan.

If borrowers are using microcredit for consumption and not only to improve a small business, how do they repay? Most borrowers are self-employed and work in the informal sector of the economy. Their incomes are often erratic; small, unexpected expenses can make repayment impossible in any given week or month. In the countryside, farmers have seasonal incomes and little cash for long periods of time.

Borrowers manage, at least in part, by relying on family members and friends to help out. In some cases, the help comes in the form of remittances from abroad. Remittances that cross national borders now total more than $300 billion yearly. A recent study in Tanzania found that microcredit borrowers get 34 percent of their income from friends and family, some of whom live abroad, but others of whom live in the city and have jobs in the formal sector. That's the most effective kind of foreign aid, targeted directly at the poor and provided by those who understand their needs.

Here again, microcredit does something that traditional banks do not. A commercial bank typically will not lend to people who work in the informal sector, precisely because their erratic incomes make them risky bets. The loan officer at a commercial bank does not care that your brother in Doha is sending money each month to help you out. But a microcredit institution cares only that you come to your weekly meeting with a small sum in hand for repayment. Because of microcredit, families can leverage one person's ability to find work elsewhere to benefit the entire group.

Sometimes microcredit leads to more savings rather than more debt. That sounds paradoxical, but borrowing in one asset can be a path toward (more efficient) saving in other assets.

To better understand this puzzle, we must set aside some of our preconceptions about how saving operates in poor countries, most of all in rural areas. Westerners typically save in the form of money or money-denominated assets such as stocks and bonds. But in poor communities, money is often an ineffective medium for savings; if you want to know how much net saving is going on, don't look at money. Banks may be a daylong bus ride away or may be plagued, as in Ghana, by fraud. A cash hoard kept at home can be lost, stolen, taken by the taxman, damaged by floods, or even eaten by rats. It creates other kinds of problems as well. Needy friends and relatives knock on the door and ask for aid. In small communities it is often very hard, even impossible, to say no, especially if you have the cash on hand.

People who have even extremely modest wealth are also asked to perform more community service, or to pay more to finance community rituals and festivals. In rural Guerrero State, in Mexico, for example, one of us (Cowen) found that most people who saved cash did not manage to hold on to it for more than a few weeks or even days. A dollar saved translates into perhaps a quarter of that wealth kept. It is as if cash savings faces an implicit "tax rate" of 75 percent.

Under these kinds of conditions, a cow (or a goat or pig) is a much better medium for saving. It is sturdier than paper money. Friends and relatives can't ask for small pieces of it. If you own a cow, it yields milk, it can plow the fields, it produces dung that can be used as fuel or fertilizer, and in a pinch it can be slaughtered and turned into saleable meat or simply eaten. With a small loan, people in rural areas can buy that cow and use

cash that might otherwise be diverted to less useful purposes to pay back the microcredit institution. So even when microcredit looks like indebtedness, savings are going up rather than down.

Microcredit *is* making people's lives better around the world. But for the most part, it is not pulling them out of poverty. It is hard to find entrepreneurs who start with these tiny loans and graduate to run commercial empires. Bangladesh, where Grameen Bank was born, is still a desperately poor country. The more modest truth is that microcredit may help some people, perhaps earning $2 a day, to earn something like $2.50 a day. That may not sound dramatic, but when you are earning $2 a day it is a big step forward. And progress is not the natural state of humankind; microcredit is important even when it does nothing more than stave off decline.

With microcredit, life becomes more bearable and easier to manage. The improvements may not show up as an explicit return on investment, but the benefits are very real. If a poor family is able to keep a child in school, send someone to a clinic, or build up more secure savings, its well-being improves, if only marginally. This is a big part of the reason why poor people are demanding greater access to microcredit loans. And microcredit, unlike many charitable services, is capable of paying for itself—which explains why the private sector is increasingly involved. The future of microcredit lies in the commercial sector, not in unsustainable aid programs. Count this as another benefit.

If this portrait sounds a little underwhelming, don't blame microcredit. The real issue is that we so often underestimate the severity and inertia of global poverty. Natalie Portman may not be right when she says that an end to poverty is "just a mouse click away," but she's right to be supportive of a tool that helps soften some of poverty's worst blows for many millions of desperate people.

Critical Thinking

1. What has made microcredit programs so popular?
2. What are the origins of microcredit and who are its biggest beneficiaries?
3. What is a major drawback of microcredit?
4. With whom do microfinanciers now compete? What are each competitor's advantages and disadvantages?
5. How does microcredit contribute to bettering people's lives?

KAROL BOUDREAUX is a senior research fellow at the Mercatus Center at George Mason University. **TYLER COWEN** is a professor of economies at George Mason University and author of *Discover Your Inner Economist: Use Incentives to Fall in Love, Survive Your Next Meeting, and Motivate Your Dentist* (2007).

Many Borrowers of Microloans Now Find the Price Is Too High

NEIL MACFARQUHAR

In recent years, the idea of giving small loans to poor people became the darling of the development world, hailed as the long elusive formula to propel even the most destitute into better lives.

Actors like Natalie Portman and Michael Douglas lent their boldface names to the cause. Muhammad Yunus, the economist who pioneered the practice by lending small amounts to basket weavers in Bangladesh, won a Nobel Peace Prize for it in 2006. The idea even got its very own United Nations year in 2005.

But the phenomenon has grown so popular that some of its biggest proponents are now wringing their hands over the direction it has taken. Drawn by the prospect of hefty profits from even the smallest of loans, a raft of banks and financial institutions now dominate the field, with some charging interest rates of 100 percent or more from their impoverished customers.

"We created microcredit to fight the loan sharks; we didn't create microcredit to encourage new loan sharks," Mr. Yunus recently said at a gathering of financial officials at the United Nations. "Microcredit should be seen as an opportunity to help people get out of poverty in a business way, but not as an opportunity to make money out of poor people."

The fracas over preserving the field's saintly aura centers on the question of how much interest and profit is acceptable, and what constitutes exploitation. The noisy interest rate fight has even attracted Congressional scrutiny, with the House Financial Services Committee holding hearings this year focused in part on whether some microcredit institutions are scamming the poor.

Rates vary widely across the globe, but the ones that draw the most concern tend to occur in countries like Nigeria and Mexico, where the demand for small loans from a large population cannot be met by existing lenders.

Unlike virtually every Web page trumpeting the accomplishments of microcredit institutions around the world, the page for Te Creemos, a Mexican lender, lacks even one testimonial from a thriving customer—no beaming woman earning her first income by growing a soap business out of her kitchen, for example. Te Creemos has some of the highest interest rates and fees in the world of microfinance, analysts say, a whopping 125 percent average annual rate.

The average in Mexico itself is around 70 percent, compared with a global average of about 37 percent in interest and fees, analysts say. Mexican microfinance institutions charge such high rates simply because they can get away with it, said Emmanuelle Javoy, the managing director of Planet Rating, an independent Paris-based firm that evaluates microlenders.

"They could do better; they could do a lot better," she said. "If the ones that are very big and have the margins don't set the pace, then the rest of the market follows."

Manuel Ramírez, director of risk and internal control at Te Creemos, reached by telephone in Mexico City, initially said there had been some unspecified "misunderstanding" about the numbers and asked for more time to clarify, but then stopped responding.

Unwitting individuals, who can make loans of $20 or more through websites like Kiva or Microplace, may also end up participating in practices some consider exploitative. These websites admit that they cannot guarantee every interest rate they quote. Indeed, the real rate can prove to be markedly higher.

Debating Microloans' Effects

Underlying the issue is a fierce debate over whether microloans actually lift people out of poverty, as their promoters so often claim. The recent conclusion of some researchers is that not every poor person is an entrepreneur waiting to be discovered, but that the loans do help cushion some of the worst blows of poverty.

"The lesson is simply that it didn't save the world," Dean S. Karlan, a professor of economics at Yale University, said about microlending. "It is not the single transformative tool that proponents have been selling it as, but there are positive benefits."

Still, its earliest proponents do not want its reputation tarnished by new investors seeking profits on the backs of the poor, though they recognize that the days of just earning enough to cover costs are over.

"They call it 'social investing,' but nobody has a definition for social investing, nobody is saying, for example, that you have to make less than 10 percent profit," said Chuck Waterfield, who runs mftransparency.org, a website that promotes transparency and is financed by big microfinance investors.

Making pots of money from microfinance is certainly not illegal. CARE, the Atlanta-based humanitarian organization, was the force behind a microfinance institution it started in Peru in 1997. The initial investment was around $3.5 million, including $450,000 of taxpayer money. But last fall, Banco de Credito, one of Peru's largest banks, bought the business for $96 million, of which CARE pocketed $74 million.

"Here was a sale that was good for Peru, that was good for our broad social mission and advertising the price of the sale wasn't the point of the announcement," Helene Gayle, CARE's president, said. Ms. Gayle described the new owners as committed to the same social mission of alleviating poverty and said CARE expected to use the money to extend its own reach in other countries.

The microfinance industry, with over $60 billion in assets, has unquestionably outgrown its charitable roots. Elisabeth Rhyne, who runs the Center for Financial Inclusion, said in Congressional testimony this year that banks and finance firms served 60 percent of all clients. Nongovernmental organizations served 35 percent of the clients, she said, while credit unions and rural banks had 5 percent of the clients.

Private capital first began entering the microfinance arena about a decade ago, but it was not until Compartamos, a Mexican firm that began life as a tiny nonprofit organization, generated $458 million through a public stock sale in 2007, that investors fully recognized the potential for a windfall, experts said.

Although the Compartamos founders pledged to plow the money back into development, analysts say the high interest rates and healthy profits of Compartamos, the largest microfinance institution in the Western Hemisphere with 1.2 million active borrowers, push up interest rates all across Mexico.

According to the Microfinance Information Exchange, a website known as the Mix, where more than 1,000 microfinance companies worldwide report their own numbers, Compartamos charges an average of nearly 82 percent in interest and fees. The site's global data comes from 2008.

But poor borrowers are often too inexperienced and too harried to understand what they are being charged, experts said. In Mexico City, Maria Vargas has borrowed larger and larger amounts from Compartamos over 20 years to expand her T-shirt factory to 25 sewing machines from 5. She is hazy about what interest rate she actually pays, though she considers it high.

"The interest rate is important, but to be honest, you can get so caught up in work that there is no time to go fill out paperwork in another place," she said. After several loans, now a simple phone call to Compartamos gets her a check the next day, she said. Occasionally, interest rates spur political intervention. In Nicaragua, President Daniel Ortega, outraged that interest rates there were hovering around 35 percent in 2008, announced that he would back a microfinance institution that would charge 8 to 10 percent, using Venezuelan money.

There were scattered episodes of setting aflame microfinance branches before a national "We're not paying" campaign erupted, which was widely believed to be mounted secretly by the Sandinista government. After the courts stopped forcing small borrowers to repay, making international financial institutions hesitant to work with Nicaragua, the campaign evaporated.

A Push for More Transparency

The microfinance industry is pushing for greater transparency among its members, but says that most microlenders are honest, with experts putting the number of dubious institutions anywhere from less than 1 percent to more than 10 percent. Given that competition has a pattern of lowering interest rates worldwide, the industry prefers that approach to government intervention. Part of the problem, however, is that all kinds of institutions making loans plaster them with the "microfinance" label because of its do-good reputation.

Damian von Stauffenberg, who founded an independent rating agency called Microrate, said that local conditions had to be taken into account, but that any firm charging 20 to 30 percent above the market was "unconscionable" and that profit rates above 30 percent should be considered high.

Mr. Yunus says interest rates should be 10 to 15 percent above the cost of raising the money, with anything beyond a "red zone" of loan sharking. "We need to draw a line between genuine and abuse," he said. "You will never see the situation of poor people if you look at it through the glasses of profit-making."

Yet by that measure, 75 percent of microfinance institutions would fall into Mr. Yunus's "red zone," according to a March analysis of 1,008 microlenders by Adrian Gonzalez, lead researcher at the Mix. His study found that much of the money from interest rates was used to cover operating expenses, and argued that tackling costs, as opposed to profits, could prove the most efficient way to lower interest rates.

Many experts label Mr. Yunus's formula overly simplistic and too low, a route to certain bankruptcy in countries with high operating expenses. Costs of doing business in Asia and the sheer size of the Grameen Bank he founded in Bangladesh allow for economies of scale that keep costs down, analysts say. "Globally interest rates have been going down as a general trend," said Ms. Javoy of Planet Rating.

Many companies say the highest rates reflect the costs of reaching the poorest, most inaccessible borrowers. It costs more to handle 10 loans of $100 than one loan of $1,000. Some analysts fear that a pronounced backlash against high interest rates will prompt lenders to retreat from the poorest customers.

But experts also acknowledge that banks and others who dominate the industry are slow to address problems.

Added Scrutiny for Lenders

Like Mexico, Nigeria attracts scrutiny for high interest rates. One firm, LAPO, Lift Above Poverty Organization, has raised questions, particularly since it was backed by prominent investors like Deutsche Bank and the Calvert Foundation.

LAPO, considered the leading microfinance institution in Nigeria, engages in a contentious industry practice sometimes referred to as "forced savings." Under it, the lender keeps a portion of the loan. Proponents argue that it helps the poor learn to save, while critics call it exploitation since borrowers do not get the entire amount up front but pay interest on the full loan.

LAPO collected these so-called savings from its borrowers without a legal permit to do so, according to a Planet Rating report. "It was known to everybody that they did not have the right license," Ms. Javoy said.

Under outside pressure, LAPO announced in 2009 that it was decreasing its monthly interest rate, Planet Rating noted, but at the same time compulsory savings were quietly raised to 20 percent of the loan from 10 percent. So, the effective interest rate for some clients actually leapt to nearly 126 percent annually from 114 percent, the report said. The average for all LAPO clients was nearly 74 percent in interest and fees, the report found.

Anita Edward says she has borrowed money three times from LAPO for her hair salon, Amazing Collections, in Benin City, Nigeria. The money comes cheaper than other microloans, and commercial banks are virtually impossible, she said, but she resents the fact that LAPO demanded that she keep $100 of her roughly $666 10-month loan in a savings account while she paid interest on the full amount.

"That is not O.K. by me," she said. "It is not fair. They should give you the full money."

The loans from LAPO helped her expand from one shop to two, but when she started she thought she would have more money to put into the business.

"It has improved my life, but not changed it," said Ms. Edward, 30.

Godwin Ehigiamusoe, LAPO's founding executive director, defended his company's high interest rates, saying they reflected the high cost of doing business in Nigeria. For example, he said, each of the company's more than 200 branches needed its own generator and fuel to run it.

Until recently, Microplace, which is part of eBay, was promoting LAPO to individual investors, even though the website says the lenders it features have interest rates between 18 and 60 percent, considerably less than what LAPO customers typically pay.

As recently as February, Microplace also said that LAPO had a strong rating from Microrate, yet the rating agency had suspended LAPO the previous August, six months earlier. Microplace then removed the rating after *The New York Times* called to inquire why it was still being used and has since taken LAPO investments off the website.

At Kiva, which promises on its website that it "will not partner with an organization that charges exorbitant interest rates," the interest rate and fees for LAPO was recently advertised as 57 percent, the average rate from 2007. After *The Times* called to inquire, Kiva changed it to 83 percent.

Premal Shah, Kiva's president, said it was a question of outdated information rather than deception. "I would argue that the information is stale as opposed to misleading," he said. "It could have been a tad better."

While analysts characterize such microfinance websites as well-meaning, they question whether the sites sufficiently vetted the organizations they promoted.

Questions had already been raised about Kiva because the website once promised that loans would go to specific borrowers identified on the site, but later backtracked, clarifying that the money went to organizations rather than individuals.

Promotion aside, the overriding question facing the industry, analysts say, remains how much money investors should make from lending to poor people, mostly women, often at interest rates that are hidden.

"You can make money from the poorest people in the world—is that a bad thing, or is that just a business?" asked Mr. Waterfield of mftransparency.org. "At what point do we say we have gone too far?"

Critical Thinking

1. Why are advocates of microfinance concerned about the direction the practice has taken?

2. What accounts for high interest rates for many microfinance loans?

3. What is needed to avoid abuses in the microfinance industry?

ELISABETH MALKIN contributed reporting from Mexico City.

Corruption Reduction

A *Foreign Policy Goal and Instrument*

AMITAI ETZIONI

Reports suggest that local populations in some of the most contested areas in Afghanistan, including Kandahar, are more troubled by corruption than by the Taliban. In these and many other parts of the country, citizens are stopped at numerous checkpoints, through which they can pass only if they pay a bribe. Businesses and professionals typically cannot get permits without greasing the palms of officials. Judges are much influenced by "donations." Drug dealers are protected by the police. The head of state, President Hamid Karzai, even admitted to receiving bags of cash from Iran, adding that, "The United States is doing the same thing, providing the cash to some of our offices." Votes are often purchased, and various layers of the military hierarchy "skim" the salaries paid to troops. More cash is carried out of Afghanistan to banks overseas than foreign aid brings in.

Curbing corruption is granted much importance these days because the United States has shifted its strategy in Iraq, and even more so in Afghanistan, from a traditional military posture to counterinsurgency (COIN), in which winning the hearts and minds of the population is essential for victory. Such a shift in the population's loyalties is, in turn, thought to require developing a native partner government that is both legitimate and effective. Curbing corruption is considered to be an important element in developing such a government. The World Bank, which for decades considered it inappropriate to circumvent national governments, is now much more inclined to collaborate directly with civic bodies or local organizations and businesses if a national government is corrupt. Fighting corruption has also become a more important element of humanitarian aid. For instance, after the earthquake in Haiti, many called for working around rather than with the corrupt Haitian government. Meanwhile, others argued for "rebuilding" the government so that it could effectively administer aid. All of these worthy endeavors are likely to fail because they set their sights too high, deal with exceedingly vague goals, and seek to change the local culture rather than build upon it.

Limitations of Long-distance Societal Engineering

Societal changes occur all the time, but these are "natural" changes in the sense that, like rivers changing their banks, no one wills or directs them. However, societal engineering—deliberate, manmade, societal change—is like making rivers reverse their flow; it is very difficult to accomplish with lasting success. Contrary to popular belief, advancing societal changes according to one's design typically requires a much greater and longer commitment of a considerable variety of resources, which is often unmet. This observation is critical for the issue at hand because curbing corruption is a form of societal engineering. Indeed, uprooting corruption, with its numerous and far-reaching foundations in society, is particularly challenging.

The sociological thesis concerning the difficulties that social engineers face gained much following in the 1980s when neoconservatives pointed out that most of the liberal Great Society programs introduced in the United States in the 1960s had failed. The government was unable to eradicate poverty, help minorities catch up, improve public schools, or stop drug abuse. More generally, neoconservatives argued that it was wrong to assume that a combination of programs fashioned by civil servants and large amounts of money could solve social problems. Even so, as of 2003, these same neoconservatives in effect maintained that what the United States could not do in Los Angeles and Washington, DC, it could do in Mosul, Sadr City, and even Marja and Kandahar.

The difficulties societal engineering encounters are particularly severe when the change agent is a foreign power with a different culture and a home base thousands of miles away; when it is prone to optimistic, even idealistic, assumptions; and when it is disinclined to commit large amounts of resources to a given course over long periods of time. In other words, long-distance societal engineering is even more failure-prone than are similar domestic endeavors.

This general thesis is well-illustrated by the difficulties which foreign aid encounters. An extensive 2006 report on the scores of billions of dollars that the World Bank has invested in economic development since the mid-1990s showed that in many countries, spending had failed to permanently increase per capita incomes. Out of 25 aid-recipient countries covered by the report, more than half (totaling 14) had the same or worsening rates of per capita income from the mid-1990s to the early 2000s. The nations that thrived, importantly, were not necessarily those that received much aid. Indeed, while the nations that received very little aid, especially China, Singapore, South Korea, and Taiwan, grew rapidly, the nations that received most

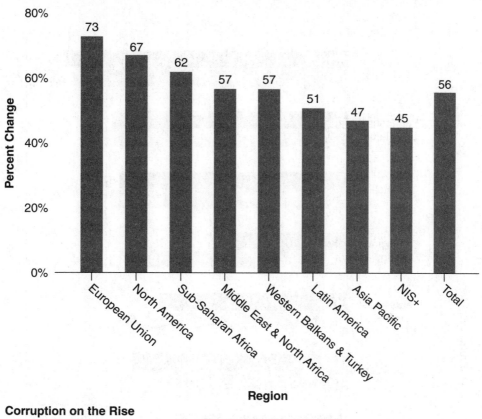

Changes in Corruption Levels, 2007–2010, by region
% of Respondents Reporting a Corruption Increase in the Past Three Years

Corruption on the Rise

Transparency International; 2010

of the aid—especially in Africa—developed least. These findings have led some to repudiate the effectiveness of foreign aid and others to argue that trade concessions are much more important. These findings show that one must scale back expectations, commit more resources for longer periods of time, and above all, incorporate local cultural practices in development strategy rather than try to change them.

All these observations apply in full measure to curbing corruption. There have been scores of anti-corruption drives in nations as diverse as Nigeria and Indonesia, Russia and India, and Greece and South Africa. Some have resulted in limited and often temporary improvements. For example, the head of Nigeria's Economic and Financial Crimes Commission, Nuhu Ribadu, prosecuted seven state governors before he was forced out. An Indian NGO issued zero rupee notes for people to hand out to demonstrate that they would neither give nor accept bribes. They enjoyed some success in shaming those who received the notes, sometimes prompting them to deliver services free of the usual bribe. However, very few endeavors created lasting, significant effects.

Examining Transparency International's annual corruption perception ranking further highlights this point. Although they cannot be used for rigid quantitative social science analysis, they parallel information from other sources, providing a preliminary way of assessing changes. Thus, one finds that most of the lowest-ranking nations of 1995, the first year of the rankings, continue to rank low some 15 years later. For instance, New

Zealand and Denmark have ranked among the top four least corrupt countries in all these years. Likewise, many countries that ranked high still maintain their troubled status, such as Nigeria and Venezuela. Indeed, very few countries have improved their scores more than a few points in the half-generation that has passed since the rankings began.

Most of the drives that were successful in curbing corruption—note, it is never eliminated—occurred in economically and politically developed nations rather late in their development. The progressive movement in the United States took place between the 1890s and the 1920s, Britain's famous political reforms were passed in the 19th century, and Hong Kong and Singapore enacted major reforms relatively recently. All of this is not to suggest that corruption cannot be reduced, but that major progress is likely to occur only as more general economic and political developments take place. These developments cannot be hurried along.

Moreover, when foreign governments function as the primary force for curbing corruption, they often do little more than fan the flames. Some consider all foreign aid to be a "poisoned gift" because it promotes dependency on foreigners, disproportionately benefits those gifted at proposal-writing and courting foreign aid representatives, rather than more deserving local entrepreneurs and businessmen, and provides more resources for corrupt agencies to exploit. Steve Knack of the World Bank, for example, showed that huge aid revenues might even spur further bureaucratization and worsen corruption.

Public Perceptions of Corruption Affecting Key Institutions
% Reporting the Sector/Institution to be Corrupt/Extremely Corrupt

Report surveys 86 countries across Asia Pacific, the European Union, Latin America,
the Middle East and North Africa, Newly Independent States, North America,
sub-Saharan Africa, the western Balkans, and Turkey.

Pessimistic Perspectives

Transparency International; 2010

All this has been exacerbated in Iraq and Afghanistan because large amounts of money were spent at a very rapid pace, with woefully insufficient accountability. American private contractors and even public officials were held to low levels of accountability, especially within the first years after the overthrow of Saddam Hussein's regime in Iraq and the Taliban in Afghanistan. Numerous reports show that funds did not serve the purposes for which they were distributed, but either simply vanished or ended up in the pockets of Iraqi and Afghani officials on the one hand—or those of insurgents on the other.

Numerous reports show that funds did not serve the purposes for which they were distributed, but either simply vanished or ended up in the pockets of Iraqi and Afghani officials on the one hand—or those of insurgents on the other.

A State Department report found the Iraqi government to be rife with corruption at all levels. Iraq's top anti-corruption investigator has looked into government misconduct totaling US$11 billion. The Inspector General for the Defense Department reported that US$15 billion of reconstruction funding could not be tracked. Similarly, a 2009 State Department report on Afghanistan revealed that "officials frequently engaged in corrupt practices with impunity," and that "corruption was endemic throughout society." This is fueled by foreign aid. Indeed, in Afghanistan, so much of the GDP ends up in overseas private bank accounts that reports estimate these amounts greatly exceed the total amounts of reconstruction aid that the United States and its allies provide to the country. The difference is drawn largely from the drug trade. However, the utility of foreign aid should not be completely dismissed. Major General Arnold Fields, the Special Inspector General for Afghan Reconstruction, estimates that about 25 to 30 cents of every US dollar spent on reconstruction in Afghanistan is actually invested in the project for which it was intended.

The preceding observations suggest that a good place to start reforms is with the Western powers that channel scores of billions of dollars into the countries at issue. These powers are much more subject to guidance by laws that seek to curb corruption than are the local partner governments. This is the case because Western nations are much more stable and effectively managed than nations such as Afghanistan, though there are limitations and weaknesses to their management. The United States, for example, has a law banning bribery overseas—the Foreign Corrupt Practices Act of 1977 (FCPA)—as do some other nations. Such laws are difficult to enforce, especially because some of the nations active in the aid-receiving areas do not follow such rules. Therefore, an agreement among all of the major donors who work in a given country to introduce such laws and enforce them vigorously would both make a dent in corruption and demonstrate that the West practices what it preaches. Indeed, in mid-2010, NATO set up a task force to control corruption perpetuated by Western companies. The UN favors forming an anti-corruption agency and requiring each civil servant to sign an oath against corruption. Those who violate the oath would be fired. Maintaining a "do not retain" list of contractors who were found to have engaged in corruption would also be a deterrent. Contractors who have been caught violating the law would be informed that they will be unable to bid for contracts in the

future. For example, though the Louis Berger Group was found to be over-billing the US government for services in Afghanistan, the head of the company was only required to pay a fine, and the group still contracts with the government. Under a "do not retain" policy, future contracts would not be allowed.

Vague Goals

Setting clear goals for many social programs and measuring progress is not necessarily a difficult task. One can seek to reduce illiteracy by a given percentage, within a defined period, decrease the rate of child mortality, raise the per-capita income of the poor to a given amount, and so on. By contrast, the anti-corruption rhetoric of the champions of foreign aid and COIN is exceedingly vague and open-ended. Secretary Clinton recently called upon Guatemala to "weed out corruption." The COIN guide calls for forming "legitimate and effective government," which requires that "corruption prevention measures should be implemented."

One of the highest-ranking US commanders in the Middle East was asked in a meeting what the United States's sociological goal in Afghanistan was. What is the non-military, "nation-building" element of COIN trying to accomplish? To turn Afghanistan into a society like, say, Jamaica, Nigeria, or India—or Chicago circa 1900? He responded that America's goal was to turn Afghanistan into Switzerland within two years. In contrast, Secretary of Defense Robert Gates has argued that the United States is not in fact trying to turn Afghanistan into a 21st century society. These short quotes highlight the analytical and political difficulties in setting a clear agenda for limiting corruption. There are no clear end-states or broadly applicable ways to measure progress. Furthermore, if either of the aforementioned officials had dared state that the United States would be content to reduce the corruption level in Afghanistan to that of Egypt, or any comparable regime, they would invite extensive criticism—both from the citizens of the country named and by those who would demand that the local government be more transparent.

When one raises this issue with US Army officers in the field and State Department representatives, they often cite a piece of conventional wisdom. They argue that all one must seek to do is to reduce corruption from the high level one encounters to a tolerably low level—a level that would not unduly burden their economies or politics. Some officials even add that low levels of corruption contribute to the "functionality" of a society because it greases the wheels of bureaucracies and helps stimulate economic development and innovation. To cite Afghanistan as an example, a nation ranked by Transparency International as the second most corrupt nation among 180, a substantial 23 percent of GDP is paid in bribes as part of the everyday cost of doing business. Additionally, a substantial part of the national GDP is derived from the illegal drug trade.

While the idea of eradicating corruption in a society makes for an attractive op-ed headline, the goal of eliminating it altogether is not sociologically viable. At the same time, campaigning to reduce corruption by a mere "x percent" does not seem to be a goal that one can readily justify in the public sphere. Nor is

Percent of People who Report Paying a Bribe in the Past 12 Months, by service

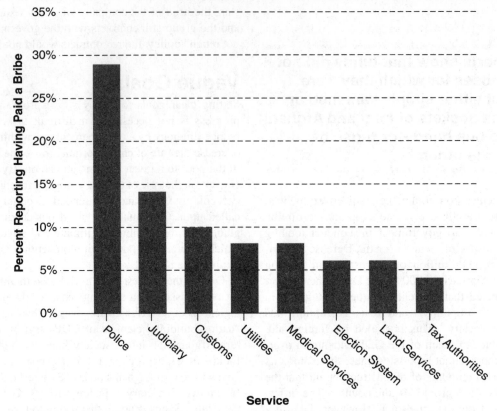

Report surveys 86 countries across Asia Pacific, the European Union, Latin America, the Middle East and North Africa, Newly Independent States, North America, sub-Saharan Africa, the western Balkans, and Turkey.

The Prevalence of Petty Bribery

Transparency International; 2010

it easy to measure the level of corruption in a given society and track changes in that level.

The best way to proceed is to allow the native population to set and reset the norms that determine what level of corruption they consider acceptable. Moreover, over time one may be able to work with them to gradually raise the level of integrity. The potential for progress will become more feasible once the role of the native culture is clearly outlined.

> **The best way to proceed is to allow the native population to set and reset the norms that determine what level of corruption they consider acceptable. . . the potential for progress will become more feasible once the role of the native culture is clearly outlined.**

Built on Culture

Implicit in the call for setting up a "legitimate and effective government" and in the ways major anti-corruption drives are forged by foreign powers is the expectation that the country at issue will develop Western-style political, economic, and civil service systems. In effect, these are typically idealized in the process. However, because these modes of governance require profound changes in practically all of the elements of the host society, this approach is bound to fail in most situations, especially in nations at early developmental stages. By contrast, building on the native culture, including native institutions, is a much more pragmatic approach.

A key issue is that Western precepts lead corruption fighters to seek to replace local controls with national ones. This tendency is based on the assumption that local leaders, often branded as warlords or tribal chiefs, typically treat their families, clans, and community members preferentially. It is also assumed that national leaders and civil servants, who have no local ties, are universalistic actors and will treat all comers equally.

This is not the case in countries in which "tribal" bonds are strong and national ones are weak. Here local leaders do tend to look after not only their cadres, supporters, and cronies, but also those within their "base" communities. They have a sense of affinity and loyalty to their people and often find that sharing the bounty, such as jobs and handouts, allows them to stay in power. This social arrangement in which the aldermen serve as the local chiefs is a pattern that was found in many major

American cities at least until the end of WWII and is still far from unknown even today in places like Chicago. By contrast, in less developed countries, civil servants who are appointed by the national government and draw their power from the center are often much more exploitative because they do not expect to stay in place for long periods of time. Consequently, they do not have a vested interest in serving local communities.

The following example illustrates the way local leaders typically function: Matiullah Khan, the local leader of Afghanistan's Oruzgan Province, formed a private security company which is the primary provider of security in the region. US and NATO forces pay Matiullah millions of dollars each month to secure roads for convoys. His militia also fights insurgents alongside American Special Forces and gathers intelligence. Like many leaders of private militias, Matiullah provides the province with more than just stability. He appoints public employees, endows scholarships, donates money for mosques, and holds weekly meetings with tribal elders. It is estimated that he employs 15,000 people in the province.

One should not overlook that these arrangements are undergirded by norms; such local leaders are expected to take care of their own kind and not to be unduly exploitative. As long as such norms are observed, there are few signs that the local population seeks to replace Matiullah and his forces, and many others like him, with the exploitative members of the national police or civil servants, who are quick to enrich themselves while failing to provide justice and services to the people. All of this is symbolized by the ostentatious homes their bosses build in Kabul, but not in the places Matiullah and his ilk reside.

One should think about these local social formations as if they were primordial elements of a civil society or as "natural" NGOs on which a nation can be built, rather than as hurdles to modernization that must be dismantled. True, there are exceptions to this rule, as there certainly may exist particularly abusive warlords who should be removed. However, often one must initially work with local leaders and only in the long run form a professional national civil service. That is, if one can build a much stronger sense of national affinity and the noblesse can oblige, national institutions can serve to further moderate local particularities and the related forms of corruption.

Finally, one cannot ignore that introducing anti-corruption measures often entails undercutting other goals. As such, the elimination of poppy—a major source of corruption—and raids of drug dealers in Afghanistan was undermined by the fact that poppy is a major source of income for large segments of the population and cannot be readily replaced with alternative crops. Also, bribery is sometimes the only way local commanders can get their supplies through contested areas. In short, raising expectations by demanding that the native partner government "eradicate" corruption or "eliminate" graft is very likely to breed cynicism. A good place to start curbing corruption is to increase accountability for the large amount of funds distributed by foreign governments and international organizations (international NGOs included). Working with local leaders rather than replacing them with national ones is often the most effective way to start curbing corruption. One must initially accept that local precepts of what makes a legitimate and effective government may differ substantially from the expectations that Western precepts contain. Over time, as general economic and political development advances, one can work to raise the standards of what is considered good governance to higher levels.

Critical Thinking

1. Why are the efforts to curb corruption likely to be unsuccessful?
2. Why is eliminating corruption an unrealistic goal?
3. How can the impact of corruption be minimized?
4. What are the difficulties in defining corruption in developing countries?

Amitai Etzioni is Professor of International Relations at George Washington University. He served as a senior advisor to the Carter White House and has authored 22 books. In 2001, Etzioni was named among the top 100 American intellectuals in a study by Richard Posner.

UNIT 3
Conflict and Instability

Unit Selections

Learning Outcomes

After reading this unit, you should be able to:

- Discuss the definitions of a failing state and the difficulties of formulating coherent policy to deal with this problem.

- Identify the sources of conflict and instability in the developing world.

- Recognize the complexity of conflict and instability in developing countries.

- Explain the connection between state weakness and conflict.

- Discuss the implications of the emergence of a new type of war in Africa.

- Analyze the connections between drug trafficking and violence in Mexico and Central America.

- Outline the consequences of global aging for stability and security.

Student Website
www.mhhe.com/cls

Internet References

The Carter Center
  www.cartercenter.org
Center for Strategic and International Studies (CSIS)
  www.csis.org
Conflict Research Consortium
  http://conflict.colorado.edu
Institute for Security Studies
  www.iss.co.za
International Crisis Group
  www.crisisgroup.org
PeaceNet
  www.igc.org/peacenet
Refugees International
  www.refintl.org

© Department of Defense photo by Airman 1st Class Kurt Gibbons III,
U.S. Air Force

Conflict and instability in the developing world remain major threats to international peace and security. Conflict stems from a combination of sources including ethnic and religious diversity, nationalism, the struggle for state control, and competition for resources. In some cases, colonial boundaries either encompass diverse groups or separate people from their ethnic kin, creating the circumstances that can lead to conflict. A state's diversity can increase tension among groups competing for scarce resources and opportunities. When some groups benefit or are perceived as enjoying privileges at the expense of others, ethnicity can offer a convenient vehicle for mobilization. Moreover, ethnic politics lends itself to manipulation both by regimes that are seeking to protect privileges, maintain order, or retain power and those that are challenging existing governments. In an atmosphere charged with ethnic and political tension, conflict and instability often arise as groups vie to gain control of the state apparatus in order to extract resources and allocate benefits. While ethnicity has played a role in many conflicts, competition over power and resources may sometimes be mistaken for ethnic warfare. Ethnic diversity and competition for resources, combined with other factors, resulted in the war that raged in the Democratic Republic of Congo between 1998 and 2004. This was a prime example of the complex causes of conflicts. The war generated economic disruption, population migration, massive casualties, environmental degradation, and drew several other countries into the fighting. This murderous competition provides evidence of the emergence of a new type of warfare in Africa, one in which profit trumps ideology and politics. Weak and failing states also contribute to conflict. States with limited capacity are unable to adequately address the poverty and deprivation that often leads to instability and conflict. Failed states also encourage warlord behavior and may also offer a haven for terrorists and criminals. The spillover from the conflict in these states can cause wider instability.

There is no shortage of conflict around the world, although the causes may differ from region to region. The Taliban poses a continuing security threat in Afghanistan as well as an increasingly dangerous challenge to the fragile government in Pakistan. Yemen has become a serious concern because of its increasing association with international terrorism. Efforts to combat this development have been complicated by deteriorating economic and political conditions. India faces a growing rebellion over land distribution while parts of Africa also continue to be conflict prone. Somalia remains the world's most prominent example of a failed state, and the chaos in the region continues. The killing in Darfur has declined, but Sudan's 2011 referendum on independence in the south threatens to spark renewed conflict in that region. Sudan highlights the difficulties of effective international peacekeeping. In Latin America, drug violence has also emerged as a serious threat to the Mexican government and the effects have spread more broadly to Central America.

Threats to peace and stability in the developing world remain complicated, dangerous, and clearly have the potential to threaten international security.

Where Life Is Cheap and Talk Is Loose

Modish jargon or a useful category? The term "failed state" conceals many tangles.

The annals of diplomacy recorded something startling in February. Saying, in effect, that it was in danger of collapse, the West African state of Guinea voluntarily turned to a United Nations agency that deals with failed or failing states. Like most of its neighbours Guinea has a history of violence, weak governance, poverty and destructive competition for natural resources. Its new government sought help from the UN Peacebuilding Commission, an unwieldy body that duly set up a task force known as a "country-specific configuration" to bolster the government in Conakry. It is already involved in shoring up half a dozen other countries, all African, at the behest of the Security Council; but this was the first time a country owned up to being at risk.

Such honesty is rare, but states that cannot control their territories, protect their citizens, enter or execute agreements with outsiders, or administer justice are a common and worsening phenomenon. Robert Gates, America's defence secretary, says "fractured or failing states" are "the main security challenge of our time." The term now extends beyond the poor world: American officials have applied it to the Italian region of Calabria.

The problem has attracted lots of wonkish experts, who have offered their expertise to the American government. As a scholar, Susan Rice used to berate the Bush administration for calling broken states a deadly threat but failing to fix them. Now she is her country's envoy to the UN. As a Princeton professor, Anne-Marie Slaughter was a leading academic authority on benighted places; till last month, she was a policy planner at the State Department.

This brainpower has yet to turn the tide of anarchy. In places where the state is chronically weak, it is not improving much. The spectre of state failure is haunting hitherto calm locations too. An annual ranking published by the Fund for Peace, a think-tank in Washington DC, always features the usual black spots: Somalia, Congo, Afghanistan, Haiti. Applying a fairly strict standard, it finds that most countries in the global South face some threat to their proper functioning.

Politics can complicate diagnosis and prescription. In a topical bit of scaremongering a Texas-based think-tank, Stratfor, has voiced fears that the drug-related mayhem engulfing parts of Mexico could end in state collapse. But the State Department would never bring that language to a delicate relationship. In some contexts, the use or non-use of words is a political choice. Last year, when Russia's President Dmitry Medvedev suggested that Kyrgyzstan was at risk of failing, he wasn't engaging in political analysis but hinting that Moscow's fatherly hand might again be needed to keep order.

Some semantic history may help. "Failed state" entered the political lexicon with the (ill-fated) American-led venture in Somalia in 1992. With cold-war patrons gone, so the theory went, many poor states were at risk of collapsing into Hobbesian anarchy, with dire results for their own inhabitants and neighbouring lands. Robert Kaplan, an American writer, captured and somewhat exaggerated an important truth by describing the chaos engulfing Liberia and Sierra Leone and warning of the "coming anarchy" in other parts of the world.

When Words Become Deeds

No sooner was the term "state failure" born than political scientists began picking it apart. "Failure" may misleadingly imply that a government is trying to function but not managing. In fact, dysfunctional statehood may suit the powerful. As Ken Menkhaus of Davidson College in North Carolina has written, the last thing a kleptocrat needs is good judges, or robust ministries that could be power bases for rival robber barons. "Where governments have become deeply complicit in criminal activities . . . perpetuation of state failure is essential for the criminal enterprise to operate."

Yet even fairly bad rulers, say African or Afghan warlords or corrupt provincial governors in Russia, may feel the need to provide certain public goods, if only to further their own interests. Such public services might range from half-decent roads to the suppression (or perhaps limitation through taxing) of petty crime. What those rulers will not do, though, is create an arena in which other economic or political players can emerge. Is that a success or a failure, then?

The English word "fail" can imply a status: a binary category into which you (or your exam paper) either fall or don't fall. Or it can be a process of indefinite duration. The second sense is more useful when discussing the welfare of states, where no bright line separates success and failure. Nor is there a continuum stretching from dismal failure to blessed success. The conditions are mixed in a variety of ways.

In the case of Mexico, it is hard to deny that governance is failing at some levels: some municipal police and councils, and authorities in certain states, have been infiltrated by the narco-mafia, becoming useless or worse in any fight against the drug trade. But the government can still marshal a formidable array of forces against the traffickers; that is quite a different situation from the anomie of Congo or Somalia.

Calling Afghanistan a failed state seems less controversial, but in a land where central power has always been weak, what does success mean? The American-led coalition's goals include the defeat of the Taliban, the interdiction of the opium business and the bolstering and cleaning up of the government in Kabul. But such aims may be hard to reconcile, argues Jonathan Goodhand of London's School of Oriental and African Studies. The drug economy may have had a stabilising effect on some parts of Afghanistan, he has written; the only plausible hope of a functioning state may rest on a compromise among regional barons whose power rests on narcotics.

If this is even half-right, then success is hard to imagine, let alone achieve. And many an outsider has grown cynical about the prospects of even partial success in establishing a clean government in Kabul. Local support for clean governance is too weak; many hidden channels link the state, the drug lords and even the Taliban.

Another category of states, hard to place on any spectrum of success or failure, could be described as "brittle" dictatorships, like the communist regime that once ruled Albania or the one that still holds sway in North Korea. Such regimes are successful in the sense that they manage, as long as they last, to make people do what they are told; but once they fall, such polities can shatter into a thousand pieces.

Beyond Good and Evil

Nor is there anything simple or Manichean about the standoff between the state on the one hand and its would-be wreckers on the other. States that are fighting either terrorist or criminal groups often respond by sponsoring their own terrorist or criminal protégés. At that point it can be hard to make any moral distinction between pro- and anti-state forces.

Moreover, anti-state forces (such as the Tamil Tigers, the IRA in Northern Ireland, or the Kosovo Liberation Army) often function rather like states in the territory they control, operating welfare services and primitive justice systems, while at the same time engaging in crime, from organ-snatching to bank heists, to keep their coffers full. Such organisations may "go straight" when they gain a degree of formal political power. Or they may not.

Given the messy intractability of state failure, who or what has a chance of solving it? Coaxing states in the direction of success, so that relatively clean institutions drive out the dirtiest ones, may be the most realistic goal. But if dozens of the world's states are in some sense failed, and may well have a stake in covering up the failure of others, then help offered by yet more governments, or inter-governmental agencies, is unlikely to be a panacea.

To see the difficulties of what pundits call a "state-centric approach", consider the history of the UN Peacebuilding Commission. It was one of the big ideas to emerge from a reflection on the UN's future by the global great and good in 2005. As first conceived, it would have had enforcement powers and tried to pre-empt state failure, not just cure it. But many governments, jealously guarding the cloak of statehood, lobbied to keep the commission weak.

To have any hope of success, state-mending efforts must tackle benighted places as they really are, says James Cockayne, who co-directs a New York think-tank called the Centre on Global Counterterrorism Co-operation. They must cope with local power-brokers with no particular link to state capitals; and also with anti-state forces with global connections that could never be trumped by a single national government, even a clean one.

Anarchy's anatomy   Failed states, 2010

Country (Population, m)	Failed States index, score[*]	Life expectancy, years	Symptoms
Somalia (9.4)	114.3	51.5	Anarchy, civil war, piracy
Chad (11.5)	113.3	50.0	Desertification, destitution, meddling neighbours
Sudan (43.2)	111.8	59.8	Ethnic, religious strife, illiteracy, tyranny
Zimbabwe (12.6)	110.2	50.4	Economic collapse, kleptocracy, oppression
Congo (67.8)	109.9	48.8	Civil war, massacres, mass rape, looting
Afghanistan (29.1)	109.3	45.5	Civil war, drugs, no infrastructure, terrorism
Iraq (31.5)	107.3	70.2	Ruined infrastructure, sectarian strife, terrorism
Central African Republic (4.5)	106.4	48.6	Desertification, destitution, disease, terrorism
Guinea (10.3)	105.0	60.1	Destitution, drugs, kleptocracy
Pakistan (184.8)	102.5	68.0	Coups, drugs, illiteracy, terrorism
Haiti (10.2)	101.6	62.1	Deforestation, destitution, crime
Côte d'Ivoire (21.6)	101.2	59.6	Incipient civil war, post-election deadlock

Sources: The Fund for Peace, *Foreign Policy*; UN; *The Economist*

[*]Out of a potential 120, based on 12 indicators

The clearest cases of such transnational state-spoilers concern the drug trade. As long as Latin American narco-lords find it easy to sell cocaine and buy guns in the United States, no government to the south can eliminate them. Whether in Latin America, in Afghanistan or in the emerging narco-states of West Africa, purely national attempts to deal with drugs can be counterproductive; they just drive up prices or create new networks.

In many other cases the wreckers are too effectively globalised for any one state to take them on, adds Mr Cockayne. Examples include Somali warlords with deep ties to the diaspora and Western passports; Congolese militia leaders who market the produce of tin and coltan mines to end-users in China and Malaysia; Tamil rebels who used émigré links to practise credit-card fraud in Britain; or Hezbollah's cigarette smuggling in the United States.

No worthy effort to train civil servants in just one capital will be of much use in neutralising these global networks. Last November the UN Security Council took a step towards recognising this. It passed a resolution telling buyers of tin not to source their raw material from mines controlled by Congolese militia leaders.

It was highly unusual for the council to issue an order to anybody except governments. Global Witness, an anti-corruption outfit, has reported that the resolution has been badly enforced, with only half-hearted efforts at self-policing by the tin industry. But at least the UN may be edging away from the fiction that governments, and people under their orders, are the only factors that determine the fate of nations.

Critical Thinking

1. What are the origins of the term "failed state"?
2. Describe the range of circumstances that this term encompasses.
3. Where should efforts to deal with state collapse be directed?

Afghanistan's Rocky Path to Peace

Even if all essential parties are interested in a negotiated settlement, getting to yes is no sure thing.

J. Alexander Thier

It is a hallmark of intractable conflicts that the distance between the status quo and the conflict's inevitable resolution can appear unbridgeable. Such is the case with today's Afghanistan.

For the first time since 2001, when the US-led intervention in Afghanistan began, a serious prospect exists for political dialogue among the various combatants, aimed at the cessation of armed conflict. Over the past few months, and highlighted by a conference on Afghanistan held in London on January 28, 2010, signs have emerged of a concerted and comprehensive effort to engage elements of the insurgency in negotiations, reconciliation, and reintegration.

In London, Afghan President Hamid Karzai repeated a previous offer to negotiate with, and reintegrate, not only low-level foot soldiers and commanders of the Afghan insurgency, but also its leadership, including the Taliban chief Mullah Muhammad Omar. Karzai went further by announcing that he would in the spring convene a national peace *jirga,* a traditional Afghan assembly, to facilitate high-level talks with the insurgency. Karzai expressed hope that Saudi Arabia would play a key role in this process.

Eight and a half years after the invasion, amid rising insecurity across Afghanistan and with a continuously expanding international troop presence in the country, the prospect of a negotiated settlement with some or all elements of the insurgency is enticing. However, a successful path toward sustainable peace in Afghanistan remains far from obvious. Fundamental questions persist about the willingness and capability of key actors, inside and outside Afghanistan, to reach agreements and uphold them. Further, the content of an agreement or series of agreements, as well as the process by which any accord would be established, is uncertain. And even if all essential parties are interested in a negotiated settlement, getting to yes is no sure thing.

Peace—Who Wants It?

Winston Churchill said "to jaw-jaw is always better than to war-war," but jaw-jaw is not always easier. In Afghanistan, the process is not off to a promising start. Already, US Secretary of State Hillary Clinton has all but ruled out negotiating with the Taliban's senior leadership. She told National Public Radio in January that the United States is "not going to talk to the really bad guys because the really bad guys are not ever going to renounce Al Qaeda and renounce violence and agree to re-enter society. That is not going to happen with people like Mullah Omar and the like."

Meanwhile, President Barack Obama took full ownership of the war in a December 1, 2009, speech at the US Military Academy. The president, after having sent 21,000 additional troops to Afghanistan in the first months of his presidency, ordered another 30,000 soldiers into the theater—a place he called the "epicenter of violent extremism," where "our national security is at stake." By the summer of 2010, the international presence will amount to about 135,000 troops, with the United States contributing 100,000 of them.

Obama's announcement came nine days before he accepted the Nobel Peace Prize in Oslo, but it was no peacemaker's gambit. Rather, he sent the troops to undergird a robust new strategy aimed at displacing the insurgency from key population centers. While this surge of forces may eventually create more propitious conditions for a negotiated settlement, it may in the near term have the opposite effect.

Even so, it is time to take seriously the idea of political reconciliation in Afghanistan, to weigh the prospects for arriving at such an outcome, and to consider the obstacles in the way. If we cannot even imagine how reconciliation might be achieved, it will be impossible either to prepare the way or to determine whether the path is worth traveling in the first place.

Every war has its own logic—and its own economy.

Is the conflict in Afghanistan ripe for resolution? In a conflict, after all, reaching a settlement can be very difficult even when the key players have decided that they want it. Every war has its own logic—and its own economy.

Peace in Afghanistan will require the stars to align. Several constellations of actors will have to participate to secure a lasting peace. These include the "progovernment Afghans"—that is, along with the government itself, those opposition groups that are not fighting the government; the insurgents (themselves composed of at least three major groupings); the United States and its partners in the International Security Assistance Force (ISAF); and regional powers like Pakistan, Iran, India, and China. Also in the mix are several spoilers—groups that likely will never want stability. These include Al Qaeda, Pakistani radical groups in solidarity with the Afghan insurgents, and the drug traffickers who move 90 percent of the world's illicit opium.

In any case, do the progovernment forces want to reconcile with the Taliban? Karzai, who sees his future and his legacy hinging on a political settlement, has been a strong advocate for such efforts, and he is using his executive power and personal prestige in support of them. He is backed by large segments of an Afghan society that is bone-tired of war and is likely willing to accept significant compromises in exchange for stability.

Many, however, including some close to Karzai, may be much more ambivalent. Assume for a moment that a deal means conceding to the Taliban control over some part of southern Afghanistan. The people around Karzai who govern these provinces, who operate construction and road-building enterprises, and who profit from the drug trade would under such a settlement lose their power and their cash cows.

Two of the enterprises that generate the most profit are transport—essential for supplying international forces—and private security, in the form of companies that guard convoys, bases, and reconstruction projects. These multibillion-dollar industries would wither rapidly if stability were established and international forces withdrew. Other Karzai allies—such as his two warlord-cum vice presidents from the Northern Alliance, Muhammad Fahim and Karim Khalili—represent constituencies that have fought the Taliban since 1994 and are not keen to see them gain any power.

Other potential opponents of a peace deal include civil society organizations that have pushed for human and especially women's rights in the post-Taliban period. Allowing the return of Taliban-style gender apartheid policies, even in limited sections of the country, would be anathema to these groups and the vocal international constituency that supports them.

Men with Guns

And what about the insurgents? The three major groupings—Mullah Omar's Taliban, directed from sites in Pakistan; the Haqqani network; and Gulbuddin Hekmatyar's Hezb-e-Islami—are not a monolith, and may treat the prospect of negotiations differently. This differentiation is often seen as a good thing, because parts of the insurgency might split off from the rest. But recalcitrant actors might also try to sabotage the process. Also, even a successful settlement with one group will not under these circumstances end the insurgency.

The harder question, though, is why the insurgency would sue for peace if it believes it is winning and the Americans are preparing to leave. Considering the Karzai government's continued loss of moral authority, the insurgency's still largely safe haven in Pakistan, and an ongoing decline in public support for the war in NATO countries, the insurgents might easily decide to wait out the next few years, meanwhile waging a very effective guerrilla campaign.

But several factors could conspire to change their calculus. The first is the war itself. Obama's deployment decisions will essentially double the number of forces in the country this year. The Afghan security forces are also growing—and some are getting better at their jobs. The bigger force numbers, moreover, are accompanied by a new counterinsurgency strategy, one that looks likely to produce effects more lasting than those generated by the Bush administration's "economy of force" strategy, which involved too few troops to secure territory won through battle.

NATO also seems finally to have figured out how to reduce Afghan civilian casualties, depriving the insurgency of a key propaganda asset at a moment when militants are killing more civilians than ever. The United Nations estimates that in 2008 the Afghan and international military forces killed 828 civilians, and the insurgents killed 1,160. In 2009, the numbers were 596 and 1,630 respectively.

The war on the Pakistani side of the border, involving drone aircraft, has also been stepped up, and both the Pakistani Taliban's top leader and his replacement have been picked off in such strikes in recent months. It is unclear whether guided missile attacks have been used against Afghan insurgent targets in Pakistan as yet, but certainly the capability exists.

If all this adds up to a change in military momentum, popular attitudes might change, costing the Taliban support and increasing the number of people willing to inform or even fight against them.

Most Afghans have had little incentive to risk their necks for a government widely viewed as corrupt and ineffective.

Increased credibility of Afghan and international civilian efforts also could have an impact on public opinion. While most Afghans do not support the Taliban, they have had little incentive to risk their necks for a government widely viewed as corrupt and ineffective. If the Afghan government and its international partners can present a compelling, plausible alternative to the Taliban, backed by significant new investments in delivery of services and good governance, the environment will become less hospitable for the insurgents. The Afghan government and NATO have also launched a massive new reintegration effort intended to lure insurgent soldiers and low-level commanders off the battlefield. If this program succeeds in demobilizing combatants and safely reintegrating them into society, prospects for defeating the rebels would brighten.

The Pakistan Factor

And finally, the insurgency would be dealt a heavy blow if it lost its sanctuary in Pakistan. The Taliban recruit, train, fundraise, convalesce, and maintain their families there. For years, the Pakistani government has denied that the insurgent leadership was present in the country, but this has begun to change. In February, the government arrested Mullah Abdul Ghani Baradar, the operational commander of the Afghan Taliban. The Pakistanis also arrested Mullahs Abdul Salam and Mir Muhammad, the Taliban's "shadow governors" for two Afghan provinces.

Pakistan has come under increasing pressure from the Obama administration to confront the Afghan Taliban, with senior US officials reportedly telling the Pakistanis that if they do not act within their own territory, the United States will. Islamabad is also grappling with an internal struggle against militants who are determined to overthrow the state, and it has learned some hard lessons after getting burned by extremist fires that it has stoked in the past. That said, Pakistan is unlikely to abandon its longstanding patron-client relationships with groups that it still considers strategic assets. But it might use its leverage to help force a political outcome in Afghanistan.

The United States, despite some hedging, seems to view an Afghan political settlement that includes the Taliban as a possible element of its plan to draw down US forces. In early 2009, the Obama administration's focus was almost exclusively on "reintegration," or coaxing insurgents off the battlefield, rather than "reconciliation," which implies a broader political settlement with insurgent leaders. According to a March 2009 statement of Obama's new Afghanistan and Pakistan strategy: "Mullah Omar and the Taliban's hard core that have aligned themselves with Al Qaeda are not reconcilable and we cannot make a deal that includes them."

It appears that eight months of bad news from Afghanistan, along with declining support for the war among the US public and some soul-searching deliberations, softened the administration's stance toward the prospect of negotiations. In his December West Point address, Obama said, "We will support efforts by the Afghan government to open the door to those Taliban who abandon violence and respect the human rights of their fellow citizens." And in January of this year, just days before the London conference, General Stanley McChrystal, Obama's hand-picked commander of the ISAF, said, "I believe that a political solution to all conflicts is the inevitable outcome."

Afghanistan's neighbors and other regional powers also have a say in the process—or at least a veto. Pakistan, Iran, India, Russia, and Saudi Arabia have all contributed to Afghan instability over the past three decades, supporting various warring factions (while also at times supporting peaceful development). Afghanistan is a poor, mountainous, landlocked country with a weak central government, and while it is difficult to control, it has always been too easily destabilized by the predations and manipulations of larger powers. An agreement among regional actors to promote mutual noninterference in Afghanistan's internal affairs would be necessary to secure the peace.

Efforts to reach such an agreement are hampered by regional and international rivalries that drive the desire to intervene. Pakistan, the most significant of the regional players, backed the Taliban in the 1990s in order to end Afghanistan's civil war, open trade routes to the newly independent states in Central Asia, and secure a friendly government in Kabul. This strategy worked for a while, but the Taliban regime proved so odious and extreme that Pakistan found itself, on September 11, 2001, on the wrong side of a great conflict engulfing the region.

The Pakistani security establishment, though it cooperated with the US invasion of Afghanistan, has found it difficult to completely break with its former clients, and has allowed the Taliban sanctuary in Pakistan. Thus Pakistan serves simultaneously as the primary supply route for the ISAF and as the base for the insurgent leadership.

The Indian Presence

Why this untenable balancing act? The Pakistani military and its intelligence apparatus still feel surrounded by India. Pakistan has lost three or four wars to India (depending on how you count them). India's superiority in economic and conventional military strength, combined with Pakistan's unresolved border issues with both India (Kashmir) and Afghanistan (the Durand Line), keeps Pakistan's guard up. Islamabad is also facing a severe domestic militancy crisis that has cost thousands of lives—and, in Baluchistan, a simmering separatist insurgency that, Pakistan charges, receives Afghan-Indo support.

India for its part maintains strong relations with the Karzai government and is training Afghan civil servants and providing hundreds of millions in aid to Kabul—despite itself having the highest number of poverty-stricken people in the world. Pakistan feels threatened by India's relationship with Afghanistan, and so continues to maintain a hedge in the Taliban.

Pakistan's attitude toward the use of militants as a strategic asset in Kashmir and Afghanistan is changing.

Many believe, as a consequence, that the road to peace in Afghanistan runs through Delhi. Yet, if Afghan stability is held hostage to a comprehensive accord between Pakistan and India, we can forget about it. In the near term, ways must be found to mitigate Pakistan's concerns about India and Afghanistan. The resumption of comprehensive talks between Pakistan and India—which were tabled after a Pakistan-based extremist group carried out a November 2008 massacre in Mumbai—could provide a critical outlet. Also, because of brutality and overreaching by the Pakistani Taliban and other groups in the past few years, Pakistan's attitude toward the use of militants as a strategic asset in Kashmir and Afghanistan is changing.

Iran's potential role also remains ambiguous. Tehran has supported the Karzai government, provided some development assistance near western Afghanistan's border with Iran, and was a strong foe of the Taliban. It has also acted consistently to combat the opium trade, which has helped create an estimated 4 to 5 million Iranian addicts—a massive public health crisis.

On the other hand, Iran is encircled by US forces in Iraq and Afghanistan, and it faces continuing confrontation with the United States over its nuclear program. A settlement in Afghanistan would allow the United States to concentrate more on dealing with Iran, and would free up US military assets as well. Tehran might prefer to see America bogged down in a costly conflict.

Art of the Deal

Prevailing on key parties to agree to a peace deal will depend heavily on the shape of the deal itself. Last year some starting positions were aired, but both sides effectively demanded the other's capitulation. The Afghan and US governments called on insurgents to reject Al Qaeda, lay down their arms, and accept the Afghan constitution. The insurgents demanded withdrawal of foreign forces, removal of the Karzai government, and revision of the Afghan constitution to create a "true" Islamic republic.

Each of the three primary parties—the Afghan government, the Taliban, and the United States—would enter negotiations with their political survival depending on one condition. For Kabul, the condition for survival is just that—survival. In other words, the Karzai government will not make a deal requiring it to step down or hand over power. Such a prospect appears to Kabul far worse than the status quo; in addition, the likelihood of the government's catastrophic collapse seems distant enough to ignore.

For the Taliban leadership, the condition is the withdrawal of foreign forces. The Taliban's success today relies not on ideology, but rather on resistance to foreign occupation and Karzai's corrupt puppet regime. It would be hard for the Taliban, perhaps impossible, to accept some sort of accommodation with Karzai—but it is nearly unimaginable that the Taliban would accept any agreement that does not include the fairly quick withdrawal of foreign forces from the Taliban heartland, and their timeline-based withdrawal from the entire country. Between this Taliban demand and the US desire to withdraw, a pleasing symmetry exists. But Afghanistan's fragility and that of neighboring Pakistan—a country that to the United States represents an even greater national security concern—will make pulling out entirely a risky endeavor.

For the Obama administration, the one completely sacrosanct condition for a peace deal with insurgents is a firm, verifiable break with Al Qaeda. Al Qaeda was the reason for going into Afghanistan to begin with, and this issue will prevent US withdrawal until it is addressed. But *can* the Taliban break with Al Qaeda? The two entities grew up together, and so did their leaders—fighting the Soviets, ruling Afghanistan from 1996 to 2001, and since 2001 returning to the fight, against the Americans. They have shared foxholes, and reportedly have established family ties through marriages.

The Taliban have made an effort to suggest they would rule without Al Qaeda. In November 2009, they released a statement claiming that the "Islamic Emirate of Afghanistan wants to take constructive measures together with all countries for mutual cooperation, economic development, and [a] good future on the basis of mutual respect." But would a ban on Al Qaeda in Taliban-controlled territory be verifiable? After all, international terrorist cells continue to operate in Pakistan, where the United States has resorted to an all-but-official drone war because of the lack of local cooperation and the inaccessibility of the territory.

Up for Discussion

Aside from these core conditions, everything is to some extent negotiable. Some groups in the "progovernment" camp have for years supported changes to the 2004 constitution and to Afghan law that would increase power sharing, decentralization, and strengthening of Islamic strictures. Many conservative political leaders, mostly former mujahideen figures, would love to see an increased role for Islamic law, or sharia. A political and legal map that allows for regional variation might make sense in such an ethnically and geographically segmented country.

Meanwhile, a process of political reconciliation with the Taliban could be used not only to mollify the insurgents, but also to address tensions still lingering from the civil war, as well as perceived inequities among Afghanistan's regions and ethnicities, which continue to cause conflict. Addressing these tensions and inequities should be a key focus of the upcoming peace jirga.

The United States, its Western allies, and the UN would come under serious political fire if a deal with the Taliban meant abandoning Afghan women—whose privations under the Taliban have served to rally international support for the intervention since 2001. But any legal changes that threatened Afghanistan's gains in human rights would likely be limited and subtle, at least on paper. Since we are not talking about a deal that would put the Taliban in charge of the national government—in the near term, at any rate—little danger exists that the constitution would be changed to ban outright girls' education or women's access to employment.

To be sure, an accommodation with the Taliban might accelerate the steady erosion of rights that Afghan women have experienced in recent years. Indeed, the democratically elected parliament passed a family law last year—signed by President Karzai—that sanctioned, among other things, marital rape under certain circumstances. And if, after the ink dried on an agreement, the Taliban imposed an unofficial ban on female employment in provinces that they controlled, no ISAF offensive would likely be triggered, even if such a ban were in contravention of the constitution or the terms of the peace agreement.

There is also a real possibility that combatants on all sides of the conflict who have committed war crimes and atrocities will not be brought to justice. Evidence from many conflicts suggests a sustainable peace is unlikely without such reckoning.

Even so, the real issue in negotiations is not likely to be the rules themselves, but rather who makes and enforces them. Power sharing is the firmament of all peace processes, and changing the Afghan political system will have to involve sharing power. What exactly would a power sharing arrangement look like? Would the Taliban (and other groups) be given control over certain provinces? Would they help fill out the ranks of the Afghan national security forces? Would they be guaranteed a number of ministries or seats in the parliament? Or would they simply be allowed to compete for such things in a (quasi) democratic process?

Peace accords that have been reached in Bosnia, Burundi, and Northern Ireland, to name a few examples, spell out such arrangements in great detail. In the end, it is even more difficult to implement such complex provisions than to agree on them.

Neighboring countries will also be looking for certain guarantees. Pakistan wants its allies to succeed, and wants to be a key player in the peace process itself. Afghans, including perhaps the Taliban, will resent a strong Pakistani role in the process, but no process will take place without Pakistan. And unless Pakistan nudges the Taliban to the table by denying them sanctuary, the insurgents can always, if the pressure gets too high in Afghanistan, retreat into Pakistan, where they can go to ground and wait out the United States for a few more years.

Iran, Russia, and the Central Asian states for their part will want guarantees that the Taliban and other groups will not harbor or export militancy. All the neighbors are likely to agree on one thing—that Afghanistan should be neutral, eschewing alliances with any of the regional powers.

Can It Happen Here?

Even if all the parties are willing to negotiate, and sufficient space exists to reach a viable agreement despite all the red lines, achieving resolution will still be enormously challenging. Between and among the various actors there is a fundamental lack of trust, and talks this year will occur amid an intense military campaign. It is unclear whether either the Karzai government or the insurgent leaders have the wherewithal to discipline their own constituencies. Strong leadership will be needed on all sides both to craft an agreement and to achieve buy-in for unpopular concessions.

The profusion of players, motivations, conditions, and potential spoilers seems to cast serious doubt on prospects for a negotiated peace. But the status quo cannot hold either. Obama has already signaled that the Afghan mission has the full support of his government until July 2011. At that point, if the trajectory of the war has not changed appreciably, US strategy will. Nobody knows what that means. It could mean abandonment of the counterinsurgency strategy, with increased focus given instead to the sort of counterterrorism strategy reportedly advocated by Vice President Joseph Biden in 2009, with few

troops on the ground and heavy reliance on drones and special forces to strike at terrorist targets. A new strategy could entail the replacement of the Karzai government.

Perhaps the most important issue affecting chances for a negotiated outcome is whether, to the various players, such an outcome looks more attractive than the alternatives. If the Taliban think they can run out the American clock without losing the war, they will do so. If the Karzai government and the Americans think they can beat the Taliban and stabilize Afghanistan without a deal, they will try. If the Pakistanis think that a weak, unstable Afghanistan that brings billions into their coffers is better, they will undermine a deal. So will the Iranians, if they decide the better alternative is a weak and unstable Afghanistan that pins down American forces.

But all of these factors might cut in more than one direction. Paradoxically, it is conceivable that the prospect of a US surge and departure could make a negotiated outcome more attractive to all parties—that is, negotiations might appear preferable to the risk of collapse and failure.

Do the Afghan people get a say? After 30 years of war they are among the poorest and most traumatized people on earth. But they are possessed of endurance and an indomitable spirit. If the indigenous, neutral leadership that supports a just peace could find its voice, that might spur a movement that presses the parties to reconcile.

Critical Thinking

1. What factors influence prospects for negotiations in Afghanistan?
2. Who are the important actors in any effort to achieve a settlement in Afghanistan?
3. What are the obstacles to such an agreement?
4. What role do Pakistan and India play in the Afghan conflict?

J. ALEXANDER THIER is the director for Afghanistan and Pakistan at the US Institute of Peace. He is the editor and coauthor of *The Future of Afghanistan* (USIP, 2009).

From *Current History*, April 2010, pp. 131–137. Copyright © 2010 by Current History, Inc. Reprinted by permission.

Civil Conflict Flares
In northern Yemen, the government has spent five years battling some 10,000 Zayidi Shiite rebels, known as Houthis. Since last August, government troops have been waging a bloody offensive called Operation Scorched Earth, with little success.

A Refugee Crisis
Some 250,000 Yemenis have fled the fighting and crowded into overwhelmed refugee camps that are rife with disease and malnutrition.

A Wider War?
Saudi Arabia entered the civil war in November, when Houthi rebels crossed into its territory. More than 100 Saudi soldiers have since been killed, and though a fragile cease-fire now holds, many fear that the war will soon expand. The Saudis have accused Iran of arming the Houthis, suggesting that the rebellion could turn into a proxy fight between the two regional powers.

A Nation on the Brink

It's not Just Al-Qaeda. Water Shortages, Collapsing Oil Supplies, War, Refugees, Pirates, Poverty—Why Yemen is Failing.

CHRISTOPHER BOUCEK AND DAVID DONADIO

Yemen—once known to Americans mainly as the site of the suicide attack on the U.S.S. *Cole* in 2000—has recently reentered the public imagination as a central front in the war on terror. An alarming number of would-be jihadists—like Nidal Malik Hasan, the Fort Hood shooter; and Umar Farouk Abdulmutallab, the Christmas Day bomber—have sought spiritual direction or logistical support there, and American security officials now consider Yemen a counterterrorism priority second only to South Asia.

But as the map at right shows, Yemen faces an astonishing confluence of other challenges that make fighting terrorism even harder. Among them: a civil war in the north, a secessionist movement in the south, dangerously depleted natural resources, rampant corruption and unemployment, and the fearsome possibility that Yemen will become the first country in modern history to run out of water.

It's also now clear that Yemen's government lacks the capacity to exert full control over much of its territory. This has created a refuge from which al-Qaeda can mount terrorist attacks across the country—and increasingly across the wider world.

At the heart of all these problems is Yemen's looming economic collapse. Already the poorest country in the Arab world, Yemen is rapidly depleting its oil reserves and lacks any options for creating a sustainable post-oil economy. Unemployment is estimated at 35 percent, higher than what the U.S. faced during the Great Depression.

Accelerating the economic decline is a protracted civil war in the north between Shia insurgents and the Sana'a-based government. The war has caused a refugee crisis and extensive damage to infrastructure, and its costs will result in a major budget deficit next year. (The government is already burning through roughly $200 million in foreign-currency reserves per month.) Even if that war subsides, the worsening economy will likely inflame a roiling secessionist movement in the south. Yemen has often teetered on the brink of collapse, but it has never faced so many interconnected challenges at once. And the stakes have never been greater.

Critical Thinking

1. Why is Yemen a counterterrorism priority?

2. How do economic and political factors affect Yemen's ability to cope with its adversity?

3. What accounts for Yemen's internal divisions?

Al-Qaeda's New Home
By some estimates, as many as 300 al-Qaeda fighters are active in Yemen, especially in the southern tribal areas of Ma'rib and Shabwah, where the government has little authority. The group's local branch, al-Qaeda in the Arabian Peninsula, has deep connections with Yemeni tribes and plenty of potential recruits among the country's jobless young men.

CHRISTOPHER BOUCEK is an associate in the Middle East Program at the Carnegie Endowment for International Peace, where DAVID DONADIO is a writer and editor.

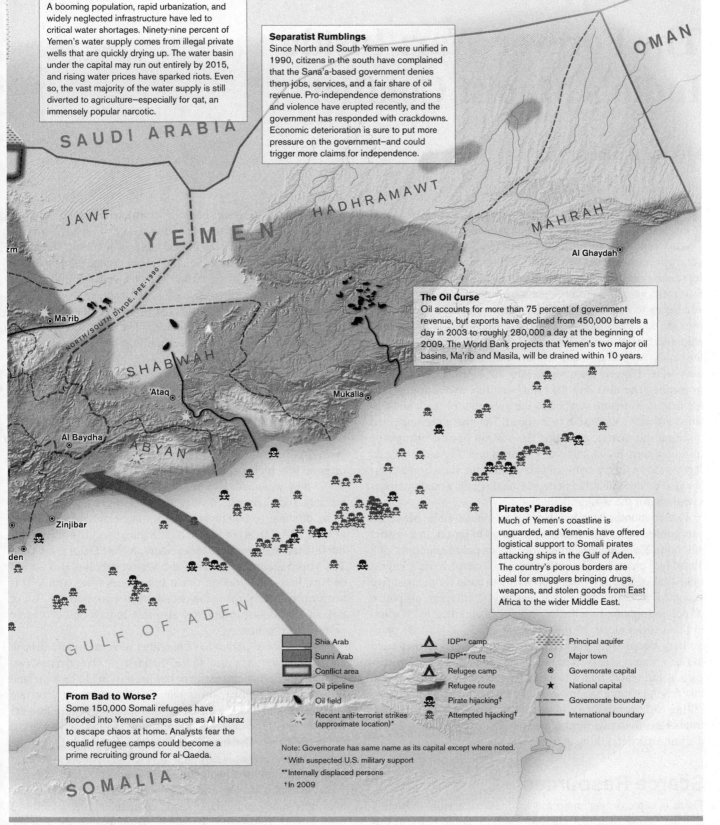

The Last Drop
A booming population, rapid urbanization, and widely neglected infrastructure have led to critical water shortages. Ninety-nine percent of Yemen's water supply comes from illegal private wells that are quickly drying up. The water basin under the capital may run out entirely by 2015, and rising water prices have sparked riots. Even so, the vast majority of the water supply is still diverted to agriculture—especially for qat, an immensely popular narcotic.

Separatist Rumblings
Since North and South Yemen were unified in 1990, citizens in the south have complained that the Sana'a-based government denies them jobs, services, and a fair share of oil revenue. Pro-independence demonstrations and violence have erupted recently, and the government has responded with crackdowns. Economic deterioration is sure to put more pressure on the government—and could trigger more claims for independence.

The Oil Curse
Oil accounts for more than 75 percent of government revenue, but exports have declined from 450,000 barrels a day in 2003 to roughly 280,000 a day at the beginning of 2009. The World Bank projects that Yemen's two major oil basins, Ma'rib and Masila, will be drained within 10 years.

Pirates' Paradise
Much of Yemen's coastline is unguarded, and Yemenis have offered logistical support to Somali pirates attacking ships in the Gulf of Aden. The country's porous borders are ideal for smugglers bringing drugs, weapons, and stolen goods from East Africa to the wider Middle East.

From Bad to Worse?
Some 150,000 Somali refugees have flooded into Yemeni camps such as Al Kharaz to escape chaos at home. Analysts fear the squalid refugee camps could become a prime recruiting ground for al-Qaeda.

SAUDI ARABIA

OMAN

JAWF

Y E M E N

HADHRAMAWT

MAHRAH

Al Ghaydah

NORTH/SOUTH DIVIDE, PRE-1990

Ma'rib

SHABWAH

'Ataq

Mukalla

Al Baydha

ABYAN

Zinjibar

GULF OF ADEN

SOMALIA

0   50 Kilometers
0   50 Miles

	Shia Arab		IDP** camp		Principal aquifer
	Sunni Arab		IDP** route	o	Major town
	Conflict area		Refugee camp	◉	Governorate capital
—	Oil pipeline		Refugee route	★	National capital
	Oil field		Pirate hijacking†	- - -	Governorate boundary
	Recent anti-terrorist strikes (approximate location)*		Attempted hijacking†	——	International boundary

Note: Governorate has same name as its capital except where noted.
* With suspected U.S. military support
** Internally displaced persons
† In 2009

Map Copyright © International Mapping. Map Sources: Adelphi Energy, Atlantic Research, Carnegie Endowment for International Peace, Central Intelligence Agency, International Chamber of Commerce, Relief Web, United Nations, World Bank.

The Forever War: Inside India's Maoist Conflict

MEGHA BAHREE

Chhattisgarh State, India—It was 4 P.M. one March afternoon in 2008. The victims were living in a relief camp in a village called Matwada. Two dozen members of a government-backed civilian militia, accompanied by at least one police officer, burst into their homes. They dragged four men out onto the street, across from a paramilitary office, and began to beat them with sticks. They paused to pour water over the Matwada men, waking them when they fainted out of pain and fear. When their wives flung themselves across their husbands' weakened bodies, they were beaten too. Then the men were dragged from sight, into the forest. One managed to escape. The next day the remaining three were found buried next to a stream, stabbed in the eyes and the neck and finished off with a knife stab to the head. The men were suspected of being informants, of aiding the nascent Maoist insurgency in the eastern Indian state of Chhattisgarh. The survivor and three widows filed a criminal case against the state, and a court decided recently that the State of Chhattisgarh would compensate them for the wrongful attacks.

Fifteen months later, a village leader named Vimal Meshram was gunned down by Maoists in a market in Bastar, in a district adjoining Matwada. Meshram was an outspoken supporter of a Tata Steel plant that the multinational—one of India's largest industrial companies—has been trying to build for the past five years. Meshram was one of at least 1,700 villagers, all police or police-supported vigilantes, who've been killed by Maoists in this district alone. In the bloodiest attack, at least 80 paramilitary troops were gunned down in early April as they tried to flush Maoist rebels from the Dantewada forests in Chhattisgarh. A little more than a month later, the rebels attacked again, this time placing a landmine on a national highway in Bastar, killing eight paramilitary troops when they ran it over in their truck. Less than two weeks later the Maoists blew up a bus in the same district, killing at least 50 civilians.

Scarce Resources

There is a proxy war underway in India's interior—a bloody conflict raging over that rare and valuable commodity in this too crowded country: land. On one side, powerful rebel groups

claim to be fighting for the poor—farmers and small agrarian tribes in particular. On the other side, the government is locking up land and the resources buried beneath it (particularly coal and bauxite) for some of India's biggest private companies. In its attempts to exterminate the Maoists, India's military and police forces have killed at least 1,300 insurgents since 2004. Trapped in the crossfire, some 2,900 villagers have also died; at least 100,000 have been displaced. The clash includes some of the most powerful industrial empires in India: Jindal Steel & Power and Tata Steel.

What began 43 years ago as a small but violent peasant insurrection in Naxalbari, a village in West Bengal, is now a full-fledged conflict and ideological movement. In 2004, the Maoists went so far as to form a political party—the Communist Party of India (Maoists). Though it was banned last year, and its entire senior leadership has since been arrested or gone into hiding, the Maoists have only grown stronger. In 2001, they were active in 56 districts in a small corner of the country. Today, they hold sway in 223 districts, boast an armed cadre of some 10,000 revolutionaries and can field a militia of at least 100,000, according to Ajai Sahni, executive director of the Institute for Conflict Management, a New Delhi think tank. The government has declared the Maoist rebels—also known as Naxalites—the greatest threat India faces from within. It is not surprising that the same decade that witnessed the rise of this violent Maoist insurgency also saw India's best economic performance in history.

"India's boom period has coincided with maximum dissent and dissatisfaction in rural India," Sahni says. Over the past two decades, the Indian government has been trying to lock up land for public projects like power plants and, more recently, private enterprises like Tata Steel. Often this means evicting farmers from the small, privately held farms their families have worked for generations. The biggest problem, Sahni says, is that the national government is abysmal at resettling people who have been stripped of their land, home and income.

In regions with dense tribal populations like Chhattisgarh, non-indigenous individuals and companies are prohibited from buying land owned by tribal members directly. But the law allows the government to acquire this land, then sell it to third parties. Hundreds of thousands of villagers have been dispossessed and displaced. Many now live in what could soon become permanent refugee camps, where they are prey to both sides in the proxy war and easy converts to radicalism. "There will always be developmental friction," says Sahni. "Of all the people displaced between 1950 and 1990, when India undertook large projects like dams, only 25 percent have been rehabilitated." In comparison, the few thousand who will be affected by Tata and Jindal's projects are so small that, according to Sahni, they "shouldn't cause friction. Rehabilitation and relief must precede dispossession."

Cleansing the Epicenter

Dantewada district, in Bastar, is the epicenter of Maoist activity. The village is 55 miles from Jagdalpur, where a factory under development by Tata will produce 5 million tons of steel a year. Iron mines nearby will feed the plant. Last fall, the federal government and the state government launched a "cleansing" operation here, to root out the Maoists. For the last five years, New Delhi has been trying to acquire 5,050 acres across ten villages, displacing some 1,750 landowners in the process. It has been met with resistance, and is accused of bullying and pressuring villagers and taking the land on Tata's behalf. Tata refuses to acknowledge these allegations. "Land acquisition is the government's job," a spokesperson said.

As he stands among his six acres of chickpeas, Hidmo Mandavi—chief of Takara Guda village—says Tata representatives have told him to sell his land. They've told other farmers this too, and have offered them jobs in the new steel factory. "We're not engineers," Mandavi says. "We may get jobs—but they'll be jobs serving water to others or sweeping the floors. Right now we live like owners. Why should we become servants?" Mehteram Kahsyap, another Takara Guda villager, refused to sell his 20 acres. "We've said [to Tata representatives] go put up your factory somewhere else," he says. "This is fertile agricultural land, why would you put up a factory here? If we get kicked out we won't survive."

Their defiance doesn't sit well, even in the world's largest democracy. Kashyap has been jailed three times on charges of disturbing the peace. Police have broken up gatherings of as few as five people, though there is no law prohibiting such activities. A few years ago two busloads of villagers were on their way to meet the governor of Chhattisgarh to complain about being bullied into selling their land for the Tata plant. The group advertised their intentions in the newspaper to drum up support, but the police stopped the buses en route and hauled the villagers off to jail. Mashre Mora, a farmer from Dabpal who refused to sell out, returned home from a weekly gathering with his fellow farmers. They discussed water supplies and crop infestations and sorted out disputes with their neighbors. That evening some 40 police officers broke the lock to Mora's house, knocked some tiles off his roof and dragged him to jail for disturbing the peace. It was his third arrest. "I've told them I won't give up my land," he says. "I'm uneducated and can't get a job in an office, so once the money runs out what will I do? I only have the support of my farming, I don't have anything

else." The police say that they have no involvement in land acquisition, they only show up to hunt Maoists.

Some villagers have found their names on lists of people who have sold their land—though they say they haven't. Kamal Gajbiya, 40, is a towering, muscular figure with a thick beard. A resident of Kumbli village, he owns eight acres with his brother, sister and mother. Gajbiya has met the same fate as Mora. On each trip to prison, he says, people he believes were Tata reps, accompanied by government officials, asked him to part with his land. "They said, 'We'll let you go; take the money,'" Gajbiya recalls. "I said, 'I'm a prisoner, and I cannot talk to you.'" Last May he discovered his name had been struck from the revenue records because he had supposedly sold his farm. Gajbiya filed multiple complaints with the Ministry of Information before he finally received a copy of the records showing that he and 1,750 other farmers had been struck from the government records as they had allegedly sold their land, even though he hadn't. He eventually obtained letters from those farmers stating their opposition to selling. There's nothing subtle about the government's threats. Retu Ram, a teacher from a neighboring village, was told he'd be transferred to another district if he didn't sell. Ram's colleague was told the same and, sure enough, got relocated. In another village, Banga Peeta Aito, a 60-year-old farmer, went to prison for a month on charges of disturbing the peace. His sons were told that until they agreed to take the check from Tata, their father would remain in jail. They finally caved in, and their father was released the next day. In its blanket denial of abuses, Tata declines to address specific incidents.

Tata claims it has been invited here by the government of Chhattisgarh, and that it is bringing economic opportunity to the area. "Although rich in mineral resources, Bastar is among the most backward regions of the country," says Sanjay Choudhry, a Tata spokesperson, who adds that the plant "will give a boost to all-round development in the region." The company, he observes, paid double the amount per acre set by the government and plans to offer a real estate exchange for up to 2.5 acres of land lost. It will also provide technical training and job-placement for one member from each affected family. Moreover, Tata says that 70 percent of the local landowners have accepted its offers, and the rest are coming around. "Youth of the area are in favor of industrialization, in which they see their future," Choudhry says.

The villagers dispute this.

Strife on a Cheerless Landscape

Some 400 miles north of Bastar, the thickly forested region of Raigarh gives way to a black, cheerless landscape. Soot blankets trees, shrubs, roads, buildings. The Jindal Steel & Power plant dominates the region. It runs a 7 million ton steel plant, a 2 million ton cement plant and a 1,600 megawatt captive power plant in the state. Its subsidiary, Jindal Power Ltd., is expanding its existing thermal power plant in a place called Tamnar with an additional $2.4 billion, 2.4-gigawatt coal-fired power plant. Naveen Jindal, executive chairman of Jindal Steel and Power and a member of India's parliament, has transformed his company from a modest performer into an international player. Naveen's mother, Savitri, is chairman of the O.P. Jindal Group and ranks 44th on Forbes's billionaires list—with an estimated net worth of $12.2 billion. Jindal Steel and Power has among the lowest production costs in the world, thanks to cheap supplies of iron ore, electric power and sponge iron, which is made from inexpensive bituminous coal rather than anthracite. To keep growing, Jindal needs more land and more resources, and the push has led to strife.

Although there have been public hearings to decide whether Jindal can build its new 2.4-gigawatt coal-fired plant, residents say they weren't allowed to voice their concerns. During one such meeting, in January 2008, several people were beaten by police and seven were hospitalized for a week. Among the abused was Harihar Patel, chief of the Khamaria village. "The company has a no-objection certificate okaying the project, but we never signed it," Patel says. Ramesh Agrawal, who runs an Internet café in Raigarh thinks that most of the public hearings are for show. Agrawal uses the profits from his café to pursue court cases against Jindal and inform villagers of their legal rights. When asked about the role his company played in the public hearings, Naveen Jindal claims, "We had no role in conducting the public hearing except for making a brief presentation about the project. I believe some people wanted to create trouble, and the police had to intervene to maintain peace."

But at times there isn't even the farce of a public hearing. According to Krishna Lal Sao, an ex-cop in Tamnar, in 2003 Jindal Power dumped 1,100 truckloads of mud on his two acres of arable land just before harvest. Sao says that his fellow officers wouldn't let him register a complaint and harassed so much that he resigned from the force in late 2005. In March 2007, a district court gave him title to his land and directed the police to restore his property. Then, without his permission, Jindal installed a cooling tower and warehouse on his farmland, and Sao gave up. He recently took out a loan and opened a stationery store.

In the Camps

Maoists need economic and human resources—money and men—to continue to spread their ideology and to strengthen their hold across the country. But anyone who comes across as a Naxal supporter will be hunted down both by the police and a government-backed civil militia known as the Salwa Judum (literally, "Purification Hunt"). Those ousted by the rebels—many of them victims of the appropriation of their lands—have ended up in relief camps. At least 45,000 are crammed into 23 camps run by the Judum that opened five years ago, when the proxy war began in earnest. The militia trains and arms its members and their enforcers—known as Special Police Officers—to secure the camps and conduct regular patrols in the surrounding forests.

There is an air of listlessness at the Dornapal camp, in the heart of this conflict-ridden area. Row after row of single-room, thatched roof mud huts are interspersed with piles of garbage. The air is filled with the acrid smoke of *bidis,* cheap cigarettes. There is no work for the farmers. A few may chance a day trip to check on the land they were forced from, and even sneak sowing a crop. But most do nothing, wasting their lives away. Kathar Ganga arrived at Dornapal just after the camp opened. Maoists held a meeting in his village, he recalls, and accused his son of being a police informant. They killed him on the spot. He was just 20 years old and newly married.

Attacks, explosions, dead bodies—such is the daily news from India.

While Ganga and others like him may eventually return to their villages and again take up farming, Markam Joge never can. He joined the Judum as a Special Police Officer four years ago. His future lies with the Judum. He's 21, married, with a five-year-old daughter. Joge earns $46 a month hunting Maoists and their supporters. "I will raise my daughter here in the camp," he says. "I do miss my village but now that I've picked up arms I can't go back." Salwa Judum members aren't merely the protectors of the villagers, as they like to claim. "There is a complete collapse of the rule of law—with the root cause of violence in the area being the Salwa Judum and Naxal counterattacks," says Nandini Sundar, a sociology professor at the Delhi School of Economics, who is researching the history and anthropology of citizenship and war in South Asia. Joge cannot simply hang up his arms and stop the fight. He has picked sides for life.

Some 15 miles from the Dornapal camp, deep in the forests, inaccessible even by mud road, is Naindra village. In 2006, the Salwa Judum raided and burned down the indigenous villagers' homes. Those who failed to escape, like Muchaki Ganga's father, were killed. "They slit his throat with a knife and left (his neck) hanging by a piece," Ganga says. "I'm too scared to go to the police. They'd finish us off if we complained." Not so, says Amresh Mishra, superintendent of police for Dantewada. "There are many incidents where Naxals have done this and blamed it on Salwa Judum and the police." After the houses were torched, Maoists came and gave the villagers clothes. The Judum returned twice more, set fire to the homes and abducted two boys and a girl who have not been seen since. The village was recently rebuilt by Himanshu Kumar, who for the past 18 years has run an ashram and a nonprofit school promoting literacy and basic hygiene in the heart of Naxal territory. An ardent supporter of the tribal people, he has carefully recorded police, Judum and government atrocities. He has supported some 600 legal complaints against these groups, while many are still grinding through the court system. The police are now trying to label him a Maoist. "The question is if this is an operation to kill Naxals or to start mining," he says. "But it's being done in a wrong way. They can't track down Naxals so they are going around killing innocent people." But Kumar thinks there is an easy solution. "If you want peace, give the tribals schools, hospitals, ration shops. The Naxals will never interfere with any of this."

Dilip Choudhary, the Additional Secretary to the Home Ministry, thinks this is easier said than done. The Maoists, he says, "have refused to respond to the simple call to give up violence"—the sole condition the government has set for talks.

Angry, Thinking People

In her book *Subalterns and Sovereigns*, Nandini Sundar observes that much of the debate in India today is not about the violence but the threat the Naxalites pose to the status quo. It's the security establishment's need to project this "threat" that justifies their often unchecked funding and use of force. The everyday, essential, but far less profitable task of improving governance—including an effective, impartial police force—plays little part in official efforts to deal with the rebels. As Sundar put it, "People are fighting against land acquisitions and the government is labeling them Naxals and then using that to suppress them. This is becoming increasingly dangerous as now (innocent) people are being fired upon." But, she adds, the Maoists have inflicted damage on industrial property, causing the companies to demand private security. The government is conflating both dilemmas. "If the Naxals were not there, the government would be able to acquire more land for the private sector."

Attacks, counter attacks, explosions, dead bodies—such is the daily news from India. And while the reasons for the carnage vary in different parts of the country—from land rights and access to hidden minerals to caste and class issues—the conflict can be broadly defined as the clash between industrialization and an older, agricultural, communal way of life. Keeping in mind India's socialist history, the urban-rural gulf only widens as one part of this diverse nation seeks to modernize and develop, and the other gets placed in camps. For India to become a true global power of any consequence, this dirty narrative of development needs to be resolved. Vast numbers of tribal citizens, many already the poorest in the country, have been rendered utterly destitute by the conflict and are suffering from severe malnutrition, Sundar says, adding, "They will not come back home unless they can be assured of peace, which will come about only if criminal prosecution is initiated against the guilty, and there is an end to the continuing displacement." The displaced, she says, fall into three categories. The largest includes those hiding in the jungles around their villages, or living at home, but periodically fleeing into the jungles after their villages are attacked by the security forces and Salwa Judum. Next are those who have fled to neighboring states because of attacks by the Salwa Judum, and live an uncertain existence on forest land at the mercy of the forest department officials or host villagers. The third category includes those in Salwa Judum camps.

Sundar has proposed a rehabilitation plan to the Supreme Court of India. It includes: individual compensation for injury, death and sexual violence; household compensation for property loss and damage; rebuilding of village infrastructures, including installation of ration shops, handpumps, schools and child care facilities; restoration of tribal society, which has suffered damage due to the breakdown of trust and fratricidal violence; and restoration of district administrative, police and judicial machinery. The plan includes contributions from the National Commission for the Protection of Child Rights for restoring village schools and rehabilitating minors who were employed as combatants and addressing the psychological trauma of children who are caught in the conflict. The National Commission of Women would be enlisted to counsel female victims of rape and sexual violence and help them file cases. "Victims' voices must be given fair representation," Sundar says.

Author Sudeep Chakravarti, who chronicles his extensive travels through the heartland of India's insurgency in his book, *Red Sun—Travels in Naxalite Country,* explains that Maoists have moved away from their earliest priorities of the 1960s, when the movement was about sharecroppers and landless peasantry. In states like Chhattisgarh and West Bengal, uprisings are concerned with tribal rights; in Orissa and Jharkhand it's over the rich mineral deposits there; in Bihar, Uttar Pradesh and parts of Haryana it's about caste and land. Now the movement is even spreading to Punjab where the area is over-farmed and undergoing a serious water crisis. The movement is growing as injustices proliferate.

"All the inequities of India are beginning to add up," Chakravarti says. "The government can't wish away resentment and rebellion. Repeatedly, since the 1960s the Maoist movement has been 'annihilated.' But from the time it started with three villages, it has come back stronger, and now it's in 223 districts. These are not your frothing individuals. There's a method to what they do. You have to accept that these are angry, yet thinking people."

Critical Thinking

1. What accounts for the increasing strength of India's Naxalite rebellion?
2. Why is the Indian government trying to secure control of land?
3. What two important trends are at odds in this struggle?
4. How has the Indian government responded to this conflict?

MEGHA BAHREE is a staff writer at *Forbes,* specializing in Asia and the India-Pakistan region.

Sudan on the Cusp

"The appointed date for southern Sudan's separation fast approaches. . . . Once separation does take place, both north and south will still face a multitude of stress points, risks, and challenges."

RICHARD S. WILLIAMSON

I
f events go as planned, southern Sudan in just weeks will separate from the north and the world's newest nation, the Republic of South Sudan, will be born. However, serious impediments to a peaceful separation still must be addressed. And even if an uneventful separation does take place, that will not be the end of the story—it will be the end of the beginning. Many challenges lie ahead both for the new independent nation and for what remains of the old Sudan, as well as for neighboring countries, the wider region, and the international community.

Seared in my memory is a visit I made in May 2008 to Abyei, a border town contested by north and south Sudan. Just days earlier thousands of families had lived, laughed, and loved there. On the day of my visit I saw only remnants of lives lost. The town's dirt roads stood empty except for three teenage soldiers wearing flip-flops and carrying Kalashnikov rifles. I saw burned-out huts, blackened chairs and bed frames, scattered fragments of clothes, the occasional charred skeleton of a truck, and the contorted remains of a child's bicycle. Here and there rose wisps of smoke, the pungent smell hanging heavy in the air.

An unknown number of innocents had been killed in the spring of 2008, and many more forced to flee their homes, in a terrible flash of violence carried out by nomadic Misseriya Arabs while Sudan's armed forces stayed in their barracks and allowed the carnage to rage on. Tens of thousands of people lost the lives they had known. They were only the latest victims of the endless violence in Sudan, a nation that has suffered more trauma and tragedy than any society could possibly digest.

Weeks later I visited Agok, a day's walk from Abyei, where over 50,000 displaced people who had fled the Abyei destruction had settled temporarily. It was the rainy season. The people were crowded under plastic sheets hung between trees. My feet sank three inches into the mud as I walked from shelter to shelter to visit the victims of yet another spasm of sense-less destruction. These people, kept alive by humanitarian aid, were hurt and angry, but determined to return to their homes and rebuild.

The final disposition of Abyei—whether it becomes part of the new Republic of South Sudan or remains part of the north—has yet to be determined. This question is one of the many consequential matters still unresolved as we approach the scheduled separation date of July 9, 2011. Abyei is just one example of how fragile things are and of how much work remains to be done before a peaceful separation can proceed.

At the Margins

Throughout much of Sudan's painful history, Arab Muslims at the center have been favored while the non-Arab, non-Muslim people at the periphery have been marginalized. Indeed such discrimination—in the economy, politics, healthcare, and education—has defined Sudan's past 200 years. The country's divisions are deep and its injustices significant; no vision unites Sudan, no sense exists that various groups share a stake in the nation, no agreement pertains on what it is to be Sudanese.

Under the Ottoman Empire in the nineteenth century and the British Empire during the first half of the twentieth century, the Arab Muslims at the center were partners in ruling this diverse land, where nearly 600 ethnic groups and tribes speak almost 400 languages. When the British left in 1956, political power was transferred to the Arab Muslims and, not surprisingly, they continued the patterns of marginalization practiced by their former imperial rulers.

Economic deprivation, political discrimination, and injustice naturally produced deep resentments. Periodic efforts by Khartoum to assert greater control over the periphery, coupled with attempts to impose sharia, led to rebellions and warfare.

No acceptable narrative for a broader Sudan has ever existed; nor a sense of nationhood; nor the harmony and tranquility associated with a normal state. Instead the country has experienced discrimination and division, strain and struggle, fragmentation and friction, bickering and brutality. These were the underlying causes of the long north-south Sudanese civil war, a conflict that began in 1955, stopped in 1972, then resumed in 1983. It was Africa's longest war, claiming 2.5 million lives and displacing more than 4 million people.

A 2005 peace agreement ended the worst violence of that war and created a six-year path toward self-determination and the independence of the south. But it is important to understand that the people of the south are not the only group on the periphery that has long been marginalized. Peoples of the east, of the central Nuba Mountains, of Darfur in the west, and elsewhere have suffered similar injustices and have rebelled from time to time. The fundamental problems between them and Khartoum will not end with the south's independence. Indeed, the danger of violence between Khartoum and these other peripheral areas may well increase.

Yes and No

President George W. Bush and Jack Danforth, a former senator and my predecessor as Bush's special envoy to Sudan, took the lead in trying to end Sudan's north-south civil war. Negotiations were long and difficult, and involved Khartoum; Juba (the city in southern Sudan that is now slated to be the capital of the new republic); countries belonging to the Intergovernmental Authority on Development, a regional grouping; and other stakeholders, such as Norway and the United Kingdom. The result was the Comprehensive Peace Agreement (CPA) between Khartoum and the leadership of the southern rebels, the Sudan People's Liberation Movement. The agreement was signed in January 2005.

Implementing the pact has been difficult and imperfect. Low-intensity fighting has continued and casualties persist. The north after the agreement was reached failed to live up to some important commitments. Leaders in southern Sudan, meanwhile—especially Salva Kiir, the president of the south—proved patient, skilled, and disciplined. They refused to respond proportionally to violence sponsored by Khartoum. They kept their focus on the prize of self-determination.

The CPA, while often in danger, proved resilient, and the parties moved toward the January 2011 referendum on southern independence that was specified in the agreement. The vote was deemed credible. Over 99 percent of southerners chose independence.

Still, it is worthwhile to examine some CPA commitments that have not been honored—for example, regarding border areas contested between the north and south. In the agreement, both parties committed to accept a border demarcation to be drawn by the Abyei Border Commission, a body of international experts who were to rely on various specified criteria.

The commission gathered information and rendered its judgment. The south did not get everything it had hoped for, but nonetheless met its obligation and accepted the border decisions. The north, however, abrogated its commitment by refusing to accept the commission's decision.

After the May 2008 flare-up in Abyei, both the north and the south made various commitments, outlined in a document called the Abyei Road Map Agreement. This agreement specified that, among other things, the contested border issues would be referred to the Permanent Court of Arbitration in The Hague and that both sides would abide by whatever decision this international body reached. In essence, the south agreed to let the north have a second bite at the apple.

Filings were made, documents were entered into evidence, and arguments were tendered to the court. The court made its decision. The new border demarcation was somewhat less favorable to the south than that rendered by the Abyei Border Commission; nonetheless, consistent with its commitment, Juba accepted the decision. The north, again in violation of its commitment, refused to accept.

Similarly, the north did not disarm and demobilize its proxy Arab militias as it had committed to do in the CPA. The north did not fully integrate joint security forces, nor did it provide transparent accounting for the sharing of oil revenues as agreed to in the CPA. The list goes on. The point is that Khartoum's failure fully to live up to its commitments has created various negative consequences.

First, the south has developed a deep distrust of Khartoum's reliability; it appears to be the north's conscious strategy to give little weight to fulfilling its obligations. Second, other marginalized peoples in Sudan have witnessed this record and taken note. Third, the international community has developed a poor record of inducing the north to honor its commitments and of holding Khartoum accountable for its breaches.

While serving as special envoy, and working with Sudan's prominent personalities and watching the maneuvering of the north, I came to believe that Khartoum had decided there was little cost to abrogating commitments. Rather, the leaders in the capital saw value in a strategy that drew things out. They liked to set up elaborate processes for consideration of critical matters. Then they would discuss, deliberate, debate, and delay. Meanwhile, the international community's attention would wander to some other pressing issue somewhere else in the world. So Khartoum would escape the immediate crisis and kick the can down the road.

Shifting Leverage

Before a peaceful separation can occur in July, a number of pressing issues must be resolved. These issues have been understood for more than six years. That they remain outstanding is a testament to the north's success at controlling the pace of deliberations.

The north's thinking seems to be that its leverage will grow as July 9 draws closer. I suspect that Khartoum believes Juba will increasingly feel that it must make a deal as that date approaches; that the south will make concessions and the north will win more-than-equitable terms on key issues.

Furthermore, given the Barack Obama administration's tilt away from Juba and toward Khartoum, the north might calculate that the United States will pressure Juba to make concessions. Based on the US government's posture over the past 28 months, that seems a reasonable perspective. But if Washington were to act in this way, it would be a grave mistake, and might imperil any chance for stability after the south's independence.

Key issues include Abyei and five other contested border areas, citizenship, various treaty commitments, security guarantees, and sharing of oil revenues. All of these matters are consequential, but the two most critical are oil-revenue sharing and the future of the Abyei region.

When President Omar Hassan al-Bashir and his regime came to power in 1989 in a coup d'état, total exports from Sudan amounted to around half a billion dollars a year. Thanks to oil, current Sudanese exports are about $9.8 billion per year. That enormous growth has helped prop up the regime, bought security, paid for various armed conflicts, and made many people in Khartoum rich. However, 70 to 80 percent of the oil comes from the south.

Southern Sudan is the size of Texas. It has no paved roads outside the capital.

Naturally, the north does not want to lose that revenue stream. The viability of the regime might even be endangered if it lost all its revenue from oil in the south. I believe the reason that the five contested border regions remain unresolved is not that Khartoum harbors a deep desire for more land, or that it feels particular loyalty to Arab nomadic tribes in those areas (some of whom have served as proxy militias for Khartoum), but because of the oil that lies under the ground.

The south, understandably, does not want to share its oil with the north, which has marginalized and brutalized it for so long. It wants the oil revenue to help build the south, to develop its economy, and to provide the peace dividend its people are hoping for. But the south has a problem. The pipeline through which the oil flows (built by the Chinese) goes through the north to oil storage facilities (also built by the Chinese); from these facilities, located near Port Sudan, the oil is exported to world markets. There is no alternative route. The south has few paved roads and receives about 50 inches of rain a year, making truck transport unfeasible. Building a pipeline to the sea through neighboring countries would take at least three years.

Consequently, both north and south have reasons to reach some accommodation, at least for the short term. The south has said it will not share revenue from the oil that rightfully belongs to the south; however, the south also has said it would be willing to pay a fee for use of the north's pipeline. So the basis for an agreement is available.

As of this writing, however, no deal has been struck. Various international partners, including the United States, are working as facilitators to help the north and south reach agreement on this and other issues. No reason exists that an agreement cannot be reached, but we can expect the north to overreach and the south to be parsimonious. The facilitators must act as honest brokers to guide the parties to a sustainable resolution of this crucial issue.

The Abyei area—a region on the border between the north and south—presents a different sort of challenge, one charged with emotion and political significance, and complicated as well by oil issues. It is the home of the Ngok Dinka, the tribe to which many of the most prominent personalities in southern Sudan belong. However, the nomadic Misseriya Arabs graze cattle there and consider it part of the north. It has been the site of clashes over the years, including the terrible violence of May 2008.

Abyei did not take part in the January referendum because the north and south could not agree on who there should have the right to vote. Since the referendum Abyei has seen some scattered clashes, as well as major armed violence in late February and early March that claimed hundreds of lives. Each side accuses the other of starting these clashes. Additional United Nations peacekeeping troops have been sent to the area. The situation remains tense, with both sides drawing lines in the sand and refusing to compromise.

Bashir's adviser for security affairs, Salah Abdallah Gosh, has warned that Abyei will remain part of the north whether through a bilateral agreement or war. For Bashir, any compromise on Abyei would be a major political victory, while for Kiir it would be a major defeat. Nonetheless, some agreement must be reached. Otherwise, it is difficult to see a path toward a peaceful separation.

Hedging Bets

Nine countries share borders with Sudan. Most, while hedging their bets, have favored unity as the safest and most stable outcome. They are concerned about the contagion of instability and the possibility of terrorists exploiting power vacuums. They also are concerned that separation might set an example for resolving disputes within their own states. In various ways, large and small, most neighboring states in the past have found ways to be supportive of Khartoum during its various clashes with marginalized peoples on Sudan's periphery.

However, each neighbor has charted its own course, and in fact most have been active within Sudan's borders. Ethiopia has generally supported Khartoum but also has provided training for the southern Sudan People's Liberation Army. Uganda, plagued by rebels known as the Lord's Resistance Army (LRA)—who have gained some support from Khartoum and found safe haven within Sudan—has supported separation in the expectation that an independent southern Sudan will be less hospitable to the LRA.

Egypt, where some Sudanese refugees have flowed, is concerned about treaties and other arrangements regarding the Nile River, which flows through southern Sudan's vast marshland, and consequently has tilted heavily toward unity. Chad has served as a safe haven and a launching site for the Justice and Equality Movement (JEM), a Darfuri rebel group. In retaliation, Khartoum has provided safe haven and a launching pad for rebels in Chad. Libya's Muammar el-Qaddafi has provided support for various Darfuri rebels. The list goes on.

The south does not want to share its oil with the north, which has marginalized and brutalized it for so long.

Within the past year, however, things reached a tipping point. In part because of a diplomatic surge by the Obama administration last fall, it became clear that separation was inevitable. Since then neighboring countries have increasingly focused on nurturing a peaceful separation supporting a stable outcome. Of course, this is better for the Sudanese people as well as their neighbors.

The African Union (AU) has long favored unity. Most African nations are multiethnic and many face ethnic and regional stresses of their own, which has led to AU concerns about Sudan splitting into two states. While it never openly opposed the CPA, for a long time the AU was neither enthusiastic about it nor particularly helpful regarding its implementation. In more than one meeting at AU headquarters in Addis Ababa, I heard concerns about the dangers of elections, referendums, and the splintering of a country.

Over time, however, the wider region has come to accept the inevitability of separation, and African nations have recently sought to help with maintaining stability. This has been a very constructive development. Such regional help could prove invaluable in the immediate aftermath of separation, when both the north and the newly independent south will confront enormous internal stresses as well as the threat of violence.

The international community beyond Africa has been divided in its dealings with Sudan. Washington, the European Union, and most others have been committed to full implementation of the CPA. These countries have spoken out about violations of the CPA, supported mechanisms for implementation of the agreement, and provided humanitarian assistance and development aid to southern Sudan in preparation for possible separation. Norway in particular has been helpful, providing expertise on a range of oil-related matters.

Some countries, however, have been less helpful. Those that sell weapons to Sudan and those that purchase its oil have favored Khartoum in ways that have not always promoted full implementation of the CPA. China in particular has been singled out as having provided cover for Khartoum when the UN Security Council has considered the slow-motion genocide in Darfur and the violence and other problems in southern Sudan. The problematic nations, however, including China, seemed at some point last year to accept the probability of the south's secession and to behave more favorably toward stability in Sudan and development of the south.

High Stress

If the key issues—revenue sharing, Abyei, the five other contested border areas, citizenship, security, and so on—are resolved so that separation can proceed as scheduled in July, a number of major problems will still have to be overcome if sustainable peace is to be achieved.

Khartoum will face a crisis of legitimacy. Some will challenge the regime on the grounds that it allowed dismemberment of the country. Opposition political parties in the north are already in consultations about unifying to challenge Bashir's National Congress Party (NCP). Khartoum will also have to contend with a substantial drop in revenues because so much oil money will go to the newly independent south. This economic shock will feed further political turbulence.

Furthermore, the political unrest that began in Tunisia and proceeded to Egypt and elsewhere has bled into Sudan. While Egypt boiled over, demonstrations took place in Khartoum. The protests were not as large or sustained as they have been in many other Arab nations, but further unrest and political

turmoil could ensue. Some commentators have suggested that this may lead the NCP to take a more Islamist tack. Many observers suspect that Bashir's recent declaration that he would not seek reelection in 2015 is a response to the unrest running through the Arab world.

During this time of great stress in the north, various rebel movements in Darfur and elsewhere may seize on Khartoum's weakness and renew demands for greater autonomy or independence. Especially problematic may be the JEM, which in May 2008 successfully advanced all the way to Omdurman, just across the Nile from Khartoum. This is the only time that any rebel group has been able to penetrate the defenses of Sudan's armed forces and strike near the heart of the regime.

From my many discussions with senior officials of the NCP, I know healthy concern exists about the military capabilities of the JEM. This may explain efforts that Khartoum has recently made to relieve tensions with Chad, Sudan's neighbor on the Darfuri border, and may also explain the deployment of more Sudanese troops to the Darfur region.

Indeed, Khartoum may be planning attacks of its own in Darfur. This would add more names to the long list of Darfuri victims, including those of innocent civilians. Moreover, attacks by Khartoum would make it very difficult if not impossible for the Obama administration to lift sanctions on Khartoum, as it has promised to do, if separation proceeds peacefully. After all, the most restrictive sanctions were imposed not because of the north-south struggle but because of the carnage in Darfur.

The south will also face enormous stress immediately after separation. President Kiir has a long history as a successful rebel general, but he is an accidental president. The dominant personality and unifier of southern Sudan's rebel movements was John Garang, the charismatic and skillful warrior-politician who drove the negotiations for the CPA, and who, it was assumed, would be the country's leader when the CPA was fully implemented. Tragically, soon after implementation began, Garang was killed in a helicopter accident—and his quieter vice president, Kiir, rose to the presidency.

I have enormous respect for Kiir. For almost six years he has been the indispensable man in keeping the CPA's implementation on track, often at considerable political cost. But he does not have a dominant personality—and during the long transition period, many other aspirants to the top post have been submerging their own ambitions. After independence, many constraints will be gone. The unifying force of a common enemy, Khartoum, will disappear, and personal ambitions will be unleashed. The jockeying for power, prestige, and position will be considerable, and Kiir's own position will be fragile.

For Peace's Sake

For the sake of stability, this natural political competition must occur within normal nonviolent boundaries. If the United States and others in the international community press Kiir to make excessive concessions on the final resolution of Abyei, or to concede too much to the north regarding oil revenues, such actions would invite a political crisis that would gravely endanger stability.

Furthermore, the new government of the Republic of South Sudan must deal with widespread expectations among southerners that a significant peace dividend will flow from independence. Southern Sudan is the size of Texas. It has no paved roads outside the capital. Most southerners live on less than a dollar per day. And while the United States and the international community have provided massive humanitarian assistance to the south, very little development has occurred.

Things must change and change quickly. Governance capacity is urgently needed. Improved education and health care are required, as are roads, bridges, and other infrastructure. And to move toward economic viability, the south must expand beyond oil extraction—it must exploit other mineral resources, establish small-scale manufacturing, and, most urgently, achieve sustainable agricultural development. For this, multilateral and bilateral development assistance is required. Assistance must be targeted and effective if stability is to be achieved in this land that for generations has been a cauldron of conflict and humanitarian crisis.

The appointed date for southern Sudan's separation fast approaches. But a great deal must be done for separation to occur peacefully. And once separation does take place, both north and south will still face a multitude of stress points, risks, and challenges. The Sudanese people, having suffered greatly, yearn for an end to the violence. It is in the interest of Sudan's neighbors, the region, and the international community to help them attain the diplomatic and material means to achieve the sustainable peace they desire.

Critical Thinking

1. What are the origins of the independence movement in southern Sudan?
2. What outstanding issues threaten peaceful independence for southern Sudan?
3. What challenges does the government in Khartoum face?
4. What must southern Sudan do to assure its success as an independent country?

RICHARD S. WILLIAMSON, a former US ambassador to the United Nations Commission on Human Rights, served as President George W. Bush's special envoy to Sudan from 2007 to 2009.

From *Current History*, May 2011, pp. 171–176. Copyright © 2011 by Current History, Inc. Reprinted by permission.

Africa's Forever Wars

Jeffrey Gettleman

There is a very simple reason why some of Africa's bloodiest, most brutal wars never seem to end: They are not really wars. Not in the traditional sense, at least. The combatants don't have much of an ideology; they don't have clear goals. They couldn't care less about taking over capitals or major cities—in fact, they prefer the deep bush, where it is far easier to commit crimes. Today's rebels seem especially uninterested in winning converts, content instead to steal other people's children, stick Kalashnikovs or axes in their hands, and make them do the killing. Look closely at some of the continent's most intractable conflicts, from the rebel-laden creeks of the Niger Delta to the inferno in the Democratic Republic of the Congo, and this is what you will find.

What we are seeing is the decline of the classic African liberation movement and the proliferation of something else—something wilder, messier, more violent, and harder to wrap our heads around. If you'd like to call this war, fine. But what is spreading across Africa like a viral pandemic is actually just opportunistic, heavily armed banditry. My job as *The New York Times'* East Africa bureau chief is to cover news and feature stories in 12 countries. But most of my time is spent immersed in these un-wars.

I've witnessed up close—often way too close—how combat has morphed from soldier vs. soldier (now a rarity in Africa) to soldier vs. civilian. Most of today's African fighters are not rebels with a cause; they're predators. That's why we see stunning atrocities like eastern Congo's rape epidemic, where armed groups in recent years have sexually assaulted hundreds of thousands of women, often so sadistically that the victims are left incontinent for life. What is the military or political objective of ramming an assault rifle inside a woman and pulling the trigger? Terror has become an end, not just a means.

This is the story across much of Africa, where nearly half of the continent's 53 countries are home to an active conflict or a recently ended one. Quiet places such as Tanzania are the lonely exceptions; even user-friendly, tourist-filled Kenya blew up in 2008. Add together the casualties in just the dozen countries that I cover, and you have a death toll of tens of thousands of civilians each year. More than 5 million have died in Congo alone since 1998, the International Rescue Committee has estimated.

Of course, many of the last generation's independence struggles were bloody, too. South Sudan's decades-long rebellion is thought to have cost more than 2 million lives. But this is not about numbers. This is about methods and objectives, and the leaders driving them. Uganda's top guerrilla of the 1980s, Yoweri Museveni, used to fire up his rebels by telling them they were on the ground floor of a national people's army. Museveni became president in 1986, and he's still in office (another problem, another story). But his words seem downright noble compared with the best-known rebel leader from his country today, Joseph Kony, who just gives orders to burn.

Even if you could coax these men out of their jungle lairs and get them to the negotiating table, there is very little to offer them. They don't want ministries or tracts of land to govern. Their armies are often traumatized children, with experience and skills (if you can call them that) totally unsuited for civilian life. All they want is cash, guns, and a license to rampage. And they've already got all three. How do you negotiate with that?

The short answer is you don't. The only way to stop today's rebels for real is to capture or kill their leaders. Many are uniquely devious characters whose organizations would likely disappear as soon as they do. That's what happened in Angola when the diamond-smuggling rebel leader Jonas Savimbi was shot, bringing a sudden end to one of the Cold War's most intense conflicts. In Liberia, the moment that warlord-turned-president Charles Taylor was arrested in 2006 was the same moment that the curtain dropped on the gruesome circus of 10-year-old killers wearing Halloween masks. Countless dollars, hours, and lives have been wasted on fruitless rounds of talks that will never culminate in such clear-cut results. The same could be said of indictments of rebel leaders for crimes against humanity by the International Criminal Court. With the prospect of prosecution looming, those fighting are sure never to give up.

How did we get here? Maybe it's pure nostalgia, but it seems that yesteryear's African rebels had a bit more class. They were fighting against colonialism, tyranny, or apartheid. The winning insurgencies often came with a charming, intelligent leader wielding persuasive rhetoric. These were men like John Garang, who led the rebellion in southern Sudan with his Sudan People's Liberation Army. He pulled off what few guerrilla leaders anywhere have done: winning his people their own country. Thanks in part to his tenacity, South

Sudan will hold a referendum next year to secede from the North. Garang died in a 2005 helicopter crash, but people still talk about him like a god. Unfortunately, the region without him looks pretty godforsaken. I traveled to southern Sudan in November to report on how ethnic militias, formed in the new power vacuum, have taken to mowing down civilians by the thousands.

Even Robert Mugabe, Zimbabwe's dictator, was once a guerrilla with a plan. After transforming minority white-run Rhodesia into majority black-run Zimbabwe, he turned his country into one of the fastest-growing and most diversified economies south of the Sahara—for the first decade and a half of his rule. His status as a true war hero, and the aid he lent other African liberation movements in the 1980s, account for many African leaders' reluctance to criticize him today, even as he has led Zimbabwe down a path straight to hell.

These men are living relics of a past that has been essentially obliterated. Put the well-educated Garang and the old Mugabe in a room with today's visionless rebel leaders, and they would have just about nothing in common. What changed in one generation was in part the world itself. The Cold War's end bred state collapse and chaos. Where meddling great powers once found dominoes that needed to be kept from falling, they suddenly saw no national interest at all. (The exceptions, of course, were natural resources, which could be bought just as easily—and often at a nice discount—from various armed groups.) Suddenly, all you needed to be powerful was a gun, and as it turned out, there were plenty to go around. AK-47s and cheap ammunition bled out of the collapsed Eastern Bloc and into the farthest corners of Africa. It was the perfect opportunity for the charismatic and morally challenged.

In Congo, there have been dozens of such men since 1996, when rebels rose up against the leopard skin-capped dictator Mobutu Sese Seko, probably the most corrupt man in the history of this most corrupt continent. After Mobutu's state collapsed, no one really rebuilt it. In the anarchy that flourished, rebel leaders carved out fiefdoms ludicrously rich in gold, diamonds, copper, tin, and other minerals. Among them were Laurent Nkunda, Bosco Ntaganda, Thomas Lubanga, a toxic hodgepodge of Mai Mai commanders, Rwandan genocidaires, and the madman leaders of a flamboyantly cruel group called the Rastas.

I met Nkunda in his mountain hideout in late 2008 after slogging hours up a muddy road lined with baby-faced soldiers. The chopstick-thin general waxed eloquent about the oppression of the minority Tutsi people he claimed to represent, but he bristled when I asked him about the warlord-like taxes he was imposing and all the women his soldiers have raped. The questions didn't seem to trouble him too much, though, and he cheered up soon. His farmhouse had plenty of space for guests, so why didn't I spend the night?

Nkunda is not totally wrong about Congo's mess. Ethnic tensions are a real piece of the conflict, together with disputes over land, refugees, and meddling neighbor countries. But what I've come to understand is how quickly legitimate grievances in these failed or failing African states deteriorate into rapacious, profit-oriented bloodshed. Congo today is home to a resource rebellion in which vague anti-government feelings become an excuse to steal public property. Congo's embarrassment of riches belongs to the 70 million Congolese, but in the past 10 to 15 years, that treasure has been hijacked by a couple dozen rebel commanders who use it to buy even more guns and wreak more havoc.

Probably the most disturbing example of an African un-war comes from the Lord's Resistance Army (LRA), begun as a rebel movement in northern Uganda during the lawless 1980s. Like the gangs in the oil-polluted Niger Delta, the LRA at first had some legitimate grievances—namely, the poverty and marginalization of the country's ethnic Acholi areas. The movement's leader, Joseph Kony, was a young, wig-wearing, gibberish-speaking, so-called prophet who espoused the Ten Commandments. Soon, he broke every one. He used his supposed magic powers (and drugs) to whip his followers into a frenzy and unleashed them on the very Acholi people he was supposed to be protecting.

The LRA literally carved their way across the region, leaving a trail of hacked-off limbs and sawed-off ears. They don't talk about the Ten Commandments anymore, and some of those left in their wake can barely talk at all. I'll never forget visiting northern Uganda a few years ago and meeting a whole group of

Africa Heats Up

Scientists have long warned that warming global temperatures and the resource scarcities that result will bring more violent conflicts. The U.S. government even directed its intelligence community to study the potential national security implications of climate change. But the evidence showing that rising temperatures cause armed conflict has been sketchy at best—until now.

In a recent study published in *Proceedings of the National Academy of Sciences,* a team of economists compared variations in temperature with the incidence of conflict in sub-Saharan Africa between 1981 and 2002 and found startling results: Just a 1 degree Celsius increase in temperature resulted in a 49 percent increase in the incidence of civil war. The situation looks even bleaker in coming decades. Given projected increases in global temperatures, the authors see a 54 percent increase in civil conflict across the region. If these conflicts are as deadly as the wars during the study period, Africa could suffer an additional 393,000 battle deaths by 2030.

The main reason for the projected violence is global warming's impact on agriculture, but there could be other factors as well. For instance, violent crime tends to increase when temperatures are high, while economic productivity decreases. In an especially depressing aside, the authors note that even under the "optimistic scenario" for economic growth and political reform in the coming decades, "neither is able to overcome the large effects of temperature increase on civil war incidence."

—Joshua E. Keating

women whose lips were sheared off by Kony's maniacs. Their mouths were always open, and you could always see their teeth. When Uganda finally got its act together in the late 1990s and cracked down, Kony and his men simply marched on. Today, their scourge has spread to one of the world's most lawless regions: the borderland where Sudan, Congo, and the Central African Republic meet.

Child soldiers are an inextricable part of these movements. The LRA, for example, never seized territory; it seized children. Its ranks are filled with brainwashed boys and girls who ransack villages and pound newborn babies to death in wooden mortars. In Congo, as many as one-third of all combatants are under 18. Since the new predatory style of African warfare is motivated and financed by crime, popular support is irrelevant to these rebels. The downside to not caring about winning hearts and minds, though, is that you don't win many recruits. So abducting and manipulating children becomes the only way to sustain the organized banditry. And children have turned out to be ideal weapons: easily brainwashed, intensely loyal, fearless, and, most importantly, in endless supply.

In this new age of forever wars, even Somalia looks different. That country certainly evokes the image of Africa's most chaotic state—exceptional even in its neighborhood for unending conflict. But what if Somalia is less of an outlier than a terrifying forecast of what war in Africa is moving toward? On the surface, Somalia seems wracked by a religiously themed civil conflict between the internationally backed but feckless transitional government and the Islamist militia al-Shabab. Yet the fighting is being nourished by the same old Somali problem that has dogged this desperately poor country since 1991: warlordism. Many of the men who command or fund militias in Somalia today are the same ones who tore the place apart over the past 20 years in a scramble for the few resources left—the port, airport, telephone poles, and grazing pastures.

Somalis are getting sick of the Shabab and its draconian rules—no music, no gold teeth, even no bras. But what has kept locals in Somalia from rising up against foreign terrorists is Somalia's deeply ingrained culture of war profiteering. The world has let Somalia fester too long without a permanent government. Now, many powerful Somalis have a vested interest in the status quo chaos. One olive oil exporter in Mogadishu told me that he and some trader friends bought a crate of missiles to shoot at government soldiers because "taxes are annoying."

Most frightening is how many sick states like Congo are now showing Somalia-like symptoms. Whenever a potential leader emerges to reimpose order in Mogadishu, criminal networks rise up to finance his opponent, no matter who that may be. The longer these areas are stateless, the harder it is to go back to the necessary evil of government.

All this might seem a gross simplification, and indeed, not all of Africa's conflicts fit this new paradigm. The old steady—the military coup—is still a common form of political upheaval, as Guinea found out in 2008 and Madagascar not too long thereafter. I have also come across a few non-hoodlum rebels who seem legitimately motivated, like some of the Darfurian commanders in Sudan. But though their political grievances are well defined, the organizations they "lead" are not. Old-style African rebels spent years in the bush honing their leadership skills, polishing their ideology, and learning to deliver services before they ever met a Western diplomat or sat for a television interview. Now rebels are hoisted out of obscurity after they have little more than a website and a "press office" (read: a satellite telephone). When I went to a Darfur peace conference in Sirte, Libya, in 2007, I quickly realized that the main draw for many of these rebel "leaders" was not the negotiating sessions, but the all-you-can-eat buffet.

For the rest, there are the un-wars, these ceaseless conflicts I spend my days cataloging as they grind on, mincing lives and spitting out bodies. Recently, I was in southern Sudan working on a piece about the Ugandan Army's hunt for Kony, and I met a young woman named Flo. She had been a slave in the LRA for 15 years and had recently escaped. She had scarred shins and stony eyes, and often there were long pauses after my questions, when Flo would stare at the horizon. "I am just thinking of the road home," she said. It was never clear to her why the LRA was fighting. To her, it seemed like they had been aimlessly tramping through the jungle, marching in circles.

This is what many conflicts in Africa have become—circles of violence in the bush, with no end in sight.

Critical Thinking

1. Why are many of Africa's wars non-traditional?
2. What are the implications of this development for peaceful settlement of these conflicts?
3. How do the current rebel groups differ from past conflicts?
4. How did the end of the cold war contribute to the emergence of this non-traditional warfare?
5. Why has the emergence of this type of conflict contributed to the use of child soldiers?

Jeffrey Gettleman is East Africa bureau chief for *The New York Times*.

The Struggle for Mexico

Its present is grim, its future uncertain—but is it a failed state?

DAVID RIEFF

From a diplomatic point of view, the U.S. military's Joint Forces Command did the incoming Obama administration no favors with the stark warning it issued in November 2008. In its annual evaluation of the threats America's armed forces were likely to face in the future, it declared that, "[i]n terms of worst-case scenarios for the Joint Force and indeed the world, two large and important states bear consideration for a rapid and sudden collapse: Pakistan and Mexico."

The report, in fairness, did go on to concede that the collapse of Mexico "may seem less likely" than the collapse of Pakistan. Still, it noted that "the government, its politicians, police, and judicial infrastructure are all under sustained assault and pressure by criminal gangs and drug cartels."

Not surprisingly, this didn't sit well with the Mexican government of Felipe Calderón. And so, Secretary of State Hillary Clinton, whose references to U.S.-Mexico relations during her Senate confirmation hearings had been so perfunctory as to be nonexistent in political terms, was obliged to make a trip to Mexico City in March 2009 to smooth relations between the two governments. This was followed the next month with a visit to Mexico City by President Obama himself. Jorge Castañeda, Mexico's former foreign minister, quipped at the time that Calderón "wants to hear [Obama] say that Mexico was never a failed state, is not a failed state today, and even in their deepest, darkest fears will never, ever be a failed state."

But was it true? Was Mexico at risk of becoming a failed state? In recent years, the U.S. military has hardly been alone in promulgating this notion. It is now common to read that Mexico is collapsing, and the daily horrors that emerge from the border city of Juárez—across the Rio Grande from El Paso—would seem to confirm this view. Five years after Calderón deployed the military against the growing dominance of the drug cartels, the city remains paralyzed by violence. The British journalist Ed Vulliamy—whose book *Amexica: Along the Border* is by far the best account of the current crisis—estimates that the total number of homicides in Juárez since late 2006 now stands at more than 8,200. Meanwhile, the usual figure given for drug-related murders in Mexico as a whole since the end of 2006 is more than 34,000.

Sandra Rodriguez of Juárez's local newspaper *El Diario* (and, given that 66 Mexican journalists were killed covering the narco wars between the end of 2006 and the end of 2010, the journalists of *El Diario* are truly heroic) summed it up for Vulliamy when she told him that impunity for murder started at the top and went all the way down "to the kids growing up in this criminal city, who never go to school, who go over to the narcos." Rodriguez pointed to the emblematic story she had written about a 16-year-old boy "who had killed his mother and sister. When I asked him why, he said, 'Because I could.'"

So far at least, the Calderón government's decision to deploy substantial military forces in the cities along the U.S. border and appoint a number of retired senior officers to reform a largely corrupt and terrified state police apparatus has only led to more violence. This is not to say that there have not been successes, with many leading cartel figures killed or captured. But, to date, militarization of the conflict has not made a dent either in the violence or the flow of drugs into the United States. The near-constant stream of reports detailing kidnappings, beheadings, and torture continues apace.

All of this would seem to suggest that the pessimism of the U.S. military back in 2008 was justified—that Mexico is in fact a failed, or at least a failing, state. And yet, as grave and as horrifying as all this is, it's worth pausing to ask whether the label "failed state" is really the most accurate, or useful, way to think about our neighbor to the south.

When people talk about Mexico as a failed state, what they seem to be discussing is not the Mexico of today but the Colombia of 20 years ago. (Generals, apparently, are not the only people always well-prepared to fight the last war.) From the 1980s to the early '90s, the Medellín and, to a lesser extent, the Cali cartel posed a genuine threat to the Colombian state. To be fair, some of the similarities between Colombia and Mexico are startling, most notably that Medellín then was what Juárez is today—the city with the highest murder rate in the world. But it is also important to consider the differences. The Colombian narco-traffickers had complicated but extremely important links with both the left-wing FARC guerrillas and the right-wing paramilitaries. The result of these connections was that the leaders of the cartels, most famously, Pablo Escobar Gaviria of the Medellín cartel—in 1989, *Forbes* magazine described him as the seventh-richest man in the world—became important actors on the political and military fronts of a two- and sometimes three-sided, low-intensity insurgency that verged on civil war. Escobar really was like a character out of a Gabriel García Márquez novel, fascinated by power and with political ambitions from the start. In 1982, he had been elected on the Colombian Liberal Party list as an alternate representative from Medellín to Congress. He never gave up his ambition to play a political role, advertising it to the media even in the last year of his life, as government forces were hunting him down.

In contrast, while Mexicans are profoundly divided about how to respond to the cartels, no one I have spoken with has ever suggested there is credible evidence that any of the cartel leaders have Escobar-like ambitions—or any national political agenda. This emphatically does not mean that what the drug lords want is not terrible enough. How else can one describe their demand that the Mexican state give them a free hand to run their domestic production and cross-border smuggling operations, as well as to go after their real and supposed enemies, and, indeed, anyone who gets in their way or who is just in the wrong place at the wrong time, with complete impunity? To do this, the cartels have not just bribed enormous numbers of policemen and local officials, but, in at least one case, helped elect someone to the Mexican Congress. Still, to say that the cartels represent a fundamental challenge to the Mexican government as a whole—a rebellion on the scale of what took place in Colombia or what is taking place now in Pakistan—would be hyperbole.

Indeed, the Mexican state is in important ways both stronger and more successful than many Americans seem to realize. In the area of public health, and, more broadly, in poverty reduction, Mexico has far more to teach than to learn. The country is generally thought to have handled the H1N1 panic better than many rich countries. And the Mexican government's social-assistance program, now known as Oportunidades—which skillfully and creatively uses a range of assistance, from conditional cash transfers to health and nutritional support—has been enormously effective in changing the status of Mexican women (who are the program's recipients), improving the health of children, and lifting large numbers of people out of poverty. Oportunidades's global reputation is such that Michael Bloomberg gave the okay for an Oportunidades pilot program in New York City. The Ministry of Social Development (SEDESOL in its Spanish acronym) is a model of what such an agency should be, and development experts around the world speak of it with a respect sometimes bordering on awe. Significantly, the corruption that bedevils Mexican law enforcement has no equivalent whatsoever in the social sphere, and, despite the drug crisis, SEDESOL goes from strength to strength.

On the economic side, while Mexico remains heavily dependent on the remittances of the millions of immigrants now working, legally or illegally, in the United States, the country also has a rising middle class. It is common to associate the Mexican economy with Pemex, the state oil company, which

the government has tended to loot—in the process, depleting oil revenue that should have been put to work on modernization of drilling infrastructure, particularly offshore, which, if Mexico is to continue as a major petroleum exporter, is where it must hunt for new resources. (The contrast with the much better-run, state-controlled Brazilian oil giant, Petrobras, or Malaysia's Petronas, is painful.) But, increasingly, there is also the Mexico of Homex, a company started in Sinaloa in 1989. Homex is now one of the leading global firms involved in the building of low- and middle-income housing, with large operations in Brazil and India as well as in 20 Mexican states. And yet, the only thing most non-Mexicans who are drawn to the failed-state hypothesis seem to know about Sinaloa is that it gave its name to a powerful drug cartel.

If one takes the long view, the clash between the Mexico of Pemex and the Mexico of Homex may be as important as the war between the cartels and the government. And, unless the Mexican economy implodes, which is highly unlikely, there is an excellent chance that the Mexico of Homex will prevail. In any case, it is a contest in which the narco-traffickers—even narco-traffickers operating right alongside the Homexes of Mexico—do not now have, and will never have, a say.

Most important of all, Mexican democracy, deformed for so long during the decades of rule by the Institutional Revolutionary Party (PRI), is now strong. This is actually quite remarkable, because what is too often forgotten is just how young a democracy it is. The great Mexican historian (and frequent NEW REPUBLIC contributor) Enrique Krauze characterized PRI rule as "a collective monarchy with the electoral forms of a republic." That monarchy disappeared in 2000 when the opposition National Action Party (PAN), led by Vicente Fox, swept into office. (Calderón, his successor, is also a member of the PAN.) In this, a strong analogy can be made to France, where, from the founding of the Fifth Republic in 1958 to the election of the Socialist François Mitterrand in 1981, it seemed somehow inconceivable that the country would ever have a president who was not from the right. Ever since Mitterrand, though, neither the French right nor the French left has been under the illusion that the Fifth Republic somehow "belongs" to them.

History suggests that, while democratic states can go through terrible periods and face daunting crises—both of which, unhappily, look to be in the cards for Mexico—they almost never become failed states. This is what makes the Joint Forces Command's linking of Pakistan and Mexico so unconvincing. If Pakistan becomes a failed state—and, while not likely, unhappily, the possibility can't be excluded—it will not only be because of the threat posed by the Pakistani Taliban, the other jihadi formations, and some separatist groups, but because Pakistani democracy is a sham.

There are other ways in which it is important to distinguish Mexico from Pakistan. The government in Islamabad has done virtually nothing, and seems to care not a whit, about the country's poor, whether in terms of their health and general nutrition, their educational opportunities, or their chances of finding work. Moreover, unlike Pakistan, Mexico is not a religiously divided country (the contest for adherents between the Catholic Church and its increasingly successful evangelical rivals is impassioned, but it is neither violent nor a challenge to the state's authority). Nor is it a country facing a population crisis: The average age in Mexico was 17 in 1980; it is 28 today, and Mexican birthrates are in free fall. Pakistan's birthrates, by contrast, continue to rise, which makes the chances of even a decent government providing reasonable levels of employment a long shot at best. Finally, Pakistan's only powerful neighbor with whom it could plausibly link its economy happens to be its chief rival, India. The Mexican economy, by contrast, is now thoroughly interconnected with America's. Which means that, barring a complete collapse of the capitalist system, Mexico's economy will always have a floor from which to build.

One reason to resist, or at least complicate, the failed-state label when talking about Mexico is that such language can lead policymakers down a disastrous path. For one thing, when we speak of failed states, we tend to imagine that the only solution is a military one—and, as the failure of the Mexican military to pacify Juárez shows, the solution to Mexico's problems cannot simply be more tanks in the streets.

But the biggest downside to labeling Mexico a failed state may be that it allows us to ignore our own complicity in the country's problems. The sad fact is that the power of the drug cartels largely reflects demand in the United States. Castañeda, who was foreign minister in the first years of the Fox presidency, has called for the immediate legalization of marijuana, and it's no surprise that many Mexicans now support him. Even those who disagree—such as Castañeda's protégé during his time as foreign minister, Arturo Sarukhan, now Mexico's ambassador to the United States—concur that U.S. demand is the basis of the entire problem. Meanwhile, America's grotesquely lax and, in any case, widely unenforced gun laws have made U.S. gun shops, particularly in Arizona and Texas, the de facto arms providers of the cartels. No doubt the cartels could find other ways to supply themselves with weapons if the United States ever did crack down on gun sales (presumably by buying them from soldiers and policemen). Still, America's insistence on easy access to guns has hardly helped the situation.

Unfortunately, rather than revisiting our approach to drugs or guns, Americans seem more disposed, as Governor Rick Perry of Texas demonstrated last year, to contemplate the possibility of U.S. military forces being committed to the fight in Mexico. Perry, to be sure, was quick to say that he would only favor such a move if the Mexican government approved it, as if Mexico's government would ever really authorize U.S. troops to effectively invade the country for a third time. But his comments illustrated the narrowness of thinking about Mexico among American policymakers. To her credit, Secretary of State Clinton did say during her fencemending visit to Mexico City in 2009 that—given America's "insatiable demand for illegal drugs" and its "inability to prevent weapons from being illegally smuggled across the border"—it was unfair "to be creating a situation where people [in the United States] are holding the Mexican government and people responsible." But, as has

so often been the case with U.S. policy toward Mexico, the secretary's rhetorical leap into richly deserved self-criticism led to virtually no substantive policy changes.

The war of the drug cartels against the state and its people is scarcely the first terrible war that Mexico has endured. The Cristero rebellion of 1926–'29—which was a response to both a real and, even where it did not actually occur, perceived repression of the Catholic faithful by a central government in Mexico City intent on pushing the historic anti-clericalism of the Mexican state to its limit—cost the lives of nearly 90,000 people and sent another 50,000 into exile, mostly to Los Angeles; this, at a time when the population of Mexico was about 15 million. Of the 4,500 priests who had served the country before the uprising, only a few more than 300 remained eight years later, most of the rest having been expelled, and some—like the priest on whom Graham Greene based his novel *The Power and the Glory*—hunted down and killed.

It took Mexico a long time to recover from that event, and, even if one is optimistic about Mexico, as I am over the longer term—and not just in the sense of the icy, comfortless certainty that, in the long run, all wars end—it is too much to hope that these drug wars will leave it unscathed. The danger is not that Mexico will become a failed state, but rather that the experience of this violence will somehow profoundly brutalize Mexican society. The cruelty with which the narco-traffickers kill, even if most Mexicans only read about it or see it on television, cannot help but be profoundly dispiriting. Cruelty is not just an act; it is a culture. As a result, Mexicans are justifiably worried about their future. "I fear the next ten years will be lost," was the way a friend of mine in Mexico City put it to me recently.

So Mexico certainly has deep and substantial problems to confront. But, while those problems are real, it would be nice if people in the United States would stop writing Mexico's obituary by declaring it a failed state. The situation is far too complicated for such sweeping pronouncements. Empty expressions of solidarity, meanwhile, as in the case of Secretary Clinton's 2009 visit—where she delivered the geo-political equivalent of a "GET WELL" card bought in the hospital gift shop—may not do any harm, but they certainly don't help. What might be of some real use would be to take a step back and actually think about how our drug and gun policies are affecting Mexico. Unfortunately, in contrast to my guarded hopes about Mexico's long-term future, it's hard to be optimistic that the United States will revisit these issues anytime soon.

Critical Thinking

1. Why has Mexico been labeled a failing state?
2. What successful Mexican policy initiatives have been overshadowed by the drugs and violence?
3. What role does the United States play in Mexico's drug and violence problems?

From *The New Republic*, April 7, 2011, pp. 15–17. Copyright © 2011 by David Reiff. Reprinted by permission of the author via The Wylie Agency.

Central America's Security Predicament

"The end of political, armed conflict 15 years ago has not been accompanied by higher levels of social peace. On the contrary, fear and lawlessness today are rampant in the region."

MICHAEL SHIFTER

In retrospect, it was probably naïve to expect that, with the signing of the last of the Central American peace accords (Guatemala, 1996), the heightened civil strife that beset the region for decades would give way to a greater measure of social peace. Although Central America can celebrate the virtual end of political violence over the past 15 years, the five countries of the isthmus that in the 1980s were in the international spotlight on account of instability—Guatemala, El Salvador, Honduras, Nicaragua, and Costa Rica—are, to varying degrees, still notably troubled.

That this is true even of Costa Rica—the Central American nation most known for (relative) tranquility, social progress, and democratic performance—speaks to the depth of the problems in the region. Indeed, at the end of 2010 Costa Rica found itself increasingly contending with drug-fueled violence and also experiencing a tense standoff with neighboring Nicaragua over a disputed border area. Yet, despite Costa Rica's difficulties, the country's position remains comparatively advantageous. It is better equipped institutionally than its more vulnerable neighbors to withstand the global pressures and strains that contribute to societal disintegration.

The region has registered, to be sure, some impressive economic, political, and social gains in recent years, including higher levels of political competition within countries. These achievements have mostly been eclipsed, however, by an overall deterioration in security conditions and by continuing economic stagnation. Unfavorable external conditions and internal decay and fragmentation have produced societies with increasingly urgent problems.

Central America has been squeezed by rising energy costs—the region has little choice but to import its oil and gas—and has suffered disproportionately from the financial and economic crisis that originated in the United States in 2008 and continues to be acutely felt. Remittance flows from the United States, which are critical to sustaining the region's economies, have sharply dropped as a result of the economic downturn.

Meanwhile, precarious political institutions and endemic poverty and inequality have rendered governance challenges daunting. The results of the 2010 Latinobarómetro report, a region-wide public opinion survey, reveal that Central Americans are particularly tepid in their support of democracy.

Such ambivalence is understandable in light of the ominous tendencies of both organized and common crime in the subregion. Pervasive fear often corresponds to objective data on violence. According to a study carried out in 2008 by the Latin American Public Opinion Project, high crime levels significantly erode interpersonal trust and tend to fray the social fabric on which democracies are constructed. The study found that, in the five Central American countries, roughly 14 percent to 19 percent of citizens said they had been victims of crime during the preceding 12 months.

Other research has highlighted the explosive growth of private security companies that often outstrip official police forces and typically function without controls or regulation. A 2009 United Nations Development Program report showed that in Guatemala and Honduras private security personnel outnumber police forces by five to ten times. No Central American country has more police than private security officers. Economic costs associated with anti-crime measures absorb an increasing share of national budgets throughout the subregion.

Regrettably, Central America is often overlooked compared with other regions within Latin America. While South America, led by Brazil, has drawn praise for its remarkable ascent, and Mexico has dominated headlines because of its unrelenting and particularly brutal criminality, Central American nations have been off the international radar and are at best treated as an afterthought.

Yet what is taking place both north and south of Central America is contributing to the deepening predicament of the region, which has become a hub for drug trafficking routes. Only recently has concern substantially increased in Washington and elsewhere regarding a set of countries that occupied center stage—and generated moderately high hopes and expectations—just two decades ago.

Guatemalan Gangland

Recent developments in Guatemala have especially alarmed observers and policy officials. Guatemala is Central America's largest country and also the one where a decades-long civil war took the greatest toll, with 200,000 dead. Longstanding inequities highlighted by sharp ethnic divisions—Guatemala's population is majority indigenous—have posed formidable challenges for governing the country. Guatemala has among the region's lowest tax rates, with notoriously fierce resistance from wealthy sectors to contributing their fair share, and this has made it even more difficult to redress the glaring disparities.

However, while political violence and old-fashioned militarism have subsided, there has been a striking surge in the penetration of organized crime in all spheres of the nation. Analysts often refer to dark forces and parallel structures that engage in illicit activities and operate with nearly assured impunity. Judicial and police institutions are riddled with corruption. The country's governance structures are too weak and ineffective to cope with such powerful pressures. In this context, the International Commission Against Impunity in Guatemala (CICIG) performs a fundamental role. A special judicial body assembled in cooperation with the United Nations, the CICIG began its work in 2007 with the aim of supporting efforts by the country's flawed criminal justice system to root out criminal networks operating inside government bodies.

A succession of murky and complicated incidents in recent years has highlighted disturbing trends in the country. In May 2009, the killing of a Guatemalan lawyer, Rodrigo Rosenberg, became a major political controversy after a video was made public in which Rosenberg, before he died, blamed President Alvaro Colom for his assassination. The CICIG investigated the Rosenberg case and in January 2010 announced detailed findings concluding that Rosenberg staged his own murder in an attempt to call attention to the killing of his son, in which Rosenberg believed Colom had had a hand.

The CICIG investigations also led to the arrest of a former president, Alfonso Portillo, on corruption charges and in response to an extradition request from the United States on money laundering charges. And the commission contributed to the arrest in March 2010 of a former national police chief, Baltazar Gómez, for involvement with drug trafficking and blocking an investigation of corrupt police officers.

In June 2010, however, the head of CICIG, a Spanish lawyer named Carlos Castresana, resigned out of frestration, complaining that the Guatemalan government had not been following the commission's recommendations and that there was an active campaign to discredit the CICIG among groups with an entrenched interest in continued impunity.

The resignation was provoked by the Colom government's appointment of Conrado Reyes as attorney general—after the CICIG had identified Reyes as having ties to drug trafficking and illegal adoption rings. Castresana's decision created a political firestorm, and the country's Constitutional Court ultimately rejected Reyes's appointment on grounds that the selection process may have been influenced by organized crime. The UN then appointed Costa Rican Attorney General Francisco Dall'Anese, a renowned advocate against organized crime, to succeed Castresana as the CICIG's head.

Another illustration of the sort of convoluted intrigue that increasingly characterizes Guatemala occurred in early December 2010, when a Guatemalan court sentenced eight people to prison for lengthy terms for involvement in the February 2007 murders of three Salvadoran members of the Central American Parliament and their driver. The CICIG had worked closely with Guatemalan prosecutors on the case, and among those sentenced was a former Guatemalan congressman charged with masterminding the killing. The court ruled that the four men had been murdered at the behest of a Salvadoran legislator who had been expelled from his party over allegations of criminal activity. The murders were actually carried out by four Guatemalan police officers, who were slain in a high-security prison just days after being arrested.

And in January 2011, a bomb attack on a bus in Guatemala City claimed seven lives. In recent years, the country's public transport has been increasingly subjected to extortion by organized crime groups (a member of the Mara 18 gang was charged in the January attack). In 2010, according to Guatemalan police, bus drivers paid out over $1.5 million in extortion money. Local rights groups report that 119 of the country's bus drivers and 51 other transport workers were murdered last year.

As if the security situation and the fragility of political institutions were not serious enough, Guatemala has been profoundly affected by the brutal and bloody cartel battles being waged in Mexico. Fighting among Mexican drug cartels and the aggressive response by the government of Felipe Calderón not only have resulted in more than 30,000 deaths since the start of the Calderón administration. They also have pushed the cartels further south, into northern Guatemala, where they increasingly wreak havoc in an already battered nation that has few defenses.

Members of Los Zetas, a Mexican drug trafficking group, and the Sinaloa drug cartel now routinely attack local law enforcement officials and control substantial swaths of territory, according to a US State Department report. As the journalist Steven Dudley has written in *Foreign Policy,* "as Mexico and Colombia cracked down on their own drug trafficking problems, the criminals sought new refuge, and Guatemala fit the bill: a weak government, a strategic location, and a bureaucracy whose allegiance came cheap." At present the homicide rate in Guatemala is four times that in Mexico.

At present the homicide rate in Guatemala is four times that in Mexico.

On December 19, 2010, the Guatemalan government, worried that the situation was spiraling out of control, declared a state of siege in the northern province of Alta Verapaz, large areas of which had reportedly been taken over by Mexican drug traffickers. As an *Associated Press* dispatch observed two days later, "Gangs roamed the streets with assault rifles and armored vehicles, attacking whomever they pleased and abducting women who caught their eye. Shootouts became so common residents couldn't tell gunfire from holiday fireworks." Local leaders from the province, which had become a prime corridor for drug trafficking from Honduras to Mexico, said they had been requesting the intervention of federal authorities for two years.

Undisciplined and fractured political parties aggravate the dire situation in a country that the International Crisis Group has called a "paradise for criminals." Colom's party, for example, holds barely a fifth of the seats in the legislature. This has made promises of greater social inclusion nearly impossible to achieve. According to the World Bank, more than half the population lives in poverty.

While it still may not be accurate (or constructive) to depict Guatemala as a "failed state" or "narco-state," mounting evidence points to conditions of rampant lawlessness that warrant considerable alarm. The real risk is that, with a presidential election scheduled for the fall of 2011, unchecked criminality could trigger reflexes for more authoritarian approaches that evoke what was widely thought to be a bygone era.

Unchecked criminality could trigger reflexes for more authoritarian approaches.

Honduras Is Murder

Together with Guatemala and El Salvador, Honduras forms part of the so-called "Northern Triangle," a doorway for cocaine traffic into Mexico. The World Drug Report of 2010, published by the UN Office on Drugs and Crime, documents that this territory has the highest murder rates of any region in the world, with more than 50 homicides each year per 100,000 people. *The Economist* notes that Honduras currently has the highest murder rate in the world, at 67 per 100,000; the murder rate in the United States, by contrast, is 5.4 per 100,000.

According to the UN report, Honduras is the Central American country that is most affected by the drug trade. With dense jungle territories and the longest Caribbean coastline, Honduras is positioned as the first corner of the triangle, leading into trade routes that eventually reach Mexico and the United States. The Mexican cartels have penetrated Honduras, as have expanding criminal gangs with readily accessible firearms. The Sinaloa cartel is reported to have assassinated Honduras's top counter-drug official in December 2009 over the seizure of a pseudoephedrine shipment. A plot by the Zetas to kill the minister of security was thwarted in early 2010.

Mexican cartels have penetrated Honduras, as have criminal gangs with readily accessible firearms.

Honduras's highly unsettling security situation has been exacerbated by a still-unresolved political crisis that has undermined governance and, in turn, has tended to benefit drug trafficking organizations and criminal gangs. More than a year and a half after Honduras suffered a military coup that dislodged the constitutionally elected government of Manuel Zelaya (who is in exile in the Dominican Republic), the country remains profoundly polarized between Zelaya's supporters and those associated with the de facto government that took control in June 2009, led by Roberto Micheletti.

In accordance with previously scheduled elections, a new government headed by Porfirio Lobo of the National Party took office in January 2010 and has struggled to navigate and overcome the country's sharp divisions. Conciliatory measures to defuse tensions have borne scant fruit. Distrust and bitterness on both sides compound the difficulties of addressing the country's daunting policy agenda, which includes not just expanding criminality but also high levels of unemployment and deepening social and economic distress.

A truth commission directed by Guatemala's former foreign minister and vice president Eduardo Stein has sought to pursue a balanced approach and heal the wounds, but the undertaking has not garnered broad support and has been criticized from both sides. A clear measure of the country's polarization can be seen in the reaction to a July 2009 diplomatic cable by US ambassador Hugo Llorens, which was leaked by Wikileaks, in which Llorens clearly called the ouster of Zelaya unconstitutional. Whereas coup supporters were upset that the United States adopted a critical stance toward a move they regarded as justified, coup opponents were puzzled that Washington failed to respond to such a depiction with more forceful action against the de facto government.

Honduras continues to be a significant source of discord and strain in inter-American relations. The coup caused member states of the Organization of American States (OAS), the hemisphere's chief political body, to expel Honduras—only the second country, after Cuba (1962), to have met such a fate. Despite substantial pressure to recognize the Lobo government that has been exerted by the United States and all but one of Honduras's Central American neighbors (Nicaragua), key players in regional political affairs still deem the government illegitimate—including Venezuela (Zelaya was an ally of Venezuela's president, Hugo Chávez) and, most crucially, Brazil (Zelaya took refuge in Brazil's embassy in Tegucigalpa, the capital of Honduras, before going into exile).

The continued ostracism of the country from regional forums has complicated Honduras's ability to secure needed funds from multilateral financial institutions and has slowed down the government's attempts to ameliorate the nation's acute socioeconomic ills.

Indeed, the economic impact of the political crisis since June 2009 has been quite significant. It is estimated that 200,000 jobs were lost as a direct result of it. Some 36 percent of the workforce was unemployed or underemployed in 2009. Not surprisingly, foreign investment also suffered, with the Honduran central bank reporting a drop of almost 50 percent from 2008 levels, though the global economic downturn surely played a part in that as well. More recently, access to international capital has eased.

One particularly troubling phenomenon in Honduras, which reflects the confluence of security and political crises, has been the killing of journalists (which is also a serious problem in Mexico, though less so in other Central American nations). In 2010, eight journalists in Honduras were murdered. Several of them reported on organized crime, whereas others, according to rights groups, may have been targets of political crimes. In any case, all of the murders have gone unpunished.

In a July 2010 report, the Committee to Protect Journalists accused the Honduran government of "fostering a climate of lawlessness that is allowing criminals to kill with impunity." Buttressing that assessment was a December 2010 report issued by Human Rights Watch, entitled "After the Coup: Ongoing Violence, Intimidation, and Impunity in Honduras." The report documented some 47 attacks or threats against journalists, human rights defenders, and political activists during Lobo's first year in office.

El Salvador Tested

El Salvador, since the two sides to the country's bitter and bloody civil war signed a peace agreement in 1992, has seen a huge upsurge in gang violence. There are an estimated 30,000 gang members in a country of just over 6 million. This phenomenon, which has become more associated with El Salvador than with other countries in Central America, has to some degree offset the welcome peace dividends that accompanied the end of political violence. The legacies of the armed conflict—along with a proliferation of firearms, enduring socioeconomic woes, and transnational contacts with US-based gangs (an element of which is increased deportations from the United States back to El Salvador)—have resulted in a toxic mix.

Many observers were hopeful that, with the election of President Mauricio Funes in 2009, El Salvador would be better able to develop the institutional capacity to cope with its monumental security and social problems. After nearly two decades of rule by the rightist Arena party, Funes is El Salvador's first elected president from the FMLN (Farabundo Martí National Liberation Front), the party of the demobilized guerrilla movement that fought in the civil conflict (1979–92). Funes's election carried enormous symbolic significance and heightened expectations for a region seeking to bridge longstanding ideological chasms.

Funes, governing largely as a moderate pragmatist, has tried to model his government after that of Luiz Inácio Lula da Silva, Brazil's hugely successful former president. Operating within significant constraints, Funes has accorded more emphasis to poverty-alleviation strategies than his predecessors, presiding over important advances in education and health care. His administration's foreign policies have been notably centrist. El Salvador's posture toward the United States has been accommodating, and regarding the Honduras controversy the Funes administration has been supportive of President Lobo, strongly urging other Latin American governments to recognize his elected government.

According to public opinion surveys, Funes's political approach has wide appeal in a country weary of partisan rancor. Yet the president faces fierce resistance from his FMLN party, which is pressing for a more radical agenda, as well as from factions of the opposition Arena, and he has yet to build a solid governing structure. To do so will require considerable political skill and a measure of luck, but most importantly concrete results in improving El Salvador's security and economic conditions. This will not be easy, especially in light of declining remittances coming from the United States to a country that relies heavily on such flows.

In confronting the security challenge, Funes has moved to criminalize gang membership and has also tried to appeal to Central American neighbors to pursue more coordinated efforts to reduce the spread of criminality, which poses the greatest threat to rule of law in the region. It is far from clear, however, that such measures, however well intentioned, will succeed in arresting the overall deterioration. The growing presence of Mexican drug trafficking organizations in El Salvador could well overwhelm efforts to deal with the gang phenomenon, which has been around since the 1990s.

Nicaragua's Strong Man

Beyond and beneath the Northern Triangle, one finds a greater measure of tranquility. With 14 murders per 100,000 citizens, Nicaragua is almost a model of social peace compared to Guatemala, Honduras, and El Salvador. Part of the explanation for this is the country's more consistently professional police force, which has been maintained since the transition from Sandinista revolutionary rule to democratic, elected government in 1990.

While crime is less rampant, however, the perpetuation in power of Daniel Ortega remains a concern. Ortega, who has led the Sandinista National Liberation Front since 1979 and was president of Nicaragua from 1985 until his defeat at the polls in 1990, was elected president in 2006 after a number of failed runs for the office. Now he is scarcely disguising his intention to stay on as president: He plans to run again in 2011 despite the fact that doing so is unconstitutional. Through shrewd manipulation of institutions (for example, illegally extending the terms of two Sandinista judges); frequent use of decree authority; cynical and convenient political pacts with prominent opposition figures (especially the former president Arnoldo Alemán); and some moderately successful social programs, Ortega appears to be in a strong position to pull it off.

This is particularly so because there is no guarantee the voting process will be free and fair. Local elections in 2008, in which no outside observers were permitted, were widely deemed to be fraudulent. Ortega's brand of strongman rule, marked by the steady erosion of checks and constraints on executive authority, recalls certain features of the dictatorship of Anastasio Somoza (1967–1979), against which Ortega and his fellow Sandinistas fought in the 1970s. To date, Ortega has been able to proceed with his blatant power grab with little response from the rest of the hemisphere, which is politically fragmented and is not focused on the Nicaraguan situation.

Despite Ortega's alliance with President Chávez, and despite Nicaragua's participation in the Chávez-led regional group ALBA (Bolivarian Alliance for the Americas), ideology has for Ortega clearly taken a back seat to sheer power politics. He appears ready to do whatever is necessary to remain in power. Ortega has, for example, been quite accommodating with international financial institutions and even parts of Nicaragua's private sector. And, occasionally harsh rhetoric notwithstanding, he has been open to dealing with the United States, even fully honoring the 2005 Central American Free Trade Agreement.

In October 2010—in a move few regard as unrelated to Ortega's quest to remain in power—some 50 Nicaraguan troops were sent to a disputed zone on the country's border with Costa Rica, presumably to help dredge the San Juan River. That led Costa Rica to mobilize some of its police force (Costa Rica abolished its military in 1948), resulting in a tense standoff. The OAS has intervened but, despite the adoption of several resolutions, has so far been unable to get Ortega to withdraw the soldiers. The Costa Rican government has also appealed to the International Court of Justice in The Hague for a resolution of the conflict.

Not surprisingly, the dispute has aroused nationalist sentiment in both countries, and has thus boosted Ortega's political standing as he prepares for the 2011 race amid intense controversy over a 2009 Supreme Court ruling that exempted him from the constitutional ban on consecutive reelection. In alliance with Alemán, Ortega also has successfully turned to the national assembly to support legislation that would provide a new framework for the country's defense and security policies, including the formation of an intelligence-gathering network.

Critics warn of further erosion of the rule of law and the prospect of growing militarization of Nicaraguan society. Some observers are also worried about the politicization of the country's police forces, which so far have been an important factor in guarding against the rise and penetration of organized crime that have afflicted Guatemala, Honduras, and El Salvador.

Vulnerable Costa Rica

Although Costa Rica on nearly all institutional and social measures is more advanced than its Central American neighbors, it is far from immune to some of the wider phenomena creating security problems in the region. At the end of 2010 the government of President Laura Chinchilla of the center-left National Liberation Party was clearly preoccupied with the tense impasse with Nicaragua.

By resorting to the OAS and the International Court of Justice, Chinchilla, Costa Rica's first woman president and a noted expert on public security matters, was pursuing diplomatic and legal options to keep the situation from getting out of control. Further, as the only Central American country with relations with China (established under the previous administration of Oscar Arias), Costa Rica is focused on attracting investment and boosting trade.

Chinchilla's professional background and expertise may turn out to be useful in addressing the problem of drug-related violence, which is putting a strain on Costa Rican institutions. Unlike its neighbors, Costa Rica does not have armed forces, so it cannot deploy military units as other countries have done to bolster police presence and combat spreading criminality. Thus, while Costa Rica does not face the risk of "militarizing" what is fundamentally a law enforcement issue, it is vulnerable to a problem that its police forces may not be fully equipped to handle.

As a result, in accordance with a Joint Maritime Agreement, the United States military, with some 46 warships and 7,000 troops off the coast, has been granted permission to enter the country should the need arise. Although the decision has generated some minor controversy in the country, for the most part the bilateral deal has not so far posed a serious political problem. For Costa Ricans, along with other Central Americans, security has become an increasingly salient concern.

Central America's Travails

Survey after survey point to the same finding: Security is the overriding issue for most Central Americans. Available data tend to bear out the widespread perception: The end of political, armed conflict 15 years ago has not been accompanied by higher levels of social peace. On the contrary, fear and lawlessness today are rampant in the region.

This situation is the product of precarious governance structures, including ineffective judicial institutions and incoherent political parties, along with a far from propitious external environment. High energy costs and the consequences of the severe economic downturn in the United States—particularly in sectors of the economy in which Hispanics are disproportionately active—have hit Central America with unusual force.

Mechanisms of integration, both within the Central American subregion and across the hemisphere, have to date not responded adequately to the worsening problems—particularly the organized crime in Guatemala, Honduras, and El Salvador, and the authoritarianism in Nicaragua. The US-backed Mérida Initiative, started under the George W. Bush administration and extended under President Barack Obama, has essentially sought to assist Mexico, through the provision of various kinds of equipment and training, in its enormously difficult fight against drug-fueled violence and organized crime. Within that package of some $1.6 billion over three years, however, relatively few resources have been directed further south, to Central America, despite the problems aggravated by drug trafficking and the war on drugs.

To its credit, the Obama administration has become increasingly concerned with the deteriorating security situation in Central America. In August 2010, the State Department launched the Central American Regional Security Initiative, which lists a set of laudable aims and proposes to devote $165 million to supporting law enforcement and judicial institutions in the region as well as an array of social and economic programs. In September the administration added Honduras, Nicaragua, and Costa Rica to the United States' list of countries with major drug trafficking or producing problems.

Given the magnitude of the challenge and the high stakes involved, however, it is not clear whether such efforts, however worthwhile, will be sufficient to deal effectively with problems that require sustained, high-level political attention and a more robust and energized multilateral system. For Washington, a broader strategy would, for example, focus seriously on stemming continuing flows of arms and money from the United States to the region; fostering more genuine cooperation among Central American governments and other Latin American countries, particularly Mexico; and rethinking an antidrug policy that has yielded such disappointing results.

Although Central America's crime problem cannot be reduced to drugs—illicit activities flourish in a number of different areas—it is a key factor in the overall situation and, if properly addressed, would help mitigate the worst consequences of criminality.

Shared Responsibility

The urgent need for a comprehensive approach was highlighted in August 2010, when 72 migrants—most of them from Central America—were executed by the Zetas, the Mexican drug trafficking group. In pursuit of profit, the Zetas help migrants from Guatemala, Honduras, and El Salvador cross the border into Mexico on the way to the United States, then hold some of them hostage and force their families to pay ransom or insist that they help with drug smuggling. If they refuse, they are often executed, as happened in this case.

Such extortion practices and human trafficking, in addition to other tragic stories associated with the narcotics trade and gang violence, are all too common among the United States' closest neighbors, whose citizens make up an increasing share of the US population. For reasons of national interest—not to mention out of a sense of shared responsibility—Washington should seek to catalyze a broader hemispheric effort, marshalling both economic and political resources to address a colossal problem, one that shows no signs of abating and indeed threatens to metastasize.

Critical Thinking

1. What accounts for Central America's security predicament?
2. How have countries in the region responded to this challenge?
3. What other political challenges do countries in the region face?

MICHAEL SHIFTER, a *Current History* contributing editor, is the president of the Inter-American Dialogue and an adjunct professor of Latin American studies at Georgetown University.

Global Aging and the Crisis of the 2020s

"The risk of social and political upheaval could grow throughout the developing world—even as the developed world's capacity to deal with such threats declines."

NEIL HOWE AND RICHARD JACKSON

From the fall of the Roman and the Mayan empires to the Black Death to the colonization of the New World and the youth-driven revolutions of the twentieth century, demographic trends have played a decisive role in many of the great invasions, political upheavals, migrations, and environmental catastrophes of history. By the 2020s, an ominous new conjuncture of demographic trends may once again threaten widespread disruption. We are talking about global aging, which is likely to have a profound effect on economic growth, living standards, and the shape of the world order.

For the world's wealthy nations, the 2020s are set to be a decade of rapid population aging and population decline. The developed world has been aging for decades, due to falling birthrates and rising life expectancy. But in the 2020s, this aging will get an extra kick as large postwar baby boom generations move fully into retirement. According to the United Nations Population Division (whose projections are cited throughout this article), the median ages of Western Europe and Japan, which were 34 and 33 respectively as recently as 1980, will soar to 47 and 52 by 2030, assuming no increase in fertility. In Italy, Spain, and Japan, more than half of all adults will be older than the official retirement age—and there will be more people in their 70s than in their 20s.

Falling birthrates are not only transforming traditional population pyramids, leaving them top-heavy with elders, but are also ushering in a new era of workforce and population decline. The working-age population has already begun to contract in several large developed countries, including Germany and Japan. By 2030, it will be stagnant or contracting in nearly all developed countries, the only major exception being the United States. In a growing number of nations, total population will begin a gathering decline as well. Unless immigration or birthrates surge, Japan and some European nations are on track to lose nearly one-half of their total current populations by the end of the century.

The working-age population has already begun to contract in several large developed countries, including Germany and Japan.

These trends threaten to undermine the ability of today's developed countries to maintain global security. To begin with, they directly affect population size and GDP size, and hence the manpower and economic resources that nations can deploy. This is what RAND scholar Brian Nichiporuk calls "the bucket of capabilities" perspective. But population aging and decline can also indirectly affect capabilities—or even alter national goals themselves.

Rising pension and health care costs will place intense pressure on government budgets, potentially crowding out spending on other priorities, including national defense and foreign assistance. Economic performance may suffer as workforces gray and rates of savings and investment decline. As societies and electorates age, growing risk aversion and shorter time horizons may weaken not just the ability of the developed countries to play a major geopolitical role, but also their will.

The weakening of the developed countries might not be a cause for concern if we knew that the world as a whole were likely to become more pacific. But unfortunately, just the opposite may be the case. During the 2020s, the developing world will be buffeted by its own potentially destabilizing demographic storms. China will face a massive age wave that could slow economic growth and precipitate political crisis just as that country is overtaking America as the world's leading economic power. Russia will be in the midst of the steepest and most protracted population implosion of any major power since the plague-ridden Middle Ages. Meanwhile, many other developing countries, especially in the Muslim world, will experience a sudden new resurgence of youth whose aspirations they are unlikely to be able to meet.

China will face a massive age wave that could slow economic growth and precipitate political crisis.

The risk of social and political upheaval could grow throughout the developing world—even as the developed world's capacity to deal with such threats declines. Yet, if the developed world seems destined to see its geopolitical stature diminish, there is one partial but important exception to the trend: the United States. While it is fashionable to argue that US power has peaked, demography suggests America will play as important a role in shaping the world order in this century as it did in the last.

Demography suggests America will play as important a role in shaping the world order in this century as it did in the last.

Graying Economies

Although population size alone does not confer geopolitical stature, no one disputes that population size and economic size together constitute a potent double engine of national power. A larger population allows greater numbers of young adults to serve in war and to occupy and pacify territory. A larger economy allows more spending on the hard power of national defense and the semi-hard power of foreign assistance. It can also enhance what political scientist Joseph Nye calls "soft power" by promoting business dominance, leverage with nongovernmental organizations and philanthropies, social envy and emulation, and cultural clout in the global media and popular culture.

The expectation that global aging will diminish the geopolitical stature of the developed world is thus based in part on simple arithmetic. By the 2020s and 2030s, the working-age population of Japan and many European countries will be contracting by between 0.5 and 1.5 percent per year. Even at full employment, growth in real GDP could stagnate or decline, since the number of workers may be falling faster than productivity is rising. Unless economic performance improves, some countries could face a future of secular economic stagnation—in other words, of zero real GDP growth from peak to peak of the business cycle.

Economic performance, in fact, is more likely to deteriorate than improve. Workforces in most developed countries will not only be stagnating or contracting, but also graying. A vast literature in the social and behavioral sciences establishes that worker productivity typically declines at older ages, especially in eras of rapid technological and market change.

Economies with graying workforces are also likely to be less entrepreneurial. According to the Global Entrepreneurship Monitor's 2007 survey of 53 countries, new business start-ups in high-income countries are heavily tilted toward the young. Of all "new entrepreneurs" in the survey (defined as owners of a business founded within the past three and one-half years), 40 percent were under age 35 and 69 percent under age 45. Only 9 percent were 55 or older.

At the same time, savings rates in the developed world will decline as a larger share of the population moves into the retirement years. If savings fall more than investment demand, as much macroeconomic modeling suggests is likely, either businesses will starve for investment funds or the developed economies' dependence on capital from higher-saving emerging markets will grow. In the first case, the penalty will be lower output. In the second, it will be higher debt service costs and the loss of political leverage, which history teaches is always ceded to creditor nations.

Even as economic growth slows, the developed countries will have to transfer a rising share of society's economic resources from working-age adults to nonworking elders. Graying means paying—more for pensions, more for health care, more for nursing homes for the frail elderly. According to projections by the Center for Strategic and International Studies, the cost of maintaining the current generosity of today's public old-age benefit systems would, on average across the developed countries, add an extra 7 percent of GDP to government budgets by 2030.

Yet the old-age benefit systems of most developed countries are already pushing the limits of fiscal and economic affordability. By the 2020s, political conflict over deep benefit cuts seems unavoidable. On one side will be young adults who face stagnant or declining after-tax earnings. On the other side will be retirees, who are often wholly dependent on pay-as-you-go public plans. In the 2020s, young people in developed countries will have the future on their side. Elders will have the votes on theirs.

Faced with the choice between economically ruinous tax hikes and politically impossible benefit cuts, many governments will choose a third option: cannibalizing other spending on everything from education and the environment to foreign assistance and national defense. As time goes by, the fiscal squeeze will make it progressively more difficult to pursue the obvious response to military manpower shortages—investing massively in military technology, and thereby substituting capital for labor.

Diminished Stature

The impact of global aging on the collective temperament of the developed countries is more difficult to quantify than its impact on their economies, but the consequences could be just as important—or even more so. With the size of domestic markets fixed or shrinking in many countries, businesses and unions may lobby for anticompetitive changes in the economy. We may see growing cartel behavior to protect market share and more restrictive rules on hiring and firing to protect jobs.

We may also see increasing pressure on governments to block foreign competition. Historically, eras of stagnant population and market growth—think of the 1930s—have been characterized by rising tariff barriers, autarky, corporatism, and other anticompetitive policies that tend to shut the door on free trade and free markets.

This shift in business psychology could be mirrored by a broader shift in social mood. Psychologically, older societies are likely to become more conservative in outlook and possibly more risk-averse in electoral and leadership behavior. Elder-dominated electorates may tend to lock in current public spending commitments at the expense of new priorities and shun decisive confrontations in favor of ad hoc settlements. Smaller families may be less willing to risk scarce youth in war.

We know that extremely youthful societies are in some ways dysfunctional—prone to violence, instability, and state failure. But extremely aged societies may also prove dysfunctional in some ways, favoring consumption over investment, the past over the future, and the old over the young.

Meanwhile, the rapid growth in ethnic and religious minority populations, due to ongoing immigration and higher-than-average minority fertility, could strain civic cohesion and foster a new diaspora politics. With the demand for low-wage labor rising, immigration (at its current rate) is on track by 2030 to double the percentage of Muslims in France and triple it in Germany. Some large European cities, including Amsterdam, Marseille, Birmingham, and Cologne, may be majority Muslim.

In Europe, the demographic ebb tide may deepen the crisis of confidence that is reflected in such best-selling books as *France Is Falling* by Nicolas Baverez, *Can Germany Be Saved?* by Hans-Werner Sinn, and *The Last Days of Europe* by Walter Laqueur. The media in Europe are already rife with dolorous stories about the closing of schools and maternity wards, the abandonment of rural towns, and the lawlessness of immigrant youths in large cities. In Japan, the government has half-seriously projected the date at which only one Japanese citizen will be left alive.

Over the next few decades, the outlook in the United States will increasingly diverge from that in the rest of the developed world. Yes, America is also graying, but to a lesser extent. Aside from Israel and Iceland, the United States is the only developed nation where fertility is at or above the replacement rate of 2.1 average lifetime births per woman. By 2030, its median age, now 37, will rise to only 39. Its working-age population, according to both US Census Bureau and UN projections, will also continue to grow through the 2020s and beyond, both because of its higher fertility rate and because of substantial net immigration, which America assimilates better than most other developed countries.

The United States faces serious structural challenges, including a bloated health care sector, a chronically low savings rate, and a political system that has difficulty making meaningful trade-offs among competing priorities. All of these problems threaten to become growing handicaps as the country's population ages. Yet, unlike Europe and Japan, the United States will still have the youth and the economic resources to play a major geopolitical role. The real challenge facing America by the 2020s may not be so much its inability to lead the developed world as the inability of the other developed nations to lend much assistance.

Perilous Transitions

Although the world's wealthy nations are leading the way into humanity's graying future, aging is a global phenomenon. Most of the developing world is also progressing through the so-called demographic transition—the shift from high mortality and high fertility to low mortality and low fertility that inevitably accompanies development and modernization. Since 1975, the average fertility rate in the developing world has dropped from 5.1 to 2.7 children per woman, the rate of population growth has decelerated from 2.2 to 1.3 percent per year, and the median age has risen from 21 to 28.

The demographic outlook in the developing world, however, is shaping up to be one of extraordinary diversity. In many of the poorest and least stable countries (especially in sub-Saharan Africa), the demographic transition has failed to gain traction, leaving countries burdened with large youth bulges. By contrast, in many of the most rapidly modernizing countries (especially in East Asia), the population shift from young and growing to old and stagnant or declining is occurring at a breathtaking pace—far more rapidly than it did in any of today's developed countries.

Notwithstanding this diversity, some demographers and political scientists believe that the unfolding of the transition is ushering in a new era in which demographic trends will promote global stability. This "demographic peace" thesis, as we dub it, begins with the observation that societies with rapidly growing populations and young age structures are often mired in poverty and prone to civil violence and state failure, while those with no or slow population growth and older age structures tend to be more affluent and stable. As the demographic transition progresses—and population growth slows, median ages rise, and child dependency burdens fall—the demographic peace thesis predicts that economic growth and social and political stability will follow.

We believe this thesis is deeply flawed. It fails to take into account the huge variation in the timing and pace of the demographic transition in the developing world. It tends to focus exclusively on the threat of state failure, which indeed is closely and negatively correlated with the degree of demographic transition, while ignoring the threat of "neo-authoritarian" state success, which is more likely to occur in societies in which the transition is well under way. We are, in other words, not talking just about a hostile version of the Somalia model, but also about a potentially hostile version of the China or Russia model, which appears to enjoy growing appeal among political leaders in many developing countries.

More fundamentally, the demographic peace thesis lacks any realistic sense of historical process. It is possible (though by no means assured) that the global security environment that emerges after the demographic transition has run its course will be safer than today's. It is very unlikely, however, that the transition will make the security environment progressively safer along the way. Journeys can be more dangerous than destinations.

Economists, sociologists, and historians who have studied the development process agree that societies, as they move from the traditional to the modern, are buffeted by powerful and disorienting social, cultural, and economic crosswinds. As countries are integrated into the global marketplace and global culture, traditional economic and social structures are overturned and traditional value systems are challenged.

Along with the economic benefits of rising living standards, development also brings the social costs of rapid urbanization, growing income inequality, and environmental degradation. When plotted against development, these stresses exhibit a hump-shaped or inverted-U pattern, meaning that they become most acute midway through the demographic transition.

The demographic transition can trigger a rise in extremism. Religious and cultural revitalization movements may seek to reaffirm traditional identities that are threatened by modernization and try to fill the void left when development uproots communities and fragments extended families. It is well documented that international terrorism, among the developing countries, is positively correlated with income, education, and urbanization. States that sponsor terrorism are rarely among the youngest and poorest countries; nor do the terrorists themselves usually originate in the youngest and poorest countries. Indeed, they are often disaffected members of the middle class in middle-income countries that are midway through the demographic transition.

Ethnic tensions can also grow. In many societies, some ethnic groups are more successful in the marketplace than others—which means that, as development accelerates and the market economy grows, rising inequality often falls along ethnic lines. The sociologist Amy Chua documents how the concentration of wealth among "market-dominant minorities" has triggered violent backlashes by majority populations in many developing countries, from Indonesia, Malaysia, and the Philippines (against the Chinese) to Sierra Leone (against the Lebanese) to the former Yugoslavia (against the Croats and Slovenes).

We have in fact only one historical example of a large group of countries that has completed the entire demographic transition—today's (mostly Western) developed nations. And their experience during that transition, from the late 1700s to the late 1900s, was filled with the most destructive revolutions, civil wars, and total wars in the history of civilization. The nations that engaged in World War II had a higher median age and a lower fertility rate—and thus were situated at a later stage of the transition—than most of today's developing world is projected to have over the next 20 years. Even if global aging breeds peace, in other words, we are not out of the woods yet.

Storms Ahead

A number of demographic storms are now brewing in different parts of the developing world. The moment of maximum risk still lies ahead—just a decade away, in the 2020s. Ominously, this is the same decade when the developed world will itself be experiencing its moment of greatest demographic stress.

Consider China, which may be the first country to grow old before it grows rich. For the past quarter-century, China has been "peacefully rising," thanks in part to a one-child-per-couple policy that has lowered dependency burdens and allowed both parents to work and contribute to China's boom. By the 2020s, however, the huge Red Guard generation, which was born before the country's fertility decline, will move into retirement, heavily taxing the resources of their children and the state.

China's coming age wave—by 2030 it will be an older country than the United States—may weaken the two pillars of the current regime's legitimacy: rapidly rising GDP and social stability. Imagine workforce growth slowing to zero while tens of millions of elders sink into indigence without pensions, without health care, and without large extended families to support them. China could career toward social collapse—or, in reaction, toward an authoritarian clampdown. The arrival of China's age wave, and the turmoil it may bring, will coincide with its expected displacement of the United States as the world's largest economy in the 2020s. According to "power transition" theories of global conflict, this moment could be quite perilous.

By the 2020s, Russia, along with the rest of Eastern Europe, will be in the midst of an extended population decline as steep or steeper than any in the developed world. The Russian fertility rate has plunged far beneath the replacement level even as life expectancy has collapsed amid a widening health crisis. Russian men today can expect to live to 60—16 years less than American men and marginally less than their Red Army grandfathers at the end of World War II. By 2050, Russia is due to fall to 16th place in world population rankings, down from 4th place in 1950 (or third place, if we include all the territories of the former Soviet Union).

Prime Minister Vladimir Putin flatly calls Russia's demographic implosion "the most acute problem facing our country today." If the problem is not solved, Russia will weaken progressively, raising the nightmarish specter of a failing or failed state with nuclear weapons. Or this cornered bear may lash out in revanchist fury rather than meekly accept its demographic fate.

Of course, some regions of the developing world will remain extremely young in the 2020s. Sub-Saharan Africa, which is burdened by the world's highest fertility rates and is also ravaged by AIDS, will still be racked by large youth bulges. So will a scattering of impoverished and chronically unstable Muslim-majority countries, including Afghanistan, the Palestinian territories, Somalia, Sudan, and Yemen. If the correlation between extreme youth and violence endures, chronic unrest and state failure could persist in much of sub-Saharan Africa and parts of the Muslim world through the 2020s, or even longer if fertility rates fail to drop.

Meanwhile, many fast-modernizing countries where fertility has fallen very recently and very steeply will experience a sudden resurgence of youth in the 2020s. It is a law of demography that, when a population boom is followed by a bust, it causes a ripple effect, with a gradually fading cycle of echo booms and busts. In the 2010s, a bust generation will be coming of age in much of Latin America, South Asia, and the Muslim world. But by the 2020s, an echo boom will follow—dashing economic expectations and perhaps fueling political violence, religious extremism, and ethnic strife.

These echo booms will be especially large in Pakistan and Iran. In Pakistan, the decade-over-decade percentage growth in the number of people in the volatile 15- to 24-year-old age bracket is projected to drop from 32 percent in the 2000s to just 10 percent in the 2010s, but then leap upward again to 19 percent in the 2020s. In Iran, the swing in the size of the youth bulge population is projected to be even larger: minus 33 percent in the 2010s and plus 23 percent in the 2020s. These echo booms will be occurring in countries whose social fabric is already strained by rapid development. One country teeters on the brink of chaos, while the other aspires to regional hegemony. One already has nuclear weapons, while the other seems likely to obtain them.

Pax Americana Redux?

The demographer Nicholas Eberstadt has warned that demographic change may be "even more menacing to the security prospects of the Western alliance than was the cold war for the past generation." Although it would be fair to point out that such change usually presents opportunities as well as dangers, his basic point is incontestable: Planning national strategy for the next several decades with no regard for population projections is like setting sail without a map or a compass. It is likely to be an ill-fated voyage. In this sense, demography is the geopolitical cartography of the twenty-first century.

Although tomorrow's geopolitical map will surely be shaped in important ways by political choices yet to be made, the basic contours are already emerging. During the era of the Industrial Revolution, the population of what we now call the developed world grew faster than the rest of the world's population, peaking at 25 percent of the world total in 1930. Since then, its share has declined. By 2010, it stood at just 13 percent, and it is projected to decline still further, to 10 percent by 2050.

The collective GDP of the developed countries will also decline as a share of the world total—and much more steeply. According to new projections by the Carnegie Endowment for International Peace, the Group of 7 industrialized nations' share of the Group of 20 leading economies' total GDP will fall from 72 percent in 2009 to 40 percent in 2050. Driving this decline will be not just the slower growth of the developed world, as workforces age and stagnate or contract, but also the expansion of large, newly market-oriented economies, especially in East and South Asia.

Again, there is only one large country in the developed world that does not face a future of stunning relative demographic and economic decline: the United States. Thanks to its relatively high fertility rate and substantial net immigration, its current global population share will remain virtually unchanged in the coming decades. According to the Carnegie projections, the US share of total G-20 GDP will drop significantly, from 34 percent in 2009 to 24 percent in 2050. The combined share of Canada, France, Germany, Italy, Japan, and the United Kingdom, however, will plunge from 38 percent to 16 percent.

By the middle of the twenty-first century, the dominant strength of the US economy within the developed world will have only one historical parallel: the immediate aftermath of World War II, exactly 100 years earlier, at the birth of the "Pax Americana."

The UN regularly publishes a table ranking the world's most populous countries over time. In 1950, six of the top twelve were developed countries. In 2000, only three were. By 2050, only one developed country will remain—the United States, still in third place. By then, it will be the only country among the top twelve committed since its founding to democracy, free markets, and civil liberties.

All told, population trends point inexorably toward a more dominant US role in a world that will need America more, not less.

Critical Thinking

1. What impact will an aging population have on the industrialized world?

2. How will demographic transition affect developing countries?

3. What are the implications of the US exception to the demographic trends in the industrialized world?

NEIL HOWE and RICHARD JACKSON are, respectively, a senior associate and a senior fellow at the Center for Strategic and International Studies. They are the authors of *The Graying of the Great Powers: Demography and Geopolitics in the 21st Century* (CSIS, 2008).

UNIT 4

Political Change in the Developing World

Unit Selections

Learning Outcomes

After reading this unit, you should be able to:

- Describe the recent trends in the progress of human rights and democracy worldwide.
- Suggest ways in which post-conflict settlements may fall short of democracy.
- Understand the factors that led to political upheaval in the Middle East and the implications of these developments.
- Analyze the prospects for peaceful change in the Middle East.
- Evaluate the prospects for democracy in Latin America.
- Discuss the factors that explain the emergence of Brazil and Indonesia.

Student Website

www.mhhe.com/cls

Internet References

Center for Research on Inequality, Human Security, and Ethnicity
www.crise.ox.ac.uk

Latin American Network Information Center—LANIC
www.lanic.utexas.edu

ReliefWeb
www.reliefweb.int/w/rwb.nsf

A recent assessment of democracy and human rights found a continuing decline in both categories worldwide. The history of authoritarian colonial rule and the failure to prepare colonies adequately for democracy at independence helps to account for the fragility of democracy and human rights in many developing countries. Even when there was an attempt to foster parliamentary government, the experiment failed frequently, largely due to the lack of a democratic tradition and a reliance on political expediency. Independence-era leaders frequently resorted to centralization of power and authoritarianism, either to pursue ambitious development programs or more often simply to retain power. In some cases, leaders experimented with socialist development schemes that emphasized ideology and the role of party elites. The promise of rapid, equitable development proved elusive, and the collapse of the Soviet Union further discredited this strategy. Other countries had the misfortune to come under the rule of tyrannical leaders who were concerned only with enriching themselves and who brutally repressed anyone with the temerity to challenge their rule. Although there are a few notable exceptions, the developing world's experiences with democracy since independence have been uneven.

The results of democracy's "third wave" have been mixed so far. While democracy has increased across the world, the pace of democratic change has slowed recently, and in some instances democratic reform has regressed. There has been a backlash against democracy in some parts of Asia. The end of the civil war in Sri Lanka and the re-election of the incumbent president resulted in a crackdown against the opposition and an indication of a turn away from democracy. The rapid rise of China and Singapore has reopened the debate about authoritarian rule and economic growth. Although Latin America has been the developing world's most successful region in establishing democracy, widespread dissatisfaction due to corruption, inequitable distribution of wealth, and the threats to civil rights have produced a left-wing, populist trend in the region's politics recently. Several countries have decided to either extend presidential terms or abolish term limits.

Africa's experience with democracy has also been varied since the third wave of democratization swept over the continent beginning in 1990. Although early efforts resulted in the ouster of many leaders, some of whom had held power for decades, and international pressure forced several countries to hold multiparty elections, the political landscape in Africa includes consolidating democracies and states still mired in conflict. Among the success stories is Ghana, which held elections in late 2008 that resulted in the opposition leader defeating the ruling party's candidate. South Africa, the continent's biggest success story, held its fourth round of democratic elections in April 2009. The elections took place amid allegations of corruption against the new president, Jacob Zuma, and featured a nasty split in the ruling

African National Congress. Although South Africa continues to face major challenges, its democracy remains vibrant. Ghana and South Africa stand in sharp contrast to the circumstances in some other parts of Africa. Ivory Coast's disputed 2010 election and the standoff that followed demonstrated some of the challenges of democratic transition on the African continent.

Political change has begun in some parts of the Middle East as a result of the revolutions in Tunisia and Egypt triggering demands for democratic reforms across the region. These demands have been met by acceptance in some places and a brutal crackdown in others.

The role of Islam in the region and its incompatibility with democracy continues to be a major issue. There is some evidence that Islamic political parties have moderated their message and that those that have not do not fare well in elections. Prospects for broader democratic reform in the region will depend on the success of efforts to reframe the political debate and the willingness of ruling elites to accept change.

While there has been significant progress toward democratic reform around the world, as the recent trend suggests, there is no guarantee that these efforts will be sustained. Although there has been an increase in the percentage of the world's population living under democracy, nondemocratic regimes still exist. Furthermore, some semi-democracies hold elections but citizens lack full civil and political rights. International efforts to promote democracy often tend to focus on elections rather than on the long-term requirements of democratic consolidation. More effective ways of promoting and sustaining democracy must be found in order to expand freedom further in the developing world.

Crying for Freedom

A disturbing decline in global liberty prompts some hard thinking about what is needed for democracy to prevail.

More than at any time since the cold war, liberal democracy needs defending. That warning was issued recently by Arch Puddington, a veteran American campaigner for civil and political rights around the world.

This week the reasons for his concern became clearer. Freedom House, a lobby group based in Washington, DC (where Mr Puddington is research director), found in its latest annual assessment that liberty and human rights had retreated globally for the fourth consecutive year. It said this marked the longest period of decline in freedom since the organisation began its reports nearly 40 years ago.

Freedom House classifies countries as "free", "partly free" or "not free" by a range of indicators that reflect its belief that political liberty and human rights are interlinked. As well as the fairness of their electoral systems, countries are assessed for things like the integrity of judges and the independence of trade unions. Among the latest findings are that authoritarian regimes are not just more numerous; they are more confident and influential.

In its report entitled "Freedom in the World 2010: Global Erosion of Freedom", the American lobby group found that declines in liberty occurred last year in 40 countries (in Africa, Latin America, the Middle East and the ex-Soviet Union) while gains were recorded in 16. The number of electoral democracies went down by three, to 116, with Honduras, Madagascar, Mozambique and Niger dropping off the list while the Maldives were reinstated. This leaves the total at its lowest since 1995, although it is still comfortably above the 1990 figure of 69.

Taken as a whole, the findings suggest a huge turn for the worse since the bubbly mood of 20 years ago, when the collapse of Soviet communism, plus the fall of apartheid, convinced people that liberal democracy had prevailed for good. To thinkers like America's Francis Fukuyama, this was the time when it became evident that political freedom, underpinned by economic freedom, marked the ultimate stage in human society's development: the "end of history", at least in a moral sense.

In the very early days after the Soviet collapse, Russia and some of its neighbours swarmed with Western advisers, disseminating not only the basics of market economics but also the mechanics of multi-party democracy. And for a short time, these pundits found willing listeners.

Today, the idea that politicians in ex-communist countries would take humble lessons from Western counterparts seems laughable. There is more evidence of authoritarians swapping tips. In October, for example, the pro-Kremlin United Russia party held its latest closed-door meeting with the Chinese Communist party. Despite big contrasts between the two countries—not many people in Russia think there is a Chinese model they could easily apply—the Russians were interested by the Chinese "experience in building a political system dominated by one political party," according to one report of the meeting.

For freedom-watchers in the West, the worrying thing is that the cause of liberal democracy is not merely suffering political reverses, it is also in intellectual retreat. Semi-free countries, uncertain which direction to take, seem less convinced that the liberal path is the way of the future. And in the West, opinion-makers are quicker to acknowledge democracy's drawbacks—and the apparent fact that contested elections do more harm than good when other preconditions for a well-functioning system are absent. It is a sign of the times that a British reporter, Humphrey Hawksley, has written a book with the title: "Democracy Kills: What's So Good About the Vote?"

A more nuanced argument, against the promotion of electoral democracy at the expense of other goals, has been made by other observers. Paul Collier, an Oxford professor, has asserted that democracy in the absence of other desirables, like the rule of law, can hobble a country's progress. Mark Malloch-Brown, a former head of the UN Development Programme, is still a believer in democracy as a driver of economic advancement, but he thinks that in countries like Afghanistan, the West has focused too much on procedures—like multi-party elections—and is not open enough to the idea that other kinds of consensus might exist. At the University of California, Randall Peerenboom defends the "East Asian model", according to which economic development naturally precedes democracy.

Whatever the eggheads may be saying, there are some obvious reasons why Western governments' zeal to promote democracy, and the willingness of other countries to listen, have ebbed. In many quarters (including Western ones), the assault on Saddam Hussein's Iraq, and its bloody aftermath, seemed to confirm people's suspicion that promoting democracy as an American foreign-policy aim was ill-conceived or plain cynical.

In Afghanistan, the other country where an American-led coalition has been waging war in democracy's name, the corruption and deviousness of the local political elite, and the flaws of last year's election, have been an embarrassment. In the Middle East, America's enthusiasm for promoting democracy took a dip after the Palestinian elections of 2006, which brought Hamas to office. The European Union's "soft power" on its eastern rim has waned as enlargement fatigue has grown.

But perhaps the biggest reason why democracy's magnetic power has waned is the rise of China—and the belief of its would-be imitators that they too can create a dynamic economy without easing their grip on political power. In the political rhetoric of many authoritarian governments, fascination with copying China's trick can clearly be discerned.

For example, Syria's ruling Baath party talks of a "socialist market economy" that will fuel growth while keeping stability. Communist Vietnam has emulated China's economic reforms, but it was one of the states scolded by Freedom House this year for curbing liberty. Iran has called in Chinese legal experts and economists. There are limits to how much an Islamic republic and a communist state can have in common, but they seem to agree on what to avoid: Western-style freedom.

Even Cuba, while clinging to Marxist ideas, has shown an interest in China's economic reforms. And from the viewpoint of many poor countries, especially in Africa, co-operating with China—both economically and politically—has many advantages: not least the fact that China refrains from delivering lectures on political and human freedom. The global economic downturn—and China's ability to survive it—has clearly added to that country's appeal. The power of China (and a consequent lessening of official concern over human rights) is palpable in Central Asia. But as dissidents in the region note, it is not just Chinese influence that makes life hard for them; it is also the dithering of Western governments which often temper their moral concerns with commercial ones.

The Argument for Open Argument

Given that democracy is unlikely to advance, these days, through the military or economic preponderance of the West, its best hope lies in winning a genuinely open debate. In other words, wavering countries, and sceptical societies, must be convinced that political freedom works best.

So how does the case in defence of democracy stand up these days? As many a philosopher has noted, the strongest points to be made in favour of a free political contest are negative. Democracy may not yield perfect policies, but it ought to guard against all manner of ills, ranging from outright tyranny (towards which a "mild" authoritarian can always slide) to larceny at the public expense.

Transparency International, a corruption watchdog, says that all but two of the 30 least corrupt countries in the world are democracies (the exceptions are Singapore and Hong Kong, and they are considered semi-democratic). Autocracies tend to occupy much higher rankings on the corruption scale (China is

somewhere in the middle) and it is easy to see why. Entrenched political elites, untroubled by free and fair elections, can get away more easily with stuffing their pockets. And strongmen often try to maintain their hold on power by relying on public funds to reward their supporters and to buy off their enemies, leading to a huge misallocation of resources.

Yet it is easy to find corrupt democracies—indeed, in a ramshackle place like Afghanistan elections sometimes seem to make things worse. Or take the biggest of the ex-Soviet republics. Russia is authoritarian and has a massive problem with corruption; Ukraine is more democratic—the forthcoming elections are a genuine contest for power, with uncertain results—but it too has quite a big corruption problem. Ukraine has no "Kremlin", wielding authority over all-comers, but that does not make it clean or well-governed.

What about the argument that economic development, at least in its early stages, is best pursued under a benign despot? Lee Kuan Yew, an ex-prime minister of Singapore, once asserted that democracy leads to "disorderly conduct", disrupting material progress. But there is no evidence that autocracies, on average, grow faster than democracies. For every economically successful East Asian (former) autocracy like Taiwan or South Korea, there is an Egypt or a Cameroon (or indeed a North Korea or a Myanmar) which is both harsh and sluggish.

The link between political systems and growth is hard to establish. Yet there is some evidence that, on average, democracies do better. A study by Morton Halperin, Joseph Siegle and Michael Weinstein for the Council of Foreign Relations (CFR), using World Bank data between 1960 and 2001, found that the average annual economic growth rate was 2.3% for democracies and 1.6% for autocracies. Other studies, though, are less clear.

Believers in democracy as an engine of progress often make the point that a climate of freedom is most needed in a knowledge-based economy, where independent thinking and innovation are vital. It is surely no accident that every economy in the top 25 of the Global Innovation Index is a democracy, except semi-democratic Singapore and Hong Kong.

China, which comes 27th in this table, is often cited as a vast exception to this rule. Chinese brainpower has made big strides in fields like computing, green technology and space flight. The determination of China's authorities to impose their own terms on the information revolution was highlighted this week when Google, the search engine, said it might pull out of China after a cyber-attack that targeted human-rights activists. Since entering the Chinese market in 2006, Google had agreed to the censorship of some search results, at the authorities' insistence.

Admirers of China's iron hand may conclude that it can manage well without the likes of Google, which was being trounced in the local market by Baidu, a Chinese rival. But in the medium term, the mentality that insists on hobbling search engines will surely act as a break on creative endeavour. And no country should imagine that by becoming as autocratic as China, it will automatically become as dynamic as China is.

What about the argument that autocracy creates a modicum of stability without which growth is impossible? In fact, it is not evident that authoritarian countries are more stable than democracies.

Quite the contrary. Although democratic politicians spend a lot of time vacillating, arguing and being loud and disagreeable, this can reinforce stability in the medium term; it allows the interests and viewpoints of more people to be heard before action is taken. On the State Fragility Index, which is produced annually by George Mason University and studies variables such as "political effectiveness" and security, democracies tend to do much better than autocracies. Tito's Yugoslavia was stable, as was Saddam Hussein's Iraq—but once the straitjacket that held their systems together came off, the result was a release of pent-up pressure, and a golden opportunity for demagogues bent on mayhem.

At the very least, a culture of compromise—coupled with greater accountability and limits on state power—means that democracies are better able to avoid catastrophic mistakes, or criminal cruelty. Bloody nightmares that cost tens of millions of lives, like China's Great Leap Forward or the Soviet Union's forced collectivisation programme, were made possible by the concentration of power in a small group of people who faced no restraint.

Liberal democratic governments can make all manner of blunders, but they are less likely to commit mass murder. Amartya Sen, a Nobel prize-winning economist, has famously argued that no country with a free press and fair elections has ever had a large famine. And research by those three CFR scholars found that poor autocracies were at least twice as likely as democracies to suffer an economic disaster (defined as a decline of 10% or more in GDP in a year). With no noisy legislatures or robust courts to hold things up, autocracies may be faster and bolder. They are also more accident-prone.

For all its frustrations, open and accountable government tends in the long run to produce better policies. This is because no group of mandarins, no matter how enlightened or well-meaning, can claim to be sure what is best for a complex society. Autocracies tend to be too heavy at the top: although decisions may be more easily taken, the ethos of autocracies—their secrecy and paranoia—makes it harder for alternative views to emerge. Above all, elections make the transfer of power legitimate and smooth. Tyrannies may look stable under one strongman; but they can slide into instability, even bloody chaos, if a transition goes awry. Free elections also mean that policy mistakes, even bad ones, are more quickly corrected. Fresh ideas can be brought in and politicians thrown out before they grow too arrogant.

But if something has been learnt from the recent backlash against democratic enthusiasm, it is that ballot boxes alone are nothing like enough. Unless solid laws protect individual and minority rights, and government power is limited by clear checks, such as tough courts, an electoral contest can simply lead to a "tyranny of the majority," as Alexis de Tocqueville, a French philosopher, called it. That point has particular force in countries where some variety of political Islam seems likely to prevail in any open contest. In such places, minorities include dissident Muslims who often prefer to remain under the relative safety offered by a despot.

Another caveat is that democracy has never endured in countries with mainly non-market economies. The existence of an overweening state machine that meddles in everything can tempt leaders to use it against their political foes. Total control of the economy also sucks the air away from what Istvan Bibo, a Hungarian political thinker, called "the little circles of freedom"—the free associations and independent power centres that a free economy allows. Free-market economies help create a middle class that is less susceptible to state pressure and political patronage.

Perhaps most important, democracy needs leaders with an inclination and ability to compromise: what Walter Bagehot, a 19th-century editor of *The Economist,* called a "disposition rather to give up something than to take the uttermost farthing." Without a propensity for tolerating and managing differences, rival groups can easily reduce democracy to a ruthless struggle for power that ultimately wears down liberal institutions.

Democracy, this suggests, is more likely to succeed in countries with a shared feeling of belonging together, without strong cultural or ethnic fissures that can easily turn political conflict into the armed sort. Better positioned are "people so fundamentally at one that they can safely afford to bicker," as Lord Balfour, a 19th-century British politician, said. Such was not the case in Yugoslavia in the 1990s or in Lebanon in the 1970s.

Even where all the right conditions are in place, democracy will not prevail unless its proponents show success at governing. No constitution can, in itself, guarantee good governance. The success of any political system ultimately depends on whether it can provide basic things like security, wealth and justice. And in countries where experiments in democracy are in full swing, daily reality is more complex than either zealous democracy-promoters or authoritarian sceptics will allow.

In Kabul a 26-year-old handyman called Jamshed speaks for many compatriots when he lists the pros and cons of the new Western-imposed order. Compared with life under the Taliban, he appreciates the new "freedom to listen to music, to go out with your wife, to study or do whatever you want." But he cannot help remembering that "under the Taliban, you could leave your shop to pray and nobody would steal anything...now the government is corrupt, they take all your money."

Jamshed has never read John Stuart Mill or Ayn Rand. But whether he is ruled by theocrats or Western-backed election winners, he knows what he doesn't like.

Critical Thinking

1. What trends are evident in the latest Freedom House survey?

2. What questions have arisen about promoting democracy worldwide?

3. How have U.S. actions contributed to skepticism about the promotion of democracy?

4. What effect has China's rise had on the promotion of democracy?

5. What advantages do democracies have in producing economic growth and good public policy?

6. What is needed to strengthen democracy's attraction?

Understanding the Revolutions of 2011

Weakness and Resilience in Middle Eastern Autocracies

Jack A. Goldstone

The wave of revolutions sweeping the Middle East bears a striking resemblance to previous political earthquakes. As in Europe in 1848, rising food prices and high unemployment have fueled popular protests from Morocco to Oman. As in Eastern Europe and the Soviet Union in 1989, frustration with closed, corrupt, and unresponsive political systems has led to defections among elites and the fall of once powerful regimes in Tunisia, Egypt, and perhaps Libya. Yet 1848 and 1989 are not the right analogies for this past winter's events. The revolutions of 1848 sought to overturn traditional monarchies, and those in 1989 were aimed at toppling communist governments. The revolutions of 2011 are fighting something quite different: "sultanistic" dictatorships. Although such regimes often appear unshakable, they are actually highly vulnerable, because the very strategies they use to stay in power make them brittle, not resilient. It is no coincidence that although popular protests have shaken much of the Middle East, the only revolutions to succeed so far—those in Tunisia and Egypt—have been against modern sultans.

For a revolution to succeed, a number of factors have to come together. The government must appear so irremediably unjust or inept that it is widely viewed as a threat to the country's future; elites (especially in the military) must be alienated from the state and no longer willing to defend it; a broad-based section of the population, spanning ethnic and religious groups and socioeconomic classes, must mobilize; and international powers must either refuse to step in to defend the government or constrain it from using maximum force to defend itself.

Revolutions rarely triumph because these conditions rarely coincide. This is especially the case in traditional monarchies and one-party states, whose leaders often manage to maintain popular support by making appeals to respect for royal tradition or nationalism. Elites, who are often enriched by such governments, will only forsake them if their circumstances or the ideology of the rulers changes drastically. And in almost all cases, broad-based popular mobilization is difficult to achieve because it requires bridging the disparate interests of the urban and rural poor, the middle class, students, professionals, and different ethnic or religious groups. History is replete with student movements, workers' strikes, and peasant uprisings that were readily put down because they remained a revolt of one group, rather than of broad coalitions. Finally, other countries have often intervened to prop up embattled rulers in order to stabilize the international system.

Yet there is another kind of dictatorship that often proves much more vulnerable, rarely retaining power for more than a generation: the sultanistic regime. Such governments arise when a national leader expands his personal power at the expense of formal institutions. Sultanistic dictators appeal to no ideology and have no purpose other than maintaining their personal authority. They may preserve some of the formal aspects of democracy—elections, political parties, a national assembly, or a constitution—but they rule above them by installing compliant supporters in key positions and sometimes by declaring states of emergency, which they justify by appealing to fears of external (or internal) enemies.

Behind the scenes, such dictators generally amass great wealth, which they use to buy the loyalty of supporters and punish opponents. Because they need resources to fuel their patronage machine, they typically promote economic development, through industrialization, commodity exports, and education. They also seek relationships with foreign countries, promising stability in exchange for aid and investment. However wealth comes into the country, most of it is funneled to the sultan and his cronies.

The new sultans control their countries' military elites by keeping them divided. Typically, the security forces are separated into several commands (army, air force, police, intelligence)—each of which reports directly to the leader. The leader monopolizes contact between the commands, between the military and civilians, and with foreign governments, a practice that makes sultans essential for both coordinating the security forces and channeling foreign aid and investment. To reinforce fears that foreign aid and political coordination would disappear in their absence, sultans typically avoid appointing possible successors.

To keep the masses depoliticized and unorganized, sultans control elections and political parties and pay their populations off with subsidies for key goods, such as electricity, gasoline, and foodstuffs. When combined with surveillance, media control, and intimidation, these efforts generally ensure that citizens stay disconnected and passive.

By following this pattern, politically adept sultans around the world have managed to accumulate vast wealth and high concentrations of power. Among the most famous in recent history were Mexico's Porfirio Díaz, Iran's Mohammad Reza Shah Pahlavi, Nicaragua's Somoza dynasty, Haiti's Duvalier dynasty, the Philippines' Ferdinand Marcos, and Indonesia's Suharto.

But as those sultans all learned, and as the new generation of sultans in the Middle East—including Bashar al-Assad in Syria, Omar al-Bashir in Sudan, Zine el-Abidine Ben Ali in Tunisia, Hosni Mubarak in Egypt, Muammar al-Qaddafi in Libya, and Ali Abdullah Saleh in Yemen—has discovered, power that is too concentrated can be difficult to hold on to.

Paper Tigers

For all their attempts to prop themselves up, sultanistic dictatorships have inherent vulnerabilities that only increase over time. Sultans must strike a careful balance between self-enrichment and rewarding the elite: if the ruler rewards himself and neglects the elite, a key incentive for the elite to support the regime is removed. But as sultans come to feel more entrenched and indispensable, their corruption frequently becomes more brazen and concentrated among a small inner circle. As the sultan monopolizes foreign aid and investment or gets too close to unpopular foreign governments, he may alienate elite and popular groups even further.

Meanwhile, as the economy grows and education expands under a sultanistic dictator, the number of people with higher aspirations and a keener sensitivity to the intrusions of police surveillance and abuse increases. And if the entire population grows rapidly while the lion's share of economic gains is hoarded by the elite, inequality and unemployment surge as well. As the costs of subsidies and other programs the regime uses to appease citizens rise, keeping the masses depoliticized places even more stress on the regime. If protests start, sultans may offer reforms or expand patronage benefits—as Marcos did in the Philippines in 1984 to head off escalating public anger. Yet as Marcos learned in 1986, these sops are generally ineffective once people have begun to clamor for ending the sultan's rule.

The weaknesses of sultanistic regimes are magnified as the leader ages and the question of succession becomes more acute. Sultanistic rulers have sometimes been able to hand over leadership to younger family members. This is only possible when the government has been operating effectively and has maintained elite support (as in Syria in 2000, when President Hafez al-Assad handed power to his son Bashar) or if another country backs the regime (as in Iran in 1941, when Western governments promoted the succession from Reza Shah to his son Mohammad Reza Pahlavi). If the regime's corruption has already alienated the country's elites, they may turn on it and try to block a dynastic succession, seeking to regain control of the state (which is what happened in Indonesia in the late 1990s, when the Asian financial crisis dealt a blow to Suharto's patronage machine).

The very indispensability of the sultan also works against a smooth transfer of power. Most of the ministers and other high officials are too deeply identified with the chief executive

to survive his fall from power. For example, the Shah's 1978 attempt to avoid revolution by substituting his prime minister, Shahpur Bakhtiar, for himself as head of government did not work; the entire regime fell the next year. Ultimately, such moves satisfy neither the demands of the mobilized masses seeking major economic and political change nor the aspirations of the urban and professional class that has taken to the streets to demand inclusion in the control of the state.

Then there are the security forces. By dividing their command structure, the sultan may reduce the threat they pose. But this strategy also makes the security forces more prone to defections in the event of mass protests. Lack of unity leads to splits within the security services; meanwhile, the fact that the regime is not backed by any appealing ideology or by independent institutions ensures that the military has less motivation to put down protests. Much of the military may decide that the country's interests are better served by regime change. If part of the armed forces defects—as happened under Díaz, the shah of Iran, Marcos, and Suharto—the government can unravel with astonishing rapidity. In the end, the befuddled ruler, still convinced of his indispensability and invulnerability, suddenly finds himself isolated and powerless.

The degree of a Sultan's weakness is often visible only in retrospect. Although it is easy to identify states with high levels of corruption, unemployment, and personalist rule, the extent to which elites oppose the regime and the likelihood that the military will defect often become apparent only once large-scale protests have begun. After all, the elite and military officers have every reason to hide their true feelings until a crucial moment arises, and it is impossible to know which provocation will lead to mass, rather than local, mobilization. The rapid unraveling of sultanistic regimes thus often comes as a shock.

In some cases, of course, the military does not immediately defect in the face of rebellion. In Nicaragua in the early 1970s, for example, Anastasio Somoza Debayle was able to use loyal troops in Nicaragua's National Guard to put down the rebellion against him. But even when the regime can draw on loyal sectors of the military, it rarely manages to survive. It simply breaks down at a slower pace, with significant bloodshed or even civil war resulting along the way. Somoza's success in 1975 was short-lived; his increasing brutality and corruption brought about an even larger rebellion in the years that followed. After some pitched battles, even formerly loyal troops began to desert, and Somoza fled the country in 1979.

International pressure can also turn the tide. The final blow to Marcos' rule was the complete withdrawal of U.S. support after Marcos dubiously claimed victory in the presidential election held in 1986. When the United States turned away from the regime, his remaining supporters folded, and the nonviolent People Power Revolution forced him into exile.

Rock the Casbah

The revolutions unfolding across the Middle East represent the breakdown of increasingly corrupt sultanistic regimes. Although economies across the region have grown in recent years, the gains have bypassed the majority of the population, being amassed instead by a wealthy few. Mubarak and his family reportedly built up a fortune of between $40 billion and $70 billion, and 39 officials and businessmen close to Mubarak's son Gamal are alleged to have made fortunes averaging more than $1 billion each. In Tunisia, a 2008 U.S. diplomatic cable released by the whistleblower Web site WikiLeaks noted a spike in corruption, warning that Ben Ali's family was becoming so predatory that new investment and job creation were being stifled and that his family's ostentation was provoking widespread outrage.

Fast-growing and urbanizing populations in the Middle East have been hurt by low wages and by food prices that rose by 32 percent in the last year alone, according to the United Nations' Food and Agriculture Organization. But it is not simply such rising prices, or a lack of growth, that fuels revolutions; it is the persistence of widespread and unrelieved poverty amid increasingly extravagant wealth.

Discontent has also been stoked by high unemployment, which has stemmed in part from the surge in the Arab world's young population. The percentage of young adults—those aged 15–29 as a fraction of all those over 15—ranges from 38 percent in Bahrain and Tunisia to over 50 percent in Yemen (compared to 26 percent in the United States). Not only is the proportion of young people in the Middle East extraordinarily high, but their numbers have grown quickly over a short period of time. Since 1990, youth population aged 15–29 has grown by 50 percent in Libya and Tunisia, 65 percent in Egypt, and 125 percent in Yemen.

Thanks to the modernization policies of their sultanistic governments, many of these young people have been able to go to university, especially in recent years. Indeed, college enrollment has soared across the region in recent decades, more than tripling in Tunisia, quadrupling in Egypt, and expanding tenfold in Libya.

It would be difficult, if not impossible, for any government to create enough jobs to keep pace. For the sultanistic regimes, the problem has been especially difficult to manage. As part of their patronage strategies, Ben Ali and Mubarak had long provided state subsidies to workers and families through such programs as Tunisia's National Employment Fund—which trained workers, created jobs, and issued loans—and Egypt's policy of guaranteeing job placement for college graduates. But these safety nets were phased out in the last decade to reduce expenditures. Vocational training, moreover, was weak, and access to public and many private jobs was tightly controlled by those connected to the regime. This led to incredibly high youth unemployment across the Middle East: the figure for the region hit 23 percent, or twice the global average, in 2009. Unemployment among the educated, moreover, has been even worse: in Egypt, college graduates are ten times as likely to have no job as those with only an elementary school education.

In many developing economies, the informal sector provides an outlet for the unemployed. Yet the sultans in the Middle East made even those activities difficult. After all, the protests were sparked by the self-immolation of Mohamed Bouazizi, a 26-year-old Tunisian man who was unable to find formal work and whose fruit cart was confiscated by the police. Educated youth and workers in Tunisia and Egypt have been carrying out local protests and strikes for years to call attention to high unemployment, low wages, police harassment, and state corruption. This time, their protests combined and spread to other demographics.

These regimes' concentration of wealth and brazen corruption increasingly offended their militaries. Ben Ali and Mubarak both came from the professional military; indeed, Egypt had been ruled by former officers since 1952. Yet in both countries, the military had seen its status eclipsed. Egypt's military leaders controlled some local businesses, but they fiercely resented Gamal Mubarak, who was Hosni Mubarak's heir apparent. As a banker, he preferred to build his influence through business and political cronies rather than through the military, and those connected to him gained huge profits from government monopolies and deals with foreign investors. In Tunisia, Ben Ali kept the military at arm's length to ensure that it would not harbor political ambitions. Yet he let his wife and her relatives shake down Tunisian businessmen and build seaside mansions. In both countries, military resentments made the military less likely to crack down on mass protests; officers and soldiers would not kill their countrymen just to keep the Ben Ali and Mubarak families and their favorites in power.

A similar defection among factions of the Libyan military led to Qaddafi's rapid loss of large territories. As of this writing, however, Qaddafi's use of mercenaries and exploitation of tribal loyalties have prevented his fall. And in Yemen, Saleh has been kept afloat, if barely, by U.S. aid given in support of his opposition to Islamist terrorists and by the tribal and regional divisions among his opponents. Still, if the opposition unites, as it seems to be doing, and the United States becomes reluctant to back his increasingly repressive regime, Saleh could be the next sultan to topple.

The Revolutions' Limits

As of this writing, Sudan and Syria, the other sultanistic regions in the region, have not seen major popular protests. Yet Bashir's corruption and the concentration of wealth in Khartoum have become brazen. One of the historic rationales for his regime—keeping the whole of Sudan under northern control—recently disappeared with southern Sudan's January 2011 vote in favor of independence. In Syria, Assad has so far retained nationalist support because of his hard-line policies toward Israel and Lebanon. He still maintains the massive state employment programs that have kept Syrians passive for decades, but he has no mass base of support and is dependent on a tiny elite, whose corruption is increasingly notorious. Although it is hard to say how staunch the elite and military support for Bashir and Assad is, both regimes are probably even weaker than they appear and could quickly crumble in the face of broad-based protests.

The region's monarchies are more likely to retain power. This is not because they face no calls for change. In fact, Morocco, Jordan, Oman, and the Persian Gulf kingdoms face the same demographic, educational, and economic challenges that the sultanistic regimes do, and they must reform to meet them. But the monarchies have one big advantage: their political structures are flexible. Modern monarchies can retain considerable executive power while ceding legislative power to elected parliaments. In times of unrest, crowds are more likely to protest for legislative change than for abandonment of the monarchy. This gives monarchs more room to maneuver to pacify the people. Facing protests in 1848, the monarchies in Germany and Italy, for example, extended their constitutions, reduced the absolute power of the king, and accepted elected legislatures as the price of avoiding further efforts at revolution.

In monarchies, moreover, succession can result in change and reform, rather than the destruction of the entire system. A dynastic succession is legitimate and may thus be welcomed rather than feared, as in a typical sultanistic state. For example, in Morocco in 1999, the public greeted King Mohammed VI's ascension to the throne with great hopes for change. And in fact, Mohammed VI has investigated some of the regime's previous legal abuses and worked to somewhat strengthen women's rights. He has calmed recent protests in Morocco by promising major constitutional reforms. In Bahrain, Jordan, Kuwait, Morocco, Oman, and Saudi Arabia, rulers will likely to be able to stay in office if they are willing to share their power with elected officials or hand the reins to a younger family member who heralds significant reforms.

The regime most likely to avoid significant change in the near term is Iran. Although Iran has been called a sultanistic regime, it is different in several respects: unlike any other regime in the region, the ayatollahs espouse an ideology of anti-Western Shiism and Persian nationalism that draws considerable support from ordinary people. This makes it more like a party-state with a mass base of support. Iran is also led by a combination of several strong leaders, not just one: Supreme Leader Ali Khamenei, President Mahmoud Ahmadinejad, and Parliamentary Chair Ali Larijani. So there is no one corrupt or inefficient sultan on which to focus dissent. Finally, the Iranian regime enjoys the support of the Basij, an ideologically committed militia, and the Revolutionary Guards, which are deeply intertwined with the government. There is little chance that these forces will defect in the face of mass protests.

After the Revolutions

Those hoping for Tunisia and Egypt to make the transition to stable democracy quickly will likely be disappointed. Revolutions are just the beginning of a long process. Even after a peaceful revolution, it generally takes half a decade for any type of stable regime to consolidate. If a civil war or a counterrevolution arises (as appears to be happening in Libya), the reconstruction of the state takes still longer.

In general, after the post-revolutionary honeymoon period ends, divisions within the opposition start to surface. Although holding new elections is a straightforward step, election campaigns and then decisions taken by new legislatures will open debates over taxation and state spending, corruption, foreign policy, the role of the military, the powers of the president, official policy on religious law and practice, minority rights, and so on. As conservatives, populists, Islamists, and modernizing reformers fiercely vie for power in Tunisia, Egypt, and perhaps Libya, those countries will likely face lengthy periods of abrupt government turnovers and policy reversals—similar to what

occurred in the Philippines and many Eastern European countries after their revolutions.

Some Western governments, having long supported Ben Ali and Mubarak as bulwarks against a rising tide of radical Islam, now fear that Islamist groups are poised to take over. The Muslim Brotherhood in Egypt is the best organized of the opposition groups there, and so stands to gain in open elections, particularly if elections are held soon, before other parties are organized. Yet the historical record of revolutions in sultanistic regimes should somewhat alleviate such concerns. Not a single sultan overthrown in the last 30 years—including in Haiti, the Philippines, Romania, Zaire, Indonesia, Georgia, and Kyrgyzstan—has been succeeded by an ideologically driven or radical government. Rather, in every case, the end product has been a flawed democracy—often corrupt and prone to authoritarian tendencies, but not aggressive or extremist.

This marks a significant shift in world history. Between 1949 and 1979, every revolution against a sultanistic regime—in China, Cuba, Vietnam, Cambodia, Iran, and Nicaragua—resulted in a communist or an Islamist government. At the time, most intellectuals in the developing world favored the communist model of revolution against capitalist states. And in Iran, the desire to avoid both capitalism and communism and the increasing popularity of traditional Shiite clerical authority resulted in a push for an Islamist government. Yet since the 1980s, neither the communist nor the Islamist model has had much appeal. Both are widely perceived as failures at producing economic growth and popular accountability—the two chief goals of all recent anti-sultanistic revolutions.

Noting that high unemployment spurred regime change, some in the United States have called for a Marshall Plan for the Middle East to stabilize the region. But in 1945, Europe had a history of prior democratic regimes and a devastated physical infrastructure that needed rebuilding. Tunisia and Egypt have intact economies with excellent recent growth records, but they need to build new democratic institutions. Pouring money into these countries before they have created accountable governments would only fuel corruption and undermine their progress toward democracy.

What is more, the United States and other Western nations have little credibility in the Middle East given their long support for sultanistic dictators. Any efforts to use aid to back certain groups or influence electoral outcomes are likely to arouse suspicion. What the revolutionaries need from outsiders is vocal support for the process of democracy, a willingness to accept all groups that play by democratic rules, and a positive response to any requests for technical assistance in institution building.

The greatest risk that Tunisia and Egypt now face is an attempt at counterrevolution by military conservatives, a group that has often sought to claim power after a sultan has been removed. This occurred in Mexico after Díaz was overthrown, in Haiti after Jean-Claude Duvalier's departure, and in the Philippines after Marcos' fall. And after Suharto was forced from power in Indonesia, the military exerted its strength by cracking down on independence movements in East Timor, which Indonesia had occupied since 1975.

In the last few decades, attempted counterrevolutions (such as those in the Philippines in 1987–88 and Haiti in 2004) have largely fizzled out. They have not reversed democratic gains or driven post-sultanistic regimes into the arms of extremists—religious or otherwise.

However, such attempts weaken new democracies and distract them from undertaking much-needed reforms. They can also provoke a radical reaction. If Tunisia's or Egypt's military attempts to claim power or block Islamists from participating in the new regime, or the region's monarchies seek to keep their regimes closed through repression rather than open them up via reforms, radical forces will only be strengthened. As one example, the opposition in Bahrain, which had been seeking constitutional reforms, has reacted to Saudi action to repress its protests by calling for the overthrow of Bahrain's monarchy instead of its reform. Inclusiveness should be the order of the day.

The other main threat to democracies in the Middle East is war. Historically, revolutionary regimes have hardened and become more radical in response to international conflict. It was not the fall of the Bastille but war with Austria that gave the radical Jacobins power during the French Revolution. Similarly, it was Iran's war with Iraq that gave Ayotallah Ruhollah Khomeini the opportunity to drive out Iran's secular moderates. In fact, the one event that may cause radicals to hijack the Middle Eastern revolutions is if Israeli anxiety or Palestinian provocations escalate hostility between Egypt and Israel, leading to renewed war.

That said, there is still reason for optimism. Prior to 2011, the Middle East stood out on the map as the sole remaining region in the world virtually devoid of democracy. The Jasmine and Nile Revolutions look set to change all that. Whatever the final outcome, this much can be said: the rule of the sultans is coming to an end.

Critical Thinking

1. What factors account for the vulnerability of sultanistic regimes?
2. Why are monarchies more likely to retain power?
3. Why is democratic transition in the Middle East likely to be a lengthy process?
4. What are the threats to these nascent revolutions?

JACK A. GOLDSTONE is Virginia E. and John T. Hazel, Jr., Professor at George Mason University's School of Public Policy.

Good Soldier, Bad Cop

The Nasser model set the groundrules for Africa's post-colonial regimes: authoritarian, nationalist, single-party and underwritten by the military.

Egypt matters as an economic power and a political exemplar. That is why the scenes from Tahrir Square resonated across Africa so powerfully. Now, Egypt's revolutionaries are asking whether the military can be trusted to manage the transition to democracy.

It was the military high command that finally pushed Hosni Mubarak and Zine el Abidine Ben Ali out, but Tunisians and Egyptians are ambivalent about whether the soldiers will promote or steal the revolution. Civilian politicians have taken centre stage in Tunisia, but the military waits in the wings. In Egypt, the military keeps control at the head of the Supreme Military Council. Field Marshal Mohamed Hussein Tantawi has issued decrees paving the way for free elections and independent political parties.

The late distinguished Egyptian diplomat Mahmoud Kassem traced the origins of authoritarian rule in Africa to the Free Officers' revolution that toppled King Farouk in 1952 and ushered in Gamal Abdel Nasser. The Nasser model, said Kassem, set the groundrules for Africa's post-colonial regimes: authoritarian, nationalist, single-party and underwritten by the military.

Tunisia and Egypt put such regimes on notice. A million-strong security apparatus in Egypt, the generals calculated, could not hold back the aspirations of a large proportion of the 80 million other Egyptians. Under Nasser's model, the secret (and unsecret) police did the spying and torturing while the army and air force stayed away from daily repression, burnishing credentials as guardians of the national interest.

Those lines blurred in Libya under Colonel Muammar Gaddafi's Jamahiriya. Fearing coups, Gaddafi weakened the military, constrained it with revolutionary committees alongside an omnipresent secret police and set up armed units run by his sons outside the formal command structure. That is why regiments in eastern Libya joined the opposition and turned on their nominal commander-in-chief.

Will Africa's other armies go the Egyptian or Libyan route? In West Africa, home to more military coups than any other region, the soldiers are back in the barracks, for now. The Ghanaian and Nigerian militaries had followed Nasser's model, but as they grew as corrupt and dysfunctional as their civilian counterparts, the generals handed over power to elected regimes.

Different dynamics are at work in states such as Algeria, Angola, Mozambique and Zimbabwe, where the national army grew out of forces that had fought colonial rule. Such armies earned kudos as national liberators but have become fused to ruling parties that are running corrupt and repressive regimes.

The question haunting presidents Abdelaziz Bouteflika and Robert Mugabe is how their militaries would react to people power on the streets of Algiers and Harare. Bouteflika looks the more worried. As a key apparatchik in the post-colonial regimes in the 1960s and 1970s, Bouteflika returned to power in the 1990s determined to reduce the strength of the military. Some scores have yet to be settled. Should opposition to the regime gather momentum in the streets, the generals would not hesitate to suggest that Bouteflika go into retirement.

Mugabe gets on with the military, whose top brass get lucrative contracts and top jobs in government. Soldiers generally stay out of the hurly-burly while the police and special units such as the Green Bombers do the political killings and torture. Mugabe, one of Africa's canniest tacticians, is lucky that few of the generals trust his main opponent, Morgan Tsvangirai.

Realists in the officers' corps see that the 87-year-old Mugabe has now reached the endgame. Like their Egyptian counterparts, they will want to steer the coming transition without losing political influence, and they will not necessarily ask Comrade Mugabe for his advice.

Critical Thinking

1. What role did the military play in the political changes in the Middle East?

2. How can rulers weaken the armed forces' ability to force political change?

3. What are the prospects that armed forces in other African countries will play a role in political reform?

"Moderates" Redefined: How to Deal with Political Islam

It is imperative for the United States to engage mainstream Islamic political parties that are committed to gradual change through the ballot box.

Emile Nakhleh

Political Islam has been part of the modern Middle East landscape for several decades, but until recently the United States has rarely perceived a need to engage it. After the attacks against New York and Washington on September 11, 2001, the administration of George W. Bush painted political Islam in the Middle East, as in the rest of the Muslim world, with the broad brush of terrorism. The administration saw no meaningful differences between the minority of Islamic activists who support violence and terrorism and the majority of activists who reject the radical message of Osama bin Laden and his Al Qaeda organization.

Partly as a result, Muslims worldwide perceived Bush's global war on terror as a war on Islam, which they rejected outright. Middle East Islamic activists in particular viewed the invasions of Iraq and Afghanistan, along with Washington's continuing strong support for Israel, as amounting to an American attack on Muslim lands. Islamic activists and mainstream Islamic political parties and movements identified, as other examples of Washington's anti-Islamic posture, the tacit US support for Israel's Lebanon war in 2006 and Gaza war in 2008–09, the abuses of prisoners at Guantánamo Bay and Abu Ghraib, and the detention of thousands of Muslims in Iraq, Afghanistan, and elsewhere.

Islamic activists also viewed the cozy relationship between the United States and Arab authoritarian regimes, as well as Washington's refusal to accept Hamas's electoral victory in Gaza in 2006, as indications of America's lack of commitment to democracy and human rights, and its lack of interest in reaching out to civil society institutions in the region.

Middle Eastern regimes, for their part, were suspicious of the Bush administration's call for democracy. Elites in the region—both Islamic and secular—viewed as hypocritical the contradiction between Washington's rhetoric of democracy and its continued coddling of dictatorial regimes. The United States was seen as uninterested in engaging Arab civil society to promote civil rights, political reform, and democratization. According to opinion polls, Arab publics perceived the United States from 2003 to 2008 as advocating regime change in any country whose policies contradicted American interests in the region. Washington's bellicose rhetoric against

Iran and Syria following the fall of Saddam Hussein's regime in 2003, and its undermining of the freely elected Hamas government in the Palestinians' Gaza territory, were cited as reasons for low favorability ratings accorded the United States and Bush's policies in the region.

Some academics, think tanks, and intelligence analysts in recent years have urged US policy makers to engage credible civil society institutions in the Middle East—despite the objections of entrenched authoritarian regimes—in order to encourage political and educational reforms in these societies and spur governments to open up public space for mainstream groups to participate in the political process. They have pointed out that regimes' repressive measures to curtail civil rights and freedoms of speech, assembly, and political organization have created, in many countries, a political landscape featuring just two paradigms—the authoritarian paradigm imposed by the regimes, and a radical paradigm promulgated by Al Qaeda, bin Laden, and his deputy, Ayman al-Zawahiri.

Consequently, these experts have argued that, in order to achieve the strategic objective of political reform and democratization in the region, it is imperative for the United States to engage mainstream Islamic political parties that are committed to gradual change through the ballot box. Examples of such parties and movements include the Muslim Brotherhood in Egypt, the Islamic Action Front in Jordan, the Islamic Constitutional Movement in Kuwait, Al Wifaq in Bahrain, Hamas in Palestine, Hezbollah in Lebanon, and the Justice and Development Party in Morocco.

In opposition to this idea, other analysts have contended that engaging Islamic groups would undercut the stability of pro-US authoritarian regimes and would embolden Islamic movements to contest—and win—elections, thereby paving the way for potentially anti-American Islamic regimes to emerge. Furthermore, Islamic regimes might impose Islamic law (*sharia*), which would restrict civil rights and personal freedoms and undermine the ability of liberal, secular organizations to participate in the political process. According to this argument, the "resistance" (*muqawama*) ideology of some of the Islamic parties would determine their behavior in government, thereby exacerbating conflicts and inviting more tension between regimes and societies.

The key belief underpinning opposition to engagement is that the United States should abandon the strategic policy goal of promoting democracy and continue to manage its bilateral relations with friendly Middle Eastern regimes based on the dictates of America's traditional national interests in the region—economic, political, and strategic. But in fact, political and social realities on the ground raise serious doubts about the validity of this view. And, fortunately for US-Muslim relations in the Middle East and elsewhere, the Barack Obama administration has adopted a more nuanced, sensible, and pragmatic approach.

Obama Extends a Hand

President Obama's post-inauguration statements on political Islam, along with two major speeches—in April 2009 in Ankara, and in June in Cairo—have resonated well in the Muslim world. The speeches reflected a willingness to move beyond the confrontational policy of the previous administration and toward a new era of "smart diplomacy." The bounce from Obama's conciliatory rhetoric among Arabs and Muslims will be long-lasting if it is followed by significant policy shifts—on human rights, political reform, democracy, war crimes, the closing of the Guantánamo prison—and by renewed efforts at the highest level to resolve the Israeli-Palestinian conflict.

The administration's recent direct contacts with Iranian officials—despite Tehran's heavy-handed silencing of dissent over the June presidential election—again signals Obama's commitment to engaging the Muslim world and moving from confrontation to diplomacy. Efforts to decouple elements of the Afghan Taliban (many of whom are just fighting the presence of foreign troops in their country) from the more globally dangerous Al Qaeda and the Pakistani Taliban are another affirmation by the Obama administration that it seeks simultaneously to fight terrorism and extend a peaceful hand to the wider Muslim world.

The bad news about Afghanistan is that the fire-fight is becoming much bloodier and the Taliban are emboldened. Still, Obama's historic Cairo speech, in which he detailed a vision of future relations with the Muslim world, helped put to rest the perception among many Muslims that the war on terror is a war on Islam. Also, in addressing "Muslim communities," not Muslim regimes, the president in Cairo seemed to signal that engagement will be broad-based, will not be funneled only through regimes, and will focus on economic and educational opportunities that will help improve quality of life in these societies and provide youth with more hope for the future.

Obama's approach to engaging the Muslim world seems to reflect several core themes. First, America is not at war with Islam. Second, all religions share certain "noble" ideas, including justice, tolerance, fairness, and a desire to make choices freely. Likewise, people worldwide aspire for dignity, respect, equality, economic opportunity, progress, and security. Third, people in different societies, regardless of race, religion, and color, should be able to select their governments freely, and these governments should be transparent, accountable, just, and committed to the rule of law.

Fourth, the United States is committed to engaging Muslim communities to help foster a tolerant and creative vision of Islam—but Muslims themselves, not America, must drive the debate. Fifth, the United States is committed to working with Muslim communities to settle regional conflicts on the basis of justice, fairness, and equity. And in the pursuit of these objectives, Washington will partner with American Muslims, who can act as a bridge between the United States and the Muslim world.

John Brennan, the assistant to the president for homeland security and counterterrorism, in an August 6, 2009, speech at the Center for Strategic and International Studies in Washington, elaborated further on the administration's approach. Brennan emphasized two points from the Cairo speech. One is that America's values and its commitment to justice, respect, fairness, and peace are the most effective weapons in its arsenal to fight the forces of radicalism and terrorism. The other is that bringing hope, educational promise, and economic opportunity to the youth in Muslim societies offers the best defense against the false promises and death and destruction promoted by Al Qaeda and its affiliates.

An engagement strategy can succeed in the long term only if it is accompanied by tangible policies that would reflect a change of direction in America's posture toward the Arab Muslim world. Examples of such policies include withdrawal from Iraq, ending the war in Afghanistan, and a serious push to halt expansion of Israeli settlements in the West Bank and to resolve the Israeli-Palestinian conflict. One Muslim interlocutor in the region once told me, "You can't sell hot air—engagement without substance will not succeed."

It is equally critical, however, that engagement include a concerted effort to communicate with Muslim society and civil society organizations by promoting economic, educational, and women's rights initiatives—and by dealing directly with Islamic political groups. In this respect, the Obama administration continues to engage regimes bilaterally in the service of national interests, but it is also exploring avenues to engage Islamic political parties and civil society religious groups. Key administration officials apparently believe that engaging these communities will help empower them to effect political reform from within.

Engaging these groups—sensibly, pragmatically, and openly—would make strategic sense for the West.

And with good reason. An examination of the recent legislative record of mainstream Islamic groups, their support within their own communities, and their opposition to the rising neo-Salafi extremist trend, clearly shows that engaging these groups—sensibly, pragmatically, and openly—would make strategic sense for the West. It would also improve America's standing among Muslims worldwide, and help foster an atmosphere of mutual trust and respect between the United States and the Muslim world.

Engaging Arguments

Several trends in political Islam support the argument for a robust engagement policy. First, the Islamization of Middle East politics has changed qualitatively and quantitatively since 9/11, as we have seen growing demands for economic, educational, political, and social justice in Muslim societies. Numerous Islamic political parties and movements have become more engaged in the political process through elections. Meanwhile, authoritarian regimes have used the specter of terrorism to thwart efforts to democratize and to still all demands for political reform, regardless of whether these demands are voiced by secular opposition groups or by Islamic parties.

Second, religious-nationalist ideology is driving Islamic politics at the state level in most Muslim states, but particularly in the greater Middle East. In fact, religion has become an ideological force motivating action by, and defining the interests of, both states and non-state actors. Because of regime corruption and repression—along with the bankruptcy and marginalization of traditional secular elites, largely due to their association with regimes—Islamic political parties have gained legitimacy as agents of reform and as advocates of transparent, accountable government and of the rule of law.

Third, the relationship between religion and politics is changing, largely because of demographic and economic stresses, globalization, the communications revolution, entrenched authoritarianism in many Muslim countries, a weak identification with the state, and the general failure of secular nationalist ideologies. Religions and religious affiliation have become drivers of the political process across the globe—from Russia to India, from Ankara to Kuala Lumpur.

Fourth, because of regimes' diminishing legitimacy and the weakening of public identification with the state, Islam has become an identity anchor for millions of Muslims. Religious programs broadcast on global satellite television networks are able to carry the "sacred word" from Mecca and other centers of Islam to the remotest villages in West Africa, Central Asia, the Indus Valley, and western China—and of course throughout the Middle East.

Fifth, Islamic political activism in the Middle East, as in the rest of the Muslim world, has become more diverse and complex. Such diversity—cultural, economic, historical, political, religious, and demographic—dictates that, before Washington engages these groups, US policy makers must understand the varied historical narratives to which different Islamic groups cling, the reasons why entrenched authoritarian regimes oppose political participation by Islamic activists, the indigenous and country-specific agendas of Islamic groups, and their legislative behavior in national assemblies.

An Energized Debate

Sixth, political ideology has become embedded in an energized debate among Muslim activists on Islamic blogs and in the media, both print and electronic. The debate has focused on at least three themes. One is the future vision of Islam that Muslims should pursue, and whether such a vision should be limited to the moral dictates of the faith or should expand to the political and social realms. Another topic is whether Islamic political parties should continue to participate in the political process through elections even under regimes that actively undermine the democratic process, or whether they should instead reject politics and return to their core mission of proselytization (da'wa). Still another issue is whether Islamic political parties, which have traditionally been committed to the implementation of sharia, can equally maintain a long-term commitment to democracy and pluralism as these terms are understood in the West.

Seventh, Middle Eastern Islamic political parties remain territorially focused and committed to indigenous agendas. They do not share the global jihadist ideology of Al Qaeda and its affiliates. The strategic goal of these parties' struggles and activism is to liberate their territories from occupation and safeguard the political, economic, and security status of their people. In fact, Al Qaeda's second-in-command, Zawahiri, in 2006 severely criticized Islamic

political parties in the region—including the Egyptian Muslim Brotherhood, the Palestinian Hamas, and the Moroccan Justice and Development Party—for participating in national elections. The parties in turn openly and forcefully rejected Al Qaeda's criticism.

Eighth, Islamic parties' disagreements with the United States and other Western powers in recent years have been driven by specific policies, not by disputes over governance issues. Public opinion polls—administered by organizations including Pew, Gallup, the BBC, and Zogby—have clearly shown that majorities of Muslims, including in the Middle East, endorse fair and free elections, transparent and accountable government, a free press, an independent judiciary, and the rule of law. Their disagreements with the United States, according to these polls, have been driven by specific policies, such as the Iraq War and US support for Israeli actions, which they consider aggressive, a threat to world peace, and anti-Islamic.

Ninth, mainstream Islamic political parties have fought the rise of the new Salafi ideology because of its conservative, intolerant, and exclusivist bent. The Salafi ideology, which in some cases has been supported by regimes as an antidote to mainstream Islamic activism, is grounded in a narrow reading of religious texts. It preaches an extremist version of Wahhabi Islam (which insists on a return to an original, purer form of the faith). It calls for the establishment of a strict version of Islamic law that imposes a rigid moral code on society, separates the sexes, and restricts women's participation in education, culture, and business.

A bloody conflict in August 2009 between Hamas and the Salafi Jund Ansar Allah group in Gaza, which featured an attack on a mosque in Rafah and the killing of the Salafi leader Shaykh Abu Mousa, illustrates the threat that mainstream Islamic parties across the Middle East are facing from the Salafi trend. Engaging mainstream Islamic political parties could help empower them to fight the Salafi movement in Middle Eastern societies, including Palestine, Egypt, Lebanon, Yemen, Morocco, Sudan, and Kuwait.

Islam and Potholes

Debate about Islamic political parties' participation in politics has focused on the question of whether their commitment to the electoral process is a tactical maneuver to get them into power, or whether they have made a strategic decision to pursue gradual political change through politics. One could ask: If these parties have espoused sharia as the basis for their existence, how strong or sustainable can their commitment to democracy and pluralism be? In fact, interviews with many Muslim activists over the years, and an examination of the electoral campaign platforms and legislative agendas of some Islamic political parties, reveal that their commitment to nationalist causes or social justice often supersedes their commitment to Islamic law.

Islamic parties in general have undergone a transformation in their religious ideology. They have moved away from their original "charters"—which usually espouse a strong commitment to sharia—and now focus instead on social, economic, and political practices. Once in a legislature, they have worked with other political parties to pass legislation dealing with roads, public utilities, and other bread-and-butter issues.

Hamas's charter, for example, which was written in the 1980s before the group's leaders even decided to form a political party, embodied the movement's religious commitment, its vision of Palestinian society and territory, and its opposition to participating in the political process. Although Lebanon's Hezbollah was launched with significant Iranian support, it has built an impressive political constituency in a community marked by impoverishment, deprivation, and dispossession.

A review of the political programs of Hamas and Hezbollah, two of the Middle East's most active political parties, shows that, although both parties initially scorned electoral politics, they subsequently became avid players in the political game and participated successfully in national elections. Hamas won Legislative Council elections in 2006, and Hezbollah has successfully competed in Lebanese parliamentary elections since 1992, including the spring 2009 elections.

The national political programs of Hamas and Hezbollah share two characteristics: a deep commitment to social justice and community development; and the embodiment of "resistance." The religious identity that each espouses is wedded to conceptions of resistance through community service and armed opposition to occupation. While they strongly draw on their Sunni (Hamas) and Shiite (Hezbollah) religious cultural heritages, neither group has made the imposition of sharia or the creation of an Islamic state its dominant objective. Hamas has not advocated reestablishment of the "caliphate." While Hezbollah officially advocates the *Vilayet-e Faqih,* or rule of Islamic judges, for many years it has accepted that the creation of such a system in religiously mixed Lebanon is infeasible and very unlikely.

Hezbollah and Hamas have been able to face down Israeli military assaults—a feat that conventional Arab armies have failed to accomplish since the creation of the state of Israel. As a result, both groups at times have enjoyed widespread popularity in the Arab world, even in more secular segments of society. According to public opinion polls, Hamas and Hezbollah symbolize for many Arabs a successful Islamic engagement in politics, a strong commitment to social justice, and a rejection of corruption and authoritarianism. Not surprisingly, Arab regimes, including the corruption-ridden Palestinian Authority in Ramallah under Mahmoud Abbas, have become wary of the success of Hamas and Hezbollah and have often opposed their rise, influence, and activities, and even turned a blind eye to Israel's recent military attempts to defeat them.

Thus Islamic parties—even beyond Hamas and Hezbollah—have over time changed their political ideologies and tempered their commitment to sharia in the face of the practical demands of electoral and legislative politics. In the early 1990s, some of these parties refused to participate in the electoral process because of the "un-Islamic" behavior of regimes; by the late 1990s, most had decided to take part in national elections and play the game of politics regardless of the nature of the government.

While Islamic parties still evince a commitment to Islamic law, sharia is so diverse and multifaceted that dedication to it need not imply a conservative Wahhabi-like or retrograde Taliban-like agenda. Political pragmatism, rather than purist religious ideology, has become the guiding principle of the Islamization of politics in Muslim-majority countries, including in the Middle East.

The Radical Element

Terrorists both in the Middle East and globally generally follow the radical paradigm of bin Laden and Al Qaeda, which claims that Islam—faith and territory—is under attack and that the "enemy" consists of the Christian Crusaders headed by the United States, the Zionists represented by Israel, and pro-Western Arab and Muslim regimes. Bin Laden further maintains that in the face of this attack, jihad by whatever means is a duty for all Muslims, and that the killing of innocent civilians and the use of weapons of mass destruction are justified.

Providing a religious justification for terrorism has been an effective recruiting strategy, especially among alienated youth with limited education and poor economic prospects. In justifying terrorism, bin Laden has presented violent jihad as a struggle between good and evil. The struggle, he argues, will continue until the "final days."

On this last point there is a disagreement between Al Qaeda, as an advocate of global jihad, and country-specific Islamist organizations such as Hamas and Hezbollah, which aspire to achieve territorial autonomy or independence. These parties do not share Al Qaeda's millenarian ideology and focus instead on their own objectives.

Although in the past decade the vast majority of Muslims worldwide has not renounced terrorism forcefully and openly, more and more Muslims in the last three years have been speaking out against terrorism and the wanton killing of innocent civilians. Moderate Muslim thinkers have argued that relations between Muslims and non-Muslims need not be full of conflict, as bin Laden has postulated. They also suggest that the Koran, revealed to the prophet Muhammad in seventh-century Arabia, must be transformed to fit Muslim life in a twenty-first–century globalized world.

Muslim thinkers in both Western and Muslim countries have argued that certain aspects of Western political culture, including parliamentary democracy, political and social pluralism, women's rights, civil society, and human rights, are compatible with Islamic scripture and traditions. As noted, according to many public opinion polls, most Muslims believe in these values. Mainstream Islamic political parties in the Middle East also endorse this view of democracy.

The radical paradigm promulgated by Al Qaeda appears to be on the wane because of its opposition to ideas that mainstream Islamic parties are promoting.

Thus, the radical paradigm promulgated by Al Qaeda appears to be on the wane today precisely because of its opposition to the ideas of tolerance, inclusion, and political participation that the mainstream Islamic parties are promoting. More and more Muslims are denouncing the killing of innocent civilians—Muslim and non-Muslim—and are beginning to question openly and publicly the logic of violence. More and more Islamic activists are choosing local and national causes over global jihad. And despite Al Qaeda's strong and persistent opposition to "man-made" democracy and elections, more and more Islamic political parties are participating in national elections and in the mundane activities of electoral politics and pragmatic governance. It is no coincidence that the radical political paradigm is declining at a time when Islamic parties have increasingly entered the political fray.

A Fraught Task

Regardless of Al Qaeda's fortunes, religious extremism and political radicalism will persist in the Middle East for years to come. This is the case because of factors having little or nothing to do with Islamic ideology—factors such as entrenched authoritarianism, weak state legitimacy, continuing disregard for civil and human rights, the rise of non-state actors and sub-state loyalties, systemic state corruption, economic stagnation, and the failure so far to find a solution to the Israeli-Palestinian conflict.

Several Arab regimes have used the fight against terrorism as an excuse to deny their peoples the right to participate in the political process freely, openly, and without harassment. Yet the record of Islamic political parties' participation in electoral politics, over several national elections, does not support the regimes' argument that such participation destabilizes society or undermines national security.

Indeed, it may be time for senior policy makers in Western countries to revisit their use of the term "moderate" when dealing with the Middle East. Policy makers have tended to bestow the "moderate" moniker on pro-Western governments despite their autocratic nature, while grouping Islamic activists generically into the "radical" category. But equating authoritarian regimes with "moderation" has resulted in a perception of hypocrisy and has helped drive the very radicalization that the West has sought to counter. Meanwhile, the effort to counter radicalization, when paired with a refusal to deal with Islamic groups, has yielded poor results. It might be more prudent, as well as honest, to describe such regimes as "friendly" or "pro-US" rather than "moderate."

> **Policy makers have tended to bestow the "moderate" moniker on pro-Western governments while grouping Islamic activists generically into the "radical" category.**

Reaching out to the vast majority of Muslims will require a long-term commitment in time, resources, and personnel. It will require a thorough knowledge of the cultures involved, sophisticated influence operations, strategically developed public diplomacy campaigns, a coherent and carefully crafted message, and utilization of credible indigenous Muslim voices.

Engaging Islamic political parties is likewise a process fraught with challenges, especially since most "friendly" regimes in the Middle East are opposed to such engagement. Some Islamic parties will pose particularly thorny dilemmas for the United States. Hamas and Hezbollah, for example, are considered terrorist organizations under US law. Some Iraqi Islamic parties are closely aligned with Iran. And a few Shiite movements in Iraq and Bahrain advocate sectarian autonomy.

As the Obama administration proceeds with implementing principles that the president enunciated in his Cairo speech, policy makers will have to find ways to convince regimes that engaging civil society institutions and non-state actors in their societies will not necessarily undermine those regimes. Policy makers must continually point out that, if the people in a particular country have the right to choose their government freely, they will be more invested in social peace and political stability, which in the long run will minimize tensions between state and society.

This amounts to a daunting task, to be sure. But in the final analysis, engagement with Muslim societies must include the Islamic parties and movements in those societies. To believe otherwise is damaging both to regional stability and to America's strategic interests and standing in the Muslim world.

Critical Thinking

1. How do many Muslims regard US involvement in the Islamic world?

2. What are the arguments for and against engaging mainstream Islamic movements?

3. How has President Obama's outreach been received in the Middle East?

4. What themes does Obama's policy reflect?

5. What trends in political Islam suggest some support for this engagement effort?

EMILE NAKHLEH is a former senior intelligence officer with the US Central Intelligence Agency, where he served as director of the Political Islam Strategic Analysis program and chief of regional analysis for the Near East and South Asia. He is the author of *A Necessary Engagement: Reinventing America's Relations with the Muslim World* (Princeton University Press, 2008).

From *Current History*, December 2009, pp. 402–404, 406–409. Copyright © 2009 by Current History, Inc. Reprinted by permission.

The Islamists Are Not Coming

Religious parties in the Muslim world are hardly the juggernauts they've been made out to be.

CHARLES KURZMAN AND IJLAL NAQVI

D o Muslims automatically vote Islamic? That's the concern conjured up by strongmen from Tunis to Tashkent, and plenty of Western experts agree. They point to the political victories of Islamic parties in Egypt, Palestine, and Turkey in recent years and warn that more elections across the Islamic world could turn power over to anti-democratic fundamentalists.

But these victories turn out to be exceptions, not the political rule. When we examined results from parliamentary elections in all Muslim societies, we found a very different pattern: Given the choice, voters tend to go with secular parties, not religious ones. Over the past 40 years, 86 parliamentary elections in 20 countries have included one or more Islamic parties, according to annual reports from the Inter-Parliamentary Union. Voters in these places have overwhelmingly turned up their noses at such parties. Eighty percent of these Islamic parties earned less than 20 percent of the vote, and a majority got less than 10 percent—hardly landslide victories. The same is true even over the last few years, with numbers barely changing since 2001.

80% Share of Islamic parties that earned 20% or less of the vote over the last 40 years.

True, Islamic parties have won a few well-publicized breakthrough victories, such as in Algeria in 1991 and Palestine in 2006. But far more often, Islamic parties tend to do very poorly. What's more, the more free and fair an election is, the worse the Islamic parties do. By our calculations, the average percentage of seats won by Islamic parties in relatively free elections is 10 points lower than in less free ones.

Even if they don't win, Islamic parties often find themselves liberalized by the electoral process. We found that Islamic party platforms are less likely to focus on sharia law or armed jihad in freer elections and more likely to uphold democracy and women's rights. And even in more authoritarian countries, Islamic party platforms have shifted over the course of multiple elections toward more liberal positions: Morocco's Justice and Development Party and Jordan's Islamic Action Front both stripped sharia law from their platforms over the last several years.

These are still culturally conservative parties, by any standard, but their decision to run for office places them at odds with Islamic revolutionaries. In many cases, they're actually risking their lives. Almost two decades ago, even before his alliance with Osama bin Laden, Egyptian jihadist Ayman al-Zawahiri wrote a tract condemning the Muslim Brotherhood's abandonment of revolutionary methods in favor of electoral politics. "Whoever labels himself as a Muslim democrat, or a Muslim who calls for democracy, is like saying he is a Jewish Muslim or a Christian Muslim," he wrote. In Iraq, Sunni Islamic revolutionaries recently renewed their campaign "to start killing all those participating in the political process," according to a warning received by a Sunni politician who was subsequently assassinated in Mosul.

What enrages Zawahiri and his ilk is that Islamists keep ignoring demands to stay out of parliamentary politics. Despite threats from terrorists and a cold shoulder from voters, more and more Islamic parties are entering the electoral process. A quarter-century ago, many of these movements were trying to overthrow the state and create an Islamic society, inspired by the Iranian Revolution. Now, disillusioned with revolution, they are working within the secular system.

But today's problems for Islamic parties may recall an earlier historical moment, the watershed period of the early 20th century when demands for democracy and human rights first gained mass support in Muslim societies from the Russian Empire to the Ottoman Empire. Then as now, violent Islamic movements such as the Ottoman-era Islamic Unity Society objected to electoral politics. But that was not what ultimately undermined democracy in Muslim societies. Instead, secular autocrats, such as Mustafa Kemal Ataturk in Turkey and Reza Shah in Iran, suppressed pro-democratic Islamic movements, driving Islamists underground and helping to radicalize them.

Today, too, dictators and terrorists are conspiring to keep Islamic political parties from competing freely for votes. Government repression has been successful in one sense—Islamic parties have won few elections. In a broader sense, however, it is failing: According to the World Values Survey, which has polled cultural attitudes around the world, support for sharia is one-third lower in countries with relatively free elections than in other Muslim societies. In other words, suppressing Islamic movements has only made them more popular. Perhaps democratization is not such a gift to Islamists after all.

Critical Thinking

1. How have Islamic parties fared in terms of voter support?
2. Under what circumstances do these parties fare the worst?
3. What impact do free elections seem to have on Islamic parties?
4. What effect does suppressing Islamic party participation have?

Charles Kurzman is professor of sociology and **Ijlal Naqvi** is a sociology graduate student at the University of North Carolina at Chapel Hill.

Reprinted in entirety by McGraw-Hill with permission from *Foreign Policy*, January/February 2010, p. 34. www.foreignpolicy.com. © 2010 Washingtonpost.Newsweek Interactive, LLC.

The Transformation of Hamas

Palestine's Islamic movement has subtly changed its uncompromising posture on Israel.

Fawaz A. Gerges

Something is stirring within the Hamas body politic, a moderating trend that, if nourished and engaged, could transform Palestinian politics and the Arab-Israeli peace process. There are unmistakable signs that the religiously based radical movement has subtly changed its uncompromising posture on Israel. Although low-key and restrained, those shifts indicate that the movement is searching for a formula that addresses the concerns of Western powers yet avoids alienating its social base.

Far from impulsive and unexpected, Hamas's shift reflects a gradual evolution occurring over the past five years. The big strategic turn occurred in 2005, when Hamas decided to participate in the January 2006 legislative elections and thus tacitly accepted the governing rules of the Palestinian Authority (PA), one of which includes recognition of Israel. Ever since, top Hamas leaders have repeatedly declared they will accept a resolution of the conflict along the 1967 borders. The Damascus-based Khaled Meshal, head of Hamas's political bureau and considered a hardliner, acknowledged as much in 2008. "We are realists," he said, who recognize that there is "an entity called Israel." Pressed by an Australian journalist on policy changes Hamas might make, Meshal asserted that the organization has shifted on several key points: "Hamas has already changed—we accepted the national accords for a Palestinian state based on the 1967 borders, and we took part in the 2006 Palestinian elections."

Another senior Hamas leader, Ghazi Hamad, was more specific than Meshal, telling journalists in January 2009 that Hamas would be satisfied with ending Israeli control over the Palestinian areas occupied in the 1967 war—the West Bank, Gaza and East Jerusalem. In other words, Hamas would not hold out for liberation of the land that currently includes Israel.

Previously Hamas moderates had called at times for a *tahdia* (a minor truce, or "calm") or *hudna* (a longer-term truce, lasting as long as fifty years), which implies some measure of recognition, if only tacit. The moderates justified their policy shift by using Islamic terms (in Islamic history *hudnas* sometimes develop into permanent truces). Now leaders appear to be going further; they have made a concerted effort to re-educate

the rank and file about the necessity of living side by side with their Jewish neighbors, and in so doing mentally prepare them for a permanent settlement. In Gaza's mosques pro-Hamas clerics have begun to cite the example of the famed twelfth-century Muslim military commander and statesman Saladin, who after liberating Jerusalem from the Crusaders allowed them to retain a coastal state in the Levant. The point is that if Saladin could tolerate the warring, bloodthirsty Crusaders, then today's Palestinians should be willing to live peacefully with a Jewish state in their midst.

The Saladin story is important because it provides Hamas with religious legitimacy and allows it to justify the change of direction to followers. Hamas's raison d'être rests on religious legitimation; its leaders understand that they neglect this at their peril. Western leaders and students of international politics should acknowledge that Hamas can no more abandon its commitment to Islamism than the United States can abandon its commitment to liberal democracy. That does not mean Hamas is incapable of change or compromise but simply that its political identity is strongly constituted by its religious legitimation.

It should be emphasized as well that Hamas is not monolithic on the issue of peace. There are multiple, clashing viewpoints and constituencies within the movement. Over the years I have interviewed more than a dozen leaders inside and outside the occupied territories. Although on the whole Hamas's public rhetoric calls for the liberation of all of historic Palestine not only the territories occupied in 1967, a healthy debate has grown both within and without.

Several factors have played a role in the transformation. They include the burden of governing a war-torn Gaza and the devastation from Israel's 2008–09 attack, which has caused incalculable human suffering and increasing public dissatisfaction in Gaza with Hamas rule.

Before the 2006 parliamentary elections, Hamas was known for its suicide bombers, not its bureaucrats, even though between 2002 and 2006 the organization moved from rejectionism toward participation in a political framework that is a direct product of the Oslo peace process of the 1990s. After the elections, the shift continued. "It is much more difficult to run a government than to oppose and resist Israeli occupation," a senior Hamas leader told me while on official business in Egypt in 2007. "If we do not provide the goods to our people, they'll disown us." Hamas is not just a political party. It's a social movement, and as such it has a long record of concern about and close attention to public opinion. Given the gravity of deteriorating conditions in Gaza and Hamas's weak performance during last year's fighting, it should be no surprise that the organization has undergone a period of fairly intense soul-searching and reassessment of strategic options.

Ironically, despite the West's refusal to regard the Hamas government as legitimate and despite the continuing brutal siege of Gaza, demands for democratic governance within Gaza are driving change. Yet Hamas leaders are fully aware of the danger of alienating more-hardline factions if they show weakness or water down their position and move toward de facto recognition of Israel without getting something substantive in return. Hamas's strategic predicament lies in striking a balance between, on the one hand, a new moderating and maturing sensibility and, on the other, insistence on the right and imperative of armed resistance. This difficult balance often explains the tensions and contradictions in Hamas's public and private pronouncements.

What is striking about Hamas's shift toward the peace process is that it has come at a time of critical challenges from Al Qaeda–like jihadist groups; a low-intensity civil war with rival Fatah, the ruling party of the PA; and a deteriorating humanitarian situation in Gaza.

Last summer a militant group called Jund Ansar Allah, or the Warriors of God, one of a handful of Al Qaeda–inspired factions, declared the establishment of an Islamic emirate in Gaza—a flagrant rejection of Hamas's authority. Hamas security forces struck instantly and mercilessly at the Warriors, killing more than twenty members, including the group's leader, Abdel-Latif Moussa. In one stroke, the Hamas leadership sent a message to foes and friends alike that it will not tolerate global jihadist groups like Al Qaeda, which want to turn Gaza into a theater of transnational jihad.

Despite the crushing of Moussa's outfit, the extremist challenge persists. The Israeli siege, in place since 2006, along with the suffering and despair it has caused among Gaza's 1.4 million inhabitants, has driven hundreds of young Palestinians into the arms of small Salafist extremist factions that accuse Hamas of forfeiting the armed struggle and failing to implement Shariah law. Hamas leaders appear to be worried about the proliferation of these factions and have instructed clerics to warn worshipers against joining such bands.

Compared with these puritanical and nihilistic groups, Hamas is well within the mainstream of Islamist politics. Operationally and ideologically, there are huge differences between Hamas and jihadi extremists such as Al Qaeda—and there's a lot of bad blood. Hamas is a broad-based religious/nationalist resistance whose focus and violence is limited to Palestine/Israel, while Al Qaeda is a small, transnational terrorist network that has carried out attacks worldwide. Al Qaeda

leaders Osama bin Laden and Ayman al-Zawahiri have vehemently criticized Hamas for its willingness to play politics and negotiate with Israel. Hamas leaders have responded that they know what is good for their people, and they have made it crystal clear they have no interest in transnational militancy. Their overriding goal is political and nationalist rather than ideological and global: to empower Palestinians and liberate the occupied Palestinian territories.

Unlike Al Qaeda and other fringe factions, Hamas is a viable social movement with an extensive social network and a large popular base that has been estimated at several hundred thousand. Given its tradition of sensitivity and responsiveness to Palestinian public opinion, a convincing argument could be made that the recent changes in the organization's conduct can be attributed to the high levels of poverty, unemployment and isolation of Palestinians in Gaza, who fear an even greater deterioration of conditions there.

A further example of Hamas's political and social priorities is its decision to agree in principle to an Egyptian-brokered deal that sketches out a path to peace with Fatah. After two years of bitter and violent division, the warring parties came very close to agreement in October. The deal collapsed at the last moment, but talks continue. There are two points to make about the Egyptian role: first, Hamas leaders say they feel somewhat betrayed by the Egyptians because after pressure from the Americans, Cairo unilaterally revised the final agreed-upon text without consulting the Hamas negotiating team. Second, many Palestinian and Arab observers think Egypt is in no hurry to conclude the Fatah-Hamas talks. They contend that faced with regional challenges and rivals (Iran, Turkey, Syria and Saudi Arabia), the Mubarak regime views its brokering process in the Palestinian-Israeli theater as an important regional asset and a way to solidify its relationship with Washington.

Despite its frequently reactionary rhetoric, Hamas is a rational actor, a conclusion reached by former Mossad chief Ephraim Halevy, who also served as Ariel Sharon's national security adviser and who is certainly not a peacenik. The Hamas leadership has undergone a transformation "right under our very noses" by recognizing that "its ideological goal is not attainable and will not be in the foreseeable future," Halevy wrote in the Israeli daily *Yediot Ahronot* just before the 2008 attack on Gaza. He believes Hamas is ready and willing to accept the establishment of a Palestinian state within the 1967 borders. The US Army Strategic Studies Institute published a similar analysis just before the Israeli offensive, concluding that Hamas was considering a shift of its position and that "Israel's stance toward [Hamas]…has been a major obstacle to substantive peacemaking."

Indeed, it could be argued that Hamas has moved closer to a vision of peace consistent with international law and consensus (two separate states in historic Palestine, divided more or less along the '67 borders with East Jerusalem as the capital of Palestine, and recognition of all states in the region) than the current Israeli governing coalition. Prime Minister Benjamin Netanyahu vehemently opposes the establishment of a genuinely viable Palestinian state in the West Bank and Gaza, and is opposed to giving up any part of Jerusalem—and

Netanyahu's governing coalition is more right wing and pro-settlement than he is.

Hamas's political evolution and deepening moderation stand in stark contrast to the rejectionism of the Netanyahu government and call into question which parties are "hardline" and which are "extremist." And at the regional level, a sea change has occurred in the official Arab position toward the Jewish state (the Arab League's 2002 Beirut Declaration, subsequently reiterated, offers full recognition and diplomatic relations if Israel accepts the international consensus regarding a two-state solution), while the attitudes of the Israeli ruling elite have hardened. This marks a transformation of regional politics and a reversal of roles.

Observers might ask, if Hamas is so eager to accept a two-state solution, why doesn't it simply accept the three conditions for engagement required by the so-called diplomatic Quartet (the United States, Russia, the European Union and the United Nations): recognition of Israel, renunciation of violence and acceptance of all previous agreements (primarily, the Oslo Accords)? In my interviews with Hamas officials, they stress that while they have made significant concessions to the Quartet, it has not lifted the punishing sanctions against Hamas, nor has it pressed Israel to end its siege, which has caused a dire humanitarian crisis. In addition, Hamas leaders believe that recognition of Israel is the last card in their hand and are reluctant to play it before talks even begin. Their diplomatic starting point will be to demand that Israel recognize the national rights of the Palestinians and withdraw from the occupied territories—but it will not be their final position.

There can be no viable, lasting peace between Israel and the Palestinians if Hamas is not consulted and if the Palestinians remain divided, with two warring authorities in the West Bank and Gaza. Hamas has the means and public support to undermine any agreement that does not address the legitimate rights and claims of the Palestinian people. Its Fatah/PA rival lacks a popular mandate and the legitimacy needed to implement a resolution of the conflict. PA President Mahmoud Abbas has been weakened by a series of blunders of his own making, and with his moral authority compromised in the eyes of a sizable Palestinian constituency, Abbas is yesterday's man—no matter how long he remains in power as a lame duck, and whether or not he competes in the upcoming presidential elections.

If the United States and Europe engaged Hamas, encouraging it to continue moderating its views instead of ignoring it or, worse yet, seeking its overthrow, the West could test the extent of Hamas's evolution. So far the strategy of isolation and military confrontation—pursued in tandem by Israel and the United States—has not appeared to weaken Hamas significantly. If anything, it has radicalized hundreds of young Palestinians, who have joined extremist factions and reinforced the culture of martyrdom and nihilism. All the while, the siege of Gaza has left a trail of untold pain and suffering.

If the Western powers don't engage Hamas, they will never know if it can evolve into an open, tolerant and peaceful social movement. The jury is still out on whether the Islamist movement can make that painful and ideologically costly transition. But the claim that engaging Hamas legitimizes it does not carry much weight; the organization derives its legitimacy from the Palestinian people, a mandate resoundingly confirmed in the free and fair elections of 2006.

To break the impasse and prevent gains by more extremist factions, the Obama administration and Congress should support a unified Palestinian government that could negotiate peace with Israel. Whatever they think of its ideology, US officials should acknowledge that Hamas is a legitimately elected representative of the Palestinian people, and that any treaty signed by a rump Fatah/PA will not withstand the test of time. And instead of twisting Cairo's arms in a rejectionist direction, Washington should encourage its Egyptian ally to broker a truce between Hamas and Fatah and thus repair the badly frayed Palestinian governing institutions. If the Obama administration continues to shun engagement with Hamas, Europe ought to take the lead in establishing an official connection. European governments have already dealt with Lebanon's Hezbollah, a group similar to Hamas in some respects, and they possess the skills, experience and political weight to help broker a viable peace settlement.

Like it or not, Hamas is the most powerful organization in the occupied territories. It is deeply entrenched in Palestinian society. Neither Israel nor the Western powers can wish it away. The good news, if my reading is correct, is that Hamas has changed, is willing to meet some of the Quartet's conditions and is making domestic political preparations for further changes. But if Hamas is not engaged, and if the siege of Gaza and Palestinian suffering continue without hope of ending the political impasse, there is a real danger of a regional war.

Critical Thinking

1. How has Hamas shifted its stance on Israel?
2. To what can this shift be attributed?
3. What is striking about this shift in attitude?
4. What are the differences between the views of Hamas and those of Islamic radicals?
5. What should be done to take advantage of this change in attitude?

FAWAZ A. GERGES is a professor of Middle Eastern politics and international relations at the London School of Economics and Political Science at the University of London. His most recent book is *Journey of the Jihadist Inside Muslim Militancy* (Harcourt).

In Sri Lanka, the Triumph of Vulgar Patriotism

Rajapaksa's patriotism merges nation and state, and it promotes a love of country based on a particular reading of the Sinhalese people's foundation myth, a reading in which all other groups . . . are present only as shadows.

NIRA WICKRAMASINGHE

On January 27, 2010, incumbent President Mahinda Rajapaksa was declared the winner of Sri Lanka's sixth presidential election. He triumphed over his main challenger, former army commander Sarath Fonseka, with a comfortable tally of 58 percent to 40 percent. The opposition immediately launched demonstrations to protest alleged election fraud.

According to a report by an independent monitoring group, the Commonwealth Expert Team, the presidential polling did not fully meet benchmarks for democratic elections. Yet most observers acknowledge that the outcome was affected not by vote rigging so much as by large-scale propaganda in the media in favor of Rajapaksa in weeks preceding the polls. State television, for example, repeatedly screened images of Uganda's notorious Idi Amin to instill fear of military dictatorship among Sinhalese voters.

A crackdown on the losers followed the release of the election results. Members of an elite army commando unit and army deserters who had supported Fonseka were arrested. Fonseka's office in Colombo was raided. On February 8, the former general himself was arrested under suspicion of conspiring to topple the government and assassinate Rajapaksa. Parliament was dissolved ahead of parliamentary elections scheduled for April.

For the longer term, the incumbent president is said to entertain hopes of consolidating family rule. His youthful son ran for parliament from Hambantota, Rajapaksa's hometown, and is expected to be groomed to become prime minister.

Sri Lanka's opposition parties have not remained silent in the face of these provocations. A number of demonstrations calling for Fonseka's release peppered the country and were violently suppressed. But as the government castigates as treason virtually any form of political opposition or criticism of official abuses, and as fears of reprisals grow, much of the public has been silenced and depoliticized.

A Result Foretold

The massive support that Rajapaksa mustered in the January election was strongest in the Sinhalese-dominated rural south, the area from where the president hails. He received more than 60 percent of the vote in that region. Tamils, especially in the north and in urban areas, along with Muslims in the east, paradoxically cast their lot with Fonseka, a well-known Sinhalese supremacist and the architect of last May's brutal military victory over the rebel Tamil Tigers.

They voted for him because, in ethnically and religiously divided Sri Lanka, the former general had become the nominal leader of the opposition, and was supported by the Tamil National Alliance, the main Tamil party in parliament. Moreover, in the Eastern Province where paramilitary Tamil armed groups, aided and abetted by the government, have been a law unto themselves since the demise of the Tamil Tigers, Tamils and Muslims saw in Fonseka the only candidate capable of restoring some degree of security for the people.

Even so, votes from urban areas, and from Tamils—who make up only 12 percent of the country's population of 21.3 million—proved not nearly sufficient for Fonseka to overcome Rajapaksa. The reason is that the incumbent regime succeeded where all others failed: It ended a debilitating, three-decades-long civil war.

Although many people in the south maintain serious concerns about Rajapaksa's government—which they recognize as grotesquely nepotistic, openly corrupt, and slow to deliver an expected peace dividend—this did not, at the crucial hour, outweigh their immense gratitude for being secure at last in their everyday lives.

When Rajapaksa decided last November to hold the presidential election two years earlier than previously scheduled, it seemed that the opposition parties would mount no real challenge. His victory appeared a certainty, a fait accompli. But Fonseka, disgruntled by the regime's dismissive attitude toward him, disturbed this scenario. Rallying around him all of Rajapaksa's political foes, the former army chief emerged as the consensus opposition candidate.

Fonseka's campaign hinged on criticizing the Rajapaksa administration for failing to carry out reconstruction, build the economy, and tackle corruption and mismanagement. Fonseka also deplored the deterioration of freedoms and rights in a country where, in recent years, a prominent editor was murdered and many others offering critical voices have been beaten up, kidnapped in notorious white vans, or detained under questionable charges. Fonseka even openly accused the secretary of defense, the president's brother, of committing war crimes during the last phase of the battle against the Tamil Tigers.

To voters, however, the anti-Rajapaksa alliance appeared fragile and divided. The Tamil National Alliance, the main Tamil party backing Fonseka, called for a merger of the Northern and Eastern provinces, the Tamils' traditional homelands, an idea that Fonseka rejected. The Marxist-nationalist Janata Vimukti Peramuna (the People's Liberation Front, or JVP) and the United National Party (UNP), the biggest opposition party, held conflicting views on the issue of granting more administrative power to the Tamils. The JVP opposed the idea of a Tamil homeland, while the UNP was more receptive to the idea of some form of self-determination for the Tamils.

In any case, in a country where the media had been beaten into submission and all state institutions had been blatantly misused over the previous two years to bolster Rajapaksa's image, it would have taken a miracle for this makeshift coalition to achieve a whirlwind victory. No miracle occurred.

The 30 Years' War

Each of the presidential candidates presented himself as the force behind the government's victory over Tamil "terrorism"—a victory that was dramatically achieved in the spring of 2009 with the death of Tamil Tiger leader Velupillai Prabhakaran and the destruction of the military edifice that he had constructed over 30 years.

Each of the presidential candidates presented himself as the force behind the government's victory over "Tamil terrorism."

The Tamil Tigers (formed in 1972 as the New Tamil Tigers, and renamed in 1976 as the Liberation Tigers of Tamil Eelam) had been fighting for a separate Tamil state (or "*eelam*") in Sri Lanka's north and east since 1977. They argued that Tamils had been victims of discrimination under successive majority Buddhist Sinhalese governments. Legislation granting primacy to the Sinhalese language and to Buddhism, together with fears of Sinhalese colonization of their lands, was invoked to justify assassinations, massacres, and countless suicide bombings on civilian as well as military targets in the south.

After the repeated failure of talks between the government and the Tigers—partly due to the Sinhalese parties' unwillingness to work together to broker a devolution deal that would be acceptable to the Tamil people—the Tigers and government forces renewed the military conflict in 2006. Rajapaksa's "war to eliminate terrorism" gained considerable international support and was provided the armament required for sustained military operations.

After liberating the Eastern Province in 2008, the Sri Lankan army headed by General Fonseka broke through rebel lines and drove the Tigers from areas in the north that they had controlled for decades. Thousands of civilians were held hostage by the Tigers in their final retreat. Eventually, after the fall of the Tigers' de facto capital, Kilinochchi, and the death of the Tamil leader, the 30-year war came to an end.

While the military phase of the conflict ended last May, the human costs of the war's conclusion will never be known. No independent media were allowed in the war zone during the final battle, but the United Nations estimates that 7,000 people died in early May and many more in the final two weeks of the fighting.

With the end of the war, another ordeal began for the quarter-million displaced Tamils who were interned in barbed-wired camps, where little access was provided to independent journalists and international agencies. The material conditions in the camps were monitored by the UN, which ensured that basic needs were provided for, but (unverifiable) stories of rape, other violence, and extortion reached the media. However, the Sinhalese people in the south appeared indifferent to the plight of their countrymen—the result of longtime exposure to government media that portrayed all Tamils as potential terrorists.

The Postwar State

Events since the end of the war have confirmed observers' fears that Sri Lanka is moving toward becoming a nepotistic state dominated by a coterie of sycophants seemingly intent on draining the coffers of state institutions. Meanwhile, the country is confronting serious economic challenges: The economy continues to totter despite a $2.8 billion bailout package from the International Monetary Fund.

According to IMF guidelines, the government is supposed to operate with a budget deficit of no more than 7 percent of GDP. But the deficit has already reached 8.5 percent of GDP and is likely to rise further. The government's claims notwithstanding, there is little foreign direct investment—the regime is spending heavily on borrowed funds.

Exports have contracted sharply, though US demand has started to pick up again. The European Union decided to suspend preferential tariff benefits for Sri Lanka following an investigation by the European Commission that concluded that the country fell short in implementing UN human rights conventions relevant to the trade benefits. Corruption and cronyism continue to depress investment.

At the same time the government, even though it no longer faces a civil war, is expanding the military, whose troop strength is already larger than that of the Israeli army. Emergency regulations remain in place, giving the regime's security forces special powers of search, arrest, and seizure of property.

And in the wake of the government's triumph over the Tamil Tigers, an insidious chauvinism has taken hold over much of the country. A few months ago the government issued a new thousand rupee note to commemorate its victory. On one side of the note is Rajapaksa's image; on the other is an Iwo Jima–like representation of Sri Lankan soldiers hoisting a flag, presumably after the fall of the Tamil stronghold of Kilinochchi. The new bill reflects the nature of the state in Sri Lanka today—patrimonial, nepotistic, nationalistic, and militarized.

To be sure, Fonseka's arrest has emboldened the previously feeble opposition. The United National Party now has a rallying cry, a cause célèbre that has resonance inside the country as well as outside. Arresting a war hero appears to have been a major miscalculation on Rajapaksa's part. Not only did it damage the country's image even further, it has elicited angry reactions from erstwhile allies such as the Buddhist clergy. The head priests of the major Buddhist sects, in a stern message to the president, called for the immediate release of Fonseka and other army personnel who had been taken into custody.

Protests immediately followed Fonseka's arrest. Hundreds of lawyers carrying placards demonstrated peacefully in front of the court complex in Colombo. Other supporters of the retired general gathered outside the supreme court, where a petition against his detention was heard. The opposition parties were gathering strength in advance of the parliamentary elections scheduled for April.

But whatever happens in current clashes between the government and the opposition, the centralized nature of Sri Lanka's state is not likely to change soon. Indeed, the regime's ideology—a form of vulgar civic patriotism that does not recognize any special rights for minorities—demands a strong centralized government along the lines of the one inherited from the colonial era.

The New Patriotism

This new patriotism has little in common with the "postnational" or "constitutional" patriotism that has been proposed as an alternative form of loyalty that is distinct from nationalism and is compatible with universal values. To the contrary, Rajapaksa's patriotism merges nation and state, and it promotes a love of country based on a particular reading of the Sinhalese people's foundation myth, a reading in which all other groups—those formally known as minorities—are present only as shadows.

Even expressions of banal nationalism can, in some cases, alienate cultural minorities. The regime and especially the president are constantly flagging Sinhalese Buddhist nationhood in public life, as well as policing the private lives of citizens. For instance, when Rajapaksa visited the sacred city of Anuradhapura last May to attend religious observances, he is reported to have offered hereditary gold ornaments to the sacred Bo tree, a ritual that ancient kings used to perform and that later was entrusted to high Buddhist officials. The president has allowed, if not encouraged, the media to portray him as another King Dutugemunu, another son of southern Sri Lanka who succeeded in seizing Anuradhapura from the Tamil king Elara.

Apart from such symbolic acts, the patriotic state is acting on society itself. Not only has it begun to monitor a long-forgotten excise law that forbids women from buying alcoholic drinks, it has also decreed that women are not permitted to enter government school premises unless clad in a sari (predominantly worn by Sinhalese women), and that liquor cannot be bought or consumed during the entire week surrounding the Buddhist Vesak festival. Being patriotic now means agreeing to abide by these rules, whether you are from the Sinhalese, Tamil, Muslim, or any other community.

The world in general appears to be moving away from the belief that pluralism and diversity are in themselves a panacea for societies' problems. But even if we accept citizenship and equality as higher values, only a principled regime can strive to protect the neutrality of the public sphere and ensure that majoritarianism and discrimination do not set in. Rajapaksa's regime has yet to display such principle.

Whatever the flaws of multiculturalism, they are still lesser evils than those faced today by Sri Lanka's minorities.

Whatever the flaws of multiculturalism and its avatar, the devolution of power—flaws that include essentializing the fragment, promoting the formation of ethnic enclaves, and denying the hybridity of communities and the possibility of multiple belongings—they are still lesser evils than those faced today by Sri Lanka's minorities, as well as by opponents of the Rajapaksa regime, as they encounter the administration's crude civic patriotism and ruthless repression.

The war is over, but journalists are still disappearing. Critics of the regime are vilified, attacked, or arrested on flimsy charges. Sri Lanka's government—which has close ties with Myanmar, Iran, Russia, China, and Pakistan—displays the type of defiant hubris that comes with the perception of being treated unfairly by the international community. But the chauvinist Sri Lankan state that is taking shape is founded on a grotesque travesty of the values it claims to champion in its critique of Western hypocrisy.

Critical Thinking

1. What has followed in the aftermath of Sri Lanka's 2010 elections?
2. What accounted for the incumbent president's reelection?
3. Who was the opposition candidate and what was his platform?
4. What challenges does Sri Lanka face?
5. What are the prospects for a multicultural society in Sri Lanka?

NIRA WICKRAMASINGHE is a professor of modern South Asian studies at Leiden University.

From *Current History*, April 2010, pp. 158–161. Copyright © 2010 by Current History, Inc. Reprinted by permission.

Indonesia's Moment

It is the world's most populous Muslim-majority nation and a highly successful democracy. How did Indonesia do it?

ROBERT PRINGLE

It is hard for a nation of 240 million, and one that is overwhelmingly Muslim and a democracy at that, to slip beneath the radar, but until recently that has been Indonesia's fate. Like dozens of other less developed countries, it has rarely come to the world's attention except when it suffered a coup or a particularly sensational natural disaster. In November, however, even as the nation's perennially active Mount Merapi was dramatically erupting again, Indonesia was in the spotlight for another reason, as a visit by President Barack Obama signaled that the country he first saw as a small child has emerged from obscurity.

Obama's decision to go to Indonesia certified a truth already recognized by informed observers. After more than a decade as an increasingly stable and genuinely free democracy, Indonesia is beginning to make its weight felt in the wider world. On Wall Street, where many have been impressed by the nation's steady economic growth, there is talk of Indonesia adding its "I" to the BRICs, as the world's largest emerging economies (Brazil, Russia, India, and China) are collectively known. With the human rights abuses that prevailed during the three-decade regime of President Suharto largely a thing of the past, there is a new warmth in relations with the United States. And even though China has become a major market for Indonesia's products—especially minerals, timber, and fish—Jakarta has been rattled by China's growing strength in Southeast Asia and its aggressive territorial claims in the South China Sea, and thus more appreciative of America's countervailing power.

Indonesia's upswing began in 1998, when B. J. Habibie, a protégé of Suharto since childhood, succeeded him as president. Habibie is a brilliant, German-educated engineer who rose to the top ranks of Germany's aeronautical industry before Suharto brought him home in 1974 and eventually made him vice president. But Habibie remained an awkward technocrat with no apparent aptitude for politics, often ridiculed for promoting improbable schemes, such as his insistence at the end of the Cold War on purchasing dozens of ships of the defunct East German navy.

Yet in less than two years as president, in the midst of a financial and political meltdown triggered by the Asian financial crisis, Habibie, supported by a robust reform movement, terminated military rule, unchained the press, and ended Indonesia's disastrous 24-year occupation of East Timor.

Most important, he inaugurated a radically decentralized democracy, transferring real power to some 470 districts and cities, instituting local elections all the way to the village level, and allocating a third of the national budget to support the new system. These were not cosmetic changes. Habibie and the reformers who supported him were convinced that a country as huge and diverse as Indonesia could not have genuine democracy without devolving real power from Jakarta. Seen in its totality, the democratic transformation Habibie authored in Indonesia, now more than a decade old, has had few rivals anywhere.

Indonesia has always been a difficult place to understand, and the surprising developments of the past dozen years have in a way made it an even more complex place. A nation strewn across thousands of islands, with dozens of major languages and innumerable ethnic groups, it is an improbable success story. New York Times columnist Thomas Friedman once described Indonesia as "too big to fail, too messy to work," and for a time its fledgling democracy made it even messier than before.

Indonesia is probably best understood in terms of dualities. Dualism Number One is embodied in the Indonesian term for "fatherland," *tanah air,* which literally means land and sea. The sea divides the islands but it also unites them. Because the island interiors are mountainous, the people of the archipelago have always had to reach across the water to connect and trade with others.

Dualism Number Two juxtaposes the fertile island of Java, home to the majority of Indonesians, against all the rest. The others are collectively known as the Outer Islands, where soils are typically poor and hard to cultivate. They are big producers of oil, rubber, spices, timber (from rapidly vanishing tropical forests), gold, copper, and, perhaps most notably, coal.

The Outer Islands include California-sized Sumatra, with the fervently Islamic province of Aceh at its northern tip; Borneo, four times the size of Java but with only one-twelfth its population; and Sulawesi, the one that on a map looks like a Rorschach inkblot, with so many arms that early explorers thought it was more than one island and called it "the Celebes."

Dualism Number Three, perhaps the most important, is Apparent Chaos vs. A Degree of Coherence. Apparent Chaos derives mainly from the sheer complexity of Indonesia's diversity and the related messiness of its politics. Indonesia's reputation for chaos also derives from its turbulent past, captured most famously in the 1982 film *The Year of Living Dangerously*, which dramatized the spasm of anticommunist killings in 1965 and 1966 after Suharto took power. (Like many Javanese, he used only a single name.) Generally suave and polite individually, Indonesians historically have had a penchant for kris-wielding mob violence. The word "amuck" is of Malay/Indonesian origin, and anthropologists once used it to describe a peculiarly Southeast Asian form of hysterical mass attack.

The Degree of Coherence results from a shared past, especially a common nationalism forged in resistance to Dutch colonialism. Trade united the archipelago, and at times parts of it were under consolidated political rule. It was blessed by linguistic unity. Most of Indonesia's languages belong to one great family, including the national language, Indonesian. (Papua, Indonesia's half of the great island of New Guinea, is the only region with significantly different linguistic and historical roots, and it is no coincidence that it has a separatist movement.)

Indonesian is a modern version of Malay, a traditional language of regional trade. The Dutch, who began to colonize Indonesia in the 17th century, made Malay into an official administrative language in order to avoid teaching the natives Dutch, which they feared might encourage dangerous notions of equality. When Indonesian nationalists emerged early in the 20th century, they realized they had been handed a national language on a silver platter, and thus avoided the plague of multiple tongues that would afflict so many other nation-builders in the developing world. Today Indonesian is spoken by the overwhelming majority of the population, but usually as a second language.

Dozens of local languages and major cultural variations remain, scattered through Indonesia's fragmented ethnic landscape, but the country's religions are layered, having arrived one on top of another. Most Indonesians were animists and ancestor worshipers until around the fifth century AD, when Indian traders and holy men introduced Hinduism and Buddhism, together with the concept of divinely endorsed monarchy. These new influences gave birth to the long-lived kingdom of Srivijaya in the seventh century and Majapahit in the late 13th century as well as some of the world's greatest "Indian" art, such as the monumental Borobudur Buddhist temple in central Java.

Islam arrived a millennium later, brought by Muslim Indians who traded in cloves and nutmeg with the people of the Spice Islands in what is now eastern Indonesia. Although Islam gradually became Indonesia's majority religion, the archipelago was never completely Islamized. Hinduism survived on the island of Bali, and important pockets of animism remained elsewhere. The Dutch introduced Christianity, which took root among animists and the economically important Chinese minority that began arriving on the heels of the Europeans.

Indonesian Islam soon began to display another dualism. In order to achieve widespread conversion of the local people, especially in Java, it was important for Islam to tolerate or incorporate powerful Hindu and animist traditions, much as the Prophet had done when he made the Kaabah, an ancient shrine in Mecca, the central holy place of Islam. But debate about precisely where the line between tradition and Islam should be drawn began early and has continued. By the 19th century, an uneven polarization had developed between those favoring doctrinal strictness—fundamentalism, if you will—and those leaning toward tolerance.

During the Japanese occupation of Indonesia in World War II, an enduring division emerged between those who wanted an Islamic state that required adherence to sharia law by all Muslims, and nationalists led by Sukarno (most of them also Muslims). The nationalists, mindful of Indonesia's diversity and bent on national unity above all else, preferred a pluralistic state, requiring only belief in One God. He was assumed by many to be Allah, but this was not enough for those who felt that Indonesia's majority religion deserved a more specific role.

When Sukarno declared independence in 1945, he enshrined his pluralistic credo in the Indonesian constitution. Advocates of Islamic statehood remain a force, but today the great majority of Indonesia's Muslims are moderates, both doctrinally and politically. Many of them belong to one of two Muslim mass organizations, Nahdlatul Ulama (NU) and Muhammadiyah, with a combined membership estimated at 60 million.

While the two organizations are internally diverse, they reflect the polarity that developed before the colonial era. NU represents a primarily Javanese tradition of relative tolerance, with strong ties to the more mystical Sufi branch of Islam, while Muhammadiyah has been more influenced by fundamentalism.

In contrast to most Islamic organizations in the Middle East, both NU and Muhammadiyah have strongly supported democracy and government development programs. Both operate schools, hospitals, and other affiliates. Neither participates directly in politics, but most members of Islamic political parties in Indonesia—there are about half a dozen major ones, as well as multireligious parties—have ties to one or the other. In line with NU's tradition of relative tolerance, some of its leaders have taken a liberal line on issues such as women's rights, helping the organization to develop a new constituency among Indonesia's burgeoning middle class. Abdurrahman Wahid, a product of NU who succeeded Habibie as president in 1999, even advocated closer ties with Israel.

Yet there is also a darker strand in Indonesian Islam. During the Suharto era, Saudi-financed religious schools promoted Wahhabi-style fundamentalism. The Saudi teachings were not explicitly violent, but they strengthened the intellectual basis for violent extremism, which had already taken root in Indonesian soil. In 1948, a Muslim extremist group calling itself Darul Islam had launched a guerilla war against Sukarno's nationalists in parts of Java and elsewhere. Not finally defeated until 1962, Darul Islam left behind remnants that provided the nuclei for later manifestations of Islamic extremism.

In 1993 two Indonesian clerics, Abdullah Sungkar and Abu Bakar Bashir, formed Jemaah Islamiyah, a regional Southeast Asian jihadist organization that recruited Indonesians to fight in Afghanistan. The jihadis returned home with motivation and bomb-making know-how, attacking hotels, embassies, and Christian churches, and stoking unrest in Sulawesi and the Malukus (as the Spice Islands are now known). Occurring at the same time that Indonesia was staggering under the impact of widespread unrest and score settling brought on by the beginning of Habibie's decentralized democracy, the attacks helped persuade many analysts that the country was falling apart.

The ugliest crime of all came in 2002, when Jemaah Islamiyah terrorists bombed a nightclub in Bali, killing more than 200 people, most of them foreign tourists. The world was shocked: Hindu Bali is supposed to be a place for eating, praying, and loving. But no one was more upset than Indonesians, who are proud of beautiful Bali and keenly appreciate the tourist revenues it generates. The slaughter left Jemaah Islamiyah discredited, and the ensuing government drive against it—Indonesia's security forces now have a deserved reputation for competence—led to a three-year stretch free of violent extremism. Though suicide bombers struck again in 2009, attacking two luxury hotels in Jakarta, the terrorism trend line is down sharply.

Indonesia's Islamic unrest feeds on a streak of paranoia that almost all Indonesian Muslims share to some extent. It has many roots, including resentment over what are seen as the anti-Muslim wars led by the United States in the Middle East and Afghanistan. Equally important is the grating reality that while Muslims are a majority of the population, Islamic activists have been unable to make headway against Indonesia's multireligious constitution.

In 1967, the hopes of Muslim conservatives were high after the army put down a bungled communist power grab and deposed the aging Sukarno. Muslim youth groups in Java had helped the army carry out the killings during "the year of living dangerously," which left thousands of nominally communist peasants dead and communism itself virtually exterminated. When the dust settled, Muslim leaders

expected recognition and political rewards for their support. The newly installed Suharto, however, had spent years as a young army officer pursuing Darul Islam rebels and continued to regard political Islam as a threat. And he also saw it as a convenient replacement for the demolished Indonesian Communist Party as a specter that could be used to justify military rule.

Suharto was not all bad. The first two decades of his reign brought near-double-digit economic growth rates, spurred by oil revenues and the president's technocratic reforms. The introduction of high-yielding rice varieties lifted farmers' incomes, while family planning programs reduced the looming threat of Malthusian disaster in Java and Bali and spurred the emergence of a village-level, motor scooter-riding middle class. From the time of its arrival with the spice trade, Islam in Indonesia had always thrived on commerce, and so it did again. Muslims grew increasingly observant, with headscarves and other forms of Islamic dress becoming more fashionable, while the more relaxed and quasi-animistic Islam of peasant Java practically disappeared.

Prosperity and globalization have nurtured new expressions of Islam, from urban intellectual discussion groups to lifestyle-centered radio ministries. One creative Internet imam caused a minor sensation when he urged his listeners to emulate the Prophet's supposed practice of taking baths with his wife. But rapid change also brought increasing secularization among Indonesia's urban youth. Religious conservatives, disturbed by pornography, nightclubs, and symptoms of female liberation, provided a new political base for a draconian understanding of sharia, including support for such practices as the stoning of adulterers, polygamy (which is legal but controversial), and even, among a small minority, acts of terrorism such as the Bali bombing.

While terrorism is in retreat, Islamic vigilantism is a serious problem, most notoriously the repeated violence by the Islamic Defenders' Front (FPI) against Ahmadiyyah, an Islamic sect that has offended other Muslims by claiming that its founder was a new prophet. The government has often chosen to look the other way. When FPI activists attacked a group of moderate Muslims and others in 2008 who had protested FPI violence, injuring a dozen, the perpetrators got off with short stays in jail. Such incidents, including violence against Christians and their churches in Muslim areas, violate Indonesia's constitutional guarantee of religious freedom. However, the country's generally admirable but very cautious president, Susilo Bambang Yudhoyono, has thus far refused to risk alienating his fundamentalist Muslim supporters by enforcing the law.

The government's reluctance to crack down on the thuggery of the FPI and others is a major blemish on Indonesia's democracy, all the more so because it is accompanied by more general weaknesses in the judicial system, which is shot through with corruption. A few years ago, I interviewed Goenawan Mohamad, a famous Indonesian journalist and Muslim liberal who has felt the sting of FPI intimidation. I asked him if the country needed more laws, perhaps a bill of rights, to control such threats. "No," he said, "we have enough laws; we need to enforce the laws that we have." Most Indonesian intellectuals would probably agree.

Public opinion polling, highly developed in Indonesia, often shows alarming degrees of support (although never majorities) for harsh interpretations of sharia, such as cutting off thieves' hands. But there is no evidence that such sentiment signifies increasing support for an Islamic state. Very different and more credible evidence is available from the results of the four truly free national elections held since Indonesia's independence, in 1955, 1999, 2004, and 2009. Despite the greatly increased level of Islamic observance over this period, about three-quarters or more of all voters have supported political parties that favor the pluralistic status quo rather than an Islamic state. In 2009, only 13 percent of voters chose parties seeking or appearing to seek a rejection of pluralism.

Indonesia has been the world's third-largest genuine democracy since 1999, and one of its few Muslim-majority ones. That is arguably the most important quality of the country, even more important than its economic potential or its role in regional affairs. More than one-third of Indonesia's national budget is devoted to supporting decentralized local governments, all of which have lively, competitive elections.

Decentralization seems to be working, despite plenty of bumps in the road. No one was surprised that it added a confusing new layer to the Indonesian policy process. People were taken unaware, however, when local initiative began to stimulate new regional nodes of economic growth in places such as Riau, in central Sumatra, and Samarinda, a coal-mining center in Borneo, reducing Jakarta's hitherto unhealthy dominance.

Indonesia's experiment could be a model for other countries, such as Turkey, that have often been too timid to release real power to local governments. Indonesia's tremendous diversity does make for a messier kind of democracy, but it also makes some kind of democracy imperative. That is an idea that should sound familiar to Americans; it is one reason why the United States has a federal system with several layers of government.

Many facets of Indonesian reality that puzzle outsiders can be understood as a healthy response to diversity. In fact, it often makes sense to look for clues to Indonesian puzzles in the United States, which frequently has forged a similar set of responses to enormous diversity. The national and local components of both the Indonesian and American political systems regularly get crosswise of each other. Both countries have a dominant religion that is not the state religion. Our respective fundamentalists are shocked by the excesses of youth and do things that worry the moderate majority. Our politicians sometimes make things worse by pandering to vocal minorities.

The Indonesian national motto, *Bhinekka Tunggal Ika,* usually translated as "unity in diversity," seems to mean almost the same thing as *E Pluribus Unum,* and may have been inspired by American precedent. But if you parse the ancient Balinese text from which it comes, there is a subtle but powerful difference. The text is concerned with the dual religions of the Majapahit Empire: Buddhism, the religion of contemplation and scholarship, and Hindu Sivaism, best understood as the religion of state affairs. The verse from which the motto is drawn reads, "They are indeed different, but they are of the same kind, as there is no division in truth." Unity, the verse suggests, is not always seen on the surface, and may sometimes be realized only through striving.

In both the United States and Indonesia, diversity tends to push politicians toward the moderate center—at least in the long run. In a handful of Indonesian localities, politicians who hoped to attract fervently Islamic voters have enacted religiously inspired regulations that forbid women to be outdoors after dark, for example, or require knowledge of the Qur'an as a prerequisite for government employment. The regulations are probably illegal, since the decentralization laws did not empower localities to regulate religion, but Jakarta has done nothing to stop them. Many foreign journalists have pointed to these measures as a sign of creeping "sharia-ization" in Indonesia. What most of them fail to mention is that such regulations have proved to be unpopular with most voters, and no new ones have been enacted since 2006.

It is easy to find portents of disaster in Indonesia's story, but one doesn't need to be an extreme optimist to imagine a fine future for this often-mystifying country. It has become a model democracy against all odds, and there is every reason to hope that it can continue to build on its recent progress. As in all healthy democracies, its problems are in plain view. For instance, the future role of political Islam remains a question mark. Another issue is uneven economic performance. Indonesia boasts one of the fastest-growing stock markets in Asia and economic growth averaging around six percent; it breezed through the recent global downturn virtually untouched. But its widespread poverty and low rate of job creation are still problematic, and the corruption of the judicial system, combined with the heavy hand of bureaucracy, still deters foreign investment.

Like Americans, Indonesians love political jokes and innuendo. My favorite example of Indonesian humor involves the vast Istiqlal Mosque in Jakarta, which President Obama visited on his recent trip. The building was commissioned long ago by President Sukarno, who once grandiosely claimed that he blended all the world's faiths and philosophies in his own person (though he certainly did not hang on the fine points of any of them). In this syncretic spirit, Sukarno selected a Protestant member of the Batak ethnic group from North Sumatra as the architect of the Istiqlal Mosque, which was to be the largest such structure in Southeast Asia.

Years later, during the Suharto regime, when the mosque was finally inaugurated, people noticed that its vast dome was supported by 12 pillars. Instant uproarious joke—the pillars obviously represented the Twelve Apostles and had been purposely smuggled into the plan by the Christian architect, probably with a wink and a nod from his less than devoutly Muslim patron!

It almost certainly wasn't true, but it was far too funny not to repeat. As long as people are laughing, one can hope, they will keep anger at bay.

Critical Thinking

1. What events led to Indonesia's emergence as an important international actor?
2. What are Indonesia's "dualities"?
3. Why has Indonesia's Islamic radicalism been limited?

ROBERT PRINGLE, a retired U.S. Foreign Service officer, is the author of *Understanding Islam in Indonesia: Politics and Diversity* (2010).

From *The Wilson Quarterly,* Winter 2011, pp. 26–33. Copyright © 2011 by Robert Pringle. Reprinted by permission of Robert Pringle and Woodrow Wilson International Center for Scholars.

Divergent Paths

The Future of One-Party Rule in Singapore

MENG CHEN

Is democracy always the most fitting model of governance, or can circumstances justify a more authoritarian approach for the sake of securing the country's material wealth? The parliamentary republic of Singapore has been under international scrutiny for its stringent one-party rule by the People's Action Party (PAP) and suppression of the media and minority parties that oppose its control of the government. However, many attribute Singapore's rapid rise to first-world status and economic prosperity to the same set of ideologies the PAP used to build up the state following independence from the United Kingdom. Since 1959, the first Prime Minister Lee Kuan Yew has had an important say in who would govern the country and how. Now, as Lee, the current leader of the PAP, approaches the age of 87 and shows signs of a worsening heart condition, many around the world have begun to question the nation's unclear future, specifically its path of succession. A public conference was even held on April 21, 2009, to discuss Singapore's path after Lee's death. Will the dynastic pattern of succession continue beyond Lee Kuan Yew's son, incumbent Prime Minister Lee Hsien Loong? Will there be changes to government practices pertaining to press freedom and political opposition? As the older Lee eventually leaves the country in the hands of younger generations, Singapore must face the decision of whether to continue Lee's legacy or embrace sociopolitical reform.

The Self-Renewal of the PAP

Although the extraordinary success of the PAP has helped Singapore rapidly grow in the past, the country now stands at a crucial juncture with this new generation. Indeed, the system may be particularly vulnerable to the internal self-renewal of the PAP itself, as Ho Kwong Ping, Chairman of Singapore Management University, suggests. Elections are held every five years in Singapore; the next election in 2011 will test the PAP's ability to maintain its grip on the government in the years to come, but Lee remains unfazed. "I don't see any problem in the next election or probably in the next one after that," he says. However, Lee does express concern that if the younger generation of politicians is unable to form a good team by then, the PAP will be at risk of being overtaken by a well-organized opposition party. Kishore Mahbubani, Dean and Professor of the Lee Kuan Yew School of Public Policy, National University of Singapore, believes that there are three scenarios post-Lee Kuan Yew: first, a smooth transition and continuation of the current political system; second, a significant reversal of Lee's legacy; third, continued domination of the government by the PAP, but with greater opposition. According to Mahbubani, destabilizing change seems unlikely due to seven factors that should perpetuate the patriarch's legacy: a quality education system, national service, strong public institutions, a victory-prone political party, ethnic harmony, meritocracy, and a firm anti-corruption policy.

A key factor pointed out by Mahbubani in the PAP's success in elections is the current lack of opposition. The party's ability to be "victory-prone" acts as a stabilizer against government reform from the outside. As a testament to the party's infallibility, the unicameral parliament currently has 82 of 84 seats occupied by PAP members, the other two held respectively by the Singapore Democratic Alliance and the Worker's Party. The current president, Sellapan Ramanathan, took office in 1999, endorsed by Lee, after all opponents were disqualified by the Electoral Committee; in 2005, the same scenario occurred and the scheduled election was never held.

Although the PAP's governing system is still less than democratic, many Singaporeans say that they do not speak against it, solely out of respect for the contributions of the country's iconic founder. Journalists have noted that even the country's youth, ignorant of the beginnings of Singapore's post-independence transformation, harbor a certain sentiment of gratitude towards Lee, thanks to the country's astonishing economic success and stability and the strength of his personality. Once Lee Kuan Yew can no longer guide the younger ruling generation, the legitimacy of the PAP will diminish without the venerated founder at its helm. Opposition is likely to grow from Singapore's minority parties, such as the Singapore Democratic Party (SDP), whose Secretary-General Chee Soon Juan is a long-standing opponent of the former prime minister. Chee has been imprisoned multiple times for public rallies and protests, among other acts banned by the government. After being sued by Lee and declared bankrupt in 2006 on a charge of slander against the former prime minister, Chee continues his activism domestically and internationally, to Lee's dismay.

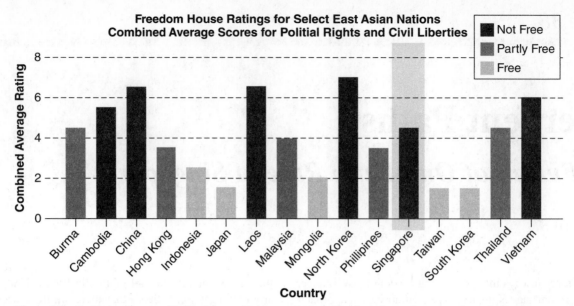

Freedom House Ratings for Select East Asian Nations
Combined Average Scores for Politial Rights and Civil Liberties

- Not Free
- Partly Free
- Free

Combined Average Rating (y-axis: 0, 2, 4, 6, 8)

Countries (x-axis): Burma, Cambodia, China, Hong Kong, Indonesia, Japan, Laos, Malaysia, Mongolia, North Korea, Phillipines, Singapore, Taiwan, South Korea, Thailand, Vietnam

Country

Disparities in Democracy   Methodology: Each country and territory is assigned a numerical rating—on a scale of 1 to 7—for political rights and an analogous rating for civil liberties; a rating of 1 indicates the highest degree of freedom and 7 the lowest level of freedom.

Freedom House; 2010

Ingredients of Singapore's Success

In response to critics such as Chee who protest that Singapore's government restricts the press and free speech, imposes over-stringent laws, and acts authoritarian on other accounts, Lee counters that his undemocratic policies were necessary to build the nation up to its current prosperity. The PAP's legitimacy in continuing these practices would be challenged without the attribution of Singapore's success to Lee—it is thus crucial to assess whether his style of heavy government involvement has truly been necessary in state-building. Lee asserts that the sense of vulnerability in the country's foundation is what keeps his fists clenched. He argues that the survival of the country depended on the adoption of his methods of governance and that Singapore's current modernity is the product of these. Without Lee's style, the country would have collapsed, he argues. Indeed, in Singapore there are almost no natural resources and no common culture, only a disharmonious mixture of Chinese, Malays, Indians, and other groups that have yet to create a strong cultural identity. So in some sense, Lee's rule consolidated a population that may otherwise have engaged in ethnic conflict.

It is undeniable that Lee's stringent government policies played a considerable role in guiding the country's rapid development from a British settlement to a city-state of material wealth far exceeding its neighbors' in less than 60 years. In the early stages of Singapore's nation-building, attracting long-term foreign investment was still a concern due to active labor unions and strikes. Such practices have destabilized the workforce of multinational corporations and fueled unsustainable inflation, as currently is the case in Argentina and several other Latin American countries. President Yusof bin Ishak announced in December 1965 that trade unions were "irresponsible" and called them unaffordable luxuries. Therefore, when the PAP won all 58 parliamentary seats in 1968, Lee's government passed new legislation that allowed longer working hours,

cut holidays, and granted employers greater control over hiring, firing, and promoting workers in order to shake the power of unions. At the same time, however, workers were also given sick leave and unemployment compensation. Due to Lee's policies of tightened control and higher employee benefits, productivity soared and 1969 passed without a single strike. The government was then able to implement policies to attract foreign investors, such as tax relief for up to five years and full repatriation of profits in certain industries. Singapore has since continued to attract foreign investment due to such favorable policies.

However, it is questionable whether the nation's success along the purportedly narrow road can be primarily attributed to Lee's "ideology-free" policies. In *Development as Freedom,* Amartya Sen attacks the "Lee thesis" as having little empirical support. Although some say denial of basic civil and political rights helps promote the economy, Sen believes that evidence for this "Lee thesis" is not strong enough.

A pertinent question, then, is which factors drove the small island country's speedy path to economic prosperity. Prior to independence, Singapore was already a crucial British settlement and thus had a head start on its infrastructure development, much as is arguably the case for Hong Kong and India. Although Singapore's neighbor, Malaysia, shared a similar history in that its origin lies in the independence of former British Malaya in 1957, its less strategic geographic location and larger land mass put it at a disadvantage in terms of both organizing the country and trade prosperity. At the eastern end of the Strait of Malacca, between western Malaysia and Indonesian Sumatra, Singapore has been one of the world's busiest ports for many decades, only bypassed by Shanghai in shipping tonnage in 2005. It is also considerably simpler for the government to optimize land use and to devise efficient property taxation laws for the city-state of Singapore with its 268 square miles (693 square km), than it is for its comparatively giant neighbor Malaysia with its 127,350 square miles (329,849 square km). Due to this large disparity in land size, it may be categorically incorrect to compare Singapore's

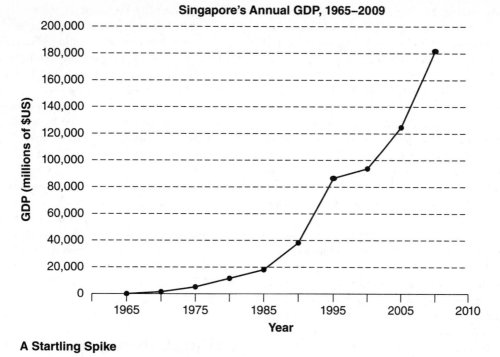

Singapore's Annual GDP, 1965–2009

A Startling Spike

Singapore Federal Department of Statistics; 2010

model of development to countries such as Malaysia. In addition, the world economy was experiencing a period of growth during the mid-1960s, and after President Suharto stepped down from power in 1966 in Indonesia, his ban on trade with Singapore was lifted and the neighboring country resumed transactions. Due to the United States' heavy involvement in Indochina at the time, Singapore soon became a major supplier. History might have slightly favored the nation's economic ascendancy.

Reform: Taking It Slow

Even if the "Lee thesis" is true in that authoritarian rule was essential to Singapore's growth, the underlying reason for limiting freedom of the press and political activism no longer seems as convincing as when Singapore was still an underdeveloped, newly independent island. Singapore has since become technologically advanced and economically prosperous.

So what is holding back reform liberalization? It is true that with Singapore's maturation, Lee Kuan Yew has gradually loosened control. In 1990, he stepped down from office and handpicked his deputy and defense minister Goh Chok Tong to succeed him. However, he left himself considerable influence in the government by remaining as Minister Mentor in Goh's cabinet and continuing to lead the PAP. Mr. Goh acknowledges the difficulties that Lee has had in restraining himself from participation in state affairs, but he chooses to accept and welcome such intervention. Under Goh's administration, Lee Hsien Loong, Lee Kuan Yew's son, became Deputy Prime Minister. It came as no surprise when he was appointed the new Prime Minister on August 12, 2004, when Goh Chok Tong switched roles with the younger Lee and became the Chairman of the Monetary Authority of Singapore. Since then, Lee Hsien Loong has slowly been relaxing restrictions on the media and

opposition parties, but at what Andrew Loh says is "the speed of a sedated sloth." Loh worries that the government's hesitation to enact socio-political change is "creating a generation of political infants" that may not be able to cope if such a change were to come in a drastic and inescapable form. However, there is little reason to worry because groundbreaking government reform is highly unlikely to occur.

One variable that prevents large scale reform is the series of tactful policies that have been set up to limit the extent to which an opposition government can enact changes. For instance, it would be required by law to gain the president's approval to withdraw from international reserves, suggesting it would not be granted.

The education system and meritocracy in government also tend toward maintaining the status quo, perhaps with minute changes. To bring the country's top scholars into the government and assure that they align themselves with the PAP, the nation's brightest crop of students are selected for generous Public Service Commission Scholarships such as the President's Scholarship, which pays for their tuition in addition to a stipend to attend the world's most prestigious universities. Upon graduation, they are required to return to Singapore and work several years in the government in one of the various tracks of their choice; given a chance to rise to high positions, many stay with the government and perpetuate the system. This is one of the factors listed by Mahbubani that continue Lee Kuan Yew's legacy—meritocracy in a Confucian sense. By educating the smartest students abroad before incorporating them into the government, new perspectives are introduced to the administration even though democratic elections are not held.

In order to compete with the private sector for those with the highest qualifications and to dissuade corruption, Singapore offers one of the highest incomes in the world for the country's

155

political leaders. According to *The Economist,* Singapore's Prime Minister's annual salary was over US$2.1 million in the latest year with data released, which is the highest in the world and second highest in terms of the ratio of political leader's pay to the national GDP per capita. In comparison, the President of the United States earns US$400,000 annually. In the case of China, while the official income of government leaders is average, their "gray income" or undisclosed earnings was reported to be 5.4 trillion yuan (about US$797.1 billion) in 2009, which exceeded a total government revenue of only 3.6 trillion yuan. The theory underlying the Singaporean government's generous compensations is that high salaries will give incentive for officials holding the desired positions to remain in those posts and produce high quality work.

Lee's meritocratic system, which diverges from common Western models of governance, can be both a hindrance and a boon to reform. The way officials are often appointed by the PAP without democratic elections reinforces the dominant party's control in Singapore and bars reform from outside the government. However, this self-selecting process within the PAP allows smooth transition of power, as seen in the past two instants when the prime ministers voluntarily stepped down for the younger generation. In addition, by recruiting the brightest scholars into the PAP after providing them with university education abroad, new ideas are brought into the government. Without a takeover by an opposition party, smaller internal reforms within the PAP, one at a time, is the most effective way to create change. These various factors indicate that minor progress towards increased socio-political freedom in the current administration, despite old political safeguards created by Lee Kuan Yew, is yet promising. The times of strong governmental control of the media and elections are slowly passing away. Ideological changes and liberalization are occurring slowly already and may even be hastened by external opposition if the PAP diminishes in influence.

In the end, it appears that Singapore post-Lee Kuan Yew will continue in his legacy due to his carefully crafted policies that prevent significant change even if an opposition party gains a majority in elections. Just as former prime ministers remain in the cabinet, vestiges of old policies are unlikely to disappear soon. However, as the reasons for Lee's strict guidelines erode due to stable economic growth, more freedom will inevitably be given, whether due to changing ideologies within the PAP or pressure from opposition parties striving to gain legitimacy.

Critical Thinking

1. What role has Lee Kuan Yew played in Singapore's rapid rise?
2. What role has Singapore's location played in its prosperity?
3. What are the obstacles to political reform in Singapore?

From *Harvard International Review,* Winter 2011, pp. 28–31. Copyright © 2011 by the President of Harvard College. Reprinted by permission via Sheridan Reprints.

Uprising Threat

The government's crackdown on an anti-government protest in Luanda last month shows that the tide is turning for Dos Santos' virtual one-party state.

CHOFAMBA SITHOLE

The announcement of anti-government protests by Angolan activists in March exposed the jitters afflicting President Jose Eduardo Dos Santos' regime in the wake of the spectacular success of the internet-fanned popular uprisings in Tunisia and Egypt.

Drumming up the spectre of the country's gruesome 27 year-long civil war, the ruling Popular Movement for the Liberation of Angola (MPLA) swiftly moved into preemptive gear with a campaign of intimidation and arbitrary arrests. For decisive effect, an outlandish show of popular support for the government was rapidly contrived to coincide with the country's annual carnival.

The organisers of the protest remained anonymous, but a Facebook page called "The Angolan People's Revolution" had been put up calling on people to demonstrate against Dos Santos, in power for 32 years, and his government. In the weeks leading up to the March 7 anti-government protest, the government warned that anyone who joined would be punished for inciting violence and attempting to return the country to civil war. On the night before the march and on the day of the planned protests, police arrested activists as well as journalists who had come out to cover the event.

Ana Margoso, one of the four journalists for the newspaper *Novo Jornal,* later told reporters that police agents had put her in an isolation cell and interrogated her through the night as they tried to link her to some opposition politicians. Police also arrested a group of 17 young rap musicians in Luanda's city centre who were reading poems and distributing pamphlets, accusing them of planning to participate in the protests later that day.

Rapper Brigadeiro Mata Frakus, who recently returned from exile, is hugely popular on the internet since he released a song criticising Dos Santos, in power since 1979.

The North African uprisings in Tunisia and Egypt, and also in Libya and a few other Arab countries, have largely been driven by disillusioned, educated and technologically savvy urban youths, hence the Angolan regime's apparent tetchiness.

Human Rights Watch expressed concern at anonymous death threats against opposition politicians and human rights lawyers, the arbitrary arrests of journalists and activists, and misuse of the state media by the MPLA government to drum up its partisan messages.

The rights body also received reports of arbitrary arrests in Cabinda city and other parts of the country, including Lunda Norte province two days before the planned protest. The regime's pursuit of opposition politicians stems from an announcement made in February by a collection of small opposition parties that they would join the demonstration. They said they wanted to raise concern about the social and economic exclusion of the majority of the Angolan population, and against corruption, intimidation, and the government's clampdown on free speech.

In the weeks prior to March 7, the planned protests had dominated conversation in Luanda, from office skyscrapers to the city's slums. The footage of angry masses in the Arab world hounding out or challenging longstanding rulers will no doubt have animated Angolans about the possibilities immanent in their own society. But, ironically, many dismissed the call to action as a government ploy and chose to stay at home.

The organisers may have failed ultimately to mobilise a mass of protesters onto the streets, and yet they can indeed claim to have scored a major victory in the form of the state's nervous response. The security apparatus was rolled out to bare its teeth, and the MPLA went for overkill.

The MPLA mobilised thousands of its supporters to attend a 'patriotic march for peace in response to the subversions to order and to the demonstrations against the government' and to repudiate 'those who would eventually want to spread political instability'.

State radio said 500,000 supporters took to the streets of Luanda waving MPLA flags. However, the Associated Press estimated a lower figure of 20,000 participants. But the numbers are hard to determine, as that Saturday also was one of the main days during the Angolan carnival, which sees hundreds of thousands celebrating in the streets.

Senior ruling party officials repeatedly reiterated the message in the state media that the march was a patriotic obligation for all citizens. MPLA spokesperson, Rui Falcão, tried to use an incident involving the seizure by the government of an alleged illegal arms shipment, now disproven, to suggest that the main opposition party and former rebel group, Union for the Total Independence of Angola (Unita), was planning a violent uprising. But Unita had long since declared itself uninterested in the protest, saying it lacked credibility because it was called by an anonymous group with an unknown agenda.

'Angola's ruling party should not scare people with renewed violence to deter them from freely expressing their views,' Daniel Bekele, Africa director at Human Rights Watch said. 'Such disrespect of basic political freedoms does not bode well for Angola's upcoming general elections in 2012.'

Local rights group Mãos Livres ('Free Hands') received anonymous death threats by phone and text messages and had two of their cars torched. The organisation provides legal aid and has been defending victims of official abuse throughout the country.

'Politically motivated death threats against opposition politicians, lawyers, and human rights defenders are a deadly serious concern,' Bekele said. 'The Angolan government should explain publicly that such threats are crimes and take all necessary steps to protect those targeted.'

The opposition to MPLA remains rudimentary, but social inequalities as well as the lopsided distribution of Angola's breathtaking oil wealth have cast a pall on President Jose Eduardo Dos Santos' virtual one-party state. The MPLA won 82 per cent of the vote two years ago and is almost certain to win the 2012 elections.

However, the ruling party looks increasingly unnerved by Unita's accusations of not putting up a sufficient fight against poverty and corruption. Social inequality is at levels comparable to those of India and Brazil.

Oil has helped Angola pick up the pieces of a devastating civil war to become sub-Saharan Africa's third biggest economy after South Africa and Nigeria. But the government is still struggling to diversify commercial activity outside oil, construction and diamonds. Poverty in Angola—where the majority lives on less than $2 a day—jars with the country's resource endowment.

An estimated 68 per cent of the population lives below the national poverty line, with 26 per cent classified as living in extreme poverty. Some of the worst poverty derives from wartime dislocations, and is concentrated in rural areas, particularly among the nonfarming population.

High unemployment in the urban areas is also of particular concern, especially among women and youth. The decades of civil war rendered education inaccessible for generations of Angolans. As such, many are unqualified for the formal economy due to insufficient education or marketable skills.

In the towns and cities of this former Portuguese colony, poverty is associated with widening social inequality. But sitting atop the piles of petro dollars and diamond wealth is a preponderantly opulent and predatory bourgeoisie within or aligned to the MPLA regime. Despite moves to diversify and invest in sectors such as agriculture, oil still accounts for 90 per cent of Angola's export income but employs less than 1 per cent of its people.

The IMF, the World Bank and ratings agencies, which have given Angola the same B+ rating as Nigeria, have all urged Angola to do more to diversify its economy.

Analysts say that should it fail to do so, it risks becoming another Nigeria, where quarrels about the distribution of oil wealth have fuelled civil unrest.

President Dos Santos has been unusually vocal about corruption after his government turned to the IMF for a loan in 2009, and his comments on zero-tolerance for graft prompted parliament to pass a law to punish corrupt officials. Pressure from multilateral institutions has compelled the government to begin to treat oil revenues, external debt and the transactions of Sonangol and Endiama, respectively the state enterprises for oil and diamonds, in a more transparent manner.

Social inequality had been, until recently, a subject discussed only among opposition ranks, civil society and in academia. However, MPLA elites growing increasingly aware of the fact that a rent-seeking economy maximising profits for a minority is not viable in the long run, have taken up the issue within the ruling class as well.

For them, widespread poverty damages prospects for economic development, leading to social inequality that will, in turn, produce social unrest and jeopardise the political system. Some analysts in Angola believe that the answer to the country's growing social inequality may yet come from conscientious leftists within the MPLA who still cherish their party's original ideals and commitment to social justice before its soul was drowned in the 'devil's excrement'—oil.

Critical Thinking

1. What issues have prompted protestors to try to organize demonstrations against Angola's ruling party?

2. What has been the government's response?

3. What challenges does Angola's oil-rich economy face?

From *NewsAfrica*, April 30, 2011, pp. 28–29. Copyright © 2011 by NewsAfrica. Reprinted by permission of TT Media Limited.

Ivory Coast: Another Asterisk for Africa's Democratization

"In the continent's political struggles . . . the fight almost always concerns access to resources, and it is access to resources that enables corrupt, inept, and occasionally illegitimate regimes to remain in power."

WILLIAM B. MILAM AND JENNIFER G. JONES

The failure of African states to create the institutions and political culture that can assure peaceful transitions for legitimately elected leaders continues to impede the continent's search for sustainable democracy. The November 28, 2010, election in Ivory Coast, the region's latest test of democratic transition, can hardly be regarded as a triumph for democracy and the rule of law. The fact that the election's winner, Alassane Ouattara, had to resort to force to take his office has sent a dangerous signal throughout Africa.

The loser, the incumbent Laurent Gbagbo, clung desperately to the presidency for four months after his defeat at the polls. He insisted that he had won despite the adamant, universal rejection of his claim by Ivory Coast's neighbors, other African states, and the international community. Gbagbo was able to ignore demands that he give up the office he lost fair and square because he could tap the government's coffers to pay for military resistance. Until he was captured and arrested after an assault on his residence by the combined forces of Ouattara and France on April 11, 2011, Gbagbo appeared prepared to go down fighting, and to take the nation with him, rather than give in.

A Military Conclusion

Gbagbo had holed up in a bunker in the presidential palace, surrounded by Ouattara's paramilitary forces. Reports from the United Nations and the French, as well as Ouattara's spokespeople, indicated that he was seeking to negotiate his departure. But those reports proved premature, as Gbagbo evidently used the talks as cover to strengthen his position and to rearm. His supporters began to push back with some success in the main Ivorian city of Abidjan.

Outside the city, however, Gbagbo's forces controlled only thin slices of territory, and some worried that he might try to expand the conflict into a wider civil war. This might very well have been his strategy, as he had deliberately stirred up ethnic and xenophobic emotions in Ivory Coast's south.

Today, Ouattara's forces control the entire country—yet the impact of the matter's having been forced to a military conclusion remains uncertain. In a nation that has been on the brink of civil war for over a decade, the military resolution of the impasse may weaken Ouattara's ability to pursue reconciliation between the north and the south, which remain divided along political, ethnic, and sectarian lines.

A civil war not only would wreak awful damage in Ivory Coast; it would destabilize the nation's already weak and fragile neighbors. Indeed, inter-African groups, especially the West African regional organization ECOWAS (the Economic Community of West African States), recognized the domino-effect potential of Gbagbo's usurpation and reacted strongly in order to promote peaceful democratic transitions.

ECOWAS's rapid and firm response was a bright spot in the crisis. It could end up aiding the still-fragile process of democratization in the region by demonstrating that inter-African organizations are willing to enforce (by political means, or in extreme cases, through force) the fundamental tenets of democracy, including that the winner of a free and fair election should be handed power peacefully and allowed to fulfill his mandate.

Pressure Drop

The issue of how to institutionalize stable democratic transitions has confounded African nations since they gained independence. Only a handful of leaders on the continent have given up power willingly in the past 50 years. It is a rare African presidential election that is not disputed by the loser, who usually claims fraud. (And the majority of elections are flawed enough to raise doubts about their outcome.) Many of these disputes have been resolved without outside help, particularly when the winner was already in office and able to employ the levers of state power to overcome such challenges—often through repression and bribery.

The issue of how to institutionalize stable democratic transitions has confounded African nations since they gained independence.

In a few cases, such as in Kenya and Zimbabwe in 2008, mediation has produced power-sharing agreements that at least temporarily resolved crises. Power-sharing agreements, however, are usually the last resort used by outside mediators in an effort to avoid, or stop, violence. Often such agreements only encourage more violence and fraud. Worse still, when an election has produced a clear winner, power sharing subverts the purpose of voting and thereby undermines democratic procedures and institutions.

Ivory Coast's election produced a clear winner, and no rationale existed for mediation that would dilute the result or produce a power-sharing arrangement. Rather, there was a clear case for action that would allow the acknowledged winner to fulfill the mandate afforded by a majority of voters.

At the beginning of the crisis in early December, leaders of the West African states and the African Union (AU), as well as the international community, exerted heavy pressure on Gbagbo to give up his office. Had this effort continued and been ratcheted up systematically, it is possible that the crisis would not have lasted so long or required, in the end, a military solution.

But the pressure was not sustained, in part because uprisings in North Africa and the Middle East diverted attention in Western capitals and among the international media away from Ivory Coast. The crisis only regained significant notice when the impasse descended into military conflict.

In fact, because Gbagbo never budged from his intention to retain power despite universal acceptance of the election results (and never ceased using state resources to stay in office), the close attention of officials in Western capitals and the UN was needed, and so were their coordinated and leveraged efforts to increase international pressure. Also, as it turned out, Western efforts were needed to keep pressure on some African nations outside the West African region. Leaders in a number of such countries were not fully on the same page as ECOWAS regarding how to handle the Ivory Coast crisis—or whether even to try.

In December 2010 and January 2011, Abidjan, Ivory Coast's de facto capital, received a procession of ECOWAS diplomatic missions searching for a formula that would persuade Gbagbo to give up power and step down. ECOWAS remained firmly in favor of diplomatic intervention, and did not take joint military action off the table. By February, however, some of the AU's more entrenched leaders—probably seeing the implications for themselves of a strong stand on Ouattara's legitimacy—backed away from anything resembling tough intervention.

The unambiguous electoral result in Ivory Coast should have lent strength to regional efforts to bring about a true democratic outcome. But such a process is never easy or simple. In Africa, as in much of the developing world, politics is all about access to resources. This is what complicates the African search for sustainable democracy and what often motivates the civil strife that causes national political systems to break down.

The Strongman's Legacy

The paternalism that characterized Africa's early decades of independence failed to establish political systems that could function stably and sustainably when nations' early leaders inevitably departed. Ivory Coast's history exemplifies this fact.

From 1960, when Ivory Coast gained independence from France, until 1993, Félix Houphouët-Boigny, one of the grand old men of the African independence movement, ran the country on much the same principles by which his father, a Baoulé tribal chief, ran his village. Houphouët-Boigny ruled with a firm hand but fairly, making sure that all groups tasted the fruits of the economic miracle that the country experienced under his leadership (with generous financial and technical assistance from a French community numbering 60,000).

Ivory Coast was easily West Africa's premier economy in the 1960s and 1970s—the world's leading exporter of cocoa and a major exporter of coffee, pineapples, palm oil, sugar, and other tropical agricultural products. For 20 years, the Ivorian economy grew at about 10 percent a year, quite a feat for an African country that did not export oil.

Houphouët-Boigny was the proverbial benign despot. Only one political party—his—was allowed to exist, and press freedom was strictly limited. When the economic miracle fell apart amid the world commodity recession of the 1980s, and with the growth of democratic aspirations around the globe, opposition to his one-man, one-party rule began to develop. (Ironically, Gbagbo was one of the early advocates of political reform.) The president was forced into some concessions, such as allowing other parties to compete in elections. But he faced no serious political challenges.

Houphouët-Boigny was always inclusive of outsiders with talent and expertise. In 1988, he appointed Ouattara, a respected international economist and a Muslim from northern Ivory Coast, as his prime minister to help address the country's economic crisis. Social and political disquiet had grown during the 1980s as the economic troubles intensified, but the aging president kept it bottled up. Multiparty politics did not produce a democratic culture, and there was little opportunity while Houphouët-Boigny was alive, even in his last feeble days, for the social and political pressures built up over the years to vent.

The cork came off the bottle when Houphouët-Boigny died in 1993. His constitutional successor was Henri Konan Bédié, the president of the National Assembly, who took office after a brief power struggle with Prime Minister Ouattara. Bédié began immediately to prepare for a general election scheduled for October 1995, in which it appeared his main challenge would come from a party based in the north, led by Ouattara.

Seeds of Conflict

To undermine Ouattara, Bédié found ways to exacerbate endemic, but heretofore quiescent, tensions between Akan ethno-linguistic groups (of the mainly Christian south) and Dioula and Senoufo immigrants, primarily from Burkina Faso, Mali, and Guinea (in the mostly Muslim north). Bédié, like Houphouët-Boigny, was from the Baoulé, a subgroup of the Akan, which was among the ethnicities that settled earliest along the western part of the Gulf of Guinea coast.

The Muslims, of which Ouattara is a product, had begun to settle in northern Ivory Coast before the Europeans arrived, but they flooded in after 1960, drawn there by the country's two decades of booming economic growth. Of course, that growth made it easier for Houphouët-Boigny to repress the tensions that this large influx generated.

Bédié's strategy called the nationality and loyalty of the northern immigrants into question, emphasizing that their language and cultural heritage came from foreign countries to the north and were not of "native" Ivorian descent. What came to be called the doctrine of *Ivoirité* (Ivorianness) measured individuals' degree of nationality through paternity. This doctrine excluded from Ivorian nationality a large number of people who had been born in Ivory Coast. Yet Bédié succeeded in getting the National Assembly to write the concept into the electoral law as a basis for voter eligibility. This forced Ouattara to withdraw from the 1995 presidential race, and Bédié was elected.

Bédié came into office in an environment characterized by economic difficulties and multiparty and multi-ethnic politics. He appeared to want to rule (like his patron) as an African strongman, but he lacked the stature and finesse of his predecessor. Instead, he relied on excluding those he considered political rivals.

This strategy became more problematic when Bédié began to exclude military officers from the circles of power. Moreover, he stopped paying the army regularly—an error that assured his downfall. A 1999 coup by disgruntled soldiers forced him out of office. General Robert Guei took over, and elections were scheduled for 2000.

Ouattara remained an omnipresent political force even though he had returned to his previous employer, the International Monetary Fund, in 1994. To counter his growing popularity among northerners, as well as to demonstrate to the outside world that Ivoirité was the choice of the Ivorian people, Guei pushed through a constitutional amendment according to which candidates for president had to be "of Ivorian origin, born of father and mother who are also of Ivorian origin." In October 2000 the Supreme Court, stacked with Guei supporters, upheld the amendment. Ouattara was excluded from the election, even though he produced documents showing that he met the test of Ivoirité.

Bédié was also barred from running in the 2000 election: The Supreme Court declared that he was unable to prove his "mental and physical" fitness to run. (Bédié, who had found temporary exile in France, was charged with embezzlement as well.) That left Gbagbo—a longtime opposition politician, the head of a small political party, and a member of the minority Beté ethnic group—as Guei's only rival. (Gbagbo had also been Houphouët-Boigny's only opponent in the 1990 election.) Much to Guei's surprise, Gbagbo emerged as the winner of the 2000 voting.

Guei immediately dissolved the nation's electoral commission and proclaimed himself president. But Gbagbo called out his party's militant youth wing, the Young Patriots, as well as a very militant student group. Three days of violent protests ensued, and Guei fled the country when the military and police abandoned him. Gbagbo became president, but clearly did not absorb any lessons about peaceful democratic transitions.

North vs. South

Ethnic tensions, which increased as President Gbagbo continued to apply Bédié's Ivoirité doctrine, ultimately brought about the division of the country into a rebel-held north and a government-controlled south. An insurgent army called the Forces Nouvelles, headed by Guillaume Soro, rallied around Ouattara's political banner and took control of the northern region. Gbagbo, safely ensconced in his presidential palace, paid his security forces high salaries to retain control of the south.

Conflict erupted in September 2002 when elements of the regular army attempted a coup. French intervention saved Gbagbo. With the country about to be engulfed in civil war, the UN sent in a peacekeeping force to augment the small French force there and to occupy neutral territory between the two regions. This kept the conflict from escalating into a full-blown war, but enmity between the two sides remained tangible.

The UN sponsored a series of inter-African regional meetings to look for a framework to resolve the impasse. This incremental process went on for about five years, focusing on both the nationality question and the problem of disarming and demobilizing the two main fighting forces. It ended in 2007 with a breakthrough agreement between Gbagbo and Ouattara, brokered by President Blaise Compaoré of Burkina Faso.

This Ouagadougou Political Agreement (OPA), named for the city in Burkina Faso where it was negotiated, fashioned a framework and machinery for establishing the nationality of populations living in Ivory Coast and for creating on that basis an approved list of voters. It also laid out provisions for establishing an independent election commission, and worked out a plan for integrating the two combatant forces into a national army. These steps promised a democratic resolution to the long political conflict.

In the meantime Gbagbo's presidential term, which was supposed to end in 2005, kept getting extended, and elections kept getting postponed. In keeping with the spirit of the OPA, further political steps to resolve the conflict were taken in 2007, when a power-sharing deal was struck between Gbagbo and Soro, according to which the rebel leader was named prime minister. In August of that year, Gbagbo announced that Ouattara would be able to run in the next presidential election. But the election continued to be postponed.

By 2010, tensions had subsided as the Forces Nouvelles were satisfied that northerners could enjoy full rights as Ivorian citizens. The situation seemed ripe for holding the long-overdue vote, and Gbagbo finally agreed to let it take place. However, in the months preceding the election, he began to renege on his agreement to abide by the process set out in the OPA. Gbagbo was quoted as saying that he "would not go to the elections like a sheep."

The president fed the flames of north-south tension as the election drew nearer, returning to the Ivoirité issue and promoting rumors about the fraudulent nationality of Muslim families. He dissolved his government and the independent election commission on February 12, 2010. However, when Prime Minister Soro formed a new government, the new election commission remained neutral, based on the strictures of the OPA.

The 2010 Election

For the October 31, 2010, election, 84 percent of the country's voters turned out. But with 14 presidential candidates, there was no clear winner in the first round. Before the runoff between Ouattara and Gbagbo, Bédié, who came in third, threw his support to Ouattara. (There is enmity between Bédié's Baoulé ethnic group and Gbagbo's Beté.) Despite ethnic violence, 81 percent of 6 million registered voters appeared at the polls for the November 28 runoff.

On December 2, the election commission declared Ouattara the clear winner with 54.1 percent of the vote. The UN on December 3 certified the result, as prescribed in the OPA. However, the Constitutional Council, a Gbagbo-controlled body that is supposed to resolve election disputes and "proclaim" the results, voided 400,000 votes arbitrarily and without investigation, and declared Gbagbo the winner.

Based on the UN's certification, the international community immediately declared its support for Ouattara. The states of ECOWAS, meeting on December 7, declared unanimously that Ouattara's status "as the legitimate leader of Côte d'Ivoire [was] nonnegotiable." France, the United States, the UN, and the AU likewise announced their support for Ouattara.

On December 24 ECOWAS met again, this time a with the Nigerian diplomat Akin Fayomi in attendance to represent the AU chairman. Not only did ECOWAS reassert its support for Ouattara; it declared that, if Gbagbo refused to step down, there would be no alternative other than "the use of legitimate force to achieve the goals of the Ivorian people."

Although not all African leaders seemed to be on the same page, Victor Gbeho—the ECOWAS president and a distinguished Ghanaian former diplomat and foreign minister—issued a statement on February 10, 2011, saying that ECOWAS was convinced "that Ouattara was the winner of the second round of presidential elections" and the military force remained an option for resolving the crisis "but only after all other peaceful avenues . . . should fail."

Money Rules the Roost

Money was both cause and effect in Ivory Coast's crisis. In the continent's political struggles, this is usually the case. The fight almost always concerns access to resources, and it is access to resources that enables corrupt, inept, and occasionally illegitimate regimes to remain in power. Gbagbo's ability to retain power as long as he did was a function of his access to the state's money, with which he could pay salaries of his supporters in the civil service, his security services, and the police. This was estimated require about $120 million a month.

The international community (through the UN Security Council) and ECOWAS immediately put a squeeze on the flow of resources to Gbagbo, imposing economic sanctions and an embargo on export of cocoa and other commodities. But Gbagbo was able to loot various government cash providers to keep the money flowing his way. He withdrew funds from the Ivorian Central Bank, which forced all the local private banks

to shut their doors. He also cut back on some state expenditures, failing in December to make a $29 million interest payment on Ivorian bonds, and reducing government salaries by half.

None of this, however, was going to see him through the longer run. Gbagbo's efforts to get cocoa and coffee producers to pay taxes early, and to tap the murky export profits of the nationalized oil company, were not sustainable. Although he did retain enough access to money to pay his hard-core security forces, he clearly was running low on cash by the time of his capture.

On the other hand, the embargo and sanctions were a double-edged sword for Ouattara and his Ivorian and international supporters. An estimated 7 million Ivorians depend on the cocoa harvest for their livelihoods. The vast majority of these are smallholder farmers with no more than a couple acres of land each, and the sanctions were hurting them severely. Ivory Coast produces about 40 percent of the world's cocoa and, of course, the embargo boosted world prices and increased smuggling for a while.

Weak Democracy

As with many of the crises of democracy in Africa, this one did not have to happen. The shortsightedness and self-aggrandizement of politicians, coupled with weak political institutions and a corrupt political culture, brought it about. Ironically, the politician most responsible, Gbagbo, was in his earlier days an admired proponent of political reform and democratization in Ivory Coast.

But after a decade in power, he believed himself anointed by the heavens and indispensable to his people. (Gbagbo and his wife, both evangelical Christians, reportedly had been convinced by their pastors that only God could remove him from power. Often these pastors appeared on state television declaring that Gbagbo had won the election and that Ouattara represented the devil. Many young, illiterate southern Ivorian Christians believed this.)

Gbagbo used state television often, while he controlled it, to inflame opinion among his southern supporters against the northern Muslims and Ouattara, and also against the French and the UN, which he accused of being imperialist hegemons that wanted to rule Ivory Coast indirectly through their agent, Ouattara. Gbagbo's strategy, as far as one could be discerned, appeared to be to outlast Ouattara's forces and the UN and France while undermining Ouattara's claim to be the legitimate president, at least in the eyes of southern Ivorians.

It was, in essence, a double-suicide strategy. He was prepared, if he went down, to see his nation go down with him. We have seen this before in history, and Gbagbo as a historian must have recognized it for what it was. What he wanted, in the end, was for the forces opposing him to grow weary of the struggle and eventually accept something less than outright victory. From the beginning of the impasse, one witness said, Gbagbo insisted he had won the election, yet was open to some form of power sharing.

Such an option would have tested ECOWAS's unity and resolve. The regional organization was reluctant to pursue joint military action—in other words, to make war on one of its members. (Its record in such efforts is poor in any case.) Nor did ECOWAS enjoy the prospect of a humiliating back-down that might have led either to an unsatisfactory mediated outcome or outright civil war, or both.

As it happened, the logic of the situation prevailed: Gbagbo's opponents realized they had to move swiftly to take him down. This required French assistance because Ouattara's fighters, though more numerous than Gbagbo's, were outgunned. On April 11, France emphasized that it was Ouattara's forces, not the French, that arrested Gbagbo after French attack helicopters had fired rockets into the presidential compound. The UN publicly endorsed the operation as necessary and proper given the illegitimate leader's refusal to recognize his defeat in a free and fair election.

It would have been best to obtain ECOWAS's prior public approval of the international military action. (A recent parallel was the Arab League's call for a UN no-fly zone over Libya.) In the absence of such an endorsement, the accusation that Ouattara is a stalking horse for the West, and particularly the French, will be harder to dodge. The only other feasible alternative was an ECOWAS joint military intervention, but time would have been required to prepare such an action—a major drawback. Another drawback was that, with Nigerian elections just around the corner, the major military power in the region might have been otherwise occupied.

Ouattara has assumed leadership of a nation essentially torn in half.

Gbagbo's arrest has to be deemed a victory of sorts. What should give the victors pause, however, is the daunting task ahead for Ouattara and his government. Not only must they repair economic damage that the political impasse caused and damage to the country's infrastructure that the ensuing conflict created. They must also deal with the fact that Gbagbo sowed seeds of ethnic and religious discord that could disrupt Ivory Coast's politics and society for many years.

Prospects for reconciliation between north and south are much dimmer than if Gbagbo had left office in accordance with democratic principles.

The prospects for reconciliation between the north and south, between Muslim and Christian, are much dimmer than if Gbagbo had left office peacefully and in accordance with democratic principles. It has not helped, moreover, that Ouattara supporters are accused of killing many civilians during the crisis. Ouattara has assumed leadership of a nation essentially torn in half. Stabilizing the situation will require a patient and healing touch and an inclusive approach to governing—qualities in short supply among leaders of Africa's struggling democracies.

Critical Thinking

1. What were the origins of the battle for the presidency in Ivory Coast?
2. What was former president Gbagbo trying to achieve by refusing to accept the election results?
3. How did the west African region respond to this crisis?
4. What challenges does the new Ouattara administration face?

WILLIAM B. MILAM, a former ambassador and career diplomat, is a senior policy scholar at the Woodrow Wilson International Center for Scholars. JENNIFER G. JONES is a research assistant at the Wilson Center.

A New Global Player

Brazil's Far-Flung Agenda

Julia E. Sweig

In the last decade, Brazil has recast itself as a global brand and a global power. It is home to the world's fifth-largest land mass and eighth-largest economy and is one of the top global producers of stuff everyone else needs: from animals, vegetables, and minerals to water, energy, and airplanes. The new conventional wisdom suggests that Brazil is now poised to make its name on the global stage and balance the other power in its neck of the woods, the United States. Brazil's ascent coincides with the relative decline of U.S. influence in Latin America and the rise of new centers of power in Asia. This dynamic reinforces Brazil's central foreign policy message: with both place and purpose for a new global player on the world stage, Brazil can be the Mac to the United States' PC—with an ethos and an international agenda to match.

Brazil's aspirations are fueled by its impressive social and economic gains and its diplomatic accomplishments, as well as the ambition, vision, and personal narratives of its two recent presidents, Fernando Henrique Cardoso and Luiz Inácio Lula da Silva (known as Lula). However, Brazil's attempts to exert its influence on a wide range of pressing international issues may dilute the legitimacy of its efforts in such areas as climate change, peacekeeping, and global governance, where Brazilian participation has been most successful. This is not the first time Brazil has generated so much breathless excitement. The challenge for Brazil now is to not let an exaggerated self-image eclipse its focus on balancing the constraints faced at home with the opportunities available abroad.

The next government has the chance to spare itself the illusory quest to be a global power—soft, hard, or otherwise—and instead relish its well-established place at the table. A more modest, although still ambitious, strategy would allow Brazil to shape and influence global institutions, and deepening investments at home would redress its domestic liabilities: glaring underinvestment in human capital and innovation and the still near absence of the state from the lives of millions of Brazilian citizens.

The country's multidimensional identity has long been vexing for U.S. policymakers. Although Brazilians share a solid consensus on the domestic priority of social inclusion, they are not of one mind about how they see themselves. Brazil is a developing country and a developed country. The state is both strong and weak. Nearly half the population identifies itself as black, or at least not white. The country shares its borders with ten South American nations but does not quite see itself as Latin American. Brazil adheres to conservative macroeconomic principles while pursuing aggressive social programs. It boasts a world-class banking and finance sector, with the third-largest stock exchange in the world, but 26 percent of its population still lives in slums. Massive infrastructure projects are under way in Rio de Janeiro, which will be home to the World Cup in 2014 and the Olympic Games in 2016; yet in the same city, more than 4,600 people died in criminal, drug, militia, and police-related violence in 2008.

However Brazil chooses to handle these domestic challenges and its newfound international clout, Washington will have to come to terms with a new power in the neighborhood and understand that Brazil defines itself in a global context.

Great Expectations

The excitement surrounding Brazil is largely based on its economic achievements and natural resources. Macroeconomic stability, inflation targeting, a floating currency, manageable debt, ample dollar reserves, rapid growth, and a climate of political stability catapulted Brazil in the global psyche from just another Latin American debtor nation to an economic powerhouse. The breathlessness about Brazil's potential picked up speed after 2003, when Goldman Sachs coined the term "BRIC" to describe the four emerging markets—Brazil, Russia, India, and China—that will make up almost half of the world's GDP growth by 2020. Brazil seized the BRIC moniker and used it to amplify its leadership role on issues from climate change and food security to global trade.

Brazilians have coalesced around what one Brazilian pollster described as the "material basis for consensus": a broad-based agreement to invest government revenue in people on the margins. This investment has produced a rapid expansion of a domestic consumer class, which, however, remains neither civically empowered nor adequately educated. Initiatives such as Bolsa Família, a conditional cash-transfer program linked to school attendance and regular medical checkups for children; subsidized loans for housing; and an increase in the minimum wage have reduced poverty by approximately 24 percent since 2003. Brazil is still the third most unequal country in Latin America, but almost 13 million Brazilians have escaped from poverty, and 12 million from extreme poverty, in the last eight years. To date, the rich in Brazil have given up a little wealth, and they may be poised to give up more through what is—for Latin America and much of the developing world—an uncharacteristically robust, yet still regressive, system for collecting and paying taxes. Brazil's impressive social gains have become the envy of the developing world, turning Brazil into a laboratory and model for globalization with a social conscience.

Outward Bound

Until the end of the twentieth century, Brazilian foreign policy was based on four primary directives: protect the country's vast territorial holdings, consolidate and strengthen its republic, avoid or settle all conflicts with its neighbors, and maintain a distant but cordial relation-ship with the United States. A founding member of the League of Nations and the UN, Brazil sent troops to fight with the Allies in World War II, but it never aspired to lead Latin America. During the period of military rule in the 1960s, 1970s, and 1980s, Brazil successfully projected itself as both a leading nonaligned country and an occasional but never intimate partner of the United States.

In the 1990s, Brazil evolved from its traditional reclusiveness. The country's success on the home front, together with radical shifts in global politics and economics, has generated a new story line—one that crystallized under the Lula administration—that Brazilians invoke to explain the country's near ubiquity on the global stage. This new narrative recalls the manifest destiny of nineteenth-century America, with a Brazilian twist.

With neither blood spilled nor territory annexed, Brazil consolidated a multiethnic and multiracial democracy, stabilized a strong market economy, and lifted millions into a growing middle class. Brazilians of all stripes argue that by virtue of these accomplishments, Brazil is entitled to be seen as a global power and to act as one.

An increasingly confident Brazil has undertaken an ambitious and far-flung foreign policy agenda. This quest has included efforts to secure a seat on an expanded UN Security Council, to organize major and minor developing countries into a stronger coalition within the Doha trade talks, and, more recently, to expand voting rights for itself and others at the World Bank and the International Monetary Fund.

Brazil also has a powerful voice in climate change negotiations. The country has an exceptionally clean energy matrix and contains approximately 60 percent of the Amazon rain forest within its borders. At the same time, Brazil's deforestation is a significant contributor of greenhouse gases. Brazil is a champion of affordable access to HIV/AIDS medications for the poor and has led the UN peacekeeping mission in Haiti since 2004. After last year's earthquake in Haiti killed 21 Brazilians, the highest loss for Brazilian troops abroad since World War II, Brazil made a $19 million contribution to the UN, announced a $205 million relief plan for Haiti, and committed an additional 1,300 rescue workers. Likewise, Brazilian troops are part of the UN missions in Liberia, the Central African Republic, Côte d'Ivoire, and East Timor, among other current peacekeeping operations. That said, with commercial and diplomatic interests in mind, Brazil has largely stayed silent on crises in Myanmar (also called Burma), Sudan, and Zimbabwe.

Notwithstanding its BRIC brotherhood, Brazil is alert to the double-edged sword represented by China's market power and resource grab. China is now Brazil's largest source of foreign investment—in ports, rail, reactors, iron, steel, and oil. China has become Brazil's largest export market for soy, oil, and iron and its biggest competitor when it comes to manufactured goods and resources in Africa. After years of remaining silent, this year Brazil joined with the other G-20 countries, including India, Russia, and the United States, to call for China to let its currency float.

Under Lula, Brazil championed a South-South agenda in its near and far abroad. Along these lines, the country promoted pan-ideological South American integration and began forging a loose coalition and dialogue with India and South Africa. Brazil has made major investments in Africa, especially in Portuguese-speaking nations and other resource-rich countries. And the Brazilian Foreign Ministry has opened 16 new embassies across the continent in as many years. The Lula government drew on Brazil's economic strength and diverse population—the country is home to approximately ten million Brazilians of Middle Eastern descent—to justify a number of high-profile and commercially driven presidential visits to Israel, the West Bank, and Jordan. Lula touted Brazil's potential as a neutral interlocutor in negotiations between the Israelis and the Palestinians. With no evident diplomatic results to show for the trips, the visits seemed a commercial exercise above all.

Lula's Persian Gamble

Lula and Foreign Minister Celso Amorim's two-year initiative to broker an alternative to UN sanctions against Iran was perhaps the single most controversial—and, to some, inexplicable—example of the new Brazil's international ambition. Joined by Turkey, Brazil attempted to revive an initiative first proposed by the Obama administration to persuade Iran to send its uranium abroad for enrichment. Following several months of talks, including often contentious consultations with the United States, Brazil and Turkey secured such an agreement in a public declaration signed by Turkish Foreign Minister Ahmet Davutoglu, Iranian Foreign Minister Manouchehr Mottaki, and Amorim. The morning after the deal was announced, U.S. Secretary of State Hillary Clinton revealed that China and Russia, both of which Brazil believed would oppose sanctions, supported the U.S.-sponsored resolution. Clinton later called the move by Brazil and Turkey a "ploy" to delay UN sanctions. Brazil and Turkey, which held rotating seats at the Security Council during this period, voted against the resolution. After an internal debate and last-minute communications between Washington and Brasília and Brasília and Tehran, Brazil voted against the United States at the Security Council for the first time ever. Although the deal could have served as a confidence-building measure between the United States and Iran, the Obama administration dismissed the Brazilian initiative outright.

The reaction was even fiercer in Brazil than abroad. The Brazilian elite and media responded sharply to images of Lula hugging and grasping the hands of Iranian President Mahmoud Ahmadinejad as the two leaders celebrated the declaration. The failed diplomatic gambit threatened to isolate Brazil from the major powers on one of the defining international security issues of the day. Critics argued that Lula had squandered the diplomatic capital and prestige Brazil had gained over the last two decades by positioning itself as an independent, influential, and responsible international actor.

Brazil had a variety of motives—historical and geopolitical—for intervening on the Iranian nuclear issue. Brazil's experience in the run-up to the Iraq war hovered over its view of the U.S. strategy on Iran. Amorim, at the time Brazil's permanent representative to the UN, also chaired the Iraq sanctions committee, and he came to regard sanctions as a slippery slope toward the use of military force. As foreign minister, Amorim sought to position Brazil as a bridge between the West and Iran and in so doing establish Brazil as a confidante and reliable interlocutor. For Brazilians, the nuclear swap deal could have been successful on a number of fronts: preventing Iran from weaponizing its nuclear program; challenging Washington's fundamental premise that sanctions could produce more serious negotiations; asserting Brazil's moral authority as the only nonnuclear member of the BRIC group; and underscoring the Foreign Ministry's insistence that the old rules governing international institutions—whether at the Security Council or within the nonproliferation regime—must be updated to more accurately reflect the emergence of new powers, starting with Brazil itself.

Lula and Amorim also projected Brazil's own nuclear history onto Iran and thus saw Brazil as uniquely positioned to convince Iran to commit to a verifiably peaceful, civilian nuclear program. After all, Brazil had tried to develop a nuclear program in the 1970s, and the effort was pushed underground by the threat of U.S. sanctions. For the Brazilian generals who ran the program and the defense intellectuals who promoted it, the bomb was intended to give Brazil the upper hand in its rivalry with Argentina and help secure its international prestige. However, Brazil's transition to democracy changed its nuclear calculus. By 1967, Brazil had signed the Treaty of Tlatelolco, which committed Brazil and Argentina to peaceful nuclear programs and created a binational verification program. Brazil's 1988 constitution banned the possession of nuclear weapons, and in 1998, Brazil became a signatory of the Nuclear Non-proliferation Treaty (NPT). Brazil had thrown off its authoritarian past, voluntarily abandoned its secret nuclear weapons program, moved from confrontation to cooperation with its neighboring rival, and acceded to the nonproliferation regime. For Lula and his foreign policy team, this history suggested that with the right diplomacy, Iran could be persuaded to follow a similar path.

Perhaps the deepest strategic rationale for Brazil to position itself as a diplomatic broker was Article 4 of the NPT—which asserts the right of signatories to "develop research, production and use of nuclear energy for peaceful purposes." Brazil is home to the world's sixth-largest proven reserves of uranium (209,000 tons), and further prospecting may turn up nearly three times this amount. According to the International Energy Agency, over the next two decades, global consumption of nuclear-powered electricity may nearly double. Brazil has two nuclear reactors and a third that will go on line in 2015; plans are in the works to build four additional reactors by 2030. Brazil still sends most of its uranium abroad (to Canada and Europe) for enrichment. Once the third reactor is complete, Brazil will possess an independent enrichment capacity that could allow it to begin exporting enriched uranium. No wonder, then, that Brazil's national security doctrine identifies the nuclear industry as one of three strategic areas of national defense. Opposing sanctions against Iran—indeed, persuading it, at least in principle, to send its fuel abroad for enrichment under the International Atomic Energy Agency's watch—may well have been about preserving a market.

A successful deal could also have shown those Brazilians nostalgic for the bomb that Brazil's moral authority and diplomatic firepower were enough to secure international prestige. But the Iran initiative instead reignited a debate over whether the country's strategic interests were served by giving up its pursuit of nuclear weapons. A nationalist sensibility on the left and the right coalesced around the inherent unfairness of the NPT. The benefits that India, Pakistan, Israel, and North Korea have accrued from staying outside of the nonproliferation regime fuel the frustration that without the bomb Brazil can never join the club of genuine first-order world powers. The constitutional and international obligations under which Brazil operates may be sufficient to limit talk of the bomb to just that. Still, frustration with the ineffectiveness and inequity of the existing nonproliferation regime, as well as Brazil's increasing assertiveness to reform it, will remain a feature of the new Brazil.

Rich Resources, Hot Commodities

Despite the collapse of the Iran deal and the harm done to Brazils image, Brazil will continue to play an influential role on the international stage. Climate change has become an area where Brazil has turned its clean-energy and environmental bona fides into a significant international voice. Yet Brazil's climate change strategy is still evolving: although the deforestation of the Amazon has contributed to global warming more than 40 percent of Brazil's energy supply is derived from renewable sources. The percentage of Brazilians ranking the environment as their top concern more than doubled between 2002 and 2007, to 85 percent, making Brazilians the most environmentally concerned citizens in the world. The Brazilian government remains protective of its sovereignty over the Amazon and, until recently, refused even to discuss deforestation in international climate change meetings. But the shift in opinion has opened the door for Brazil to place stewardship of the Amazon at the top of its agenda.

Brazil's National Plan on Climate Change now outlines a strategy to eliminate the net loss of forest coverage by 2015 and reduce the average deforestation rate by 70 percent before 2017. Its national development bank also administers a $1 billion international fund to finance the preservation and sustainable development of the Amazon. And it has committed to a national greenhouse gas reduction of 36–39 percent by 2020 and positioned itself as a representative of and a bridge to the developing world in climate talks. Although the Copenhagen accord is only a modest step forward on climate change, Brazil's participation and willingness to compromise proved how serious the country is about this issue.

In the coming years, Brazil will play a fundamental role in ensuring international food security. Pastureland covers nearly a quarter of the country, and 150 million acres of arable land remain uncultivated, promising enormous potential for increasing agricultural production in a nation that is already the world's fourth-largest food exporter. Brazil is the largest producer of sugar cane, coffee, and beef. Although China and India lead Brazil in wheat, rice, and corn production, Brazil's agricultural GDP growth between 2000 and 2007 surpassed that of both countries, as well as the global average. In unequal Brazil, however, abundance and deprivation coexist. The Zero Hunger program, which began in 2003, and other initiatives have decreased the number of people who suffer from hunger by 28 percent. This progress, along with Brazil's technological success in adapting mass agricultural production to tropical conditions, has made Brazil a reference point and model for food security programs in Africa and Latin America.

Brazil is home to an astounding 18 percent of the world's available freshwater resources—thanks to its many rivers, lakes, and aquifers. Indeed, hydropower generates 40 percent of the country's energy. Although the global water market is still developing, projections of drought and heightened demand make water one of the world's most valued and scarce natural resources. Access to water for Brazilians themselves remains inadequate—only 2.5 million of 28 million rural Brazilians have access to running water. Nonetheless, UN predictions that climate change could lead to armed conflicts over water mean that Brazil stands to translate this soon-to-be scarce resource into influence well beyond its borders.

Brazil is now preparing to cash in on another gusher: oil. In 2007, Brazil discovered massive oil reserves 150 miles off its southern coast, 16,000 feet below sea level, and buried beneath more than one mile of unstable salt—known as pre-salt reserves. The find could give Brazil the eighth-largest oil reserves in the world, up from 24th (its current ranking), and produce billions of dollars of oil wealth. Petrobras, the parastatal Brazilian oil company—already a major international player in the industry, with operations in 27 countries—expects to be producing a total of 5.4 million barrels of oil per day by 2020.

Extracting this oil has become even more expensive and complex since the 2010 Deepwater Horizon spill in the Gulf of Mexico. Petrobras' reputation for expertise in deep-water oil exploration and extraction is based on its state-of-the-art safety and environmental program. However, insurance premiums have risen 50 percent for deep-water rigs, and Brazil's spill-containment technology, which is the same as Deepwater Horizon's, now requires additional investments. The cost of turning pre-salt oil deposits into revenue to finance infrastructure, education, and social spending has soared since the initial discovery.

Despite the few countervailing voices raising the environmental drawbacks of big oil, Brazil is placing a heavy bet on oil to drive its domestic agenda. Petrobras is likely to capitalize a $224 billion, five-year investment with a share offering this fall. Orchestrated by the presidential candidate Dilma Rousseff, who served as minister of energy and as Lula's chief of staff, the new legal framework governing pre-salt oil deposits would give the state greater control of new reserves, shifting from Petrobras' concession-based foreign investment model to a revenue-sharing model for a new entity, Petrosal. These laws would allocate 50 percent of the state's share of Petrosal's revenues to financing education in science and technology. Some Brazilians—leading intellectuals and those in the "green" movement or nongovernmental organizations—rightly caution against the corruption, politicization, and environmental consequences of placing oil at the heart of Brazil's development model. But far more powerful political and economic players argue that the country's acute structural liabilities—poverty, inequality, and poor education and infrastructure—make the direct and spinoff benefits of an oil boom irresistible.

Domestic Liabilities

Brazil has begun to address some of these perennial burdens. In 2001, inequality began dropping for the first time ever; between 2003 and 2008, ten percent of Brazil's population rose out of poverty; a majority of Brazilians now belong to the lower middle class; and Brazil weathered the 2008 global financial crisis better than most. Investments in infrastructure have picked up: the Suape industrial complex in the northeast and the 1,600-mile Interoceanic Highway, connecting eastern Brazil to Peru, both under construction, are just two examples.

Still, Brazil remains the tenth most unequal country in the world—and more than one-quarter of Brazilians live below the poverty line. Although Bolsa Família has put almost all students in the classroom, the quality of education remains poor, with Brazilian primary education ranking 119th in the world. In a study of countries selected by the Organization for Economic Cooperation and Development, Brazilian students ranked 54th out of 57 countries in mathematics (ahead of only Tunisia, Qatar, and Kyrgyzstan); they ranked 48th out of 61 in reading ability.

Creating the opportunity for poor Brazilians to join the professional and technocratic work force will mean, as Brazilians themselves have long argued, reengineering the paradoxically exclusive public education system. The state now overspends on higher education, funding public universities that primarily benefit students who were able to afford private education in the early years and were thus prepared to pass the rigorous qualifying exams. Multinational and Brazilian companies poised to profit from Brazil's boom have a long history of training workers directly and raiding one another for the country's scant engineers. To be sure, Brazil is now harvesting the dividends of investments in science and technology made by its military governments in the 1960s and 1970s; Embrapa (the agroscience innovator), Embraer (Brazil's world-class aircraft manufacturer), and Petrobras are three examples. Brazil's international competitiveness now depends on a political decision to spend public resources to transform those lower-class and lower-middle-class Brazilians who have recently become consumers into literate producers in an increasingly knowledge-based economy.

Along with educational deficits, violence and insecurity still plague many Brazilian cities. The northeastern region of Brazil, historically the most economically underdeveloped and the most politically feudal, has the fastest economic growth in the country. Yet the region also has the country's highest homicide rate. Although some in Brazil complain that the government can be overly intrusive, in Brazil's favelas—sprawling shantytowns that snake around the margins of the country's major cities—the state is either absent or seen as a threat.

In Rio de Janeiro, more than one million people (nearly one-fifth of the city's population) live in favelas. Many of these neighborhoods—some new, some decades old—are now run by gangs. Easy access to arms contributes to high levels of violence. So-called resistance killings—police killings attributed to self-defense—annually exceed 1,000 in São Paulo and Rio de Janeiro combined. Seven favelas have been "pacified" since Rio was awarded the 2016 Olympics. Pacification entails occupation and armed raids, along with the provision of basic goods, including water and sanitation infrastructure, thoroughfares, street lighting, health and education services, Internet communication, and housing upgrades. This is just the start of an aggressive push to occupy and bring greater safety to 40 favelas surrounding Rio. But the problems of the favelas—weak institutions, informal economic activity, and poverty, to name just a few—require more than pacification and temporary occupation. The intractability of the favelas, despite decades of public policies aimed to redress it, is a permanent reminder that the health and legitimacy of Brazil's democracy depend on its fulfilling its still illusory promises to the millions of Brazilians living on the margins.

Beyond Samba, Sun, and Soccer

The United States is no longer the only go-to power for resolving crises, providing security, or setting the development agenda for Latin America. Most Americans still cling to the visceral but incorrect notion that Brazil should behave primarily as a Latin American country. Washington needs to understand that Brazilians think of themselves less as Latin Americans and more as Brazilians: a hodgepodge of African, European, Middle Eastern, Asian, and indigenous cultures. Brazil's strategic thinkers recognize that the nature and quality of its relations with its neighbors will define Brazil in the twenty-first century as much, if not more, than the bilateral relationship with the United States.

Brazil brings plenty of historical baggage to its relationship with the United States. Many Brazilians who came of age during the political struggles to unseat the generals running the country in the 1960s, 1970s, and 1980s saw the United States as an obstacle to Brazilian democracy and now lead Brazil's most important political parties, social movements, state institutions, and businesses. Even Brazilians with deep ties to the United States share an underlying belief that Brazil has little to gain from an old-fashioned alliance with Washington.

Despite their very real ideological differences on foreign policy, both Cardoso and Lula kept Brazil's distance from the U.S. agenda in Latin America. Through the 1990s, when Latin America generally followed Washington's free-trade, democracy, and counternarcotics agenda, Cardoso's government refused to participate in the Clinton administration's Plan Colombia, resisted the Free Trade Area of the Americas proposal, and opposed the U.S. embargo against Cuba and the 2002 attempted coup against Hugo Chávez in Venezuela, which was initially applauded by the White House.

Like Cardoso, Lula sought to distance Brazil from the United States on regional issues while also putting a Brazilian stamp on a number of regional institutions, including Mercosur, the Union of South American Nations, the South American Defense Council, and, most recently, the Community of Latin American and Caribbean States. But with drugs and violence becoming a Brazilian problem, too, Lula's government provided intelligence and other material support to the government of Álvaro Uribe in Colombia. Still, Brazil denounced the renewal and expansion of the U.S. presence at military bases in Colombia, opposed the coup in Honduras and the U.S. decision not to back the ousted president's return to power, and pushed Washington to lift the embargo against Cuba.

Regardless of whether the next government aligns with or distances itself from U.S. policy in the region, the permanent expansion of Brazil's own interests in Latin America is now paramount. Well beyond its historic and commercial ties with Argentina or its political and economic hegemony in Paraguay, its commercial and financial participation in the economies of its neighbors has taken off. Between 2000 and 2009, Brazilian trade with Mercosur countries rose 86 percent, its trade with the Andean Community grew by 253 percent, and its trade with Mexico increased by 121 percent. Often with preferential financing from the Brazilian Development Bank, Brazil's global companies have become major actors in infrastructure projects throughout the region—including investments in Colombia's mining and oil sectors; oil-refinery modernization and highway construction in Peru; and transit, construction, oil extraction, and soybean planting in Venezuela. Unlike Chávez, who distributes his country's petro-largess for explicitly political and ideological purposes, Brazil has translated its investments and economic prowess in Latin America into influence on the global stage.

The informality of the economies along Brazil's borders makes them a breeding ground for organized criminal gangs and for trafficking in people, guns, drugs, and other contraband. Conscious of the vast asymmetries in the neighborhood, Brazil has recently begun to build an elaborate network of military bases along the country's extremely porous 9,000-mile border.

In Latin America, the competition for diplomatic leverage and political influence is just getting started. Indeed, Lula and Rousseff's foreign policy architects argue that Brazil's interests in Latin America necessarily propel the country into low-intensity competition with the United States. After decades of taking its cues about how to think about the region primarily from U.S.-oriented elites, the United States is playing catch-up to acquaint itself with a substantially changed region. Latin American governments are now accountable first and foremost to a newly empowered electorate—including the poor, the working class, the new middle class, indigenous groups, and social movements—and not to Washington. Proximity and interests have likewise compelled the new Brazil to learn to live with this changed political environment.

It is unlikely that either Brazil or the United States will succeed in dominating diplomacy in Latin America. Old multilateral institutions such as the Organization of American States are struggling to recover from the distortions of U.S. hegemony and the ambivalence and outright defiance of some member countries. Without appearing to desire leadership over institutions in the region, which could possibly induce an anti-Brazil backlash from lesser powers, Brazil is proceeding gingerly to maximize its interests and minimize conflict.

On some issues, real conflict will continue to exist between the United States and Brazil. But on balance, Brazil is neither fundamentally anti-American nor pro-American. While Brazil was challenging the United States from Honduras to Colombia to Iran, for example, it was simultaneously negotiating the first defense cooperation agreement with the United States since 1977, working with the Obama administration to resolve a dispute over the cotton market, and maintaining an open channel of communication on climate change and international economic institutions.

The bilateral relationship is likely to hover in this undefined space of neither friend nor adversary. The Obama and Lula governments have coined the term "global partnership dialogue," a fuzzy way of acknowledging some interest in building up

layers of scaffolding around a house in the very early stages of construction. The missed opportunity and mixed signals of the Iran episode reflect strategic differences between the two countries. But global issues still provide fertile ground for them to cooperate, especially on climate change, in the G-20, through modest joint efforts in alleviating poverty, and in treating infectious diseases in Haiti and Africa.

The biggest and most immediate test for the next Brazilian president will be to balance an ambitious domestic agenda with the need to secure Brazil's international position. Indeed, Brazil is in the catbird seat of global powers: it can afford to modernize its defense and security establishment without being forced to make wrenching guns-versus-butter choices. To substantially deepen the investments in its people—on which its new social contract is based—Brazil may well have to lower its near-term sights regarding global leadership. Ultimately, the outcome could be the same: a strong, self-confident Brazil that makes a sizable contribution to peace and prosperity, not just in the region but globally. Perhaps the single most important way the United States can influence Brazilian foreign policy is to make clear, in word and deed, that Washington regards Brazil's rise not as a zero-sum game that threatens U.S. interests but rather as the emergence of a not-quite-natural, albeit sometimes necessary, global partner.

Critical Thinking

1. What has propelled Brazil into the position of rising global player?

2. What domestic challenges does Brazil face?

3. What was Brazil trying to accomplish by engaging Iran on its nuclear program?

4. What issues are likely to increase Brazil's influence in the future?

Julia E. Sweig is Nelson and David Rockefeller Senior Fellow and Director for Latin America Studies and the Global Brazil Initiative at the Council on Foreign Relations. She is the author of *Friendly Fire: Losing Friends and Making Enemies in the Anti-American Century*.

Perilous Times for Latin America

THEODORE J. PICCONE

Latin America has suffered more than its fair share of economic crises, but the global recession of 2008–2009 was supposed to be different. Because this crisis was triggered not by fiscal mismanagement in Latin America but by a combination of risky lending and lax regulation in the United States, some experts and politicians in the region proclaimed it a moment of "de-linkage" from the North. Yet early predictions of a soft landing—following a six-year economic bonanza for the region, which was largely driven by China's thirst for natural resources—proved incorrect.

Indeed, the prognosticators' pendulum has now swung in the opposite direction. We hear warnings about a long, slow, painful recovery in many of the region's nations. Reductions in poverty, unemployment, and inequality are not expected to be achieved until long after economic growth returns. Many expect to see populist, autocratic leaders once again pushing protectionism and resource nationalism.

Latin America is likely to muddle through the current economic turbulence. The bigger story in the region is an unfolding, longer-term crisis of democracy.

In reality, though, Latin America is likely to muddle through the current economic turbulence. The bigger story in the region is an unfolding, longer-term crisis of democracy.

First, the required caveat: Latin America and the Caribbean form a diverse region that is increasingly divided along a number of subregional and ideological lines. Mexico, Central America, and the Caribbean, with their higher dependence on the North American economy and on immigrant remittances, are experiencing more serious effects from the recession than are other areas. The volatile Andean region is torn between the Bolivarian ambitions of Venezuelan President Hugo Chávez and the democratic security message of Colombian President Álvaro Uribe. The Southern Cone, led by Brazil, is flexing its muscles in the Group of 20 and diversifying its trade and political relations with Asia, Europe, Africa, and even Iran.

Regional integration by most accounts is dead, notwithstanding Brazil's effort to establish a Union of South American Nations. Old tensions between neighbors are apparent again as talk of arms races gets louder.

Before the recession hit, different countries varied in their fiscal, trade, and debt situations. As a result, some will return to growth faster than others. States that before the crisis accumulated capital reserves and kept their spending in check, such as Chile and Brazil, have been able to carry out countercyclical spending policies. These policies include further investments in the social safety net, which will, at a minimum, soften the impact of the crisis on the poorest. States in a weaker fiscal position, such as Venezuela and Mexico, are in for a much tougher ride.

Politics Is Back

One direct political consequence of the global recession is that it has driven the final nail in the coffin of the neoliberal "Washington Consensus." What will take its place remains to be seen, but certainly Latin America's leaders are looking to reassert the state's role in regulating economic affairs.

As former Chilean President Ricardo Lagos put it at a recent Club of Madrid gathering on the political implications of the economic crisis, "Politics is back." And given the weakness of governments in the region, a consensus in favor of strengthening the state would on balance be a good thing. But will a stronger state be more or less democratic?

The answer depends largely on how leaders tackle longstanding structural challenges that have burdened the region with the world's highest rates of inequality and public insecurity. Latin America's persistent dependence on natural resource extraction and exports, reinforced by China's thirst for raw materials, means that the region will remain highly vulnerable to boom-and-bust cycles and external shocks. At the same time, continuing underinvestment in education, infrastructure, public services, and technology means that Latin America will fall further behind other regions in the global race for comparative advantage.

At the crux of these problems is that Latin America's economies are notoriously illicit and under-taxed, which leaves governments without the fiscal resources necessary to invest in a brighter future. Unless today's political leaders, and the special interests that support them, are willing to come to terms with the need to pay taxes, Latin America is doomed to remain a second-tier region.

A related economic and political challenge facing the region is respect for the rule of law. To attract private investment in today's competitive global market, states must maintain judicial systems and police institutions that are capable of protecting citizens and enterprises. While some progress in this arena has been made—witness the impressive prosecutions of former presidents and other senior officials on graft and human rights charges in Peru, Costa Rica, Chile, and Argentina—corruption remains a serious drag on the region's political economy. Trust in the social contract is frayed, and this leads small and large businesses alike to evade paying taxes whenever possible.

Short Term, Long Term

Every crisis has a silver lining—at least to the extent that crises can compel a fundamental rethinking of policy and facilitate progress toward achieving much-needed reforms. So perhaps the current crisis will prompt Latin American political leaders to make some hard decisions: Do they raise taxes, redistribute income, and invest in high-quality education and other public goods? Or do they borrow from the future by incurring new debt and relying on the usual export-led economic model, which seems only to reinforce chronic underdevelopment?

In essence, do they govern for short-term political gain, or with a long-term view toward putting their societies on a more sustainable and equitable growth path, even at the risk that they serve just one term? Does democracy, as it is now practiced in Latin America, allow a longer-term perspective? Or will the region's politicians be jarred into action only by another crisis?

While some of Latin America's democratization trends are positive—free elections, alternation of power, burgeoning civil society, and independent media are evident across the region—the underlying patterns of strong-man rule, elite control, corruption, and weak civic education still predominate.

To make matters worse, illicit networks such as those centered around drug trafficking are, in a vicious cycle of illegality, increasingly contaminating political and judicial systems in the region. These developments do not bode well for building consensus within nations around long-term goals.

The economic crisis if anything has exacerbated the difficulties involved in reaching such a consensus. Painful cuts in public services, and increasing crime and social tensions, have made coalition building all the more challenging. This in turn has increased the chances that populist and nationalist appeals to voters will succeed in a number of Latin American countries.

A proliferation of cross-border rivalries and of full-throated attacks against old enemies (Ecuador-Colombia, Peru-Chile, Venezuela-Colombia, Argentina-Uruguay, for example) demonstrates the tendency of politicians to change the subject when economic times turn sour.

The ongoing political crisis in Honduras following a military coup last summer demonstrates what can happen when key actors take matters into their own hands rather than pursuing some form of reconciliation.

Latin America's democrats, if they are to overcome their inherent tendency to govern for short-term gain, must build coalitions and undertake national dialogues to construct long-term visions for their countries. In this way they might establish some basic, common understandings about citizens' responsibility to honor the rule of law in exchange for their governments' delivery of public goods.

Crises Ahead?

Elections are one way to build consensus and hold incompetent leaders accountable—but, as Assistant Secretary of State for Western Hemisphere Affairs Arturo Valenzuela recently explained, they are insufficient by themselves to resolve a constitutional crisis.

We are likely to see more political crises in Latin America as leaders on both the left and the right, with support from key allies, continue to attempt to revise constitutions to extend their hold on power. The Organization of American States, riven by internal conflict, is proving itself incapable of resolving these emergencies, let alone preventing them.

So we are left with a rather downbeat forecast for democratic politics in the region. Even if the major economies continue to climb out of the recession and return to a path of growth in the short term, few benefits will accrue to the average person's economic status. This will raise social and political tensions for years to come.

Even as economic growth resumes, Latin America's great democratic experiment of the past two decades faces considerable peril unless the region's political and civic leaders invest themselves in constructing new forms of national dialogue and reconciliation and begin governing for the long haul.

Critical Thinking

1. What were the effects of the 2008–2009 global recession for Latin America?

2. In what ways has the recession affected the politics of the region?

3. What are the short-and long-term governing options for Latin American political leaders?

4. What developments would reduce the tendency to govern for short term gains?

THEODORE J. PICCONE, a senior fellow and deputy director for foreign policy at the Brookings Institution, is an adviser to the Club of Madrid and has served on the staff of the National Security Council, the State Department, and the Pentagon.

Human Rights Last

China's diplomats have the ear of the world's bad guys. So what are they telling them?

GARY J. BASS

On Feb. 21, 2010, the Chinese Embassy in Harare threw a birthday party for Robert Mugabe, Zimbabwe's heavy-handed and increasingly erratic octogenarian despot, complete with cake, almost 100 guests, and a "Happy 86th birthday" sign. Xin Shunkang, China's dapper ambassador, led the embassy staff in singing the Zimbabwean national anthem in the Shona language. The embassy invited local students to sing Chinese folk songs. "The Chinese people sing the Zimbabwean national anthem in Shona; Zimbabwean people sing Chinese songs in Chinese," recalled Xin when we met in Harare some months later. "It's harmonious." It was the first time Mugabe had visited a foreign embassy since Zimbabwe became independent in 1980. "It's not easy to get a president to come to your embassy," said Xin with a bit of pride. "Not every ambassador can do this, but I could do it."

In Zimbabwe and many other countries far from Beijing, China's hand is increasingly conspicuous these days, and its choice of friends, like the thuggish Mugabe, is increasingly under scrutiny. It used to be that the Western world lectured China most extensively about its poor human rights record at home, for detaining dissenters and silencing free speech. But as China's power and influence grow, the Chinese government now finds itself weathering criticism for its support of cruel regimes around the world—from accusations, as *New York Times* columnist Nicholas Kristof and others have put it, that "Beijing is financing, diplomatically protecting and supplying the arms for the first genocide of the 21st century" in Darfur, to the recent warning by Win Tin, co-founder of Aung San Suu Kyi's National League for Democracy, that if Chinese leaders "praise the [Burmese] regime" without helping the public, then "China will fail to win the hearts of the people." Chinese officials are newly sensitive to such reproaches, if not exactly responsive. As one Foreign Ministry official told me with surprise in the run-up to the 2008 Beijing Olympics, "For the first time, China's foreign position on human rights outweighs the world's concern for China's domestic human rights."

Certainly, as Chinese trade and commerce have exploded over the last decade, they have been an economic boon to many developing countries, correspondingly boosting China's clout in countries as remote from Beijing as Angola, Ethiopia, and Uzbekistan. But in many of those places, China has purchased its clout at the cost of maintaining warm ties with murderous governments, from Burma to North Korea to, perhaps most prominently, Sudan—where two U.S. presidents, George W. Bush and Barack Obama, have accused Omar Hassan al-Bashir's regime of genocide.

Yet it is much less obvious how the Chinese government thinks about these awkward relationships. How does a generation of Chinese who opened up their own country to the world square China's ongoing transformations with such ties to some of the most closed societies on Earth? How does a country haunted by awful memories of the Great Leap Forward and the Cultural Revolution overlook suffering in other countries? Is the Chinese government defending its long-standing principle that national sovereignty should reign supreme, seeking natural resources to fuel its red-hot economic growth, or offering a new model of international development and diplomacy? Is there any way the United States can more effectively engage with China on these issues? Above all, what do China's complex attitudes toward its rogue friends say about the kind of great power China will become?

How does a country haunted by awful memories of the Great Leap Forward and the Cultural Revolution overlook suffering in other countries?

It is almost impossible to report on what China's top rulers think and say behind secure doors in the Zhongnanhai leadership complex. But over the course of multiple trips to Beijing in the last several years, I was able to interview about a dozen Chinese Foreign Ministry officials from various departments, some repeatedly, about China's dealings with outlaw governments. They seemed well briefed that I write about human rights—ordinarily a topic much avoided in Beijing

Having documented what the historic rise of liberal great powers like Britain and America meant for human rights, I wanted to know how Chinese officials see their own impact.

When asked about human rights, Chinese officials invariably start with a principled defense of national sovereignty. Dating back to the 1949 revolution, this tenet recalls China's own searing experience of colonial oppression by the West and Japan. But defending sovereignty may be Chinese diplomats' only guiding ideology today. Since Deng Xiaoping, China has given up on sponsoring Maoist revolutions, as it did in Africa during the 1960s and 1970s. Chinese officialdom remains deeply wary of most of the tools that Western governments have used to promote human rights, not least because the Chinese state has been on the receiving end of many of them.

Chinese authorities recoil at the prospect of humanitarian military intervention, as the West undertook in Kosovo in 1999. Criticizing the use of force in general, a Chinese official drew a stark contrast toward the end of 2008: "This year we had two big events. China had the Olympic Games; Russia attacked Georgia." Another Foreign Ministry official told me, "Sometimes we think what's caused by intervention could be even more thorny than the reality before, like what [the Americans] have in Afghanistan and Iraq. Out of some emotion, [the Americans] initiated those two wars. But it becomes very difficult to get out." When I raised Rwanda as an example of a terrifyingly fast genocide that the outside world failed to stop, one Chinese official rather lamely suggested that the African Union should have been allowed to mediate. Another, asked about Rwanda, uneasily hinted at personal dissatisfaction with the official line, but wouldn't say anything more.

Chinese officials are equally appalled by economic sanctions, which were imposed on their own country after the June 1989 Tiananmen Square crackdown. "In Myanmar, you give more sanctions, but the leaders have a very happy life," argued a Foreign Ministry official. "Why do you just make people suffer, but you cannot change the regime?" Even the tactic of naming and shaming human rights violators is too much for the Chinese state—itself frequently singled out for its own human rights abuses. "It is maddening to be rebuked by foreign countries in a high-profile way," a Chinese Foreign Ministry official told me. Instead, this official boasted, "We usually convince the other parties in a most subtle manner."

Whatever their private misgivings, Chinese officials can be determinedly unwilling to publicly criticize even their most outrageous partners. When, in an unsubtle manner, I pointed out that North Korea had starved a million of its own people to death, as well as sunk the South Korean corvette *Cheonan* and shelled South Korean civilians on Yeonpyeong Island in recent days, a Chinese diplomat would go no further than saying, "We encourage them to have better living standards for their people." According to this official, when Kim Jong Il visited China recently, his hosts were impressed with his desire to develop the North Korean economy. This official, while questioning whether North Korea had really sunk the *Cheonan*, said, "Generally speaking, North Korea is a normal state. It's a nation that has its own right to choose how to govern."

Reluctant to publicly condemn even the baddest of bad actors, Chinese officials champion a diplomacy based on trade and engagement, rather than on military, political, or economic leverage. As one Chinese diplomat told me in Beijing in October 2008, the North Koreans "want to talk to the U.S. The U.S. won't talk to them. Then they develop nuclear weapons; then the U.S. talks to them." The official added jokingly, "But still the U.S. is reluctant to talk to Myanmar officials, perhaps because they did not develop nuclear weapons."

With the outbreak of violence in Darfur in 2003, even some of the most sophisticated Chinese officials were startled to find themselves facing blistering Western criticism over their support for Bashir's government. In 2007, a puzzled Chinese Foreign Ministry official asked me whether Bush had latched onto Darfur as a potential "legacy issue," like the North Korean nuclear negotiations, on which China and the United States cooperated closely and effectively. The official said, "For many Chinese, it's a surprise. Two years ago, people, even academics, would say, 'What is Darfur? Where is Darfur?'" A Foreign Ministry official told me, "One or two years ago, we didn't realize that Darfur was so important."

Nobody has borne the brunt of foreign outrage over China's Sudan policy more than Liu Guijin, China's first-ever special representative for Darfur. Liu is the model of an old Africa hand: an influential veteran diplomat who served in Kenya and Ethiopia, as ambassador to South Africa, and as director of the Africa department in the Foreign Ministry. He is a sprightly man with owlish glasses, a ready smile, and a gracious manner. He's steeped in Western literature, recommending to me *Saviors and Survivors,* a book by Columbia University professor Mahmood Mamdani that shows, Liu said, how the "Darfur issue has been highly politicized." When he gets going, he has the air of a man who's not used to being interrupted.

Liu, who met with me at the gargantuan stone-and-glass Foreign Ministry building in Beijing in August 2009 and again in December 2010, was unembarrassed about China's economic stake in Sudan. It is, he said, "a matter of fact that China does have a great interest there." He defended the state-owned China National Petroleum Corp.'s $7 billion investments in Sudan's oil sector over protests from human rights campaigners: "I say that to get oil that way is not so rare. Lots of multinational corporations do that too. And not everywhere the multinational corporations go have that good a human rights record. So to have economic dealings in countries like Sudan, that the Western countries do not love, that is something normal." Even Liu, a sophisticated character, doesn't register that this might not be the most winning banner for Chinese foreign policy: as principled as a multinational corporation.

During the worst of the slaughter in Darfur, in 2003 and 2004, China was the Sudanese government's most powerful supporter. It used its U.N. Security Council power to block or water down tough measures against Sudan, like the imposition of sanctions or peacekeeping troops. Western accusations of genocide caused a particular headache because China is a party to the Genocide Convention, which obliges states to prevent and punish killings and persecutions "committed with intent to destroy, in whole or in part, a national, ethnical, racial or religious group." To dodge that obligation, Chinese diplomats deny that Darfur meets the definition. One Chinese official did tell me, "If there is a widely agreed opinion that there is a genocide, I think that the international community has the obligation to prevent or to help end it." But the official then downplayed claims from the likes of Bush and activist Mia Farrow ("the star lady") that Darfur counts as genocide.

During the worst of the slaughter in Darfur, China was the Sudanese government's most powerful supporter.

A Foreign Ministry staffer remembered a colleague returning from a trip to Darfur and giving a PowerPoint presentation about the refugee camps. While admitting that Sudan might have stage-managed the trip, this official said, "We didn't see anyone dying. It's serious, but how serious? We have some doubts." Although credible human rights groups estimate that several hundred thousand people have died in Darfur, Chinese officials and elites are skeptical. "I don't know how many people died," a Chinese Foreign Ministry official told me. Another asked: "There are so many crises that need attention. Why this one? We think it's because of the strategic interest of Western countries."

But as the death toll mounted and the U.S. government repeatedly accused Sudan of genocide, Chinese policy quietly began to shift. Liu, who has met with Darfur activists, told me he was impressed with their effectiveness: "They are so successful, the Save Darfur Coalition and Enough." In a September 2005 speech that got Beijing's attention, Robert Zoellick, then the U.S. deputy secretary of state, urged China to become a "responsible stakeholder" in the world system and specifically rebuked China over its support for Sudan. In February 2007, Hu Jintao became the first Chinese president to visit Khartoum, offering loans, partnership accords, and financing for a new presidential palace. But in a break with past practice, China also privately pressured Bashir to accept new peacekeepers, according to Chinese officials. In public, Hu called for creativity in Darfur peacekeeping, as well as a U.N. role there. In July 2007, China for the first time joined the Security Council in voting to deploy a joint African Union and U.N. peacekeeping mission to Darfur, known as UNAMID. Liu bluntly said, "We played a key role in convincing Khartoum to accept UNAMID," and pointed out that China also sent about 300 Chinese engineers to help the peacekeepers.

In another step aimed at heading off Western criticism, in May 2007 China announced Liu's appointment to his unusual envoy position. Liu, in a remarkable statement by the standards of Chinese officialdom, told me being named as "special envoy for a country which is thousands of miles far away from

China—that is something unprecedented, the first time in history. It shows that China feels, though we still adhere to the principle of noninterference in the affairs of a sovereign state, we have a more flexible interpretation than 10 or 20 years before."

After the International Criminal Court (ICC) issued an arrest warrant for Bashir in March 2009, China bristled and tried to neutralize the tribunal's action. Even so, Liu said that behind the scenes, China's "strong advice" to the Khartoum government was "please do not stop your cooperation with UNAMID or expel UNAMID. The consequences will be devastating." He warned the Khartoum government not to retaliate against foreigners living in Sudan, he said. His account is borne out by a confidential U.S. State Department cable released by WikiLeaks, recounting that in September 2008, before the arrest warrant, Zhai Jun, China's assistant foreign minister (as paraphrased by a U.S. diplomat), "expressed grave concern" about ICC charges but "strongly counseled" the government of Sudan to "remain prudent."

Human rights activists argue that China's shift hasn't gone far enough. When I asked Liu about a U.N. request for Chinese helicopters to help more with Darfur peacekeeping, he replied that the Sichuan earthquake had shown China "so seriously lacking in necessary helicopters" of the kind needed in the vast spaces of western Sudan. He noted that, before the sanctions imposed after the Tiananmen Square massacre, a U.S. arms maker had sold Black Hawk helicopters to China, which are now grounded for lack of spare parts. He wryly told a story about a Chinese leader who, visiting the United States, was asked for helicopters for Darfur. The Chinese leader pointedly replied that China didn't have enough helicopters, but "if you could sell us some, we will pay you in cash, and immediately we are going to send them to Darfur."

Today, China is showing flexibility in another part of Sudan, the oil-rich south. As a January referendum on the secession of Southern Sudan approached, which a Chinese official admitted would inevitably mean southern independence, China nimbly built up ties with the southerners. A senior Obama administration official told me that Obama, Secretary of State Hillary Clinton, and other top officials energetically enlisted China's backing for the referendum, with many specific requests. "President Obama is raising it in every meeting with Hu Jintao," said this official, so that Bashir faced united American and Chinese support for the referendum. So long as the referendum was "free, transparent, and credible," Liu told me beforehand, China would accept it—an unusual solicitude about fair voting from a Chinese official.

But China has not abandoned its support of Sudan, only modified it. Beijing remains a powerful backer of Bashir, albeit with fresh reservations. Still, China's changes in Sudan policy lend some credence to those who argue that Western engagement with China can have benefits for human rights even in China's worst client states. "Publicly we are very cautious," acknowledged Liu. "But when we engage with our Sudanese brothers, I am sometimes quite straightforward." Liu said, "Our strict principle is that we do not interfere. But we do not regard giving advice, suggestions, as interference." When I pointed out that when a country of 1.3 billion people suggests something smaller governments are going to listen, he laughed in agreement. Another time, he said flatly, "When we give advice to Sudan, it has to consider it seriously. Because China is one of the few friends of that country."

Sudan was a rare case for China: where international pressure, not least U.S. engagement, was overwhelming. But China is less impressed with American clout today, and most places where China is investing and cultivating friendships, from Burma to Angola, haven't made it onto the Western agenda in the same way. In these neglected places, China is free to stick closer to its own view of its influence. In particular, Chinese officials point to a success story for their softer kind of diplomacy, with a case that would startle many Westerners: Zimbabwe.

"Zimbabwe is a good example for us," said a senior Chinese official. As seen from Beijing, Zimbabwe exemplifies a model of inclusive compromise, with two local rivals coming together without thundering military or economic threats from self-interested superpowers. In September 2008, the dictatorial Mugabe and opposition leader Morgan Tsvangirai made a quiet deal to move forward. The brokers were fellow Africans, not the meddling hegemonists of Washington and London. "It proves once again that it is a good way of countries to solve issues by themselves," said a Chinese official in Beijing. This official suggested that Zimbabwe made a good precedent for other troubled countries: "In light of what happened in Zimbabwe, we should still give time to the Sudanese government and parties in Sudan to make a new accomplishment." But there's an obvious problem with this pleasant vision: Mugabe has repeatedly and brazenly violated the power-sharing pact, maintaining his grip on power while China continues its happy talk.

China has supported Mugabe since his revolutionary struggle against British colonialism and white supremacy. "He led the Zimbabwean people to win their independence," Xin, the Chinese ambassador, told me in May 2010 over dinner at a Hunanese restaurant in a low-density area of crumbling, ravaged Harare. "Just like Chairman Mao."

This friendship endured even as Mugabe drove Zimbabwe into economic collapse after 2000, with at least 80 percent unemployment, hyperinflation reaching 231 million percent, a quarter of the population fleeing, and female life expectancy plummeting to 34 years, the lowest on Earth. Chinese officials admit frankly that, unlike in oil-rich Sudan, they have little economic stake in Zimbabwe; "it's just one drop in the sea," as one put it. But even so, "China did not stop our normal economic relations, as Western countries did," said Liu Guijin, himself a former ambassador to Zimbabwe. Another Chinese official said, "The West is suspicious: Why do you have such good relations with Zimbabwe? Is there a secret deal? I don't know of any secret deal at all."

The key test for China came in March 2008, when the opposition Movement for Democratic Change (MDC), led by Tsvangirai, claimed victory over Mugabe's party in presidential and parliamentary elections. Tsvangirai's movement endured widespread government-backed violence, in which

some 200 people died. When I asked Xin about this bloodshed, he replied, "If they say the president beat some people, did you see that with your own eyes? People could believe it or not."

Tsvangirai, shaken by the carnage, pulled out of a second, decisive round of voting scheduled for June 2008. Neighboring African states refused to accept Mugabe's assertions of victory. Finally, South Africa helped broker a power-sharing arrangement, with Tsvangirai becoming prime minister while Mugabe held on as president. Despite loud MDC claims that Mugabe stole the elections, Chinese officials in Beijing are sanguine: "The Zimbabwe issue is by its nature a domestic issue; like in the U.S. you also in 2000 had this controversy."

This, for Chinese officials, stands out as the proper way to handle an African political crisis. A Chinese diplomat told me, "Many people in the West think it's better to intervene in the domestic situation of the Zimbabwean election. We advocated that the Zimbabweans should solve the issue themselves, with what is good for the nation itself in mind. They went through some zigzags on the road, but the result is much better." A Chinese Foreign Ministry official praised Mugabe's statesmanship: "For a hero of the liberation struggle to make such a big compromise is not an easy thing."

A Chinese Foreign Ministry official praised Mugabe's statesmanship: "For a hero of the liberation struggle to make such a big compromise is not an easy thing."

Now, Chinese officials are full of praise for the joint Mugabe-Tsvangirai government. One Foreign Ministry official said (without evident irony), "That agreement is a great leap forward." In Harare, a city that still suffers frequent power and water outages, Xin told me, "Things are getting better and better." The two parties, he claimed, are like siblings: "For ZANU-PF, there is a new brother, so they have to get used to discussing things." As for Tsvangirai's movement, "The MDC is like a younger brother; they don't have experience in running the country. They try to learn how to cooperate with the older brother."

China balks at using its considerable influence to pressure the regime. One Chinese official told me, "We cannot put a gun to Mugabe and say that you have to accept this or accept that." Liu argued that sanctions would be counterproductive: "It's the ordinary people who suffer from sanctions or embargoes. That is not Mugabe."

It was particularly important to China that the deal be done without superpower interference. "We still see it as a domestic affair," said a Chinese diplomat. "It's not something that needs the intervention of the U.N. Security Council." China usually reserves its Security Council veto for core security issues like Taiwan. In Zimbabwe, one Foreign Ministry official told me, "there is no direct [Chinese] interest involved, no vital interest involved."

But on July 10, 2008, just after Mugabe was sworn in for a sixth term as president, China vetoed a U.S.-sponsored Security

Council resolution imposing an arms embargo on Zimbabwe and a travel ban and asset freeze on Mugabe and some of his top aides. Russia joined China, as did South Africa. Liu said that the African Union had asked China to veto the sanctions. "Because China is the only developing country" in the permanent five members of the Security Council, "that veto belongs to the developing countries," said a Chinese Foreign Ministry official, adding, "No matter how serious it is, it is their internal affair. If the U.N. Security Council really adopts a resolution to sanction Zimbabwe, it maybe sets a very bad precedent; it may set a precedent to have the U.N. interfere in the domestic affairs of a sovereign country."

The reality in Zimbabwe—devastating levels of unemployment, infrastructure in collapse, Mugabe squarely in control—is miserably different from China's rosy official version. It's true that Zimbabwe halted its economic free-fall by adopting the U.S. dollar as its base currency, ending hyperinflation. But Mugabe has trampled the power-sharing deal repeatedly. He named loyalists to all 10 of the regional governorships, though they were supposed to be distributed among the rival factions. He grabbed the most important ministries. Without consulting Tsvangirai, Mugabe appointed a stooge as attorney general and reappointed the central bank governor who had presided over the country's economic meltdown. In May 2010, to the MDC's shock, Mugabe appointed the controversial former electoral chief, accused of helping rig the 2008 election, as the president of Zimbabwe's high court. Tsvangirai's finance minister, Tendai Biti, has complained, "ZANU-PF cannot continue to urinate on us."

When I asked Xin about these vehement complaints, he said, "First, I didn't hear such comments from any ministers from the MDC. Second, I want to say that such a thing is just like in the past 30 years ago; there was a lot of not very accurate criticism of China." It's hard to believe that Chinese officials are truly naive about Mugabe. Liu, who knows the old dictator well from his posting as ambassador in Harare, was unsurprised at the thought of Mugabe violating the power-sharing deal: "I could imagine it. He's such a senior leader, well established, controls everything." Still, with Mugabe and Tsvangirai now jockeying over the prospect of new elections, Chinese diplomats seem to be among the last to publicly assert faith in a shotgun marriage that has overwhelmingly benefited Mugabe.

My most recent trip to China coincided with the awarding of the Nobel Peace Prize to Liu Xiaobo, the Chinese writer and democracy activist sentenced in December 2009 to 11 years in prison for inciting subversion. A few days before the prize was placed in Liu Xiaobo's empty chair, an urbane, worldly Chinese official in Beijing, who usually emphasizes his country's peaceful cooperation with the United States, vented some of his government's fury: "If a million or even a hundred million people listened to Liu Xiaobo's call and make moves to overthrow this government, what could happen to China?" This official heatedly warned that Liu Xiaobo risked igniting an "endless quarrel" like the Cultural Revolution, a dreaded memory among reformist Chinese elites:

"How can China stand it? China will fall into a chaotic situation. Then China cannot pull people out of poverty. Nobody cares for China but us. The basic law helps us enjoy this kind of stability. We can prevent this country falling into the abyss."

This kind of scorched-earth response makes it tempting to explain China's friendships with dictatorships as a simple affinity with China's own resilient authoritarianism. After all, China has taken a hard line on domestic dissent over the past several years, including Liu Xiaobo's stiff jail sentence. But Chinese officials style themselves as a different kind of government: one that has lifted hundreds of millions of its people out of poverty, reached out to the world, allowed limited openness at home, and played a helpful role on the global stage. They point with pride to their role in pressing North Korea on its nuclear weapons and to China's considerable contributions to U.N. peacekeeping operations.

This self-presentation makes China's support for radical tyrants like Robert Mugabe and Kim Jong Il more than a little awkward. Mugabe drove his economy into the ground, and Kim rages against the international system; Chinese diplomats are proud of doing none of those things. Liu Guijin recalls sitting in on summits with African leaders, where "our paramount leader Deng Xiaoping said, 'I don't wish you to take up socialism.'" Liu, remembering China's own experiences, told me he warns Africans against revolutionary excess: "If you go a more drastic revolutionary way, you will destroy infrastructure; you will undermine what you have achieved. You will have more resistance. And you may be faced with embargoes or sanctions."

That softer kind of thinking may yet leave an opening for people who care about human rights. After all, it's easier for China to engage with the West on the human rights situation—couched in suitably diplomatic terms—in a faraway country like Sudan than within China itself. Even before the Sudan experience, Liu noted, China had become more open in its view of sovereignty: "Twenty years ago, we regard[ed] U.N. peacekeeping as a kind of interference in internal affairs. But now we are active participants." And the Sudan example demonstrates that smart, sustained Western engagement with China can pay off. China's shift, however belated or inadequate, puts the lie to the notion that China will never pressure a friendly government about its domestic abuses.

Yet, getting China to reconsider its rogue relationships takes an enormous amount of effort and skill. Other issues—Taiwan, renminbi undervaluation, Iran—will threaten to crowd out America's concerns about China's record on human rights abroad, just as they do on China's domestic human rights record. "I'd put Sudan in the same category of currency, Iran, and North Korea," a senior Obama administration official told me.

The Chinese government excels at spotting weaknesses in foreign pressure. Chinese officials are full of praise for Scott Gration, Obama's special envoy on Sudan, who prefers offering inducements to Bashir. "There is a new approach of Scott Gration," Liu said after the Obama team took charge. "It's no longer 'You do this; we do that.'" In August 2009, when I told a Chinese Foreign Ministry official that Darfur was an important personal and moral issue for Obama, the official replied, "In the character of President Obama, we not only find his morality bu lso his pragmatism." (This was meant as a compliment.) But more recently, after a surge of sustained engagement on Sudan from the highest levels of the Obama administration, Liu noted that "not everyone in Washington agrees with [Gration's] moderate policy." A senior Obama administration official told me, "We've seen them step up in surprising ways" on Sudan.

Yet America's influence over a more assertively nationalist China is already on the wane. At a moment when many elites in today's more self-confident China, particularly in the military, believe that the American system is in decline, dragged down by bitterly deadlocked politics and a stagnant economy, it will not be easy for the United States to engage with Beijing on its human rights impact abroad.

But a more responsible Chinese attitude toward its pariah friends would actually benefit China. By cozying up to Mugabe, China stands to alienate generations of ordinary Zimbabweans, not to mention the millions of other Africans looking on helplessly from outside. In April 2008, dockworkers at the South African port of Durban, with the backing of their powerful labor unions, refused to unload weapons bound for Zimbabwe from a Chinese ship. That could be but a taste of enduring African resentment of Chinese influence.

China risks falling into the same trap that America fell into during—and even after—the Cold War. In places like Pakistan and Argentina, Egypt and Tunisia, the United States championed convenient tyrants and thereby embittered ordinary citizens against America for decades. "Even when we are economically stronger, in the middle of this century, I hope China's behavior will not be the same as the superpowers," Liu Guijin said. "We have such a unique history that is so similar with the developing countries." It is an admirable sentiment. There are some reasons to hope that China will get more responsible. But so far, there are few Darfuris or Zimbabweans who would see much to cheer in China's growing global influence. China would not be the first big power to grow both strong and cold.

Critical Thinking

1. How does China justify its reluctance to criticize the human rights records of countries like Zimbabwe and North Korea?

2. What policy decisions show flexibility in China's thinking?

3. How do China's economic interest influence its willingness to criticize human rights violations?

GARY J. BASS, a professor of politics and international affairs at Princeton University, is the author of *Freedom's Battle* and *Stay the Hand of Vengeance*.

Reprinted in entirety by McGraw-Hill with permission from *Foreign Policy*, March/April 2011, pp. 81–82, 84, 86, 88–89. www.foreignpolicy.com. © 2011 Washingtonpost. Newsweek Interactive, LLC.

Not Ready for Prime Time

Why Including Emerging Powers at the Helm Would Hurt Global Governance

JORGE G. CASTAÑEDA

Few matters generate as much consensus in international affairs today as the need to rebuild the world geopolitical order. Everyone seems to agree, at least in their rhetoric, that the makeup of the United Nations Security Council is obsolete and that the G-8 no longer includes all the world's most important economies. Belgium still has more voting power in the leading financial institutions than either China or India. New actors need to be brought in. But which ones? And what will be the likely results? If there is no doubt that a retooled international order would be far more representative of the distribution of power in the world today, it is not clear whether it would be better.

The major emerging powers, Brazil, Russia, India, and China, catchily labeled the BRICS by Goldman Sachs, are the main contenders for inclusion. There are other groupings, too: the G-5, the G-20, and the P-4; the last—Brazil, Germany, India, and Japan—are the wannabes that hope to join the UN Security Council and are named after the P-5, the council's permanent members (China, France, Russia, the United Kingdom, and the United States). Up for the G-8 are Brazil, China, India, Mexico, and South Africa. The G-8 invited representatives of those five states to its 2003 summit in Evian, France, and from 2005 through 2008, this so-called G-5 attended its own special sessions on the sidelines of the G-8's.

Others states also want in. Argentina, Egypt, Indonesia, Italy, Mexico, Nigeria, Pakistan, and South Africa aspire to join the UN Security Council as permanent members, with or without a veto. But with little progress on UN reform, none of them has been accepted or rejected (although China is known to oppose admitting Japan and, to a lesser degree, India). After the G-8 accommodated the G-5, other states, generally those close to the countries hosting the summits, also started to join the proceedings on an ad hoc basis. When the global economic crisis struck in 2008, matters were institutionalized further. The finance ministers of the G-20 members had already been meeting regularly since 1999, but then the heads of state started participating. Today, the G-20 includes just about everybody who wishes to join it: the P-5 and the P-4, the G-8 and the G-5, as well as Argentina, Australia, the European Union, Indonesia,

Nigeria, Saudi Arabia, South Korea, and Turkey. Still, despite the express wishes of some—and because of the tacit resentment of others—the G-20 has not replaced the G-8. Earlier this year, the smaller, more exclusive group met at a luxury resort in Muskoka, a lake district in Canada, while the larger assembly was treated to demonstrations and tear gas in downtown Toronto.

There is some overlap in this alphabet soup. France, Russia, the United Kingdom, and the United States belong to both the P-5 and the G-8; China is in the P-5, the G-5, and the G-20; Brazil and India desperately want to join everything in sight. At the end of the day, the world's inner sanctum will be expanded to include only the few states that possess the ambition to enter it and at least one good reason for doing so—such as geographic, demographic, political, or economic heft. That means the short list boils down to Brazil, China, Germany, India, Japan, and South Africa.

Bric-A-Brac

The Chief rationale for inviting these states to join the world's ruling councils is self-evident: they matter more today than they did when those bodies were created. India will soon be the most populous nation on earth, just before China. In current dollars, Japan is the world's second-largest economy, with China and Germany gaining on it rapidly. Brazil combines demographic clout (it has about 200 million inhabitants) with economic power (a GDP of almost $1.6 trillion) and geographic legitimacy (Latin America must be represented), and in fact, it has already begun to play a greater role in international organizations such as the International Monetary Fund and the World Bank. Africa cannot be altogether excluded from the world's governing councils, and only South Africa can represent it effectively.

Germany and Japan are a case of their own. The two defeated powers of World War II already work closely with the permanent members of the UN Security Council (when it comes to policy having to do with Iran, for example, Germany acts together with the P-5, forming the P-6), and both belong to the Nuclear Suppliers Group, which promotes the enforcement of nuclear nonproliferation by monitoring exports of nuclear material, among other things. Germany is participating in the NATO operation in Afghanistan (as it did in the mission in Kosovo in the late 1990s); Japan supported the U.S.-led invasion and occupation of Iraq with logistical assistance on the high seas. The values and general conduct of these two highly developed democracies are indistinguishable from those of the powers already at the helm of international organizations. These states would thus provide additional clout and talent to the Security Council—the only membership at stake for them—if they joined it, but they would hardly transform it. Meanwhile, since including Germany and Japan and not others is unimaginable, for now they will have to accept the status quo: de facto participation in lieu of formal membership.

The argument for admitting Brazil, China, India, and South Africa to the helm rests on the general principle that the world's leadership councils should be broadened to include emerging powers. But unlike the case for Germany and Japan, this one raises some delicate questions. Over the past half century, a vast set of principles—the collective defense of democracy, nuclear nonproliferation, trade liberalization, international criminal justice, environmental protection, respect for human rights (including labor, religious, gender, ethnic, and indigenous peoples' rights)—have been enshrined in many international and regional treaties and agreements. Of course, this system is not without problems. A Eurocentric, Judeo-Christian tint pervades—a flaw one can acknowledge without approving of female circumcision, child soldiers and child labor, or amputation as a punishment for robbery—and the Western powers have often flagrantly and hypocritically violated those values even while demanding that other states respect them.

The United States has been an especially reluctant participant in the current world order. It has opposed the International Criminal Court, the Kyoto Protocol, and the convention to ban antipersonnel land mines, and it has undermined progress in the Doha Round of international trade negotiations by refusing to suspend its agricultural subsidies. Still, the world is a better place today thanks to the councils and commissions, the sanctions and conditions that these values have spawned—from the human rights mechanisms of the UN, the European Union, and the Organization of American States (OAS) to the International Criminal Court; from the World Trade Organization to the Nuclear Nonproliferation Treaty (NPT); from international cooperation on combating HIV/AIDS to the International Labor Organization's conventions on labor rights and the collective rights of indigenous peoples; from UN sanctions against apartheid in South Africa and the African Union's attempt to restore democracy in Zimbabwe to the OAS' condemnation of a military coup in Honduras.

Constructing this web of international norms has been slow and painful, with less overall progress and more frequent setbacks than some have wished for. Many countries of what used to be called the Third World have contributed to parts of the edifice: Mexico to disarmament and the law of the sea; Costa Rica to human rights; Chile to free trade. But now, the possible accession of Brazil, China, India, and South Africa to the inner sanctum of the world's leading institutions threatens to undermine those institutions' principles and practices.

Weak Links

Brazil, China, India, and South Africa are not just weak supporters of the notion that a strong international regime should govern human rights, democracy, nonproliferation, trade liberalization, the environment, international criminal justice, and global health. They oppose it more or less explicitly, and more or less actively—even though at one time most of them joined the struggle for these values: India wrested its independence from the United Kingdom, South Africa fought off apartheid, and Brazilian President Luiz Inácio Lula da Silva (known as Lula) opposed the military dictatorship in Brazil.

Consider these states' positions on the promotion of democracy and human rights worldwide. Brazil, India, and South Africa are representative democracies that basically respect human rights at home, but when it comes to defending democracy and human rights outside their borders, there is not much difference between them and authoritarian China. On those questions, all four states remain attached to the rallying cries of their independence or national liberation struggles: sovereignty, self-determination, nonintervention, autonomous economic development. And today, these notions often contradict the values enshrined in the international order.

It is perfectly predictable that Beijing would support the regimes perpetuating oppression and tragedy in Myanmar (also known as Burma) and Sudan. The Chinese government has never respected human rights in China or Tibet, and it has always maintained that a state's sovereignty trumps everything else, both on principle and to ward off scrutiny of its own domestic policies. Now that China wants to secure access to Myanmar's natural gas and Sudan's oil, it has used its veto in the UN Security Council to block sanctions against those states' governments.

India's stance—to say nothing of Brazil's or South Africa's—is not much better. India once promoted democracy and human rights in Myanmar, but in the mid-1990s, after seeing few results, it started to moderate its tone. In 2007, when the military junta in Myanmar cracked down more violently than usual on opposition leaders, dissenters, and monks, New Delhi issued no criticism of the repression. It refused to condemn the latest trial and conviction of the opposition leader Aung San Suu Kyi and opposed any sanctions on the regime, including those that the United States and the European Union have been enforcing since the mid-1990s. India has its reasons for responding this way—reasons that have little to do with human rights or democracy and everything to do with Myanmar's huge natural gas reserves; with getting the junta to shut down insurgent sanctuaries along India's northeastern border; and, most important, with making sure not to push the Myanmar regime into Beijing's hands. New Delhi's official support for what in 2007 it called "the undaunted resolve of the Burmese people to achieve democracy" has been more rhetorical than anything else.

India has also adopted a problematic approach toward refugees and Tamil Tiger ex-combatants in Sri Lanka. Today, a year after the civil war in Sri Lanka ended, more than 100,000 of the Tamil Tigers' supporters (and, by some accounts, as many as 290,000) remain in displaced persons camps that are virtual prisons. According to Human Rights Watch, India—together with Brazil, Cuba, and Pakistan—blocked a draft resolution by the UN Human Rights Council that would have condemned the situation; instead, it supported a statement commending the government of Mahinda Rajapaksa. New Delhi has been looking the other way, knowing full well that Sri Lanka would have bowed under pressure from India to allow displaced Sri Lankans to return home. There are perfectly logical explanations for India's stance, including the fact that India has its own social and political problems in the southern state of Tamil Nadu; the Indian politician Sonia Gandhi's husband, Rajiv, was assassinated there by a Tamil suicide bomber in 1991. New Delhi prefers to turn a blind eye toward the Sri Lankan government's violations of human rights rather than risk taking a principled stand on an issue too close to home.

One could argue, of course, that this kind of cynical pragmatism is exactly what the Western powers have practiced for decades, if not centuries. France and the United Kingdom in their former colonies, the United States in Latin America and the Middle East, even Germany in the Balkans—all readily sacrificed their noble principles on the altar of political expediency. But the purpose of creating a network of international institutions, intergovernmental covenants, and nongovernmental organizations to promote democracy and human rights was precisely to limit such great-power pragmatism, as well as to ensure that authoritarian regimes do not get away with committing abuses and that civil society everywhere is mobilized in defense of these values. India's stance does nothing more to advance these goals than does China's. In fact, given its prestige as the world's largest democracy and founder of the Non-Aligned Movement, it might be undercutting them even more when it fails to uphold them.

This last point is even truer for South Africa. No other African country enjoys such moral authority as South Africa does, thanks to Nelson Mandela's struggle against apartheid and his work on behalf of national reconciliation. But the African National Congress remains a socialist, anti-imperialist national liberation organization, and Mandela's successors at the head of the party and the country, Thabo Mbeki and Jacob Zuma, still basically endorse those values. Partly for that reason, the South African government opposed censuring the government of President Robert Mugabe in Zimbabwe even after it cracked down especially brutally on the Zimbabwean opposition following the contested elections of March 2008. Mbeki, who was then president, was unwilling to challenge his former national liberation comrade and the principal goal of not intervening in neighbors' affairs. Working through the African Union and the South African Development Community, Pretoria did help broker a power-sharing deal between the government and the opposition in Zimbabwe. But as an April 2008 editorial in *The Washington Post* argued, Mugabe managed to stay in office thanks to the support of then South African President Mbeki.

The South African government, like nearly every regime in Africa, is wary of criticizing the internal policies of other countries, even if they are undemocratic or violate human rights. Unlike other African states, however, South Africa is a thriving democracy that aspires to a regional and even an international role. So which is it going to choose: nonintervention in the domestic affairs of its neighbors in the name of the passé ethos of national liberation and the Non-Aligned Movement or the defense—rhetorical at least and preferably effective—of universal values above national sovereignty, as would befit a new member of the world's ruling councils?

Brazilian Lulabies

And which way will it be for Brazil, for whose leaders the issues of democracy and human rights were once especially dear? Like his predecessor, Lula opposed the military dictatorship that ruled Brazil between 1964 and 1985. At the time, he was an advocate of human rights, free and fair elections, and representative democracy; he often sought out foreign governments to support his cause and censure the people who were torturing members of the Brazilian opposition. But since he has been in office, he has not paid much heed to these issues. Although he has repeatedly flaunted Brazil's entry into the great-power club, he has been dismissive of the importance of democracy and human rights throughout Latin America, particularly in Cuba and Venezuela, and in places as far afield as Iran. He has reinforced the Brazilian Foreign Ministry's tendency to not meddle in Cuba's internal affairs. Earlier this year, he traveled to Havana the day after a jailed Cuban dissident died from a hunger strike. Speaking at a press conference, he practically blamed the prisoner for dying and said he disapproved of that "form of struggle." Just hours later, he posed, beaming, for a photograph with Fidel and Raúl Castro.

Lula also gave Iranian President Mahmoud Ahmadinejad a hero's welcome in Brasília and São Paulo (the latter home to a majority of Brazil's significant Jewish community) just a few months after Ahmadinejad stole his country's 2009 election and the Iranian government violently suppressed the resulting public demonstrations. Within a few months of that visit, Lula traveled to Tehran. To Venezuelan President Hugo Chávez's increasingly heavy hand, Lula has also turned a blind eye. He never questions the jailing of political opponents; crackdowns on the press, trade unions, and students; or tampering with the electoral system in Venezuela. Brazilian corporations, especially construction companies, have huge investments there, and Lula has used his friendship with Chávez and the Castro brothers to placate the left wing of his party, which is uncomfortable with his orthodox economic policies. He systematically cloaks his pragmatic—some would say cynical—approach in the robes of nonintervention, self-determination, and Third World solidarity.

Recently, Brazil seems to have changed its tune somewhat, moving slightly away from its traditional stance of nonintervention after a coup in Honduras last year. When Honduran President Manuel Zelaya was ousted from office in June 2009, Lula suddenly became a stalwart defender of Honduras' democracy. Together with allies of Zelaya, such as Raúl Castro, Chávez, and the presidents of Bolivia, Ecuador, and Nicaragua,

Lula convinced other members of the OAS, including Mexico and the United States, to suspend Honduras from the organization. Lula subsequently granted Zelaya asylum in the Brazilian embassy in Tegucigalpa, allowing him to mobilize his followers and organize against the coup's instigators from there. But since Porfirio Lobo Sosa was chosen to be Honduras' new president in free and fair elections late last year and several Latin American countries and the United States have recognized his government, Brazil's enduring support for Zelaya has increasingly come to seem intransigent and quixotic. One wonders whether Lula's position expresses the reflexive solidarity of a state that once suffered military coups itself, signals a new willingness to stand up for democratic principles, or is yet another concession to Chávez and his friends in an effort to quiet the restless and troublesome left wing of Lula's party by defending its disciple in Tegucigalpa. But this much seems clear: Brazil's first attempt to take a stance on an internal political conflict in another Latin American country did not turn out too well, and Brazil does not yet feel comfortable with leaving behind its traditional policy of nonintervention in the name of the collective defense of human rights and democracy.

It's the Bomb!

These States' ambivalence on so-called soft issues, such as human rights and democracy, tends to go hand in hand with their recalcitrance on "harder" issues, such as nuclear proliferation. With the exception of South Africa, which unilaterally gave up the nuclear weapons it had secretly built under apartheid, Brazil, China, and India have opposed the international nonproliferation regime created by the NPT in 1968. India has not deliberately helped or encouraged other countries with their nuclear ambitions. But it has never ratified the NPT, and the very fact that it went nuclear in 1974 led Pakistan, its neighbor and enemy, to do the same in 1982. Pakistan has since become one of the world's worst proliferators, thanks to the shenanigans of the rogue nuclear scientist A. Q. Khan. India cannot rightly be faulted for the actions of Pakistan, but it can be for not signing the NPT, for not doing more to assist the Nuclear Suppliers Group, and for not sanctioning states that aspire to get the bomb. It has coddled Tehran even as Tehran has seemed increasingly determined to build a nuclear weapon; it has repeatedly rejected imposing sanctions. In opposing the last batch in June of this year, Indian Prime Minister Manmohan Singh stated that Iran had every right to develop a peaceful nuclear industry and that there was scant evidence that any military intent was driving its program. He did not need to say that India is developing an important energy relationship with Iran and is seeking to build gas and oil pipelines from Iran all the way to New Delhi.

China, for its part, has an "execrable" record on proliferation, according to *The Economist* earlier this year—or rather it did until it joined the NPT in 1992 (after that, it at least nominally began to improve). The Chinese government helped Pakistan produce uranium and plutonium in the 1980s and 1990s, and it gave Pakistan the design of one of its own weapons. Beijing has not been especially constructive in trying to hinder North Korea's efforts to acquire nuclear weapons, and it has been downright unhelpful regarding Iran, systematically opposing or undermining sanctions against Tehran and threatening to use its veto on the UN Security Council if the Western powers go too far. Its recent decision to sell two new civilian nuclear power reactors to Pakistan will ratchet up the nuclear rivalry between India and Pakistan and undercut the work of the Nuclear Suppliers Group by making it easier for Islamabad to build more bombs.

Neither China nor India can be counted on to defend the nonproliferation regime. Both states seem too attached to the recent past, especially to the notion that they, huge developing nations once excluded from the atomic club, were able to challenge the nuclear monopoly held by the West and the Soviet Union thanks to the genius, discipline, and perseverance of their scientists. Not that there is anything wrong with being faithful to the past. But perhaps those states that remain faithful to the past best belong there—and not among those that will build a new international order.

Nostalgia is not the problem when it comes to Brazil. Brazil cannot be counted on when it comes to nuclear nonproliferation either, but for reasons having less to do with its past than its future. In the 1960s, it signed the Treaty of Tlatelolco, which banned nuclear weapons from Latin America, and in the 1990s, together with Argentina, it agreed to dismantle its enrichment program. When it finally ratified the NPT, in 1998, Brazil was perceived as a strong supporter of nonproliferation. But this May, eager to cozy up to Iran and wanting to be treated as a world power, it suddenly teamed up with Turkey to propose a deal that would lift sanctions on Iran if Iran took its uranium to Turkey to be enriched. Tehran nominally accepted the arrangement; the rest of the world did not. Lula and Turkish Prime Minister Recep Tayyip Erdogan claimed that the arrangement simply replicated a proposal previously put forth by the P-6 and that Obama supported their effort. Washington nonetheless called for stronger sanctions against Iran. Twelve of the UN Security Council's 15 members, including China and Russia, voted for the sanctions; only Brazil and Turkey opposed them. (Lebanon abstained.) In the end, the episode was widely seen as a clumsy scheme to get Tehran off the hook and a gambit by Lula to get the world to take Brazil more seriously. (Turkey was also deemed to be a spoiler, but at least it has real interests in the Middle East.) What Lula achieved instead was to show that Brazil is still more interested in Third World solidarity than in international leadership. Worse, now some are speculating that Brazil is laying the groundwork to resurrect its own nuclear program.

One might say that in behaving in these ways, the emerging powers of today are acting no differently from the established powers—and that this is the best proof that they have come of age. They are rising powers, and—just like the states that came before them—they act increasingly on the basis of their national interests, and those national interests are increasingly global and well defined. But unlike the existing global players, they are not subject to enough domestic or international safeguards, or checks and balances, or, mainly, pressure from civil society—all forces that could limit their power and help them define their national interests beyond the economic realm and the short term. Their discourse and conduct may seem to be as legitimate as those of the traditional powers, but they are in fact far more self-contradictory. On the one hand, the rising powers still see themselves as members of and spokespeople for the developing world, the Non-Aligned Movement, the world's poor, and so on; on the other hand, they are staking their reputations on having become major economic, military, geopolitical, and even ideological powers, all of which not only distinguishes them from the rest of the Third World but also involves subscribing to certain universal values.

To Be or Not to Be

The stance of these countries on climate change also illustrates this persistent ambivalence about what role they are ready to assume. Brazil, China, and India are among the world's top emitters of carbon dioxide (China and India are among the top five). Last December, at the Copenhagen conference on climate change, they, along with South Africa (and Sudan, which was chairing the UN's Group of 77, or G-77, a coalition of developing nations), put forward a position that they said reflected the interests and views of "the developing nations." Building on a statement they had made at the 2008 G-8 summit, they called for assigning states' responsibilities for fighting climate change according to states' capacities. They believe that reducing emissions is above all the responsibility of the developed countries. They are willing to do their share and reduce their own emissions, they say, but rich countries will have to do more, such as make deeper, legally binding emissions cuts and help the most vulnerable nations pay for the expenses of mitigating and adapting to the effects of global warming. Their case rests on a strong foundation: after all, it was over a century of the rich countries' industrial growth and unrestricted emissions that led to climate change, and the poorer countries are only now beginning to develop strongly. Placing proportional limits on the emissions of all states, the reasoning goes, would amount to stunting the economic growth of developing countries by imposing on them requirements that did not exist when the developed countries were first growing.

Perhaps, but this argument also raises the question of whom these countries are speaking for and what role they envision for themselves. Brazil's emissions are mainly the byproduct of extensive agricultural development, deforestation, and degradation; India's, like China's, come from industrialization, which both countries claim they have a right to pursue despite the pollution it causes. These are not traits common to the vast majority of the world's poor nations. On the eve of the Copenhagen summit, Jairam Ramesh, India's environment minister, described India's position clearly: "The first nonnegotiable is that India will not accept a legally binding emission cut. . . . We will not accept under any circumstances an agreement which stipulates a peaking year for India." He did say that India was prepared to "modulate [its] position in consultation with China, Brazil, and South Africa" and to "subject its mitigation actions to international review." But he added, apparently in all earnestness, that India's acceptance of such a review would depend on how much "international financing and technology" the country got.

Do the emerging powers identify more with the rich polluters whose ranks they want to join or with the poor nations, which are both potential victims of and contributors to climate change? The groups overlap (the rich nations also are victims, and the poor ones also pollute), and Brazil, China, India, and South Africa have much in common with both groups, but they cannot be part of both at once. For now, these states seem to have chosen to side with the poor countries. Partly because of that decision, the Copenhagen summit failed, and the Cancún climate summit scheduled for the end of 2010 will probably fail, too. Marina Silva, a former environment minister under Lula who is running for president against her former boss' chosen candidate, seems to have grasped the contradiction in Brazil's official position more clearly than Lula. She has made the case that Brazil should do more. "It must admit global goals of carbon dioxide emissions reduction," she said a few weeks before the Copenhagen summit last year, "and contribute to convincing other developing countries to do the same."

Some candidates for emerging power status are beginning to understand this, but just barely. Mexico, for example, had originally subscribed to the joint stance of Brazil, China, India, and South Africa on emissions caps in 2008 and 2009, but by the time of the Copenhagen summit, it realized that its $14,000 per capita income (in 2008 purchasing parity prices) placed it closer to the states of the Organization for Economic Cooperation and Development (to which it already belongs) than to those of the G-77 or the Non-Aligned Movement (to which it does not belong) and stopped signing their common documents. Similarly, during the Doha Round of trade negotiations, Mexico grasped that its myriad free-trade agreements and low levels of agricultural exports put it in the camp of the industrialized nations rather than the camp of Brazil, China, India, and South Africa. Those states presented something of a common front on behalf of, as Lula put it, "the most fragile economies," although Brazil was more interested in opening up agricultural markets and China and India were more concerned with protecting small farmers. But these are exceptions, like Turkey's attempt to join the European Union, accepting all of its conditions regarding values and institutions. None of the emerging countries, democratic or otherwise, richer or poorer, more integrated into regional groups or not, has truly undergone its political or ideological aggiornamento.

Pay to Play

The ongoing discussion about whether emerging powers should be admitted to the helm of the world geopolitical order emphasizes the economic dimension of their rise and its geopolitical consequences. Not enough attention has been paid to the fact that although these countries are already economic powerhouses, they remain political and diplomatic lightweights. At best, they are regional powers that pack a minuscule international punch; at worst, they are neophytes whose participation in international institutions may undermine progress toward a stronger international legal order. They might be growing economic actors, but they are not diplomatic ones, and so as they strive to gain greater political status without a road map, they fall back on their default option: the rhetoric and posturing of bygone days, invoking national sovereignty and nonintervention, calling for limited international jurisdiction, and defending the application of different standards to different nations.

Given this, granting emerging economic powers a greater role on the world stage would probably weaken the trend toward a stronger multilateral system and an international legal regime that upholds democracy, human rights, nuclear nonproliferation, and environmental protection. An international order that made more room for the BRICS, for Mexico and South Africa, and for other emerging powers, would be much more representative. But it would not necessarily be an order whose core values are better respected and better defended.

The world needs emerging powers to participate in financial and trade negotiations, and it would benefit immensely from hearing their voices on many regional and international issues, such as the killings in Darfur, instability in the Middle East, repression in Myanmar, or the coup in Honduras. For now, however, these states' core values are too different from the ones espoused, however partially and duplicitously, by the international community's main players and their partners to warrant the emerging powers' inclusion at the helm of the world's top organizations.

These states still lack the balancing mechanisms that have helped curb the hypocrisy of great powers: vibrant and well-organized civil societies. This lack is more obvious in some countries (China, South Africa) than in others (Brazil, India),

but there is a fundamental difference between the terms of their inclusion into the inner sanctum and that of those countries that are already there (although this difference obviously applies to Russia also). Before a serious debate takes place within these countries regarding their societies' adherence to the values in question, it might not be such a good idea for them to become full-fledged world actors. Maybe they should deliberate more prudently over whether they really want to pay in order to play, and the existing powers should ponder whether they wish to invite them to play if they will not pay.

Critical Thinking

1. What countries are likely contenders for leadership roles in international institutions?

2. What are the issues that raise questions about these countries' leadership?

3. What positions on these issues are the most troubling?

4. What are the arguments in favor of admitting these emerging countries to leadership positions in international institutions?

Jorge G. Castañeda was Mexico's Foreign Minister in 2000–2003. He teaches at New York University and is a member of the Board of Directors of Human Rights Watch and a Fellow at the New America Foundation.

From *Foreign Affairs,* September/October 2010, pp. 109–122. Copyright © 2010 by Council on Foreign Relations, Inc. Reprinted by permission of Foreign Affairs. www.ForeignAffairs.com

UNIT 5

Population, Resources, Environment, and Health

Unit Selections

Learning Outcomes

After reading this unit, you should be able to:

- Describe the environmental challenges facing the industrialized and developing countries.
- Discuss the implications of these challenges.
- Outline the connections between environment and security.
- Explain the threats associated with water insecurity.
- Evaluate the arguments for a right to water.
- Comprehend the factors that drive increases in food prices.
- Trace the links between higher food prices and the potential for conflict.

Student Website

www.mhhe.com/cls

Internet References

Earth Pledge Foundation
www.earthpledge.org

EnviroLink
http://envirolink.org

Greenpeace
www.greenpeace.org

Linkages on Environmental Issues and Development
www.iisd.ca/linkages

Population Action International
www.populationaction.org

World Health Organization (WHO)
www.who.ch

The Worldwatch Institute
www.worldwatch.org

The developing world's population continues to increase at an annual rate that exceeds the world average. The average fertility rate (the number of children a woman will have during her life) for all developing countries is 2.9, while for the least developed countries the figure is 4.9. Although growth has slowed considerably since the 1960s, world population is still growing at the rate of over 70 million per year, with most of this increase taking place in the developing world. Increasing population complicates development efforts, puts added stress on the ecosystem, and threatens food security. World population surpassed 6 billion toward the end of 1999 and, if current trends continue, could reach 9 billion or more by 2050. Even if, by some miracle, population growth was immediately reduced to the level found in industrialized countries, the developing world's population would continue to grow for decades.

Almost one-third of the population in the developing world is under the age of 15, with that proportion jumping to 40 percent in the least developed countries. The population momentum created by this age distribution means that it will be some time before the developing world's population growth slows substantially. Some developing countries have achieved progress in reducing fertility rates through family planning programs, but much remains to be done. At the same time, reduced life expectancy, especially related to the HIV/AIDS epidemic, is having a significant demographic impact especially in sub-Saharan Africa.

Over a billion people live in absolute poverty, as measured by a combination of economic and social indicators. Economic development has not only failed to eliminate poverty but has actually exacerbated it in some ways. Ill-conceived economic development plans have diverted resources from more productive uses and contributed to environmental degradation. Large-scale industrialization, sometimes unsuitable to local conditions, also increases pollution. If developing countries try to follow Western consumption patterns, sustainable development will be impossible. Furthermore, economic growth without effective environmental policies can lead to the need for more expensive clean-up efforts in the future. As population increases, it becomes more difficult to meet the basic human needs of the citizens of the developing world. Indeed, food scarcity looms as a major problem as the world struggles with a global food crisis, triggered by higher demand, skyrocketing oil prices, and the diversion of agricultural production to biofuels. The world's capacity to increase food production is limited and food shortages are likely to be more common perhaps triggering conflict. Larger populations of poor people also places greater strains on scarce resources and fragile ecosystems. Trade disputes, resource scarcity, and the uncertainties of alternative energy supplies potentially make the world's efforts toward a greener

© The McGraw-Hill Companies, Inc./Barry Barker, photographer

environment a significant security challenge. Growing demand for water is rapidly depleting available supplies. Competition for scarce water resources not only affects agricultural production, but it also threatens to spark conflict. By some estimates, over the next 20 years, a gap of over 40 percent will exist between global demand and reliable water supplies. Greenhouse gas emissions are accelerating climate change; the adverse effects will be felt first by the developing world. Up until now, little has been done to prepare for the inevitable climate refugees that are certain to result from climate change.

Divisions between the North and the South on environmental issues became evident at the 1992 Rio Conference on Environment and Development. The conference highlighted the fundamental differences between the industrialized world and developing countries over the causes of, and the solutions to, global environmental problems. Developing countries pointed to consumption levels in the North as the main cause of environmental problems and called on the industrialized countries to pay most of the costs of environmental programs. Industrialized countries sought to convince developing countries to conserve their resources in their efforts to modernize and develop. These divisions have deepened on the issues of climate and greenhouse gas emissions. The Johannesburg Summit on Sustainable Development, a follow-up to the Rio conference, grappled with many of these issues, achieving some modest success in addressing water and sanitation needs. The Copenhagen Climate Conference aimed at establishing a new limit on greenhouse gases further demonstrated this rift between industrial and developing countries.

Is a Green World a Safer World?

Not Necessarily

A guide to the coming green geopolitical crises yet to come.

David J. Rothkopf

Greening the world will certainly eliminate some of the most serious risks we face, but it will also create new ones. A move to electric cars, for example, could set off a competition for lithium—another limited, geographically concentrated resource. The sheer amount of water needed to create some kinds of alternative energy could suck certain regions dry, upping the odds of resource-based conflict. And as the world builds scores more emissions-free nuclear power plants, the risk that terrorists get their hands on dangerous atomic materials—or that states launch nuclear-weapons programs—goes up.

The decades-long oil wars might be coming to an end as black gold says its long, long goodbye, but there will be new types of conflicts, controversies, and unwelcome surprises in our future (including perhaps a last wave of oil wars as some of the more fragile petrocracies decline). If anything, a look over the horizon suggests the instability produced by this massive and much-needed energy transition will force us to grapple with new forms of upheaval. Here's a guide to just a few of the possible green geopolitical tensions to come.

1. The Green Trade Wars

One source of international friction is far more certain to be a part of our energy future than many of the new technologies being touted as the next big thing. Consider the new U.S. approach in the energy and climate bill recently passed by the House of Representatives, which contains provisions for erecting trade barriers to countries that do not adopt measures to limit emissions. Proponents say these are necessary to reduce the chances of companies relocating to countries with lower emissions standards in order to get an unfair competitive edge. Such tariff regimes are also seen as keeping corporations from relocating to places where climate laws may be more lax, such as China.

Green protectionism is already a growth business. When the European Union considered restricting entry of biofuels based on a range of environmental standards, eight developing countries on three continents threatened legal action in the fall of 2008. In fact, there is a long tradition of such disputes (dolphin-safe tuna, anyone?), but the business community is worried that green protectionism could be a defining feature of international markets in the decades ahead. And of course, the prospect of green trade wars or even just opportunistic fiddling with trade laws to "protect" local jobs suggests a period of related international tensions, especially between developed countries and the emerging world.

2. The Rise and Fall of the Oil Powers

We're also going to witness the complex consequences of the simultaneous rise and decline of petrostates. First, the soaring price of oil—which could skyrocket to $250 a barrel, according to some recent Wall Street estimates—will fill their coffers. Sovereign wealth funds will grow fat again, and with the dollar likely to be weak for years to come, oil fat cats will be buying cheap U.S. assets and making American nationalists uncomfortable all the while.

Those fat cats still have a few good decades ahead of them. Twenty years from now, the world will still be getting at least three quarters of its energy from oil, coal, and natural gas. Today's energy infrastructure took years to develop, and even with revolutionary technological change, the energy mix can shift only marginally in the short term. So, as much as the West may wish to reduce its dependence on the likes of OPEC—because it's not good to be too dependent on anyone, because oil is dirty and killing the environment, because Providence has seen fit to identify the world's most dangerous regions by locating oil beneath them, and because oil is a drug that has corrupted the character of many of its producing nations—these countries will have considerable power for the foreseeable future.

But even as these states reach an apotheosis of power due to the price and scarcity of oil, the writing is on the wall. There is no return to oil once the supply peak has eventually been reached, and it is likely that the demand peak will come even before then. Burning oil at today's rate is just not a sustainable course unless you live inland or in far northern latitudes or own a company that manufactures hip waders.

So, the oil states will be rich, influential, and, paradoxically, in decline. The forward-looking among them might use the time they have to plan, to hedge their bets. But the slow death of the oil economy will undoubtedly lead to flare-ups as social pressures translate into political fractures and opportunistic politicians cling to wealth the old-fashioned way—by grabbing it from their neighbors.

Predicting just where these fractures will occur is difficult. But it doesn't take much imagination to conclude that a Russia dependent on oil exports but faced with declining demand, dwindling reserves, and an unprecedented demographic meltdown will feel diminished in ways that are likely to be dangerous for its neighbors. Or consider how oil's inevitable decline will impact the succession struggle in Saudi Arabia, and that's if the current structure hasn't already collapsed under the weight of the ruling family's mismanagement and neglect of its people. Economic powers with a geological death sentence on their heads are likely to be erratic. One way or another, they will make the rest of us feel their pain.

3. Aftershocks of the Coming Nuclear Boom

…[T]here is simply no way to reverse the effects of climate change without much more broadly embracing nuclear energy. Not only is it essentially emissions free, scalable, and comparatively energy efficient, but just 1 metric ton of uranium produces the same amount of energy as approximately 3,600 metric tons of oil (about 80,000 barrels). It is a far more sophisticated and proven technology than virtually all of the other emerging alternatives. These facts have already led to a very real renaissance in nuclear energy, one that is concentrated in the energy-hungry developing world (more than two thirds of announced projects are in developing countries).

Unfortunately, nuclear power is also fraught with real and perceived risks. Plant-safety hazards are pretty minimal, if history is any indicator. However, two real issues loom. One is how to safely dispose of spent fuel, a dilemma still hotly debated by environmentalists. And another is how to ensure the security of the fuel at every other stage of its life cycle, particularly in comparatively cash-strapped emerging countries, which are often in regions scarred by instability and home to terrorist organizations with their own nuclear ambitions.

With each new program, the chances of a security breach increase. Nor is the danger of a bad actor diverting fuel to produce an atomic bomb the only nuclear nightmare we're facing. Radioactive waste could be used to produce a dirty bomb with devastating impact. And fiddling with weapons programs behind closed doors might be the greatest security risk of all.

A nuclear event would have broad global aftershocks affecting areas as diverse as civil liberties and trade.

Nuclear-weapons expert Robert Gallucci once told me that, considering these growing risks, a deadly nuclear terrorist incident was "almost certain." Such an event would have broad global aftershocks affecting areas as diverse as civil liberties and trade. Imagine, for example, trying to ship anything anywhere in the world the day after. To give just one example, only 5 percent of shipping containers today are subject to visual inspection in the United States. Pressure to make inspection absolute in the wake of a nuclear event could easily lead to the buildup of millions of goods at U.S. ports, driving up consumer-goods prices as market supplies dwindle.

A new nuclear nonproliferation treaty is already on the drawing board, but even as U.S. President Barack Obama works to fulfill his dream of a world free of nuclear weapons, it is already clear that the risks posed by old-fashioned national stockpiles are being eclipsed by those associated with small groups exploiting cracks in an increasingly complex worldwide nuclear infrastructure.

4. Water Wars and Worse

Today, 1.1 billion people don't have ready access to clean water, and estimates suggest that within two decades as many as two thirds of the Earth's people will live in water-stressed regions. It has become a new conventional wisdom that water will become "the new oil," as Dow Chemical Chief Executive Andrew Liveris has said, both because of the new value it will have and the new conflicts it will generate.

Ironically, the hunt for energy alternatives to replace oil could make the water problem much worse. Some biofuels use significant amounts of water, including otherwise efficient sugar cane (unlike rain-soaked ethanol giant Brazil, most sugarcane producers have to irrigate). Similarly, the various technologies that are seen as essential to the clean use of coal are water hogs. Plug-in hybrid cars also increase water use because they draw electricity, and most types of power plants use water as a coolant. Even seemingly unrelated technologies, such as silicon chips (key to everything from smart-grid technologies to more efficient energy use) require a great deal of water to produce.

Many countries could begin to address this by working out schemes to charge for water, the single best way to grapple with this problem. Alternatively, they may build nuclear desalination plants that make saltwater drinkable. Neither course is perfect. A de facto privatization of water has occurred throughout the world, with low-income populations forced to purchase bottled water to avoid contamination, but even so, the ideal of the right to free water has held firm and governments have found it politically untenable to charge even nominal sums. And those nuclear desalination plants? As countries that have deployed this technology, such as India, Japan, and Kazakhstan, have found, they're bloody expensive, at hundreds of millions of dollars a pop.

5. The Great Lithium Game

In Asia, Europe, and the United States, people are getting excited about the electric car—and for good reason. Electric cars will enable greater independence from oil and could play a significant role in lowering carbon dioxide emissions. But the major fly in the ointment for the electric car is the battery.

Many solutions are being considered, including "air" batteries that produce electricity from the direct reaction of lithium metal with oxygen. The most likely option for now, though, is the lithium-ion battery used in cameras, computers, and cellphones. Lithium-ion batteries offer better storage and longer life than the older nickel-metal hydride models, making them ideal for a space-constrained, long-running vehicle.

All this means that lithium is likely to be a hot commodity in the years immediately ahead. It so happens that about three quarters of the world's known lithium reserves are concentrated in the southern cone of Latin America-to be precise, in the Atacama Desert, which is shared by two countries: Chile and Bolivia. Other than these reserves and the Spanish language, the one thing these two countries have in common is a historical animosity, cemented by their late 19th-century War of the Pacific. Chile was able to cut off Bolivia's access to the sea, a maneuver that rankles bitterly in La Paz to this day.

Bolivia's lack of coastline could become an issue again if the two lithium powerhouses start jostling to attract investors. Competition between Bolivian and Chilean lithium mines and, potentially, over domestic production of lithium batteries could very well bring about a second War of the Pacific—to say nothing of the huge environmental costs that lithium mining incurs. Any such tension could jeopardize U.S. efforts to adopt electric vehicles, as the United States already gets 61 percent of its lithium imports from Chile. China and Russia, which also hold significant reserves, would be poised to ride out and profit from such an event. Further, conflict between the two Latin American states would likely bolster the fortunes of batteries made from less efficient resources, such as those used in nickel-metal hydride batteries, or boost other technologies that use different substances with their own drawbacks. And in any event, the possibility of a regional lithium rush reminds us that whatever technologies take hold, demand will emerge for the scarce commodities on which they depend...and we know well where that can lead.

Critical Thinking

1. How might concern for the environment increase trade tensions?
2. What are the implications of continued dependence on oil?

These are just a few, fleeting glimpses of the future, but many geopolitical ramifications of moving toward green energy are very much with us already. In India, anxiety among some in the business community is growing as the United States and China meet secretly and not-so-secretly to try to hammer out an agreement on climate change. It's fast dawning on some Indians that their government's tough stance (resisting mandated emissions caps and offering only to keep India's per capita emissions at or below the average emissions in developed countries) could effectively keep it from having a seat at the table when the core elements of a global deal are worked out in the conversation between the world's two leading emitters and a handful of others. Brazil has a very different view on where such talks should come out because it wants credit for its role as the world's largest absorber of carbon. Russia also has its particular stance, that of an energy provider, and, as with other countries in northern climes, global warming could increase Russia's tourism income, boost its agricultural output, and produce other economic benefits.

Add in the tensions associated with differing views on green protectionism, the shape of relevant international institutions, and the competition for resources, and you can easily see how this contentious climate conversation is going to increasingly reshape the world. And who knows which new technologies could make much of today's speculation moot?

The bottom line: A shift away from dirty old fuels is the only path toward reducing several of the greatest security threats the planet faces, but we must step carefully and avoid letting our optimism run away with us. By acknowledging that a greener world will hardly be devoid of geopolitical challenges and preparing accordingly, we may find a path to defusing our threats today, while largely avoiding the inadvertent drawbacks of desperately needed innovation.

3. What are the obstacles to greater reliance on nuclear power?
4. How might the search for alternative fuels worsen the water crisis?
5. How could the rising demand for lithium increase tensions?

DAVID J. ROTHKOPF, a Foreign Policy blogger, is president and chief executive of Garten Rothkopf, a Washington-based advisor firm specializing in energy, climate, and global risk-related issues. He is a visiting scholar at the Carnegie Endowment for International Peace and author most recently of *Superclass: The Global Power Elite and the World They Are Making.*

The Last Straw

If you think these failed states look bad now, wait until the climate changes.

STEPHAN FARIS

Hopelessly overcrowded, crippled by poverty, teeming with Islamist militancy, careless with its nukes—it sometimes seems as if Pakistan can't get any more terrifying. But forget about the Taliban: The country's troubles today pale compared with what it might face 25 years from now. When it comes to the stability of one of the world's most volatile regions, it's the fate of the Himalayan glaciers that should be keeping us awake at night.

> **When it comes to the stability of one of the world's most volatile regions, it's the fate of the Himalayan glaciers that should be keeping us awake at night.**

In the mountainous area of Kashmir along and around Pakistan's contested border with India lies what might become the epicenter of the problem. Since the separation of the two countries 62 years ago, the argument over whether Kashmir belongs to Muslim Pakistan or secular India has never ceased. Since 1998, when both countries tested nuclear weapons, the conflict has taken on the added risk of escalating into cataclysm. Another increasingly important factor will soon heighten the tension: Ninety percent of Pakistan's agricultural irrigation depends on rivers that originate in Kashmir. "This water issue between India and Pakistan is the key," Mohammad Yusuf Tarigami, a parliamentarian from Kashmir, told me. "Much more than any other political or religious concern."

Until now, the two sides had been able to relegate the water issue to the back burner. In 1960, India and Pakistan agreed to divide the six tributaries that form the Indus River. India claimed the three eastern branches, which flow through Punjab. The water in the other three, which pass through Jammu and Kashmir, became Pakistan's. The countries set a cap on how much land Kashmir could irrigate and agreed to strict regulations on how and where water could be stored. The resulting Indus Waters Treaty has survived three wars and nearly 50 years. It's often cited as an example of how resource scarcity can lead to cooperation rather than conflict.

But the treaty's success depends on the maintenance of a status quo that will be disrupted as the world warms. Traditionally, Kashmir's waters have been naturally regulated by the glaciers in the Himalayas. Precipitation freezes during the coldest months and then melts during the agricultural season. But

if global warming continues at its current rate, the Intergovernmental Panel on Climate Change estimates, the glaciers could be mostly gone from the mountains by 2035. Water that once flowed for the planting will flush away in winter floods.

Research by the global NGO ActionAid has found that the effects are already starting to be felt within Kashmir. In the valley, snow rarely falls and almost never sticks. The summertime levels of streams, rivers, springs, and ponds have dropped. In February 2007, melting snow combined with unseasonably heavy rainfall to undermine the mountain slopes; landslides buried the national highway—the region's only land connection with the rest of India—for 12 days.

Normally, countries control such cyclical water flows with dams, as the United States does with runoff from the Rocky Mountains. For Pakistan, however, that solution is not an option. The best damming sites are in Kashmir, where the Islamabad government has vigorously opposed Indian efforts to tinker with the rivers. The worry is that in times of conflict, India's leaders could cut back on water supplies or unleash a torrent into the country's fields. "In a warlike situation, India could use the project like a bomb," one Kashmiri journalist told me.

Water is already undermining Pakistan's stability. In recent years, recurring shortages have led to grain shortfalls. In 2008, flour became so scarce it turned into an election issue; the government deployed thousands of troops to guard its wheat stores. As the glaciers melt and the rivers dry, this issue will only become more critical. Pakistan—unstable, facing dramatic drops in water supplies, caged in by India's vastly superior conventional forces—will be forced to make one of three choices. It can let its people starve. It can cooperate with India in building dams and reservoirs, handing over control of its waters to the country it regards as the enemy. Or it can ramp up support for the insurgency, gambling that violence can bleed India's resolve without degenerating into full-fledged war. "The idea of ceding territory to India is anathema," says Sumit Ganguly, a professor of political science at Indiana University. "Suffering, particularly for the elite, is unacceptable. So what's the other option? Escalate."

"It's very bad news," he adds, referring to the melting glaciers. "It's extremely grim."

The Kashmiri water conflict is just one of many climate-driven geopolitical crises on the horizon. These range from possible economic and treaty conflicts that will likely be resolved peacefully—the waters of the Rio Grande and Colorado River have long been a point of contention between the United States and Mexico, for instance—to possible outright wars. In 2007, the London-based

NGO International Alert compiled a list of countries with a high risk of armed conflict due to climate change. They cited no fewer than 46 countries, or one in every four, including some of the world's most gravely unstable countries, such as Somalia, Nigeria, Iran, Colombia, Bolivia, Israel, Indonesia, Bosnia, Algeria, and Peru. Already, climate change might be behind the deep drought that contributed to the conflict in the Darfur region of Sudan and hundreds of thousands of deaths.

Rising global temperatures are putting the whole world under stress, and the first countries to succumb will be those, such as Sudan, that are least able to adapt. Compare the Netherlands and Bangladesh: Both are vulnerable to rises in sea levels, with large parts of their territory near or under the level of the waves. But the wealthy Dutch are building state-of-the-art flood-control systems and experimenting with floating houses. All the impoverished Bangladeshis can do is prepare to head for higher ground. "It's best not to get too bogged down in the physics of climate," says Nils Gilman, an analyst at Monitor Group and the author of a 2006 report on climate change and national security. "Rather, you should look at the social, physical, and political geography of regions that are impacted."

Indeed, with a population half that of the United States crammed into an area a little smaller than Louisiana, Bangladesh might be among the most imperiled countries on Earth. In a normal decade, the country experiences one major flood. In the last 11 years, its rivers have leapt their banks three times, most recently in 2007. That winter, Cyclone Sidr, a Category 5 storm, tore into the country's coast, flattening tin shacks, ripping through paddies, and plunging the capital into darkness. As many as 10,000 people may have died.

Bangladesh's troubles are likely to ripple across the region, where immigration flows have been historically accompanied by rising tensions. In India's northeastern state of Assam, for instance, rapidly changing demographics have led to riots, massacres, and the rise of an insurgency. As global warming tightens its squeeze on Bangladesh, these pressures will mount. And in a worst-case scenario, in which the country is struck by sudden, cataclysmic flooding, the international community will have to cope with a humanitarian emergency in which tens of millions of waterlogged refugees suddenly flee toward India, Burma, China, and Pakistan.

Indeed, the U.S. military has come to recognize that weakened states—the Bangladeshes and Pakistans of the world—are often breeding grounds for extremism, terrorism, and potentially destabilizing conflict. And as it has done so, it has increasingly deployed in response to natural disasters. Such missions often require a warlike scale of forces, if not warlike duration. During the 2004 Indian Ocean tsunami, for instance, the United States sent 15,000 military personnel, 25 ships, and 94 aircraft. "The military brings a tremendous capacity of command-and-control and communications," says retired Gen. Anthony Zinni, the former head of U.S. Central Command. "You have tremendous logistics capability, transportation, engineering, the ability to purify water."

As the world warms, more years could start to look like 2007, when the U.N. Office for the Coordination of Humanitarian Affairs announced it had responded to a record number of droughts,

Life in a Failed State

Pakistan

"I remember being in high school when the Taliban took over in Afghanistan. I remember thinking to myself, 'Oh God, it's so close. Could that ever happen here?' and thinking that it wasn't possible. And now, 10 years later, I see the same thing happening in my own country."

— Fatima Bhutto, Pakistani commentator

floods, and storms. Of the 13 natural disasters it responded to, only one—an earthquake in Peru—was not related to the climate.

Worryingly, some analysts have suggested the United States might not fully grasp what it needs to respond to this challenge. The U.S. military has been required by law since 2008 to incorporate climate change into its planning, but though Pentagon strategic documents describe a climate-stressed future, there's little sign the Department of Defense is pivoting to meet it. "Most of the things that the military is requesting are still for a conventional war with a peer competitor," says Sharon Burke, an energy and climate change specialist at the Washington-based Center for a New American Security. "They say they're going to have more humanitarian missions, but there's no discussion at all of 'What do you need?'" The rate at which the war in Iraq has chewed through vehicles and equipment, for instance, has astonished military planners. "Is this a forewarning of what it's like to operate in harsher conditions?" Burke asks.

To be sure, some of the more severe consequences of climate change are expected to unfold over a relatively extended time frame. But so does military development, procurement, and planning. As global warming churns the world's weather, it's becoming increasingly clear that it's time to start thinking about the long term. In doing so, the West may need to adopt an even broader definition of what it takes to protect itself from danger. Dealing with the repercussions of its emissions might mean buttressing governments, deploying into disaster zones, or tamping down insurgencies. But the bulk of the West's effort might be better spent at home. If the rivers of Kashmir have the potential to plunge South Asia into chaos, the most effective response might be to do our best to ensure the glaciers never melt at all.

Critical Thinking

1. How will climate change affect Pakistani-Indian relations over Kashmir?
2. What threats does climate change pose for Bangladesh?
3. How does climate change affect U.S. military missions and planning?

STEPHAN FARIS is the author of *Forecast: The Consequences of Climate Change, from the Amazon to the Arctic, from Darfur to Napa Valley*, from which reporting for this article is drawn.

The World's Water Challenge

If oil is the key geopolitical resource of today, water will be as important—if not more so—in the not-so-distant future.

Erik R. Peterson and Rachel A. Posner

Historically, water has meant the difference between life and death, health and sickness, prosperity and poverty, environmental sustainability and degradation, progress and decay, stability and insecurity. Societies with the wherewithal and knowledge to control or "smooth" hydrological cycles have experienced more rapid economic progress, while populations without the capacity to manage water flows—especially in regions subject to pronounced flood-drought cycles—have found themselves confronting tremendous social and economic challenges in development.

Tragically, a substantial part of humanity continues to face acute water challenges. We now stand at a point at which an obscenely large portion of the world's population lacks regular access to fresh drinking water or adequate sanitation. Water-related diseases are a major burden in countries across the world. Water consumption patterns in many regions are no longer sustainable. The damaging environmental consequences of water practices are growing rapidly. And the complex and dynamic linkages between water and other key resources—especially food and energy—are inadequately understood. These factors suggest that even at current levels of global population, resource consumption, and economic activity, we may have already passed the threshold of water sustainability.

An obscenely large portion of the world's population lacks regular access to fresh drinking water or adequate sanitation.

A major report recently issued by the 2030 Water Resources Group whose members include McKinsey & Company, the World Bank, and a consortium of business partners) estimated that, assuming average economic growth and no efficiency gains, the gap between global water demand and reliable supply could reach 40 percent over the next 20 years. As serious as this world supply-demand gap is, the study notes, the dislocations will be even more concentrated in developing regions that account for one-third of the global population, where the water deficit could rise to 50 percent.

It is thus inconceivable that, at this moment in history, no generally recognized "worth" has been established for water to help in its more efficient allocation. To the contrary, many current uses of water are skewed by historical and other legacy practices that perpetuate massive inefficiencies and unsustainable patterns.

The Missing Links

In addition, in the face of persistent population pressures and the higher consumption implicit in rapid economic development among large populations in the developing world, it is noteworthy that our understanding of resource linkages is so limited. Our failure to predict in the spring of 2008 a spike in food prices, a rise in energy prices, and serious droughts afflicting key regions of the world—all of which occurred simultaneously—reveals how little we know about these complex interrelationships.

Without significant, worldwide changes—including more innovation in and diffusion of water-related technologies; fundamental adjustments in consumption patterns; improvements in efficiencies; higher levels of public investment in water infrastructures; and an integrated approach to governance based on the complex relationships between water and food, water and economic development, and water and the environment—the global challenge of water resources could become even more severe.

Also, although global warming's potential effects on watersheds across the planet are still not precisely understood, there can be little doubt that climate change will in a number of regions generate serious dislocations in water supply. In a June 2008 technical paper, the Inter governmental Panel on Climate Change (IPCC) concluded that "globally, the negative impacts of climate change on freshwater systems are expected to outweigh the benefits." It noted that "higher water temperatures and changes in extremes, including droughts and floods, are projected to affect water quality and exacerbate many forms of water pollution."

Climate change will in a number of regions generate serious dislocations in water supply.

As a result, we may soon be entering unknown territory when it comes to addressing the challenges of water in all their dimensions, including public health, economic development, gender equity, humanitarian crises, environmental degradation, and global security. The geopolitical consequences alone could be profound.

Daunting Trends

Although water covers almost three-quarters of the earth's surface, only a fraction of it is suitable for human consumption. According to the United Nations, of the water that humans consume, approximately 70 percent is used in agricultural production, 22 percent in industry, and 8 percent in domestic use. This consumption—critical as it is for human health, economic development, political and social stability, and security—is unequal, inefficient, and unsustainable.

Indeed, an estimated 884 million people worldwide do not have access to clean drinking water, and 2.5 billion lack adequate sanitation. A staggering 1.8 million people, 90 percent of them children, lose their lives each year as a result of diarrheal diseases resulting from unsafe drinking water and poor hygiene. More generally, the World Health Organization (WHO) estimates that inadequate water, sanitation, and hygiene are responsible for roughly half the malnutrition in the world.

In addition, we are witnessing irreparable damage to ecosystems across the globe. Aquifers are being drawn down faster than they can naturally be recharged. Some great lakes are mere fractions of what they once were.

And water pollution is affecting millions of people's lives. China typifies this problem. More than 75 percent of its urban river water is unsuitable for drinking or fishing, and 90 percent of its urban groundwater is contaminated. On the global scale, according to a recent UN report on world water development, every day we dump some 2 million tons of industrial waste and chemicals, human waste, and agricultural waste (fertilizers, pesticides, and pesticide residues) into our water supply.

Over the past century, as the world's population rose from 1.7 billion people in 1900 to 6.1 billion in 2000, global fresh water consumption increased six-fold—more than double the rate of population growth over the same period. The latest "medium" projections from the UN's population experts suggest that we are on the way to 8 billion people by the year 2025 and 9.15 billion by the middle of the century.

The contours of our predicament are clear-cut: A finite amount of water is available to a rapidly increasing number of people whose activities require more water than ever before. The UN Commission on Sustainable Development has indicated that we may need to double the amount of freshwater available today to meet demand at the middle of the century—after which time demand for water will increase by 50 percent with each additional generation.

Why is demand for water rising so rapidly? It goes beyond population pressures. According to a recent report from the UN Food and Agriculture Organization, the world will require 70 percent more food production over the next 40 years to meet growing per capita demand. This rising agricultural consumption necessarily translates into higher demand for water. By 2025, according to the water expert Sandra Postel, meeting projected global agricultural demand will require additional irrigation totaling some 2,000 cubic kilometers—roughly the equivalent of the annual flow of 24 Nile Rivers or 110 Colorado Rivers.

Consumption patterns aside, climate change will accelerate and intensify stress on water systems. According to the IPCC, in coming decades the frequency of extreme droughts will double while the average length of droughts will increase six times. This low water flow, combined with higher temperatures, not only will create devastating shortages. It will also increase pollution of fresh water by sediments, nutrients, pesticides, pathogens, and salts. On the other hand, in some regions, wet seasons will be more intense (but shorter).

In underdeveloped communities that lack capture and storage capacity, water will run off and will be unavailable when it is needed in dry seasons, thus perpetuating the cycle of poverty.

Climatic and demographic trends indicate that the regions of the world with the highest population growth rates are precisely those that are already the "driest" and that are expected to experience water stress in the future. The Organization for Economic Cooperation and Development has suggested that the number of people in water-stressed countries—where governments encounter serious constraints on their ability to meet household, industrial, and agricultural water demands—could rise to nearly 4 billion by the year 2030.

The Geopolitical Dimension

If oil is the key geopolitical resource of today, water will be as important—if not more so—in the not-so-distant future. A profound mismatch exists between the distribution of the human population and the availability of fresh water. At the water-rich extreme of the spectrum is the Amazon region, which has an estimated 15 percent of global runoff and less than 1 percent of the world's people. South America as a whole has only 6 percent of the world's population but more than a quarter of the world's runoff.

At the other end of the spectrum is Asia. Home to 60 percent of the global population, it has a freshwater endowment estimated at less than 36 percent of the world total. It is hardly surprising that some water-stressed countries in the region have pursued agricultural trade mechanisms to gain access to more water—in the form of food. Recently, this has taken the form of so-called "land grabs," in which governments and state companies have invested in farmland overseas to meet their countries' food security needs. *The Economist* has estimated that, to date, some 50 million acres have been remotely purchased or leased under these arrangements in Africa and Asia.

Although freshwater management has historically represented a means of preventing and mitigating conflict between countries with shared water resources, the growing scarcity of water will likely generate new levels of tension at the local, national, and even international levels. Many countries with limited water availability also depend on shared water, which increases the risk of friction, social tensions, and conflict.

The Euphrates, Jordan, and Nile Rivers are obvious examples of places where frictions already have occurred. But approximately 40 percent of the world's population lives in more than 260 international river basins of major social and economic importance, and 13 of these basins are shared by five or more countries. Interstate tensions have already escalated and could easily intensify as increasing water scarcity raises the stakes.

Within countries as well, governments in water-stressed regions must effectively and transparently mediate the concerns and demands of various constituencies. The interests of urban and rural populations, agriculture and industry, and commercial and domestic sectors often conflict. If allocation issues are handled inappropriately, subnational disputes and unrest linked to water scarcity and poor water quality could arise, as they already have in numerous cases.

Addressing the Challenge

Considering the scope and gravity of these water challenges, responses by governments and nongovernmental organizations have fallen short of what is needed. Despite obvious signs that we overuse water, we continue to perpetuate gross inefficiencies. We continue to skew consumption on the basis of politically charged subsidies or other supports. And we continue to pursue patently unsustainable practices whose costs will grow more onerous over time.

The Colorado River system, for example, is being overdrawn. It supplies water to Las Vegas, Los Angeles, San Diego, and other growing communities in the American Southwest. If demand on this river system is not curtailed, there is a 50 percent chance that Lake Mead will be dry by 2021, according to experts from the Scripps Institution of Oceanography.

Despite constant reminders of future challenges, we continue to be paralyzed by short-term thinking and practices. What is especially striking about water is the extent to which the world's nations are unprepared to manage such a vital resource sustainably. Six key opportunities for solutions stand out.

First, the global community needs to do substantially more to address the lack of safe drinking water and sanitation. Donor countries, by targeting water resources, can simultaneously address issues associated with health, poverty reduction, and environmental stewardship, as well as stability and security concerns. It should be stressed in this regard that rates of return on investment in water development—financial, political, and geopolitical—are all positive. The WHO estimates that the global return on every dollar invested in water and sanitation programs is $4 and $9, respectively.

Consider, for example, how water problems affect the earning power of women. Typically in poor countries, women and girls are kept at home to care for sick family members inflicted with water-related diseases. They also spend hours each day walking to collect water for daily drinking, cooking, and washing. According to the United Nations Children's Fund, water and sanitation issues explain why more than half the girls in sub-Saharan Africa drop out of primary school.

Second, more rigorous analyses of sustainability could help relevant governments and authorities begin to address the conspicuous mismanagement of water resources in regions across the world. This would include reviewing public subsidies—for water-intensive farming, for example—and other supports that tend to increase rather than remove existing inefficiencies.

Priced to Sell

Third, specialists, scholars, practitioners, and policy makers need to make substantial progress in assigning to water a market value against which more sustainable consumption decisions and policies can be made. According to the American Water Works Association, for example, the average price of water in the United States is $1.50 per 1,000 gallons—or less than a single penny per gallon. Yet, when it comes to the personal consumption market, many Americans do not hesitate to pay prices for bottled water that are higher than what they pay at the pump for a gallon of gasoline. What is clear, both inside and outside the United States, is that mechanisms for pricing water on the basis of sustainability have yet to be identified.

Fourth, rapid advances in technology can and should have a discernible effect on both the supply and demand sides of the global water equation. The technology landscape is breathtaking—from desalination, membrane, and water-reuse technologies to a range of cheaper and more efficient point-of-use applications (such as drip irrigation and rainwater harvesting). It remains to be seen, however, whether the acquisition and use of such technologies can be accelerated and dispersed so that they can have an appreciable effect in offsetting aggregate downside trends.

From a public policy perspective, taxation and regulatory policies can create incentives for the development and dissemination of such technologies, and foreign assistance projects can promote their use in developing countries. Also, stronger links with the private sector would help policy makers improve their understanding of technical possibilities, and public-private partnerships can be effective mechanisms for distributing technologies in the field.

Fifth, although our understanding of the relationship between climate change and water will continue to be shaped by new evidence, it is important that we incorporate into our approach to climate change our existing understanding of water management and climate adaptation issues.

Sixth, the complex links among water, agriculture, and energy must be identified with greater precision. An enormous amount of work remains to be done if we are to appreciate these linkages in the global, basin, and local contexts.

In the final analysis, our capacity to address the constellation of challenges that relate to water access, sanitation, ecosystems, infrastructure, adoption of technologies, and the mobilization of resources will mean the difference between rapid economic development and continued poverty, between healthier populations and continued high exposure to water-related diseases, between a more stable world and intensifying geopolitical tensions.

Critical Thinking

1. What are the dimensions of the world's water crisis?

2. What changes are required to cope with the challenge of diminishing water resources?

3. What are the consequences of unequal, inefficient, and unsustainable water consumption?

4. What accounts for the rapid increase in water demand?

5. What steps should the international community take to address this crisis?

ERIK R. PETERSON is senior vice president of the Center for Strategic and International Studies and director of its Global Strategy Institute. **RACHEL A. POSNER** is assistant director of the CSIS Global Water Futures project.

From *Current History*, January 2010, pp. 31–34. Copyright © 2010 by Current History, Inc. Reprinted by permission.

Water Warriors

Declaring water a right, not a commodity, a global water justice movement is growing.

MAUDE BARLOW

Thousands have lived without love, not one without water.

—W.H. Auden, *First Things First*

A fierce resistance to the corporate takeover of water has grown in every corner of the globe, giving rise to a coordinated and, given the powers it is up against, surprisingly successful water justice movement. "Water for all" is the rallying cry of local groups fighting for access to clean water and the life, health and dignity that it brings. Many of these groups have lived through years of abuse, poverty and hunger. Many have been left without public education and health programs when their governments were forced to abandon them under World Bank structural adjustment policies. But somehow, the assault on water has been the great standpoint for millions. Without water there is no life, and for thousands of communities around the world, the struggle over the right to their own local water sources has been politically galvanizing.

A mighty contest has grown between those (usually powerful) forces and institutions that see water as a commodity, to be put on the open market and sold to the highest bidder, and those who see water as a public trust, a common heritage of people and nature, and a fundamental human right. The origins of this movement, generally referred to as the global water justice movement, lie in the hundreds of communities around the world where people are fighting to protect their local water supplies from pollution, destruction by dams and theft—be it from other countries, their own governments or private corporations such as bottled water companies and private utilities backed by the World Bank. Until the late 1990s, however, most were operating in isolation, unaware of other struggles or the global nature of the water crisis.

Latin America was the site of the first experiments with water privatization in the developing world. The failure of these projects has been a major factor in the rejection of the neoliberal market model by so many Latin American countries that have said no to the extension of the North American Free Trade Agreement to the Southern Hemisphere and that have forced the big water companies to retreat. A number of Latin American countries are also opting out of some of the most egregious global institutions. This past May Bolivia, Venezuela and Nicaragua announced their decision to withdraw from the World Bank's arbitration court, the International Centre for the Settlement of Investment Disputes (ICSID), in no small measure because of the way the big water corporations have used the center to sue for compensation when the countries terminated private delivery contracts.

Latin America, with its water abundance, should have one of the highest per capita allocations of water in the world. Instead, it has one of the lowest. There are three reasons, all connected: polluted surface waters, deep class inequities and water privatization. In many parts of Latin America, only the rich can buy clean water. So it is not surprising that some of the most intense fights against corporate control of water have come out of this region of the world.

The first "water war" gained international attention when the indigenous peoples of Cochabamba, Bolivia, led by a five-foot, slightly built, unassuming shoemaker named Oscar Olivera, rose up against the privatization of their water services. In 1999, under World Bank supervision, the Bolivian government had passed a law privatizing Cochabamba's water system and gave the contract to US engineering giant Bechtel, which immediately tripled the price of water. In a country where the minimum wage is less than $60 a month, many users received water bills of $20 a month, which they simply could not afford. As a result, La Coordinadora de Defensa del Agua y de la Vida (Coalition in Defense of Water and Life), one of the first coalitions against water privatization in the world, was formed and organized a successful referendum demanding the government cancel its contract with Bechtel. When the government refused to listen, many thousands took to the streets in nonviolent protest and were met with army violence that wounded dozens and killed a 17-year-old boy. On April 10, 2000, the Bolivian government relented and told Bechtel to leave the country.

The Bolivian government had also bowed to pressure from the World Bank to privatize the water of La Paz and in 1997 gave Suez, a French-based multinational, a thirty-year contract to supply water services to it and El Alto, the hilly region surrounding the capital, where thousands of indigenous peoples live. From the beginning, there were problems. Aguas del Illimani, a Suez subsidiary, broke three key promises: it did not deliver to all the residents, poor as well as rich, leaving about 200,000 without water; it charged exorbitant rates for water hookups, about $450, equivalent to the food budget of a poor family for two years; and it did not invest in infrastructure repair or wastewater treatment, choosing instead to build a series of ditches and canals through poor areas of La Paz, which it used to send garbage, raw sewage and even the effluent from the city's abattoirs into Lake Titicaca, considered by UNESCO a World Heritage site. To add insult to injury, the company located its fortresslike plant under the beautiful Mount Illimani, where it captured the snowmelt off the mountain and, after rudimentary treatment, piped it into the homes of families and businesses in La Paz that could pay. The nearest community, Solidaridad, a slum of about 100 families with no electricity, heat or running water, had its only water supply cut off. Its school and health clinic, built with foreign-aid money, could not operate because of a lack of water. It was the same all through El Alto.

An intense resistance to Suez formed. FEJUVE, a network of local community councils and activists, led a series of strikes in January 2005, which crippled the cities and brought business to a halt. This resistance was a prime factor in the ousting of presidents Gonzalo Sánchez de Lozada and Carlos Mesa. Their replacement, Evo Morales, the first indigenous president in the country's history, negotiated Suez's departure. On January 3, 2007, he held a ceremony at the presidential palace celebrating the return of the water of La Paz and El Alto after a long and bitter confrontation. "Water cannot be turned over to private business," said Morales. "It must remain a basic service, with participation of the state, so that water service can be provided almost for free."

Although they have received less international attention, similar battles over privatized water have raged in Argentina. Río de la Plata (Silver River) separates Buenos Aires, the Argentine capital, from Montevideo, the capital of Uruguay. For 500 years, it has also been called Mar Dulce (Sweet Sea) because its size made people think it was a freshwater sea. Today, however, the river is famous for something else: it is one of the few rivers in the world whose pollution can be seen from space. On March 21, 2006, the Argentine government rescinded the thirty-year contract of Aguas Argentinas, the Suez subsidiary that had run the Buenos Aires water system since 1993, in no small part because the company broke its promise to treat wastewater, continuing to dump nearly 90 percent of the city's sewage into the river. In another broken promise, the company repeatedly raised tariffs, for a total increase of 88 percent in the first ten years of operation. Water quality was another issue; water in seven districts had nitrate levels so high it was unfit for human consumption. An April 2007 report by the city's ombudsman stated that most of the population of 150,000 in the southern district of the city lived with open-air sewers and contaminated drinking water.

Yet as Food and Water Watch reports, the Inter-American Development Bank continued to fund Suez as late as 1999, despite the mounting evidence that the company was pulling in 20 percent profit margins while refusing to invest in services or infrastructure. Outrageously, with the backing of the French government, Suez is trying to recoup $1.7 billion in "investments" and up to $33 million in unpaid water bills at the ICSID. Suez had just (in December 2005) been forced out of the province of Santa Fe, where it had a thirty-year contract to run the water systems of thirteen cities. The company is also suing the provincial government at the ICSID for $180 million. Close on the heels of the Buenos Aires announcement, Suez was forced to abandon its last stronghold in Argentina, the city of Córdoba, when water rates were raised 500 percent on one bill.

In all cases, strong civil society resistance was key to these retreats. A coalition of water users and residents of Santa Fe, led by Alberto Múñoz and others, actually organized a huge and successful plebiscite, in which 256,000 people, about a twelfth of the population of the province, voted to rescind Suez's contract. They convened a Provincial Assembly on the Right to Water with 7,000 activists and citizens in November 2002, which set the stage for the political opposition to the company. The People's Commission for the Recovery of Water in Córdoba is a highly organized network of trade unions, neighborhood centers, social organizations and politicians with a clear goal of public water for all, and was instrumental in getting the government to break its contract with Suez. "What we want is a public company managed by workers, consumers and the provincial government, and monitored by university experts to guarantee water quality and prevent corruption," says Luis Bazán, the group's leader and a water worker who refused employment with Suez.

Mexico is a beachhead for privatization across the region, with its elites having access to all the water they need and also controlling governments at most levels of the country. Only 9 percent of the country's surface water is fit for drinking, and its aquifers are being drawn down mercilessly. According to the National Commission on Water, 12 million Mexicans have no access to potable water whatsoever and another 25 million live in villages and cities where the taps run as little as a few hours a week. Eighty-two percent of wastewater goes untreated. Mexico City has dried up, and its 22 million inhabitants live on the verge of crisis. Services are so poor in the slums and outskirts of the city that cockroaches run out when the tap is turned on. In many "colonias" in Mexico City and around the country, the only available water is sold from trucks that bring it in once a week, often by political parties that sell the water for votes.

In 1983 the federal government handed over responsibility for the water supply to the municipalities. Then in 1992 it passed a new national water bill that encouraged the municipalities to privatize water in order to receive funding. Privatization was supported by former President Vicente Fox, himself a former senior executive with Coca-Cola, and is also favored by the current president, Felipe Calderón. The World Bank and the Inter-American Development Bank are actively promoting water privatization in Mexico. In 2002 the World Bank provided $250 million for infrastructure repair with conditions that municipalities negotiate public-private partnerships. Suez is deeply entrenched in Mexico, running the water services for part of Mexico City, Cancún and about a dozen other cities. Its wastewater division, Degremont, has a large contract for San Luis Potosí and several other cities as well. The privatization of water has become a top priority for the Mexican water commission, Conagua. As in other countries, privatization in Mexico has brought exorbitant water rates, broken promises and cutoffs to those who cannot pay. The Water Users Association in Saltillo, where a consortium of Suez and the Spanish company Aguas de Barcelona run the city's water systems, reports that a 2004 audit by the state comptroller found evidence of contractual and state law violations.

A vibrant civil society movement has recently come together to fight for the right to clean water and resist the trend to corporate control in Mexico. In April 2005 the Mexican Center for Social Analysis, Information and Training (CASIFOP) brought together more than 400 activists, indigenous peoples, small farmers and students to launch a coordinated grassroots resistance to water privatization. The Coalition of Mexican Organizations for the Right to Water (COMDA) is a large collection of environmental, human rights, indigenous and cultural groups devoted not only to activism but also to community-based education on water, its place in Mexico's history and the need for legislation to protect the public's right to access. Their hopes for a government supportive of their perspective were dashed when conservative candidate Calderón won (many say stole) the 2006 presidential election over progressive candidate Andrés Manuel López Obrador. Calderón is working openly with the private water companies to cement private control of the country's water supplies.

Other Latin American cities or countries rejecting water privatization include Bogotá, Colombia (although other Colombian cities, including Cartagena, have adopted private water systems); Paraguay, whose lower house rejected a Senate proposal to privatize water in July 2005; Nicaragua, where a fierce struggle has been waged by civil society groups and where in January 2007 a court ruled against the privatization of the country's wastewater infrastructure; an Brazil, where strong public opinion has held back the force of water privatization in most cities. Unfortunately, resistanc in Peru, where increased rates, corruption and debt plague th system, has not yet reversed water privatization. Likewise, i Chile, resistance to water privatization is very difficult becaus of the entrenched commitment to market ideology of the rulin elites, although there is hope that the center-left government o Michelle Bachelet will be more open to arguments for publi governance of Chile's water supplies.

From thousands of local struggles for the basic right t water—not just throughout Latin America but in Asia-Pacifi countries, Africa and the United States and Canada—a highl organized international water justice movement has been forge and is shaping the future of the world's water. This movemer has already had a profound effect on global water politics, forc ing global institutions such as the World Bank and the Unite Nations to admit the failure of their model, and it has helpe formulate water policy inside dozens of countries. The move ment has forced open a debate over the control of water an challenged the "Lords of Water" who had set themselves up a the arbiters of this dwindling resource. The growth of a dem cratic global water justice movement is a critical and positi development that will bring needed accountability, transparenc and public oversight to the water crisis as conflicts over wat loom on the horizon.

Critical Thinking

1. What are the two views of water as a resource?
2. What are the origins of the movement to make water a fundamental right?
3. Why does Latin America, with substantial water resources, have one of the worst per capita water allocations?

MAUDE BARLOW is the author of *Blue Covenant: The Global Wat Crisis and the Coming Battle for the Right to Water* (New Press), fro which this article was adapted.

The New Geopolitics of Food

From the Middle East to Madagascar, high prices are spawning land grabs and ousting dictators. Welcome to the 21st-century food wars.

LESTER R. BROWN

In the United States, when world wheat prices rise by 75 percent, as they have over the last year, it means the difference between a $2 loaf of bread and a loaf costing maybe $2.10. If, however, you live in New Delhi, those sky-rocketing costs really matter: A doubling in the world price of wheat actually means that the wheat you carry home from the market to hand-grind into flour for chapatis costs twice as much. And the same is true with rice. If the world price of rice doubles, so does the price of rice in your neighborhood market in Jakarta. And so does the cost of the bowl of boiled rice on an Indonesian family's dinner table.

Welcome to the new food economics of 2011: Prices are climbing, but the impact is not at all being felt equally. For Americans, who spend less than one-tenth of their income in the supermarket, the soaring food prices we've seen so far this year are an annoyance, not a calamity. But for the planet's poorest 2 billion people, who spend 50 to 70 percent of their income on food, these soaring prices may mean going from two meals a day to one. Those who are barely hanging on to the lower rungs of the global economic ladder risk losing their grip entirely. This can contribute—and it has—to revolutions and upheaval.

Already in 2011, the U.N. Food Price Index has eclipsed its previous all-time global high; as of March it had climbed for eight consecutive months. With this year's harvest predicted to fall short, with governments in the Middle East and Africa teetering as a result of the price spikes, and with anxious markets sustaining one shock after another, food has quickly become the hidden driver of world politics. And crises like these are going to become increasingly common. The new geopolitics of food looks a whole lot more volatile—and a whole lot more contentious—than it used to. Scarcity is the new norm.

Until recently, sudden price surges just didn't matter as much, as they were quickly followed by a return to the relatively low food prices that helped shape the political stability of the late 20th century across much of the globe. But now both the causes and consequences are ominously different.

In many ways, this is a resumption of the 2007–2008 food crisis, which subsided not because the world somehow came together to solve its grain crunch once and for all, but because the Great Recession tempered growth in demand even as favorable weather helped farmers produce the largest grain harvest on record. Historically, price spikes tended to be almost exclusively driven by unusual weather—a monsoon failure in India, a drought in the former Soviet Union, a heat wave in the U.S. Midwest. Such events were always disruptive, but thankfully infrequent. Unfortunately, today's price hikes are driven by trends that are both elevating demand and making it more difficult to increase production: among them, a rapidly expanding population, crop-withering temperature increases, and irrigation wells running dry. Each night, there are 219,000 additional people to feed at the global dinner table.

More alarming still, the world is losing its ability to soften the effect of shortages. In response to previous price surges, the United States, the world's largest grain producer, was effectively able to steer the world away from potential catastrophe. From the mid-20th century until 1995, the United States had either grain surpluses or idle cropland that could be planted to rescue countries in trouble. When the Indian monsoon failed in 1965, for example, President Lyndon Johnson's administration shipped one-fifth of the U.S. wheat crop to India, successfully staving off famine. We can't do that anymore; the safety cushion is gone.

That's why the food crisis of 2011 is for real, and why it may bring with it yet more bread riots cum political revolutions. What if the upheavals that greeted dictators Zine el-Abidine Ben Ali in Tunisia, Hosni Mubarak in Egypt, and Muammar al-Qaddafi in Libya (a country that imports 90 percent of its grain) are not the end of the story, but the beginning of it? Get ready, farmers and foreign ministers alike, for a new era in which world food scarcity increasingly shapes global politics.

The doubling of world grain prices since early 2007 has been driven primarily by two factors: accelerating growth in demand and the increasing difficulty of rapidly expanding production. The result is a world that looks strikingly different from the bountiful global grain economy of the last century. What will the geopolitics of food look like in a new era dominated by scarcity? Even at this early stage, we can see at least the broad outlines of the emerging food economy.

On the demand side, farmers now face clear sources of increasing pressure. The first is population growth. Each year the world's farmers must feed 80 million additional people, nearly all of them in developing countries. The world's population has nearly doubled since 1970 and is headed toward 9 billion by midcentury. Some 3 billion people, meanwhile, are also trying to move up the food chain, consuming more meat, milk, and eggs. As more families in China and elsewhere enter the middle class, they expect to eat better. But as global consumption of grain-intensive livestock products climbs, so does the demand for the extra corn and soybeans needed to feed all that livestock. (Grain consumption per person in the United States, for example, is four times that in India, where little grain is converted into animal protein. For now.)

At the same time, the United States, which once was able to act as a global buffer of sorts against poor harvests elsewhere, is now converting massive quantities of grain into fuel for cars, even as world grain consumption, which is already up to roughly 2.2 billion metric tons per year, is growing at an accelerating rate. A decade ago, the growth in consumption was 20 million tons per year. More recently it has risen by 40 million tons every year. But the rate at which the United States is converting grain into ethanol has grown even faster. In 2010, the United States harvested nearly 400 million tons of grain, of which 126 million tons went to ethanol fuel distilleries (up from 16 million tons in 2000). This massive capacity to convert grain into fuel means that the price of grain is now tied to the price of oil. So if oil goes to $150 per barrel or more, the price of grain will follow it upward as it becomes ever more profitable to convert grain into oil substitutes. And it's not just a U.S. phenomenon: Brazil, which distills ethanol from sugar cane, ranks second in production after the United States, while the European Union's goal of getting 10 percent of its transport energy from renewables, mostly biofuels, by 2020 is also diverting land from food crops.

This is not merely a story about the booming demand for food. Everything from falling water tables to eroding soils and the consequences of global warming means that the world's food supply is unlikely to keep up with our collectively growing appetites. Take climate change: The rule of thumb among crop ecologists is that for every 1 degree Celsius rise in temperature above the growing season optimum, farmers can expect a 10 percent decline in grain yields. This relationship was borne out all too dramatically during the 2010 heat wave in Russia, which reduced the country's grain harvest by nearly 40 percent.

While temperatures are rising, water tables are falling as farmers overpump for irrigation. This artificially inflates food production in the short run, creating a food bubble that bursts when aquifers are depleted and pumping is necessarily reduced to the rate of recharge. In arid Saudi Arabia irrigation had surprisingly enabled the country to be self sufficient in wheat for more than 20 years; now, wheat production is collapsing because the non-replenishable aquifer the country uses for irrigation is largely depleted. The Saudis soon will be importing all their grain.

Saudi Arabia is only one of some 18 countries with water based food bubbles. All together, more than half the world's people live in countries where water tables are falling. The politically troubled Arab Middle East is the first geographic region where grain production has peaked and begun to decline because of water shortages, even as populations continue to grow. Grain production is already going down in Syria and Iraq and may soon decline in Yemen. But the largest food bubbles are in India and China. In India, where farmers have drilled some 20 million irrigation wells, water tables are falling and the wells are starting to go dry. The World Bank reports that 175 million Indians are being fed with grain produced by overpumping. In China, overpumping is concentrated in the North China Plain, which produces half of China's wheat and a third of its corn. An estimated 130 million Chinese are currently fed by overpumping. How will these countries make up for the inevitable shortfall when the aquifers are depleted?

Even as we are running our wells dry, we are also mismanaging our soils, creating new deserts. Soil erosion as a result of overplowing and land mismanagement is undermining the productivity of one-third of the world's cropland. How severe is it? Look at satellite images showing two huge new dust bowls: one stretching across northern and western China and western Mongolia; the other across central Africa. Wang Tao, a leading Chinese desert scholar, reports that each year some 1,400 square miles of land in northern China turn to desert. In Mongolia and Lesotho, grain harvests have shrunk by half or more over the last few decades. North Korea and Haiti are also suffering from heavy soil losses; both countries face famine if they lose international food aid. Civilization can survive the loss of its oil reserves, but it cannot survive the loss of its soil reserves.

Beyond the changes in the environment that make it ever harder to meet human demand, there's an important intangible factor to consider: Over the last half-century or so, we have come to take agricultural progress for granted. Decade after decade, advancing technology underpinned steady gains in raising land productivity. Indeed, world grain yield per acre has tripled since 1950. But now that era is coming to an end in some of the more agriculturally advanced countries, where farmers are already using all available technologies to raise yields. In effect, the farmers have caught up with the scientists. After climbing for a century, rice yield per acre in Japan has not risen at all for 16 years. In China, yields may level off soon. Just those two countries alone account for one-third of the world's rice harvest. Meanwhile, wheat yields have plateaued in Britain, France, and Germany—Western Europe's three largest wheat producers.

In this era of tightening world food supplies, the ability to grow food is fast becoming a new form of geopolitical leverage, and countries are scrambling to secure their own parochial interests at the expense of the common good.

The first signs of trouble came in 2007, when farmers began having difficulty keeping up with the growth in global demand for grain. Grain and soybean prices started to climb, tripling by mid-2008. In response, many exporting countries tried to control the rise of domestic food prices by restricting exports. Among them were Russia and Argentina, two leading wheat exporters. Vietnam, the No. 2 rice exporter, banned exports entirely for several months in early 2008. So did several other smaller exporters of grain.

With exporting countries restricting exports in 2007 and 2008, importing countries panicked. No longer able to rely on the market to supply the grain they needed, several countries took the novel step of trying to negotiate long-term grain-supply agreements with exporting countries. The Philippines, for instance, negotiated a three-year agreement with Vietnam for 1.5 million tons of rice per year. A delegation of Yemenis traveled to Australia with a similar goal in mind, but had no luck. In a seller's market, exporters were reluctant to make long-term commitments.

Fearing they might not be able to buy needed grain from the market, some of the more affluent countries, led by Saudi Arabia, South Korea, and China, took the unusual step in 2008 of buying or leasing land in other countries on which to grow grain for themselves. Most of these land acquisitions are in Africa, where some governments lease cropland for less than $1 per acre per year. Among the principal destinations were Ethiopia and Sudan, countries where millions of people are being sustained with food from the U.N. World Food Program. That the governments of these two countries are willing to sell land to foreign interests when their own people are hungry is a sad commentary on their leadership.

By the end of 2009, hundreds of land acquisition deals had been negotiated, some of them exceeding a million acres. A 2010 World Bank analysis of these "land grabs" reported that a total of nearly 140 million acres were involved—an area that exceeds the cropland devoted to corn and wheat combined in the United States. Such acquisitions also typically involve water rights, meaning that land grabs potentially affect all downstream countries as well. Any water extracted from the upper Nile River basin to irrigate crops in Ethiopia or Sudan, for instance, will now not reach Egypt, upending the delicate water politics of the Nile by adding new countries with which Egypt must negotiate.

The potential for conflict—and not just over water—is high. Many of the land deals have been made in secret, and in most cases, the land involved was already in use by villagers when it was sold or leased. Often those already farming the land were neither consulted about nor even informed of the new arrangements. And because there typically are no formal land titles in many developing-country villages, the farmers who lost their land have had little backing to bring their cases to court. Reporter John Vidal, writing in Britain's *Observer,* quotes Nyikaw Ochalla from Ethiopia's Gambella region: "The foreign companies are arriving in large numbers, depriving people of land they have used for centuries. There is no consultation with the indigenous population. The deals are done secretly. The only thing the local people see is people coming with lots of tractors to invade their lands."

Local hostility toward such land grabs is the rule, not the exception. In 2007, as food prices were starting to rise, China signed an agreement with the Philippines to lease 2.5 million acres of land slated for food crops that would be shipped home. Once word leaked, the public outcry—much of it from Filipino farmers—forced Manila to suspend the agreement. A similar uproar rocked Madagascar, where a South Korean firm, Daewoo Logistics, had pursued rights to more than 3 million acres of land. Word of the deal helped stoke a political furor that toppled the government and forced cancellation of the agreement. Indeed, few things are more likely to fuel insurgencies than taking land from people. Agricultural equipment is easily sabotaged. If ripe fields of grain are torched, they burn quickly.

Not only are these deals risky, but foreign investors producing food in a country full of hungry people face another political question of how to get the grain out. Will villagers permit trucks laden with grain headed for port cities to proceed when they themselves may be on the verge of starvation? The potential for political instability in countries where villagers have lost their land and their livelihoods is high. Conflicts could easily develop between investor and host countries.

These acquisitions represent a potential investment in agriculture in developing countries of an estimated $50 billion. But it could take many years to realize any substantial production gains. The public infrastructure for modern market-oriented agriculture does not yet exist in most of Africa. In some countries it will take years just to build the roads and ports needed to bring in agricultural inputs such as fertilizer and to export farm products. Beyond that, modern agriculture requires its own infrastructure: machine sheds, grain-drying equipment, silos, fertilizer storage sheds, fuel storage facilities, equipment repair and maintenance services, well-drilling equipment, irrigation pumps, and energy to power the pumps. Overall, development of the land acquired to date appears to be moving very slowly.

So how much will all this expand world food output? We don't know, but the World Bank analysis indicates that only 37 percent of the projects will be devoted to food crops. Most of the land bought up so far will be used to produce biofuels and other industrial crops.

Even if some of these projects do eventually boost land productivity, who will benefit? If virtually all the inputs—the farm equipment, the fertilizer, the pesticides, the seeds—are brought in from abroad and if all the output is shipped out of the country, it will contribute little to the host country's economy. At best, locals may find work as farm laborers, but in highly mechanized operations, the jobs will be few. At worst, impoverished countries like Mozambique and Sudan will be left with less land and water with which to feed their already hungry populations. Thus far the land grabs have contributed more to stirring unrest than to expanding food production.

And this rich country-poor country divide could grow even more pronounced—and soon. This January, a new stage in the scramble among importing countries to secure food began to unfold when South Korea, which imports 70 percent of its grain, announced that it was creating a new public-private entity that will be responsible for acquiring part of this grain. With an initial office in Chicago, the plan is to bypass the large international trading firms by buying grain directly from U.S. farmers. As the Koreans acquire their own grain elevators, they may well sign multiyear delivery contracts with farmers, agreeing to buy specified quantities of wheat, corn, or soybeans at a fixed price.

Other importers will not stand idly by as South Korea tries to tie up a portion of the U.S. grain harvest even before it gets to market. The enterprising Koreans may soon be joined by China, Japan, Saudi Arabia, and other leading importers. Although South Korea's initial focus is the United States, far and away the world's largest grain exporter, it may later consider brokering deals with Canada, Australia, Argentina, and other major exporters. This is happening just as China may be on the verge of entering the U.S. market as a potentially massive importer of grain. With China's 1.4 billion increasingly affluent consumers starting to compete with U.S. consumers for the U.S. grain harvest, cheap food, seen by many as an American birthright, may be coming to an end.

No one knows where this intensifying competition for food supplies will go, but the world seems to be moving away from the international cooperation that evolved over several decades following World War II to an every-country-for-itself philosophy. Food nationalism may help secure food supplies for individual affluent countries, but it does little to enhance world food security. Indeed, the low-income countries that host land grabs or import grain will likely see their food situation deteriorate.

After the carnage of two world wars and the economic missteps that led to the Great Depression, countries joined together in 1945 to create the United Nations, finally realizing that in the modern world we cannot live in isolation, tempting though that might be. The International Monetary Fund was created to help manage the monetary system and promote economic stability and progress. Within the U.N. system, specialized agencies from the World Health Organization to the Food and Agriculture Organization (FAO) play major roles in the world today. All this has fostered international cooperation.

But while the FAO collects and analyzes global agricultural data and provides technical assistance, there is no organized effort to ensure the adequacy of world food supplies. Indeed, most international negotiations on agricultural trade until recently focused on access to markets, with the United States, Canada, Australia, and Argentina persistently pressing Europe and Japan to open their highly protected agricultural markets. But in the first decade of this century, access to supplies has emerged as the overriding issue as the world transitions from an era of food surpluses to a new politics of food scarcity. At the same time, the U.S. food aid program that once worked to fend off famine wherever it threatened has largely been replaced by the U.N. World Food Program (WFP), where the United States is the leading donor. The WFP now has food-assistance operations in some 70 countries and an annual budget of $4 billion. There is little international coordination otherwise. French President Nicolas Sarkozy—the reigning president of the G-20—is proposing to deal with rising food prices by curbing speculation in commodity markets. Useful though this may be, it treats the symptoms of growing food insecurity, not the causes, such as population growth and climate change. The world now needs to focus not only on agricultural policy, but on a structure that integrates it with energy, population, and water policies, each of which directly affects food security.

But that is not happening. Instead, as land and water become scarcer, as the Earth's temperature rises, and as world food security deteriorates, a dangerous geopolitics of food scarcity is emerging. Land grabbing, water grabbing, and buying grain directly from farmers in exporting countries are now integral parts of a global power struggle for food security.

With grain stocks low and climate volatility increasing, the risks are also increasing. We are now so close to the edge that a breakdown in the food system could come at any time. Consider, for example, what would have happened if the 2010 heat wave that was centered in Moscow had instead been centered in Chicago. In round numbers, the 40 percent drop in Russia's hoped-for harvest of roughly 100 million tons cost the world 40 million tons of grain, but a 40 percent drop in the far larger U.S. grain harvest of 400 million tons would have cost 160 million tons. The world's carryover stocks of grain (the amount in the bin when the new harvest begins) would have dropped to just 52 days of consumption. This level would have been not only the lowest on record, but also well below the 62-day carryover that set the stage for the 2007–2008 tripling of world grain prices.

Then what? There would have been chaos in world grain markets. Grain prices would have climbed off the charts. Some grain-exporting countries, trying to hold down domestic food prices, would have restricted or even banned exports, as they lid in 2007 and 2008. The TV news would have been dominated not by the hundreds of fires in the Russian countryside, but by footage of food riots in low-income grain-importing countries and reports of governments falling as hunger spread out of control. Oil-exporting countries that import grain would have been trying to barter oil for grain, and low-income grain importers would have lost out. With governments toppling and confidence in the world grain market shattered, the global economy could have started to unravel.

We may not always be so lucky. At issue now is whether the world can go beyond focusing on the symptoms of the deteriorating food situation and instead attack the underlying causes. If we cannot produce higher crop yields with less water and conserve fertile soils, many agricultural areas will cease to be viable. And this goes far beyond farmers. If we cannot move at wartime speed to stabilize the climate, we may not be able to avoid runaway food prices. If we cannot

accelerate the shift to smaller families and stabilize the world population sooner rather than later, the ranks of the hungry will almost certainly continue to expand. The time to act is now—before the food crisis of 2011 becomes the new normal.

Critical Thinking

1. Why have international food prices continued to increase?
2. What factors are likely to limit the expansion of food production?
3. Where are the more affluent countries turning for greater food security?
4. What challenges do overseas land acquisition deals face?

LESTER R. BROWN, president of the Earth Policy Institute, is author of *World on the Edge: How to Prevent Environmental and Economic Collapse.*

Reprinted in entirety by McGraw-Hill with permission from *Foreign Policy,* May/June 2011, pp. 56–58, 61–62. www.foreignpolicy.com. © 2011 Washingtonpost.Newsweek Interactive, LLC.

UNIT 6
Women and Development

Unit Selections

Learning Outcomes

After reading this unit, you should be able to:

- Describe the challenges that women face in developing countries.
- Identify the benefits of educating girls.
- Explain why women are particularly vulnerable in conflict situations.
- Recognize the importance of including women in post-conflict settlements.
- Describe the consequences of climate change for women.
- Discuss the ways that multinational corporations can contribute to the empowering women in the developing world.

Student Website
www.mhhe.com/cls

Internet References

WIDNET: Women in Development NETwork
    www.focusintl.com/widnet.htm
Women Watch/Regional and Country Information
    www.un.org/womenwatch

There is widespread recognition of the crucial role that women play in the development process. Women are critical to the success of family planning programs, bear much of the responsibility for food production, account for an increasing share of wage labor in developing countries, are acutely aware of the consequences of environmental degradation, and can contribute to the development of a vibrant, civil society and good governance. Despite their important contributions, however, women lag behind men in access to health care, nutrition, and education while continuing to face formidable social, economic, and political barriers. Women's lives in the developing world are invariably difficult. Often female children are valued less than male offspring, resulting in higher female infant and child mortality rates. In extreme cases, this undervaluing leads to female infanticide.

Those females who do survive face lives characterized by poor nutrition and health, multiple pregnancies, hard physical labor, discrimination, and in some cases violence. Clearly, women are central to any successful population policy. Evidence shows that educated women have fewer and healthier children. This connection between education and population indicates that greater emphasis should be placed on educating women. In reality, female school enrollments are lower than those of males because of state priorities, insufficient family resources to educate both boys and girls, female socialization, and cultural factors. Education is probably the largest single contributor to enhancing the status of women and promoting development, but access to education is still limited for many women. Sixty percent of children worldwide not enrolled in schools are girls. Education for women leads to improved health, better wages, and greater influence in decision making, which benefits not only women but the broader society as well. Educated women contribute more to their families, are less likely to subject their daughters to female genital mutilation, and are three times less likely to contract HIV.

Women make up a significant portion of the agricultural workforce. They are heavily involved in food production right from planting to cultivation, harvesting, and marketing. Despite their agricultural contribution, women frequently do not have adequate access to advances in agricultural technology or the benefits of extension and training programs. They are also discriminated against in land ownership. As a result, important opportunities to improve food production are lost when women are not given access to technology, training, and land ownership commensurate with their agricultural role.

The industrialization that has accompanied the globalized production has meant more employment opportunities for women, but often these are low-tech, low-wage jobs. The lower labor costs in the developing world that attract manufacturing facilities are a mixed blessing for women. Increasingly, women are recruited to fill these production jobs because wage differentials allow employers to pay women less. On the other hand, expanding opportunities for women in these positions contribute to family income. The informal sector, where jobs are small scale, more traditional, and labor-intensive, has also attracted more women. These jobs are often their only employment option, due to family responsibilities or discrimination.

© blue jean images/Getty Images

Women also play a critical role in the economic expansion of developing countries. Nevertheless, women are often the first to feel the effects of an economic slowdown. The consequences of the structural adjustment programs that many developing countries have to adopt have also fallen disproportionately on women. When employment opportunities decline because of austerity measures, women lose jobs in the formal sector and face increased competition from males in the informal sector. Cuts in spending on health care and education also affect women, who already receive fewer of these benefits. Currency devaluations further erode the purchasing power of women. The global economic crisis is only going to worsen the plight of working women. Because of the gender division of labor, women are often more aware of the consequences of environmental degradation. Depletion of resources such as forests, soil, and water are much more likely to be felt by women, who are responsible for collecting firewood and water and who raise most of the crops. As a result, women are an essential component of successful environmental protection policies, but they are often overlooked in planning environmental projects.

Enhancing the status of women has been the primary focus of several international conferences. The 1994 International Conference on Population and Development (ICPD) focused attention on women's health and reproductive rights, and the crucial role that these issues play in controlling population. The 1995 Fourth World Conference on Women held in Beijing, China, proclaimed women's rights to be synonymous with human rights. Along with the Convention on the Elimination of All Forms of Discrimination against Women, these developments represent a turning point in women's struggle for equal rights and have prompted efforts to pass legislation at the national level to protect women's rights.

There are indications that women have made progress in some regions of the developing world. The election of Ellen John-Sirleaf as president of Liberia and Africa's first female head of state is the most visible indicator of a trend toward greater political involvement of women in Africa. In the Middle

East, the 2002 Arab Human Development Report highlighted the extent to which women in the region lagged behind their counterparts in other parts of the world. Women were important actors in the demands for political reform in the region, and this may open further opportunities to increase women's political participation. It remains the case that women in conflict zones are particularly vulnerable to violence. In Afghanistan, not only are women subject to the violence that comes with war, but a recent family law has set back the progress on women's rights made after the ouster of the Taliban. There continues to be a wide divergence in the status of women worldwide, but the recognition of the valuable contributions they can make to society is increasing the pressure to enhance their status. Reflecting this recognition, multinational corporations are increasingly seeking to empower women and enhance their status.

The Women's Crusade

The oppression of women worldwide is the human rights cause of our time. And their liberation could help solve many of the world's problems, from poverty to child mortality to terrorism. A 21st-century manifesto.

NICHOLAS D. KRISTOF AND SHERYL WUDUNN

In the 19th century, the paramount moral challenge was slavery. In the 20th century, it was totalitarianism. In this century, it is the brutality inflicted on so many women and girls around the globe: sex trafficking, acid attacks, bride burnings and mass rape.

Yet if the injustices that women in poor countries suffer are of paramount importance, in an economic and geopolitical sense the opportunity they represent is even greater. "Women hold up half the sky," in the words of a Chinese saying, yet that's mostly an aspiration: in a large slice of the world, girls are uneducated and women marginalized, and it's not an accident that those same countries are disproportionately mired in poverty and riven by fundamentalism and chaos. There's a growing recognition among everyone from the World Bank to the U.S. military's Joint Chiefs of Staff to aid organizations like CARE that focusing on women and girls is the most effective way to fight global poverty and extremism. That's why foreign aid is increasingly directed to women. The world is awakening to a powerful truth: Women and girls aren't the problem; they're the solution.

One place to observe this alchemy of gender is in the muddy back alleys of Pakistan. In a slum outside the grand old city of Lahore, a woman named Saima Muhammad used to dissolve into tears every evening. A round-faced woman with thick black hair tucked into a head scarf, Saima had barely a rupee, and her deadbeat husband was unemployed and not particularly employable. He was frustrated and angry, and he coped by beating Saima each afternoon. Their house was falling apart, and Saima had to send her young daughter to live with an aunt, because there wasn't enough food to go around.

"My sister-in-law made fun of me, saying, 'You can't even feed your children,'" recalled Saima when Nick met her two years ago on a trip to Pakistan. "My husband beat me up. My brother-in-law beat me up. I had an awful life." Saima's husband accumulated a debt of more than $3,000, and it seemed that these loans would hang over the family for generations. Then when Saima's second child was born and turned out to be a girl as well, her mother-in-law, a harsh, blunt woman named Sharifa Bibi, raised the stakes.

"She's not going to have a son," Sharifa told Saima's husband, in front of her. "So you should marry again. Take a second wife." Saima was shattered and ran off sobbing. Another wife would leave even less money to feed and educate the children. And Saima herself would be marginalized in the household, cast off like an old sock. For days Saima walked around in a daze, her eyes red; the slightest incident would send her collapsing into hysterical tears.

It was at that point that Saima signed up with the Kashf Foundation, a Pakistani microfinance organization that lends tiny amounts of money to poor women to start businesses. Kashf is typical of microfinance institutions, in that it lends almost exclusively to women, in groups of 25. The women guarantee one another's debts and meet every two weeks to make payments and discuss a social issue, like family planning or schooling for girls. A Pakistani woman is often forbidden to leave the house without her husband's permission, but husbands tolerate these meetings because the women return with cash and investment ideas.

Saima Muhammad, lives near Lahore, Pakistan. She was routinely beaten by her husband until she started a successful embroidery business.

Saima took out a $65 loan and used the money to buy beads and cloth, which she transformed into beautiful embroidery that she then sold to merchants in the markets of Lahore. She used the profit to buy more beads and cloth, and soon she had an embroidery business and was earning a solid income—the only one in her household to do so. Saima took her elder daughter back from the aunt and began paying off her husband's debt.

When merchants requested more embroidery than Saima could produce, she paid neighbors to assist her. Eventually 30 families were working for her, and she put her husband to work as well—"under my direction," she explained with a twinkle in her eye. Saima became the tycoon of the neighborhood, and she was able to pay off her husband's entire debt, keep her daughters in school, renovate the house, connect running water and buy a television.

Goretti Nyabenda Musiga Commune, Burundi

In Burundi, which is one of the poorest countries in the world, Goretti Nyabenda used to be largely a prisoner in her hut. In keeping with tradition in the region where she lived, she could not leave without the permission of her husband, Bernard. Her interactions with Bernard consisted in good part of being beaten by him. "I was wretched," she remembers. Then Goretti joined an empowerment program run by CARE, taking out a $2 microloan to buy fertilizer. The result was an excellent crop of potatoes worth $7.50—and Goretti began to build a small business as a farmer, goat breeder, and banana-beer brewer. When Bernard fell sick with malaria, it was Goretti who was able to pay the bill. Today Goretti is no longer beaten, and she comes and goes freely. Her children, including her second daughter, Ancilla, have been able to afford school with Goretti's earnings.

"Now everyone comes to me to borrow money, the same ones who used to criticize me," Saima said, beaming in satisfaction. "And the children of those who used to criticize me now come to my house to watch TV."

Today, Saima is a bit plump and displays a gold nose ring as well as several other rings and bracelets on each wrist. She exudes self-confidence as she offers a grand tour of her home and work area, ostentatiously showing off the television and the new plumbing. She doesn't even pretend to be subordinate to her husband. He spends his days mostly loafing around, occasionally helping with the work but always having to accept orders from his wife. He has become more impressed with females in general: Saima had a third child, also a girl, but now that's not a problem. "Girls are just as good as boys," he explained.

Saima's new prosperity has transformed the family's educational prospects. She is planning to send all three of her daughters through high school and maybe to college as well. She brings in tutors to improve their schoolwork, and her oldest child, Javaria, is ranked first in her class. We asked Javaria what she wanted to be when she grew up, thinking she might aspire to be a doctor or lawyer. Javaria cocked her head. "I'd like to do embroidery," she said.

As for her husband, Saima said, "We have a good relationship now." She explained, "We don't fight, and he treats me well." And what about finding another wife who might bear him a son? Saima chuckled at the question: "Now nobody says anything about that." Sharifa Bibi, the mother-in-law, looked shocked when we asked whether she wanted her son to take a second wife to bear a son. "No, no," she said. "Saima is bringing so much to this house. . . . She puts a roof over our heads and food on the table."

Sharifa even allows that Saima is now largely exempt from beatings by her husband. "A woman should know her limits, and if not, then it's her husband's right to beat her," Sharifa said. "But if a woman earns more than her husband, it's difficult for him to discipline her."

What should we make of stories like Saima's? Traditionally, the status of women was seen as a "soft" issue—worthy but marginal. We initially reflected that view ourselves in our work as journalists. We preferred to focus instead on the "serious" international issues, like trade disputes or arms proliferation. Our awakening came in China.

After we married in 1988, we moved to Beijing to be correspondents for *The New York Times*. Seven months later we found ourselves standing on the edge of Tiananmen Square, watching troops fire their automatic weapons at prodemocracy protesters. The massacre claimed between 400 and 800 lives and transfixed the world; wrenching images of the killing appeared constantly on the front page and on television screens.

Yet the following year we came across an obscure but meticulous demographic study that outlined a human rights violation that had claimed tens of thousands more lives. This study found that 39,000 baby girls died annually in China because parents didn't give them the same medical care and attention that boys received—and that was just in the first year of life. A result is that as many infant girls died unnecessarily every week in China as protesters died at Tiananmen Square. Those Chinese girls never received a column inch of news coverage, and we began to wonder if our journalistic priorities were skewed.

A similar pattern emerged in other countries. In India, "bride burning" takes place approximately once every two hours, to punish a woman for an inadequate dowry or to eliminate her so a man can remarry—but these rarely constitute news. When a prominent dissident was arrested in China, we would write a front-page article; when 100,000 girls were kidnapped and trafficked into brothels, we didn't even consider it news.

Amartya Sen, the ebullient Nobel Prize-winning economist, developed a gauge of gender inequality that is a striking reminder of the stakes involved. "More than 100 million women are missing," Sen wrote in a classic essay in 1990 in *The New York Review of Books,* spurring a new field of research. Sen noted that in normal circumstances, women live longer than men, and so there are more females than males in much of the world. Yet in places where girls have a deeply unequal status, they vanish. China has 107 males for every 100 females in its overall population (and an even greater disproportion among newborns), and India has 108. The implication of the sex ratios Sen later found, is that about 107 million females are missing from the globe today. Follow-up studies have calculated the number slightly differently, deriving alternative figures for "missing women" of between 60 million and 107 million.

The U.N. has estimated that there are 5 thousand honor killings a year, the majority in the Muslim world.

Girls vanish partly because they don't get the same health care and food as boys. In India, for example, girls are less likely to be vaccinated than boys and are taken to the hospital only when they are sicker. A result is that girls in India from

1 to 5 years of age are 50 percent more likely to die than boys their age. In addition, ultrasound machines have allowed a pregnant woman to find out the sex of her fetus—and then get an abortion if it is female.

The global statistics on the abuse of girls are numbing. It appears that more girls and women are now missing from the planet, precisely because they are female, than men were killed on the battlefield in all the wars of the 20th century. The number of victims of this routine "gendercide" far exceeds the number of people who were slaughtered in all the genocides of the 20th century.

For those women who live, mistreatment is sometimes shockingly brutal. If you're reading this article, the phrase "gender discrimination" might conjure thoughts of unequal pay, underfinanced sports teams or unwanted touching from a boss. In the developing world, meanwhile, millions of women and girls are actually enslaved. While a precise number is hard to pin down, the International Labor Organization, a U.N. agency, estimates that at any one time there are 12.3 million people engaged in forced labor of all kinds, including sexual servitude. In Asia alone about one million children working in the sex trade are held in conditions indistinguishable from slavery, according to a U.N. report. Girls and women are locked in brothels and beaten if they resist, fed just enough to be kept alive and often sedated with drugs—to pacify them and often to cultivate addiction. India probably has more modern slaves than any other country.

Another huge burden for women in poor countries is maternal mortality, with one woman dying in childbirth around the world every minute. In the West African country Niger, a woman stands a one-in-seven chance of dying in childbirth at some point in her life. (These statistics are all somewhat dubious, because maternal mortality isn't considered significant enough to require good data collection.) For all of India's shiny new high-rises, a woman there still has a 1-in-70 lifetime chance of dying in childbirth. In contrast, the lifetime risk in the United States is 1 in 4,800; in Ireland, it is 1 in 47,600. The reason for the gap is not that we don't know how to save lives of women in poor countries. It's simply that poor, uneducated women in Africa and Asia have never been a priority either in their own countries or to donor nations.

Abbas Be, a beautiful teenage girl in the Indian city of Hyderabad, has chocolate skin, black hair and gleaming white teeth—and a lovely smile, which made her all the more marketable.

Money was tight in her family, so when she was about 14 she arranged to take a job as a maid in the capital, New Delhi. Instead, she was locked up in a brothel, beaten with a cricket bat, gang-raped and told that she would have to cater to customers. Three days after she arrived, Abbas and all 70 girls in the brothel were made to gather round and watch as the pimps made an example of one teenage girl who had fought customers. The troublesome girl was stripped naked, hogtied, humiliated and mocked, beaten savagely and then stabbed in the stomach until she bled to death in front of Abbas and the others.

Abbas was never paid for her work. Any sign of dissatisfaction led to a beating or worse; two more times, she watched girls murdered by the brothel managers for resisting. Eventually Abbas was freed by police and taken back to Hyderabad. She found a home in a shelter run by Prajwala, an organization that takes in girls rescued from brothels and teaches them new skills. Abbas is acquiring an education and has learned to be a bookbinder; she also counsels other girls about how to avoid being trafficked. As a skilled bookbinder, Abbas is able to earn a decent living, and she is now helping to put her younger sisters through school as well. With an education, they will be far less vulnerable to being trafficked. Abbas has moved from being a slave to being a producer, contributing to India's economic development and helping raise her family.

Perhaps the lesson presented by both Abbas and Saima is the same: In many poor countries, the greatest unexploited resource isn't oil fields or veins of gold; it is the women and girls who aren't educated and never become a major presence in the formal economy. With education and with help starting businesses, impoverished women can earn money and support their countries as well as their families. They represent perhaps the best hope for fighting global poverty.

In East Asia, as we saw in our years of reporting there, women have already benefited from deep social changes. In countries like South Korea and Malaysia, China and Thailand, rural girls who previously contributed negligibly to the economy have gone to school and received educations, giving them the autonomy to move to the city to hold factory jobs. This hugely increased the formal labor force; when the women then delayed childbearing, there was a demographic dividend to the country as well. In the 1990s, by our estimations, some 80 percent of the employees on the assembly lines in coastal China were female, and the proportion across the manufacturing belt of East Asia was at least 70 percent.

The hours were long and the conditions wretched, just as in the sweatshops of the Industrial Revolution in the West. But peasant women were making money, sending it back home and sometimes becoming the breadwinners in their families. They gained new skills that elevated their status. Westerners encounter sweatshops and see exploitation, and indeed, many of these plants are just as bad as critics say. But it's sometimes said in poor countries that the only thing worse than being exploited in a sweatshop is not being exploited in a sweatshop. Low-wage manufacturing jobs disproportionately benefited women in countries like China because these were jobs for which brute physical force was not necessary and women's nimbleness gave them an advantage over men—which was not the case with agricultural labor or construction or other jobs typically available in poor countries. Strange as it may seem, sweatshops in Asia had the effect of empowering women. One hundred years ago, many women in China were still having their feet bound. Today, while discrimination and inequality and harassment persist, the culture has been transformed. In the major cities, we've found that Chinese men often do more domestic chores than American men typically do. And urban parents are often not only happy with an only daughter; they may even prefer one, under the belief that daughters are better than sons at looking after aging parents.

Why do microfinance organizations usually focus their assistance on women? And why does everyone benefit when women enter the work force and bring home regular pay checks? One reason involves the dirty little secret of global poverty: some of the most wretched suffering is caused not just by low incomes but also by unwise spending by the poor—especially by men. Surprisingly frequently, we've come across a mother mourning a child who has just died of malaria for want of a $5 mosquito bed net; the mother says that the family couldn't afford a bed net and she means it, but then we find the father at a nearby bar. He goes three evenings a week to the bar, spending $5 each week.

Our interviews and perusal of the data available suggest that the poorest families in the world spend approximately 10 times as much (20 percent of their incomes on average) on a combination of alcohol, prostitution, candy, sugary drinks and lavish feasts as they do on educating their children (2 percent). If poor families spent only as much on educating their children as they do on beer and prostitutes, there would be a breakthrough in the prospects of poor countries. Girls, since they are the ones kept home from school now, would be the biggest beneficiaries. Moreover, one way to reallocate family expenditures in this way is to put more money in the hands of women. A series of studies has found that when women hold assets or gain incomes, family money is more likely to be spent on nutrition, medicine and housing, and consequently children are healthier.

In Ivory Coast, one research project examined the different crops that men and women grow for their private kitties: men grow coffee, cocoa and pineapple, and women grow plantains, bananas, coconuts and vegetables. Some years the "men's crops" have good harvests and the men are flush with cash, and other years it is the women who prosper. Money is to some extent shared. But even so, the economist Esther Duflo of M.I.T. found that when the men's crops flourish, the household spends more money on alcohol and tobacco. When the women have a good crop, the households spend more money on food. "When women command greater power, child health and nutrition improves," Duflo says.

Such research has concrete implications: for example, donor countries should nudge poor countries to adjust their laws so that when a man dies, his property is passed on to his widow rather than to his brothers. Governments should make it easy for women to hold property and bank accounts—1 percent of the world's landowners are women—and they should make it much easier for microfinance institutions to start banks so that women can save money.

Of course, it's fair to ask: empowering women is well and good, but can one do this effectively? Does foreign aid really work? William Easterly, an economist at New York University, has argued powerfully that shoveling money at poor countries accomplishes little. Some Africans, including Dambisa Moyo, author of "Dead Aid," have said the same thing. The critics note that there has been no correlation between amounts of aid going to countries and their economic growth rates.

Our take is that, frankly, there is something to these criticisms. Helping people is far harder than it looks. Aid experiments often go awry, or small successes turn out to be difficult to replicate or scale up. Yet we've also seen, anecdotally and in the statistics, evidence that some kinds of aid have been enormously effective. The delivery of vaccinations and other kinds of health care has reduced the number of children who die every year before they reach the age of 5 to less than 10 million today from 20 million in 1960.

Abbas Be was held captive in a Delhi brothel. After she was freed, she returned to her home city of Hyderabad, became a bookbinder and now puts her sisters through school.

In general, aid appears to work best when it is focused on health, education and microfinance (although microfinance has been somewhat less successful in Africa than in Asia). And in each case, crucially, aid has often been most effective when aimed at women and girls; when policy wonks do the math, they often find that these investments have a net economic return. Only a small proportion of aid specifically targets women or girls, but increasingly donors are recognizing that that is where they often get the most bang for the buck.

In the early 1990s, the United Nations and the World Bank began to proclaim the potential resource that women and girls represent. "Investment in girls' education may well be the highest-return investment available in the developing world," Larry Summers wrote when he was chief economist of the World Bank. Private aid groups and foundations shifted gears as well. "Women are the key to ending hunger in Africa," declared the Hunger Project. The Center for Global Development issued a major report explaining "why and how to put girls at the center of development." CARE took women and girls as the centerpiece of its anti-poverty efforts. "Gender inequality hurts economic growth," Goldman Sachs concluded in a 2008 research report that emphasized how much developing countries could improve their economic performance by educating girls.

98 percent of people in Egypt say they believe that 'girls have the same right to education as boys.'

Bill Gates recalls once being invited to speak in Saudi Arabia and finding himself facing a segregated audience. Four-fifths of the listeners were men, on the left. The remaining one-fifth were women, all covered in black cloaks and veils, on the right. A partition separated the two groups. Toward the end, in the question-and-answer session, a member of the audience noted that Saudi Arabia aimed to be one of the Top 10 countries in the world in technology by 2010 and asked if that was realistic. "Well, if you're not fully utilizing half the talent in the country," Gates said, "you're not going to get too close to the Top 10." The small group on the right erupted in wild cheering.

Policy makers have gotten the message as well. President Obama has appointed a new White House Council on Women and Girls. Perhaps he was indoctrinated by his mother, who was one of the early adopters of microloans to women when she worked to fight poverty in Indonesia. Secretary of State Hillary Rodham Clinton is a member of the White House Council, and she has also selected a talented activist, Melanne Verveer, to direct a new State Department Office of Global Women's Issues. On Capitol Hill, the Senate Foreign Relations Committee has put Senator Barbara Boxer in charge of a new subcommittee that deals with women's issues.

Yet another reason to educate and empower women is that greater female involvement in society and the economy appears to undermine extremism and terrorism. It has long been known that a risk factor for turbulence and violence is the share of a country's population made up of young people. Now it is emerging that male domination of society is also a risk factor; the reasons aren't fully understood, but it may be that when women are marginalized the nation takes on the testosterone-laden culture of a military camp or a high-school boys' locker room. That's in part why the Joint Chiefs of Staff and international security specialists are puzzling over how to increase girls' education in countries like Afghanistan—and why generals have gotten briefings from Greg Mortenson, who wrote about building girls' schools in his best seller, "Three Cups of Tea." Indeed, some scholars say they believe the reason Muslim countries have been disproportionately afflicted by terrorism is not Islamic teachings about infidels or violence but rather the low levels of female education and participation in the labor force.

So what would an agenda for fighting poverty through helping women look like? You might begin with the education of girls—which doesn't just mean building schools. There are other innovative means at our disposal. A study in Kenya by Michael Kremer, a Harvard economist, examined six different approaches to improving educational performance, from providing free textbooks to child-sponsorship programs. The approach that raised student test scores the most was to offer girls who had scored in the top 15 percent of their class on sixth-grade tests a $19 scholarship for seventh and eighth grade (and the glory of recognition at an assembly). Boys also performed better, apparently because they were pushed by the girls or didn't want to endure the embarrassment of being left behind.

Another Kenyan study found that giving girls a new $6 school uniform every 18 months significantly reduced dropout rates and pregnancy rates. Likewise, there's growing evidence that a cheap way to help keep high-school girls in school is to help them manage menstruation. For fear of embarrassing leaks and stains, girls sometimes stay home during their periods, and the absenteeism puts them behind and eventually leads them to drop out. Aid workers are experimenting with giving African teenage girls sanitary pads, along with access to a toilet where they can change them. The Campaign for Female Education, an organization devoted to getting more girls into school in Africa, helps girls with their periods, and a new group, Sustainable Health Enterprises, is trying to do the same.

Claudine Mukakarisa Kigalf, Rwanda

Claudine Mukakarisa spent much of the genocide in Rwanda imprisoned in a rape house. She escaped, and afterward she found that she was the only one left alive in her family—she was pregnant, homeless, and 13 years old. Claudine gave birth in a parking lot, and hating the child because its father was a rapist, she initially left him to die. But then she returned to the parking lot, picked up her son and nursed him. She survived by begging and washing laundry; eventually, another child followed—the father was a man who raped her after offering her shelter. Claudine, with her two children, received help from an aid organization called Women for Women International, which paired her with Murvelene Clarke, a bank employee from Brooklyn. Clarke began donating $27 a month, and that money (together with training in making beadwork, which can be sold) helped Claudine educate her children.

And so, if President Obama wanted to adopt a foreign-aid policy that built on insights into the role of women in development, he would do well to start with education. We would suggest a $10 billion effort over five years to educate girls around the world. This initiative would focus on Africa but would also support—and prod—Asian countries like Afghanistan and Pakistan to do better. This plan would also double as population policy, for it would significantly reduce birthrates—and thus help poor countries overcome the demographic obstacles to economic growth.

But President Obama might consider two different proposals as well. We would recommend that the United States sponsor a global drive to eliminate iodine deficiency around the globe, by helping countries iodize salt. About a third of households in the developing world do not get enough iodine, and a result is often an impairment in brain formation in the fetal stages. For reasons that are unclear, this particularly affects female fetuses and typically costs children 10 to 15 I.Q. points. Research by Erica Field of Harvard found that daughters of women given iodine performed markedly better in school. Other research suggests that salt iodization would yield benefits worth nine times the cost.

We would also recommend that the United States announce a 12-year, $1.6 billion program to eradicate obstetric fistula, a childbirth injury that is one of the worst scourges of women in the developing world. An obstetric fistula, which is a hole created inside the body by a difficult childbirth, leaves a woman incontinent, smelly, often crippled and shunned by her village—yet it can be repaired for a few hundred dollars. Dr. Lewis Wall, president of the Worldwide Fistula Fund, and Michael Horowitz, a conservative agitator on humanitarian issues, have drafted the 12-year plan—and it's eminently practical and built on proven methods. Evidence that fistulas can be prevented or repaired comes from impoverished Somaliland,

209

Do-It-Yourself Foreign AID

People always ask us: How can I help the world's needy? How can I give in a way that will benefit a real person and won't just finance corruption or an aid bureaucracy? There are innumerable answers to those questions, but it's becoming increasingly clear that many of them involve women. From among the examples in our book "Half the Sky," here are a handful:

Choose a woman to lend to on kiva.org. The minimum amount is $25, and you can choose from people all over the world. The money will be used to support a business and will be paid back. Or go to globalgiving .com, find a woman abroad whose cause you identify with and make a small gift. On GlobalGiving, for example, we have supported a program to prevent runaway girls from being trafficked into brothels.

Sponsor a girl abroad through one of the many child-sponsorship organizations. We do so through Plan USA (planusa.org), but there are many other great ones, including Women for Women International (womenforwomen.org).

Become an advocate for change by joining the CARE Action Network at care.org. CARE is now focused on assisting women and girls for the pragmatic reason that that is where it can get the best results. The network helps people speak out and educate policy makers about global poverty.

Find a cause that resonates with you, learn more about it and adopt it. For example, we send checks to support an extraordinary Somali woman, Edna Adan who has invested her savings and her soul in her own maternity hospital in Somaliland (ednahospital.org).

Even school kids can make a difference. Jordana Confino, an eighth grader in Westfield N.J., started an initiative with friends to help girls go to school in poor countries. The effort grew to become Girls Learn International (girlslearn.org), which now pairs American middle schools and high schools with needy classrooms in Africa, Asia and Latin America. An expanded list of organizations that specialize in supporting women in developing countries is at nytimes.com/magazine.

— N.D.K. and S.W.D.

a northern enclave of Somalia, where an extraordinary nurse-midwife named Edna Adan has built her own maternity hospital to save the lives of the women around her. A former first lady of Somalia and World Health Organization official, Adan used her savings to build the hospital, which is supported by a group of admirers in the U.S. who call themselves Friends of Edna Maternity Hospital.

For all the legitimate concerns about how well humanitarian aid is spent, investments in education, iodizing salt and maternal health all have a proven record of success. And the sums are modest: all three components of our plan together amount to about what the U.S. has provided Pakistan since 9/11—a sum that accomplished virtually nothing worthwhile either for Pakistanis or for Americans.

One of the many aid groups that for pragmatic reason has increasingly focused on women is Heifer International, a charitable organization based in Arkansas that has been around for decades. The organization gives cows, goats and chickens to farmers in poor countries. On assuming the presidency of Heifer in 1992, the activist Jo Luck traveled to Africa, where one day she found herself sitting on the ground with a group of young women in a Zimbabwean village. One of them was Tererai Trent.

Tererai is a long-faced woman with high cheekbones and a medium brown complexion; she has a high forehead and tight cornrows. Like many women around the world, she doesn't know when she was born and has no documentation of her birth. As a child, Tererai didn't get much formal education, partly because she was a girl and was expected to do household chores. She herded cattle and looked after her younger siblings. Her father would say, Let's send our sons to school, because they will be the breadwinners. Tererai's brother, Tinashe, was forced to go to school, where he was an indifferent student. Tererai pleaded to be allowed to attend but wasn't permitted to do so. Tinashe brought his books home each afternoon, and Tererai pored over them and taught herself to read and write. Soon she was doing her brother's homework every evening.

The teacher grew puzzled, for Tinashe was a poor student in class but always handed in exemplary homework. Finally, the teacher noticed that the handwriting was different for homework and for class assignments and whipped Tinashe until he confessed the truth. Then the teacher went to the father, told him that Tererai was a prodigy and begged that she be allowed to attend school. After much argument, the father allowed Tererai to attend school for a couple of terms, but then married her off at about age 11.

Tererai's husband barred her from attending school, resented her literacy and beat her whenever she tried to practice her reading by looking at a scrap of old newspaper. Indeed, he beat her for plenty more as well. She hated her marriage but had no way out. "If you're a woman and you are not educated, what else?" she asks.

Yet when Jo Luck came and talked to Tererai and other young women in her village, Luck kept insisting that things did not have to be this way. She kept saying that they could achieve their goals, repeatedly using the word "achievable." The women caught the repetition and asked the interpreter to explain in detail what "achievable" meant. That gave Luck a chance to push forward. "What are your hopes?" she asked the women, through the interpreter. Tererai and the others were puzzled by the question, because they didn't really have any hopes. But Luck pushed them to think about their dreams, and reluctantly, they began to think about what they wanted.

Tererai timidly voiced hope of getting an education. Luck pounced and told her that she could do it, that she should write down her goals and methodically pursue them. After Luck and her entourage disappeared, Tererai began to study on her own, in hiding from her husband, while raising her five children. Painstakingly, with the help of friends, she wrote down her goals on a piece of paper: "One day I will go to the United States of America," she began, for Goal 1. She added that she would earn a college degree, a master's degree and a Ph.D.—all exquisitely absurd dreams for a married cattle herder in Zimbabwe who had less than one year's formal education. But Tererai took the piece of paper and folded it inside three layers of plastic to protect it, and then placed it in an old can. She buried the can under a rock where she herded cattle.

Then Tererai took correspondence classes and began saving money. Her self-confidence grew as she did brilliantly in her studies, and she became a community organizer for Heifer. She stunned everyone with superb schoolwork, and the Heifer aid workers encouraged her to think that she could study in America. One day in 1998, she received notice that she had been admitted to Oklahoma State University.

Some of the neighbors thought that a woman should focus on educating her children, not herself. "I can't talk about my children's education when I'm not educated myself," Tererai responded. "If I educate myself, then I can educate my children." So she climbed into an airplane and flew to America.

At Oklahoma State, Tererai took every credit she could and worked nights to make money. She earned her undergraduate degree, brought her five children to America and started her master's, then returned to her village. She dug up the tin can under the rock and took out the paper on which she had scribbled her goals. She put check marks beside the goals she had fulfilled and buried the tin can again.

In Arkansas, she took a job working for Heifer—while simultaneously earning a master's degree part time. When she had her M.A., Tererai again returned to her village. After embracing her mother and sister, she dug up her tin can and checked off her next goal. Now she is working on her Ph.D. at Western Michigan University.

Tererai has completed her course work and is completing a dissertation about AIDS programs among the poor in Africa.

She will become a productive economic asset for Africa and a significant figure in the battle against AIDS. And when she has her doctorate, Tererai will go back to her village and, after hugging her loved ones, go out to the field and dig up her can again.

Edna Adan A former first lady of Somalia and World Health Organization official, she built her own maternity hospital in the enclave of Somaliland.

There are many metaphors for the role of foreign assistance. For our part, we like to think of aid as a kind of lubricant, a few drops of oil in the crankcase of the developing world, so that gears move freely again on their own. That is what the assistance to Tererai amounted to: a bit of help where and when it counts most, which often means focusing on women like her. And now Tererai is gliding along freely on her own—truly able to hold up half the sky.

Critical Thinking

1. What abuses do women often suffer in developing countries?

2. What impact does empowering women have on their families?

3. How might governments and donor countries help to improve women's lives?

4. Aside from the economic benefits, what other reasons are there to educate and empower women?

5. What steps are needed to more fully involve women in the fight against poverty?

NICHOLAS D. KRISTOF is a *New York Times* Op-Ed columnist and SHERYL WUDUNN is a former *Times* correspondent who works in finance and philanthropy. This essay is adapted from their book *"Half the Sky: Turning Oppression Into Opportunity for Women Worldwide,"* which will be published next month by Alfred A. Knopf. You can learn more about *Half the Sky* at nytimes.com/ontheground.

Women in Developing Countries 300 Times More Likely to Die in Childbirth

UN report reveals 500,000 women in developing world die each year as a result of pregnancy.

SARAH BOSELEY

Women in the world's least developed countries are 300 times more likely to die during childbirth or because of their pregnancy than those in the UK and other similarly developed countries, a UN report says today.

The death toll is more than half a million women a year, according to Unicef, the UN children's emergency fund. Some 70,000 who die are girls and young women aged 15 to 19. Although it is the subject of one of the millennium development goals, the death toll is not going down.

The reasons are multiple, according to Unicef's annual state of the world's children report on maternal and newborn health. "The root cause may lie in women's disadvantaged position in many countries and cultures and in the lack of attention to, and accountability for, women's rights," it says.

"Saving the lives of mothers and their newborns requires more than just medical intervention," said Ann Veneman, Unicef's executive director. "Educating girls is pivotal to improving maternal and neonatal health and also benefits families and societies."

Women die as a result of infection and of haemorrhage. Some have obstructed labour and cannot get a caesarean section. Others die of preventable complications.

Both mothers and babies are vulnerable in the weeks after birth, the report points out. They need post-natal visits, proper hygiene and counselling about the danger signs for themselves and their baby.

Many developing countries have succeeded in reducing the death rate for children under five, but have failed to make much progress on mothers. Niger and Malawi, for example, cut under-five deaths by nearly half between 1990 and 2007.

In the developing world, a woman has a one-in-76 risk of dying because of pregnancy or childbirth in her lifetime. In developed countries, that risk is only one in 8,000.

Having a child in a developing country is one of the most severe health risks for women. For every woman who dies, another 20 suffer illness or injury, which can be permanent.

The 10 countries with the highest risk of maternal death, says Unicef, are Niger, Afghanistan, Sierra Leone, Chad, Angola, Liberia, Somalia, the Democratic Republic of Congo, Guinea-Bissau and Mali.

Deaths of newborns have also received too little attention, the report says. A child born in one of the least developed countries is nearly 14 times more likely to die within the first 28 days of life than one in an industrialised country such as the UK.

Critical Thinking

1. What accounts for higher death rates during pregnancy and childbirth in developing countries?
2. Why are newborns also vulnerable to preventable death in poor countries?
3. Where is the risk of maternal mortality greatest?

Girls in War

Sex Slave, Mother, Domestic Aide, Combatant

RADHIKA COOMARASWAMY

"The attackers tied me up and raped me because I was fighting. About five of them did the same thing to me until one of the commanders who knew my father came and stopped them, but also took me to his house to make me his wife. I just accepted him because of fear and didn't want to say no because he might do the same thing to me too." This is the testimony of a young girl of 14 from Liberia as told to the *Machel Review* in a focus group conducted jointly by the United Nations Children's Fund (UNICEF) and the Office of the Special Representative of the Secretary-General for Children and Armed Conflict (OSRSG/CAAC).

This story shows how vulnerable girls are in armed conflict. Actually, they can be affected by war in five different ways. Firstly, they are often direct victims of violence—killed, maimed or sexually violated as war crimes are committed against them. Secondly, they can be recruited and used as combatants for fighting in the battlefield. Thirdly, as refugees and internally displaced persons (IDPS), they remain in insecure environments, often deprived of basic amenities. Fourthly, they are frequently trafficked and exploited, as perpetrators abuse their vulnerability. Finally, when they become orphans, some of them have to manage child-headed households, eking out a living for themselves and their siblings.

Direct Violence

The number of children who are victims of direct violence, especially killings, has greatly increased in the last few years. Many have lost their lives in the confrontation between terrorism and counter terrorism. We have seen the phenomenon of children being used as suicide bombers and we have seen children as victims of aerial bombardment, a part of what is euphemistically called "collateral damage".

In Afghanistan I met Aisha, a girl whose home had been destroyed during an air raid which killed many of her family members, and whose school had been attacked by insurgents opposing education for girls. But Aisha was determined to go on with her studies so that she could become a school teacher.

Sexual Violence

Girls are often raped or violated in situations of conflict. Raping girls and women is often a military strategy aimed at terrorizing the population and humiliating the community. At other times,

the climate of impunity in war zones leads to rape and exploitation by individual soldiers who know they will not be punished. Eva was a young girl I met in the Democratic Republic of the Congo. She and her friend were walking to school when they were waylaid by armed members of the Democratic Liberation Forces of Rwanda. They were taken to the camp, repeatedly raped, compelled to live in a state of forced nudity and assigned to domestic chores for the members of the group. Eva finally escaped and found shelter in Panzi hospital, a refuge for victims of sexual violence, where she found out that she was pregnant. She was 13 years old. When I met her, Panzi hospital was taking care of her child while she was attending school. They were trying to trace her family, even though they knew that girls who are victims of rape are often shunned by their next of kin.

Girl Soldiers

Increasingly, girls are being recruited into fighting forces as child soldiers. Some are abducted and have to play the dual role of sex slave and child combatant. This was particularly true in the wars of Sierra Leone and Liberia. In other cases, girls join the fighting forces for a multitude of reasons because they identify with the ideology, they want to run away from home or they have no other option for survival. Maria was a former girl child soldier whom I met in Colombia. She joined the rebel groups because her brothers had joined before her. Subjected to domestic violence at home, she ran away. She fought with the rebels and was then captured during one of the confrontations. Today she feels very lost. She does not want to go back home and she feels she has neither the education nor the skills to survive alone. When I met her, she was being taken care of by a foster parent. She felt boys were frightened of her because of her past. She also told me that many girls who had left the movement finally end up in sex work as a survival strategy.

Internally Displaced

Eighty percent of the world's refugees and internally displaced are women and children. Displaced children are perhaps one of the most vulnerable categories. In many parts of the world they are separated from their families while fleeing, becoming orphans overnight. And living in camps, they are often recruited into the fighting forces. Displaced children also suffer from high rates of malnutrition and have little access to medical services. Many girls are victims of violence in the camp or when they leave the camp to gather firewood and other necessities. For those who advocate for the rights of displaced children, the first priority should be security. The objective is to ensure that children are safe, protected from sexual violence and recruitment, and that there are child-friendly spaces in the camp. The second priority is education. Recently, UN agencies and non-governmental organizations (NGOS) have partnered to advocate strongly that education is an integral part of emergency response and not a luxury development. This was one of the key messages of the General Assembly debate on Education in Emergencies, in March 2009. It is important to plan for schools and play areas for children as the camp is constructed and provisions are made for families to be settled. It gives children a sense of normalcy and routine when they live in the camps.

Trafficking and Sexual Exploitation

Another concern we have for girl children in situations of armed conflict is that they are often trafficked and sexually exploited. At the international level, commentators have always pointed to "waves" of trafficking: that is, particular groups being trafficked in large numbers at a particular time. These waves often occur in areas of armed conflicts; women flee in large numbers, and being sex workers is their only survival strategy. They become victims of terrible exploitation by ruthless international criminal gangs. So many of these stories have been chronicled and a great deal of effort has been made over the last two decades to tackle the phenomenon. Nevertheless, the ground realities of conflict still lead to the sexual vulnerability of girls and women. Our own peacekeepers have not been immune to these situations. The UN Department of Peacekeeping Operations has made it a priority through their zero tolerance policy and code of conduct and discipline to ensure that this type of activity ceases and that peacekeepers will only be seen as protectors.

In areas of armed conflicts women flee in large numbers, and being sex workers is their only survival strategy. They become victims of terrible exploitation by ruthless international criminal gangs.

Orphans and Child-Headed Households

The terrible toll of war also makes many children into orphans overnight. In many parts of the world, we are seeing child-headed households where children have to fend for themselves as well as for other children. This happens especially to girl children who have to take over the role of parents. Parentless children often live in deplorable conditions such as broken-down buildings with leaky roofs, or no roofs at all. They sleep together under torn plastic sacks and cook with old rusty cans and broken pottery. They are susceptible to all manner of diseases and their situation is terribly vulnerable and heartbreaking. UN agencies are trying ways of giving these children a future without institutionalizing them in centres. It is their aim to keep children in the community and make it the responsibility of the community to take care of its children. Through schemes that find foster homes and foster mothers, they hope to let the children enjoy the benefit of family life.

The terrible toll of war also makes many children into orphans overnight. In many parts of the world, we are seeing child-headed households where children have to fend for themselves and also other children. This happens especially to girl children who have to take over the role of parents.

The International Tribunals and the Fight against Impunity

How has the international community responded to these devastating descriptions of what girl children suffer during war time? Recently things are slowly beginning to change, especially in the fight against impunity. The first breakthrough for children was the establishment of international tribunals which began to hold perpetrators accountable for international crimes. The cases before the tribunals of the Former Yugoslavia and Rwanda that dealt with sexual violence, created a framework of international jurisprudence that will help us in the future. Individual women found justice, and there is always the deterrent effect that cannot be measured in an empirical manner. Recently, the Special Court for Sierra Leone found several commanders of the Revolutionary United Front guilty of 16 charges of war crimes and crimes against humanity including conscription and enlistment of children under 15 into the fighting forces. The setting up of the International Criminal Court was the culmination of this trajectory. Their first case, the Thomas Lubanga case, involved the recruitment and use of children as child soldiers, strengthening the cause for children. Our office submitted an amicus curiae to the court in that case, arguing that girl children should be brought into the ambit of protection. We advocate for the young, abducted girls who play multiple roles in camps, to receive the protection of the law against being recruited, used, as well as forced to participate in the hostilities. We hope to get our day in court to argue this point of view so that the enormous suffering of girl children does not remain invisible.

Involvement of the Security Council

In the area of children in armed conflict, another mechanism that has begun to chip away at impunity is Security Council resolution 1612. The resolution, passed in 2005, created a Working

Group on Children and Armed Conflict. It also established a monitoring and reporting mechanism involving a Task Force at the national level made up of all the UN agencies, assigned to report on the violations. The Task Force is chaired by either the Resident Co-ordinator or the Special Representative and is often co-chaired by UNICEF. Through this mechanism, OSRSG/CAAC receives bimonthly reports on grave violations against children in war zones. The Security Council process is informed by the Annual Report of the Secretary-General to the Council which lists parties that recruit and use child soldiers. Resolution 1612 recommends the prospect of targeted measures against persistent violators of children's rights. The hope in 2009 is to extend these measures, beyond the recruitment and use of child soldiers, to include sexual violence against children, such that those who persistently use sexual violence in war be listed, shamed and face the possibility of sanctions. Having received the full support of the UN system, it is hoped that Member States, especially those in the Security Council, will help our office deliver on this promise.

In a world where there is so much abuse against women and children, one may become cynical about these small steps that the international community has begun to take to fight impunity, but we must not underestimate their effects. Recently, I was in the Central African Republic and met three generations of women in one family who had been raped when Jean-Pierre Bemba's troops attacked the capital, Bangui. They were getting ready to go to The Hague to testify against him. Their elation at the possibility of justice, and their gratitude that these things have come to pass has convinced me that we are on the right path. Grave violations, war crimes and crimes against humanity must be taken seriously, so that the culture of impunity that often hangs over warfare be broken.

Reintegration of Former Child Soldiers

Another area where the international community can help is the field of rehabilitation and reintegration. Reintegrating children affected by war is a major task facing governments, UN agencies and NGO partners working in the field. The Paris Principles give us a framework on how to reintegrate children associated with armed groups, but these principles are also a guide to reintegrating all children. The call for community-based programming that works with the child, while developing the family and the community in an inclusive manner, must be the starting point for child-based programming. And yet, some children need special attention. Research shows that children who were forced to commit terrible crimes and children who were victims of sexual violence need special care and attention. Girl children often have different needs from boys. Treating children as important individuals while, at the same time, developing the community in a holistic manner, is the only sustainable way forward.

Finally we cannot even begin to speak of the psychological toll that war takes on children. When I was in Gaza, I went to a school and entered a classroom of nine year-old girls, who were drawing in an art class. I moved from one to the other, and then I just looked down at one girl's drawing, Ameena's. She had drawn a house and she explained to me that the two figures in the house were her mother and herself. Above the house there was a mangled object which I gather was a helicopter gunship; to the left of the house there was an imposing looking tank and to the right of the house, a soldier. All these were firing at the home. Her sad, dull eyes on her beautiful face told the rest of the story. Meeting the day to day reality of war is a terrible calling for all of my colleagues working in the field. But rebuilding the shattered lives of children is an even more daunting task; to make them smile again, care again and live with purpose is the challenge of the hour.

Critical Thinking

1. In what ways are girls vulnerable in conflict situations?
2. How are internal displacement and vulnerability linked?
3. How has the international community responded to this vulnerability?

RADHIKA COOMARASWAMY is the Special Representative of the UN Secretary-General for Children and Armed Conflict (www.un.org/children/conflict).

From *UN Chronicle*, No. 1&2, 2009, pp. 50, 52–53. Copyright © 2009 by United Nations Publications. Reprinted by permission.

Remember the Women?

Women belong at the center of the debate over the Afghan war, not on the margins.

ANN JONES

Women are made for homes or graves.

—Afghan saying

Gen. Stanley McChrystal says he needs more American troops to salvage something like winning in Afghanistan and restore the country to "normal life." Influential senators want to increase spending to train more soldiers for the Afghan National Army and Police. The Feminist Majority recently backed off a call for more troops, but it continues to warn against US withdrawal as an abandonment of Afghan women and girls. Nearly everyone assumes troops bring greater security; and whether your touchstone is military victory, national interest or the welfare of women and girls, "security" seems a good thing.

I confess that I agonize over competing proposals now commanding President Obama's attention because I've spent years in Afghanistan working with women, and I'm on their side. When the Feminist Majority argues that withdrawing American forces from Afghanistan will return the Taliban to power and women to house arrest, I see in my mind's eye the faces of women I know and care about. Yet an unsentimental look at the record reveals that for all the fine talk of women's rights since the US invasion, equal rights for Afghan women have been illusory all along, a polite feel-good fiction that helped to sell the American enterprise at home and cloak in respectability the misbegotten government we installed in Kabul. That it is a fiction is borne out by recent developments in Afghanistan—President Karzai's approving a new family law worthy of the Taliban, and American acquiescence in Karzai's new law and, initially, his theft of the presidential election—and by the systematic intimidation, murder or exile of one Afghan woman after another who behaves as if her rights were real and worth fighting for.

Last summer in Kabul, where "security" already suffocates anything remotely suggesting normal life, I asked an Afghan colleague at an international NGO if she was ever afraid. I had learned of threatening phone calls and night letters posted on the gates of the compound, targeting Afghan women who work within. Three of our colleagues in another city had been kidnapped by the militia of a warlord, formerly a member of the Karzai government, and at the time, as we learned after their release, were being beaten, tortured and threatened with death if they continued to work.

"Fear?" my colleague said. "Yes. We live with fear. In our work here with women we are always under threat. Personally, I work every day in fear, hoping to return safely at the end of the day to my home. To my child and my husband."

"And the future?" I said. "What do you worry about?"

"I think about the upcoming election," she said. "I fear that nothing will change. I fear that everything will stay the same."

Then Karzai gazetted the Shiite Personal Status Law, and it was suddenly clear that even as we were hoping for the best, everything had actually grown much worse for women.

Why is this important? At this critical moment, as Obama tries to weigh options against our national security interests, his advisers can't be bothered with—as one US military officer put it to me—"the trivial fate of women." As for some hypothetical moral duty to protect the women of Afghanistan—that's off the table. Yet it is precisely that dismissive attitude, shared by Afghan and many American men alike, that may have put America's whole Afghan enterprise wrong in the first place. Early on, Kofi Annan, then United Nations secretary general, noted that the condition of Afghan women was "an affront to all standards of dignity, equality and humanity."

Annan took the position, set forth in 2000 in the landmark UN Security Council Resolution 1325, that real conflict resolution, reconstruction and lasting peace cannot be achieved without the full participation of women every step of the way. Karzai gave lip service to the idea, saying in 2002, "We are determined to work to improve the lot of women after all their suffering under the narrow-minded and oppressive rule of the Taliban." But he has done no such thing. And the die had already been cast: of the twenty-three Afghan notables invited to take part in the Bonn Conference in December 2001, only two were women. Among ministers appointed to the new Karzai government, there were only two; one, the minister for women's affairs, was warned not to do "too much."

The Bonn agreement expressed "appreciation to the Afghan mujahidin who...have defended the independence, territorial integrity and national unity of the country and have played a major role in the struggle against terrorism and oppression, and whose sacrifice has now made them both heroes of jihad and champions of peace, stability and reconstruction of their beloved homeland, Afghanistan." On the other hand, their American- and Saudi-sponsored "sacrifice" had also made many of them war criminals in the eyes of their countrymen. Most Afghans surveyed between 2002 and 2004 by the Afghan Independent Human Rights Commission thought the leaders of the mujahedeen were war criminals who should be brought to justice (75 percent) and removed from public office (90 percent). The mujahedeen, after all, were Islamist extremists just like the Taliban, though less disciplined than the Taliban, who had risen up to curb the violent excesses of the mujahedeen and then imposed excesses of their own. That's the part American officials seem unwilling to admit: that the mujahedeen warlords of the Karzai government and the oppressive Taliban are brothers under the skin. From the point of view of women today, America's friends and America's enemies in Afghanistan are the same kind of guys.

Though women were excluded from the Bonn process, they did seem to make strides in the first years after the fall of the Taliban. In 2004 a new constitution declared, "The citizens of Afghanistan—whether man or woman—have equal rights and duties before the law." Westerners greeted that language as a confirmation of gender equality, and to this day women's "equal rights" are routinely cited in Western media as evidence of great progress. Yet not surprisingly, Afghan officials often interpret the article differently. To them, having "equal rights and duties" is nothing like being equal. The first chief justice of the Afghan Supreme Court, formerly a mullah in a Pakistani madrassa, once explained to me that men have a right to work while women have a right to obey their husbands. The judiciary—an ultraconservative, inadequate, incompetent and notoriously corrupt branch of government—interprets the constitution by its own lights. And the great majority of women across the country, knowing little or nothing of rights, live now much as they did under the Taliban—except back then there were no bombs.

In any case, the constitution provides that no law may contravene the principles of Sharia law. In effect, mullahs and judges have always retained the power to decide at any moment what "rights" women may enjoy, or not; and being poorly educated, they're likely to factor into the judgment their own idiosyncratic notions of Sharia, plus tribal customary laws and the size of proffered bribes. Thus, although some women still bravely exercise liberty and work with some success to improve women's condition, it should have been clear from the get-go that Afghan women possess no inalienable rights at all. Western legal experts who train Afghan judges and lawyers in "the law" as we conceive it often express frustration that Afghans just don't get it; Afghan judges think the same of them.

The paper foundations of Afghan women's rights go beyond national law to include the Universal Declaration of Human Rights, the International Treaty of Civil and Political Rights, and the Convention on the Elimination of All Forms of Discrimination Against Women (CEDAW). All these international agreements that delineate and establish human rights around the world were quickly ratified by the Karzai government. CEDAW, however, requires ratifying governments to submit periodic reports on their progress in eliminating discrimination; Afghanistan's first report, due in 2004, hasn't appeared yet. That's one more clue to the Karzai government's real attitude toward women—like Karzai's sequestration of his own wife, a doctor with much-needed skills who is kept locked up at home.

Given this background, there should have been no surprise when President Karzai first signed off in March on the Shiite Personal Status Law or, as it became known in the Western press, the Marital Rape Law. The bill had been percolating in the ultraconservative Ministry of Justice ever since the Iranian-backed Ayatollah Asif Mohseni submitted it in 2007. Then last February Karzai apparently saw the chance to swap passage of the SPSL for the votes of the Shiites—that is, the Hazara minority, 15–20 percent of the population. It was just one of many deals Karzai consolidated as he kept to the palace while rival presidential candidates stomped the countryside. The SPSL passed without alteration through the Parliamentary Judicial Committee, another little bunch of ultraconservative men. When it reached the floor of Parliament, it was too late to object. Some women members succeeded in getting the marriageable age for girls—age 9—revised to 16. Calling it victory, they settled for that. The Supreme Court reviewed the bill and pronounced it constitutionally correct on grounds the justices did not disclose.

The rights Afghan women stood to lose on paper and in real life were set forth in the SPSL. Parliamentarian Shinkai Karokhail alerted a reporter at the *Guardian,* and the law was denounced around the world for legalizing marital rape by authorizing a husband to withhold food from a wife who fails to provide sexual service at least once every four days. (The interval assumes the husband has four wives, a practice permitted by Islam and legalized by this legislation.) But that's not all the law does. It also denies or severely limits women's rights to inherit, divorce or have guardianship of their own children. It forbids women to marry without permission and legalizes forced marriage. It legalizes marriage to and rape of minors. It gives men control of all their female relatives. It denies women the right to leave home except for "legitimate purposes"—in effect giving men the power to deny women access to work, education, healthcare, voting and whatever they please. It generally treats women as property, and it considers rape of women or minors outside marriage as a property crime, requiring restitution to be made to the owner, usually the father or husband, rather than a crime against the victim. All these provisions are contained in twenty-six articles of the original bill that have been rendered into English and analyzed by Western legal experts. No doubt other regressive rules will be discovered if the 223 additional articles of the law ever appear in English.

In April a few women parliamentarians spoke out against the law. A group of women, estimated to number about 300, staged a peaceful protest in the street, protected by Kabul's police officers from an angry mob of hundreds of men who pelted them with obscenities and stones, shouting, "Death to the enemies of Islam!" Under pressure from international diplomats—President Obama called the law "abhorrent"—Karzai withdrew it for review. The international press reported the women's victory. In June, when a large group of women MPs and activists met with Karzai, he assured them the bill had been amended and would be submitted to Parliament again after the elections.

Instead, on July 27, without public announcement, Karzai entered the SPSL, slightly revised but with principal provisions intact, into the official gazette, thereby making it law. Apparently he was betting that with the presidential election only three weeks away, the United States and its allies would not complain again. After all, they had about $500 million (at least half of that American money) riding on a "credible" outcome; and they couldn't afford the cost of a runoff or the political limbo of an interregnum. In August,

Brad Adams, Asia director of Human Rights Watch, observed that such "barbaric laws were supposed to have been relegated to the past with the overthrow of the Taliban in 2001, yet Karzai has revived them and given them his official stamp of approval." No American official said a word.

But what about all the women parliamentarians so often cited as evidence of the progress of Afghan women? With 17 percent of the upper house and 27 percent of the lower—eighty-five women in all—you'd think they could have blocked the SPSL. But that didn't happen, for many reasons. Many women parliamentarians are mere extensions of the warlords who financed their campaigns and tell them how to vote: always in opposition to women's rights. Most non-Shiite women took little interest in the bill, believing that it applied only to the Shiite minority. Although Hazara women have long been the freest in the country and the most active in public life, some of them argued that it is better to have a bad law than none at all because, as one Hazara MP told me, "without a written law, men can do whatever they want."

The human rights division of the UN's Assistance Mission in Afghanistan (UNAMA) published a report in early July, before the SPSL became law, documenting the worsening position of Afghan women, the rising violence against them and the silence of international and Afghan officials who could defend them. The researchers' most surprising finding is this: considering the risks of life outside the home and the support women receive within it, "there is no clear distinction between rural and urban women." Commentators on Afghanistan, myself included, have assumed—somewhat snobbishly, it now appears—that while illiterate women in the countryside might be treated no better than animals, educated urban Afghan women blaze a higher trail. The debacle of the Shiite Personal Status Law explodes that myth.

The UNAMA report attributes women's worsening position in Afghan society to the violence the war engenders on two domestic fronts: the public stage and the home. The report is dedicated to the memory of Sitara Achakzai, a member of the Kandahar Provincial Council and outspoken advocate of women's rights, who was shot to death on April 12, soon after being interviewed by the UNAMA researchers. She "knew her life was in danger," they report. "But like many other Afghan women such as Malalai Kakar, the highest-ranking female police officer in Kandahar killed in September 2008, Sitara Achakzai had consciously decided to keep fighting to end the abuse of Afghan women." Malalai Kakar, 40, mother of six, had headed a team of ten policewomen handling cases of domestic violence.

Women's worsening position is a result of the violence the war engenders on two fronts: the public stage and the home.

In 2005 Kim Sengupta, a reporter with the London *Independent,* interviewed five Afghan women activists; by October 2008 three of them had been murdered. A fourth, Zarghuna Kakar (no relation to Malalai), a member of the Kandahar Provincial Council, had left the country after she and her family were attacked and her husband was killed. She said she had pleaded with Ahmed Wali Karzai, head of the Kandahar Provincial Council, for protection; but he told her she "should have thought about what may happen" before she stood for election. Kakar told the reporter, "It was his brother [President Karzai], the Americans, and the British who told us that we women should get involved in political life. Of course, now I wish I hadn't."

Women learn to pull their punches. MPs in Kabul confessed that they are afraid of the fundamentalist warlords who control the Parliament; so they censor themselves and keep silent. One said, "Most of the time women don't dare even say a word about sensitive Islamic issues, because they are afraid of being labeled as blasphemous." Many women MPs have publicly declared their intention to quit at the end of the term. Women journalists also told UNAMA that they "refrain from criticizing warlords and other power brokers, or covering topics that are deemed contentious such as women's rights."

Other women targeted for attack are civil servants, employees of international and national organizations, including the UN, healthcare workers and women in "immoral" professions—which include acting, singing, appearing on television and journalism. When popular Tolo TV presenter Shaima Rezayee, 24, was forced out of her job in 2005, she said "things are not getting better . . . . We have made some gains, but there are a lot of people who want to take it all back. They are not even Taliban, they are here in Kabul." Soon after, she was shot and killed. Zakia Zaki, 35, a teacher and radio journalist who produced programs on women's rights, was shot to death in her home in Parwan Province on June 6, 2007. Actress Parwin Mushtakhel fled the country last spring after her husband was gunned down outside their house, punished for his failure to keep her confined. When the Taliban fell, she thought things were getting better, but "the atmosphere has changed; day by day women can work less and less." Setara Hussainzada, the singer from Herat who appeared on the Afghan version of *American Idol* (and in the documentary *Afghan Star*) also fled for her life.

Threats against women in public life are intended to make them go home—to "unliberate" themselves through voluntary house arrest. But if public life is dangerous, so is life at home. Most Afghan women—87 percent, according to Unifem—are beaten on a regular basis. The UNAMA researchers looked into the unmentionable subject of rape and found it to be "an everyday occurrence in all parts of the country" and "a human rights problem of profound proportions." Outside marriage, the rapists are often members or friends of the family. Young girls forced to marry old men are raped by the old man's brothers and sons. Women and children—young boys are also targets—are raped by people who have charge of them: police, prison guards, soldiers, orphanage or hospital staff members. The female victims of rape are mostly between the ages of 7 and 30; many are between 10 and 20, but some are as young as 3; and most women are dead by 42.

Women rarely tell anyone because the blame and shame of rape falls on them. Customary law permits an accused rapist to make restitution to the victim's father, but because the question of consent does not figure in the law of sexual relations, the victim is guilty of *zina,* or adultery, and can be punished accordingly: sent to jail or murdered by family members to preserve family honor. The great majority of women and girls in prison at any time are charged with *zina;* most have been raped and/or have run away from home to escape violence. It's probably safe to say, in the absence of statistics, that police—who, incidentally, are trained by the American for-profit contractor DynCorp—spend more time tracking down runaway women and girls than real criminals. Rapists, on the other hand, as UNAMA investigators found, are often "directly linked to power brokers who are, effectively, above the law and enjoy immunity from arrest as well as immunity from social condemnation." Last year Karzai pardoned political thugs who had gang-raped a woman before witnesses, using a bayonet, and who had somehow been convicted despite their good connections. UNAMA researchers conclude: "The current reality is that . . . women are denied their most fundamental human rights and risk further violence in the course of seeking justice for crimes perpetrated against them." For women, "human rights are values, standards, and entitlements that exist only in theory and at times, not even on paper."

Caught in the maelstrom of personal, political and military violence, Afghan women worry less about rights than security. But they complain that the men who plan the country's future define "security" in ways that have nothing to do with them. The conventional wisdom, which I have voiced myself, holds that without security, development cannot take place. Hence, our troops must be fielded in greater numbers, and Afghan troops trained faster, and private for-profit military contractors hired at fabulous expense, all to bring security. But the rule doesn't hold in Afghanistan precisely because of that equation of "security" with the presence of armed men. Wherever troops advance in Afghanistan, women are caught in the cross-fire, killed, wounded, forced to flee or locked up once again, just as they were in the time of the Taliban. Suggesting an alternative to the "major misery" of warfare, Sweden's former Defense Minister Thage Peterson calls for Swedish soldiers to leave the "military adventure" in Afghanistan while civilians stay to help rebuild the country. But Sweden's soldiers are few, and its aid organizations among the best in the world. For the United States even to lean toward such a plan would mean reasserting civilian control of the military and restoring the American aid program (USAID), hijacked by private for-profit contractors: two goals worth fighting for.

Wherever troops advance, women are caught in the cross-fire, killed, wounded, forced to flee or locked up just as they were under the Taliban.

Today, most American so-called development aid is delivered not by USAID, but by the military itself through a system of Provincial Reconstruction Teams (PRTs), another faulty idea of former Defense Secretary Donald Rumsfeld. Soldiers, unqualified as aid workers and already busy soldiering, now shmooze with village "elders" (often the wrong ones) and bring "development," usually a costly road convenient to the PRT base, impossible for Afghans to maintain and inaccessible to women locked up at home. Recent research conducted by respected Afghanistan hands found that this aid actually fuels "massive corruption"; it fails to win hearts and minds not because we spend too little but because we spend too much, too fast, without a clue. Meanwhile, the Taliban bring the things Afghans say they need—better security, better governance and quick, hard-edged justice. US government investigators are looking into allegations that aid funds appropriated for women's projects have been diverted to PRTs for this more important work of winning hearts and minds with tarmac. But the greatest problem with routing aid through the military is this: what passes for development is delivered from men to men, affirming in the strongest possible terms the misogynist conviction that women do not matter. You'll recognize it as the same belief that, in the Obama administration's strategic reappraisal of Afghanistan, pushed women off the table.

So there's no point talking about how women and girls might be affected by the strategic military options remaining on Obama's plate. None of them bode well for women. To send more troops is to send more violence. To withdraw is to invite the Taliban. To stay the same is not possible, now that Karzai has stolen the election in plain sight and made a mockery of American pretensions to an interest in anything but our own skin and our own pocketbook. But while men plan the onslaught of more men, it's worth remembering what "normal life" once looked like in Afghanistan, well before the soldiers came. In the 1960s and '70s, before the Soviet invasion—when half the country's doctors, more than half the civil servants and three-quarters of the teachers were women—a peaceful Afghanistan advanced slowly into the modern world through the efforts of all its people. What changed all that was not only the violence of war but the accession to power of the most backward men in the country: first the Taliban, now the mullahs and mujahedeen of the fraudulent, corrupt, Western-designed government that stands in opposition to "normal life" as it is lived in the developed world and was once lived in their own country. What happens to women is not merely a "women's issue"; it is the central issue of stability, development and durable peace. No nation can advance without women, and no enterprise that takes women off the table can come to much good.

Critical Thinking

1. What is the status of women's rights in Afghanistan?
2. What has acted as a constraint upon women's rights as outlined in the 2004 Afghan constitution?
3. How did the Shiite Personal Status Law further undermine women's rights?
4. How are women in public life affected by a lack of status in Afghanistan?
5. In what ways are women vulnerable at home?

ANN JONES, author of *Kabul in Winter,* does humanitarian work in postconflict zones with NGOs and the United Nations.

Women in the Shadow of Climate Change

Balgis Osman-Elasha

Climate change is one of the greatest global challenges of the twenty-first century. Its impacts vary among regions, generations, age, classes, income groups, and gender. Based on the findings of the Intergovernmental Panel on Climate Change (IPCC), it is evident that people who are already most vulnerable and marginalized will also experience the greatest impacts. The poor, primarily in developing countries, are expected to be disproportionately affected and consequently in the greatest need of adaptation strategies in the face of climate variability and change. Both women and men working in natural resource sectors, such as agriculture, are likely to be affected.[1] However, the impact of climate change on gender is not the same. Women are increasingly being seen as more vulnerable than men to the impacts of climate change, mainly because they represent the majority of the world's poor and are proportionally more dependent on threatened natural resources. The difference between men and women can also be seen in their differential roles, responsibilities, decision making, access to land and natural resources, opportunities and needs, which are held by both sexes.[2] Worldwide, women have less access than men to resources such as land, credit, agricultural inputs, decision-making structures, technology, training and extension services that would enhance their capacity to adapt to climate change.[3]

> **Worldwide, women have less access than men to resources such as land, credit, agricultural inputs, decision-making structures, technology, training and extension services that would enhance their capacity to adapt to climate change.**

Why Women Are More Vulnerable

Women's vulnerability to climate change stems from a number of factors—social, economic and cultural.

Seventy percent of the 1.3 billion people living in conditions of poverty are women. In urban areas, 40 percent of the poorest households are headed by women. Women predominate in the world's food production (50–80 percent), but they own less than 10 percent of the land.

Women represent a high percentage of poor communities that are highly dependent on local natural resources for their livelihood, particularly in rural areas where they shoulder the major responsibility for household water supply and energy for cooking and heating, as well as for food security. In the Near East, women contribute up to 50 percent of the agricultural workforce. They are mainly responsible for the more time-consuming and labour-intensive tasks that are carried out manually or with the use of simple tools. In Latin America and the Caribbean, the rural population has been decreasing in recent decades. Women are mainly engaged in subsistence farming, particularly horticulture, poultry and raising small livestock for home consumption.

Women have limited access to and control of environmental goods and services; they have negligible participation in decision-making, and are not involved in the distribution of environment management benefits. Consequently, women are less able to confront climate change.

During extreme weather such as droughts and floods, women tend to work more to secure household livelihoods. This will leave less time for women to access training and education, develop skills or earn income. In Africa, female illiteracy rates were over 55 percent in 2000, compared to 41 percent for men.[4] When coupled with inaccessibility to resources and decision-making processes, limited mobility places women where they are disproportionately affected by climate change.

In many societies, socio-cultural norms and childcare responsibilities prevent women from migrating or seeking refuge in other places or working when a disaster hits. Such a situation is likely to put more burden on women, such as travelling longer to get drinking water and wood for fuel. Women, in many developing countries suffer gender inequalities with respect to human rights, political and economic status, land ownership, housing conditions, exposure to violence, education and health. Climate change will be an added stressor that will aggravate women's

Oxfam International reported disproportional fatalities among men and women during the tsunami that hit Asia at the end of 2004. According to an Oxfam briefing, females accounted for about three quarters of deaths in eight Indonesian villages, and almost 90 percent of deaths in Cuddalore, the second most affected district in India. Of the 140,000 who died from the 1991 cyclone disasters in Bangladesh, 90 percent were women.[6]

Women and girls in many rural societies spend up to three hours per day fetching water and collecting firewood. Droughts, floods, and desertification exacerbated by climate change make women spend more time on these tasks, diminishing their ability to participate in wage-earning activities.[7]

During natural disasters, more women die (compared to men) because they are not adequately warned, cannot swim well, or cannot leave the house alone.

Moreover, lower levels of education reduce the ability of women and girls to access information, including early warning and resources, or to make their voices heard. Cultural values could also contribute to women's vulnerability in some countries. For example, in Bangladesh, women are more calorie-deficient than men (the male members in a family have the "right" to consume the best portions of the food, and the female members have to content themselves with the left-overs) and have more problems during disasters to cope with.

In Sudan, the increase in the migration of men from the drought-hit areas of western Sudan increased the number of female-headed households, and consequently their responsibilities and vulnerabilities during natural disasters.

—Balgis Osman-Elasha

In Africa, for example, old women represent wisdom pools with their inherited knowledge and expertise related to early warnings and mitigating the impacts of disasters. This knowledge and experience that has passed from one generation to another will be able to contribute effectively to enhancing local adaptive capacity and sustaining a community's livelihood. For this to be achieved, and in order to improve the adaptive capacity of women worldwide particularly in developing countries, the following recommendations need to be considered:

- Adaptation initiatives should identify and address gender-specific impacts of climate change particularly in areas related to water, food security, agriculture, energy, health, disaster management, and conflict. Important gender issues associated with climate change adaptation, such as inequalities in access to resources, including credit, extension and training services, information and technology should also be taken into consideration.

- Women's priorities and needs must be reflected in the development planning and funding. Women should be part of the decision making at national and local levels regarding allocation of resources for climate change initiatives. It is also important to ensure gender-sensitive investments in programmes for adaptation, mitigation, technology transfer and capacity building.

- Funding organizations and donors should also take into account women-specific circumstances when developing and introducing technologies related to climate change adaptation and to try their best to remove the economic, social and cultural barriers that could constrain women from benefiting and making use of them. Involving women in the development of new technologies can ensure that they are adaptive, appropriate and sustainable. At national levels, efforts should be made to mainstream gender perspective into national policies and strategies, as well as related sustainable development and climate change plans and interventions.

vulnerability. It is widely known that during conflict, women face heightened domestic violence, sexual intimidation, human trafficking and rape.[5]

According to the IPCC in Africa, an increase of 5–8% (160–90 million hectares) of arid and semiarid land is projected by the 2080s under a range of climate change scenarios.

Improving Women's Adaptation to Climate Change

In spite of their vulnerability, women are not only seen as victims of climate change, but they can also be seen as active and effective agents and promoters of adaptation and mitigation. For a long time women have historically developed knowledge and skills related to water harvesting and storage, food preservation and rationing, and natural resource management.

Notes

1. ILO, 2008. Report of the Committee on Employment and Social Policy, Employment and labour market implications of climate change, Fourth Item on the Agenda, Governing Body, 303rd Session (Geneva), p. 2.

2. Osman-Elasha, 2008 "Gender and Climate Change in the Arab Region", Arab Women Organization, p. 44.

3. Aguilar, L., 2008. "Is there a connection between gender and climate change?", International Union for Conservation of Nature (IUCN), Office of the Senior Gender Adviser.

4. Rena, Ravinder and N. Narayana (2007) "Gender Empowerment in Africa: An Analysis of Women Participation in Eritrean Economy", New Delhi: *International Journal of Women, Social Justice and Human Rights,* vol. 2. no. 2, pp. 221–237 (Serials Publishers).

5. Davis, I. et. al. 2005, "Tsunami, Gender, and Recovery".

6. IUCN 2004 (a), "Climate Change and Disaster Mitigation: Gender Makes the Difference". Intergovernmental Panel on Climate Change, 2001. Climate Change: Impacts, Adaptation and Vulnerability, Contribution of Working Group II to the Third Assessment Report of the IPCC.

7. IUCN 2004 (b), "Energy: Gender Makes the Difference". Gender Action, 2008. Gender Action Link: Climate Change (Washington, D.C.), www.genderaction.org/images/Gender%20Action%20Link%20-%20Climate%20Change.pdf

8. Third Global Congress of Women in Politics and Governance, 2008. Background and Context Paper for the Conference, Manila, Philippines, 19–22 October, www.capwip.org/3rdglobalcongress.htm IUCN 2007, "Gender and Climate Change: Women as Agents of Change"

Critical Thinking

1. Why are women particularly vulnerable to climate change?

2. Why are they less able to deal with the consequences of climate change?

3. How do socio-cultural norms affect women's ability to meet the challenge of climate change?

BALGIS OSMAN-ELASHA is Principal Investigator with the Climate Change Unit, Higher Council for Environment and Natural Resources, Sudan; and a lead author of the Intergovernmental Panel on Climate Change's Fourth Assessment Report.

The Global Glass Ceiling

Why Empowering Women Is Good for Business

ISOBEL COLEMAN

Over the last several decades, it has become accepted wisdom that improving the status of women is one of the most critical levers of international development. When women are educated and can earn and control income, a number of good results follow: infant mortality declines, child health and nutrition improve, agricultural productivity rises, population growth slows, economies expand, and cycles of poverty are broken.

But the challenges remain dauntingly large. In the Middle East, South Asia, and sub-Saharan Africa, in particular, large and persistent gender gaps in access to education, health care, technology, and income—plus a lack of basic rights and pervasive violence against women—keep women from being fully productive members of society. Entrenched gender discrimination remains a defining characteristic of life for the majority of the world's bottom two billion people, helping sustain the gulf between the most destitute and everyone else who shares this planet.

Narrowing that gulf demands more than the interest of the foreign aid and human rights communities, which, to date, have carried out the heavy lifting of women's empowerment in developing countries, funding projects such as schools for girls and microfinance for female entrepreneurs. It requires the involvement of the world's largest companies. Not only does the global private sector have vastly more money than governments and nongovernmental organizations, but it can wield significant leverage with its powerful brands and by extending promises of investment and employment. Some companies already promote initiatives focused on women as part of their corporate social-responsibility programs—in other words, to burnish their images as good corporate citizens. But the truly transformative shift—both for global corporations and for women worldwide—will occur when companies understand that empowering women in developing economies affects their bottom lines.

The majority of global population growth in the coming decades will occur in those countries where gender disparities are the greatest and where conservative religious traditions and tribal customs work against women's rights. As multinational corporations search for growth in the developing world, they are beginning to realize that women's disempowerment causes staggering and deeply pernicious losses in productivity, economic activity, and human capital. Just as many corporations have found that adopting environmentally sensitive business practices is not only good public relations but also good business, companies that embrace female empowerment will see their labor forces become more productive, the quality of their global supply chains improve, and their customer bases expand. They will also help drive what could be the greatest cultural shift of the twenty-first century.

Benefits Package

In 2006, General Electric was facing a growing disaster. Its ultrasound technology had spread to India, and Indian human rights groups and gender activists began to accuse the company of being complicit in female feticide. This was a burgeoning public relations nightmare that also threatened GE's profitable Indian ultrasound business.

In India, as in many other countries in South and East Asia, the heavy burden of dowry payments and/or patriarchal traditions make parents prefer male children to female ones. The spread of GE's portable sonogram machines to clinics across rural India brought low-cost fetal sex screening to millions—which meant that parents could now easily abort unwanted girls. Although in 1994 the Indian government passed a law prohibiting sex-selective abortion, the problem persists. In some parts of the country, as many as 140 boys are born for every 100 girls. Comparing the cost of an abortion to a future dowry, abortion clinics lure customers with advertisements warning that it is better to "pay 500 rupees now, save 50,000 rupees later." Because abortion providers have continued to flout the 1994 law, in 2002 the Indian government amended it to make the manufacturers and distributors of sonogram equipment responsible for preventing female feticide.

To protect its ultrasound business and avoid legal damages, GE created a series of training programs, sales-screening procedures, and post-sale auditing processes designed to detect misuse, and it also put warning labels on its equipment. Nonetheless, GE was caught off-guard by the media campaign launched by Indian activists, who accused it of enabling female feticide. Before long, GE realized that if it hoped to continue to dominate the country's ultrasound market, it would have to confront the low status of women in Indian society. It met with activist groups and launched a poster campaign to change attitudes about women's rights. At the same time, it began to fund education for girls and to sponsor a hip, young Indian female tennis star as a progressive role model.

As often happens when the private sector gets involved in the touchy subject of women's rights in the developing world, the case of GE in India was disappointingly reactive. Too often, companies act only after they face a public relations problem, whether being charged with female feticide or with hiring underage girls in sweatshops. Perhaps it is not surprising that multinational companies tend to approach the topic gingerly and belatedly, given the cultural sensitivities regarding women in many emerging markets and the fact that the senior management of local subsidiaries is often overwhelmingly male.

Slowly, however, attitudes are beginning to change. Partly in response to shareholder demands, some companies are becoming increasingly proactive regarding women's empowerment. In addition, investors have put more than $2 trillion into socially responsible investment funds, which weigh both financial returns and societal impact. Although supporting women's rights is not yet a primary concern of most such funds, it is becoming an increasingly high-profile component of the larger social justice agenda that dictates how and where socially responsible investment funds invest. Meanwhile, the rise of female senior managers, board members, and CEOs in Western companies is also raising the profile of women's rights in the global corporate agenda.

Nike is one company that has decided to take a proactive approach to women's empowerment. Having been regularly hit in the 1990s with accusations of relying on sweatshop labor abroad, Nike instituted an elaborate inspection system to root out the worst labor practices among its suppliers. Along the way, it realized that many of its overseas factories were overwhelmingly staffed with female workers, meaning that the problems of oppressed girls and women—including a lack of education and access to health care, child marriage, vulnerability to HIV/AIDS, human trafficking, and domestic violence—were its problems, too. In 2004, the company created the Nike Foundation, which invests in health, education, and leadership programs for adolescent girls in the developing world. So far, it has distributed close to $100 million. Perhaps more important, Nike has deployed its powerful brand and marketing skills in support of young girls. In 2008, it launched *The Girl Effect,* a dramatic, smartly produced video that has since gone viral on the Internet.

In 2008, Goldman Sachs put its own recognizable brand and considerable resources behind female empowerment when it launched a program called 10,000 Women, a five-year, $100 million global initiative to invest in business and management education for female entrepreneurs in developing countries. The initiative helps make up for the lack of business education available to women in the developing world: in all of Africa, for example, there are fewer than 3,000 women enrolled in local MBA courses. Goldman touts the program on the economic grounds that closing employment gender gaps in emerging markets stimulates growth. The company's CEO, Lloyd Blankfein, says that the program is a way of "manufacturing global GNP," which, in the long run, is good for Goldman. Early assessments in the press indicate that graduates of the program have seen increases in the revenues of their businesses and have hired more employees, thus growing local GNP and raising the economic stature of women. The 10,000 Women program is also funding new teachers and curricula to educate future generations of female entrepreneurs in Africa, Asia, Latin America, and the Middle East. Just as governments and international development organizations have realized that empowering women is much more than a human rights issue, leaders in the private sector, such as Goldman Sachs and Nike, are starting to understand that enhancing women's economic power is good business.

Rani the Riveter

A 2009 McKinsey survey of corporations with operations in emerging markets revealed that less than 20 percent of the companies had any initiatives focused on women. Their executives have simply not made the issue a strategic priority. Perhaps they should reconsider. According to the same study, three-quarters of those companies with specific initiatives to empower women in developing countries reported that their investments were already increasing their profits or that they expected them to do so soon. Such investments pay off by improving a company's talent pool and increasing employee productivity and retention. Corporations also benefit as new markets are created and existing ones expand. In the developing world especially, networks of female entrepreneurs are becoming increasingly important sales channels in places where the scarcity of roads and stores makes it difficult to distribute goods and services.

One example of how a corporation can simultaneously expand its business and empower women is Hindustan Unilever, India's largest consumer goods company. It launched its Shakti Entrepreneur Program in 2000 to offer microcredit grants to rural women who become door-to-door distributors of the company's household products. This sales network has now expanded to include nearly 50,000 women selling to more than three million homes across 100,000 Indian villages. Not only do these women benefit from higher self-esteem and greater status within their families, but they invest their incomes in the health, nutrition, and education of their children, thereby helping lift their communities out of poverty. Hindustan Unilever, for its part, was able to open up a previously inaccessible market.

Training women as local distributors of goods and services is important, of course, but so is incorporating women-owned businesses into global supply chains. As giant retailers such as Walmart and Carrefour move aggressively into emerging markets, they are trying to buy more of their products, particularly food, directly from local producers—both to lower prices and to improve quality. With more than $400 billion in annual sales, Walmart is the world's largest retailer, so its purchasing decisions have a cascading effect throughout the global supply chain. Its recent sensitivity to environmental issues, for example, is starting to transform how companies around the world produce goods. This February, it announced a plan to reduce the greenhouse gas emissions produced by its global supply chain by 20 million metric tons within five years; it plans to do this by forcing its suppliers to adjust how they source, manufacture, package, and transport their products.

Similarly, there are signs that Walmart is beginning to understand the importance of women's empowerment in the developing world, where it projects that most of its future growth will take place. Since almost 75 percent of its employees are women, the company has a clear interest in promoting women's economic empowerment in its new markets. Working alongside CARE, a humanitarian organization that combats global poverty, Walmart has launched several pilot programs to teach literacy and workplace skills in the developing world. In Peru, it is helping female farmers meet the company's quality-control standards. In Bangladesh, it is training local women in the garment industry to move up from fabric sorters to seamstresses and cutters. Similarly, it is developing the skills of female cashew farmers in India so that they can progress from low-level pickers to high-end processors. Walmart expects to see increased productivity, higher quality, and greater diversity in its supply chain as a result. "We aren't engaging with Walmart solely for the financial resources they bring to the table," says Helene Gayle, president and CEO of CARE. "We are working together to make change on a global level. Walmart has enormous potential to transform women's lives in the emerging markets in which it operates."

It is ironic, of course, that Walmart is embracing women's empowerment in emerging markets even as it fights the largest class-action sex-discrimination lawsuit in U.S. history. (Walmart is accused of discriminating against women in pay and promotions.) Undoubtedly, its women's empowerment initiatives could have multiple motivations, including diverting negative public attention. But Walmart's efforts will be sustainable only to the extent that the company considers them central to its long-term growth and profitability and not just part of a public relations strategy. The potential for its female employees and suppliers in the developing world is enormous: if Walmart sourced just one percent of its sales from women-owned businesses, it would channel billions of dollars toward women's economic empowerment—far more than what international development agencies could ever muster for such efforts.

Interestingly, one organization that seems to understand the power of using its supply chain to further women's economic empowerment is the U.S. military. In Afghanistan, the United States has made strengthening the role of women in Afghan society a central element of its counterinsurgency strategy. To this end, the U.S. military is experimenting with setting aside some contracts for Afghan women entrepreneurs to supply uniforms for the national police and army. Initial results in the fall of 2009 were disastrous, however: proposals came back with mistakes and with product samples in the wrong color, fabric, and sizes. In response, the U.S. military has held several training courses to educate Afghan businesswomen on how to meet quality standards and navigate the complicated "request for proposal" process. It is too early to tell if any women-owned companies will be able to fill large military orders—the minimum is for $300,000 worth of goods—but according to news reports, the women who have participated in the program say that the experience has been invaluable.

Attitude Adjustment

Companies that are interested in women's empowerment—whether driven by corporate social responsibility or by business strategy—now have more tools and support available to guide their investments than ever before. The World Bank is one example of an institution that is partnering with private-sector firms in this effort. For two decades, economists at the World Bank have been making the case that girls' education and women's economic empowerment are among the best investments that the developed world can make to reduce poverty and stimulate growth in the developing world. As Robert Zoellick, president of the World Bank, frequently says, "Gender equality is smart economics." The World Bank's Gender Action Plan invests in infrastructure in the developing world, in areas such as energy, transportation, agriculture, water, and sanitation, in ways that are specifically focused on promoting women's economic empowerment. But the plan is short on resources, with only $60 million in funding over four years. Not surprisingly, then, the World Bank is looking for other ways to steer funding toward women in the developing world. In April 2008, it launched the Global Private Sector Leaders Forum to engage corporate executives in developing countries. Already, the 23 member companies in the forum and the World Bank itself have committed to spending $3 billion on goods and services from women-owned businesses over the next three years. Initially, much of this procurement will take place in developed economies, where women-owned business are more established and the commitments are easier to track. But these conditions are beginning to change, thanks to organizations such as WEConnect International, which certifies the operations of women-owned businesses in the developing world according to international standards. Although the Global Private Sector Leaders Forum is composed largely of blue-chip companies based in the United States, such as Boeing, Cisco, ExxonMobil, and Goldman Sachs, it also has a sprinkling of prominent companies from emerging-market economies, such as Egypt, India, Peru, and Turkey.

Governments in emerging-market countries are beginning to understand that to be competitive, they will need to respond to the growing demands of the global economy regarding women's empowerment. For example, in 2008, Morocco retracted its reservations about the UN's Convention on the Elimination of All Forms of Discrimination Against Women—the leading international treaty to protect women's rights—partly so that it would become more attractive to foreign companies. Even Saudi Arabia, an oil-rich state that has rejected any international standards on women's rights, is finding it harder to resist the demands of the global economy. In 2009, recognizing that it must upgrade its educational system to produce enough skilled professionals to fuel growth, it opened a new $10 billion university for science and technology—and, for the first time in the country's history, enrolled women alongside men.

The Five-Point Plan

Five principles should guide the efforts of those corporations that are just now beginning to consider women's empowerment as a strategic aspect of their emerging-market operations.

First, success must be defined and measured appropriately. Success cannot be reduced to the types of metrics now familiar in Western corporate suites, such as how many women are in senior management positions. Instead, corporations must track the most basic information about their female employees, suppliers, and customers in emerging markets. For example, do their female employees have access to financial services so that they can actually control their incomes? Do they have identity cards that allow them to be counted as citizens? Do they need a male family member's permission to work? Since obstacles to female empowerment differ across regions, companies should rely on local market studies and workforce surveys to identify the relevant issues for corporate growth in each market.

Second, although donating money to women's empowerment initiatives is a good start, incorporating such objectives into actual business practices is even better. Bringing female farmers into the global supply chain probably has the most potential in this regard. In sub-Saharan Africa and South Asia, for example, although farm labor is more than 70 percent female, women tend to focus on subsistence crops rather than cash crops, a sector that men still dominate. Using women to increase sales also holds great possibility, as the experience of Hindustan Unilever shows. Even

sectors that employ a low percentage of women, such as the extractive industries, could target women-owned businesses for support services, such as catering, laundry, office cleaning, and transportation.

Third, companies should concentrate on providing skills and resources to female entrepreneurs and business leaders. For some firms, this could mean expanding their financial services to female clients—not just credit but savings products, too. Or it could take the form of supporting an existing local organization that helps women obtain access to health care, identity cards, or property rights. Leadership training, as well as secondary and university education, is central to developing the next generation of female business leaders and managers.

Fourth, even though companies are understandably wary of being associated with controversy, they cannot deny that they have an interest in the outcome of conflicts taking place over the role of women in many developing countries. Important and growing markets, such as Indonesia, Nigeria, and Pakistan, are home to protracted debates between moderates and extremists. Such thorny subjects as child marriage, domestic violence, and women's access to reproductive health may seem off-limits to corporations. But consider just one example: rapid population growth in Nigeria, already Africa's most populous state, will strain the country's resources and threaten its stability, thus jeopardizing substantial Western investments. Similarly, decades of research have shown that societies with a disproportionately high number of men—as is the case where families prefer male children to female ones—are less stable and more prone to violence, which hinders economic growth.

Fifth, corporations should not try to reinvent methods that have already been perfected by others simply to appear innovative and committed. Instead, they should look to partner with the many excellent nonprofit organizations that have been working on issues of women's empowerment for decades. Organizations such as CARE, Vital Voices, and Women's World Banking are eager to work with the private sector to develop programs that can take advantage of corporations' expertise and assets, including their brands, employees, supplier bases, technology, and funding. Nike and ExxonMobil have formed a number of such partnerships. Likewise, Goldman Sachs is working with more than 70 academic institutions and nongovernmental organizations around the world to develop its 10,000 Women initiative. Walmart, meanwhile, is working with CARE in Bangladesh, where the organization has more than 50 years of on-the-ground experience.

Closing the gender gap and improving women's rights in the Middle East, South Asia, and sub-Saharan Africa may take many generations, but the benefits will be huge—not only for the individual women and their families but also for global markets. As companies seek new sources of revenue in emerging economies, they will find that gender disparities ose an obstacle to doing business. The sooner the private ector works to overcome gender inequality, the better off he world—and companies' own bottom lines—will be.

Critical Thinking

1. How do women's empowerment efforts improve the image and productivity of multinational business?

2. What types of programs have multinationals initiated to enhance women's empowerment?

3. How have international financial institutions supported efforts to empower women?

4. What principles should guide corporate efforts to empower women?

ISOBEL COLEMAN is Senior Fellow for U.S. Foreign Policy and Director of the Women and Foreign Policy Program at the Council on Foreign Relations. She is the author of *Paradise Beneath Her Feet: How Women Are Transforming the Middle East*. For an annotated guide to this topic, see "What to Read on Gender and Foreign Policy" at www .foreignaffairs.com/readinglists/gender.

Test-Your-Knowledge Form

We encourage you to photocopy and use this page as a tool to assess how the articles in *Annual Editions* expand on the information in your textbook. By reflecting on the articles you will gain enhanced text information. You can also access this useful form on a product's book support website at www.mhhe.com/cls.

NAME: DATE:

_____

TITLE AND NUMBER OF ARTICLE:

_____

BRIEFLY STATE THE MAIN IDEA OF THIS ARTICLE:

_____

LIST THREE IMPORTANT FACTS THAT THE AUTHOR USES TO SUPPORT THE MAIN IDEA:

_____

WHAT INFORMATION OR IDEAS DISCUSSED IN THIS ARTICLE ARE ALSO DISCUSSED IN YOUR TEXTBOOK OR OTHER READINGS THAT YOU HAVE DONE? LIST THE TEXTBOOK CHAPTERS AND PAGE NUMBERS:

_____

LIST ANY EXAMPLES OF BIAS OR FAULTY REASONING THAT YOU FOUND IN THE ARTICLE:

_____

LIST ANY NEW TERMS/CONCEPTS THAT WERE DISCUSSED IN THE ARTICLE, AND WRITE A SHORT DEFINITION:

We Want Your Advice

ANNUAL EDITIONS revisions depend on two major opinion sources: one is our Advisory Board, listed in the front of this volume, which works with us in scanning the thousands of articles published in the public press each year; the other is you—the person actually using the book. Please help us and the users of the next edition by completing the prepaid article rating form on this page and returning it to us. Thank you for your help!

ANNUAL EDITIONS: Developing World 12/13

ARTICLE RATING FORM

Here is an opportunity for you to have direct input into the next revision of this volume.
We would like you to rate each of the articles listed below, using the following scale:

1. **Excellent: should definitely be retained**
2. **Above average: should probably be retained**
3. **Below average: should probably be deleted**
4. **Poor: should definitely be deleted**

Your ratings will play a vital part in the next revision.
Please mail this prepaid form to us as soon as possible.
Thanks for your help!

RATING	ARTICLE	RATING	ARTICLE
	1. The New Face of Development		27. The Struggle for Mexico
	2. How Development Leads to Democracy: What We Know about Modernization		28. Central America's Security Predicament
			29. Global Aging and the Crisis of the 2020s
	3. The New Population Bomb: The Four Megatrends That Will Change the World		30. Crying for Freedom
			31. Understanding the Revolutions of 2011: Weakness and Resilience in Middle Eastern Autocracies
	4. Best. Decade. Ever.		
	5. And Justice for All: Enforcing Human Rights for the World's Poor		32. Good Soldier, Bad Cop
			33. "Moderates" Redefined: How to Deal with Political Islam
	6. The Case against the West: America and Europe in the Asian Century		
			34. The Islamists Are Not Coming
	7. The Post-Washington Consensus: Development after the Crisis		35. The Transformation of Hamas
			36. In Sri Lanka, the Triumph of Vulgar Patriotism
	8. The Poor Man's Burden		37. Indonesia's Moment
	9. A Tiger Despite the Chains: The State of Reform in India		38. Divergent Paths: The Future of One-Party Rule in Singapore
	10. Welcome to Minegolia		39. Uprising Threat
	11. The African Miracle		40. Ivory Coast: Another Asterisk for Africa's Democratization
	12. The New Mercantilism: China's Emerging Role in the Americas		
			41. A New Global Player: Brazil's Far-Flung Agenda
	13. Cotton: The Huge Moral Issue		42. Perilous Times for Latin America
	14. Taking the Measure of Global Aid		43. Human Rights Last
	15. The New Colonialists		44. Not Ready for Prime Time: Why Including Emerging Powers at the Helm Would Hurt Global Governance
	16. A Few Dollars at a Time: How to Tap Consumers for Development		
			45. Is a Green World a Safer World?: Not Necessarily
	17. The Fertile Continent: Africa, Agriculture's Final Frontier		46. The Last Straw
			47. The World's Water Challenge
	18. The Micromagic of Microcredit		48. Water Warriors
	19. Many Borrowers of Microloans Now Find the Price Is Too High		49. The New Geopolitics of Food
			50. The Women's Crusade
	20. Corruption Reduction: A Foreign Policy Goal and Instrument		51. Women in Developing Countries 300 Times More Likely to Die in Childbirth
	21. Where Life Is Cheap and Talk Is Loose		52. Girls in War: Sex Slave, Mother, Domestic Aide, Combatant
	22. Afghanistan's Rocky Path to Peace		
	23. A Nation on the Brink		53. Remember the Women?
	24. The Forever War: Inside India's Maoist Conflict		54. Women in the Shadow of Climate Change
	25. Sudan on the Cusp		55. The Global Glass Ceiling: Why Empowering Women Is Good for Business
	26. Africa's Forever Wars		

ABOUT YOU

Name

Date

_____

Are you a teacher? ☐ A student? ☐
Your school's name

_____

Department

_____

Address   City   State   Zip

_____

School telephone #

_____

YOUR COMMENTS ARE IMPORTANT TO US!

Please fill in the following information:
For which course did you use this book?

_____

Did you use a text with this ANNUAL EDITION? ☐ yes ☐ no
What was the title of the text?

_____

What are your general reactions to the Annual Editions concept?

_____

Have you read any pertinent articles recently that you think should be included in the next edition? Explain.

_____

Are there any articles that you feel should be replaced in the next edition? Why?

_____

Are there any World Wide Websites that you feel should be included in the next edition? Please annotate.

_____

May we contact you for editorial input? ☐ yes ☐ no
May we quote your comments? ☐ yes ☐ no

NOTES

NOTES

NOTES

NOTES

NOTES

NOTES